Encyclopedia of Diversity and Social Justice

Encyclopedia of Diversity and Social Justice

Volume I

SHERWOOD THOMPSON

ROWMAN & LITTLEFIELD

Lanham • Boulder • New York • London

Published by Rowman & Littlefield
A wholly owned subsidiary of The Rowman & Littlefield Publishing Group, Inc.
4501 Forbes Boulevard, Suite 200, Lanham, Maryland 20706
www.rowman.com

Unit A, Whitacre Mews, 26-34 Stannary Street, London SE11 4AB

British Library Cataloguing in Publication Information Available

Library of Congress Cataloging-in-Publication Data

Encyclopedia of diversity and social justice / [edited by] Sherwood Thompson.
    volumes cm
Includes bibliographical references and index.
ISBN 978-1-4422-1604-4 (cloth : set : alk. paper)—ISBN 978-1-4422-1606-8 (electronic)
1. Cultural pluralism—Encyclopedias. 2. Social justice—Encyclopedias. I. Thompson, Sherwood.
HM1271.E485 2015
305.8003—dc23   2014028212

∞™ The paper used in this publication meets the minimum requirements of American National Standard for Information Sciences—Permanence of Paper for Printed Library Materials, ANSI/NISO Z39.48-1992.

Printed in the United States of America

Contents

Advisory Board

Dr. Christine Clark
Professor and Senior Scholar in Multicultural
    Education
Founding Vice President for Diversity and
    Inclusion
Department of Teaching and Learning
College of Education
University of Nevada, Las Vegas

Dr. Chinaka S. DomNwachukwu
Professor of Education
Associate Dean for Academic Affairs
School of Education
Azusa Pacific University

Dr. Pamela S. Gates
Dean
Professor of English
College of Humanities and Social
    and Behavioral Sciences
Central Michigan University

Dr. Sandy Hunter
Professor
Emergency Medical Care Program
Eastern Kentucky University

Dr. Eric R. Jackson
Associate Professor
Director—Black Studies Program
Editorial Board and Book Review Editor
    —*Journal of Pan African Studies*
Department of History and Geography
Northern Kentucky University

Dr. Dianne Mark
Department of Foundation, Literacy,
    and Technology
Spadoni College of Education
Coastal Carolina University

Dr. James L. Moore III
Educational Services
College of Education and
    Human Ecology
The Ohio State University

Dr. Philliph M. Mutisya
Professor
Department of Curriculum, Instruction,
    and Professional Studies
North Carolina Central University

Dr. R. C. Saravanabhavan
Professor
Educational Administration and Policy
School of Education
Howard University

Dr. William Strickland
Professor
African American Studies
University of Massachusetts at Amherst

Dr. Hazel Symonette
Program Development and
    Assessment Specialist
University of Wisconsin–Madison
Multicultural Student Center

Dr. Aaron Thompson
Senior Vice President for Academic Affairs
Kentucky Council on Postsecondary Education

Aminah M. Thompson
Judge
Raleigh/Durham District

Preface

> For a life worthy to be lived is one that
> is full of active aspiration, for something
> higher and better; and such a contempla-
> tion of the world we call meliorism.
>
> —Paul Carus, *Monism and Meliorism*, 1885

Basic human rights, which should guarantee social justice for all individuals, are being eroded. The twenty-first century has witnessed more reckless disregard for individual rights than what social analysts would have predicted in the proceeding twentieth century. Something has gone wrong.

I echo today what Jim Wallis wrote in 1994 in his book *The Soul of Politics*; then, he declared that "the world isn't working. Things are unraveling, and most of us know it" (p. xv). Sure, there are signs that confirm that the world is a mess, and instead of people fixing it, the world is spiraling downward in a drain of repugnance. It's all about people: the push by some to control and dictate to others and the resistance of people expressing their voices of bonding, mutual respect, vision, and possibilities. Concern for diversity and social justice is one movement that provides tools to individuals and groups to break the imprisonment of old beliefs and practices. It is a revelation of renewed spirits and informed sensibilities. Diversity and social justice transform society by transforming individuals and liberating the human spirit.

There is an ongoing battle to keep structural injustice out of the world's press. Denying the existence of sorrowful human situations around the globe will not make those situations go away. People of conscience, those individuals who believe in human rights and individual freedom, are compelled to speak out and bring attention to the limitations of society, but more than just pointing at the problems, people of conscience must be in the vanguard of changing the troubling ideologies that devalue the human spirit.

The start of 2014 witnessed the outcry of individuals from around the world seeking supporters from every walk of life to raise their voices and condemn the unfair punishment that individuals are suffering in certain regions of the world because they are gay. Most recently, the United Nations' AIDS task force (UNAIDS), the Malawi Law Society, and human rights groups plan to take Malawi to court over its antigay laws. These coalition groups will petition the high court to overturn as unconstitutional laws banning same-sex relationships. Homosexuality carries a maximum prison sentence of fourteen years in Malawi. Human rights groups report that there are eighty-three countries with criminal laws against persons identified as lesbian, gay, bisexual, transgender, or intersex (LGBTIs).

There have been numerous incidents that have occurred that have caused people of conscience to question whether or not certain groups of individuals are valued and their actual existence respected. One such case involved a homeless man diagnosed with schizophrenia who lived on the streets of Fullerton, California. A Fullerton County police officer was charged with one count of second-degree murder and one count of involuntary manslaughter after the officer and two other officers tasered the homeless man repeatedly and beat him with a flashlight, and all the while he cried out for his father. He was taken to a hospital and treated for his injuries, but he never regained consciousness and died five days later. A judge declared that the officers used excessive and unreasonable force; however, after a lengthy legal battle, a jury found the police officers not guilty on all charges.

Recently, Islamist militants kidnapped more than two hundred schoolgirls from a school in the northern Borno State of Nigeria. Boko Haram militants seized the schoolgirls, and they maintain that the girls won't be freed until imprisoned Boko Haram fighters are released. The kidnapping has leaders and celebrities from around the world calling for the children's release. The United States, United Kingdom, France, China, and an Israeli counterterrorism team are working with the Nigerian government to rescue the kidnapped girls.

Diversity and social justice are not just meaningless terms; they are ways of life. The *Encyclopedia of Diversity and Social Justice* is a comprehensive and systematic collection of designated entries that describe in detail a number of important subjects that relate to and reference diversity and social justice themes. This work is a discussion of individual freedom and justice.

The purpose of this encyclopedia is to reveal the unique nature of the language of diversity and social justice in our everyday lives and how this language makes the connection between human influences—negatively and positively—among society and institutions within society. The selections of terms and topics have been carefully chosen in order to present the common usage of familiar and not-so-familiar themes that dominate our daily conversations about people, places, and events. The value of this encyclopedia is to provide readers with a reference book that serves as a centralized source for discussions on relevant diversity and social justice topics. Transcending the conventional model of encyclopedias, this work includes a broad array of popular topics that are commonplace in today's society. The encyclopedia provides insight into topics of interest for a wide audience of readers and offers various viewpoints gathered from a network of contributors and consultants.

The language used in diversity and social justice conversations is not a subject that is formally talked about on a regular basis because most people assume they already know everything there is to know about the terms and phrases they use. Often, they believe they are using these terms and phrases correctly. Unfortunately, this is not true in many cases.

People struggle with diversity and social justice language in all aspects of life; oftentimes, their unfamiliarity with typical terms results in ambiguity. These terms cause some to feel uncomfortable and confused. All one has to do is to listen to cable or network news to get an idea of why this encyclopedia is necessary. News commentators can be heard using phrases and terms that misrepresent the true sense of the words or phrases used. This attempt at communicating, in turn, misrepresents the true nature

and reality of the topics discussed. They are trying to connect with a wide audience; however, because of the wrong usage of terms, they oftentimes offend the very people they are trying to reach. This confusion causes individuals to be swayed into thinking a certain way based solely on the choice of words that are spoken or read. This influence has a monumental impact on the choices an individual makes, their worldview, the way individuals think, and the political persuasion the individual embraces.

The *Encyclopedia of Diversity and Social Justice* exposes readers to relevant discussions on diversity and social justice topics. This encyclopedia is a reference work that contains over three hundred entries alphabetically arranged for straightforward and convenient use by scholars and general readers alike. The entries range from original research to synopses of existing scholarship. Reading the discussions provided, the reader will come to understand the proper usage of key diversity and social justice terms. These discussions provide alternative views to the popular doctrines and philosophical truths and their assumed legitimate meanings. The encyclopedia by no means contains an exhaustive list of the terms and phrases associated with diversity and social justice; however, it does include many of the most popular phrases and terms used in current, everyday conversations.

The *Encyclopedia of Diversity and Social Justice* is a select collection of diversity and social justice terms that characterizes and informs—vernacular of understanding culture, communities, organizations, and individuals' freedoms. It is designed to help the reader understand and appreciate the complex nature of living in a world of differences. These terms offer a baseline that helps in the process of turning inequality into equality. These terms are in fact discussions, and as such, these discussions on diversity and social justice seek to support individual freedoms and to unmask misunderstandings pertaining to topics of equity that are commonplace in society. By practicing and sustaining these ideals, it is the hope of many of the contributors that these topics, particularly in the United States, will become inherent in our understanding and lead to an appreciation of their values and also strengthen our commitment to a more pluralistic society. It is also hoped that as a world community, we will learn to adopt a common language that helps us to fully understand and appreciate the uniqueness of our diverse planet.

Liberating our spirits also frees our minds from the contemporary commonly held beliefs and customs that restrict us and keep us in bondage to myopic viewpoints. This encyclopedia is intended to expand our awareness and encourage us to resist the temptation of being self-imprisoned in a contracting reality. This reference tool strives to offer individuals a deeper appreciation and a clearer understanding of diversity and social justice in all of its dimensions. It also strives to provide the proper tools to lift the individual from the tensions that naturally occur among and between individuals and groups that fail to acknowledge and promote the advantages of diversity and social justice. This is not done serendipitously—it takes work, and lots of it, to change individuals' personal values and cultural practices. This reference book is a tool that is designed to provide some parameters for overcoming the complexities of the meaning and function of diversity and social justice realities.

Some individuals may find the thought of gaining awareness of diversity and social justice inhibitory—they would rather live secure in their own compressed world than live in a world of differences. Chávez and O'Donnell (1998) suggest that those who refuse to participate in, and attitudinally remain uncommitted to, multicultural issues are practicing a form of nonengagement—a process, the authors argue, about which individuals can be unconsciously or consciously conscious. This state of numbness seems to be an escape from reality and a defense mechanism used when one refuses to accept the personal and social reality of individuals that do not fit the image of the status quo.

As a young child, I would wonder about the big canopy of the night sky above my head. Like most children, especially those who live in the country where the night sky are not blinded by bright city lights, I tried to map the constellations. As I grew older, I was amazed at the fact that the same location where I so meticulously mapped the constellations decades ago has now been replaced by another, quite different constellation. This experience taught me that the spectacular universe gets its strength from changing, and the astronomical dimensions of

the universe produce its beautiful array of uniqueness and strength through diversity. Being sensitive to this beauty has laced and deeply grounded my appreciation for understanding the benefit of diversity and social justice in a world of differences. Just as a good guide to the constellations can deepen one's understanding of the sky, the *Encyclopedia of Diversity and Social Justice* is an important contribution to the understanding of diversity and social justice.

The *Encyclopedia of Diversity and Social Justice* is intended to provide readers with an opportunity to open their minds to the promising possibilities of different realities within the vast human existence. Instead of indoctrinating individuals with the same old inadvertently exhausted explanations of information about power relations and inappropriate worldviews, conversational, well-structured entries are particularly designed to jump-start the thinking of individuals and stimulate new possibilities and realities. We are at our best when we seek to be aware, be educated, and to not be afraid of a world of differences.

In the science of psychophysics, the term *Just Noticeable Difference* (JND) is used to identify the difference threshold or the minimum level of stimulation that a person can detect during a certain portion of time between two objects or things. The concept of JND has been integrated into many different disciplines representing the science and business communities. There is an obvious JND benefit from reading the various entries in the *Encyclopedia of Diversity and Social Justice*. The more one concentrates on the entries and their meanings, the greater the threshold of understanding and engagement one can project when using these terms in daily conversations.

Working on this project has allowed me to realize a fine difference between the common usage of diversity and social justice terms—limited definitions of diversity and social justice that one comes to recognize in daily interaction with organizations and individuals—and the refreshing and noticeable difference in the discussions present in this work that demonstrate a rich understanding of the history and usage of relevant diversity and social justice language. The topics present interesting discussions filled with brilliantly relevant information based on a clear understanding of how diversity and social justice exist in society. A good example is the term *multiculturalism*, which is today's common buzzword in diversity circles. From the earliest days when the common usage was intergroup, to today when the acceptable usage is twenty-first-century populations, the popular term *multiculturalism* continues to evolve and expand as a result of the political and social changes in society throughout the world. Multiculturalism has evolved into a word with many different meanings, all intended to respect individuals' various cultures and personal customs. The same can also be said about the terms *diversity* and *equity*, *scapegoating* and *persecution*, and *individual philosophy* and *worldview*. The language of diversity and social justice is rich and always evolving and manifesting unique attitudes, norms, customs, beliefs, personal experiences, spiritual aspirations, and affirmations.

In essence, the *Encyclopedia of Diversity and Social Justice* has a particular agenda: to stimulate a discussion of diversity and social justice that arouses a curiosity about other cultures, gender, social classes, individual differences, languages, and the broader cultural elements found throughout the world. In part, the critics of diversity and social justice have been successful in convincing the general public to view diversity and social justice as a political correctness discussion that has gone too far. But most of the critics of diversity and social justice, and to a large extent, the general public as a whole, many of whom subscribe to network news and cable talk shows, are simply misinformed. This encyclopedia, therefore, is designed to create a dialogue for those with no working knowledge of this subject and for those with a tremendous background and knowledge about this subject. The *Encyclopedia of Diversity and Social Justice* is organized to engage the reader in a reflective conversation on epistemological constructs that instruct and inform while simultaneously inculcating the reader to become proficient in building personal resources that will lead to a greater interpretation and undergird a clearer perspective of the literature on diversity and social justice topics.

Again, the selected entries that are listed in the encyclopedia are by no means an exhaustive list of diversity and social justice terms and topics, nor is an understanding of these terms and topics an end in itself. The universe of terms grows every day; therefore, this encyclopedia does not claim to be a comprehensive guide to every diversity and social justice term. What it does claim to do is to provide an avenue for diverse contributors to discuss their experience and knowledge about major themes that are relevant to them and to society. In many ways, the contributors are advocates for social and cultural change, and their voices are powerful instruments elucidating themes of awareness about the multiple perspectives of diversity and social justice in the twenty-first century.

This encyclopedia is designed to provide readers with a meaningful understanding of a living and breathing language that identifies the daily characteristics of everyday people from various cultural groups. It is universally accepted that every member of a cultural group has the right to be respected as an individual. There's no hiding the fact that our twenty-first-century world is a diverse, global society composed of people of many ethnicities, religions, political persuasions, ages, sexual orientations, and physical abilities. These differences cannot be overlooked; in fact, they constitute the beauty of our world; the richness of our differences is the fuel that advances our heterogeneous society—a society comprised of the diversity and multicultural characteristics that represents our practices and lifestyles.

The *Encyclopedia of Diversity and Social Justice* offers more than just words; it provides the reader with a window into a world that maintains that all individuals have certain beliefs, customs, rights, rituals, values, and knowledge that support individuals' uniqueness and life philosophies. In keeping with this belief, this work has incorporated experts from around the globe to write about their experiences, their values, their viewpoints related to their experiences and research on diversity and social justice issues.

Awareness and increased knowledge of diversity and social justice terms and topics gives an advantage in understanding the complex world in which we live. It gives individuals a common language, a mutual worldview, and insight into how to treat people with dignity and respect. The need to improve our communication and understanding of differences among individuals and cultural groups in the world today is imperative. I firmly believe we must learn to live together in order to save the planet.

Confucius wrote an essay titled *The Great Learning* (Runes, 1955), in which he suggests that a concept needs to be investigated before knowledge is complete. Written in clear and informative language, this encyclopedia is a compilation of topics that list a series of phrases and terms that are persuasive, significant, and widely used among academics as well as the general public. The compilation of terms and topics includes documentation of cultural, social, and political vernacular used in popular discourse; also topics and terms from an historical perspective are covered. In my effort to present a broad range of topics, I have invited a number of experts to share their research for this project. I understand that there are many other topics that could have been included in this encyclopedia. Nevertheless, I hope that the substance of these select topics, and the discussions that ensue, will be fruitful and progressive. It is my hope that greater understanding and increased knowledge about diversity and social justice will grow from this major work.

Indeed, the failure of society to seek and embrace a bonding force among all humanity is one of the causes of the paranoia and fear that are gripping the world. Appreciation of human diversity and social justice is an important and worthwhile goal to work towardand pursue. In a global community, individuals are the only ones who can make the vital transition from the culture of fear to the culture of freedom. This is done by respecting one another. Our survival on this small planet urgently requires that individuals and groups from all walks of life collectively search for ways to communicate our commonalities and fundamental qualities. To sustain a healthy and peaceful world, individuals must accept diversity and hunger for justice. This yearning becomes an incessant struggle predicated on reshaping society and valuing individuals no matter who they are, or what they have, in ways that will enhance our mortal existence on Earth.

The *Encyclopedia of Diversity and Social Justice* includes essential information about all aspects of diversity and social justice from ageism to xenophobia, and the entries consist of topics that represent a wide context among a diverse community of people from every walk of life. Contributions were made by experts in various fields and include a true analysis and explanation of specific phrases, terms, and topics pertinent to diversity and social justice. This reference guide will be of particular interest to those who intrinsically use the language of diversity and social justice in their professional lives, political organizations, media groups, and classrooms including writers, journalists, policymakers, and the general public, as it provides a centralized source and convenient way to discover the modern meaning, richness, and significance of diversity and social justice language.

The wide-ranging selection of entries creates a work that is both fascinating and informative. The contributors shed great wisdom on the definition and descriptions of detailed diversity and social justice topics. These topics are works in progress, and to that end, they continue to evolve as society continues to mature and accept the value of diversity among individuals and groups. May this encyclopedia encourage ongoing investigation and research on diversity and social justice topics and a realization that diversity and social justice are not bad things; they are the very basic strength of our collective society.

Sherwood Thompson

References
Chávez, R. C. & O'Donnell, J. (1998). *Speaking the unpleasant: The politics of (non)engagement in the multicultural education terrain.* Albany, NY: State University of New York Press.

King, Rodney. (2014). *Rodney King quotes.* Brainy Quotes. Retrieved from http://www.brainyquote.com/quotes/authors/r/rodney_king.html.

Runes, D. D. (1955). *Treasury of philosophy.* New York: Philosophical Library.

Wallis, J. (1994). *The soul of politics.* New York & Maryknoll: The New Press & Orbis Books.

Acknowledgments

The assistance and support of many individuals are necessary to produce a work as comprehensive as an encyclopedia. Without the assistance of a large number of people—advisory board members, editors, graduate assistants, consultants, and contributors—this project would not have been possible. As a result of this collaboration, the encyclopedia has set a standard that attempts to contribute to individual freedom and social justice. I cherish the advice, counseling, guidance, and suggestions offered during the composition and writing of this encyclopedia. I also appreciate the support and assistance from the editors and publisher at Rowman & Littlefield Publishing Group.

I am especially grateful to Janice Clayton, who spent countless hours working to ensure the correctness and proper formatting of the entries. Her gifted talents were simply outstanding. Many thanks to Rachel Richardson for her assistance with proofreading. I would like to express my sincere appreciation to the advisory board members, especially Dr. Christine Clark, whose scholarly assistance, motivation, feedback, and continual support during the development and completion of this project were highly valuable. A special thanks to Dr. Natasha Pratt-Harris for her assistance with editing a select number of entries.

A special expression of appreciation is extended to Dr. William "Bill" Phillips, former dean of the College of Education at Eastern Kentucky University. He supported this project without hesitation and provided much-needed resources that allowed me to retain a graduate assistant throughout this process. Special thanks to Yamini Rudraraju, educational technologist, for setting up and maintaining the encyclopedia website. Appreciation is expressed to my loving daughter, Aminah Malika Thompson, whose counsel, critical evaluation, and guidance made this project so much more enjoyable.

I would like to express my deep gratitude for the time and expertise of the contributors and consultants who generously gave of their involvement, knowledge, scholarship, support, and talents to this project. Their contributions are insightful and exciting; their voices encourage ongoing dialogue and engagement of diversity and social justice themes.

Finally, and most importantly, without my faith and trust in the Great and Mighty Creator Most High, none of this would have been possible.

Introduction: Diversity

Aaron Thompson, PhD, and Joe Cusseo, PhD

Authors of *Diversity and the College Experience, Humanity, Diversity and the Liberal Arts*, and *Infusing Diversity and Cultural Competence into Teacher Education*

The word *diversity* derives from the Latin root *diversus*, meaning "various." Thus, human diversity refers to the variety of differences that exist among people who comprise humanity (the human species). The relationship between humanity and human diversity may be viewed as similar to the relationship between sunlight and the spectrum of colors. Similar to how sunlight passing through a prism is dispersed into the variety of colors that comprise the visual spectrum, the human species spanning planet Earth is dispersed into the variety of groups that comprise the human spectrum (humanity). Human diversity expresses itself in a multiplicity of ways, including differences in external features, national origins, cultural backgrounds, and sexual orientations. Some of these dimensions of diversity are obvious; others are subtle, and some are invisible.

Equal rights and social justice are key aspects of diversity; however, they are not the only aspects. In fact, in a national survey of American voters, the vast majority of respondents agreed that diversity is more than just political correctness (National Survey of Voters, 1998). While diversity may still be viewed narrowly by some people as strictly a "political" issue, we take a broader view of diversity that includes the political issue of equal rights and social justice, but also considers diversity to be an essential *educational* issue—an integral element that enriches the learning, personal development, and career success of all students.

While humans may display diversity in the color or tone of their outer layer of skin, the reality is that all members of the human species are remarkably similar at an underlying biological level. More than 98 percent of the genes that make up humans from different racial groups are exactly the same (Bridgeman, 2003; Molnar, 1991). This large amount of genetic overlap among humans accounts for the many similarities that exist among us regardless of what differences in color appear at the surface of our skin. For example, all of us have similar external features that give us a "human" appearance and clearly distinguish us from other animal species; all humans have internal organs that are similar in structure and function; and whatever the color of our outer layer of skin, when it's cut, we all bleed in the same color.

Although humans have been classified into different cultural groups, all of these groups are still cultivated from the same soil—they are all grounded in the common experience of being human. Thus, cultural diversity represents variations on the common theme of *humanity*. Human variety and human similarity coexist and complement each other. To appreciate human diversity is to appreciate both differences and *similarities* (Public Service Enterprise Group, 2009). It includes appreciating the unique perspectives of different groups of people as well as the universal aspects of the human experience that are common to all groups—whatever their particular cultural backgrounds may be. For example, despite our racial and cultural differences, all of us experience and express the same human emotions with the same facial expressions. Understanding these similarities opens up opportunities for creating a more enlightened self and lifelong learning. Thus:

- **Diversity enhances self-awareness.** Learning from people whose backgrounds and experiences are diverse sharpens your self-knowledge and self-insight by allowing you to compare and contrast your life experiences with others whose life experiences differ sharply from your own.

- **Diversity stimulates social development.** Interacting with people from a variety of groups widens your social circle, expanding the pool of people with whom you interact and strengthening your ability to relate to people with different experiences and interests.

- **Diversity enriches the multiple perspectives developed by a college education.** Diversity magnifies the power of a college education, liberating you from the tunnel vision of an ethnocentric and egocentric (self-centered) viewpoint, while enabling you to move beyond yourself to gain a panoramic perspective of the world around you and attain a more holistic view of yourself. You acquire the ability to see how you, as a whole person, fit into the "big picture"—the whole world.

- **Diversity deepens learning and elevates thinking.** Human knowledge is socially constructed—it is built up through interpersonal interaction and dialogue with others. Widening the variety of conversations you have with others deepens your learning and elevates the quality of your thinking. If you have multiple conversations with humans from a rich diversity of backgrounds, the nature of your thinking becomes richer and more nuanced as well. Research consistently shows that we learn more from people who differ from us than we do from people who are similar to us.

- **Diversity stimulates creative thinking.** Experiencing diversity increases your exposure to a wider variety of thinking styles, which empowers you to think outside the box or boundaries of a single cultural framework. Once you acquire diverse perspectives, these viewpoints can also be combined or rearranged in ways that lead to unique or innovative solutions to problems. When you draw on ideas from people of diverse backgrounds and bounce your ideas off them, you generate mental energy, synergy, and serendipity—an unanticipated discovery of creative insights.

- **Diversity enhances career preparation and career success.** Learning about and from diversity better prepares you for today's work world. America's workforce is now more diverse than at any other time in the nation's history, and it will grow increasingly diverse. Moreover, work today takes place in a global economy characterized by greater economic interdependence among nations, more international trading (imports/exports), more multinational corporations, more international travel, and almost instantaneous worldwide communication. As a result of these trends, employers of college graduates are now seeking job candidates who possess international knowledge, foreign language skills, sensitivity to human differences, and the ability to relate to people from different cultural backgrounds. Both employers and the American public agree that diversity education is *career preparation*.

In short, the case for experiencing diversity is clear and compelling. The benefits of diversity include not only the noble and global goals of social justice, national stability, and international harmony but also include a host of educational, vocational, and personal benefits for anyone who intentionally seeks out and capitalizes on the power of diversity.

References

Bridgeman, B. (2003). *Psychology and evolution: The origins of mind*. Thousand Oaks, CA: SAGE Publications.

Molnar, S. (1991). *Human variation: Races, types, and ethnic groups* (3rd ed.). Englewood Cliffs, NJ: Prentice-Hall.

National Survey of Voters. (1998). *National survey of voters*. Ford Foundation Campus Diversity Initiative Public Information Project. New York: Ford Foundation. Retrieved from http://www.diversity-web.org/research_and_trends/research_evaluation_impact/campus_community_connections/national_poll.cfm.

Public Service Enterprise Group (PSEG). (2009). *Diversity*. Retrieved from www.pseg.com/info/environment/sustainability/2009/.../diversity.jsp.

Thompson, A. & Cuseo, J. B. (2009). *Diversity & the college experience*. Dubuque, IA: Kendall Hunt.

Thompson, A. & Cuseo, J. B. (2012). *Infusing diversity and cultural competence into teacher education*. Dubuque, IA: Kendall Hunt.

Introduction: Social Justice

Louis Tietje

People frequently use the term *social justice*, but they have different understandings of its meaning and may not be able to define it clearly. The plurality of interpretations can be understood as differences between a basic set of norms: equality, desert, or choice. In principle, any norm can be the ideal of social justice. Depending on the norm, social justice can be a libertarian, liberal, conservative, socialist, or communist concept. However, the most common assumption is that social justice belongs on the left wing of the political spectrum. In this entry, the reasons for the plurality and association of the term with the left are explained.

Each of the norms has been subjected to criticism, but philosophers have been most critical of the desert norms. Despite the criticisms, many people intuitively support these norms. All of the norms continue to be in play in Western societies, and the result is a pattern of irresolvable conflicts between the equality and desert norms. Both the equality and desert norms are in conflict with choice. These conflicts will be illustrated in the policy areas of income, education, homeownership, and discrimination in employment.

HISTORICAL ORIGINS

The idea of justice as desert is ancient. It is found in the three major Western religions, as expressed in the Christian version, "Whatever a man sows that shall he also reap" (Galatians 6:7). At judgment day, each one of us will be rewarded or punished according to our good or bad works. The first philosophical definition is found in Book I of Plato's *Republic*: "Justice consists in rendering to each his due." Plato's republic was a meritocracy: natural ability was the basis of the three classes: guardians (rulers), auxiliaries (warriors), and producers (farmers, artisans). According to Aristotle, rewards and punishments should be distributed in proportion to merit

(*Nicomachean Ethics*). The Roman view, which is found in Ulpian's *Corpus Juris*, is that "justice is the constant and perpetual will to give every man his due." In these early understandings, character traits are fundamental to desert. Louis Pojman (2006) says that giving every man his due means "giving every person what he or she deserves, based on the person's character traits, including ability, virtues and vice. If you are excellent, you merit a suitable reward. If you are vicious, you deserve punishment; if mediocre, a mediocre benefit" (p. 17).

This understanding of justice as desert can be classified under Aristotle's category of distributive justice. He had two other categories of particular justice: rectificatory justice, setting right injuries inflicted by one person on another; and commercial justice, reciprocity in market exchanges. Universal justice encompassed these particular kinds of justice and referred to general moral virtue (Miller, 1999, p. 269). Proportionality is central to all forms of particular justice: distribution should be in proportion to virtue or vice, punishment should fit the crime, and profit should be proportional to investment. Two assumptions here are noteworthy. First, desert is a matter of individual responsibility. Early adherents of justice as desert would not have imagined that society should be held responsible for a person's character traits, abilities, works, actions, or behavior. Second, distributive justice is "traditionally applied to burdens and benefits directly distributed by political authorities, such as appointed offices, welfare doles, taxes, and military conscription" (Feinberg, 1973, p. 107). It may have included the "distribution of benefits within clubs and other such private societies" (Miller, 1999, p. 2), but not class differences in the distribution of income or wealth.

Aristotle's organization of the subject matter of justice and the classical concept of justice as desert remained unchanged until the nineteenth century. In the previous century, "the expression 'social justice' was occasionally used to describe the enforcement of rules of just conduct within a given society" (Hayek, 1976, p. 175), but it remained for the Jesuit Luigi Taparelli d'Azeglio to engage in a truly sustained discussion of the concept in 1840 (Burke, 2011, p. 31). Taparelli's conception, however, neither applied to the economy nor departed in any significant way from the classical understanding of Aristotle, St. Thomas, and Kant (Burke, 2011, pp. 38–39).

In *Utilitarianism*, published in 1861, John Stuart Mill was the first to suggest that social and distributive justice are identical and that society might be responsible for the distribution: "Society should treat all equally well who have deserved equally well of it, that is, who have deserved equally well absolutely. This is the highest abstract standard of social and distributive justice" (1861/1979, p. 60). Mill did not depart from the concept of justice as desert, but he added the justification that distribution according to desert produces the highest social utility.

Karl Marx did not say anything about social justice, and he identified justice only as part of bourgeois ideology that he argued would disappear with the end of capitalism. He is famous for the communist slogan, "From each according to his ability, to each according to his need," which appeared in the *Critique of the Gotha Program* published in 1875. In the same letter, he also articulated a lesser-known socialist slogan, "From each according to his ability, to each according to his contribution" (1875/1972). These slogans should be understood as descriptive, not normative, propositions. For Marx, they are not meant to be norms of social or distributive justice but rather factual statements about distribution under successive historical social systems—first socialism and then communism. Despite what Marx meant, the slogans introduced contribution, which will later be understood as a basis of desert, and lead into discussions of the meaning of social justice. In his 1922 book, *The Elements of Social Justice*, L. T. Hobhouse, who was a self-described "liberal socialist," included need and desert as morally equivalent grounds of social justice (Burke, 2011, p. 61).

Mill linked social and distributive justice but only implied that society is ultimately responsible for the distribution of goods in society. Hobhouse argued directly that at least a part of the distributive result can be attributed to society and justly redistributed (Burke, 2011, p. 61). The shift from individual to social responsibility is clearly apparent in Pius XI's 1931 encyclical, *Quadragesimo anno*. As Burke (2011) notes, "Pius took the critical step of expanding the idea of injustice so that it no longer needed to refer to the actions or inactions of an individual, for which that individual would be accountable, but could be applied to an impersonal state of affairs, namely inequality in the distribution of this world's goods, that can occur by accident, without anyone having done anything wrong" (p. 72). Pius also shifted the focus of distribution from political authorities to the economy and introduced equality as the norm of social justice: "With Pius, 'social justice,' and often simple 'justice' by itself, *means* economic equality, and those phenomena that are associated with economic equality" (Burke, 2011, p. 72).

Pius's concept of social justice was widely disseminated as official Catholic social teaching. Franklin Roosevelt quoted Pius in a campaign speech in 1932 and claimed "that he was just as radical as the pope was" (Burke, 2011, p. 75). This is one reason for the association of social justice with the left. Another reason is the dominance of the views of philosopher John Rawls in intellectual circles in the twentieth century. Rawls (1999) argued that income and wealth should be distributed equally unless economic inequalities are "to the greatest benefit of the least advantaged," which is his well-known Difference Principle (p. 266). He also accepted the attribution of injustice to impersonal states of affairs and offered a critique of desert as an acceptable principle of social justice that persuaded many philosophers. Equality became the assumed norm of social justice for progressives and welfare liberals.

Robert Nozick (1974), who was critical of Rawls's *A Theory of Justice* three years earlier, introduced choice as an alternative norm of social justice. He used Marx's formula to create his own slogan, "From each as they choose, to each as they are chosen" (p. 161). Nozick's book spawned an extensive debate (Paul, 1981), but, except for libertarians, most philosophers continue to reject Nozick's theory in favor of some version of egalitarianism, if not Rawls's. Nozick also argued against the desert norm but for individual responsibility.

THE NORMS OF SOCIAL JUSTICE

Despite its association with the left, social justice can be defined by any of the historical norms identified above: desert, equality, and choice. As we have seen, desert has the longest history, although equality has been a significant norm since the nineteenth century. One might argue that choice was the norm for classical liberals, but it is only expressed as an explicit norm in the twentieth century with the emergence of libertarianism. The following critical review of the norms is based on the work of Joel Feinberg (1973). The term *norm* will be used throughout the exposition. Feinberg uses the term *principle*, as do others (Miller, 1999). Terms such as *criterion* and *standard* are possible, but *norm* more clearly conveys the moral force associated with social justice.

Desert is a complex concept with several facets. Feinberg adopts the term *base* to differentiate the different facets. The four bases are merit as virtue and skill, merit as achievement, contribution, and effort. Merit as virtue is the oldest version of desert, going all the way back to Plato, Aristotle, and the Roman philosopher, Ulpian. Virtue might refer to the classical virtues of faith, hope, love, courage, or wisdom. It might also include more contemporary virtues such as generosity and conscientiousness. Basing economic distributions on virtue probably does not hold much appeal in the twenty-first century. There are also the practical problems of deciding upon the "correct" virtues and measuring them in order to make the distributions. Merit as skill is more plausible. In fact, every time we present a resume for employment, we are asking a potential employer to give us a job based at least in part on the skill we have developed in the past to do the current job.

Merit as achievement is a familiar basis of desert. In this case, the focus is not on a person's character traits or skills but on what the person has done. People gain merit through sports contests, such as competing for a medal in the Olympics, or achievement in some other area of human activity, such as winning a Nobel Prize in science or Pulitzer Prize in journalism. We all recognize many kinds of academic achievement, such as getting a good grade on an exam or a degree.

There are two bases of desert that are especially relevant to the workplace. The first one is contribution. Individuals are keenly aware of what they have contributed to a product or service, even if the contribution is not tangible. For example, a person might believe that sales would not be very high without his or her idea for marketing a product. We are also aware of the part we played in producing a tangible product or service: I added a significant part on the assembly line, I developed the annual budget for the company, I sold more shoes than anyone else in the store, I wrote a report, or I developed the curriculum for a college program. Effort is the other basis relevant to the workplace. In this case, effort refers to the time and energy devoted to work. At least one criterion of salary increases or promotion should be how hard one works, and we are resentful, despite contributions, if someone who tries to do as little as possible receives more money or a promotion. Effort, however, is not exclusive to the workplace. Teachers are repeatedly confronted by students who say they should receive a better grade because they tried very hard. When it comes to allowances, parents are likely to hear the same plea from children. There are many places in our daily lives in which effort and contribution are invoked in the distribution of some good, benefit, or reward.

Desert norms are primordial in the popular imagination, but they have been subjected to withering criticism by philosophers. Louis Pojman (2006) has reduced the criticisms to three fundamental problems, one with the criterion, one with epistemology, and one with metaphysics (p. 28).

Criterion: This problem involves the difficulty, and in some cases the impossibility, of determining exactly what the desert base should be. This is evident in the prior discussion of effort and contribution. Pojman (2006) gives the example of individuals cooperating to push a car up a steep hill: "Three people are pushing the car. A is putting in the greatest effort, but B is the most effective, since he is the strongest, while C has made the greatest sacrifice to push the car, leaving his lucrative job for the afternoon in order to help out. How do we determine the relative values of these kinds of acts?" (pp. 28–29). If a reward, or even just praise, is given, should A receive it based on effort, B based on contribution, or C based on virtue? How should the reward or praise be divided? The question of the relative value of skill also arises in merit as skill. Merit as achievement seems to be the clearest, although disputes often arise about criteria, measurement, and judgment by those making the decisions.

Epistemology: The problem is that we don't know how to determine the merit, effort, and contribution of each person in today's cooperative production process that involves many people. Most of the individuals involved are only aware of a small number of other people who participate in the production of even simple products and services. For complex cooperative ventures, such as building a skyscraper, how would we measure each person's merit, effort, and contribution? And even if we could, would it be practical to do it? The desert norms are usable in an agrarian economy in which individuals are responsible for their own plot of land (whatever a man sows that shall he also reap) or in an economy dominated by artisans who make tables and chairs, but they are unusable in our current complicated economy.

Metaphysics: The problem is that desert requires free will. Many philosophers, including John Rawls, hold that our actions are determined by genetic and environmental factors over which we have no control. We lack autonomy. The assumption is that we cannot deserve anything if we are not authors of our selves. Even our effort to make something out of the traits acquired by the genetic and social lottery is determined by prior causes. One response is that at least some of our acts are caused by the self, not external factors. We might also argue that desert does not require free will. We deserve what we get if we act voluntarily; that is, without internal or external coercion. One concern here is that if we don't deserve anything we are not responsible for anything either (Pojman, 2006, pp. 30–31). These prodesert arguments have not persuaded a majority of philosophers, who prefer one of the equality norms that do not entail individual responsibility.

There are two equality norms. The first is equal shares of the economic pie. Individuals are not required to have any particular trait, moral or otherwise, or do anything. The assumption is that they should receive equal shares because they are all equally human. This assumption seems to be intuitively correct in many contexts: we should all have equal protection of the laws, the same number of votes in democratic elections, and equal rights as citizens. In the economic context, distribution according to equal shares is controversial because of the conflicting intuition that individuals should receive what they deserve based on who they are and what they have done. Another problem is that equal shares will result in an unequal distribution of economic goods because people's needs are not equal. Some will receive more, some less than what they need. This suggests the second equality norm.

Need is a more profound equality norm. It represents burdens or deficiencies that differ among individuals. Individuals become equals when their needs are met. Meeting each individual's needs seems like an impossible task. This is the reason that philosophers argue that it is more plausible to meet basic needs for such goods as food, clothing, shelter, and medicine. A major problem, even with this limitation, is that needs are "extremely elastic" and difficult to separate from wishes and desires (Feinberg, 1973, p. 111). Two solutions have been proposed. In an ideal communist society, individuals are allowed to define their own needs. This solution requires economic abundance, which has not occurred historically. Many believe that this condition will never be achieved because human needs are limitless. The other solution is the practice, for the most part, in social democracies: governments use existing standards to define the needs they will meet (Miller, 1991, p. 262). This solution is also controversial because people disagree about the kind and extent of economic goods that the government should provide. Since redistribution through taxation will be required, equality as need and desert norms will conflict: those who are taxed often object to the government's redistributive decisions.

Choice is the final norm for consideration. Libertarian Robert Nozick first introduced this norm, which has not received the same level of attention as the other norms. In this libertarian perspective, owners, managers, and any economic actors who are in a position to make decisions about the distribution of economic resources and benefits are free to decide based on any criteria they choose. This means that an employer might decide to hire only the sexiest applicants. As a practical matter, employers probably would not use sexiness as the sole criterion because they would go broke if employees were sexy but unable to do the job. The employer most likely will try to base hiring decisions on merit. One difficulty with choice as a norm is that it does not have the same intuitive appeal as the desert and equality norms. The norm of choice is also subject to the same criticism directed at the desert norms: choice is determined by the genetic and social lottery. Privileged individuals will end up in positions of authority and make decisions based on their own self-interests. Less-privileged individuals will be left out of the decision-making calculus, and the society will be threatened by wide inequalities of income and wealth. Those who advocate equality norms will find this result morally unacceptable.

IDEOLOGICAL FORMULATIONS OF SOCIAL JUSTICE

Historically, as we have seen, social justice became associated with liberalism in which equality is the ideal, but, in principle, any norm can be the ideal of social justice. Depending on the norm, social justice can be a libertarian, liberal, conservative, socialist, or communist concept. Using Marx's formula, the norms and political ideologies are related in the following way:

Libertarian: From each as they choose, to each as they are chosen.
Liberal: From each as they choose, to each an equal share.
Conservative: From each according to ability, to each according to desert (merit, contribution, effort).
Socialist: From each according to ability, to each according to contribution.
Communist: From each according to ability, to each according to need.

The libertarian formulation is taken from Nozick; the socialist and communist formulations are from Marx. The liberal and conservative formulations are the author's. Contrary to popular opinion, Marx was not opposed to the classical notion of justice. In fact, he thought that in the absence of economic abundance a socialist society would be regulated by contribution, which is a desert norm. Libertarians and liberals share the first part of the formula, from each as they choose, because they belong to the same family. Their common ancestor is classical liberalism, represented by such historical figures as John Locke and Adam Smith. Libertarianism is the twentieth-century child of classical liberalism. What is today called "liberalism" is a reformed version of classical liberalism and sometimes known as modern or welfare liberalism (Ball & Dagger, 2011). Liberals have usually not insisted upon absolute equality; that is, exactly the same share of economic goods for everyone, but they believe that wide disparities in income and wealth can lead to economic instability and stagnation (Stiglitz, 2013). For liberals, equal shares is an ideal toward which we should strive. Liberals also support distribution according to basic needs.

SOCIAL JUSTICE AS AN ESSENTIALLY CONTESTED CONCEPT

Which of the norms of social justice is correct? The majority of philosophers favor equality as the norm and assume that society, not individuals, is responsible for distributive outcomes. Some philosophers, however, have recently begun to reconsider the merits of desert (Olsaretti, 2003). Aside from philosophers, there is significant popular support for the desert norms and individual responsibility. Based on cross-cultural research, moral psychologist Jonathan Haidt (2012) offers an explanation for the popularity of desert norms: our evolved moral intuition is that justice is a matter of "proportionality." "People should get what they deserve, based on what they have done" (p. 169). Our moral intuition is also that individuals should be held responsible for what they have done: "People should reap what they sow. People who work hard should get to keep the fruits of their labor. People who are lazy and irresponsible should suffer the consequences" (p. 169).

W. B. Gallie (1964) says that concepts like social justice are "essentially contested." This means that "there is no one use of any of them which can be set up as its generally accepted and therefore correct or standard use" (p. 157). It is not as if there are no arguments for each of the interpretations or that the endless disputes between adherents are not genuine. Rather, the disputes are "not resolvable by argument of any kind" (Gallie, 1964, p. 158). Social justice meets all of Gallie's conditions of an essentially contested concept: it is "appraisive" (evaluative), complex, open to new interpretations, defended as valuable in different ways, and recognized as disputed (p. 161; Gaus, 2000, p. 29).

Gallie (1964) claims that social justice seems to be involved in only a single rivalry between an "individualist" and a "collectivist" conception (p. 181). This rivalry developed historically. Almost everyone in the West before the nineteenth century supported the individualist conception with its desert norms and assumption of individual responsibility. Since the nineteenth century, the collectivist conception of equality norms and social responsibility has been dominant. The individualist conception focuses on individual transactions, but the collectivist conception focuses on results, de facto states of affairs, or the overall pattern of distribution in society.

Theoretically, these conceptions do not necessarily conflict, but in practice they routinely do. Economic actors may distribute benefits according to any norm they choose. If most of them distribute benefits equally then the overall result in society will be a relatively equal distribution. Individualist and collectivist conceptions do not conflict. In practice, most economic actors distribute benefits according to one or a combination of the desert norms, intentionally or not, in order to ensure the motivation of workers and success in business. The overall result is some degree of social inequality. Individualist and collectivist conceptions do conflict. Liberals who condemn the unequal distribution of income and wealth in society imply that producers act immorally by distributing individual benefits according to desert or choice. This implication seems to be obscured by the assumption that individual decisions about distribution are not morally relevant and society as a whole, not individuals, is responsible for the result. If society is responsible, it is also a collective responsibility to correct the maldistribution through governmental redistribution.

Since it is an essentially contested, abstract concept, social justice is subject to a wide variety of meanings, interpretations, and uses. Rawls calls his theory "justice as fairness" and uses the terms *justice* and *fairness* synonymously, but these terms can be distinguished (Pojman, 2006, p. 9). *Justice* is the application of norms to personal characteristics, actions, or states of affairs, whereas *fairness* is the consistent application of norms to similarly situated individuals or groups. For example, suppose Bill receives a C on an assignment, which he deserves, but Mary does the same quality of work and receives an A. It is not fair that Mary gets an A, but Bill was not treated unjustly. *Equity* is a term that is often used interchangeably with fairness, but it also refers to meeting needs as a condition of equality. Someone in a wheelchair needs a larger door than others in order to have equal access to a movie theater. Treating this person equitably means making a door wide enough to accommodate the wheelchair. When such an accommodation is assumed to be a collective responsibility, it may be considered a matter of social equity or social justice, with need as the norm.

IDEOLOGICAL CONFLICTS IN SOME POLICY AREAS

In the rivalry between the individualist and collectivist conceptions of social justice, we can discern the basic pattern of ideological conflict between liberals and conservatives in arguments about just distributions. Liberals assume the equality norms of equal shares or need, while conservatives assume the desert norms of merit, contribution, or effort. Because these assumptions are not always clearly articulated, it is often difficult to understand exactly why liberals and conservatives find themselves in interminable disagreements. Libertarians advocate the norm of choice, which conflicts with both the liberal and conservative norms, but they believe that the choice of conservative norms is usually necessary to foster a thriving economy. Thus, for many economic issues, it makes sense to group libertarians and conservatives together at the right end of the political spectrum.

The basic pattern of ideological conflict is visible in irresolvable disputes in a number of policy areas. The most fundamental area is income. Assuming an equality norm, liberals argue that everyone should have a good-paying job. Such a job will make it possible to at least meet basic needs and probably some wishes and desires, too. Good-paying jobs mean a higher level of consumer spending, which increases effective demand in the economy. In contrast, conservatives, who assume a desert norm, argue that jobs should be awarded on the basis of educational achievement and ability or contribution to the product or service. Guaranteeing everyone a good-paying job will only decrease motivation to work hard. Disregarding merit, contribution, and effort will also result in ineffective job performance. Businesses will be less successful, and economic growth will slow down.

We see the same conflict between the norms of equality and desert in the area of education. Liberals believe that everyone should have a college degree, which will flatten the social pyramid. Higher education is fundamental to upper mobility. Increasing everyone's knowledge and ability, that is, social capital, will increase everyone's income and contribute to economic growth. On the other hand, conservatives believe that the level of education should be based on merit—ability and other traits like conscientiousness—needed to achieve a degree and upward social mobility. Conservatives do not think it is possible to equalize social capital because there are natural differences in individual ability. A college education will be wasted on many who will not be able to develop the knowledge and skill necessary to acquire the kind of good-paying jobs that liberals want for everyone. Simply having a college degree will not guarantee a high-paying job in a knowledge-based, high-tech economy.

Another area of conflict between the norms of equality and desert is homeownership. Liberals want everyone to be able to own their own home. Homeownership is a part of the American dream. Of course, not everyone can afford to buy a home. Government should make homeownership possible by regulating mortgage interest rates and other qualifications. Conservatives believe that homeownership should be based on achievement of a high-enough mortgage score and traditional qualifying factors. Individuals should not be encouraged to take out a mortgage they cannot afford it in the long run. They risk losing their homes and being saddled with a mortgage debt they cannot repay.

Discrimination in employment is another volatile area of conflict between liberals and conservatives. In a well-publicized case, *Ricci v. DeStefano* (2009), which has been called a "reverse discrimination" case, liberals and conservatives clashed again over the norms of equality and desert. A group of white firefighters charged that the city of New Haven, Connecticut, discriminated against them by discarding the results of a test for promotion in 2003. The white firefighters passed the test at a 50 percent greater rate than blacks. None of the blacks would have been promoted if the city accepted the test results. The city of New Haven argued that promotion on the basis of the test results would have a disparate impact on the minority firefighters. The city also argued that the test results were not scientifically valid.

In a 5–4 decision, the Supreme Court ruled against the city, holding that "fear of litigation alone cannot justify an employer's reliance on race to the detriment of individuals who passed the examination and qualified for promotions." The Court's reasoning aside, a conflict between the norms of equality and desert underlies differences of opinion about how the case should be decided. Liberals believe in the promotion of an equal number of blacks and whites. At least, the promotions should be proportionate to the percentage of whites and blacks in the New Haven community. Conservatives, on the other hand, would promote firefighters, white or black, on the basis of merit; that is, the score achieved on the test.

CONCLUSION

The various norms of social justice emerged historically. Desert norms prevailed in the premodern world. Since the nineteenth century, philosophers have argued for the liberal and libertarian norms of equality and choice, but desert norms continue to be part of the popular imagination. Interpretations of social justice are essentially contested. There is no true or core meaning of the concept. A basic pattern of conflict between liberals and conservatives underlies a host of policy disputes. We have strong feelings about the norms of social justice, which is evident in the heated exchanges between liberals, conservatives, and libertarians. Policy disputes seem to be interminable and irresolvable, and the prospects for consensus are grim.

References

Ball, T. & Dagger, R. (2011). *Political ideologies and the democratic ideal* (8th ed.). Boston, MA: Longman.

Burke, T. P. (2011). *The concept of justice: Is social justice just?* London, England: Bloomsbury.

Feinberg, J. (1973). *Social philosophy.* Englewood Cliffs, NJ: Prentice-Hall.

Gallie, W. B. (1964). *Philosophy and the historical understanding.* London, England: Chatto & Windus.

Gaus, G. F. (2000). *Political concepts and political theories.* Boulder, CO: Westview Press.

Haidt, J. (2012). *The righteous mind: Why good people are divided by politics and religion.* New York: Pantheon Books.

Hayek, F. A. (1976). *Law, legislation and liberty: A new statement of the liberal principles of justice and political economy: Vol. 2. The mirage of social justice.* Chicago, IL: University of Chicago Press.

Marx, K. (1972). Critique of the Gotha program. In R. C. Tucker (Ed.), *The Marx-Engels reader* (pp. 382–98). New York: W. W. Norton. (Original work published 1875.)

Mill, J. S. (1979). *Utilitarianism.* Edited by G. Sher. Indianapolis, IN: Hackett. (Original work published 1861.)

Miller, D. (1991). Justice. In *The Blackwell encyclopaedia of political thought* (pp. 260–63). Oxford, England: Basil Blackwell.

Miller, D. (1999). *Principles of social justice.* Cambridge, MA: Harvard University Press.

Nozick, R. (1974). *Anarchy, state, and utopia.* New York: Basic Books.

Olsaretti, S. (Ed.). (2003). *Desert and justice.* New York: Oxford University Press.

Paul, J. (Ed.). (1981). *Reading Nozick: Essays on anarchy, state, and utopia.* Totowa, NJ: Rowman & Littlefield.

Pojman, L. P. (2006). *Justice.* Upper Saddle River, NJ: Prentice Hall.

Rawls, J. (1999). *A theory of justice* (Rev. ed.). Cambridge, MA: Belnap Press.

Ricci v. DeStefano, 557 U.S. 557. U.S. Supreme Court (2009).

Stiglitz, J. E. (2013). *The price of inequality: How today's divided society endangers our future.* New York: W. W. Norton.

ABLE-ISM

Able-ism is a form of discrimination or prejudice against individuals with disabilities (mental,
emotional, and/or physical). Able-ism maintains
an assumption that people with physical and/or
mental disabilities are not normal individuals. An
able-ism society is said to be one that treats nondisabled individuals as the standard of "normal living," which results in public and private places and
services, education, and social work that are built to
serve "standard, normal" people, thereby inherently
excluding those with various disabilities. Examples
of able-ism include inaccessible public buildings,
inflexible height of tables and counters, unusable
transportation systems, and segregated education.
Examples of ability privilege include the certainty
that theaters, mass transportation, and entertainment venues will provide comfortable and convenient seating arrangements for "normal" people.

Able-ism is an unrecognized form of prejudice
that is common in society but often overlooked
when analyzing why people with disabilities have
difficulty being included. The norm is to act as
though everybody has the same opportunities and
access even when such a belief is known to be false.
Many people conveniently look the other way, often
failing to assist individuals with disabilities because
accommodating the able-bodied seems so simple to
do. The prevailing attitude is that those who need
help should work things out themselves and not
burden the majority of able-bodied persons. Of
course, this treatment and attitude is oppressive to
individuals with disabilities.

People with disabilities are as varied in their backgrounds, interests, goals, and skills as able-bodied
individuals. However, their conditions do outfit
them with different experiences, different expectations, and different preferences; what works for one
person might not work for everyone with the same
disability or for people with other disabilities. People
can better understand individuals with disabilities
by not assuming that feedback from one person with
a disability applies to all people with disabilities. In
this case, one size does not fit all, as the saying goes.
As such, it is proper to allow each person to pursue
his or her own individual preference and choice.

Society needs to learn to accommodate people
with disabilities as a natural response. This includes
building ramps to make people's homes wheelchair
accessible, creating accessibility and comfort in
public places, providing centers inside and outside
of schools that offer suggestions in terms of ability awareness and acting against able-ism, developing its disability literature, hiring disabled teachers,
sponsoring good role models, and including disability content in curricula and school activities.
Of course, assistance should be provided rather
than imposed on individuals.

Sherwood Thompson

Reference

Lawton, S. (2007). *Just ask: Integrating accessibility
throughout design.* Retrieved from http://www.
uiaccess.com/accessucd/analysis.html.

ABOLITIONISM

In the United States, abolitionism is most commonly referenced as a reform movement to abolish
or eradicate the institution of slavery. However, the
term *abolitionism* can also refer to the movement
to abolish the African slave trade in Great Britain,
which prefigured the institutionalized enslavement
of persons of African descent in the United States
(Finkleman, Prince, & Newman, 2008). Like many
large movements, abolitionism was not a singular, unchanging movement, nor did abolitionists
enforce its tenets using uniform methods. Further,
abolitionists themselves cannot be identified as a
monolithic community.

Time Period

Abolitionism dates to Great Britain in the eighteenth century. In the 1700s the abolitionist movement focused on the eradication of the African slave trade in Great Britain (Finkleman, Prince, & Newman, 2008). As many scholars have discussed in their own studies, abolitionism took on various forms from this early period through to the ratification of the Thirteenth Amendment, which legally abolished slavery (Mitchell, 2005). In general, it is important to recognize that abolitionism in the United States focused, in its various instantiations, on the eradication and abolition of the institution of slavery from the 1700s, prior to the American Revolution through the end of the American Civil War, in 1865.

Religion and Morality

Abolitionism is often associated with Christian morality and the practice of promoting the abolition of slavery through moral suasion. For example, the Garrisonians, led by William Lloyd Garrison, espoused moral suasion and the recognition of slavery as a sin as the groundwork for the rhetoric of their abolitionism. Some of the most fervent years of the movement coincided with the religious reform movements related to the Great Awakening during the 1830s and 1840s (Sellman, 2005). Religious reform movements colluded with efforts to eradicate slavery by employing moral suasion as the foremost method for change. Thus, the power and growth of American Protestantism and Evangelicalism engaged a number of Christian Americans in the movement against the enslavement of African Americans based in social reform concerned with the immoral treatment of black persons. For example, the Garrisonians posited slavery as a sin consistently throughout the rhetoric of their abolitionism, often published in Garrison's abolitionist newspaper, *The Liberator*.

The complexity of abolitionism as a movement arises with the clarification that this concern for the immoral treatment of black persons did not translate to an argument that black people should be considered equal to whites, but rather that it was immoral and a sin to keep black people in physical bondage and to perpetuate chattel slavery (Mitchell, 2005). Abolitionism is further complicated by the notion that while Christian religious organizations were often the most visible or recognizable in the movement, supporters of the movement certainly were not monolithic.

American Republicanism

In many places and communities, abolitionism also took on the tenets of American Republicanism, with its supporters investing in the proclamations of the American Revolution and the building of a post-American-Revolution nation founded, according to the language of Jeffersonian government and the philosophy of the French Revolution, in freedom, equality, and equal human rights for mankind. The tenets of freedom so often cited and recited from the Declaration of Independence and the U.S. Constitution were similarly invoked in abolitionism, citing enslaved peoples' right to freedom from bondage in the United States. Not only was this reform movement promulgated vis-à-vis print periodicals and pamphlets, but it was also advanced through making speeches. For example, Frederick Douglass's well-known 1852 speech, "What to the Slave Is the Fourth of July?" forwarded abolitionism by using and signifying Republican rhetoric.

Abolitionism operated in a wide variety of forms, on which volumes have been written, but abolitionism based in Christian morality and abolitionism based in U.S. constitutional rights represent two of the most popular ideological and rhetorical forms of this major reform movement (Sellman, 2005).

Black Abolitionism

The ways that black abolitionists promoted the reform movement are as varied as those used in white abolitionism. Black abolitionism operated by arranging public speeches and circulating pamphlets and newspapers by black individuals. Black abolitionism also invoked Christian morality and American Republicanism. At times black abolitionism intersected with white abolitionism, where a number of black individuals published their writings in Garrison's *Liberator*, or gave speeches to "promiscuous audiences" (Foster, 1993) including and often arranged by white abolitionists. For example, black women such as Frances E. W. Harper, Sojourner Truth, and Maria W. Stewart gave public speeches decrying the institution of slavery to audiences comprised of black and white men and women. Additionally, Harper published antislavery poetry in Garrison's *Liberator* and Frederick Douglass's newspapers.

However, black abolitionism further included radical invectives for reform that indicted the racial superiority often posited by white abolitionists. For example, David Walker's 1829 radical jeremiad, *Appeal to the Coloured Citizens of the World*, traveled throughout the southern United States in the form of an easily transportable pamphlet, enabling a vast number of individuals to read and pass it along (Hinks, 2000). Its call for the end of the institution of slavery blended the rhetoric of Christian morality and that of American Republicanism to form an argument for the immediate abolition of slavery, and to invoke the prophetic threat of the downfall of white communities if the institution continued. This tactic simultaneously emphasized both the moral and political hypocrisy regarding slavery prevalent throughout the United States. Walker's *Appeal* further ensured that the location of the majority of abolitionist work took place in the North, as his radical jeremiad incited negative reactions to the abolitionist cause in the South. Additionally, Frederick Douglass's weekly newspaper *The North Star* (1847–1851), which later became *Frederick Douglass' Paper* (1851–1863), represented some of the foremost (and most-read) black abolitionist writing in the antebellum era. Douglass's paper printed antislavery literature by prominent black authors such as Frances E. W. Harper and Martin Delany.

White Abolitionism

Some of the earliest forms of abolitionism were led by the Quakers, a religious community consistently associated with their peaceful antislavery position. The Quakers also notably supported the eradication of the institution of slavery using gradual methods intended to resolve the problematic relationship between master and slave generated by centuries of enslavement (Mitchell, 2005).

Later, William Lloyd Garrison's radical Christian abolitionism pushed not only for the abolition of slavery but also the upheaval of the sociopolitical order entirely, where society and its interactions would be driven by Christian morality and

an aversion to sin rather than by political government. Garrison, and what became known as Garrisonian abolitionism, published one of the most well-known abolitionist newspapers, *The Liberator* (1831–1865), which supported the abolitionist cause and included antislavery publications by both black and white authors. White abolitionism often perpetuated racial hypocrisies by supporting the eradication of slavery while simultaneously reinforcing ideologies of white racial superiority and paternalism. White women contributed to this component of abolitionism as they pushed to abolish an institution that they argued was an affront to Christian morality and the tenets of nineteenth-century white respectability while also maintaining a sociopolitical distinction between their rights as U.S. citizens and those of African Americans.

Elizabeth Cali

References

Finkelman, P., Prince, C. E., & Newman, R. (2008). Abolitionism. In P. Finkleman (Ed.), *Encyclopedia of African American history, 1619–1895: From the colonial period to the age of Frederick Douglass* (pp. 2–9). New York: Oxford University Press.

Foster, F. S. (1993). *Written by herself: Literary production by African American women, 1746–1892*. Bloomington, IN: Indiana University Press.

Hinks, P. P. (2000). *David Walker's appeal to the coloured citizens of the world*. University Park, PA: Pennsylvania State University Press.

Mitchell, B. E. (2005). *Black abolitionism: A quest for human dignity*. Maryknoll, NY: Orbis Books.

Sellman, J. (2005). Abolitionism in the United States. In K. A. Appiah and H. L. Gates Jr. (Eds.), *Africana: The encyclopedia of the African and African American experience (2nd ed.)* (pp. 8–15). New York: Oxford University Press.

ACADEMIC FREEDOM

Since the early twentieth century, academic freedom—defined as the right of professors to be free from outside interference in their research and teaching—has been a central tenet of higher education in the United States. In the context of academic freedom, "outside interference" generally refers to institutional authorities—such as the state, the board of trustees, or the university administration—that have the power to coerce members of the academic community. Unlike political rights and freedoms that are granted to all citizens, academic freedom is a principle grounded in the aims of higher education generally and in the role of the university faculty in particular. That role is based on professors' production of knowledge and on their search for truth, through unbiased inquiry, in service of the public good. This framework for academic freedom was first made explicit in the landmark 1915 *Declaration of Principles on Academic Freedom and Tenure* published by the American Association of University Professors (AAUP):

> It is highly needful, in the interest of society at large, that what purport to be the conclusions of men trained for, and dedicated to, the quest for truth, shall in fact be the conclusions of such men, and not echoes of the opinions of the lay public, or of the individuals who endow or manage universities. To the degree that professional scholars, in the formation and promulgation of their opinions, are, or by the character of their tenure appear to be, subject to any motive other than their own scientific conscience and a desire for the respect of their fellow experts, to that degree the university teaching profession is corrupted . . . and society at large fails to get from its scholars . . . [the] necessary service which it is the office of the professional scholar to furnish. (pp. 294–95)

The AAUP's *Declaration of Principles* was an important promulgation of academic freedom, providing an influential explanation of this evolving concept that had not yet been officially recognized. The notion of academic freedom, accompanied by scholarly self-governance, gained wider acceptance in ensuing decades, although it failed to protect the academic community from Senator Joseph McCarthy's campaign against communism during the 1950s. In the post-McCarthy era, however, numerous academic institutions officially endorsed the right of professors to be free in their teaching and research. Universities drew upon the work of the AAUP to codify academic freedom as part of their institutions' core principles, often inserting verbatim passages from the 1940 *Statement of Principles*

on Academic Freedom and Tenure into their handbooks (Brown & Kurland, 1993). In conjunction with the growth of tenure in the 1960s and 1970s, academic freedom solidified within the academy.

Historical Roots

The rise of academic freedom in the United States can be traced to several factors. The latter part of the nineteenth century witnessed the rapid expansion of postsecondary education and the development of the modern research university in the United States. During this period, increasing numbers of American college graduates began pursuing graduate studies in Germany—where the model of the research university had first been adopted roughly a half century earlier—and returned home with the goal of developing similar institutions in the United States. As graduate students in Germany, many American scholars became accustomed to academic freedom, or more precisely its German counterpart, *Lehrfreiheit*, defined as "the right of the university professor to freedom of inquiry and to freedom of teaching, the right to study and to report on his findings in an atmosphere of consent" (Tierney & Lechuga, 2005, p. 8). These scholars saw the creation and dissemination of knowledge as central to the purpose of the academy—and to their role in it. In light of this view, scholars came to see academic freedom as a fundamental and necessary right that would protect them from potential repression by the U.S. government as well as by university trustees and administrators.

Challenges to academic freedom have traditionally taken the following form: "[A] professor said something pertaining to his or her academic specialty, someone became upset, and that . . . [professor] was fired" (Tierney & Lechuga, 2005, p. 10). Examples of this kind of incident were frequent, as professors vied for greater autonomy within the academy. The *cause célèbre* for advocates of academic freedom was Edward A. Ross, a professor of sociology at Stanford University from 1893 to 1900. Stanford president David Jordan fired Ross in 1900 at the urging of Jane Stanford, the widow of Stanford's founder and prominent businessman Leland Stanford, because of Ross's public support of labor unions and his opposition to the use of cheap migrant labor. "I must confess I am weary of

Professor Ross," Jane Stanford wrote, "and I think he ought not to be retained at Stanford University" (Washburn, 2008, p. 38). The firing was widely criticized by the academic community and resulted in an exodus of Stanford faculty members who resigned in protest. Ross's case was not an isolated incident. In 1908, Charles William Eliot, Harvard University's president at the time, described the hostile environment toward academic freedom created by "barbarous boards," which he felt "have everything to learn with regard to academic freedom":

> These barbarous boards exercise an arbitrary power of dismissal. They exclude from the teachings of the university unpopular or dangerous subjects. In some states they even treat professors' positions as common political spoils; and all too frequently, in both state and endowed institutions, they fail to treat the members of the teaching staff with that high consideration to which their functions entitle them. (As cited in AAUP, 1915, p. 294)

Thus, demands for policies that would enshrine academic freedom took shape against the backdrop of an authoritarian environment that was common on college campuses during the early twentieth century.

Current Challenges

More recently, debates over freedom in the academy have centered not on the threat of dismissal or censorship of an individual faculty member, but rather on the rapidly changing institutional structure of the university itself. That structure has been significantly shaped by the demands of the marketplace, with administrators seeking to implement changes to the university aimed at increasing productivity and efficiency—often accompanied by rhetoric about the need to lower soaring overhead and tuition costs. This has created new areas of contention that concern the AAUP and other advocates of academic freedom, as well as new questions about the proper scope and boundaries of academics' autonomy. Specifically, these debates have focused on distance education and tenure.

The combination of rising tuition and the ubiquity of the Internet has fueled more than a decade of prophecies about the "coming tsunami" of online

learning in higher education (Durden, 2012). While the ultimate impact of this trend is up for debate, the growth of online education and its integration into traditional colleges and universities is undeniable. According to a 2011 report from the Sloan Consortium, from 2002 to 2010 student enrollment in online courses increased by 10 percent compared to a 1 percent increase in total enrollment in higher education (Allen & Seaman, 2011). The report further indicated that three out of every ten students take an online course during their undergraduate education. This growth has given rise to complicated questions that often pit the interests of university administrators and faculty members against each other, such as: Who owns the intellectual property and materials developed for online courses? Who decides standards, curricula, and pedagogy of online courses? And at the most basic level, is teaching online courses voluntary or mandatory? It is clear that these questions constitute an issue of academic freedom insofar as they concern faculty members' authority and autonomy in their teaching. Yet administrators' motivation to exercise control over these aspects of teaching is not meant to curtail dissent or enforce a particular ideology at the institution, but rather is driven by market forces, the financial stability of the university, and concern for future profits. Whether, and to what extent, policies in this arena constitute a breach of academic freedom is a contested question.

William Bowen, the former president of Princeton University, has recently argued that academic freedom does not confer complete autonomy in teaching, and that invoking academic freedom in response to administrative initiatives to implement online education is misguided. He stated that

> [M]istakenly equating "academic freedom" with unbridled faculty discretion, including control over methods of delivering classroom instruction, is dangerous and even self-defeating. The use of overly sweeping "academic freedom" arguments to block reasonable efforts to innovate puts the core principles of academic freedom at risk. (2012, p. 48)

This perspective does not discount the importance of academic freedom in research and teaching, but it contends that there are limits to the scope of this freedom, particularly with regard to teaching. It has been generally understood, even by the AAUP, that academic freedom does not protect the right of a professor to refuse an assigned location or class time, the right to repeatedly skip classes, or the right to "[refuse] to teach the classes or subject matter assigned" (Nelson, 2010, part 2: 10). Bowen's line of reasoning might be extended to ask: Why should decisions related to the implementation of online education be any different from those relating to location or class time?

The AAUP, on the other hand, has stated that academic freedom as outlined in its 1940 *Statement* should remain unaltered by new educational mediums. While "[accepting] the reality of distance education programs," the AAUP asserts that discretion over it lies with the faculty:

> Faculty members engaged in distance education shall have academic freedom as teachers and researchers in full accordance with the provisions of the 1940 Statement of Principles on Academic Freedom and Tenure, including "freedom in the classroom in discussing their subject" . . . Methods of presentation and course materials are to be under the control of the faculty member assigned to develop and/or teach the distance education course. (AAUP, n.d., para. 6)

Moreover, the AAUP has suggested that instructors' decisions about whether to engage in distance education should ideally "be voluntary, not mandatory" (Euben, 2000, sect. IV: A, para. 5). When that is not possible, the assigning of a distance education course should happen at the department level and follow clearly stated policy, according to the AAUP. By locating decision-making authority within the academic department, the AAUP can respond to the charge that it is exaggerating the scope of academic freedom by noting that class assignments and classroom methods have always fallen under the purview of chairs and academic peers, not administrators.

An additional issue related to academic freedom that has been created by the growth of online education concerns the ownership of online course materials and intellectual property. In general, professors are granted ownership of their work, and thus fall outside the "work-made-for-hire" doctrine that entitles an employer to the copyright of anything created during the course of an employee's work. Several legal decisions during the 1970s and 1980s reinforced an exception to this standard labor policy for academic work, although it is unclear if these precedents are still applicable to contemporary copyright law (Twigg, 2000). The line of thought for an academic exception, however, is fairly straightforward: "If all work belonged to the administration, then its content would also have to be controlled or at least accepted by the administration, which would vitiate any freedom of thought or inquiry" (Springer, 2005, sect. IV: C3a). It would also appear that this line of reasoning would apply to online course material. Yet many universities have adopted policies claiming that the institution, rather than faculty members, owns the intellectual property of online course materials. A study of forty-two public and private Carnegie Doctoral Research Universities documented that in 2005, "a substantial majority of universities claim the intellectual property rights for materials that faculty are given specific assignments to produce (76%), are specifically hired to produce (76%), or are commissioned to produce (67%)" (Kromrey et al., 2005, p. 15). Whether the academic exception to "work-made-for-hire" holds up in the context of distance education is largely an open legal question.

The decline of tenure and the corresponding rise of part-time faculty and adjuncts is another major institutional trend that is redefining higher education. From 1970 to 2009, the ratio of full-time to part-time faculty members at postsecondary institutions went from more than three-to-one in 1970 to nearly one-to-one in 2009 (Snyder & Dillow, 2012). Part of this drastic decline can be explained by the growth of community colleges and the for-profit postsecondary sector, which rely less on full-time faculty. Nevertheless, the declining number of faculty members with tenure or tenure-track appointments working at universities with a tenure system has also been significant. This population has dropped from 62 percent of all faculty members in 1992 to 48 percent in 2009 (Snyder & Dillow, 2012).

It is not difficult to see why this decline poses a concern for advocates of academic freedom. For one, the tenure system is a means of securing professors' autonomy in teaching and research. Those without tenure—especially part-time faculty—are far more vulnerable than their tenured peers. Additionally, the principle of academic freedom provides the conceptual underpinning for a system that, in effect, grants employment until retirement and significantly restrains the university's ability to fire or cut the wages of those with tenure. Furthermore, tenure engenders a distribution of authority within the university by depriving administrators of the usual management tools to shape employee behaviors and practices, thus it helps to foster a system of shared governance in which faculty members are the primary authority in teaching and research (McPherson & Schapiro, 1999).

It may be argued that tenure has always been central to academic freedom; therefore, the view that its decline is an important academic-freedom issue does not suggest any shift in the concept. However, the notion that tenure functions as protection against abuses of power by institutional authorities and is necessary for keeping the profession uncorrupted—which is the position expressed by the AAUP's 1915 *Declaration* and its 1940 *Statement*—does not fully capture the current "attack" on tenure. For one, many of the current arguments against tenure focus on its economic cost. One commonplace argument, which has proved largely empirically unjustified, is that by providing a form of lifetime employment, tenure fosters unproductive workers who lack incentives (McPherson & Schapiro, 1999). A further argument holds that the tenure system creates organizational inefficiency and institutional rigidity, making the traditional postsecondary model unadaptable to market forces and ultimately unsustainable. Whether arguments about tenure's economic cost are correct, they suggest that business-minded ends rather than ideological suppression are at the heart of the challenge to tenure.

Tenure helps protect the professional status of academics, and the increase in adjunct faculty members has supported a bifurcation between two conceptions of academic labor: knowledge producers and knowledge transmitters. As Martin (2011) notes, "a basic distinction used to delineate tenurable from non-tenurable faculty positions is increasingly crafted between knowledge producers and knowledge transmitters—or researchers who teach and teachers who disseminate what others are said to have discovered" (p. 94). It is not simply that part-time faculty members may be more vulnerable to infringement of their academic freedom, but when viewed as "knowledge transmitters," these faculty members are considered traditional labor, for which academic freedom is not necessary or applicable. This bifurcation is an important outgrowth of the restructuring of higher education and converges with online education, since part-time faculty members are more likely to teach online courses than their tenured and tenure-track peers (Allen & Seaman, 2011).

Conclusion

There is no denying that faculty autonomy has been eroding due to powerful shifts within universities. Depending on where one stands, online education and the decline of tenure represent either a new kind of unfreedom that often violates the principle of academic freedom or a means of increasing the efficiency and economic viability of universities without compromising academic freedom. From the former perspective, the threats to faculty members' autonomy and to the integrity of the academy are more pernicious than ever. The combination of economic trends in higher education (including the defunding of public universities and the growth of the for-profit postsecondary sector) and the push toward what some have called the "corporatization of universities" pose a very different challenge to faculty autonomy than dismissals based on arbitrary or ideological confrontations between faculty members and administrators or trustees (Chomsky, 2011). From the latter perspective, academic freedom only protects against dismissal due to the conclusions of one's scholarship or the tenets of one's teachings. This is a different matter entirely than trying to implement policies in order to develop a more sustainable business model. There is, perhaps, a middle ground to be found between these two perspectives.

It should be noted that high-profile cases of faculty dismissals remain an important linchpin of academic freedom. For example, the case of Ward Churchill, whose controversial essay "On the Justice of Roosting Chickens: Reflections on the Consequences of U.S. Imperial Arrogance and Criminality" caused national attention and a University of Colorado investigation, raised concerns of potential violations to his academic freedom (Bousquet, 2008). Yet while cases like Churchill's often attract considerable attention, their impact on faculty autonomy is far less significant than either the decline of tenure or the growth of online education. It is within the context of these shifts that the scope, meaning, and relevance of academic freedom are being redefined.

Amato Nocera
Diana Hess

References
Allen E. & Seaman J. (2011). *Going the distance: Online education in the United States, 2011*. Retrieved from http://sloanconsortium.org/publications/survey/going_distance_2011.
American Association of University Professors. (1915). *1915 Declaration of principles on academic freedom and academic tenure*. Retrieved from http://www.aaup.org/AAUP/pubsres/policydocs/contents/1915.htm.
American Association of University Professors. (2006). *1940 Statement of principles on academic freedom and tenure with 1970 interpretive comments*. Retrieved from http://www.aaup.org/NR/rdonlyres/EBB1B330-33D3-4A51-B534-CEE0C7A90DAB/0/1940StatementofPrinciplesonAcademicFreedomandTenure.pdf.
American Association of University Professors. (n.d.). *Sample intellectual property policy & contract language*. Retrieved from http://www.aaup.org/aaup/issues/de/sampleDE.htm.
Bousquet, M. (2008, July 20). The AAUP and Ward Churchill [web log message]. Retrieved from http://chronicle.com/blogs/brainstorm/the-aaupward-churchill/6144.
Bowen, W. G. (2012, October). The "cost disease" in higher education: Is technology the answer? *The Tanner Lectures*. Retrieved from http://edf.stanford.edu/sites/default/files/Bowen%20lectures%20SU%20102.pdf.
Brown, R. S. & Kurland, J. E. (1993). Academic tenure and academic freedom. In W. W. Van Alstyne (Ed.), *Freedom and tenure in the academy* (pp. 325–55). Durham, NC: Duke University Press.
Chomsky, N. (2011, April). Academic freedom and the corporatization of universities. Lecture conducted from University of Toronto, Scarborough. Retrieved from http://www.chomsky.info/talks/20110406.htm.
Durden, W. G. (2012, June 11). The real tsunami. *Insider Higher Ed*. Retrieved from http://www.insidehighered.com/views/2012/06/11/essay-changes-may-most-threaten-traditional-higher-education.
Euben, D. R. (2000). *Distance learning and intellectual property: Ownership and related faculty rights and responsibilities*. Washington, DC: American Association of University Professors. Retrieved from http://www.aaup.org/AAUP/issues/DE/dl-ip-ownership.htm.
Kromrey, J., Barron, A., Hogarty, K., Hohlfeld, T., Loggie, K., Schullo, S., . . . Sweeney, P. I. (2005, June). *Intellectual property and online courses: Policies at major research universities*. Paper presented at the National Educational Computing Conference, Philadelphia, PA.
Martin, R. (2011). *Under new management: Universities, administrative labor, and the professional turn*. Philadelphia, PA: Temple University Press.
McPherson, M. S. & Schapiro, M. O. (1999). Tenure issues in higher education. *Journal of Economic Perspectives*, *13*(1), 85–98. Retrieved from http://net.educause.edu/ir/library/pdf/ffp9904.pdf.
Nelson, C. (2010, December 21). Defining academic freedom. *Insider Higher Ed*. Retrieved from http://www.insidehighered.com/views/2010/12/21/nelson_on_academic_freedom.
Snyder, T. D. & Dillow, S. A. (2012). *Digest of education statistics: 2011*. Retrieved from National Center for Education Statistics, Institute of Education Sciences, U.S. Department of Education. Retrieved from http://nces.ed.gov/pubsearch/pubsinfo.asp?pubid=2012001.
Springer, A. (2005). *Intellectual property legal issues for faculty and faculty unions*. Washington, DC: American Association of University Professors. Retrieved from http://www.aaup.org/NR/exeres/517C85B6-CC13-4A47-AE3E-5C1763713B02.htm.
Tierney, W. G. & Lechuga, V. M. (2005). Academic freedom in the 21st century. *Thought and Action*, *21*, 7–22. Retrieved from http://hin.nea.org/assets/img/PubThoughtAndAction/TAA_05_02.pdf.
Twigg, C. (2000). *Who owns online courses and course materials? Intellectual property policies for a new learning environment*. New York: Centre for

Academic Transformation, Renesselaer Polytechnic Institute.

Washburn, J. (2008). *University, inc.: The corporate corruption of higher education*. New York: Basic Books.

ACCESS TO EDUCATION

Access to education refers to an individual's right and ability to obtain a quality education throughout life. Here, education refers to both formal schooling and informal learning opportunities beginning with preschool preparation and continuing through K–12 and higher education, also known as postsecondary or tertiary education. Availability and utilization of adult learning and workforce development must also be acknowledged in this definition. A high-quality education is a necessary component of access to education whereby members of a society are not (un)intentionally excluded from learning opportunities that serve to foster more inclusive and just societies.

International Origins

In 1948, the Universal Declaration of Human Rights as put forth by the United Nations stated, "Everyone has the right to an education" (UNESCO, 2011). Thus, light was shed on access to education on the world stage. By 1960, the United Nations Educational, Scientific, and Cultural Organization (UNESCO) commissioned the Convention against Discrimination in Education in an effort to eradicate discrimination and to provide for equity of opportunity within educational realms. UNESCO additionally initiated the 1989 Convention on the Rights of the Child, which delineated that compulsory and free primary education be available to all children. All of these international human rights treaties called for nations to examine educational practices that could exclude or limit individuals' access to education opportunities. Individuals may experience such exclusion or limitation based on actual or perceived cultural differences in any given society. Furthermore, these differences are exacerbated by the fact that formalized schooling is a construct of the social and political environment of the mid-to-late nineteenth century (Merton, 1968). The advent of the digital revolution during the early to mid-1980s ushered in an unprecedented age of technology. However, the schooling system remains largely unchanged, and advocates point to the ineffectiveness of this unchanged system as a stumbling block to accessing learning.

Geography as Manifestation of Exclusion

The manner in which individuals are excluded from proper access to education manifest themselves in a variety of ways dictated by the confines of the society in which an individual exists. In particular, geographic location influences access to education on a variety of levels. Social science theorists note that access to education is severely impaired in economically, politically, and/or socially developing countries where events outside of an individual's control such as armed conflict, famine, or socio-political oppression constrict access to education (UNESCO, 2012). Geographic location also contributes to possible exclusion caused by isolation in both rural, remote areas and urban settings. Even a location's propensity for natural disasters such as earthquakes, flooding, drought, and more can contribute to an entire society's disruption of access to education.

Demography as Manifestation of Exclusion

A myriad of demographics, such as socioeconomic status (SES), social background, gender, as well as political and/or religious affiliations also affects an individual's access to education. While social scientists disagree on whether societies are becoming more open to class mobility with the advent of the digital revolution and economy, there is consensus around the concept that educational systems are key in either the promotion or impediment of social mobility (Marks, 2005). Low SES in conjunction with other related socio-cultural factors can totally obliterate access to education.

For instance, numerous scholars point to how one's national origin and ethnic background are determinant factors in accessing education. In particular, a society's construct of minority racial background and identity can proscribe educational opportunity. Additionally, an individual's family background plays a role in accessing education. The value placed on obtaining a formalized degree as well as a family's physical ability to initially and continually provide the resources necessary to access education become crucial. The intersectionality of demographics is also apparent when gender is inserted into equations of exclusion. According to the UNESCO Institute for Statistics (2012), two-thirds of the world's countries exhibit a gender gap that privilege patriarchal power structures, thereby excluding girls and women, especially by the secondary level, from obtaining formal and informal education opportunities. Lastly, ascribed demographic characteristics such as political or religious affiliations of individuals can affect their access to education.

Educational Quality

Critical research from the educational field identifies issues with the varying levels of the quality of education provided to learners. Teacher (mis-) conceptions of students influence their pedagogical practices and, in turn, their students' access to meaningful learning (Apple, Au, & Gandin, 2009). In particular, teachers' notions regarding exceptionalities can narrow curriculum and classroom practices that would otherwise create engaging and stimulating learning experiences. Exceptionalities can run the gamut from students with severe and profound mental and/or physical disabilities to those students who are high achievers, gifted, and/or talented (MacFarlane & Stambaugh, 2009). An educator can also fail to recognize students with twice-exceptionalities from either end of this continuum, therefore inhibiting learning. Additional barriers arise when a student experiences education not in his/her preferred language or learning preference. Appropriate materials and curriculum should be provided and differentiated to ensure a high level of educational quality. Lastly, the climate of a school itself can disrupt a student's educational experience. UNESCO (2012) cites violence, bullying, and other forms of discrimination as detrimental to a child's ability to learn when personal safety is threatened and/or violated.

Addressing Exclusion in Education

As millions of the world's children, youths, and adults continue to experience exclusion from education, numerous independent scholars research access to education at varying levels from local to global. UNESCO is the primary international organization charged by the United Nations to address exclusion in education on a global scale. However, the ability to access education is also studied by sociologists, historians, psychologists, economists, political scientists, pedagogues, and other innumerable disciplines as a primary indicator of the social equity of a given region. Therefore, many local governmental and nonprofit agencies concerned with human rights and social justice have access to lifelong educational services as at least one component of their mission. Thus, while lack of access to education is a pervasive crisis worldwide, efforts to improve individuals' access to both formal and informal learning opportunities continue on a centralized to international scale.

Leah Katherine Saal
Desiree R. Lindbom-Cho

References

Apple, M. W., Au, W., & Gandin, L. A. (Eds.). (2009). *The Routledge international handbook of critical education*. New York: Routledge.

MacFarlane, B. & Stambaugh, T. (Eds.). (2009). *Leading change in gifted education: The festschrift of Dr. Joyce VanTassel-Baska*. Waco, TX: Prufrock Press.

Marks, G. N. (2005). Cross-national differences and accounting for social class inequalities in education. *International Sociology, 20*(4), 483–505.

Merton, R. K. (1968). *Social theory and social structure*. New York: The Free Press.

UNESCO. (2011). *UNESCO and education: "Everyone has the right to education."* Retrieved from http://unesdoc.unesco.org/images/0021/002127/212715e.pdf.

UNESCO. (2012). *Addressing exclusion in education: A guide to assessing education systems towards more inclusive and just societies*. Retrieved from unesdoc.unesco.org/images/0021/002170/217073e.pdf.

ACCESSIBILITY

The Challenges of Accessibility: Issues of Diversity and Social Justice

The legal definition of accessibility refers to a site, facility, work environment, service, or program that is easy to approach, enter, operate, participate in, and/or use safely and with dignity by a person with a disability. A person with a disability is hereafter defined as an individual with a physical or mental impairment that substantially limits the function of an individual in one or more facets of life. This definition stands either in having a formal record of impairment or being regarded as having said impairment. People with disabilities are entitled to auxiliary aids and services that may include any of the following: qualified interpreters or accommodations for those with hearing disabilities, qualified readers for the visually impaired, acquisition or modification of devices, or other similar services or actions that level the playing field. If an organization meets all of these requirements, the institution can legally be considered accessible (Americans with Disabilities Act; ADA, 1990). People with disabilities face significant challenges in day-to-day life that accessibility can help address. However, accessibility must be tailored to individuals in order to address needs without patronizing the population.

The Components of Accessibility

PHYSICAL SPACE The most common understanding of the term *accessibility* relates to physical space, allowing comfortable entry, passage, and exit for persons with disabilities. Accessibility can be profoundly impacted by physical access to a building. ADA guidelines dictate a variety of architectural requirements required to be cleared by the federal government as a public building. Common regulations for accessible routes include walking surface dimensions, doors and gateways, ramps, elevators, and platform lifts.

These regulations typically address the needs of those with physical disabilities. As these are federally mandated in most public facilities, physical space needs are typically addressed. However, there are loopholes in the legal definition that allow older buildings to continue operating; for example, if a building was designed before the law and never renovated, there are exceptions to the legal expectations of accessibility. Furthermore, if the building is labeled historic at the local level or above, accessible routes may be limited (ADA, 1990, § 4.1.7).

ACCOMMODATIONS To be ADA compliant, an institution must offer feasible alternative means of access for persons with disabilities through auxiliary aids and services. These resources are offered to prevent persons with disabilities from being excluded from the job or service that the public facility provides. Examples of auxiliary aids and services include but are not limited to sign language interpreters for those with hearing disabilities, qualified readers for the visually impaired, assistants for individuals with motor impairments, and assistive technology to accommodate specific challenges faced by these individuals. These accommodations are meant to promote effective communication, remove barriers, and increase access for all populations.

However, if a particular auxiliary aid or service would result in a "fundamental alteration in the nature of the goods, services, facilities, privileges, advantages or accommodations" or introduce an unfair burden on the facility, the facility is required to present their own alternative accommodations (ADA, 1990, § 6.303). This would ensure that the person with a disability was included and involved to the maximum extent possible.

INDIVIDUAL NEEDS The spirit of accessibility extends beyond physical considerations. A facility must make accommodations for people at an individual level. The degree of functioning varies between persons with disabilities, so an organization must be dedicated to addressing every instance to the best of their ability. There are several types of disabilities that an organization must commit to accommodating: physical, mental, learning, and beyond.

The degree of functioning for any of these disabilities may vary in an individual. For example, certain disabilities may be demanding disorders, such as organic brain syndrome, or less inhibiting to function, such as dyslexia. As such, accommodations must necessarily vary in order to produce an effective result. The issues many face each day may be compounded by disabilities, such as writing notes, speaking on the phone, or operating machinery. But not all individuals face the same obstacles, and it is important for an organization to discern these barriers to inclusion and productivity. For a list of possible resources to address these regulations, the U.S. Department of Labor's Office of Disability Employment Policy has created a Searchable Online Accommodation Resource (ODEP, 2014) complete with text and electronic primers for work and educational settings.

The Challenges of Accessibility: Diversity and Social Justice

There are rules and regulations set forth by the federal government to protect accessibility for persons of all backgrounds. However, while these requirements address concerns by those with disabilities, they only remedy these obstacles if the legal definition is followed both in the letter and spirit of the law. Like most challenges of diversity, addressing disability concerns takes considerable effort and attention, especially as most people do not have these impairments. The unique challenge of being unable to hear an instructor or read the chapters necessary to pass a class rarely weighs upon an able-bodied student's mind. However, it is a reality that some (but not nearly all) persons with disabilities must face.

In essence, one major challenge is that not all accessibility solutions affect every individual with a disability, even when grouped similarly. For example, members with a physical disability differ, including individuals with hearing loss, visual impairments, or motor problems. The barriers facing a person with obsessive-compulsive disorder will be different from those experienced by an individual with bipolar disorder, even though both are categorized as mental health impairments. While accessibility in the legal sense accommodates these individuals adequately, the responsibility of seriously pursuing the ideal falls to the institution; after a certain point, it's up to the organization to decide how accessible it wants to be.

MARGINALIZATION Organizations typically consist of majority nondisabled members, and, unfortunately, evidence suggests that individuals develop prejudices against disabled members as early as childhood (Anderson, 1988). Barriers to accessibility likely extend beyond physical considerations; they are also social in nature. Prejudicial treatment in peers make persons with disabilities feel unwanted, feeling they are unacceptable to society (Weeber, 1999); meanwhile, research finds they are typically avoided or socially ostracized, defined as ignored and excluded (Williams, 1997), by able-bodied peers, who act as though their symptoms are communicable (Hebl & Kleck, 2000; Schaller & Neuberg, 2012; Schaller & Park, 2011). The

perception of persons with mental disabilities is considerably more negative than physical counterparts (Gouvier, Sytsma-Jordan, & Mayville, 2003). A typical person without a disability perceives less about mental relative to physical disabilities, and they may view others with them as unpredictable or even dangerous, hindering progress toward accessibility. A simple way to avoid these misunderstandings is through education and discussion with parents about various disabilities from a young age onward (Sue, 2010); however, this is not typically advocated until far later, through diversity-related initiatives or interventions (Whitney & Kite, 2010).

ABLE-ISM Ultimately, able-ism, defined as prejudice against persons with disabilities, is linked to another challenge of accessibility: fighting discrimination. Biases in peers or superiors may limit the career choices of persons with disabilities who are subject to considerable hiring discrimination (Ren, Paetzold, & Colella, 2008; Wang, Barron, & Hebl, 2010). Accessibility problems may also be exacerbated if the stereotype content of a person with a disability conflicts with the setting. For example, these groups have considerable difficulty with accessibility in upper-scale venues. As this population is not typically stereotyped as competent (Fiske et al., 2002), its members are not often considered for privileges allotted to prosperous, able-bodied individuals. Because high-end infrastructure is typically marketed to the able-bodied, it can be difficult to find accommodations in privileged settings. For example, skyboxes in stadiums denote special privilege and are often inaccessible to persons with disabilities (Jones, Dovidio, & Vietze, 2013); likewise, it can be difficult to imagine finding a dignified way to claim courtside seats in a wheelchair. This counters both the ADA's aim and the inclusive nature of accessibility, preventing them from meaningfully pursuing their goals.

However, an equally prevalent obstacle for persons with disabilities is overzealous helping. Juni and Roth (1981) found that confederates pretending to be disabled were helped significantly more than nonhandicapped confederates in helping tasks. While this initially seems positive, over-helping has become a struggle that disabled participants must contend with: being infantilized, perceived as incompetent, or always in need of help. This has a discernable effect on cognition; disabled students primed with their disability status and high in stigma-consciousness activated less autonomy-related thoughts. This suggests that feelings of low autonomy characterize the experience of a person with disabilities (Wang & Dovidio, 2011). In reality, these individuals are quite adept at navigating around their disabilities in life without aid in combination with accessible options. If they need help, they will ask for it.

Conclusion

Not being accommodating hinders the spirit of accessibility, but too much help can belittle citizens with disabilities. Like other challenges of diversity, accessibility must find balance between empowering the individual and not patronizing them. Though it may prove difficult to provide an accessible environment for individuals of all disabilities, it is a goal worth pursuing. Accessibility is much broader than a physical location. Each of these disabilities must be assessed according to the person's needs so that he or she can have full access to a situation, physical and social. Institutions must be open to providing necessary accommodations according to law and participating in the inclusion of this often-stigmatized and ostracized group. Preserving autonomy by asking and not forcing help can open the necessary dialogue between able individuals and individuals with disabilities to promote understanding and progress.

Thomas P. Tibbett
Adrienne R. Carter-Sowell
Donna Williams

References

Americans with Disabilities Act of 1990 (ADA), Pub. L. No. 101–336, 104 Stat. 328 (1990).

Anderson, P. M. (1988). American humor, handicapism, and censorship. *Journal of Reading, Writing, & Learning Disabilities International, 4*(2), 79–87.

Fiske, S. T., Cuddy, A. J. C., Glick, P., & Xu, J. (2002). A model of (often mixed) stereotype content: Competence and warmth respectively follow from perceived status and competition. *Journal of Personality and Social Psychology, 82*(6), 878–902.

Gouvier, W. D., Sytsma-Jordan, S., & Mayville, S. (2003). Patterns of discrimination in hiring job applicants with disabilities: The role of disability type, job complexity, and public contact. *Rehabilitation Psychology, 48*(3), 175–81.

Hebl, M. R. & Kleck, R. E. (2000). *The social consequences of physical disability* (pp. 419–39). New York: Guilford Press.

Jones, J. M., Dovidio, J. F., & Vietze, D. L. (2013). *The psychology of diversity: Beyond prejudice and discrimination.* Hoboken, NJ: Wiley-Blackwell.

Juni, S. & Roth, M. M. (1981). Sexism and handicapism in interpersonal helping. *Journal of Social Psychology, 115*(2), 175–81.

Office of Disability Employment Policy (ODEP). (2014). *Searchable online accommodation resource* (SOAR). Retrieved from http://askjan.org/soar/index.htm.

Ren, L. R., Paetzold, R. L., & Colella, A. (2008). A meta-analysis of experimental studies on the effects of disability on human resource judgments. *Human Resource Management Review, 18*(3), 191–203.

Schaller, M. & Neuberg, S. L. (2012). Beyond prejudice to prejudices. *Behavioral and Brain Sciences, 35*(6), 445–46.

Schaller, M. & Park, J. H. (2011). The behavioral immune system (and why it matters). *Current Directions in Psychological Science, 20*(2), 99–103.

Sue, D. W. (2010). *Microaggressions in everyday life: Race, gender, and sexual orientation.* Hoboken, NJ: John Wiley & Sons.

Wang, K., Barron, L. G., & Hebl, M. R. (2010). Making those who cannot see look best: Effects of visual resume formatting on ratings of job applicants with blindness. *Rehabilitation Psychology, 55*(1), 68–73.

Wang, K. & Dovidio, J. F. (2011). Disability and autonomy: Priming alternative identities. *Rehabilitation Psychology, 56*(2), 123–27.

Weeber, J. E. (1999). What could I know of racism? *Journal of Counseling and Development, 77*(1), 21–23.

Whitley, B. E. & Kite, M. E. (2010). *The psychology of prejudice and discrimination.* Belmont, CA: Wadsworth.

Williams, K. D. (1997). *Social ostracism.* In R. M. Kowalski (Ed.), *Aversive impersonal behaviors* (pp. 133–70). New York: Plenum Press.

ACCOMMODATION

Accommodation in Education

Accommodation is an agreement among groups of people to work together despite other attending difficulties or disagreements. Historically, in the United States, accommodation served as a guiding principle in early educational reform, particularly in the South. While accommodation creates the perception of unity, it can mask the interaction of extreme philosophical differences within groups, and even within an individual—which was often the case in post-Reconstruction America. In education, it led to school superintendents who worked to improve schools for all students—but in separate systems.

Booker T. Washington (1856–1915) was the man most identified with industrial schooling and Negro accommodationism. Washington's rise to fame began in 1881 with his appointment as head of an institutional experiment in black self-education in Alabama, the Tuskegee Institute, and grew following his momentous "Atlanta Compromise" address at the Cotton States and International Exposition and with the death of Fredrick Douglass, both in 1895. Washington quickly became the most prominent black figure in America and remained so until his death in 1915.

Washington believed that the future for black people depended upon their value as laborers rather than their desire for civil rights. In that sense, Washington embodied the industrial schooling philosophy of Negro submission. He believed that African Americans should fashion a coalition with whites and make themselves an indispensable element of prosperity for those who held power not only in the South but across the entire nation. In his address, he advised against blacks joining labor unions, instead encouraging them to become the most dependable, reliable, and economically profitable labor source in America (Spivey, 1986, p. 3):

> The wisest among my race understand that the agitation of questions of social equality is the extremest folly, and that progress in the enjoyment of all the privileges that will come to us must be the result of severe and constant struggle rather than of artificial forcing. No race that has anything to contribute to the markets of the world is long in any degree ostracized. It is important and right that all privileges of the law be ours, but it is vastly more important that we be prepared for the exercise of these privileges. The opportunity to earn a dollar in a factory just now is worth infinitely more than the opportunity to spend a dollar in an opera-house. (Harlan, 1974, p. 586)

Washington's ten-minute address, the Atlanta Compromise, called for patience, accommodation, and self-help. He de-emphasized equal political rights for blacks in favor of vocational education as the best avenue for African American advancement. "In all things that are purely social," Washington said, "we can be as separate as the fingers, yet one as the hand in all things essential to mutual progress" (Harlan, 1974, p. 585). He argued that African Americans should accommodate themselves to racial prejudice and concentrate on economic self-improvement. In exchange for blacks remaining peaceful and separate from whites socially, Washington said that whites should help and encourage blacks to exercise the privileges of the law. His critics saw this as a capitulation to segregation. W. E. B. Du Bois rejected Washington's ideas in *The Souls of Black Folk* (1903), writing, "Mr. Washington represents in Negro thought the old attitude of adjustment and submission. . . . [His] program practically accepts the alleged inferiority of the Negro races" (Tischauser, 2012, p. 176).

In some ways, the very idea of public schooling was antithetical to the Southern political economy with its sharp social divisions and view of education as a private matter. However, the emancipation of blacks and the following Reconstruction seemed to spur a great educational awakening in the South, one focused on creating an adequate system of education for white children while starving schools for blacks (Tyack & Hansot, 1982).

Among white Southerners, the two dominant approaches to the education of blacks at the turn of the twentieth century were racial exclusion—the abandonment of black instruction altogether—and racial accommodation—maintaining white superiority while instructing blacks in order to mitigate the negative effects of ignorance.

The accommodationist approach was bolstered by a belief in scientific racism, which had gained credence during the 1880s and 1890s, and provided common ground with Northern philanthropists whose money financed the work of the influential Southern Education Board and General Education Board (Leloudis, 1996, pp. 177–82).

The most progressive Southern white educators, who adopted the accommodationist perspective, tended to develop school systems driven by a set of social politics that were at once progressive and paternalistic, concerned but condescending (Waller, 1995). Such politics blurred the line between religious motivations to help the least of these among us and a tacit acceptance of white supremacy as a matter of science. The resulting politics were a confused, yet comfortable, fit for the white Democratic majority, which valued warm personal relationships with individual blacks while embracing Washington's notion of separate societies.

While Southern progressive educators differed from their Northern counterparts, writers such as Dewey Grantham (1983) in *Southern Progressivism* remarked that "it was not altogether clear how [Southern] progressivism paralleled or differed from contemporary reform in other sections" (pp. 246–47). While the South shared the national reform ethos with dozens of educators launching campaigns for public education, its "distinctive institutions, one-party politics, and perennial concern with the 'race question' no doubt gave a special color to its social reform" (pp. 246–47).

Over the decades, the South remained a great exception to the educational development seen in the northern and central United States. Widespread illiteracy, low school attendance rates, tuition-based schools, the South's conservative Protestantism, its tortured racial history, and its peculiar economic structure all contributed to a sharp perceptual divide between Southern schools and others across the country (Tyack & Hansot, 1982). In the 1890s the typical Kentucky schoolhouse had one room, about forty pupils, and one teacher whose general fitness for duty varied widely as moral concerns over some teachers' gambling, drunkenness, philandering, and thievery stood beside concerns over teacher competence (Tapp & Klotter, 1977, p. 197).

As progressive ideas slowly gained purchase in the South, it was local superintendents who exerted the most influence on the public school districts through the implementation of ideas acquired in their association meetings (Tyack & Hansot, 1982, p. 113). The most progressive white school superintendents embraced Washington's accommodationist views and set to work improving conditions for African American students while harboring an attitude of polite white supremacy. The long career (1886–1928) of Superintendent Massillon Alexander Cassidy in Lexington, Kentucky, provides a useful illustration.

Cassidy was directly involved with the Southern and General Education Boards and exemplified the transition of public school leadership in the South from noneducators who held religious ideologies to professional educators who sought to improve the schools' efficiency through expertise and scientific management. They saw themselves as the teachers and guardians of subordinate African Americans in whom they would cultivate "some measure of collaboration and consent" (Leloudis, 1996, p. 179; see also Cremin, 1961; Tyack & Hansot, 1982). He cooperated with black leaders; improved black schools; provided teacher training and innovative programs for students; created a black teacher association; conducted periodic black teacher institutes; and increased professionalism, policy development, and teacher testing all while preaching the gospel of literacy and expanding educational opportunity to an increasing number of children. Under his watch, the schools in Lexington became early adopters of progressive reforms and grew to enjoy a national reputation for quality (Day & DeVries, 2012, pp. 107–8).

In a 1919 study of the Lexington schools, the U.S. Department of the Interior, Bureau of Education, was surprised at every turn to see what had been accomplished in laying the foundations of a progressive school system. It was particularly struck by the fact that Lexington, in contrast to many cities of the South, had made no discrimination in its school facilities between whites and Negroes. The facilities included: open-air schools; the penny lunch; community center schools with a swimming pool, showers, and auditoriums; manual training and domestic economy in the fifth and sixth grades of all schools; rest rooms for the anemic and poorly nourished children; opportunity classes in some schools for irregular children; a junior high school organization throughout; kindergarten in all white schools and in some of the Negro schools; laundries in the basements of schools for use by both children and parents; moving picture apparatus in some schools; the opening of the buildings to the use of citizens; and, for the most part, clean and well-kept buildings were some of the things that belonged to the progressive school systems and that the school authorities of Lexington had secured in the face of a very meager income. Thus again, the statement is vindicated that vision and good management go far toward compensating for a thin purse (Day & DeVries, 2012, p. 115).

But sustained efforts at improving educational opportunity tended to mask the underlying racial attitudes that would reveal themselves from time to time in white gatherings. In 1906, Cassidy delivered the state address on educational progress in Kentucky at the meeting of the Southern Education Association in Montgomery, Alabama. In his speech, Cassidy argued for federal assistance in advancing the educational opportunities for blacks, saying:

> Ignorant and poverty-stricken, the Negro was made a citizen, by no fault of ours, and the federal government should aid us, who are doing our best, in making him a good citizen. . . . Now I maintain that the Negro should be educated. It is right and proper that he should have those advantages. . . . What we need is intelligent men to administer the Negro schools, just as the white schools are administered; and until the Negroes have been educated up to that point, they should by no means have the supervision of their own education. (Day & DeVries, 2012, p. 116)

Cassidy's abiding attachments to the Confederacy and its idealized, genteel Southern code of conduct led to his banning a history text that he believed mischaracterized the actions of Confederate brigadier general John Hunt Morgan and his endorsement of the controversial film *Birth of a Nation* (1915). He praised the film for its educational qualities, while the Colored Ministers Alliance and the Women's Christian Temperance Union protested against the film that they believed "glorified the Lost Cause and the Ku Klux Klan, condemned Reconstruction, and demonized and disparaged blacks at every turn" (Morelock, 2008, pp. 154–56; Marshall, 2010, pp. 170–71).

These apparent philosophical conflicts of accommodationism fall into place once we see progressive school superintendents, like Cassidy, as public officials who necessarily had to work closely with the local constituency to achieve their goals; as change agents who used the bully pulpit to extol the virtues of literacy and a proper education; as Christians in the Social Gospel tradition who saw a duty to the least of these among us; and as superintendents who used a sense of Southern gentility to attract more citizens to the enterprise. In Lexington, under Jim Crow, Cassidy's Southern sympathies and attendant racial attitudes put him in good standing with the state's dominant political forces. According to Yale historian David Blight, in Kentucky, sentiment won over ideology as "reconciliation joined arms with white supremacy in Civil War memory" (Blight, 2001, p. 397).

Justified by the twin notions of *equality of educational opportunity* and *meritocracy*, and confident that professional educators were best suited to devise solutions to social problems, this new breed of progressive educator joined with the business community to declare that a modest amount of schooling would prepare all for a life of equality, not by restructuring society, but by making each individual better (Tyack & Hansot, 1982, pp. 105–12).

Richard Day

References

Blight, D. W. (2001). Race and reunion: The Civil War in American memory. Cambridge: Harvard University Press.

Coleman, J. W. (1968). *Lexington during the Civil War*. Lexington, KY: The Henry Clay Press.

Cremin, L. A. (1961). *The transformation of the school: Progressivism in American education 1876–1957*. New York: Knopf.

Day, R. E. & DeVries, L. N. (2012). A Southern progressive: M. A. Cassidy and the Lexington schools, 1886–1928. *American Education History Journal*, 39(1), 107–25.

Du Bois, W. E. B. (1903). *The souls of black folk*. New York: Oxford University Press.

Grantham, D. W. (1983). *Southern progressivism: The reconciliation of progress and tradition.* Knoxville: University of Tennessee Press.

Harlan, L. R. (Ed.). (1974). *The Booker T. Washington papers* (Vol. 3). Urbana: University of Illinois Press.

Kelley, V. D. (1927). *A history of the public school system of Lexington, Kentucky.* Lexington, KY: University of Kentucky Press.

Kerr, J. C. (1922). Massillon Alexander Cassidy. *History of Kentucky* (Vol. 4). Chicago, IL: American Historical Society.

Knight, G. C. (1935). *James Lane Allen and the genteel tradition.* Chapel Hill: University of North Carolina Press.

Leloudis, J. (1996). *Schooling in the new south.* Chapel Hill: University of North Carolina Press.

Marshall, A. E. (2010). *Creating a confederate Kentucky: The lost cause and Civil War memory in a border state.* Chapel Hill: University of North Carolina Press.

Morelock, K. T. (2008). *Taking the town: Collegiate and community culture in the bluegrass, 1880–1917.* Lexington, KY: University Press of Kentucky.

Spivey, D. (1986). *The politics of miseducation: The Booker Washington Institute of Liberia, 1929–1984.* Lexington, KY: University Press of Kentucky.

Tapp, H., & Klotter, J. (1977). *Kentucky: Decades of discord, 1865–1900.* Frankfort, KY: Kentucky Historical Society.

Tischauser, L. V. (2012). *Jim Crow laws.* Santa Barbara: Greenwood.

Tyack, D. & Hansot, E. (1982). *Managers of virtue: Public school leadership in America, 1820–1980.* New York: Basic Books.

Wall, M. J. (2010). *How Kentucky became southern: A tale of outlaws, horse thieves, gamblers and breeders.* Lexington, KY: University Press of Kentucky.

Waller, G. A. (1995). *Main street amusements: Movies and commercial entertainment in a southern city, 1896–1930.* Washington: Smithsonian Institution Press.

ACCULTURATION

The concept of acculturation generally refers to the process by which outsiders—both ethnic groups as a whole and individual members of those groups—adapt to the mainstream culture and structure of a society. That mainstream is sometimes labeled the common, dominant, or hegemonic culture. The adapting groups or individuals may be newcomers (for example, immigrants or refugees) or internally marginalized or subordinate groups (usually racial, ethnic, and religious groups that are either not part of the statistical majority or are considered low in a nation's social, economic, or political structure).

While this is the basic concept, there are many theories and interpretations of acculturation. According to Richard Harris (2013), the term was introduced in 1880 by explorer and ethnologist J. W. Powell. Focusing his attention on Native Americans who were adopting such aspects of Anglo-American culture as language and clothing, Powell defined acculturation as psychological changes that resulted from the process of engaging in cross-cultural imitation.

In 1936, anthropologists Robert Redfield, Ralph Linton, and Melville Herskovits weighed in with their reformulation of the concept. According to them, acculturation should be construed as the process of change that occurs when cultures come into continuous contact. They posited the idea that acculturation might cause changes in both groups, not just one of them.

In recent years, however, the prevailing use of the word has been to describe acculturation as essentially a one-directional process. They (newcomers and outsiders) adapt to Us (the mainstream). They, for the most part, should give up much of what They have been and try to become more like Us, in some cases dissolving and disappearing into Us. Moreover, according to this traditional view of acculturation, throughout this process We and our culture remain basically unchanged.

In practice, however, such acculturation of dissolving and disappearing into Us has been a limited option for many. This is particularly true for people of color, meaning those who do not share a nation's dominant ethnoracial identity or have been subordinated in a nation's social, economic, and political structure.

The Berry Paradigm

Probably the most widely cited framework for analyzing acculturation is the model proposed by John W. Berry (2009). Berry posits that individuals from different ethnocultural groups are likely to fall into one of four general categories as their primary way of dealing with the challenge of acculturation.

1. *Assimilation*: People seek constant interaction with the mainstream culture while abandoning or making little effort to preserve their own ethnocultural identity. This process sometimes occurs in response to societal pressures to surrender their heritage culture and identity.
2. *Separation*: People emphasize the preservation of their ethnocultural identities and practices while also avoiding interaction with the mainstream culture. Sometimes this separation is forced upon the ethnic group by societal forces, such as legal or de facto segregation.
3. *Integration*: People attempt to maintain their ethnocultural identities while simultaneously becoming integral to mainstream society. Sometimes this leads to the formation of bicultural or multicultural identities.
4. *Marginalization*: People both lose their ethnocultural moorings and also fail to integrate or show little interest in integrating effectively into mainstream society. Sometimes this occurs because of such societal forces as discrimination and exclusion.

While Berry's formulation has been subject to modification and critique over the years (Ward & Kus, 2012), it remains the touchstone for most discussions of acculturation. However, even Berry's critics and most other acculturation theorists continue to operate basically from the premise of one-directional acculturation.

Multiculturation
In contrast to the traditional one-directional acculturation framework, competing interpretive frameworks have emerged. For example, there is the concept of multiculturation (Cortés, 2013), which combines the words *multiple* and *acculturation*. In its most concise iteration, *multiculturation* simply means "multiple acculturation." Rather than treating acculturation as a one-way street, it posits that acculturation may occur continuously in multiple directions. Within multiculturation, there are five major dimensions: individual, group, intragroup, intergroup, and societal.

1. *Individual Acculturation*: This dimension of multiculturation follows traditional acculturation theory. For example, individuals might

fall into any of Berry's four general acculturation orientations.
2. *Group Acculturation*: This dimension also falls within traditional acculturation theory patterns but focuses on groups as collectives, not just individuals. Some ethnic groups virtually disappear, leaving only traces of their heritage, such as food patterns or limited fluency in ancestral languages. Other ethnic groups vigorously maintain their ethnic cultures, including their languages, even as they adapt to the larger society.

Beyond these first two dimensions, the concept of multiculturation adds three additional dynamics usually not emphasized in traditional acculturation theories: intragroup, intergroup, and societal.

1. *Intragroup Acculturation*: Ethnic groups may emphasize important intragroup distinctions, often based on such factors as religion, language, race, geographical origin, historical roots, and sometimes historical animosities. Operating within the context of the new society in which the group finds itself, such factors may precipitate new or continuing intragroup dynamics, including conflict and intermarriage. As a result, new cultural blendings or expressions may develop.
2. *Intergroup Acculturation*: Ethnic groups acculturate not just to the society at large but also to other ethnic groups. Sometimes this has involved ethnic groups living in adjoining neighborhoods or creating multiethnic communities, in which groups mutually adapt to each other in ways that can be constructive or destructive. This acculturation process may lead to conflict based on such factors as language barriers, cultural misunderstanding, racial animosities, and struggles over turf. It may also lead to intergroup cooperation, alliances, and marriage, with resulting offspring who carry the intergroup acculturation process down through the generations.
3. *Societal Acculturation*: In most traditional presentations of the acculturation process, ethnic individuals and groups acculturate while the mainstream remains basically the same. The concept of multiculturation, however, posits that ethnic, racial, and religious diversity may also bring profound changes to

the society itself. Put another way, the society acculturates to diversity, for better and for worse. This dynamic has also been referred to by such terms as *mutual accommodation*.

For example, laws, court decisions, or executive actions may open doors of inclusion or reinforce barriers of exclusion for those of certain ethnic, racial, and religious groups. That process may lead to the establishment of new institutions or organizations or the changing of core societal mores and practices.

Consider the U.S. Supreme Court's 1967 *Loving v. Virginia* decision, which annulled state-level antimiscegenation laws. As a result of that decision, interracial marriages have increased and societal opposition to interracial marriage has steadily declined. Other examples of societal acculturation are changes in a nation's position on citizenship (who may or may not become a citizen) and language policy (ranging from official multilingualism to officializing a single language). In short, acculturation is a complex process, both in its traditional formulations and in newer formulations such as multiculturation.

Carlos E. Cortés

References

Berry, J. W. (2009). A critique of critical acculturation. *International Journal of Intercultural Relations*, *33*(5), 361–71.

Chun, K. M., Organista, P. B., & Marín, G. (Eds.) (2008). *Acculturation: Advances in theory, measurement, and applied research*. Washington, DC: American Psychological Association.

Cortés, C. E. (2013). Introduction. In C. E. Cortés (Ed.), *Multicultural America: A multimedia encyclopedia* (pp. xliii–xlviii). Thousand Oaks, CA: Sage.

Harris, R. (2013). Acculturation/assimilation. In C. E. Cortés (Ed.), *Multicultural America: A multimedia encyclopedia* (pp. 111–17). Thousand Oaks, CA: Sage.

Padilla, A. M. (Ed.) (1980). *Acculturation: Theory, models and some new findings*. Boulder, CO: Westview.

Ward, C. & Kus, L. (2012). Back to and beyond Berry's basics: The conceptualization, operationalization and classification of acculturation. *International Journal of Intercultural Relations*, *36*(4), 472–85.

AFFIRMATIVE ACTION

Affirmative Action in Higher Education

ORIGIN Affirmative action refers to a set of policies that were put in place to promote equal access and representation for women and minority groups, specifically with regard to education, business, and employment opportunities. These policies sought to remedy long-standing discrimination directed at these specific groups, despite the establishment of civil rights laws and constitutional promises. They were also dedicated to ensuring that all citizens received equal consideration without regard to race, ethnicity, gender, religious affiliation, and age (Anderson, 2005).

President John F. Kennedy first introduced the term *affirmative action* in 1961 through Executive Order 10925, which created the Committee on Equal Employment Opportunity. The committee was responsible for studying and critiquing the employment practices of federal agencies. More specifically, it mandated "affirmative action to ensure that the applicants are employed, and that employees are treated during employment without regard to race, color, creed, or national origin" (Executive Order No. 10925, 1961). Although not using the phrase *affirmative action*, President Lyndon Johnson expanded this policy by issuing Executive Order 11246, which demanded that all executive departments and agencies establish and maintain a program that promotes equal employment opportunity (Fullinwider, n.d.).

In 1964, the Civil Rights Act (CRA) was enacted, applying this prohibition of race discrimination by statute. For example, Title VII of the Act prohibited employers from discriminating on the basis of race, gender, and/or religion. While the Act did not speak directly to "affirmative action," the spirit of the act echoed similar sentiments. Prohibiting discrimination, the CRA was instrumental in raising the level of consciousness surrounding the importance of "affirmative action" policies and programs to meet this statute. The act specifically opened up the door for positive steps toward remedying a legacy of discrimination while promoting diversity. While seemingly a step in the right direction, such race-conscious affirmative action programs have been the source of much controversy and have even resulted in violent protests.

Higher Education

At the university level, higher-education institutions were mandated to diversify their student demographics along racial and gender lines. More specifically, they were to achieve this diversity through the establishment of "goals" and "timetables" for "full utilization" of educational opportunities for minorities and women (McBride, 2006). Prior to 1972, the concerns for the integration of racial/ethnic or gender diversity at learning institutions were nonexistent.

These mandates, however, prompted spirited debates as to the legitimacy of affirmative action. University officials questioned the "fairness" and ultimately the legality of forcing higher education to take race and gender preferences into consideration in their selection process, naming it "reverse discrimination." As the debates heated, ties between "goals" and "timetables" began to be associated with the idea of "quotas." In *Regents of the University of California v. Bakke* (1978), Allan Bakke, a prospective medical student, was denied admission to the University of California at Davis Medical School. The Supreme Court ruled that a university's use of racial "quotas" in its admissions process was unconstitutional, but a school's use of "affirmative action" to diversify its minority applicants was, in fact, constitutional (Curry & West, 1996).

Allan, a thirty-two-year-old white male, applied to UC-Davis School of Medicine in 1973 and 1974, but he was rejected in both years, even though his application was more competitive than those of some minority applicants who were admitted. The medical school reserved sixteen out of one hundred seats in its entering class for minority applicants, including blacks, Hispanics, Asians, and American Indians. A special school committee administered this rigid admissions quota.

Bakke sued the University of California arguing that the medical school's admission policy violated Title VI of the Civil Rights Act of 1964 and the Fourteenth Amendment's Equal Protection Clause. The Supreme Court found that the quotas were unconstitutional, thus no applicant can be rejected because of their race in favor of someone who is less qualified (McBride, 2006). The Court, however, ruled that race could be used as a factor in promoting education diversity.

While racial quotas have always been unconstitutional, affirmative action programs are applicable only when race is considered as one of many admissions factors and used to promote diversity. In the years following this ruling, higher education learning institutions have designed their affirmative action programs around this statue. For example, in *Grutter v. Bollinger* (2003), the Supreme Court upheld the University of Michigan Law School's admission policy arguing that it "reaffirmed *Bakke's* basic approach and ruled that the University of Michigan Law School's policy of giving significant but non-determinative weight to its applicants' race was 'neutral' enough, and Michigan's interest in a diverse student body was 'compelling' enough, to meet constitutional standards of equality" (*Grutter v. Bollinger*, 2003). However, in a related but separate decision—*Gratz v. Bollinger* (2003)—the Court found Michigan's undergraduate affirmative action program unconstitutional, arguing that using a point system to reward and rank minority applicants was prohibited (*Gratz v. Bollinger*, 2003).

Royel M. Johnson

References

Anderson, T. H. (2005). *The pursuit of fairness: A history of affirmative action*. New York: Oxford University Press.

Curry, G. E. & West, C. (1996). *The affirmative action debate* (1st ed.). Reading, MA: Addison-Wesley Publishing Company.

Exec. Order No. 10925, C.F.R. 1977 (1961).

Fullinwider, R. (n.d.). *Equal employment opportunity*. Retrieved from http://www.eeoc.gov/eeoc/history/35th/thelaw/eo-11246.html.

Gratz v. Bollinger, 539 U.S. 244 (2003).

Grutter v. Bollinger, 539, U.S. 306 (2003).

Kennedy, J. (1961). *Executive Order 10925: Establishing the president's committee on equal employment opportunity*. Retrieved from Equal Employment Opportunity Committee, http://www.eeoc.gov/eeoc/history/35th/thelaw/eo-10925.html.

McBride, A. (2006, December). Regents of University of *California v. Bakke* (1978). *Supreme Court History: Expanding Civil Rights—Landmark Cases*. Retrieved from http://www.pbs.org/wnet/supremecourt/rights/landmark_regents.html.

Regents of the University of California v. Bakke, 438 U.S. 265 (1978).

AFRICAN AMERICAN

African American: An Ethnic Rather Than Racial Distinction

Race has been aptly defined as "the framework of ranked categories segmenting the human population developed by western Europeans following their global expansion beginning in the 1400s" (Sanjek, 1994, p. 1). Races as demonstrably existing biological indicators do not exist. Racial classification exists for the purposes of (1) categorizing, and (2) propagating messages of superiority and inferiority (Guthrie, 1976), where white was made synonymous with superiority and black with inferiority. In his historical account of how psychology as a discipline has engaged the topic of race, Richards (1997) writes, "In the European mind blackness, it is said, symbolizes sin, the Devil, dirt, faeces and death, and Europeans projected these connotations onto peoples with highly melanised skin" (p. 5). As such, these symbolic meanings have played a central role in the perceptions of Africans by European Americans. While race-based classifications (even self-identified) can be attributive and subsequently (marginally) informative, it begs that we are astute in our attention to their historical context and connotations, as they are emotionally laden and charged.

Although assertions of biological race-based differences existing between racial groups have been widely refuted in the literature, racial classifications remain ensconced (almost irrevocably) in the literature. Despite there being immeasurable evidence to dispel the biological utility of race-based classification systems, it does little to dispel or alter the racialized life experiences of persons of color, particularly those of African descent. Racial ordering has tangible social, cultural, and political consequences for those ranking low in this social order.

Ethnicity, then, captures common geographic origins, ancestry, family patterns, language, cultural norms, and traditions (Williams, 2005). Culture is the manifestation of one's ethnic identity (or ethnicity) and provides a general design for living and a pattern for interpreting reality (Nobles, 1986).

Parham (1993) has noted that maintaining a sense of cultural integrity in a world that does not support or affirm the humanity of African Americans continues to be central to the struggle for identity. Thus, to be understood as African American is to see, acknowledge, and begin to understand the truly complex existence of African-descended people, to honor the connections to Africa and African peoples, and to move away from such reductionist classifications as *black*.

Within many cultural groups, group terminology preference can be noted and may be reflective of one's own cultural/racial/ethnic identity and/or group membership. Stated differently, an ethnic identity of African American may be an assertion of and an embracing of both one's African lineage (known or unknown) and American culture. To the contrary, while *African American* continues to be the politically correct terminology, some persons of African descent (e.g., Caribbean-born Africans) find the term exclusionary and thus offensive. Similarly, a racial preference of *black* may be a reflection for one's preference for their American heritage while eschewing ties to any African lineage, or may be their preferred identification in that its lack of ties to continent or place (or lineage) feels more inclusive.

Both racial and ethnic (black and African American, respectively) classifications have since been used interchangeably (and haphazardly) in the literature when referencing persons of African descent across the diaspora. Often, both ethnic and racial levels of analyses are necessary to honor the deep structure of culture and its influence on individual behavior as well as the racialized experiences of African-descended people.

Delishia M. Pittman

References

Guthrie, R. V. (1976). *Even the rat was white: A historical view of psychology*. New York: Harper & Row.

Nobles, W. W. (1986). *African psychology: Toward its reclamation, reascension, and revitalization*. Oakland, CA: Institution for the Advanced Study of Black Family Life and Culture.

Parham, T. A. (1993). *Psychological storms: The African American struggle for identity*. Chicago: African American Images.

Richards, G. (1997). *Race, racism, and psychology: Toward a reflexive history*. New York: Routledge.

Sanjek, R. (1994). The enduring inequalities of race. In S. Gregory & R. Sanjek (Eds.), *Race* (pp. 1–17). New Brunswick, NJ: Rutgers University Press.

Williams, D. R. (2005). The health of U.S. racial and ethnic populations. *Journals of Gerontology: SERIES B, 60B*(2), 53–62.

AFRICAN INDEPENDENCE MOVEMENT

The African Independence Movement was the progressive response of African peoples demanding freedom and self-rule from Western colonialists such as Great Britain, France, and Germany. The colonization of Africa began in the fifteenth century and lasted into the second half of the twentieth century (Eze, 1997). The period is described as "marked by the horror and violence of the transatlantic slave trade, the imperial occupation of most parts of Africa and the forced administrations of its peoples, and the resilient and enduring ideologies and practices of European cultural superiority (ethnocentrism) and 'racial' supremacy (racism)" (Eze, 1997, p. 4).

The colonization of Africa was institutionalized and globalized in 1884 when the ministers of fourteen European powers met in a conference room at the Berlin residence of German chancellor Otto von Bismarck and partitioned Africa among themselves (de Blij & Muller, 2003). This partition initiated the political, moral, and cultural fragmentation that has plagued Africa until today. It happened long before many Africans were exposed to the Western political systems, policies, and ideologies. For many years, the West exploited Africa, raping it of its resources and cultural identity until a combination of factors led Africans to rise up and challenge the European powers, leading to the independence of many African nations. Some of those causative factors toward the independence movement include Western education, Africa's exposure to the enslavement and dehumanization of their brothers and sisters held in slavery in Europe and America, and the involvement of Africa in World War I and World War II.

Western Education

Colonization brought with it Western education, which was pioneered by Christian missionaries whose primary intent was to Christianize the new colonies. It is recorded that while Christian missionary work started in earnest in the mid-1700s in a place like Ghana, by 1881 they had already established 139 primary schools with twenty teachers and five thousand students (Kilson, 1970). Western education exposed the Africans to the Western mind-set, Western political philosophies, and general worldviews. Western education enabled the African to critique Western ideologies and determine that those ideologies were neither perfect nor superior to African ideologies, contrary to colonial-imposed patterns the West used to entrench their authority among Africans. This was enhanced as young African men and women began to travel outside of Africa to Europe and America to further their education and obtain diplomas and degrees. As they arrived into these Western educational settings, they saw themselves competing healthily with native speakers of the English language, Dutch, German, and other Western languages in all subject areas: mathematics, physics, history, classics, and even political science. Upon graduation, these Africans came home questioning the rights of these Westerners to lord power over them in their own African lands.

Exposure to the Enslavement and Dehumanization of Africans in Diaspora

The very same Africans who had traveled out to the Western world also took notice of the extreme treatment of their brothers and sisters who had been taken in slavery to Europe and America. That awareness predisposed them to be intolerant of similar treatments toward them in their own lands by Western colonial authorities, who ruled the African continent with absolute sway. These early African elites were confronted with the burden for their freedom and the freedom of their people. Given that their numbers were very small and their opportunities for social mobility, even in their own countries of birth, were dependent upon the colonial authorities, their progress was rather slow and painful, yet they were persistent and strategic in their search for independence. Dr. Nnamdi Azikiwe, a Nigerian, and Kwame Nkrumah, a Ghanaian, both of whom were educated at Lincoln University in the United States, were among the elites who had to work painstakingly slowly but steadily to secure independence for their people. Responding to a colonial action in Enugu, Nigeria, where twenty-one Nigerian coal miners were shot by the colonial police in 1949, Azikiwe spoke at a rally in Trafalgar Square in London (December 4, 1949). In his speech, he stated,

> The people of Nigeria cannot continue to accept as their destiny the denial of human rights . . . The struggle for African freedom may be long and gloomy, but behind the cloud of suffering and disappointment loom the rays of hope and success on the distant horizon. (Collins, 1990, p. 240)

Collins noted that this speech by Azikiwe was the "the first speech, on the subject of freedom for Africa" (p. 238). The threat that African elites posed to colonial authorities led to the Belgian colonial administration closing up any opportunities for higher education for nationals in their territories and forbidding them from going elsewhere to obtain it. Their slogan was, "No elites, no problems" (Grimes, 1981, p. 4).

Effect of the World Wars
The two world wars had an unusual effect on Africa. The European countries with colonies in Africa (especially France and Britain) recruited their African subjects to fight their wars. This mass recruitment of able-bodied African men with little or no Western education opened the door for a larger number of Africans to encounter the West. Oliver (1991) records that during World War I about three hundred thousand Africans from the French territories alone were recruited to fight outside of Africa. These Africans were exposed to "modern technology, large organizations and ethnic mixing. These were the new experiences on which the future (of the continent) would be built" (p. 218). When these Africans returned from the wars where they had fought side by side with Europeans afflicted by the same human weaknesses and limitations they experienced, the colonial masters expected them to quickly return to their traditional lives as the servants, gardeners, and cooks to the colonial masters.

In the southern part of Africa where apartheid was already rearing its ugly head, colonial powers enacted land laws that took land away from the nationals and assigned up to 87 percent of them to the colonial and/or expatriate white powers, which left the nationals with little or nothing to live on (Collins, 1990, p. 218). The distress that arose from these colonial actions provided the African elites a ready group of allies in the world war veterans, who quickly banded with them in the education of the rest of their peoples on the evils of colonialism and forged alliances to root it out. It must be noted also that both world wars may have made their own independent contributions toward the independence of African nations. The Western nations were expending their energies and resources fighting the world wars and were temporarily distracted from establishing entrenched policies and institutions that would have made the African struggle for independence even more difficult. When they turned their attention back to Africa, it was too late to stem the tide of revolution (Frost, 1970).

Brownlie (1971) noted that the political drive for the African Independence Movements had rested on the principle of self-determination. He pointed out that when, on December 14, 1960, eighty-nine states of the UN General Council voted on UN General Assembly Resolution 1514 (XV), "Declaration on Granting of Independence to Colonial Countries and People," eight countries that voted against the resolution included the United States of America, United Kingdom, Portugal, Spain, Australia, the Union of South Africa, and France (p. 365). It should be noted that this vote to deny Africans their rights to independence by these named parties was after countries like Ghana, Sudan, Nigeria, and others had fought and won their independence. Both the prime minister of the United Kingdom and the president of the United States had earlier, in 1941, accepted the principles of the Atlantic Charter, which affirmed its respect for the rights of people to freely choose the form of government they would live by. This affirmation made at the height of World War I is now something these two nations were willing to walk away from after the war had ended.

The African Independence Movement practically accomplished its goal of self-rule for Africans in the

1970s. Some countries remained under the chains of Western imperialism. Countries such as Zimbabwe did not gain independence until April 18, 1980, when Robert Mugabe assumed the presidency of that young nation (Ndlovu, 2007). Cooper (2005) writes, "By the 1970s, colonialism had been banished from the realm of legitimate forms of political organization. What remained 'colonial' in world politics passed itself off as something else" (p. 33).

Chinaka Samuel DomNwachukwu

References

Brownlie, I. (1971). *Basic documents on African affairs*. Oxford: The Clarendon Press.

Collins, R. O. (1990). *Western African history vol. I of African history: Text readings*. Princeton: Markus Wiener Publishers.

Cooper, F. (2005). *Colonialism in question: Theory, knowledge, history*. Berkeley: University of California Press.

De Blij, H. J. & Muller, P. O. (2003). *Geography: Realms, regions and concepts*. Hobeken, NJ: John Wiley & Sons, Inc.

Eze, E. C. (1997). Introduction: Philosophy and the (post) colonial. In Emmanuel Chukwudi Eze (Ed.), *Postcolonial African philosophy: A critical reader* (pp. 1–22). Oxford: Blackwell Publishers, Ltd.

Frost, K. W. J. (1970). British policy and representative government in West Africa 1920 to 1951. In L. H. Gann & P. Duignan (Eds.), *Colonialism in Africa 1870–1960* (vol. 2) (pp. 31–57). Cambridge: Cambridge University Press.

Grimes, J. R. (1981). African developments in historical perspective. *Political trends in Africa: Development arms race human Rights*. Reports and Papers of Regional Consultation of the CCIA/WCC in Collaboration with the AACC, Nairobi, Kenya, November 17–21, 1980.

Kilson, M. (1970). The emergent elites of Black Africa, 1900 to 1960. In L. H. Gann & P. Duignan (Eds.), *Colonialism in Africa 1870–1960* (vol. 2) (pp. 351–98). Cambridge: Cambridge University Press.

Ndlovu, A. (2007). Post-Independence violence in Zimbabwe. In D. E. Miller, S. Holland, L. Fendall, & D. Johnson (Eds.), *Seeking peace in Africa: Stories from African peacemakers* (pp. 76–80) Telford, PA: Cascadia Publishing House.

Oliver, R. (1991). *The African experience: Major themes in African history from earliest times to the present*. New York: HarperCollins Publishers.

AFRICAN TRADITIONAL RELIGION(S)

African Traditional Religion (ATR) is a generic term used within academic circles to describe rather than define the varieties of religious experiences across the continent of Africa. Religion in traditional African societies can be said to share certain common elements, yet retain wide variations that make it difficult to lump them into one common designation of philosophical classification. According to King (1986), the religion of one African group may differ as much from that of its neighboring village or town as Christianity differs from Judaism. Central to religion in traditional African societies, however, is the concept of one Supreme Being, God. This concept is entrenched and fully established among all African peoples (Imasogie, 1982, pp. 14–29). The early Western intellectuals that went to Africa came away with a misguided opinion of the African traditional religions as polytheistic, a designation many African scholars have worked hard to refute and dismiss over the years (Idowu, 1973; Mbiti, 1975). ATRs are theocentric and scholars and students tend to prefer a view of them that acknowledges a hierarchy of spiritual authorities with God at the peak. While acknowledging the major roles played by deities and other spiritual mediators in ATR, these scholars would prefer that their roles are seen as mediatory and subordinate to that of God, who is supreme and unequaled. The Roman Catholic version of the Christian faith, with God as supreme, the Virgin Mary, and a host of saints, who are deceased humans, as mediators between man and God presents the best typology for conceptualizing the African traditional religions.

Religion is an essential aspect of the African psyche. All traditional African peoples have a clearly established religious belief system (Awolalu, 1979, p. 67; Imasogie, 1982, p. 1). Religion has been to the African peoples the primary lenses through which they viewed reality, life, and life's experiences. Religious views and expressions are natural and inherent in the African experience. Individuals inherit the religious expressions of their own particular African peoples and religious expressions. Individuals, while holding on to the religious expressions of his or her own African peoples, could occasionally seek aid from other African religious structures and deities outside of his or her own, if the foreign deity is known to effectively deal with the issues confronting the individual in question. Such search for spiritual support does not suggest a rejection of one's own local religious structures, but an addition or enhancement of what one already has available to him or her through the local religious structures (Mbiti, 1975, p. 12). Due to the fact that religion in Africa is more communal than it is personal, the individual has little or no leverage to personally reject the religious faith of his or her people. For most African traditional societies, to reject one's communal religious faith is to ostracize one's self from his or her people. This was an issue early Christian missions to Africa had to deal with. In many cases, new converts to Christianity had to be removed from their communities for their own safety and to sustain the new faith they had embraced.

Religion is the means by which Africans establish a clear expression of who they are, how to act, and how to respond to varying situations and experiences of life. It guides them on how to solve the myriad of life's problems, and it is the means for finding answers and direction along life's journey. Religion was the cord that held African peoples together, as it shaped the cultures, norms, and practices. The traditional African societies did not see any separation between the sacred and the secular; rather, reality was one continuum bound by the concept of the sacred.

Unlike the Middle Eastern monotheistic religions of Islam and Christianity, the African traditional religions have no sacred scriptures, except those tenets closely and boldly written in the hearts and experiences of the African peoples. ATR has been both evolutionary and dynamic in its forms. It seems to adapt to the changing cultural landscapes and experiences of the African people (Mbiti, 1975, p. 15). According to Mbiti, African traditional religions cannot be labeled as ancestral worship, a designation commonly used by Western scholars. Ancestral veneration among Africans does not rise to the ranks of worship as an African would intend

for God Almighty, so that designation is considered inadequate in describing African religions. ATR also cannot be labeled superstitious because embedded in the African traditional religions is a long history of deep reflections, experiences, and guarded responses to divine revelations. Mbiti argues that it also cannot be termed *animism* or *paganism*, terms that significantly limit the scope and efficacy of the African traditional religious experiences. Whereas animism points to a belief in the veneration of various inanimate objects and phenomena, paganism is a broad, derogatory term used for religious experiences outside of the traditional Christian and Islamic religious faiths (1975, pp. 16–18). African scholars and Africans who subscribe to the African traditional religions see those two terms as wrong and demeaning in describing their religious experiences. They reject the attempt to tag it magic or fetish, but demand that their religious experiences be seen as credible experiences based on a long history and tradition of deep reflections, philosophy, and calculated response to the divine and divine encounters (Hallen, 2002).

Idowu (1973) itemized the basic structure of the ATR as encompassing five major elements: belief in God, belief in the divinities, belief in spirits, belief in ancestors, and the practice of magic and medicine (pp. 137–202).

The resilience of the African traditional religions amid centuries of Christian and Islamic assault on the African continent stand to prove the fact that the Western designations of ATR have been inadequate and wanting in clearly defining and articulating these religious expressions. Abimbola (1991), writing about the resilience of the African traditional religions among the Yorubas of Nigeria, stated, "Despite the devastating effects of Islam and Christianity on the autochthonous religion of the Yoruba, the religion continues to hold its own and is regarded in modern Nigeria as one of the three major religions in the country" (p. 51). This is not just the case in Yoruba land, but is the same among the Igbos of Nigeria, where there is a strong resurgence in the influence of traditional deities such as Amadioha Ozuzu, Orasi Okija, and other deities of Igbo land. In West Africa and some parts of Southern Africa, the faces of both Islam and Christianity have been changed considerably by the influence of

African traditional religions. Even the Pentecostal churches in West Africa have inculcated very strong elements of the traditional African religions, giving the African version of this faith movement a unique face. These influences are more prominent in the African Independent Churches of West Africa and the Zionist Churches of East and Southern Africa. Beyond its inroads into the established Christian and Islamic religious structures, African Traditional Religion has seen resurgence among many African peoples. The likelihood is that this resurgence will continue amid contemporary failings of Islamic and Christian faiths seen in extreme intolerance and moral lapses. A result of the overwhelming Western influence on Africa has led Africans to a blind adoption of Western ethical norms characterized by Mbon (1991) as ethics of "personal comfort and personal influence" (p. 105). Recent events have caused some Africans to begin to rethink their adoption of Western Christianity and Islamic faith and to desire for the "good old days" of the ATR climate of African traditional ethics of communal welfare and intrinsic right and wrong. The degree in which this appeal to return to authentic African religions is reflected in a new African religion known as Chiism (Godianism). This religion, which was established by western Igbo elites from eastern Nigeria, is only one of such nativity movements (Wikipedia, 2013).

Chinaka Samuel DomNwachukwu

References

Abimbola, W. (1991). The place of African Traditional Religion in contemporary Africa: The Yoruba example. In J. K. Olupona (Ed.), *African traditional religion in contemporary society* (pp. 51–58). New York: Paragon House.

Awolalu, J. O. (1979). *Yoruba beliefs and sacrificial rites.* Essex, UK: Longman Group Limited.

Hallen, B. (2002). *A short history of African philosophy.* Bloomington: Indiana University Press.

Idowu, E. B. (1973). *African traditional religion: A definition.* London: SCM Press Ltd.

Imasogie, O. (1982). *African traditional religion.* Ibadan, Nigeria: University Press Limited.

King, N. Q. (1986). *African cosmos: An introduction to religion in Africa.* Belmont, CA: Wadsworth Publishing Company.

Mbiti, J. S. (1975). *Introduction to African religion.* London: Heinemann.

Mbon, F. M. (1991). African traditional socio-religious ethics and national development: The Nigerian case. In J. K. Olupona (Ed.), *African traditional religion in contemporary society* (pp. 101–9). New York: Paragon House.

Wikipedia. (2013, March 18). Godianism. Retrieved from http://en.wikipedia.org/wiki/Godianism.

AFRO-SEMINOLE

Looking for Angola

From 1812 to 1821, the maroon community of 750 formerly enslaved, free Africans, and Seminole Indians lived off the Florida Gulf Coast in the Sarasota-Bradenton area in a settlement known as Angola. The community of men, women, and children enslaved on Southern plantations came to Southwest Florida in search of freedom. Using innate skills, the community flourished until a raid by the Lower Creek Indian War Party indirectly ordered by Florida's provisional governor Andrew Jackson destroyed it in 1821. The survivors of the Angola settlement escaped throughout Florida. Some of the escapees made their way to present-day Key Biscayne, crossed the treacherous gulf stream in dugout canoes, and settled in Red Bays, Andros Island, Bahamas. British custom documents identified ninety-seven of them upon arrival in Nassau.

In 2003, journalist and documentarian Vickie Oldham organized a team of scholars from Florida, Georgia, and South Carolina and formed the Looking for Angola project to document the existence of an 1800s Black Seminole community in the Sarasota-Bradenton area. An interdisciplinary team of scholars, including archaeologists, an anthropologist, historians, and educators, are exploring the historical, anthropological, and archaeological background of free blacks, enslaved Africans, and Seminoles who established a haven of safety for their families near Tampa Bay. The scholars are working to compile evidence about the origins, location, and descendants of the early nineteenth-century Florida maroon community known as Angola. This relatively unknown community served to keep alive "colonial Florida's status as a refuge of freedom in the aftermath of Fort Mose's closure and the Negro Fort's destruction" (Brown, 2005, p. 6) in 1763.

As a result of the instability of the area and Great Britain taking possession of the former Spanish region, many black inhabitants scattered throughout Florida to escape capture, and they often associated with Seminole Indians (Brown, 2005). By 1812, the Angola settlement along the Manatee River was home to approximately 750 (escaped and free) Africans, Red Stick Creek, and Seminole Indians (USF Africana Heritage Project & IDEAS4, 2006). The location of the site provided access to waterways and defense that allowed the community to trade with Cuban fisherman and to communicate with officials in Havana (Brown, 2005). The settlement became a site for trading and military recruitment, and it provided refuge for its diverse inhabitants, until the Lower Creek Indian War Party raided their settlement in 1821 (Brown, 2005) and three hundred inhabitants were killed or captured. However, not all of Angola's residents suffered death or returned to slavery. Several hundred survivors escaped to the Florida Keys, crossed the gulf stream, and made it safely to the Bahamas. The refugees settled in Red Bays, Andros Island, where researchers have found their descendants living today (Brown, 2005).

The survivors who escaped to Red Bays are believed to have arrived between 1821 and 1837. The first two documented envoys to Providence, Bahamas, were initially returned to Florida. The third envoy, which avoided Providence and used dugout canoes and wreckers, mostly settled in Red Bays, Andros Island. Customs records indicate the arrival of these settlers. The settlement of Red Bays became residence to a critical mass of the black Seminole descendants. Today, many inhabitants of Red Bays, Andros Island, have provided oral histories that have helped document the existence of the Angola settlement and their ancestors' escape through the Florida peninsula to safety and freedom (Howard, 2002).

The history of Angola brings together the heritage of Africans in America, the Spanish in Florida, Seminoles on the Gulf Coast, and American expansion into the Florida interior. The settlement highlights Florida's role as a beacon of freedom for refugees from slavery in America. It hosted possibly the largest "maroon" community in North America during 1812 to 1821, and it represents a crucial element to understanding the course of nineteenth-century Florida history.

Although earlier sites, such as Fort Mose near St. Augustine and the Negro Fort on the Apalachicola River, have received much attention, no such site specific to the southern half of the Florida peninsula has received attention. Preserving the memory of Angola deepens the understanding of students and the community about Florida's rich African American heritage in a region where more than half the state's population resides.

The project continues to collect evidence of the Angola settlement through archaeological digs at local sites. Although nothing was found during the first exploratory dig and shovel tests, the existence of the settlement is documented in *Go Sound the Trumpet! Selections in Florida's African American History* by David H. Jackson Jr. and Canter Brown Jr. and *Black Seminoles in the Bahamas* by Rosalyn Howard. The project also seeks community involvement through public archaeology opportunities for teachers and is part of the Public Archaeological Lab research of Dr. Uzi Baram at New College of Florida.

Tashia Bradley
Vickie Oldham

References
Brown, C., Jr. (2005). Tales of Angola: Free blacks, Red Stick Creeks, and international intrigue in Spanish Southwest Florida, 1812–1821. In D. H. Jackson & C. Brown Jr. (Eds.), *Go Sound the Trumpet! Selections in Florida's African American History* (pp. 5–21). Tampa, FL: University of Tampa Press.
Howard, R. (2002). *Black Seminoles in the Bahamas*. Gainesville, FL: University Press of Florida.
USF Africana Heritage Project & IDEAS4. (2006). Looking for Angola: The search for an 1800's black settlement. The Looking for Angola Project. Retrieved from http://www.lookingforangola.org/about.asp.

AFROCENTRIC EDUCATION

One of the central purposes of Afrocentric education is to train African American students to learn, understand, and appreciate the history, culture, and geography of people either in Africa or of African descent. This training method is conducted in Afrocentric schools, regular public and private schools, community centers, charter schools, homes, or faith-based organizations. The purpose of this education is to help African American students develop an appreciation of cultural artifacts, practices, and beliefs that are African American and black. It is a transformational learning experience that helps build confidence and self-worth in African American students. The curriculum builds on the legacies of black people and instructs students to learn about the African life and culture, helping them to gain a perspective about themselves and the world that reaches beyond the Eurocentric worldview. The Afrocentric education environment is designed to create an atmosphere that is inspiring and comfortable.

During the 1960s and 1970s, Afrocentric education gained a foothold in the African American community as the Black Power movement gained influence across urban neighborhoods in the United States. This period witnessed the call from African American parents and community leaders to seek control of neighborhood schools, alongside Afrocentric scholars questioning the singular-focused curriculum of Eurocentric ideas in schools (Giddings, 2001; Kifano, 1996). The Afrocentric scholars maintained that teaching African American students about their history would inspire them to want to learn, which would enhance their overall academic performance in schools. Giddings (2001) reported that, although there was no established formal Afrocentric curriculum during the early 1960s and 1970s, there were five standards that collectively outlined what an Afrocentric curriculum would strive toward:

1. Assist students in developing the necessary intellectual, moral, and emotional skills for accomplishing a productive, affirming life in this society.
2. Provide such educational instruction as to deconstruct established hegemonic pillars and to safeguard against the construction of new ones.
3. Provide students of African descent with educational instruction that uses techniques that are in accordance with their learning style.
4. Assist students of African descent in maintaining a positive self-concept, with the goals of achieving a sense of collective accountability.
5. Serve as a model for the [James A.] Banks [model for curriculum reform] "Transformation" and "Social Action" approaches to multicultural education. (Giddings, 2001, p. 463)

The supporters of Afrocentric education believe that this style of education can have significant positive effects on African American students. They also believe that this style of education helps to lower poor school performance among such students. Through this education, they argue, the black community can achieve greater school autonomy and provide students with an Afrocentric perspective (Kifano, 1996).

Many proponents of Afrocentric education believe that this educational program works best within a regular school system—a school within a school concept. Kifano (1996) argues:

The financial, material, and personal requirements for staff development and management, program coordination, and physical plant maintenance are often inaccessible to and unharnessed by large numbers of stakeholders in the African American community. Consequently, African American parents, educators, and community members have increasingly turned to the creation of supplementary schools as a means of providing academic support and cultural enrichment to African American youth after the public school day ends, on weekends [. . .]. (p. 210)

Today, the Afrocentric education concept may have a new financial reservoir to pull from in some states, especially those states that support charter schools. Afrocentric educators may want to consider starting an Afrocentric charter school. In order to start a charter school, an application process for opening a new charter school must be fully completed. These applications can be hundreds of pages and in most cases, take years to research and complete. When the application has been approved, the school receives resources for its operation, mostly in the form of payments per student enrolled in the school. For some communities, the charter school concept might provide the necessary resource to sustain the Afrocentric education program.

Afrocentric education has a solid place in the educational experience of African American students. This learning experience has proven to elevate students' passion for learning, but there exist many challenges to overcome (Scott, 2009). The Afrocentered education system uses a blend of cross-discipline teaching that must meet the state's core educational requirements. This blended educational experience allows students to be socialized in an environment that helps them to counter stereotypes. In many ways, the blended approach gives students the best of both worlds, allowing them to integrate Afrocentric knowledge with conventional knowledge.

As the Afrocentric education movement continues, the debate over whether Afrocentric education is the best practice for African American students endures, but the most compelling question remains the same: Who can best teach black children, and what is the best curriculum for them to learn?

Sherwood Thompson

References

Binder, A. J. (2000). Why do some curricular challenges work while others do not? The case of three Afrocentric challenges. *Sociology of Education, 73*(2), 69–91.

Giddings, G. J. (2001). Infusion of Afrocentric content into the school curriculum: Toward an effective movement. *Journal of Black Studies, 31*(4), 462–82.

Kifano, S. (1996). Afrocentric education in supplementary schools: Paradigm and practice at the Mary McLeod Bethune Institute. *Journal of Negro Education, 65*(2), 209.

Scott, S. (2009). *African American students are thriving in Afrocentric schools.* Jacksonville.com. Retrieved from http://jacksonville.com/interact/blog/stanley_ scott/2009-05-06/african_american_students_are_ thriving_in_afro-centric_school.

AGE DIFFERENCES

Modernity has generated and increased age differences, through the growth of global population, the increased survival rates from birth, and the longevity of life. There are both familiar and new social constructs of age differences and their social effects. Such changes project an increasing age diversity of people as well as challenges to social justice based on age differences and inequality. Social scientists, including anthropologists, demographers, psychologists, sociobiologists, sociologists, economists, and political scientists have theorized and formulated ways of understanding age differences. These ideas have been empirically informed and have had policy implications in education, social welfare/health services, and criminal justice programs. Age differences are often reflected in popular culture and the media, adding to our understanding that age differences are social constructs in popular culture and in the social scientific study of differences.

Ways to Study Age Differences

The study of age and age differences as an explicit concept has varied in the social science disciplines. As a social category for the analysis of place in society, age cohorts, age stratification, and demographic profiles have given us macro-level topics. Age cohorts describe the aggregate group born during the same period, while age stratification is the hierarchical ranking of age groups in society. Demographers and others have generated profiles of countries and regions based on age cohort and stratification statistics. Demographic profiles have enabled policymakers to see comparative differences between nation-states and regions over time. They can chart whole societies in terms of "young" (majority of people under the age of fifteen) and those that are "aging" (increasing numbers of people living to sixty-five years and older.) This age-based data enables policymakers to make recommendations on social programs in education, health care, and social services that would adequately address the needs of the population at large. Policy work is informed by such profiles and is improved with more nuanced uses of age data.

Social, psychological, and behavioral social sciences have studied age differences to understand human growth, development, and learning. The biological attributes of age, particularly chronological age, influenced generations of learning theorists. Socialization theories helped us to see the developmental stages from infancy, through adolescence, to adulthood. The idea of aging now incorporates the human growth potential of all individuals throughout the life course. Studies of the human brain at different ages in the cognitive sciences view the growth and developmental capacities at all ages. Stages and phases of learning are still analyzed, particularly within educational environments that seek to develop "age appropriate" learning materials. The "readiness" and "maturation" levels of students as learners add to chronological age grading and challenge assumptions of age differences.

Anthropologists and other cultural theorists enable us to see comparative social differences in age differences. Whole cultures value youth or value the old more or less comparatively. One approach to this study has traditionally been through analysis of the life course and aging to connect people's personal attributes, the roles they occupy, the life events they experience, and the social and historical aspects of these events. Familiar phases of the life course are: childhood, youth and adolescence, adulthood, and old age. These age-based phases define life's significant events: birth, marriage, retirement, death. Studies often consider the intersection of age with such other attributes as class, gender, race, and ethnicity, which helps to see the increasing diversity of age differences within and across different cultures.

Generational analysis is based on the notion of age difference and seeks to explain age groups and behavioral differences across generations and over time. An early study, *From Generation to Generation* (Eisenstadt, 1956), pursued a sociological analysis of youth rebellion as a product of generational (age) differences. The study developed the idea of intergenerational problems and relations. Generational analysis emerged as a popular explanation of youth movements by journalists and polemics as well as scholars seeking to explain youth rebellions and revolts starting in the late 1950s. Writings by psychologists included the psychological or sociopsychological aspects of adolescence in various social and educational settings; a newer approach emerged in the study of identity formation among youth in modern societies, drawing upon Erik Erikson's contributions. Popular culture's commercial marketers today use generational analysis to neatly categorize whole age groups. Familiar are the "baby boomers," Y Yuppies, and Generation X. Modern-day "millennials" in the corporate world tend to be young people who are narcissistic, digital multitaskers. Such generational projections often use stereotypical and prejudicial views that lead to forms of age discrimination without creating much knowledge or understanding of the meaning of these age differences. For example, a study on the agenda-setting differences between those aged eighteen to thirty-four and two older generations used two surveys with statewide random samples and content analysis for each. The study found that the agenda of issues important to young adults was correlated with the media's issue agenda. For the heaviest Internet users, who were more likely to be in the two youngest age groups, the correlation was high. Although the youngest generation used traditional media, such as newspapers and television, significantly less frequently than older generations and used the Internet significantly more often, this differential media use did not eliminate the agenda-setting difference. The authors assumed that every new generation of young adults is different from the one that came before (Coleman & McCombs, 2007).

Another complex age-based study of generations and collective memory revisited race, region, and the memory of civil rights. The author concluded that the past seems salient, as both memory and historical significance to people whose identities and social awareness were shaped during and because of historical events. Memory is spatialized and cohort specific. The analysis suggests the memory processes other than autobiographical or generational, suggesting that civil rights memory may have become institutionalized in public memory, permitting those who came of age after the dramatic happenings of 1954 to 1970 to remember the movement at high rates. Regions matter. The American South may be compared to the Northeast in structuring the awareness and significance of the past civil rights case. Generational identity formation is place specific as well as age dependent. Region as well as race, gender, and other social factors, together with age, matter in the construction of collective memories. Sociologists address the communal significance of collective memories (Griffin, 2004). Sources of generational inequities and potential conflict that are not addressed in these studies are topics in economic and political science.

Age Differences Are Social Constructs

Sociologists along with social historians, economists, and political scientists study age differences as a social construct and are less concerned with the biological attributes of chronological age. Age is a social construct, and the new sociology of childhood (Corsaro, 1997) views the study of children and childhood as worthy of study in its own right. New empirical work done by scholars advocate the conceptual autonomy of children and childhood, where children and childhood become the center of analysis and are no longer linked to other categories such as families or schools upon which they are supposedly dependent. Micro (socio psychological) and macro (structural) approaches to the sociology of childhood are employed with an emphasis on an interpretive reproduction of child development, which is in contrast to traditional approaches to socialization and child development. Corsaro (1997) understands this age group and the orb web model of children's developing memberships in their cultures. Doing so, there is an emphasis on peer cultures. The symbolic and material aspects of peer culture in families and from the media are central institutions. Macro-level issues are understood by learning about the extent of social problems of children (including global trends in poverty, family instability, and violence) in order to understand the growing levels of anxiety about children's potential victimization and the tendency to blame some children, especially poor children and youth, for their own vulnerabilities.

The model of human development as universal stages, the epigenetic principle asserted by Erikson, is often challenged in research that treats age as a social construct with a diversity of meanings across cultures in which age groups, generational patterns, and cohort analysis are challenged. For example, a study by Chatterjee, Bailey, and Aaronoff (2001) on adolescence and old age in twelve communities found that the more complex the technological structure of a society, the higher the life expectancy. Also, the higher the placement of a community group in a social hierarchy within a society, the higher the life expectancy. While tasks to be mastered by infancy are nearly universal, by the middle school age period more differences emerge. In some cultures, children enter the world of work by age twelve; in other community groups, children of that age going to work is a norm violation. In technological societies and communities, labor contribution may not only be accepted but also required in terms of social norms and material survival. Another finding from this research indicates that old age is the attribution of witch status among older Santal. This form of collective attribution also occurred among the Navajo. Thus, living longer than one's peers may become a form of norm violation and impact on the redistributive elements of the society. Considerable debate occurs today on the fluidity of age and normative expectations and violations.

Not seeing childhood or old age as a common and universal biological phase in the life course is part of the social construct of age and age difference. Similar to the study of childhood, the study of aging includes constitutive attributes and cultural diversity. How old age is defined and the images of aging have an impact on the options people have in later life. Studies include changing norms of filial piety, younger people's anxiety about so-called childish behavior in old age, historic changes in defining old age from being defined as a medical condition without a cure in nineteenth-century America to one of century-long life spans as a desired possibility with improved health and lifestyle choices. Changes in identity and across generations are documented. For example, the oldest black Americans use racial and ethnic identity as a source of strength, social support, and pride. Work, retirement, and security are policy areas requiring research on the changing concepts of aging and old age. Family, social relationships, and intergenerational reciprocity also reflect aging and age difference understandings. The gerontology field faces challenges in understanding the multifaceted aspects of aging within diverse populations (Markson & Hollis-Sawyer, 2000).

Stereotypes, as well as constraining social norms, dictate that people "act their age" whether they are young, old, or in between. Acting your age as an expression suggests that age is a performance, one that gives meaning to one's own age and to other ages in our actions, interactions, beliefs, words, and social policies (Laz, 1998). Social constructionists develop the framework of age-as-accomplished to show its potential to organize what we have learned about age and aging. The denaturalizing of age, like that of race and gender, widens the field of study on age and age differences. Age, while shaped by social forces, is an act, and it is constituted in interaction and gains its meaning in interaction and in the context of larger social forces. This view allows a firmer social understanding of age as a great source of diversity.

The institutionalization of age differences, including the age-graded structure of educational systems, has significant consequences on human and social development. The extensive literature in the field of education cannot be reviewed here. Of interest are some of the alternative movements over the years for open education models that diffuse the age-graded structure as well as consider other learning factors such as maturation. Other institution settings have real consequences by using age differences as legal definitions. The criminal justice field and legal distinctions between minors and adults structure social practices in major ways. An example of the complexity of this age-based difference is a study of statutory rape laws. The study explores how, throughout U.S. history, the regulation of sexual behavior was seized upon as a means to alleviate larger problems. The laws implemented today, and changes made to the statutory rape laws since the 1970s, include prosecutions under the laws. These laws prohibit sexual activity with an unmarried person under a certain age. The law views underage youth as incapable of giving valid consent to sexual activity. While age is used for legal purposes, the author argues that age is not the most salient operative category. She found that underage youth who are married are exempt, both as victims and as perpetrators. Also, evidence suggests that prosecutors have targeted male homosexual relationships. Same-age perpetrators are frequently charged for felonies or misdemeanors depending on the state. Some states continue to allow defendants to claim the "mistake-of age defense," which was often paired with the claim that the female victim was sexually experienced. The categories of victim and perpetrator have proved to be fluid. Age-span provisions are studied, and decriminalized sex between teens of similar ages, while supported by some, troubles others who fear that youth are then unprotected (Cocca, 2004). Ideological understandings of youth influence efforts to legislate and control a category

of sexually vulnerable teens. The intersection of age, gender, and sexuality reveals how powerful institutions are perpetuating existing power relations. If age and age differences are a proxy for consent, such laws as statutory rape laws may fail as many youths as they protect. The treatment of youthful offenders, minors in terms of judicial proceedings and incarceration, is another large area for further study on the salience of age and age differences and the service of social justice. One useful approach might be the application of the life-course perspective in criminology (Piquero & Mazerolle, 2001).

People of all ages may find greater social justice when the study and policies determined by age and age differences are more fully understood. Life expectancy, life choices, life span, growth and development, and better social relations for all people would benefit from more nuanced studies and comprehension of meaningful age differences.

Diana Papademas

References

Chatterjee, P., Bailey, D., & Aronoff, N. (2001). Adolescence and old age in twelve communities. *Journal of Sociology and Social Welfare, XXVIII*(4), 121–59.

Cocca, C. E. (2004). *Jailbait: The politics of statutory rape laws in the United States.* Albany: State University of New York Press.

Coleman, R. & McCombs, M. (2007). The young and agenda-less? Exploring age-related differences in agenda setting on the youngest generation, baby boomers, and the civic generation. *Journalism & Mass Communication Quarterly, 84*(3), 495–508.

Corsaro, W. A. (1997). *The sociology of childhood.* Thousand Oaks, CA: Pine Forge Press.

Eisenstadt, S. N. (1956). *From generation to generation.* New York: The Free Press.

Griffin, L. J. (2004). "Generations and collective memory" revisited: Race, region, and memory of civil rights. *American Sociological Review, 69*(4), 544–57.

Laz, C. (1998). Act your age. *Sociological Forum, 13*(1), 85–113.

Markson, E. W. & Hollis-Sawyer, L. A. (Eds). (2000). *Intersections of aging.* Los Angeles, CA: Roxbury Publishing Company.

Piquero, A. & Mazerolle, P. (Eds). (2001). *Life-course criminology.* Belmont, CA: Wadsworth/Thomson Learning.

AGEISM

Ageism and Adultism

Identities related to age are deeply impacted by the values and assumptions a society holds about different age groups. It is therefore important to take those identities into account in social justice praxis. The oppression of young people is at the root of the oppressions social justice educators and activists seek to transform. Young people are constructed as dependent, innocent, immature, and incomplete, while elders are constructed as irrelevant, inflexible, and past their prime. Middle-aged adults are constructed as the "norm" of society. A prevailing assumption is that middle age is the pinnacle of human development and represents the height of maturity and productivity. Middle-aged adults maintain a hierarchy in which they occupy the position to exercise power over young people and elder adults.

It is through the experience of adultism, or the oppression of young people, that young people learn and practice the roles of dominant and subordinant. Young people learn to be in a subordinant role through society's requirement that they submit to middle-aged adult authority on a daily basis. This spelling of *subordinant* is preferred because it parallels the term used to refer to dominants. The term *dominate* is not used to refer to those in the dominant role. The use of the term *subordinate*, which is a modifying adjective, seems to contribute to the reduction and objectification of members of the group to which this term is applied. The dominant society is structured to support this power dynamic. Developmental paradigms, conceptualized by adults, suggest that this subordination is for the good and safety of young people. These paradigms lead to policies in which young people are legally relegated to a subordinant position in relation to adults.

Young people learn quickly that age has everything to do with exercising power. Older young people are given more leeway and are often encouraged to police other younger people. Older young people are given roles to exercise their power over younger people, and in this way, the position and role of dominant is learned and practiced.

Examining Adultism

Some authors and educators use the term *ageism* to describe youth oppression. We use different terms to describe the oppression of young people and the oppression of elders because of the different ways the oppression is carried out and the different messages that are internalized about people in those age groups.

Adultism is conceptualized for this discussion as "the systematic subordination of younger people as a targeted group, who have relatively little opportunity to exercise social power in the United States through restricted access to the goods, services, and privileges of society and are denied access to participation in the economic and political life of the society" (DeJong & Love, forthcoming). For example, young people must have adult permission to participate in a wide variety of everyday activities, which include participating in community organizations and research; leaving school; playing on sports teams; having a bank account, email account, and Facebook account; drinking, smoking, voting, traveling, and working; getting a loan; owning property; and making choices regarding their own bodies and health care. However, it is assumed that when a person turns eighteen (or twenty-one) they are mature enough to make decisions for themselves even though they have been denied the opportunity to practice making those decisions until the moment of their majority.

The most visible examples of this subordination of young people can be viewed in compulsory education. While not all young people are treated the same, and some young people have more opportunity to exercise power than others, particularly when they are white, male, and wealthy, young people, as a group they are excluded from participation in decision making related to the education in which they are required to participate. For the most part, young people have very little choice in most schools. They are required to line up, sit still, ask permission to go to the bathroom, and are told when they can move and speak. They are told what they should be interested in and what they must know. They are told what to read and what to watch on television. Young people are expected to engage in critical thinking, but then are disciplined for questioning adults.

They are encouraged to "act like adults" but must do so within the bounds of adult authority. Young people who are not viewed as leaders by adults and are not involved in "youth empowerment" organizations and exercises are rarely consulted about their thinking and opinions. For example, in a recent study in which young people were interviewed about their experiences as young people, a number of the interviewees described a situation in which a student was elected to a position on their district's school committee (DeJong, forthcoming). The student position does not include the right to vote on personnel decisions, and the student's voice is not regarded in the same manner as an adult school committee member.

Young people have very few institutionalized opportunities to exercise social power in the political and economic spheres of society in the United States. This is legislated by restricting young people from the rights of full citizenship, like voting, before the age of eighteen. Not only are young people required to attend school during most of the day, thereby eliminating the opportunity to earn money at a day job, but the hours they are permitted to work after school are often legislated. This practice keeps young people economically dependent on adults. In addition, many young people are not permitted to work because they are not yet "of age." Young people must secure the permission of parents and other adults at their school to obtain a work permit. The age at which young people are "of age" is determined by adults without the input of young people, who are marginalized and excluded from participating in political processes. The fact that young people do not have their own money is then used to further marginalize and exploit them. Without the right to vote, without the means to engage "purchasing power," and without the permission to make decisions about their own lives, young people's access to the goods, services, and privileges of society are limited.

Examining Ageism

Like adultism, ageism is also the systematic subordination and mistreatment of people as a group because of their age. Ageism includes the "stereotyping of and discrimination against elder people" (DeJong & Love, forthcoming). It is based on the assumption that cognitive capacities and the ability to effectively participate in organizational and institutional life automatically diminishes because of age. Ageism assumes that people automatically lose the capacity to grow, learn, and change as they age. Because of ageism, people are stereotypically treated as members of a group rather than on the basis of individual ability. This mistreatment includes the loss of power and voice and restricted opportunities for participation in society from a basis of equity.

There are a variety of ways that ageism affects the daily lives of elders. Mandatory retirement age is one manifestation of ageism. Though the U.S. Civil Service Retirement System (CSRS) or Federal Employees Retirement System (FERS) has removed its mandatory retirement age (ADS Chapter 494, Civil Service Retirement), many state and local organizations along with corporations retain age-based retirement mandates. Many people maintain the capacity for effective organizational and societal participation for many years beyond the age at which they are required to retire. The banking industry currently preys on elders with reverse mortgage schemes. Reverse mortgage schemes eliminate the potential financial flexibility on which many elders depend. The constant barrage of advertisements offering products to keep people from growing old or to look like they are not aging is another manifestation of ageism. The greeting card industry provides daily reminders of society's fear of and revulsion toward growing old and the accompanying attitudes toward those who age. "Antiaging" products are advertised to everyone by the beauty industry depicting aging as something to be avoided, typically at great cost.

The growing use of such epithets as "greedy geezer" and "silver tsunami" promote images of elders as "greedy, selfish, and constitute a serious threat to U.S. economic well-being" (Kingsley, 2011). These metaphors encourage others to think of the elderly as worthless and less than human and prepare people to accept negative, harmful, and sometimes violent treatment of the elderly. A visible manifestation of these attitudes is reflected in the high incidence of elder abuse in nursing homes (National Center on Elder Abuse, 2012). These metaphors are also used to justify current assaults on programs designed to provide social safety nets for the elderly such as social security, Medicare, and Medicaid.

Adult Supremacy

Actions of individuals, cultural norms, attitudes, and values, along with a range of institutional and organizational policies and practices, maintain an ideology of adult supremacy that supports the subordination of young people and elders. Adult supremacy posits that adult thinking is superior to the thinking of young people; therefore, it is assumed that adults should make decisions for young people and elders without their participation or agreement. Denying young people access to power, privilege, and opportunities for participation in society from a position of equity maintains the targeted status of young people. This targeted status is rationalized by the tenets of adult supremacy.

Maintaining Adultism

Power and privilege are reserved for middle-aged adults who, knowingly or unknowingly, are the primary beneficiaries of ageism and adultism. No-tolerance policies in schools, stereotyping of young people, and the blurring of the line between school and the judicial system are some examples of societal policies and practices that collectively reinforce and maintain ageism and adultism for the benefit of middle-aged adults.

The criminalization of young people creates jobs for police and social workers, creates the justification for building prisons, and creates profits for adults. For example, young people are targeted by no-tolerance policies in schools where the guidelines for determining what is acceptable depends on the environment adults want. No-tolerance policies punish young people for any infraction of a rule, regardless of context, ignorance, or extenuating circumstances. The stereotypes that young people are violent, irresponsible, and out-of-control have led to the increased presence of law enforcement personnel in schools. Where there are more police, there will be more arrests. These no-tolerance policies have led to people as young as six years old being handcuffed and arrested, thus entering the "classroom to prison pipeline." Issues that were formerly dealt with in the school become legal cases in which adults who don't have relationships with young people send them into the criminal justice system. Adults have turned what used to be "teachable moments" into an increased likelihood that young people's behavior and young people themselves will be criminalized. In this way, young people are blamed for the existence of a "juvenile justice" system that targets and oppresses. This system, from which middle-aged adults benefit, requires young people to misbehave in order to maintain the existence of this very system. In other words, if young people don't misbehave, an entire sector of the economy would disappear.

Another example of adultism is the student debt crisis. Middle-aged adults in banks and universities make a huge profit by targeting young people and young adult students to assume enormous debt. It is the subordinated status of young people that creates the conditions for adultism to lead to debt accrual for young people and profits for middle-aged adults. This is another situation in which middle-aged adults don't have to face the reality that they benefit from the oppression of young people.

Maintaining Ageism

A range of organizations and institutions including banks, housing, the beauty industry, the medical establishment, and even the greeting card industry benefit from ageism. These industries prey on fears that young and middle-aged people hold about elders, fears everyone holds about their own aging, and the fears that elders hold about their well-being during old age.

The banking industry benefits from ageism in a variety of ways. Banks demonstrate entitlement to deny loans to elders and to charge higher interest rates on mortgages and other loans for which elders apply. Reverse mortgages prey on elders' fears of not being able to take care of themselves in older age. A reverse mortgage loan is a special type of mortgage loan for seniors (generally age sixty-two and older) that pays a homeowner proceeds from a loan drawn from their home's accumulated equity. Unlike a traditional home equity loan or second mortgage loan, no repayment is required until the borrower(s) no longer uses their home as their principal residence. Elders receive a monthly payment from the bank based on the reverse mortgage. This money can be used as flexible income for daily living expenses and is attractive for elders living on a fixed income. The problem is that interest on a reverse mortgage loan is calculated as compound interest (Division of Banks, 2012). This results in the steady decrease in the amount of home equity.

Funds from home equity that elders would have used to go into a retirement home or nursing home are no longer available. Elders are paying more for reverse mortgage loans than other people are paying for conventional loans because the interest is compounded. The banks use elders' fear of not having enough money to live on to increase their revenue at elders' expense. As is the case with adultism, these practices collectively maintain elder oppression while directing benefit and profit to middle-aged adults.

Internalized Ageism and Adultism

The ideas and attitudes that maintain ageism and adultism are internalized by all members of society. Middle-aged adults internalize a sense of the rightness and normality of their power and dominance over young people and elders. Constant bombardment with messages of powerlessness, helplessness, and hopelessness result in young people and elders believing that they deserve the subordinant status to which they have been relegated. There are a variety of ways that the internalization of adultism is manifested in young people. A few examples include: (1) participating in the targeting of and practice of subordinating other younger people. Younger people accept treatment from older young people that they would not accept from people younger than themselves; (2) believing that adults know best even when the ideas of the adults are clearly not in the best interest of the young person and/or when the young person has a different and better idea; (3) believing that young people should be quiet, seen and not heard; (4) being told that when young people get older they will understand themselves and the world, and that they will be able to make their own decisions, as if that capacity is somehow connected to age.

Some of the ways that internalized ageism is manifested in elders include: (1) believing that being old means being disabled; (2) accepting a marginalized status and a diminished life, such as feeling guilty and inappropriate for wanting to have sex or whatever it is they want to do; (3) feeling

that they can't question the expertise of professionals from whom they seek services, including medical professionals, social service providers, financial advisors, and others.

Summary and Conclusions

Any curriculum focusing on issues of social justice should include these integral issues. The failure to address these issues significantly diminishes the effectiveness of our efforts toward social justice. We are building the broad consensus that ageism and adultism are social justice issues. This consensus will help us to collectively work to end ageism, adultism, and other forms of oppression as a society. Understanding the ways that adultism serves as a learning foundation for the enactment of other oppressions can help build this consensus. Understanding the way that ageism keeps people living in fear of the presumed inevitable oppression that will be directed toward them as they age can help to build this consensus. Transforming our attitudes and practices related to ageism and adultism can also increase the effectiveness of our work on other forms of oppression.

Barbara Love
Keri DeJong

References

DeJong, K. (forthcoming). *On being and becoming: Young people's perspectives on status and power in childhood.* Manuscript in preparation.

DeJong, K. & Love, B. (forthcoming). Ageism and adultism. In M. Adams, W. J. Blumenfeld, R. Castaneda, H. W. Hackman, M. L. Peters, & X. Zuniga (Eds.). *Readings for diversity and social justice* (3rd ed.). New York: Routledge. Manuscript submitted for publication.

Division of Banks. (2012). *Reverse mortgage loans: What borrowers need to know.* Retrieved from the Massachusetts Office of Consumer Affairs and Business Regulation, http://www.mass.gov/ocabr.

Kingsley, D. (2011, June). Welfare queens, greedy geezers & the silver tsunami. *Gray Panthers: Age and youth in action.* Retrieved from https://graypanthers.org.

National Center on Elder Abuse. (2012). *Statistics at a glance.* Retrieved from http://www.ncea.aoa.gov/.

AGEISM

Training against Ageism in the Twenty-First Century

The concept of ageism first appeared in Max Lerner's 1957 book, *America as a Civilization*, but the term *ageism* was not coined until 1969, when the psychiatrist Robert Butler used it to explain why Washington, D.C., citizens opposed the construction of public housing for older people (Bytheway, 2005; Cohen, 2001). Narrowly defined, ageism is a process of systematic stereotyping, prejudice, and/or discrimination against a category of people based on their age (Butler, 2006; Bytheway, 2005; Palmore, 2001). According to this narrow definition, ageism is similar to other "-isms," such as sexism, which disadvantages and oppresses women, and racism, which disadvantages and oppresses minority ethnic groups, because younger groups of people often use stereotyping, prejudice, avoidance, and discrimination when interacting with aging individuals (Butler, 2006; Bytheway, 2005; Rupp, Vodanovich, & Credé, 2005).

According to Bytheway (2005), ageism's effect on older individuals manifests itself through discrimination and prejudice based on a person's chronological age and his/her body image. For instance, society has discriminated against older individuals by including age bars in insurance plans that make policies available only to adults under the age of sixty-five and by formally rejecting the images of older individuals in many advertising campaigns (Bytheway, 2005). In addition, society's prejudice against the aging population has been demonstrated by the inclusion of age in the calculation of statistical priorities and by the common occurrence of younger individuals avoiding contact with older individuals at social events (Bytheway, 2005).

However, the narrow definition of ageism does not take into account the complicated nature of this concept. Expressions of ageism can range from the subtle to the overt and both formally and informally affect systems and individuals (Rosowsky, 2005). In a broader context, Bytheway (2005) defined ageism as "a set of beliefs about how people vary biologically as a result of the aging process" (p. 339). This broader definition includes how this set of beliefs can generate and reinforce a lifelong fear of the aging process, how the fear of aging can

lead individuals to unconsciously project presumed associations between age and competence onto other age groups, and how such projections can underpin the actions of both individuals and organizations toward different age groups (Bytheway, 2005; Terry, 2008). In this context, ageism differs from other forms of prejudice and discrimination in two ways; for one, every person (no matter their sex or ethnic background) can become the target of ageism, and second, because ageism is a relatively recent and subtle concept, many people are unaware of its existence and implications on society (Bytheway, 2005; Palmore, 2001; Terry, 2008).

The broader definition portrays ageism as a double-sided phenomenon, with younger people projecting beliefs about older individuals (to rationalize their fears of aging) and older people projecting beliefs about younger individuals (to diminish their fears of becoming helpless and/or dependent) (Terry, 2008). Moreover, unlike racism and sexism, ageism has not been brought to the public's consciousness through extensive media attention or massive social action campaigns; therefore, individuals may be unconscious of their ageist beliefs, and such beliefs may be more difficult to detect because these views have been inadvertently woven into the very thread of our society (Bytheway, 2005; Rupp, Vodanovich, & Credé, 2005). For example, ageism has not only included the negative assessments of an individual's capacity based on his/her age, it has also included the dismissive or absolving attitudes, known as "benign" or "compassionate ageism" (Hendricks, 2005, p. 5). Many of the positive stereotypes about age groups (especially those held about older individuals) can be just as dehumanizing as the negative stereotypes because in both cases people have been placed into extreme categories that result in invisibility of the individual (Hendricks, 2005).

Research on Ageism

Research has found that most people either know very little about, or have many misconceptions about, aging (Bressler, 1996; Coe, Miller, Prendergast, & Grossberg, 1982; Damron-Rodriguez, Villa, Tseng & Lubben, 1997; Gellis, Sherman, & Lawrance, 2003; Kabacoff, Shaw, Putman, & Klein, 1983; Levy & West, 1985; Palmore, 1998; West & Levy,

1984). According to Palmore (1998), the average individual with a high school or less education has as many misconceptions about aging as they do correct conceptions. Even graduate and professional college students, including gerontology students, have been found to have high levels of misconceptions about aging. For example, graduate students in gerontology missed about one-third of the questions when given the Palmore Facts on Aging Quiz. In addition, Damron-Rodriguez, Villa, Tseng, and Lubben (1997) reported that only 2 percent of graduate social work students, who were not specializing in gerontology, reported taking any aging related graduate courses. In another study, Gellis, Sherman, and Lawrance (2003) found that first-year graduate social work students had low levels of knowledge about aging and older adulthood as well as very negative ideas about older adults. In addition, research has found that once educational levels were controlled, the levels of aging knowledge did not vary significantly between different sexes, ethnicities, or occupations, and the aging knowledge levels of individuals who had high contact with older adults did not vary greatly from the levels of individuals who had low contact with older adults (Bressler, 1996; Coe, Miller, Prendergast, & Grossberg, 1982; Kabacoff, Shaw, Putman, & Klein, 1983; Levy & West, 1985; West & Levy, 1984).

In his extremely influential research, which led to the development of the Palmore Facts on Aging Quiz (first published in 1977), Dr. Erdman B. Palmore (1998) of Duke University's Center for the Study of Aging and Human Development, found that most ageist beliefs were rooted in misconceptions about aging; most of the misconceptions about aging represented negative stereotypes. These findings led Palmore to conclude that neither the general public nor college-level students (including graduate-level students specializing in gerontology) had been adequately educated about the basic processes of aging and that most individuals needed formal educational experiences specifically designed to teach aging facts in order to gain accurate, fact-based knowledge.

A study by Palmore (2001) found that the majority of older respondents' surveyed felt that ageism was frequent and widespread. In fact, over 77 percent of the older adults (aged sixty and older) in his study (N = 84) reported experiencing ageism "one or more times," with more than half of the respondents reporting incidents that had occurred "more than once" (p. 573). The ageist events varied from the relatively benign, such as being told a joke that made fun of older people, to more serious incidents, such as being treated with less dignity and respect, being ignored, and being denied employment, promotion, and medical care. In addition, Ragan and Bowen (2001) contended that ageism was a major problem for society as we entered into the twenty-first century. They noted that one major hindrance in combating ageism was the fact that many older individuals tended to see age-related discrimination as coming from other causes, such as being a part of a minority group.

While much of the earlier research on ageist beliefs and the problems caused by ageism made claims of widespread implications, according to Kane (2006), the vast majority of the past research that has been done in regard to ageism has focused much more on the experiences of men rather than women. Researchers have only recently begun to consider older women's experiences with ageism, and unfortunately, much of that research has been founded on trait theory, which only focuses on stereotypical female traits, such as emotional expressiveness, low self-esteem, interdependence, connectedness, and submissiveness (Kane, 2006). Kane argues that these traditional perceptions of women need to be challenged by a twenty-first century, postmodern, feminist appraisal of power, sexuality, and gender-role expectations. Based on Kane's research, one could conclude that in addition to experiencing ageism in a similar way to their male counterparts, women may experience additional prejudice if they are seen to behave in a way that is outside of their supposed appropriate gender role for their age group.

The Aging Population
By the beginning of the twenty-first century, trends in life expectancy had changed drastically from the previous century. During the early twentieth century, life expectancy increased due to reductions in mortality of younger individuals, with life expectancy rising from 47.3 years of age in 1900 to 68.2 years of age in 1950; however, because of the reductions in mortality of older individuals, life

expectancy reached an all-time high of 76.9 years of age by 2000 (He, Sengupta, Velkoff, & DeBarros, 2005; National Center for Health Statistics, 2007). Additionally, in recent decades, developments in disease prevention, such as cancer screenings, vaccinations, diet, and physical activity, coupled with improvements in the treatment of chronic illnesses, such as heart disease, have caused a further reduction in the mortality rate of older individuals, resulting in longer life expectancies for individuals in the future (Federal Interagency Forum on Aging-Related Statistics, 2008; He et al., 2005).

A person born in the United States at the turn of the twentieth century could have expected to only live to around the age of forty-seven, and in 1900, the population of seniors (persons sixty-five years of age and older) numbered 3.1 million; however, throughout the twentieth century, the senior population was the largest expanding population in the United States, with the growth of the older population far surpassing the growth of other age groups (He et al., 2005; U.S. Bureau of Census, 2000). In 2000, the senior population in America included 35 million people, and with the advantages in health care, researchers project that this population would continue to grow at a much faster rate than younger age cohorts (He et al., 2005). Anyone, then, who plans to work in any professional field, should expect to deal frequently with older individuals; therefore, professionals in all fields should be equipped with the knowledge and skills necessary to successfully care for the needs of and/or provide services to this growing population of potential clients/consumers.

Common Expressions of Ageism

Ageism has manifested itself in ageist discourse, age discrimination, and faulty ageist beliefs, expressed through verbal and nonverbal language rooted in intentional and nonintentional biases of aging and aging persons (Rupp et al., 2005). Various prejudice behaviors, such as the antilocution and avoidance of older persons, have been prevalent characteristics of ageist practices based on ageist beliefs (Rupp et al., 2005).

Examples of Antilocution

- "Many old people are stingy and hoard their money and possessions."
- "Most old people should not be trusted to take care of infants."
- "Teenage suicide is more tragic than suicide among the old."
- "Complex and interesting conversation cannot be expected from most old people."

Examples of Avoidance

- "It is best that old people live where they don't bother anyone."
- "There should be special clubs set aside within sports facilities so that old people can compete at their own level."
- "I don't like it when old people try to make conversation with me."

(Rupp et al., 2005, pp. 343–45)

The Current Aging Cohort

The current aging cohort is made up of two aging populations: a younger aging population, known as the Silent Generation (individuals born between 1925 and 1945), and an older aging population, known as the GI Generation or the Greatest Generation (individuals born between 1901 and 1924) (Egri & Ralston, 2004; Strauss & Howe, 1991; Thau & Heflin, 1997). Because individuals in these generational groups came of age during times that demanded great sacrifice—namely, the Great Depression and World War II—they developed conservative spending habits, which demonstrated their need for security, and as they have aged, they have become even more conservative (Egri & Ralston, 2004; Strauss & Howe, 1991; Thau & Heflin, 1997). For example, as individuals in this cohort entered their fifties, they began saving more and spending less, which reflected their desire to age in a secure world where they could avoid the dangers and catastrophes that they had experienced during their early years (Hung, Gu, & Yim, 2007).

The current cohort of older adults (aged sixty-five and older) is conservative in moral matters as well. The ultraconservatism of the 1950s was a reflection of this groups' belief system, since a majority of the individuals in the current cohort were young and middle-aged adults in that decade (Sutherland, Poloma, & Pendleton, 2003). These individuals not only respected the authority of the government (demonstrated by their extreme patriotism and support of the "American way"), but they also respected the authority of traditional religion, which resulted in the large surge of church construction and growth during the 1950s (Gronbach, 2008; Sutherland et al., 2003). Along the same lines, during the 1950s, church attendance reached new heights (Sutherland et al., 2003). These individuals attended church, and they took their children with them; as a matter of fact, as children, 95 percent of baby boomers (people born between 1946 and 1964) participated in some form of traditional religious services during the postwar years (Sutherland et al., 2003). It is no surprise, then, that as the current cohort of seniors have aged, they have continued to cling to conservative values.

The Emerging Aging Cohort

The emerging cohort of aging individuals differs from the current cohort in many ways. First, the emerging cohort is much larger than the current cohort. The emerging cohort of older adults primarily consists of the baby boom generation, which is the largest generational cohort in American history (Egri & Ralston, 2004; Strauss & Howe, 1991, Thau & Heflin, 1997). According to U.S. Census Bureau projections, with baby boomers entering the sixty-five and older age bracket, the senior population is expected to increase substantially during the years 2010 to 2030 (He et al., 2005; Mellor & Rehr, 2005). By the year 2030, the senior population is projected to double what it was in 2000, reaching an astounding number of seventy-two million people, or one in five Americans, and representing nearly 20 percent of the total U.S. population (Federal Interagency Forum on Aging-Related Statistics, 2008; He et al., 2005).

Not only is the baby boomer cohort of aging individuals expected to be larger than the current cohort, it is also expected to be the healthiest aging cohort in American history; therefore, people in this cohort are expected to live longer than the current group of seniors (Czaja, 2006). The longer life expectancy of this future cohort will influence the aging population further. With baby boomers living longer, the U.S. Census Bureau projects a substantial increase in the future population of "the oldest-old" (individuals aged eighty-five and older) (He et al., 2005, p. 11). In 2003, there were 4.7 million people aged eighty-five or older in the United States, and the Census Bureau projects that number to double to 9.6 million people by the year 2030 (He et al., 2005). Furthermore, the Census Bureau projects that nine million (or one in nine) of the eighty million baby boomers would endure into their late nineties, and three million (or one in twenty-six) would live to be one hundred years of age (Population Reference Bureau, 2006). By 2050, when a majority of baby boomers have moved into the "oldest-old" age group, that population is expected to double yet again to 20.9 million people, accounting for 24 percent of the aging population (nearly one of every four older individuals) (He et al., 2005).

In addition to living longer, the baby boomer population is also more liberal than the current cohort in both spending habits and belief systems. First, in contrast to the current aging cohort, the baby boomers came of age during the period that followed World War II; the 1950s and 1960s were periods of unprecedented economic prosperity for Americans (Egri & Ralston, 2004). Because of their reasonably affluent upbringing, boomers developed more consumerist patterns of living than their parents had, and unlike their parents, they have maintained their spending habits into their later life, continuing to spend and take out loans even after they've entered the fifty-year-old age bracket (Hung, Gu, & Yim, 2007).

Another difference between the current and emerging cohorts is found in the way the two groups identify and participate in religious and social matters, with the emerging cohort being much more liberal in religious and social matters. Although a majority of baby boomers participated in church when they were children, many began to redefine themselves as they entered their teens and early twenties. During the mid-1960s, the boomers began questioning their parents' ideologies, while at the same time breaking away from traditional, institutionalized beliefs, choosing instead a more individualistic form of spirituality that combined elements of Eastern religion, meditation, Native

American practices, and drugs (Sutherland, Poloma, & Pendleton, 2003). Green (2003) proclaimed that as these individuals started to reach their late sixties, they did not adhere to their parents' religiosity and spirituality; they chose instead to hold fast to their consumerist habits by seeking products and services that empower, such as communication tools, motivational programs, and educational travel.

Training against Ageism in the Twenty-First Century

In twenty-first-century America, ageism frequently manifests itself in ageist discourse, age discrimination, and faulty ageist beliefs expressed through verbal and nonverbal language rooted in intentional and nonintentional biases toward aging and aging persons (Rupp et al., 2005). Various prejudice behaviors, such as the antilocution and avoidance of older persons, are all-too-prevalent characteristics of ageist practices based on ageist beliefs. With the aging population growing larger at an exponential rate in coming years, there will be a dramatic increase in the need for adequately trained professionals of all educational backgrounds, including those trained to work with mental-health-related disabilities, substance-use disorders (SUDs), physically disabling conditions, and those disabilities that co-occur or present in ways that are connected and/or interrelated (Dotson, 2012). The good news is that education works! There is plethora of consistent and reliable evidence suggesting that a person's knowledge about aging reflects his or her attitude toward older individuals, and when a person has a great deal of correct knowledge about aging, he or she tends to hold more positive beliefs toward older individuals (Allen, 1981; Ausherman, 1991; Ferrario, Freeman, Nellett, & Scheel, 2008; Jones, 1993; Klemmack, 1978; Linn & Zeppa, 1987; Palmore, 1977; Palmore, 1998; Patwell, 1991). In fact, education was the main variable that Palmore (1998) found that made a consistent, significant difference when it came to reducing ageist beliefs as well as in reducing negative bias toward older adults.

In conclusion, no matter what educational background we may have, or what professional group we may belong to, there is a very pressing need to start developing and delivering relevant, fact-centered educational interventions that are based on the research that has been done (or will be done) with members of the emerging cohort of older adults for best practices in working with members of the emerging aging cohort (as opposed to research based on data collected from the current cohort of older adults). It is important to remember the many substantial and purposeful differences among the two groups. As more is learned about what the wants, needs, problems, and preferences are of the emerging cohort in their later life, it will not be surprising if we discover that it will be more important to consider how these cohorts differ than to focus on the ways they are the same. After all, who knows what new, amazing medical breakthroughs await us? Who says that how we define "old" or "older adult" today will be how we define it in the future?

D. Gent Dotson
Holly R. Dotson
J. Chad Duncan
Shawn Ricks

References

Allen, B. (1981). Knowledge of aging: A cross-sectional study of three different age groups. *Educational Gerontology*, 6(1), 49–60.

Ausherman, J. (1991). Junior high health teachers' knowledge and attitudes about aging and implementation of aging education. *Educational Gerontology*, 17(4), 391–401.

Bressler, D. (1996). Occupational therapists' knowledge on aging. Master's Thesis, Levin School of Health Sciences, Touro College.

Butler, R. N. (2006). Ageism. In R. Schulz (Ed.), *The encyclopedia of aging* (pp. 41–42). New York: Springer Publishing Company.

Bytheway, B. (2005). Ageism. In M. Johnson (Ed.), *The Cambridge handbook of age and ageing* (pp. 338–45). Cambridge, UK: Cambridge University Press.

Coe, R., Miller, D., Prendergast, J., & Grossberg, G. (1982). Faculty resources for teaching geriatric medicine. *Journal of the American Geriatrics Society*, 30(1), 63–66.

Cohen, E. S. (2001). The complex nature of ageism: What is it? Who does it? Who perceives it? *The Gerontologist*, 41(5), 576–77.

Czaja, S. J. (2006). Employment and the baby boomers: What can we expect in the future? In S. K. Whitbourne (Ed.), *The baby boomers grow up:*

Contemporary perspectives on midlife (pp. 283–98). Mahwah, NJ: Laurence Erlbaum Associates, Inc., Publishers.

Damron-Rodriguez, J., Villa, V., Tseng, H. F., & Lubben, J. E. (1997). Demographic and organizational influences on the development of gerontological social work curriculum. *Gerontology and Geriatrics Education, 17*(3), 3–18.

Dotson, D. G. (2012). "The effects of an educational intervention on the aging knowledge of graduate counseling students" (2012). Dissertations. Paper 461. http://opensiuc.lib.siu.edu/dissertations/461.

Egri, C. P. & Ralston, D. A. (2004). Generation cohorts and personal values: A comparison of China and the United States. *Organization Science, 15*(2), 210–20.

Federal Interagency Forum on Aging-Related Statistics. (2008). *Older Americans 2008: Key indicators of well-being.* Washington, DC: U.S. Government Printing Office.

Ferrario, C. G., Freeman, F. J., Nellett, G., & Scheel, J. (2008). Changing nursing students' attitudes about aging: An argument for the successful aging paradigm. *Educational Gerontology, 34*(1), 51–66.

Gellis, A., Sherman, S., & Lawrence, F. (2003). First year graduate social work students' knowledge of and attitude toward older adults. *Educational Gerontology, 29*(1), 1–16.

Green, B. (2003). *Marketing to leading-edge baby boomers.* Lincoln, NE: iUniverse.

Gronbach, K. W. (2008). *The age curve: How to profit from the coming demographic storm.* New York: AMACOM.

He, W., Sengupta, M., Velkoff, V. A., & DeBarros, K. A. (2005). U.S. Census Bureau, Current Population Reports. (2005). *65+ in the United States: 2005* (P23–209). Washington, DC: Government Printing Office.

Hendricks, J. (2005). Ageism: Looking across the margin in the new millennium. *Generations, 29*(3), 5–7.

Hung, K. H., Gu, F. F., & Yim, C. K. (2007). A social institutional approach to identifying generation cohorts in China with a comparison with American consumers. *Journal of International Business Studies, 38,* 836–53.

Jones, V. (1993). Attitudes and knowledge level of nursing personnel toward elderly persons. Master's Thesis at Russell Sage College.

Kabacoff, R., Shaw, I., Putman, E., & Klein, H. (1983). Comparison of administrators and direct service workers in agencies dealing with the elderly. *Psychological Reports, 52*(3), 979–85.

Kane, M. N. (2006). Ageism and gender among social work and criminal justice students. *Educational Gerontology, 32*(10), 859–880.

Klemmack, D. (1978). An examination of Palmore's FAQ. *The Gerontologist, 18*(4), 403–6.

Levy, W. & West, H. (1985, October 19). *Knowledge of aging in human service professions.* Paper presented at the annual meeting of the Texas chapter, National Association of Social Workers, Dallas, TX.

Linn, B. & Zeppa, R. (1987). Predicting third year medical students' attitudes toward the elderly and treating the old. *Gerontology & Geriatrics Education, 7*(3–4), 167–75.

Mellor, M. J. & Rehr, H. (Ed.). (2005). *Baby boomers: Can my eighties be like my fifties?* New York: Springer Publishing Co.

National Center for Health Statistics. (2007). *United States, 2007 with chartbook on trends in the health of Americans* (76–641496). Hyattsville, MD: U.S. Government Printing Office.

Palmore, E. (1977). Facts on aging: A short quiz. *The Gerontologist, 17*(4), 315–20.

Palmore, E. (1998). *The Facts on Ageing Quiz* (2nd ed.). New York: Springer.

Palmore, E. (2001). The ageism survey: First findings. *The Gerontologist, 41*(5), 572–75.

Patwell, T. (1991). Attitudes toward and knowledge about the elderly among acute-care nursing staff. Master's Research Paper, University of Wisconsin-Madison of Nursing.

Population Reference Bureau, Research Highlights in the Demography and Economics of Aging. (2006). *The future of human life expectancy: Have we reached the ceiling or is the sky the limit?* Retrieved from http://www.prb.org/pdf06/NIA_Futureof LifeExpectancy.pdf.

Ragan, A. M. & Bowen, A. M. (2001). Improving attitudes regarding the elderly population: The effects of information and reinforcement for change. *The Gerontologist, 41*(4), 511–15.

Rosowsky, E. (2005). Ageism and professional training in aging: Who will be there to help? *Generations, 29*(3), 55–58.

Rupp, D. E., Vodanovich, S. J., & Credé, M. (2005). The multidimensional nature of ageism: Construct validity and group differences. *Journal of Social Psychology, 14*(3), 335–62.

Strauss, W. & Howe, N. (1991). *Generations: The history of America's future, 1584–2069.* New York: William Morrow and Company, Inc.

Sutherland, J. A., Poloma, M. M., & Pendleton, B. F. (2003). Religion, spirituality, and alternative health practices: The baby boomer and cold war cohorts. *Journal of Religion and Health, 42*(4), 315–38.

Terry, P. (2008). Ageism and projective identification. *Psychodynamic Practice, 14*(2), 155–68.

Thau, R. D. & Heflin, J. S. (1997). *Generation apart: Xers vs. boomers vs. the elderly.* New York: Prometheus Books.

U.S. Bureau of Census. (2000). *Statistical abstract of the U.S.* Washington: Government Printing Office.

West, H. & Levy, W. (1984). Knowledge of aging in the medical profession. *Gerontology and Geriatrics Education, 4*(4), 23–31.

AGNOSTICISM

Agnosticism and Knowledge Acquisition

The term *agnosticism* is derived from the prefix *a*, meaning "without," and the Greek word *gnosis*, meaning "knowledge." Hence, the literal translation: "lacking knowledge." The concept of agnosticism, also known as skepticism, is central to the history of Western and Eastern philosophical thought.

The agnostic doubts the possibility of human knowledge in one or more domains of inquiry, especially the domain of metaphysics (the field that attempts to determine the nature of ultimate reality). In this sense, the term *agnostic* is synonymous with *skeptic*, *doubter*, and so forth.

Examples will help clarify the concept. In India, Siddhartha Gautama, or the Buddha, was doubtful about the reality of the ego (the self) and other such metaphysical notions (e.g., the eternality of the world) evident in many of his followers, including the Indian philosopher Nagarjuna (Berger, n.d.). In the west, Cicero's *Academica* (Book 1, section 1) ascribes to Socrates, the ancient Greek philosopher, the famous proclamation, "I know one thing: that I know nothing." Similarly, the ancient Greek philosopher and self-proclaimed skeptic, Sextus Empiricus, in *Outlines of Pyrrhonism*, maintains that any philosophical thesis can be countered by a counterthesis of equal argumentative strength; from this he concluded that a rational person suspends judgment (epoche) on all philosophical matters.

Two kinds of agnosticism may be distinguished. The first kind, characteristic of the Pyrrhonian skeptics and some Buddhist philosophers, involves a suspension of judgment regarding some metaphysical proposition *p* (e.g., "The soul exists"). Call this negative agnosticism. The negative agnostic neither affirms nor denies *p*, but suspends all judgment on the matter. This form of agnosticism is comparable to the answer of one who is asked, "How much change do I have in my pocket?" The answer will likely be, "I don't know." To say that one does not know is not to commit oneself to any particular view—certainly not to the view that it is impossible to know. Rather, neither the belief that *p* nor the belief that not-*p* plays a significant role in one's life. This form of agnosticism stands in contrast to the positive agnostic who affirms that *p* is unknowable. A positive agnostic will likely have arrived at it after having considered and rejected some arguments for *p* or because of some principled reason for thinking it impossible to settle the issue (e.g., the belief that human knowledge is too finite and limited to make such a determination).

Within a religious context, the agnostic either suspends judgment regarding the existence of God (negative agnosticism) or positively believes that God's existence is unknowable (positive agnosticism). Agnosticism, in either case, constitutes one of three major positions on the issue of whether God exists—the others being theism and atheism, belief and disbelief in God, respectively. Agnosticism about God thus falls under the domain of metaphysics.

Agnosticism can range over any and all conceptions of god, or extend only to some particular conception. For example, one can be agnostic about the God of traditional monotheism but affirm theism or atheism in respect to the Greek gods. The God of Judaism, Christianity, and Islam is the deity of primary conceptual and philosophical interest among Western scholars. For all three Abrahamic faiths, God—note the capital *G*—is a personal being who is all-knowing (omniscient), all-powerful (omnipotent), all-good (omnibenevolent), and everywhere present (omnipresent). God is the supreme and sole creator of the universe, who created human beings for a special purpose. In Eastern tradition, the term *God* primarily refers to the Dao of ancient China or Brahman, the God of Hinduism. In either case, God is conceived in pantheistic fashion, as an impersonal and nonmoral being that permeates the entire cosmos (Geden, 1908b, pp. 284–85). Brahman is conceived as the source of personal liberation from maya (unreality and illusion) and hence from earthly and bodily bondage (p. 285). Monotheism and pantheism provide the context for most contemporary discussions of theism, atheism, and agnosticism.

Agnosticism and Knowledge Acquisition

Skepticism as a vehicle to knowledge acquisition has ancient roots. The skeptical role is that of raising objections to substantive theses and theories. The skeptic's objections essentially become tests of truth. A good objection determines a standard to be met by any belief purporting to be reasonable.

In ancient India, the format known as destructive (vitanda) debate, devised by Buddhist Logicians of the Nyaya school, encouraged skeptical methods as a means of identifying true beliefs (Prets, 2000, pp. 374–75). According to this debating style, the first debater bears the burden of defending a substantive thesis, while the second bears the burden of casting doubt on it by refuting its supporting arguments. This style stands in contrast to the style of debate (jalpa) more common in the West (e.g., Oxford-style debate), according to which the second debater offers a counter thesis along with supporting arguments; in jalpa, both sides are required to "prove" their respective theses. By contrast, in vitanda, the second debater is not permitted to appeal to any substantive theses or theories; the only valid method permitted is the effective deployment of standard and well-known logical methods, such as teasing out logical fallacies (or errors in reasoning) in opponents' arguments (e.g., infinite regress, circularity and vacuous principle). The underlying premise is that a true thesis should be capable of meeting the strongest and most sophisticated objections that can be raised against it.

This method of debate shares important affinities with the method of refutation advanced by Socrates (e.g., in Plato's *Republic* and *Euthyphro*), formally known, in logic, as reductio ad absurdum—which is Latin for reducing one's opponent to absurdity. This style of argument assumes the truth of an opponent's position and draws out its implications (by asking follow-up questions) until a formal contradiction is derived; the opponent's position is thereby disproved. Socrates' method of refutation only puts forth premises that are accepted by the opponent. It is incorrect, however, to think that skepticism was

Socrates' goal. Just as the destructive style of debate in the East was designed to arrive at truth, the same is true for Socrates. For him, the only way to arrive at truth—i.e., to distinguish knowledge from mere opinion—is via process of elimination; that is, subjecting popular philosophical doctrines and beliefs to the method of reductio ad absurdum so that false doctrines are removed, and only true propositions remain. Near the end of his life, Socrates concluded that he had not yet come across a thesis that satisfied his criterion; hence, he remained agnostic.

That skepticism or doubt as an excellent tool of knowledge acquisition is at the heart of the term's coinage. It is commonly believed that the term *agnostic* originated with biologist and freethinker Thomas H. Huxley in the late 1800s, who used it as a method of evaluating beliefs according to their probability.

Huxley contemplated the popular thinking and defined methods of creating and dedicating oneself to a particular belief. He wanted to break down the multitude of unanswered questions, especially the question of the existence of God. He stated:

> Agnosticism is not a creed but a method, the essence of which lies in the vigorous application of a single principle. Positively the principle may be expressed as, in matters of the intellect, follow your reason as far as it can carry you without other considerations. And negatively, in matters of the intellect, do not pretend the conclusions are certain that are not demonstrated or demonstrable. It is wrong for a man to say he is certain of the objective truth of a proposition unless he can produce evidence which logically justifies that certainty.

The *agnostic* subscribes to agnosticism, a term which may be used to denote the suspension of belief in god or the positive belief that god's existence is unknowable. Agnosticism is one of three major positions on the issue of whether a god exists, the others being *theism* and *atheism*, belief and disbelief in god, respectively. Theism promotes belief in the existence of a higher power, a belief in one Supreme Being. Atheism, conversely, promotes a lack of belief in a Supreme Being.

Noteworthy is the fact that the terms *a* and *gnosis* in the etymological definition make no reference to a deity. This fact partly explains why it is popular, in common usage, to use the term outside a theistic context. Thus, atheism is not a denial of Supreme Being, as one might believe; rather, it is a lack of belief that a Supreme Being exists that sets atheism apart from other beliefs. Therefore, it is unquestionable that atheism is simply not a religion. Atheism is profoundly the belief in a *lack* of a Supreme Being; this argument disbelieves that such gods and supernatural beings exist. People should not try to make atheism a religion—it is not.

The term *agnostic* was first coined by biologist and freethinker Thomas H. Huxley in the late 1800s.

> When I reached intellectual maturity and began to ask myself whether I was an atheist, a theist, or a pantheist; a materialist or an idealist; a Christian or a freethinker; I found that the more I learned and reflected, the less ready was the answer; until, at last, I came to the conclusion that I had neither art nor part with any of these denominations, except the last. The one thing in which most of these good people were agreed was the one thing in which I differed from them. They were quite sure they had attained a certain "gnosis,"—had, more or less successfully, solved the problem of existence; while I was quite sure I had not, and had a pretty strong conviction that the problem was insoluble. (Huxley, 1902/2005, para. 43)

Huxley's reference to the "insoluble problem" of acquiring knowledge about religious matters might lead one to conclude that he defines agnosticism as the position that god's existence is unknowable. But this is not intended to be a definition of agnosticism, for agnosticism, in his view, is not a substantive position but a method of inquiry. As stated previously:

> Agnosticism, in fact, is not a creed, but a method, the essence of which lies in the rigorous application of a single principle ... Positively the principle may be expressed: In matters of the intellect, follow your reason as far as it will take you, without regard to any other consideration. And negatively: In matters of the intellect do not pretend that conclusions are certain which are not demonstrated or demonstrable. (Huxley, 1902/2005, para. 56)

Understood to be a mere method, agnosticism is compatible with theism, since a theist might apply

Huxley's methodology of "following reason as far as it will take you" and conclude that reason establishes theism. Today, common usage of *agnosticism* clearly expands its meaning to include the positive belief that knowledge of god is impossible. In this sense, the ancient Greek philosopher, Protagoras (Poster, n.d.), expressed agnosticism when he wrote, "Concerning the gods, I have no means of knowing whether they exist or not or of what sort they may be. Many things prevent knowledge including the obscurity of the subject and the brevity of human life" (DK80b4).

Although agnosticism has historically been a minority position, its numbers seem to be steadily growing (Zuckerman, 2007). The Freethought movement of the nineteenth and twentieth centuries stressed the conviction that beliefs should not be based on authority, but on reason and argument, including knowledge from experience, logic, and science. Although some freethinkers were atheists and Christians, many others, including Thomas Huxley (2005), Robert Ingersoll (2012), and W. E. B. Du Bois (Johnson, 2008), were committed agnostics.

As a distinctive doctrine or theory, atheism does not provide a roadmap for how people should conduct their lives or offer celebrations and rituals like most religious beliefs. It postulates a thesis that a higher power does not exist. As a result, it would be wrong to consider atheism a philosophy or a lifestyle or a particular belief system. Atheism is the belief in the absence of a god. It is not anti-religious ideology. It is this conception that provides the context for contemporary discussions of theism, atheism, and agnosticism. Hence, this conception is assumed throughout this entry.

Agnosticism in Theological Context: An Argument

It is helpful to situate agnosticism in the context of philosophical discussions over the existence of God. Philosophers since medieval times have developed arguments for God's existence. These arguments grew out of Natural Theology, a field that attempts to understand the nature of God by rational means. Christians believed that many truths about God could be known by means of the "natural light" of reason and experience—that is, without the aid of divine revelation. Natural theology stands in contrast to Revealed Theology, a field that attempts to understand the nature of God by divine revelation (i.e., sacred religious texts). St. Thomas Aquinas believed that certain facts about God, including God's existence, could be rationally demonstrated, whereas other facts about God (e.g., that Jesus is the Son of God) could not, and required the divine revelation and grace of God.

Although there are numerous arguments for God, the most important of these, historically speaking, are the Ontological, Cosmological, and Teleological arguments. For our purposes, it is sufficient that we consider Aquinas's Cosmological Argument in *Summa Theologia* (1: 2, 3), which appeals to the experience of cause and effect and argues that the universe demands a "first cause." His argument from efficient causation maintains that every event has a cause and that this chain of causes and effects cannot go on forever; therefore, there must be a first cause that began the entire chain of events. One might object that no first cause is necessary since the entire cause-effect series might be infinite. But, argues Aquinas, the concept of an infinite past entails a logical contradiction, for without a first cause there would be no second cause and hence no third cause, etc. and hence no present moment. Additionally, the universe cannot be the cause of its own existence, for it must exist prior to causing itself in order to do so. Therefore, since it is self-contradictory to believe in an infinite universe or a self-caused universe, there must be an uncaused first cause (i.e., God).

Philosophers have criticized the classic theistic arguments (e.g., Martin, 1992); the Cosmological Argument is no exception. David Hume (1779/1947) and Immanuel Kant's (1781/1929) criticisms are held by many to be decisive. Additionally, atheists have devised independent arguments against God's existence (see **Atheism**). Such debates, however, continue within the contemporary philosophy of religion.

What is the significance of this philosophical context for understanding agnosticism? It is undeniable that intellectual disagreement over God's existence persists. Very intelligent philosophers from diverse historical and ethnic backgrounds and cultures, spanning over two thousand years, diverge on this issue despite their appeal to rational argumentation (Martin, 1992; Swinburne, 2004). This glaring fact, one might think, should lead one to pause. The agnostic might use the history of philosophical controversy to argue that it is impossible to rationally settle the matter (Oppy, 2006).

Varieties of Agnosticism: Negative-Positive and Committed-Uncommitted

POSITIVE AGNOSTICISM Philosophers of religion have taken an interest in two kinds of agnosticism: positive and negative agnosticism. Positive agnosticism takes the affirmative position that the fact of whether a particular god exists is unknowable. For our purposes, let us remain focused on the traditional God of monotheism. Two or more agnostics may affirm the positive conclusion that God's existence is unknowable with varying degrees of strength. As it appears that no one has raised this distinction in the literature before, let us coin the terms *uncommitted* and *committed* forms of positive agnosticism, respectively. The *committed* positive agnostic asserts that God's existence is unknowable in principle, whereas the *uncommitted* agnostic asserts that God's existence is unknowable as of now—that is, given the current state of the evidence. The uncommitted agnostic, in other words, is open to the possibility that the current state of the evidence may change, tipping the balance in favor of either theism or atheism. What unifies both forms as positive forms of agnosticism is the fact that each of them involves a positive assertion. Moreover, in both cases, the conclusion of agnosticism is reached by means of a critical assessment of the arguments for and against God's existence.

UNCOMMITTED AND COMMITTED POSITIVE AGNOSTICISM *Uncommitted* positive agnostics maintain that the fact of whether God exists is knowable, in principle, even though the available evidence to make such a determination is insufficient. The agnostic may be philosophically interested in discovering the truth of the matter. Hence, this brand of agnosticism is akin to skepticism. Like Socrates, the agnostic is committed to pursuing truth, wherever it leads. However, like Sextus Empiricus, such optimism is curbed by the recognition that a rational conclusion must await further and better evidence.

Committed positive agnosticism is less optimistic about discovering whether theism or atheism is true. The committed agnostic is convinced that it is impossible, in principle, to know whether God exists. It is conceivable that some positive agnostics may have an independent argument for their position—e.g., along the lines of Sextus's mode of argumentation. One may feel, for instance, that given the fact that future arguments for theism and atheism are likely to be variants and updated versions of older ones, it is safe to conclude that similar criticisms and counterarguments will ultimately lead to a stalemate; therefore, the question of God's existence is likely to remain unsettled. Consequently, reasons the committed agnostic, as the arguments on both sides have been examined, the rational conclusion to draw is that they are in principle inadequate; that reason cannot settle the matter; and that the rational person suspends judgment and remains firm in the conclusion that God's existence is unknowable.

To sum up the characteristic differences of uncommitted and committed agnosticism: Whereas the uncommitted agnostic weighs the evidence and concludes that it is not *yet* possible to reach a verdict (so that one must continue suspending judgment until further notice), the committed agnostic believes that sufficient evidence is in and the verdict more or less conclusive: God's existence is in principle unknowable.

Positive agnosticism, in either of its forms, carries a *burden of proof*. The positive agnostic asserts a positive claim about what is—or, rather, what is not—knowable. He or she must, therefore, substantiate this claim by rational argumentation, if his or her position is to be justified. The most obvious way to do this is via critical examination of the arguments for and against God's existence; such a study would aim to prove that neither theism nor atheism is justified.

NEGATIVE AGNOSTICISM *Negative agnosticism* is not a substantive view or position, but the lack thereof. The negative agnostic asserts that one, personally, does not know whether God exists. This form of agnosticism is comparable to the answer of one who is asked, "How much change do I have in my pocket?" The answer will likely be, "I don't know." To say that one does not know is

not to commit oneself to any particular view on the matter—certainly not to the view that it is impossible to know. The same logic may apply to knowledge of God, for the negative agnostic affirms *no* view on the matter. He or she may suspend judgment for one of three reasons:

1. The agnostic has no knowledge of the evidence for and against God.
2. The agnostic has little or no interest in examining the evidence.
3. The agnostic is not persuaded by the evidence and prefers to suspend judgment.

Not all agnostics find the issue of God's existence important or serious enough to merit attention. This has led some to count among the number of agnostics those who take no interest in religious matters as well as those who have never been exposed to the idea of God. The argument for this is that all such persons lack sufficient knowledge to come to any reasonable conclusion; therefore, they satisfy the definition of an agnostic. Even more controversial is the claim that infants and young children are agnostics because they have no beliefs about God.

One objection to counting the aforementioned individuals as agnostics is that they are actually atheists. If a person lacks a concept of God and therefore cannot believe in God, he or she satisfies the definition of an atheist. One reply is that atheism and agnosticism are not mutually exclusive; which is to say, an individual can be both. After all, negative atheism is a view about what a person fails to *believe*, negative agnosticism is a view about what a person fails to *know*. Consequently, one may not know whether God exists and still believe or fail to believe. For this reason, following Robert Flint (1903), let us coin the term *atheist-agnostic*: this is a person who does not believe in God because he or she lacks knowledge of God's existence (i.e., has no reason to believe). On this analysis, many atheists may be surprised to discover they are also agnostics, and vice versa.

Among agnostics who find the issue of God's existence worthy of consideration are those who adamantly refuse to commit to any position. For even if they have examined the relevant evidence, they are not prepared to assent to any thesis; not even the thesis that God's existence is unknowable. The negative agnostic prefers to suspend judgment.

The Jamesian Objection to Agnosticism

Of the many objections to agnosticism, only one can be considered here. William James's "The Will to Believe" (1897/2009) argues that individuals are sometimes justified in believing religious claims on insufficient evidence, provided that the evidence is inconclusive one way or the other and the individual has a will to believe. In developing this argument, James (almost in passing) suggests that his contemporaries cannot be agnostic about God's existence because remaining undecided is effectively deciding in favor of atheism. A reasonable interpretation of this assertion is that atheism and agnosticism are not two but one and the same position. If this is correct, agnosticism is identical to atheism. One might agree with James on this point if one thinks that atheism and agnosticism are practically indistinguishable. One cannot tell from the lives of practicing atheists and agnostics that there is any difference between them. Most atheists and agnostics do not attend religious services and events, nor do they pray and worship a deity. In short, the concept of God plays absolutely no religious role in the lives of atheists and agnostics.

If atheists and agnostics live indistinguishable lives, what are we to make of the distinction between atheist and agnostic? It could be argued that the reason why some people self-identify as agnostics, when they are really atheists, is that they do not want to face up to the consequences of being atheists; others may want to distance themselves from the stigma and negative connotations of the term. Atheists are often accused of being closed-minded and just as dogmatic as theists. Thus, for many, the term *agnostic* is more appealing than *atheist* because it suggests a sense of open-mindedness and distance from dogmatism. Whatever the reason, atheists who prefer the label *agnostic* do not want to be identified as atheists. But, so the argument goes, the mere fact that one does not wish to be *called* an atheist does not change the fact that one *is* an atheist.

The agnostic may want to combat this argument by insisting on a cognitive difference. Is it really true that the difference between atheism and agnosticism is purely definitional? Is it really true that the atheist is simply more courageous than the agnostic because he or she is willing to face up to what he or she believes? One reply to these allegations is that the Jamesian makes too much of similarities in the lifestyles of the atheist and agnostic. Whether there are practical differences between the two is beside the point. It may be true that atheists and agnostics both live nontheistic lifestyles, but why should this suggest that there is no cognitive difference between them? The difference between them is plain to see: one disbelieves in God (the positive atheist) while the other suspends judgment or claims it is impossible to know (the agnostic). Is this not difference enough? If so, then the objection to agnosticism fails because it mistakenly conflates practical similarity with cognitive similarity.

Another possible reply to James is that the suggestion that no differences in form of life can be found among atheists and agnostics is false. To be sure, the atheist and agnostic share a nontheistic lifestyle, but one need not reflect for long to discover that positive atheism differs practically from some forms of agnosticism. Agnosticism, understood as methodological skepticism, involves a life of questioning and searching for the truth, of actively seeking out arguments for and against God. But many atheists do not live this way, for they are convinced that God does not or cannot exist; for them, the truth is already known, and the question settled. More radical differences between the agnostic and atheist surface if we compare a skeptic-like agnostic, such as Socrates, to a dogmatic atheist, such as a so-called New Atheist. New Atheists actively reject and speak out against religion and its moral ills. New Atheists, one might say, live a life that is *anti*-God, whereas many agnostics do not. Thus, agnosticism, like atheism, is compatible with a variety of distinct forms of life.

Alberto G. Urquidez

References

Berger, D. (n.d.). Nagarjuna (c. 150–c. 250). In J. Fieser & B. Dowden (Eds.), *Internet encyclopedia of philosophy*. Retrieved from http://www.iep.utm.edu/nagarjun/.

Flint, R. (1903). *Agnosticism. The Croall lecture for 1887–88*. Edinburgh: William Blackwood and Sons.

Geden, A. S. (1908). God (Hindu). In J. Hastings, J. A. Selbie, & L. L. Gray (Eds.), *Encyclopædia of religion and ethics* (vol. 6, pp. 282–290). Retrieved from https://archive.org/details/encyclopaediaofr01 hastuoft.

Hume, D. (1947). In N. K. Smith (Ed.), *Dialogues concerning natural religion* (2nd ed.). Edinburgh: Nelson & Sons. (Original work published 1779.)

Huxley, T. H. (2005). VII: Agnosticism. *Collected essays: Volume V science and Christian tradition* (pp. 209–62). New York: D. Appleton & Company. Retrieved from http://www.gutenberg.org/files/ 15905/15905-h/15905-h.htm#VII. (Original work published in 1902.)

Ingersoll, R. G. (2012). Why am I an agnostic? In Dresden (Ed.), *The works of Robert G. Ingersoll*, 11. Retrieved from http://www.gutenberg. org/files/38811/38811-h/38811-h.htm#link0010. (Original work published in 1900.)

James, W. (2009). *The will to believe. The will to believe and other essays in popular philosophy* (pp. 1–31). New York: Longmans, Green, and Co. Retrieved from http://www.gutenberg.org/ebooks/26659. (Original work published in 1897.)

Johnson, B. L. (2008). *W. E. B. Du Bois: Toward agnosticism, 1868–1934*. Lanham, MD: Rowman & Littlefield Publishers.

Kant, I. (1929). *Critique of pure reason.* (N. Kemp Smith, Trans.). New York: St. Martin's Press. (Original work published 1781.)

Martin, M. (1992). *Atheism: A philosophical justification.* Philadelphia, PA: Temple University Press.

Oppy, G. (2006). *Arguing about gods.* Cambridge, NY: Cambridge University Press.

Poster, C. (n.d.). Protagoras (fl. 5th C. BCE). In J. Fieser & B. Dowden (Eds.), *Internet encyclopedia of philosophy.* Retrieved from http://www.iep.utm.edu/ protagor.

Prets, E. (2000). *Theories of debate, proof and counter-proof in the early Indian dialectical tradition* (pp. 369–382). Paper presented at the International Conference on Sanskrit and Related Studies to Commemorate the Centenary of the Birth of Stanislaw Schayer, Warsaw, Poland. Retrieved from https://www.istb.univie.ac.at/caraka/file_down load/56.

Swinburne, R. G. (2004). *The existence of god* (2nd ed.). New York: Oxford University Press.

Zuckerman, P. (2007). Atheism: Contemporary numbers and patterns. In M. Martin (Ed.), *The Cambridge companion to atheism* (pp. 47–68). Cambridge: Cambridge University Press.

ALLY

In the education literature concerned with social justice and diversity, conceptions of the term *ally* generally use the term to reflect a relationship between people or relationships that people have to a cause or struggle for change. In other words, the term *ally* generally reflects a person-centered, principle-centered relationship, or both. In an essay from 1993 that was later published, Gloria Anzaldúa (2000) described the dynamics she experienced while working to forge alliances (as relationships of action) that included working toward certain goals. She discussed the many positions and experiences that one might bring to an alliance (i.e., gender, sexual identity, professional status) and stressed the importance of communicating a stance when forging an alliance. In discussing antiracist allies in particular, Tatum (1994) has stressed the need for antiracist education to shift from understandings of victims and victimizers to reframe *ally* as a social identity that includes: (1) understanding allies as people of color who enact a stance, and (2) identifying the position in the racial stratification through which one works as an ally (i.e., white allies). She described allies as a relationship defined by stance over identity, which suggests that alliances are principle centered rather than person centered. An understanding of ally as principle and person centered has been described by Kendall (2006), who defined *ally* as "a person [who] is associated with another or others for some common cause or purpose" (p. 142). She differentiates between ally to a principle or issue and ally to a person: "I realized I am basically an ally to issues" (p. 144), and "[w]hen I ally to a person I act in support of the person's ideology" (p. 146).

In contrast to these conceptualizations of ally, regardless of social position, are those that define *ally* as a person in a position of social privilege. This conceptualization of ally has become prevalent among Lesbian, Gay, Bisexual, Transgender, Queer/ Questioning, and Intersex (LGBTQI) activists and advocates concerned with the development of allies, with *ally* defined as being a member of the dominant or majority group who works to end oppression and as an advocate with and for the oppressed. Drawing on the idea that allies are members of privileged groups, education literature has begun to focus on white students and educators who advocate for social justice in schools or communities. The association of ally with a position of privilege has been challenged in recognition that people from less privileged social positions serve as allies (in the struggles) for social justice (Agosto, 2010).

Vonzell Agosto

References

Agosto, V. (2010). Incongruent conceptualizations: Prospective teachers of color as social justice allies. *Teacher Education & Practice, 23*(4), 507–21.

Anzaldúa, G. (2000). Allies. In M. Adams, W. J. Blumenfeld, R. Castañeda, H. W. Hackman, M. L. Peters, & X. Zúñiga (Eds.), *Readings for diversity and social justice: An anthology on racism, anti-Semitism, sexism, heterosexism, ableism, and classism* (pp. 475–77). New York: Routledge.

Kendall, F. (2006). *Understanding white privilege: Creating pathways to authentic relationships across race.* New York: Routledge.

Tatum, B. (1994). Teaching white students about racism: The search for allies and the restoration of hope. *Teachers College Record, 95*(4), 462–76.

ANARCHISM

Anarchism is a political ideology that advocates a stateless society comprised of self-governing communities in voluntary association. Anarchists view the state as an agent of oppression, typically working in conjunction with capital to exploit vulnerable elements of society. The basic precept of anarchism is individual freedom and rejection of hierarchal systems. Under such principles, anarchism represents a varied and contradictory philosophy, remade constantly to fit the social context of the era and rarely united in purpose. Furthermore, anarchism shares values with other leftist groups resulting in substantial movement between anarchists and other political movements.

Early anarchist philosophies emerged during the 1500s as heretical Reformation movements seeking to destroy the existing religious order along with the established social and political institutions. The Age of Revolution, however, provided the background to establish anarchism as a legitimate political philosophy. William Godwin, writing during the 1790s, linked the need for justice and equality as essential for the happiness of people and proposed the abolition of property and state. Godwin lacked the revolutionary fervor of later anarchists and espoused a largely individualist form of anarchy, but he laid important ideological foundations concerning the constraints state and property places upon the development of society. Philosopher Pierre-Joseph Proudhon expanded upon the anarchist ideology, attacking property but blending the line between collectivist and individualist forms of anarchy (Joll, 1979). The Russians Mikhail Bakunin and Peter Kropotkin developed the two primary strains of anarchy of the late nineteenth and early twentieth centuries. Despite advocating competing forms of anarchism, both sought the abolition through revolution of the state and private ownership of production. Bakunin argued in favor of a collectivist approach, where means of production would be owned by the people, but he stopped short of communist beliefs held by Kropotkin, who supported communal property and the abolition of wage systems. Both rejected the Marxist principle of the dictatorship of the proletariat (Joll, 1979; Skirda, 2002).

By the late nineteenth century, anarchism spread within the nascent labor movements in Europe and the Americas, where anarchists envisioned labor unions as the revolutionary vehicle to eliminate the state and capital interests. Unlike Marxists who sought change within the political system, anarchists avoided political action and feared the power of any political party as ultimately hierarchal. Syndicalist movements sought to organize noncompetitive federations, but they became more anarchist as the movement noted the government support of capital. Anarcho-syndicalism informed much of the labor movement in Europe, particularly in locations of developing economy such as Spain and Italy. In the United States, anarcho-syndicalism influenced radical labor groups such as the International Workers of the World. Anarcho-syndicalism sought worker self-management through direct action such as strikes, violence, and boycotts. Most notoriously, several anarchist leaders preached "propaganda of the deed," in which violence and terror against the bourgeois state would call attention to the struggles of the world's workers. By the turn of the twentieth century, anarchist violence through assassinations and bombings stigmatized the movement as sociopathic and ultraviolent. State attempts to curtail propaganda by the deed led to a cycle of retaliatory violence. The vast majority of anarchist violence took place in Europe, resulting in numerous assassinations and random terror. The United States, also struggling with labor unrest, witnessed a number of events attributed to anarchism, including the Haymarket Square bombing and the assassination of President McKinley. Fears of anarchist violence and socialist ideologies fueled xenophobia toward poor European immigrants who Americans blamed as agents of radicalism. The fear of radical immigrants prompted stricter immigration laws and intense government oppression that culminated in the persecution of the Industrial Workers of the World, arrest and deportation of radicals such as Emma Goldman, and the ultimately the Palmer Raids upon leftist groups in the United States. Following World War I and the Marxist Revolution in Russia, anarchism became more provincial and isolated. Communism absorbed the anarchist groups in industrial societies, but anarchism remained strong in nations with little industry and strong peasantry, such as Italy and Spain. Spanish anarcho-syndicalists fought a bitter civil battle against fascist right-wing forces. The Spanish revolution in Catalonia collectivized agrarian production and placed factory work under worker control, but anarchism gave ground to socialism as support from the Soviet Union supported the antifascist forces. Ultimately, the victory of fascism pushed anarchists back underground, but anarcho-syndicalist groups exist to this day (Joll, 1979).

Anarchism, socialism, and communism share many ideologies, resulting in the transfer of ideas and movement between the groups and occasional unification for a cause, such as the leftist forces in the Spanish Civil War. The multiple forms of anarchism, ranging from individual philosophies to complex, stateless utopias, reflect the core individualism behind the anarchist movements. The desire for individual freedom from both state control and social rules supported the early movements for social justice. Free love, feminism, and gay rights all found early support in the individualist anarchism of the early twentieth century. In the United States, leading anarchists Emma Goldman, Alexander Berkman, and later Paul Goodman and Robert Duncan all wrote about and debated extensively the right of individuals to make choices about sexuality without social or state oppression (Kissack, 2008; Shively, 1990). These early controversies about sexuality informed later counterculture movements, particularly the Beats of the 1950s and the New Left in the 1960s. Pacifism became an important element of anarchist ideology following the incredible violence of the two world wars and the rise of the atomic age. Threat of atomic annihilation and the terrible power of a nuclear-armed state pushed post–World War II anarchists toward anti-bomb and antiwar stances, a position that only became reinforced by the Cold War. As such, it is important to note that by the postwar era, anarchism had abandoned revolutionary violence. Terror, once embraced as a method of attaining revolution, lost favor and was denounced as counterproductive. By the 1960s, the American division over Vietnam, civil rights, the free speech movement, environmentalism, gay rights, and feminism pushed American anarchist philosophies back into prominence, but in a transformed manner. No longer focusing upon labor and collectivism, the reemergence of anarchism emphasized social and environmental injustice (Apter & Joll, 1971).

The radicalism of the 1960s and 1970s retreated in the 1980s and early 1990s as conservatives and moderates reestablished social and political dominance. The cultural wave that supported anarchism weakened in the face of reactionary criticism, regulating anarchism to a cultural youth movement in places of high unemployment and postindustrial economies. Most notably, the United Kingdom originated a punk rock culture that adopted anarchist values but lacked the positivist approach of earlier anarchism. Nihilism and youth apathy further marginalized anarchism as a social force in the United States and Western Europe. The rapidly disappearing industrial economies, renewed Cold War tensions, and the lack of political goals removed anarchism from cultural relevancy during this period.

However, anarchist challenges to capitalism reemerged in the late 1990s as a reaction to the effects of globalization. The 1999 World Trade Organization protests in Seattle typify the new wave of anarchism as anarchist groups helped organize the demonstration working alongside student groups, labor unions, and religious organizations (Cockburn & St. Clair, 2000). Unexpected violence occurred as a result of anarchist participation as young radicals clashed with police and destroyed property owned by multinational corporations. By using "Black Bloc" methods of violent protest, anarchists claimed to draw attention to the inequality and violence done by both state and corporation engaged in world business (Epstein, 2001). The Western response to the 9/11 attacks and the subsequent war in Iraq and Afghanistan further fueled anarchist protest as anarchists associated corporate war profiteering with state violence.

Contemporary anarchism is egalitarian and socialist in nature, emphasizing direct democracy and responsible individual behavior. The old debates between collectivist/Marxist and syndicalist factions have subsided, leaving instead a morally charged, emotional anarchism that draws heavily from the student movements and counterculture of the 1960s. The New Left tradition, of which anarchists played a crucial role, continues to inform the current anarchist trends. Ecological concerns, racial and sexual liberation, and the enduring socioeconomic struggles fall under what prominent anarchist philosopher Simon Critchley (2007) describes as an ethically committed political anarchism. Social media and the Internet allows the new anarchists to spread their message much more effectively than in the past, but simultaneously it has resulted in a more diffuse, fluid identification of anarchism. Through such flexibility, anarchism finds broader support from groups who avoided such radicalism in the past. The Occupy Movement of 2011 to 2012 used modern media and networking to organize the protests against social and economic inequality created by the global financial system. Commentators acknowledge the anarchist roots of the Occupy Movement, and several of the early organizers identified themselves as self-proclaimed anarchists (Berrett, 2011). The majority of the Occupy Movement, however, remained a varied conglomeration of concerned citizens, not necessarily anarchist nor radical. The rejection of violence, particularly propaganda by the deed, and the pursuit of economic,

social, and environmental justice have broadened the appeal of anarchism beyond the traditional strongholds of impoverished workers and utopian ideologists (Epstein, 2001). The rapid proliferation and publicity of the protest movement in recent years, in conjunction with the ongoing economic crisis since 2008 and the increasing criticism of military intervention abroad, provides contemporary anarchists with optimism toward the future of the movement.

James S. Barber

References

Apter, D. & Joll, J. (1971). *Anarchism today*. Garden City, NY: Doubleday & Co.

Berrett, D. (2011). Intellectual roots of Wall St. protest lie in academe. *Chronicle of Higher Education*. Retrieved from http://chronicle.com/article/Intellectual-Roots-of-Wall/129428/

Cockburn, A. & St. Clair, J. (2000). *5 days that shook the world*. London: Verso Publishers.

Critchley, S. (2007). *Infinitely demanding: Ethics of commitment, politics of resistance*. London: Verso Publishers.

Epstein, B. (2001). Anarchism and the anti-globalization movement. *Monthly Review, 54*(4), 1–14.

Joll, J. (1979). *The anarchists*. London: Methuen & Co.

Kissack, T. (2008). *Free comrades: Anarchism and homosexuality in the United States, 1895–1917*. Oakland, CA: AK Press.

Shively, C. (1990). Anarchism. In W. Dynes, W. Johansson, & W. Percy (Eds.), *Encyclopedia of homosexuality* (pp. 50–52). New York: Garland.

Skirda, A. (2002). *Facing the enemy: A history of anarchist organisation from Proudhon to May 1968*. Oakland, CA: AK Press.

ANDROCENTRISM

Androcentrism is a practice akin to sexism in which males (or masculine perspectives) are treated as the center of cultural practice and historical perspective (Dictionary.com, 2014). Androcentric behavior, with its emphasis on male domination and male interests, obviously favors the masculine over the feminine; the implication being that most women are weaklings who lack the adventurous nature and strength of men.

Sociologists have described androcentrism as an act of fulfilling traditional codes of masculinity, such as playing sports, serving in the military, holding high-status positions, or drinking hard liquor in bars. Fotiou (2002) claims that the androcentric view paints a dualistic picture of "higher versus lower, strong versus weak, and public versus private." Meanwhile, Duran (2010) offers a theoretical view of androcentrism as having its origins in contemporary aesthetics. While these discussions have been useful, the feminist philosophy needs to conduct and support an even more critical exploration of how androcentric thought emerges in the twenty-first century and what impact the conceptual framework of androcentrism has on social justice.

A healthy and open discussion on androcentrism can help foster positive attitudes about women's roles in and contributions to society, which can hopefully steer men away from gender prejudice and discrimination. To continue allowing males the unspoken right to use negative language about women is to accept a tradition in which male power is abused and women's intelligence and abilities are suffocated by stereotypes.

Sherwood Thompson

References

Androcentrism (2014). *Dictionary.com.* Retrieved from http://dictionary.reference.com/browse/androcentrism?s=ts.

Duran, J. (2010). Gender and the thought of Cornel West. *Philosophia Africana, 13*(1), 23–33.

Fotiou, S. S. (2002). The complex of androcentrism and the mystery of omoousion other. *Theology & Sexuality: The Journal of the Institute for the Study of Christianity & Sexuality, 9*(1), 56.

ANGLO-CONFORMITY

Immigrants to the United States face many difficult challenges such as adopting to new customs, adjusting to a new language, learning the laws governing the country and the protocol of employment practices, just to name a few. Of all the adjustment challenges, social scientists maintain that the most demanding challenge is Anglo-conformity, an expectation that presumes that immigrants, upon arriving on American shores, should discard their cultures and languages in favor of mainstream American culture and the English language (Dicker, 2008).

Among some U.S. politicians, there is a deeply held belief that if new citizens are acculturated to the customs, rituals, holidays, language, and culture of America, they will have a more productive and promising life. While this perspective seems to have merit—it is certainly easier to survive in an environment that one understands and has control over—there is an unnerving implication at its core: namely, that individual immigrants should divorce themselves from their familiar ways of living—their languages, customs, foods, and their worldviews. The strain of such potentially radical change should not be understated.

In a general sense, the Anglo-conformity overlaps significantly with the melting pot theory. Both of these theories rely on the belief that immigrants must abandon their cultures and language in order to acquire the language and culture of the United States. But why not both? The prevailing thought by many Americans is that if one fails to accept and adopt the "American way" of doing things, then said failure surely represents the immigrant's lack of allegiance to the United States. Dicker (2008) maintains that one's rejection of the American ethos and patriotism to the country, while continuing to rely on one's heritage and language, is widely considered a roadblock to the acquisition of English. Without that language and its accompanying values, scholars argue, "anglo-conformity holds out the promise, if not the guarantee, of success in America" (Dicker, 2008, p. 68).

The idea of Anglo-conformity outlines what is expected of immigrants, especially ethnic minority immigrants. The spirit of this expectation was to prevent non-Anglo cultures from maintaining separate ethnic communities within the United States (Rodriguez, 1990). Due to a number of social and political factors, however, this expectation did not materialize entirely as it was intended: now across the United States, especially in large urban settings, one can find communities and enclaves of immigrant groups living together, separate from the broader American population.

Despite the realities of urbanization and selective acculturation, Anglo-conformity persists as an ideal in America. Its scrutiny is not equally distributed, however; it makes particular targets of low-skilled, low-wage immigrants whose status in the domains of labor and education is especially tenuous. What the Anglo-conformity theory fails to acknowledge is that the myriad cultures of the United States contribute to the democratic fabric of the country. This diversity is a strength that promotes a strong and rich cultural pluralism in the United States.

Sherwood Thompson

References

Dicker, S. J. (2008). US immigrants and the dilemma of Anglo-conformity. *Socialism & Democracy, 22*(3), 52–74. doi:10.1080/08854300802361539

Rodriguez, F. (1990). *Equity in education: Issues and strategies*. Dubuque, IA: Kendall/Hunt Publishing Company.

Valdez, Z. (2006). Segmented assimilation among Mexicans in the Southwest. *Sociological Quarterly, 47*(3), 397–424. doi:10.1111/j.1533-8525.2006.00051.x

ANTEBELLUM

Antebellum refers to anything existing before a war. As Edward Ayers (2008) has pointed out, nearly every time period in U.S. history can be considered an antebellum era, as many narratives suggest that the trajectory of U.S. history can be traced according to successive wars. However, this general interpretation of antebellum elides the specific signification of the term within a U.S. historical and sociopolitical context.

In the United States, the term *antebellum* refers to, in most contexts, the period of time existing prior to the Civil War, which began in 1861. We should pay attention to the fact that not only is the period of time antebellum, but all of the political, social, and historical events during this period of time will be modified by the term *antebellum* as well. So antebellum operates as an important modifier for social, religious, political, and literary practices that existed prior to the war, suggesting that they were influenced by prewar atmospheres, tensions, and anxieties.

Within the U.S. context, some refer to any time following the end of the Revolutionary War in the

United States (1776) and leading up to the beginning of the Civil War as antebellum. However, it is important to be aware that the time period following a war, particularly the Revolutionary War, would have been decidedly considered a postwar era for many U.S. citizens and communities. Thus, the consideration of a particular time period as antebellum takes into account the social, political, and historical events that combine to position that time as prewar, or anticipating war (Volo & Volo, 2004). For example, in the case of the Civil War, the term *antebellum* might more specifically refer to the mid-1840s or 1850s up to the start of the war, as the climate of social and political unrest created an environment that was specifically prewar while looking toward the coming of a war.

Elizabeth Cali

References

Ayers, E. L. (2008). Antebellum era. In P. S. Boyer (Ed.), Antebellum era (pp. 37–38). New York: Oxford.

Volo, J. M. & Volo, D. D. (2004). *The antebellum period*. Westport, CT: Greenwood Press.

ANTIRACISM

Racism: The Challenge of Dismantling Lies in the Dilemma of Definition

THE CHALLENGES Some of the greatest challenges of dismantling racism are related to defining, interpreting, and detecting racism, but also deciding what the work of antiracism should connote. The work of dismantling racism is challenging because of the varied definitions and interpretations of this illusive construct. The challenge lies in the different understandings and uses of the word *racism*. Barndt (2007) states that because we use the word *racism* in many confusing and contradictory ways, we are often speaking about different products and experiences (p. 55). One of the initial steps to dismantling racism is to have some shared understanding and analysis of how racism is produced, manifested, and maintained.

This entry is grounded in critical race theory with the understanding that racism is ordinary, an everyday occurrence, and should be defined, interpreted, and addressed by its individual elements, but more so, by the structural articulations of everyday racism. For scholars of critical race theory, racism is almost always articulated as an everyday occurrence, as pedestrian rather than spectacular, although we have seen evidence of its *gendered spectacularity* (Holland, 2012, p. 3) through historical watersheds that span from Ku Klux Klan rallies and lynching to the Trayvon Martin shooting and the Donald Sterling audiotapes. The rhetoric of the present dominant discourse argues that racism is less prevalent today. One of the problems with contemporary racism is that it morphs and transforms its presentation and definition. Quite similar to a chameleon, before racism can be aptly recognized and deconstructed, its morphology changes. These shifts and transformations in shape and definition make it challenging for scholars, educators, practitioners, and the general public to arrive at, and transact around, some general consensus of cause, effect, and meaning.

The term *people of whiteness* (POW) is used in this entry instead of *white people* or *whites* as it lends some level of equality around language and race vernacular. For most academics, the term *black people* connotes some form of *color caste hierarchy* (hooks, 1995), a term that is an adaptation of bell hooks's explanation of the social stratification that exists as a result of skin color variation among people of African descent. Since the term *black people* has evolved, and they are sometimes collectively referred to as people of color, the term *people of whiteness* is more symbolic of a group of people, and its use adds a level of balance and equity to race vernacular. The term *people of whiteness* provides awareness of the systemic race hierarchy, but for transformative purposes, it allows the group to be viewed from horizontal dimensions that lend some idea of leveling and equality.

Fundamental to the discussion on the challenges of dismantling racism is the notion that POW still hold the position that racism is solely related to its overt forms, such as physical and verbal attacks, the work of white supremacist groups, or deliberate and overt discrimination (Tyson, 2006). POW tend to be oblivious to how ubiquitous everyday racism is, and they fail to inherently see other forms of everyday racism that people of color experience. These experiences of racism include encounters with patronizing attitudes, being spoken down to, being hired as tokens, contact avoidance, being accused of oversensitivity about race and racism, being told that one's color is not seen, or that color blindness is ideal. Consequently, being unable to see everyday racism establishes a level of blindness that perpetuates an even larger problem. The challenge is further exacerbated by the inability or the *weak will* (West, 2001, p. 3) of POW to understand how the power that they hold and assert cannot be used to benefit or advance the dismantling of racism and to realize racial justice if they are blind to how racism is played out in multiple, everyday social contexts.

The Role of Critical Race Theory

Critical race theory (CRT) is a scholarly and political approach to examining race that leads to a consequential analysis and profound understanding of racism. It argues, as a starting point, that the axis of American social life is fundamentally constructed in race. As a result, the economic, political, and historical relationships and arrangements that social actors have to institutions and social processes are all race based. CRT also argues that, as a whole, this idea has been purposefully ignored, subdued, and marginalized in both the dominant and public discourse and that there are serious repercussions that arise from this *structural blindness* (Mills, 1997, p. 153). The work of CRT was initiated by the efforts of Derrick A. Bell Jr. as a response to the ceasing political and social influence of the civil rights movement of the 1950s and 1960s. Lois Tyson (2006) argues that critical race theory could be thought of as "a new approach to civil rights" (p. 368). Though times have changed, and overt forms of racial violence seem to be atrocities of the past, CRT emphasizes that overt expressions of racism have gone underground and are now expressed through insidious and covert methods.

One of the important tenets of CRT is the assertion that race is socially constructed, yet it denotes explicitly and implicitly how power is used and appropriated in society. Professionals in the natural sciences have removed the concept of race from their discipline since there is no empirical evidence to support that it is a biological concept. Of interest, however, is that neither natural scientists nor anyone with power or influence has made an "organized effort to bring this rejection to the attention of schools, government, the general public or even related disciplines" (Muir, 1993, p. 102). Very often in the discussion on racism, the principle object of power is missing. In vast contrast to the dominant discourse that assumes that racism is a euphemism for racial prejudice and racial discrimination, CRT postulates that racism occurs at the macro level while racial prejudice and discrimination are experiences from an individual level. CRT posits that racism occurs both at a micro and macro level. That is, racism transcends the behavior of individual agents who are framed as bad people, who have bad thoughts, and engage in bad actions. Instead, CRT brings to light the purposeful obscurity that institutions, such as law and education, have placed on racism by failing to highlight the systematic and structural nature of racism. Building on these elements, CRT also focuses on how the component of power is used systemically and collectively to oppress people of color, benefit POW, create blindness to empirical truths, and thus maintain a status quo that supports white supremacy.

The above idea of the systemic and collective use of power is explained by the concept *interest convergence* (Bell, 2004). Derrick Bell (2004) points out that racism converges with the goals, desires, and interests of POW who have and exert collective power in many institutions and social structures that are fundamental for transactions that occur in everyday life. Bell further asserts that these interests are played out as the desire to advance in the material or social world and to position oneself and one's group as innately superior. These are some of the hidden ways that racism is practiced, upheld, and reinforced by the prevailing status quo. Though these practices are not defined as racism, the implicit power that follows material and psychosocial superiority gives the holders of this power privileges that appear ascribed, though in essence they are socially achieved. Interest convergence is played out in all aspects of social life, and it is argued that all apparent successes that people of color benefit from, even those that involve the passage of huge legislation, are wrapped up in white self-interest (Delgado & Stefancic, 2001).

Response of Scholarship and Academics

The canon of the work in CRT is wide-ranging and heterogeneous due to the various disciplinary frameworks of the scholars involved in this field. The key axis, on which the work revolves, even from its inception, was to challenge the dominant discourse on race and to point out the structural nature and oppressive consequences of race-based laws and social assumptions.

Scholars are sometimes co-opted and forget to advance the true purpose of the scholarship we create. Apart from theorizing, and at times pontificating, it is the role of scholars involved in CRT or antiracism work to advance change through praxis. The term *pracademic* refers to academics that have one foot in the academic world and the other in practical, action-related practice. This orientation is seen as lending an ability to not only advance the understanding and unraveling of the definition and meaning of racism but also to use the theory to inform some type of meaningful transformative action. Short of this, the theory resides in the cognitive annals of the academic and serves no significant purpose to those most impacted by racism. This orientation is congruent with the objectives of CRT, and it ultimately serves to animate, and at times agitate, scholarship and scholars.

Praxis is understood as practical activity, in practical revolutionary action, which goes beyond interpretations of the world but also seeks to change it. Marx's work on human potential argued that social transformation, and eventually the emancipation from oppression, requires concrete action. This action is meaningless unless it is informed by theory. Praxis denotes that scholars should not be content with mere philosophizing about social ills, such as racism, but must rather develop mechanisms and critical intellectual stances that bring about the action needed to change society. In terms of praxis, CRT supports the methodology of reflective engagement that informs the work we do and how this work is used for education and transformative action related to the definition and understanding of racism.

Researchers have examined the role of story in reproducing racial ideas and stereotypes and in perpetuating racism (Bell, 2003; Van Djik, 1993, 1999). As a form of transformative scholarship, the methodology of storytelling also serves as a powerful vehicle that examines how racial ideas and racism are produced, manifested, and perpetuated. Storytelling uses different levels of stories, which range from the ubiquitous stories that are told by the dominant groups to the new narratives that are constructed to create awareness and foster change. CRT provides a *resistance story* (Bell, 2003), which is a new narrative, both historical and contemporary, that tells about how people have resisted racism, challenged the dominant discourse that supports it, and fought for more equal and inclusive social arrangements of power, rights, and interests. The resistance story also articulates a new narrative that contests that racism is just a product of ill-willed people. Instead, it sheds light on the idea that racism is both individual in its concrete expression and structural in its intention and production. The stories can be a conduit from which racism is viewed and accessed and can provide a channel to examine how racism is produced and manifested at the individual and systemic level. The power of storytelling is its ability to create a bridge between abstract dimensions of racism discourse and concrete experiences of victims and perpetrators of racism (Bell, 2003). Storytelling can act as a mechanism to constantly reintegrate and recreate an antiracism discourse into the public consciousness.

Defining Racism

A definition is important because it produces explanations, understandings, actions, and solutions. Thus far, racism in the United States is viewed from either one of two categories: individual actions or systems of power (Barndt, 2007). The first approach has descriptions that are related to bigotry, favorable or unfavorable race prejudice, stereotypes, personal dislikes, and biases. This approach describes categories that fall into individual attitudes and the actions of individual agents. As a result, when racism is discussed from this framework, it is done within the context of individual attitudes. This framework is narrow and misses some of the important tenets that make up racism. The second approach to describing racism is done in terms of the systems of power that are structural in nature. These include the education, financial, political, legal, criminal justice, and economic systems. Definition

is problematic because these two approaches are usually used in isolation. Barndt (2007) argues that "the individual approach is heard mostly from white people and the systemic approach is heard mostly from people of color" (p. 57). Since definitions produce explanations, understandings, and solutions, these differing approaches to definition realize two very different and possibly opposing solutions. Barndt shares that his antiracism work pointed out that POW seemed content in the belief that racism can be eliminated and dismantled if they changed their prejudices, attitudes, and individual actions. They often felt that racism would be addressed by cross-racial contact and relationship building. The belief that racism can be dismantled by having POW forge personal relationships with people of color is superficial and limited. The limitation lies in this strategy ignoring the power of systemic realities that are capable of producing, manifesting, and perpetuating racism.

Barndt (2007) supports the work of CRT by calling on definitions to pay attention to the stories of people of color who can articulate their experiences of racism within the confines of the collective actions of systems and institutions. To date, Barndt has produced the most user-friendly definition of racism, which has two stringent criteria. He defines racism as "race prejudice plus the misuse of power by systems and institutions" (p. 83). Each of these will be examined in more detail.

Race Prejudice

Prejudice is defined as a feeling, favorable or unfavorable, toward a person or thing without sufficient warrant (Allport, 1979, p. 7). Prejudice is best understood as a bias or holding opinions that are based on little empirical evidence. Barndt (2007) argues that race prejudice is the least difficult to understand, the least controversial in nature, but the most misinterpreted and overused concept of racism. As an important point of departure, it should be admitted that all people exhibit race prejudice; that is, we all have favorable or unfavorable unsubstantiated opinions about people from our own race or those of other racial backgrounds (Allport, 1979). Though unfavorable race prejudice can be terribly painful and should be abhorred, it has to be distinguished from racism. Race prejudice is a subset of racism, but in and of itself it does not constitute racism. "What makes race prejudice so volatile is not the word *prejudice* but the word *race*" (Barndt, 2007, p. 61). Throughout the history of the United States, the word *race* has always determined how resources are allocated, and the word has existed solely to categorize people into a hierarchy of superior or inferior (Mills, 1997). It is for this reason that race prejudice produces such a volatile reaction, for it is reminiscent of the evil purposes for which the word *race* was created. Consequently, people accused of race prejudice react defensively because they despise being associated with being unjust, inhumane, or a judge of the human worth of someone else.

Misuse of Power

One of the key components of racism is systemic power. The power that racism exercises is not possessed by the individual as in one's ability to get what one wants, but instead, the power of racism is shared and expressed through collective systems such as the economy, education, culture, and religion. The collective nature of this type of power is a product of the collective conscience, core value, and groupthink of the system as a whole.

Barndt (2007) offers a practical formulation of the misuse of power and frames it from three determinants that are seen as *power-to-nth-power*. The first determinant he refers to as *Power¹*, which is power to the first power. This is power that is misused to have power over, destroy, and oppress people of color (p. 77). Destruction may range from collective practices, such as unemployment to unequal education, housing, or health care opportunities. Because this power is exercised in conjunction with beliefs about a person that are based on their racial group membership, this should be validated and defined as a form of racism. Far too often, issues related to the systemic misuse of power are omitted from the discussion and analysis of racism. The second expression of the collective power of racism, power to the second level, is described as *Power²* and is outlined as the systemic and collective power that benefits POW (Barndt, 2007, p. 79). The misuse of this power determinant is based on the assertion that having membership in a certain racial category enables members to have access to

resources for itself. *Power²* also affords members a right to exert collective or institutional power to exploit others with the end of helping themselves or members of their racial group. This expression of power has given rise to the racial effect, white privilege, which is an achieved system of rewards, benefits, and services that POW are privy to only because of their racial group membership. The third and most potent expression of the misuse of power is racism's ultimate power to destroy all, and it is power to the third power. This type of power is referred to as *Power³* and destroys both people of color and POW in the execution of its collective will (p. 81). In this sense, *Power³* is able to make everyone willingly or unwittingly submit to its will. An example of this would be the manner in which collective systems are able to shape one's ideology and understanding of facts. This can be demonstrated by examining the education system, which has the collective power and capability to shape curriculum and determine what students perceive as truth and fact. A system exercising *Power³* is able to choose what texts, ideas, and methods are used to educate and evaluate. As a result, all constituents of the system, including administrators, teachers, and students, regardless of their racial group membership, have little or no power to combat this form of racism and are left with no choice but to abide by the will of the system.

Pathway to Dismantling Racism

Below is a proposal for a precursory roadmap to dismantling racism. This roadmap is a framework of three initial sets of actions that provide ideas for a next set of steps. The roadmap is limited and presents ideas that may not sustain us through the entire journey of dismantling racism; however, no one has all the answers to ending racism, but this roadmap opens the gates to the pathway of this journey. In addition, the steps of the roadmap should be seen as interconnected, as all parts need to work in tandem if the gates to dismantling are to be opened.

The roadmap begins with a shift in social consciousness. This shift represents a concrete effort to challenge the dominant discourse related to racism by shifting the false notions of social consciousness that make up the social realities of members of society. The need for this shift comes from the knowledge that those who possess and exert power are able to control and manipulate social consciousness. These shifts need to occur at all levels of society, and in multiple contexts, so that they can combat all the embedded and emerging ways that social truths, access to resources, and discourses about the other are understood and perpetuated.

The second step in the roadmap calls for the creation of communities that unlearn white supremacy. These communities must exist on all societal levels: micro, meso, and macro. Constituents should include POW and people of color. In these communities, POW will divest and diversify their power and privilege. By unlearning white supremacy, people of whiteness will not give up their power and privilege, but will instead use it to benefit all, including people of color. By diversifying, they will use their new knowledge, achieved from the shift in consciousness, to teach other members of their racial group as well as the systems and institutions they have access to. People of color also have a role to play in the process of unlearning white supremacy. In their case, they must transform their internalized feelings and attitudes about being less than. The actions of people of color and POW in unlearning white supremacy have critical intersectionality and cannot be done in isolation, as the success of one is contingent on the success of the other.

The third and final aspect of the roadmap points to creating accountability through consensus. It requires that POW become accountable and are also held accountable for the power and privilege they possess and the ways that these are used. Very similar to a social bank account, POW need to be required to make a justification of how their power and privilege are spent. It should be duly noted that this accountability has to occur as education and not as accusations, to avoid roadblocks such as defensiveness, guilt, or stonewalling. As alluded to earlier, though this is the last step, it can also be seen as a catalyst to generating a shift in social consciousness and a beginning in the formation of a community that can work in concert to begin the process to dismantling racism.

Michelle M. Cromwell

References

Adams, G., Salter, P. S., Pickett, K. M., Kurtis, T., & Philips, N. L. (2010). Behavior as mind-in-context: A cultural psychology analysis of "paranoid" suspicion. In L. F. Barrett, B. Mesquita, & E. R. Smith (Eds.), *The mind in context* (pp. 277–306). New York: Guilford.

Allport, G. W. (1979). *The nature of prejudice* (3rd ed.). Boston: Basic Books.

Barndt, J. (2007). *Understanding and dismantling racism: The twenty-first century challenge to white America*. Minneapolis, MN: Fortress Press.

Bell, D. (2004). *Silent covenants:* Brown v. Board of Education *and the unfulfilled hopes for racial reform*. Oxford: Oxford University Press.

Bell, L. (2003). Telling tales: What stories can teach us about racism. *Race Ethnicity and Education, 6*(1), 8–25.

Crenshaw, K. W. (2011). Twenty years of critical race theory: Looking back to move forward. *Connecticut Law Review, 43*(5), 1253–352.

Delgado, R. (1989). Storytelling for oppositionists and others: A plea for narrative. *Michigan Law Review, 87*(8), 2411–41.

Delgado, R. & Stefancic, J. (2001). *Critical race theory: An introduction*. New York: New York University Press.

Feagin, J. R. (2006). *Systemic racism: A theory of oppression*. New York: Routledge.

Holland, S. P. (2012). *The erotic life of racism*. Durham, NC: Duke University Press.

hooks, b. (1995). *Killing rage: Ending racism*. New York: Holt Paperback.

Jones, J. M. (1997). *Prejudice and racism*. New York: McGraw-Hill.

Mills, C. W. (1997). *The racial contract*. Ithaca: Cornell University Press.

Muir, D. E. (1993). Race: The mythical root of racism. In N. Gates (Ed.), *Critical race theory: The concept of "race" in natural and social science* (pp. 93–104.). New York: Garland.

Ritzer, George. (2000). *Sociological theory*. New York: McGraw-Hill.

Torres, G. (2013). Critical race theory. In P. L. Mason (Ed.), *Encyclopedia of race and racism* (2nd ed., vol. 1, pp. 462–65). Detroit: Macmillan Reference USA. Retrieved from http://go.galegroup.com/ps/i.do?id=GALE%7CCCX4190600130&v=2.1&u=novaseu_main&it=r&p=GVRL&sw=w&asid=0a28ff1880ab51e88806ea9b9daca79a.

Tyson, L. (2006). *Critical theory today: A user-friendly guide*. New York: Routledge.

Van Dijk, T. A. (1993). *Elite discourse and racism*. Newbury Park, CA: Sage.

Van Dijk, T. A. (1999). Discourse and the denial of racism. In A. Jaworski & N. Coupland (Eds.), *The discourse reader* (pp. 541–58). London: Routledge.

West, C. (2001). *Race matters* (2nd ed.). Boston, MA: Beacon Press.

ANTI-SEMITISM

Anti-Semitism is a negative and hostile attitude toward Jews and the Jewish religion. Actions that discriminate, show prejudice, or display a set of beliefs that incorrectly potray Jews are characteristics of anti-Semitism. This form of discrimination against Jews is usually embodied by a combination of religious, racial, cultural, and ethnic biases. For example, the stereotype that Jewish men are moneylenders and control all the money in the countries they live in stems from medieval times. During this period, Jews were not allowed to own businesses, operate farms, or enter high-paying professions. However, they could collect interest and taxes from Christians, which spurred their entry into related fields such as banking (Jewface, n.d.). Their involvement with money (arguably forced upon them) fueled the belief that Jews are greedy, yet miserly—a notion that lingers in the phrase *to Jew [someone] down*, which implies that Jews always try to bargain for lower prices.

Anti-Semitism is deeply rooted in history; Jews have been subject to discrimination and persecution for hundreds of years. As such, anti-Semitism has manifested itself in many ways, ranging from individual expressions of hatred and discrimination against individual Jews to organized violent attacks by hate groups against entire Jewish communities. The most extreme instance of persecution was the Holocaust under Adolf Hitler's Nazi Germany.

In order to combat anti-Semitism, it is important to first acknowledge Jewish history and culture. Jewish lifestyle includes a religious, cultural, and ethnic group experience that originated in the land that is now called Israel. The Jewish state of Palestine was destroyed in the year 70 CE by the Romans, and Jews were scattered throughout the world.

In the year 312 CE, Christianity became the sole established religion of the Roman Empire. During this time, Christianity had separated itself from its Jewish roots, believing itself to be a successor of Judaism according to some historical accounts (Thompson, 2000).

As with many racial, ethnic, or religious groups, assumptions or generalizations are sometimes made about Jews. Comments are made about their celebrations, dress, music, and religious rituals. These assumptions are often based on confusion or misunderstanding of group behavior, belief, or custom. To better understand the roots of anti-Semitism, facts about Jews are important markers that provide greater understanding of their history and struggles. Becoming aware of this history helps to broaden the understanding and increases awareness by creating education and cultural remembrances.

Individuals can play a critical role in combating anti-Semitism by participating in human rights activities, being positive advocates and policymakers, and becoming familiar with the long history and contemporary manifestations of Jewish people. A call to local and national law enforcement agencies to monitor hate crimes and enact legislation to protect vulnerable Jews from hateful attitudes and hurtful behaviors is one way non-Jews can be allies to Jews. An aggressive and deliberate campaign to combat the stereotypes that oppress Jews must also be waged through the media, protest movements, and awareness campaigns. It is hoped that people will unlearn the hatreds of previous generations and become the engineers of greater cultural understanding about Jews.

Sherwood Thompson

References

Jewface. (n.d.) Racist Jewish stereotypes. Retrieved from http://jewface.us/.

Thompson, S. (2000). *Community, diversity and harmony: Minority services and program handbook*. Athens, GA: University of Georgia Minority Services and Program.

United States Holocaust Memorial Museum. (2008). Voices on Anti-Semitism. Retrieved from http://www.ushmm.org/museum/exhibit/focus/antisemitism/voice/?page=1.

APPALACHIA

The Birth of Appalachia

The Appalachian Mountains are the oldest mountain chain in North America and among the oldest on Earth. They form a broad belt that stretches almost 2,000 miles (3,200 kilometers) across the eastern section of the continent from Newfoundland to Alabama, but the name *Appalachia* is applied only to the central and southern highlands (USGS, 2014).

Named for the Apalachee Indians, the much-eroded Appalachian Mountains are made up of ridges and valleys, including the central Blue Ridge Mountains that extend from Georgia to Pennsylvania, and the southern Great Smoky Mountains that run from Tennessee to North Carolina. Together they form a natural barrier between the Atlantic coast and the interior lowlands of the United States and are rich in coal, iron, petroleum, and natural gas. Appalachian geology reveals elongated belts of folded and thrust-faulted marine sedimentary rocks, volcanic rocks, and slivers of ancient ocean floor. The U.S. Geological Survey asserts that these rocks were deformed during plate collision some 480 million years ago. The mountains played an important role in U.S. history. Crossed by only a few, the Appalachians effectively blocked early westward expansion as woodsmen found travel through the highlands difficult. Major east-west routes including the Cumberland Gap in Kentucky and the Mohawk Trail in New York followed river valleys or mountain notches.

In *Appalachia on our Mind*, Henry Shapiro (1978) credits Dr. Will Wallace Harney as the first to describe the "otherness" of Cumberland Mountain people in an 1873 article in *Lippincott's Monthly Magazine* titled, "A Strange Land and Peculiar People." Seeming to employ physiognomy—a pseudoscientific assessment of a person's character drawn from his or her face—Harney wrote that the natives are "characterized by marked peculiarities of the anatomical frame . . . elongation of the bones, the contour of the facial angle . . . loose muscular attachment . . . and the harsh features" (p. 431). Harney also described an exotic mountain region, touching eight states, which seemed interesting because it was so different from the familiar world of mainstream America. Shapiro (1978) argues that it was numerous stories in popular magazines of the 1870s through the 1890s that established the otherness of the mountain region as "a strange land inhabited by a peculiar people" (p. 18) in the American consciousness.

According to Shapiro (1978) two stories from James Lane Allen (Kentucky's first important novelist), "Through the Cumberland Gap on Horseback," and "The Bluegrass Region of Kentucky," published in *Harper's Magazine*, also added to this perception and established the fact of "two Kentuckys" separate in "occupations, manners and customs, dress, views of life, civilization" (pp. 27–28). Allen saw the "alien Kentucky within the borders of the Commonwealth" as a problem in need of a solution (pp. 27–28).

Central to discussions of Appalachia is Berea College, which was founded in Berea, Kentucky, in 1855 with the express purpose of demonstrating that blacks and whites from the mountain region could be educated together successfully. It seems unlikely that such a school could even exist in that place and time—and the school did suffer greatly throughout the Civil War—but Berea, with its Social Gospel traditions, was able to reestablish itself and operate in relative calm until the strictures of the Jim Crow era dismantled racial coeducation until the 1950s (Day, Cleveland, & Hyndman, 2103, pp. 35–46).

In the wake of the Civil War, those northern Protestant churches that sought a unified and homogeneous Christian nation through the integration of unassimilated populations began to see mountain people as "unchurched" and in need of "Americanization." The mountains were seen as a wide-open field for home missionary efforts. Initially, most southern churches lacked a national vision and failed to be aroused by the "plight" of the mountaineer—until mountain sections of southern states became targets for evangelism and a field of competition with northern churches. By the 1920s, this mission work would plant more than two hundred church schools in the mountains.

Berea College president Charles Fairchild noted that missions among the mountaineers would satisfy the demands of those who wished southern congregationalism to compete more actively with other northern denominations without compromising the school's historic anticaste, antiracism mission. Fairchild's main concern lay with the future of Berea College, especially continuing to be identified by the American Missionary Association as a suitable recipient of congregational benevolence (Shapiro, 1978, pp. 32–48).

Interestingly, the term *Appalachia* was first coined by Berea College president William Goodell Frost, who also saw in the mountains a coherent region with a homogeneous population possessing a uniform culture (Shapiro, 1978). In that sense, *Appalachia* described an identifiable cultural group whose lives have been mitigated by remote rural mountain conditions and who have suffered various inequities, a marginal economy, and in the consideration of progressives, were in need of assistance from educated elites (Shapiro, 1978).

But by the late 1880s, Bereans found the support for racial coeducation, as well as contributions, waning due to a shift in public sympathies. This was the most violent period in Kentucky history with its duels, feuds, nightriders, klansmen, and lynchings. Berea would soon have to address a financial crisis. At the same time, the difficulties of the region were becoming more apparent as educational opportunities that were advancing in other sections appeared to be ignored by too many in the eastern mountains. Schools were generally poor and in short supply.

When Frost assumed the presidency of Berea College in 1892, a gradual shift of the school's primary mission toward educating the poor in the Appalachian region commenced (Heckman & Hall, 1968, pp. 35–52; see also Klotter, 1996, p. 153). It was the start of the Progressive Era, a time of social activism and political reform in America. A major theme of this activism was "efficiency," the idea that educated individuals should use scientific principles to improve health and modernize the old ways of doing things.

Frost was captivated by the anachronistic communities of Appalachia and viewed the readily apparent gaps in educational opportunity in rural areas as an opportunity for Berea College to alleviate the appallingly low educational level of the region while cultivating future students in the process. Frost emphasized the privations of the region, resulting in a newfound interest in establishing Appalachia as a viable and unique culture. Rather than attempting to eliminate or subsume

Appalachia into the mainstream American culture, Frost spearheaded the movement to assist the communities in areas of necessity while still preserving the unique crafts, songs, and traditions of the culture (Shapiro, 1978, pp. 119–28).

Frost continued to advocate for the mountain people of Appalachia throughout his tenure at Berea College. In 1915, his son Norman authored a statistical study that showcased the educational shortcomings and challenges of Appalachia. President Frost's main concern was the lack of structure characteristic of previous attempts to alleviate the problems plaguing rural Appalachian schools (Frost, 1915, p. 29). He chided county superintendents for their tendency to artificially inflate enrollment rates to create the illusion that rural schools in their county were more successful than they actually were. Consistent with the traditionalistic political culture of the South, these superintendents typically only agreed to construct new schools or make repairs to existing buildings when citizens pushed for such improvements regardless of the real needs within the region. School terms were also extremely short in Appalachian counties. In 1910, the average length of a school term nationwide for rural schools was 137 days a year. This was nearly a month longer than the 104-day average term in the mountain counties of Appalachia.

No doubt, geographical hindrances of the region, the practice of students enrolling in multiple schools during the same term, and the lack of available schools also contributed to this problem. Frost reported that, in 1912, there were seventeen counties in the state of Kentucky that did not contain a high school. The rural schools that did exist were often rundown and lacking the necessary resources for effective teaching. Because state laws requiring schools to provide books for students who couldn't afford them were rarely enforced, and school budgets were small, children who lived outside of large cities could only obtain textbooks if they were furnished by their parents (Frost, 1915, p. 20).

Social scientists have grappled with the enigmas of Appalachia for decades while searching for a model that helps explain the regional dynamics. Some see Appalachia as a place of backward, impoverished conditions and unusual people. Others extol the beauty and artistry of the region and seek to preserve its values. In "Central Appalachia: Internal Colony or Internal Periphery?" Sonoma State University sociology professor Davis Walls (1978) explored several sociological models and noted that Harry Caudill made only one passing reference to the colonialism in his seminal 1965 study, *Night Comes to the Cumberlands*. But by 1965, when he began to speak of colonialism, the theme was quickly adopted by activists who drew parallels to the colonialization of black Americans. While Walls found the Internal Colonialization Model somewhat useful, he also found it to be strained at several key points. It has focused attention on the acquisition of the raw materials of the region by outside corporate interests and on the exploitation of the local workforce, and community at large, resulting from the removal of the region's natural resources for the benefit of absentee owners. He ultimately concluded that Central Appalachia is best characterized as a peripheral region within an advanced capitalist society. The deception and fraud used by agents of timber and minerals, which suggested a colonial model, may well have contributed to the insular nature of the culture with its profound distrust of outsiders, but it was not different from the techniques generally used by capitalists elsewhere during the period of industrial expansion (Walls, 1978).

Over time, the boundaries of Appalachia have been construed variously. Frost initially identified 194 counties in nine states as the Berea College service area. Within Kentucky, he identified forty-four counties. Other authors have identified 190 counties, and 254 counties. By 2014, the Appalachian Regional Commission had identified 397 Appalachian counties in thirteen states from New York to Mississippi.

Richard Day

References

Day, R., Cleveland, R. and Hyndman, J. (2013). Berea College—coeducationally and racially integrated: An unlikely contingency in the 1850s. *Journal of Negro Education*, 82(1), 35–46.

Frost, N. (1915). A statistical study of the public schools of the southern Appalachian Mountains. *United States Bureau of Education Bulletin*, 11, 29.

Harney, W. W. (1873). A strange land and a peculiar people. *Lippincott's Monthly Magazine, XII*(31), 429–38. Retrieved from http://www.gutenberg.org/files/13964/13964-h/13964-h.htm#strange.

Heckman, R. A. & Hall, B. J. (1968). Berea College and the day law. *The Register of the Kentucky Historical Society*, 66, 35–52.

Klotter, J. C. (1996). *Kentucky: Portrait in paradox, 1900–1950* (Frankfort: Kentucky Historical Society), 153.

Shapiro, H. D. (1978). *Appalachia on our mind: The southern mountains and mountaineers in the American consciousness, 1870–1920*. Chapel Hill: University of North Carolina Press.

USGS. (2014). *America's volcanic past*. Retrieved from http://vulcan.wr.usgs.gov/LivingWith/VolcanicPast/Places/volcanic_past_appalachians.html.

Walls, D. (1978). Internal colony or internal periphery? In H. Matthews Lewis, L. Johnson, & D. Askins (Eds.), *Colonialism in modern America: The Appalachian case* (n.p.). Boone, NC: Appalachian Consortium Press. Retrieved from http://www.sonoma.edu/users/w/wallsd/pdf/Internal-Colony.pdf.

Additional Reading

Abbey, E. & Porter, E. (1970). *Appalachian wilderness*. Arrowood Press.

Brooks, M. (1986). *The Appalachians*. Seneca Books.

Caudill, H. M. (1971). *My land is dying*. New York: E. P. Dutton.

ASCRIBED STATUS

Status, or social position in relation to others in society, is an inherent part of social life. Individuals typically have multiple statuses at any given time. An ascribed status, in sociological terms, refers to characteristics about an individual that are involuntary. Examples of this include, but may not be limited to, both mental and physical characteristics such as gender, race, ethnicity, age, genetics, parent's socioeconomic class, and various types of disabilities. Not all ascribed statuses are attained at birth; some ascribed statuses can be attained later in life, but still involuntarily (such as illnesses or disabilities). Commonly, the concept of ascribed status is contrasted with the concept of achieved status, which is status acquired by an individual voluntarily and through efforts of their own. Examples of achieved status may include things such as education level attainment, occupation, and marital status.

Function of Ascribed Status

Initial conception of the notion of ascribed status was by Linton (1936). Linton used the notion of ascribed status to describe "those which are assigned to individuals without reference to their innate differences or abilities. They can be predicted and trained for from the moment of birth" (p. 115). Later use of the concept by Parsons (1951) supported the idea that ascribed status is used in society as a socialization mechanism. Individuals are assigned statuses at birth originating from certain characteristics that have meaning already attached. Socialization based on these ascribed statuses begins with an individual's caregivers, usually their family of origin, which is necessary to enfold individuals into an already functioning society. This socialization is necessary to ensure common understanding and agreement as to expectations and rights associated with certain statuses within the social system. This agreement and shared understanding is what makes social life and societies possible. This socialization will be a lifelong process and will be reinforced continually from many different sources such as family, education, religious institutions, and peers. A female will be taught how a female should act and what is expected of her; an individual born into a low economic position will be taught what will be expected of them in terms of education and occupational attainment. In short, ascribed status informs individuals of their place in society and the expectations of that place, thereby presenting a social identity to the individual.

Blurred Lines between Ascribed and Achieved Status

The line between ascribed and achieved status is not distinct. In many ways ascribed status may, and does, influence achieved status. It is very likely that an individual's ascribed status, whether physical, mental, or social in nature, will provide an advantage or disadvantage in pursuit of achieved status (Bourdieu, 1977; Bourdieu & Passeron, 1990). The starting position of an individual who is born with a certain privileged ascribed status may be closer to the desired achieved status than that of a

person born into a nonprivileged ascribed status. An example of this is that an individual who is born into a higher socioeconomic class will have more resources to obtain a college degree, and therefore a desired occupation, than someone who is born into a low socioeconomic class who will have fewer resources in pursuit of the same college degree and occupation.

Cultural Relevance

Ascribed statuses are not universal and depend heavily on the context that a society places on them. The value of any characteristic depends on what is valued in a society; different societies may have different values attached to different characteristics. Another feature of cultural relevance related to ascribed status is the fact that societies can, and do, change over time. This means that there is a chance that an ascribed status can come to mean something different for a person throughout their lifetime; that the role and expectations of an ascribed status can change over time. An example of this could be what it is meant to be a woman before, during, and after the women's rights movement; or what it meant to be an African American before, during, and after the civil rights movement. Today, the same could be said for gender issues.

While the value of an individual ascribed status can vary by societies, the value that a society places on ascribed statuses in general can also vary. Some societies place lower values on ascribed statuses, which means that individuals have the opportunity to gain achieved statuses in spite of ascribed statuses. Examples of this type of society may include the United States and the United Kingdom; however, as mentioned above, there is a relationship between ascribed and achieved status. Other societies strictly adhere to social organization based on ascribed status, such as those that have a caste system. In this type of society, an individual has no chance of altering their social position, which is inherited from their parents. A common example of this type of society is India.

Summary

Ascribed status refers to characteristics about an individual that are involuntary; these characteristics have a meaning already attached to them that have nothing to do with an individual's efforts or input. Ascribed statuses are part of any society. They work as a socialization mechanism that allows society to function without having to recreate roles and expectations with each new person or generation. Although the value of an ascribed status can vary by society, culture, and change over time, they will be a factor that guides how an individual is socialized and what that socialization entails.

Amber Thompson

References

Bourdieu, P. (1977). *Outline of a theory of practice.* Oxford: Cambridge University Press.

Bourdieu, P. & Passeron, J. C. (1990). *Reproduction in education, society and culture* (2nd ed.). Thousand Oaks: Sage Publications.

Linton, R. (1936). *The study of man.* New York: Appleton Century.

Parsons, T. (1951). *The social system.* Glencoe: Free Press.

ASIAN AMERICAN

Korean American Transracial Adoptees and Their Identity Development

Transracial adoptees form a student population that commonly experiences a range of difficulties in transitioning into higher education. Transracial adoption has created a hidden identity for this population, which in turn has had a profound impact on their understanding of self, especially their racial and ethnic identity. One aspect of identity that transracial adoptees explore is their racial and ethnic identity. This is the due to the fact that they are adopted overseas and have adoptive parents who often look different from them and identify with a different race (Woon, 2004). Transracial adoptees vary in their racial identity development depending on their experiences, exposure, and comfort level with their race and ethnic identity.

Identity development is crucial to an individual because researchers believe that transracial adoptees that develop a positive racial and ethnic identity will result in high self-esteem (Friedlander, 2003). Transracial adoptees' "hidden" identity refers to the notion that without their adoptive parents next to them to contrast differences in racial and ethnic identity, their transracial adoptee status is not visible (Samuels, 2009). The "hidden" nature of the adoptee's identity status may ultimately affect and hinder their identity development.

A segment of students in higher education will have a more complex time in asking the questions "Who am I?" "Who am I in relation to others?" and "Where do I fit in?" (Kroger, 2007). For transracial adoptees, the questions "Who am I?" and "Where do I fit in?" may not be simply answered (Kroger, 2007). Specifically, Korean transracial adoptees have to integrate their racial, ethnic, and adopted identity together and ask the question "Who am I as an adoptee and how does being adopted fit in with being Korean?" (Lieberman, 2001, p. 107). Additionally, for many, these are questions that have been pondered their whole lives.

The topic of adoption is both a sensitive and complicated issue. When a second layer of being transracially adopted is added, the topic becomes that much more complex. It is important to recognize that not all cases and experiences of adoptees or transracial adoptees are generalizable. Therefore, some people believe professionals need to encourage students to tell their individual stories and allow them to find their own voice. Each individual brings many unique aspects in forming and developing their identity. Others encourage student affairs professionals to look at the key ingredients and ask key questions in order to better serve the students who may be faced with the challenge of working through multiple identities within a dual culture.

Chong Sun Kim

References

Friedlander, M. (2003). Adoption: Misunderstood, mythologized, and marginalized. *Counseling Psychologist, 31*(6), 745–52.

Kroger, J. (2007). *Identity development: Adolescence through adulthood.* Thousand Oaks, CA: Sage Publications.

Lieberman, K. (2001). *The process of racial and ethnic identity development and search for self in adult Korean transracial adoptees* (Doctoral Dissertation). Newton, MA: Massachusetts School of Professional Psychology.

Samuels, G. (2009). Being raised by white people: Navigating racial difference among adopted multiracial adults. *Journal of Marriage and Family, 71*(1), 80–94.

Woon, L. K. (2004). Socialization of transracially adopted Korean Americans: A self-analysis. *Journal of the Sociology of Self-Knowledge, 3*(1), 78–84.

ASPIRATIONAL CAPITAL

Aspirational capital is a form of community cultural wealth; a theoretical model conceptually derived from Tara Yosso's (2005) critique of Pierre Bourdieu's theory of cultural capital. Drawing from tenets within critical race theory (CRT) and building upon her research into the lived experiences and perspectives of Chicano/Chicana families, Yosso (2005) argued that community cultural wealth expands the concept of cultural capital to include "unnamed," undermined, and underutilized resources valued by American-born minoritized groups such as African Americans, Asian Americans, Chicanos/Chicanas, and ethnic immigrants as well as those living in communities disenfranchised by class-based inequalities. Within these communities, certain ways of knowing and being carry as much value as monetary currency and serve as sources of strength and support. Community cultural wealth includes six mutually constitutive processes that build upon each other and include: aspirational, linguistic, navigational, familial, resistant, and social capital. Yosso described aspirational capital as the "ability to maintain hopes and dreams for the future, even in the face of real and perceived barriers" (p. 77). Aspirational capital is an asset that fosters a "culture of possibility" (p. 77) and hope in educational and a variety of other pursuits. It counters the discourse of apathy and cultural-deficit-oriented perspectives that assert that family and community structures of support, as well as aspirations in minoritized and low-income communities, are either lacking or nonexistent. Social and oral histories, as well as contemporary counterstories, have chronicled how collective efficacy, high expectations, ancestral pride, familial bonds, extended kinships, and spiritual connections have informed and empowered marginalized populations and helped to build a culture of resiliency and collective courage. Aspirational capital is used to navigate institutional barriers and discriminatory practices that can curtail economic advancement and limit opportunities in housing, education, occupational, and leisure pursuits, among others. It includes a spirit of resolve, intellect, creativity, and spirituality, each of which serve in the interests of political, economic, and social equality.

Roberta P. Gardner

Reference

Yosso, T. (2005). Whose culture has capital? A critical race theory discussion of community cultural wealth. *Race, Ethnicity and Education, 8*(1), 69–91.

ASSIMILATION

The massive immigration to the United States of more than thirty-one million people that occurred between the 1820s and 1920s initiated much concern and debate. The goal of initial social theorizing, dominant popular opinion, and early public policy regarding this first wave of immigration emphasized assimilation, the more or less orderly adaptation of a migrating group to the ways and institutions of an established host society. The English word *assimilate* comes from the Latin *assimilare*, meaning "to make similar." As the United States undergoes assimilation, the implication is that people will become more similar and differences among groups will eventually decrease. To study assimilation from a social science perspective involves understanding the dynamics and processes through which assimilation occurs as well as the extent to which it has happened for different groups in the United States. It also poses the related question: To what extent should we become like everyone else, and in what ways should we remain different?

Park's Race Relations Cycle

Many theories of assimilation are grounded in the work of Robert E. Park (1864–1944), an influential American sociological scholar who argued that all racial and ethnic groups go through a "race relations cycle" consisting of four stages: contact, competition, accommodation, and eventual assimilation. Park (1924) explained that groups first come into contact through exploration, migration, or conquest. Initial contact subsequently leads to competition for land, jobs, and other resources, a competition that is often characterized by instability and overt conflict. Out of competition eventually emerges a more stable form of accommodation among groups in which one group establishes forced dominance over the other. This stage may possibly take the form of a caste system and could be long lasting. However, as groups continue to live together, the final stage is assimilation that is "a process of interpenetration and fusion in which persons and groups acquire the memories, sentiments, and attitudes of other persons or groups, and, by sharing their experience and history, are incorporated with them in to a common cultural life" (Park and Burgess, 1921, p. 735). While Park recognized that the assimilation of racial or ethnic groups might involve major barriers and take a substantial period of time to complete, he also noted that the race relations cycle was "apparently progressive and irreversible" (Park, 1950, p. 150).

Although Park's ideas have been extremely influential, they are not without their shortcomings. While Park's race relations cycle seems to describe fairly accurately the experiences of many European immigrant groups in the United States, it does not hold equally relevant for those physically distinct groups and those that have entered the United States involuntarily. Others have pointed out that assimilation is not inevitable and, instead, interethnic contact can lead to perpetual exclusion, pluralism, or continued ethnic stratification rather than assimilation. And unlike Park, who argues that assimilation is irreversible, more recent theorists have argued that later generations might possibly reverse the assimilation process. Finally, Park's theory has been criticized for its lack of specificity in the time frame required for the completion of assimilation and in its lack of detail with regard to the nature of the assimilation process. However, Park's model, despite its limitations, stands as a precursor to subsequent, more comprehensive theories of assimilation such as Milton Gordon's.

Gordon's Stages of Assimilation

Since Park's seminal analysis in the 1920s, many writers have adopted an assimilationist perspective. Similar to Park, Milton Gordon (1918), an American sociologist and author of the widely cited work *Assimilation in American Life* (1964), also

explains assimilation as a series of stages through which various groups pass. But rather than following a straight line leading directly from contact to eventual assimilation, Gordon perceived a variety of initial encounters between racial and ethnic groups and an array of possible assimilation outcomes. He made the point that it is useful to view assimilation as a collection of several different but related subprocesses rather than as a single process. Milton Gordon is primarily known for having identified seven stages of assimilation: cultural assimilation, structural assimilation, marital assimilation, identificational assimilation, attitude receptional assimilation, behavior receptional assimilation, and civic assimilation. The distinction Gordon made between the first two, cultural assimilation and structural assimilation, are, however, the most important.

According to Gordon, cultural assimilation, also known as acculturation, involves a change of cultural patterns to those of the core society. For instance, newcomers may adopt the language, dress, diet, values, beliefs, and daily customs of the host society while simultaneously relinquishing their native racial or ethnic group's ways of life. Although some people may make this complete cultural transformation in their own life, more often it's a gradual shift that takes several generations. And yet others may experience so many barriers to assimilation that they may remain indefinitely at this stage. However, Gordon argued that an immigrant would not be able to assimilate any further if he or she had not embraced the dominant group's culture and, therefore, cultural assimilation must precede or at least occur in conjunction with structural assimilation.

Although acculturation is a prerequisite for structural assimilation, it is important to note that it does not necessarily lead to the next stage. This is in sharp contrast to Park's view that assumes that each stage inevitably leads to the next. Gordon argues that groups may become very much like the dominant group in terms of their culture, but if they are not integrated into the host society's institutions, social networks, and primary relations, they will remain structurally and indefinitely segregated. Gordon additionally acknowledged that not only is "acculturation without integration" possible, it is also quite common, especially for racial minorities who may experience geographic isolation, residential segregation, and persistent educational or occupational discrimination.

The second stage, structural assimilation, involves large-scale entrance into the cliques, clubs, organizations, and institutions of mainstream society. Gordon saw this subprocess as occurring in two stages. At first, integration occurs in the secondary sector consisting of larger groups and organizations that are public and more task oriented. Integration typically begins in a formal way between acquaintances interacting in schools, workplaces, and other public sectors but then progresses into the primary sector through personal friendships and informal and recreational social groupings. Gordon explains that once a group has entered the institutions and public sectors of the larger society, not only will integration into the primary sector follow but also all the other stages of assimilation will also inevitably occur. Therefore, in Gordon's theory, movement from acculturation to integration, especially the primary stage, is the most critical step in the assimilation process, and it is the key to all remaining stages.

According to Gordon, if structural assimilation occurs, all other stages including marital assimilation, identificational assimilation, attitude receptional assimilation, behavior receptional assimilation, and civic assimilation will inevitably follow. To explain, as people of minority and dominant groups become friends and interact in close, intimate, social settings, marital assimilation will naturally follow. And as large-scale intermarriage and childrearing occurs, identificational assimilation, in which individuals relinquish their ethnic identities and instead develop a sense of peoplehood based exclusively on the dominant society, comes next. This is followed by attitude receptional assimilation, or a lack of prejudice against minority groups, and behavior receptional assimilation, involving little or no remaining discrimination against the minority groups. And then, civic assimilation, characterized by the absence of group conflict over power or values, is the final stage.

Over fifty years after Gordon first published his theory of assimilation in 1964, some of his conclusions have, not surprisingly, been called into question. To begin, the subprocesses of assimilation that Gordon saw as linked in a particular order are

often found to occur in a variety of other ways. A group may integrate or intermarry before culturally assimilating, for example, or combine the individual processes in a multitude of different ways. After a certain point, and similar to Park, Gordon also assumes assimilation to be unidirectional, yet others have since argued that it is possible to reverse the assimilation process by reinvesting oneself in one's ethnicity. At times Gordon also seems to suggest that if minorities do not enter into primary relationships with the dominant group, it is because the dominant group has excluded them or barred the group's entry. However, others have noted that such social segregation may be largely voluntary. That is, racial or ethnic groups may simply not want to assimilate. When it comes to assimilation, it is important to remember that not all groups seek assimilation, and not all groups who seek assimilation attain it.

Although Gordon's theory has its share of critics, nonetheless, his analysis has been a major contribution to the field of race and ethnic relations. And despite the fact that most scholars do not entirely agree with his theory of assimilation, many continue to use parts of his theory as a springboard in their own work on ethnic and racial relations. Minimally, Gordon should be credited for showing the complexity of the assimilation process and for noting that there is a multitude of ways to assimilate.

Catherine M. Petrissans

References

Gordon, M. M. (1964). *Assimilation in American life: The role of race, religion, and national origins.* New York: Oxford University Press.

Park, R. E. (1924). The concept of social distance. *Journal of Applied Sociology, 8,* 339–44.

Park, R. E. (1950). *Race and culture.* Glencoe, IL: Free Press.

Park, R. E. & Burgess, E. W. (1921). *Introduction to the science of sociology.* Chicago: University of Chicago Press.

ATHEISM

There are three major positions on the controversial question of whether a god of any sort exists. *Theism* is the view that a god exists. *Atheism* is the negation of theism. *Agnosticism* is the suspension of judgment.

The term *atheism* is derived from two Greek words: the prefix *a* means "without" and the word *theos* means "god." The literal translation, "without god," suggests that an atheist is a person without a belief in a god. Call this the etymological meaning of the term.

Historically, many persons, including historical figures, have self-identified as atheists (Bremmer, 2007; Hyman, 2007). Atheists' contributions have a long and distinguished history; however, determining the approximate number of atheists worldwide is problematic for various reasons (Zuckerman, 2007). One historical reason is the fear of religious persecution. Furthermore, surveys about belief in gods and the supernatural are plagued by various methodological difficulties, including the stigma associated with the terms *atheist* and *atheism*. Many people who do not believe in a god prefer the labels *nonreligious* or *agnostic*.

Atheism is intelligible only in relation to theism. But this is problematic, for although most cultures have affirmed one or more gods, radically different conceptions abound. *Deism* is the view that a personal god created the world and let it run its course without taking an active interest or concern in human affairs. Moreover, many gods were believed to be finite in their power and limited in various ways. The Greek gods were believed to be immortal and have extraordinary powers but were otherwise very much like human beings. Sometimes *theism* is defined as the belief in one god and *polytheism* as the belief in many, but some consider polytheism to be a special case of theism (defining theism as the belief in at least one god). Finally, not all gods have been conceived as essentially personal deities. *Impersonal* conceptions characterize god as a nonperson, having no mind, desires, intelligence, or will. *Pantheism*—the view that god is identical to all there is—is an example of an impersonal conception of god.

An atheist can be understood in reference to any of the aforementioned conceptions. Thus, it is easy to understand why the early Christians were criticized for being atheists (the Christians rejected the Roman deities). Furthermore, it seems likely that everyone is an atheist with respect to

some conception of the divine. For this reason it is helpful to distinguish, as Michael Martin (1992, pp. 464–65) does, between broad and narrow atheism. Atheism in the *narrow sense* is the rejection of some particular conception of god. Atheism in the *broad sense* is the rejection of every conception of god; that is, the rejection of gods in general. This entry focuses on atheism in the broad sense. Thus, an atheist is defined as someone who is not a theist, polytheist, deist, pantheist, and who does not affirm any personal or impersonal god.

Since contemporary discussion and debate about theism/atheism presupposes a specific conception of god, "God" (with uppercase *G*) will be used to refer to the God of traditional, Abrahamic, monotheism, of Judaism, Christianity, and Islam: a personal being who is, among other things, *omniscient* (all-knowing), *omnipotent* (all-powerful), *omnibenevolent* (all-loving), creator of all things, and who designed humans for a special purpose.

The Ethics of Belief and Two Kinds of Atheism

ETHICS OF BELIEF AND BURDEN OF PROOF Upon what sorts of reasons should belief in God be based? The branch of ethics that studies how beliefs ought to be formed is the ethics of belief. Most philosophers (theists and atheists) subscribe to *evidentialism*, the view that only claims supported by evidence should be believed, otherwise one should suspend judgment. William K. Clifford (1877/1999) defends evidentialism by means of the moral argument that beliefs based on insufficient evidence, especially in religious contexts, result in terrible and regrettable consequences (death, suffering, etc.). William James famously objects that this principle is too restrictive and rules out many beneficial beliefs (1897/2009). He argues that, in certain circumstances, belief in God may be justified on insufficient evidence.

Antony Flew (1984), by contrast, argues that theists have the burden of proof. *Burden of proof* is the notion that a certain side of a debate must argue for its position; otherwise, the other side wins. So one side is presumed correct, and the other incorrect. Suppose that the evidence for and against theism is at a stalemate. Then, argues Flew, atheism prevails. Flew calls this *the presumption of atheism*. His argument is one from analogy. In a court of law the presumption is that the defendant is innocent until

Table A.1 Differences between Negative and Positive Atheism

Negative Atheism	Positive Atheism
Negative belief: has no belief in god	Positive belief: believes god does not exist
Rejects the arguments for theism	Rejects the arguments for theism
Makes no claim to knowledge (agnostic)	Makes a claim to knowledge
Bears no burden of proof	Bears a burden of proof
No independent argument for atheism is necessary	Some impossibility or improbability argument for atheism is necessary

proven guilty, for the prosecution is the side that affirms the guilt of the defendant. Similarly, in the theistic debate, the theist makes the positive affirmation that God exists; therefore, he or she bears the burden of proof.

NEGATIVE ATHEISM AND POSITIVE ATHEISM Flew's argument is grounded in the etymological meaning of *atheism*. This definition has come to be known as *negative atheism*. The negative atheist does not claim, positively, that no gods exist; he or she merely rejects the proposition that they exist—that is, he or she lacks belief. This position is compatible with negative agnosticism, for one may reject the belief in a god precisely because no reason to believe in one exists. Hence, negative atheism is sometimes called *agnostic-atheism* or *atheist-agnosticism* (Flint, 1903).

The negative atheist is analogous to the individual who does not believe in aliens. Asked why one does not believe in aliens, one replies, "There's no convincing evidence." One need not have a positive argument *against* aliens in order to reject the arguments *for* them. Similarly, one need not have positive arguments against the gods in order to reject the arguments for them. If this is correct, the only task of the negative atheist is to raise objections to the positive arguments offered by theists.

Negative atheism implies that many atheists are unaware of their atheism. Some atheists have never been introduced to the concept of god, and many more are infants who have no cognitive ability to ascertain such a concept. Therefore, these individuals satisfy the definition of one who lacks a belief in god (because they lack the requisite concept to form such a belief).

Many philosophers who challenge the presumption of atheism reject a more positive version of atheism. Most people, theists and atheists alike, lack a belief in virtually all known conceptions of god. However, some atheists take a further step,

claiming to know that a particular conception of god does not exist; some would even allege that theists are irrational. Such atheists have the burden of proving that this particular god does not exist. This position, known as *positive atheism*, is the view that a particular god does not exist (Martin, 1992, pp. 463–64). Whereas the negative atheist merely *denies* the existence of a god, the positive atheist *affirms* that no god exists. If the negative atheist is like the person who does not believe in aliens because he or she has not been presented with sufficiently good evidence, the positive atheist is like the person who asserts that aliens do not exist because there is good evidence to the contrary.

RUSSELL'S TEAPOT ARGUMENT There are many arguments for positive atheism. However, as most have no bearing on the issue of burden of proof, they will be considered in the next section. Bertrand Russell's argument is a notable exception (Russell, 1952/1997). Suppose Jose asserts that a teapot orbits the sun, but he adds that it is too small to be detectable by the most advanced technology. Would you believe Jose or remain agnostic on the issue? According to Russell, neither alternative would do, for the idea of a flying teapot is unsubstantiated. However, consistency demands that the same logic be applied to god. Lacking adequate evidence, rational persons should conclude that no god exists. Hence, the argument attempts to undermine theism and agnosticism on the grounds that absence of evidence is evidence of absence.

One might object that positive atheists bear their own burden of proof. Norwood Hanson replies that this charge confuses two uses of the word *proof* (Parsons, 1989, pp. 21–28). The atheist can "disprove" God's existence, but not in the way he or she disproves an impossible being, for possible and impossible beings are disproved differently. We know that round squares are impossible, not by having conducted an exhaustive search, but by linguistic analysis. Given the definitions of *round* and *square*, we note their incompatibility and conclude that the concept of a round square is impossible. By contrast, a unicorn is a possible being, even if we know from experience that no unicorns exist. Similarly, says Hanson, God is a possible being. Therefore, if it can be shown that the evidence for God fails, God's existence has effectively been disproved. Hanson does not offer this as an argument against theism and agnosticism but as an argument for the reasonableness of atheism.

Atheism and Competing Worldviews

Atheism is sometimes wrongly misconstrued as a religion or worldview. One argument is that the label *atheism* must denote a positive belief because all labels refer (*Muslim*, *string theorist*, etc.). But negative labels—for example, *atheism*—don't refer. The label *a-unicornist* provides no information about what one believes. Second, theism and atheism are components of worldviews, not worldviews as such. Thus, theism is a component of Islam and Hinduism, atheism of Buddhism and naturalism.

Another bad argument claims that atheists must be committed to naturalism if theists are committed to supernaturalism. It runs as follows. If the universe is a closed system, *naturalism* obtains. If the universe is open to nonnatural realities (such as gods or heaven), *supernaturalism* obtains. Since these are mutually exclusive positions and atheism is the rejection of supernatural realities, atheists are committed to naturalism. Therefore, if atheism is not a worldview, it implies one. Therefore, atheists carry the burden of proving the superiority of naturalism to supernaturalism.

The definition of atheism as the rejection of any and all supernatural realities is mistaken, for atheism is no more than a rejection of gods. Furthermore, atheism is a *fundamentally negative position*—that is, it provides no information about what is believed outside a theistic context. Even in regard to positive atheism, the positive belief that God does not exist implies no further beliefs outside this context. For this reason, atheism is compatible with naturalism *and* supernaturalism. For example, an atheist may believe in an afterlife. This explains why atheism has been associated with such diverse historical movements as freethought, humanism, feminism, communism, and utilitarianism.

One may object that the meaning of *atheism* has evolved in ordinary discourse, for contemporary atheists often define it as the rejection of all things supernatural. However, defining atheism in this way makes it identical to naturalism. Atheism is turned into a competing worldview at the expense of losing the distinction between atheism and naturalism. Second, by making them identical, the ability to associate atheism with religious worldviews is lost. For example, belief in a transcendent soul becomes impossible for the atheist. For these reasons, the rejection of theism should not be confused with the acceptance of any particular worldview.

Arguments for Positive Atheism

Many atheists do not find it necessary to wait on the refutation of theistic arguments in order to buttress their own arguments for atheism. If any such argument is sound, then, even if atheists have a burden of proof, their burden has been met. Atheistic arguments are categorized into two kinds: impossibility and improbability arguments. This section does not attempt a general survey of all atheistic arguments.

IMPOSSIBILITY ARGUMENTS Some arguments for atheism explicitly reject Hanson's assumption that God is a possible being. Incoherency or *impossibility arguments* attempt to prove that a particular kind of god is logically impossible (Martin & Monnier, 2003). An impossible being cannot exist; so it does not exist. These arguments stand in contrast to *improbability arguments*, which attempt to show that a particular kind of god probably or very likely does not exist. Impossibility arguments are not attempts to demonstrate that *every* conception of god is impossible. Rather, they are strategically designed to undermine a commonly held or sophisticated definition of god. Most atheistic philosophers target the most widely held conception: the God of traditional monotheism.

The atheist's goal is to demonstrate that belief in God entails a contradiction. Incoherency arguments can be categorized into three types. Let us say that a conception or definition of God is impossible if it is (i) logically incompatible with itself (self-contradictory); (ii) logically incompatible with some commonly believed religious story or doctrine; or (iii) logically incompatible with human knowledge and experience.

Consider an example of (iii). J. L. Mackie's "Evil and Omnipotence" (2003, pp. 61–72) argues that an omnipotent and omnibenevolent being is incompatible with pain and suffering (*Logical Problem of Evil*). He uses the term *evil* to refer to the experience of pain and suffering. If an omnipotent being can do anything that is logically possible, it can eliminate evil. If an omnibenevolent being infinitely loves its creation, it eliminates as much evil as it can. Therefore, if God is omnipotent and omnibenevolent, evil does not exist. But evil does exist. So God cannot exist.

IMPROBABILITY ARGUMENTS Improbability arguments argue that God's existence is highly improbable; that is, given certain premises, God's existence is very unlikely. *The evidential problem of evil* is the most widely influential argument for atheism. Mackie's logical version states that any amount of pain and suffering implies God's nonexistence (see Beebe, n.d.). However, the evidential problem focuses on the vast amounts and various kinds of pain and suffering that exist. According to some (Trakakis, n.d.), *horrendous evils*—babies dying from cancer, genocide, and torture—render God's existence unlikely. For others, *gratuitous evils*—pointless suffering or suffering that does not appear to serve any meaningful purpose—count as evidence against God.

Theists have devised various objections and replies to the evidential problem of evil. They typically point out that God is not the author of evil. Most of it is the consequence of human choices (*moral evil*). Atheists counter that even if God does not *create* evil, God nevertheless *permits* it, for humans were created with free will, which is the potential for evil. Furthermore, free will does not account for pain and suffering created by hurricanes, tsunamis, and more (*natural evil*).

Atheism and Morality

Can atheism account for morality? Are all things permitted, if God does not exist? Can atheism explain why moral laws are binding? It is often claimed that that atheists are committed to a naturalistic account of morality. Michael Martin (2002, pp. 21–26), however, argues that atheists do not

carry some special burden to explain morality. For atheists are not, in virtue of their atheism, committed to any particular worldview. Thus, they are not committed to any particular account of morality. If atheists have a burden to explain morality (the origin of the universe, for example), they carry it in virtue of their commitment to some positive worldview, not in virtue of their atheism. As such, every rational person shares this burden, theists and atheists alike. It is the task of philosophical ethics—not of atheists—to give an account of morality. Having said that, many *secular* (nonreligious) accounts of ethics are available for atheists to choose from (e.g., utilitarianism, duty ethics, and virtue ethics).

Atheists reject the religious contention that moral laws are binding because they are divine commands (*Divine Command Theory*). Plato's *Euthyphro* raises the question: What makes all morally good things good and all morally bad things bad? Suppose we say that whatever is commanded by God is good and whatever God condemns is bad. Then Socrates's question arises: Are God's commandments good because God commands them, or does God command them because they are good? If a command is good *because* God commands it, it is arbitrary and changeable. Suppose God commands against murder so that murder is bad. Had God commanded otherwise, murder would be good. That murder is wrong, therefore, is arbitrary. It is wrong for no other reason than that God happened to condemn it. Indeed, God could change the command and make murder good. On the other hand, if God commands certain things because they are good, then God's choice must be based on some moral principle. Therefore, the command against murder is not the basis for its being wrong, and morality must be explained in terms of the independent moral reason.

New Atheism

The struggle against religious dogma has a distinguished history. The "New Atheism," the latest addition to this history, is growing in the United States and other English-speaking countries. Richard Dawkins (2008), Daniel Dennett (2006), Sam Harris (2004), and the late Christopher Hitchens (2007) are among its most celebrated and outspoken proponents. This form of atheism has attempted to revive and popularize atheistic critiques of theism and religion, including the claim that religious extremism is a violent force and a danger to basic moral truisms, scientific progress, and freedom of (and from) religion.

A primary goal of this movement is to raise consciousness about religious ills. Most of their arguments are not new, although some are. For example, Sam Harris (2004) challenges religious moderates to question the respectability of religious values and beliefs. He argues that such respectability, shielded by political correctness, effectively protects religion from rational criticism, creating a cover for religious extremism. In a public talk, Harris (2005) says: "It is fundamentally taboo to criticize someone's religious beliefs. Faith is really a conversation stopper." Religious assertions should be as open to intellectual and rational scrutiny as any other claims, within both the public and academic arenas.

Alberto G. Urquidez

References

Beebe, J. R. (n.d.). Logical problem of evil. In J. Fieser & B. Dowden (Eds.), *Internet encyclopedia of philosophy*. Retrieved from http://www.iep.utm.edu/evil-log/.

Bremmer, J. N. (2007). Atheism in antiquity. In M. Martin (Ed.), *The Cambridge companion to atheism* (pp. 11–26). Cambridge: Cambridge University Press.

Clifford, W. K. (1999). The ethics of belief. In T. Madigan (Ed.), *The ethics of belief and other essays* (pp. 70–96). Amherst, MA: Prometheus. (Original work published 1877.s)

Dawkins, R. (2008). *The god delusion*. New York: Mariner Books. (Original work published 2006.)

Dennett, D. (2006). *Breaking the spell: Religion as a natural phenomena*. London: Penguin Group.

Flew, A. G. (1984). The presumption of atheism. In *God, freedom, and immortality* (pp. 13–30). Buffalo, NY: Prometheus Books.

Flint, R. (1903). *Agnosticism (The Croall lecture for 1887–1888)* (pp. 49–51). Edinburgh: William Blackwood and Sons.

Harris, S. (2004). *The end of faith: Religion, terror, and the future of reason*. New York: W. W. Norton & Company.

Harris, S. (2005, June 24). *The end of faith* [lecture]. Presented at the Idea City Conference Toronto.

Hitchens, C. (2007). *God is not great: How religion poisons everything*. Toronto: McClelland & Stewart.

Hyman, Gavin. (2007). Atheism in modern history. In M. Martin (Ed.), *The Cambridge companion to atheism* (pp. 27–46). Cambridge: Cambridge University Press.

James, W. (2009). *The will to believe. The will to believe and other essays in popular philosophy* (pp. 1–31). New York: Longmans, Green, and Co. Retrieved from http://www.gutenberg.org/ebooks/26659 (Original work published in 1897.)

Leslie, S. (1832–1904). (n.d.). In J. Fieser & B. Dowden (Eds.), *Internet encyclopedia of philosophy*. Retrieved from http://www.iep.utm.edu/Stephen.

Mackie, J. L. (2003). Evil and omnipotence. In M. Martin & R. Monnier (Eds.), *The impossibility of god* (pp. 61–72). Amherst, NY: Prometheus Books.

Martin, M. (1992). *Atheism: A philosophical justification*. Philadelphia, PA: Temple University Press.

Martin, M. (2002). Introduction [*sic*] the nonreligious foundation of morality. In *Atheism, morality, and meaning* (pp. 21–26). Amherst, NY: Prometheus Books.

Martin, M. & Monnier, R. (Eds.). (2003). *The impossibility of god*. Amherst, NY: Prometheus Books.

Parsons, K. M. (1989). Plantinga and the rationality of theism. In *God and the burden of proof: Plantinga, Swinburne, and the analytic defense of theism* (pp. 19–62). Buffalo, NY: Prometheus Books.

Russell, B. (1997). Is there a god? In J. G. Slater & P. Kollner (Eds.), *Volumes of the collected papers of Bertrand Russell: Vol. 11: Last philosophical testament, 1943–1968* (pp. 547–48). London: Routledge. Retrieved from russell.mcmaster.ca/cpbr11p69.pdf (Original work published in 1952.)

Trakakis, N. (n.d.). The evidential problem of evil. In J. Fieser & B. Dowden (Eds.), *Internet encyclopedia of philosophy*. Retrieved from http://www.iep.utm.edu/evil-evi/.

Zuckerman, P. (2007). Atheism: Contemporary numbers and patterns. In M. Martin (Ed.), *The Cambridge companion to atheism* (pp. 47–68). Cambridge: Cambridge University Press.

ATHEISM

The lack of belief in God generally known as *atheism* is a much-maligned viewpoint both historically and in recent times. General suspicion then follows concerning its ability to address questions concerning diversity and social justice. Recent sociological data challenges this long-standing view by establishing close links between secularism and social well-being. The recent popularity of the "New Atheism" has also served to sharpen our understanding of atheism, secularism, and their possible connections to questions of social justice. Some commentators see the need for a synthesis of atheism with the socially progressive agenda often assigned to secular humanism. When combined with a fuller recognition of the empirical data that connects atheism with social wellness, the promotion of such a synthesis may help to gradually remove the negative social stigma commonly associated with atheism.

Definitions, Issues, and Data

In the strictest sense, an atheist is someone who does not believe in God, while an agnostic is someone who remains unsure concerning God's existence. Other terms such as freethinker, humanist, and skeptic are also sometimes associated with atheism and agnosticism. Secular individuals are nonreligious or generally uninterested in religious beliefs, rituals, and activities (Zuckerman, 2009, p. 950; Kettell, 2013, p. 62). Such sharp distinctions mask a more complicated reality. Someone might be secular but not an atheist, since although never attending religious events or participating in its rituals, they still believe in something they call God. One might be an atheist and yet still be religious; such a person has no belief in God but still finds value in the social and psychological functions of religious commitment. Here we have an example in which the religious might be replaced with what is called "the spiritual" (Zuckerman, 2009, p. 950). Differences in atheist attitudes can even vary across cultures, as has been documented in a recent comparative study of atheism in the United States and Scandinavia (Zuckerman, 2012). If we adhere to a strict definition of atheism as simply nonbelief in God, then this position does not directly imply any specific viewpoint on issues of social justice. However, as we are about to see, when discussions of atheism turn to real-life examples and sociological data, it becomes unavoidably caught up with such issues.

Focusing on the question of social justice and its possible connection to atheism reveals three significant points. The first highlights how atheists themselves have a long history of experiencing discrimination and forms of social injustice. To cite a few examples: The Bible portrays nonbelievers as corrupt individuals incapable of performing good deeds (Zuckerman, 2009, p. 949). Even the British philosopher John Locke, in his compelling and moving defense of religious toleration, remained unwilling to extend such toleration to atheists (1983). This negative view persists today, with many Americans finding atheists to be the most problematic minority group. Here, public opinion can have real-life consequences. For example, divorced parents have had custody rights denied or limited because of their professed atheism (Zuckerman, 2009, p. 949). A second point often cited as the source of this general distrust of atheism is the view that nonbelievers are simply incapable of effectively addressing issues involving political, ethical, and social justice. The faithless or godless are here depicted as morally bankrupt and without redemption. They cannot then be trusted in providing any sort of moral foundation for issues of broader social and moral concern. This negative formulation of the issue is often made by theists, but as a basic question concerning the ethical and political credentials of atheism has recently appeared as a controversial issue debated within the atheism camp itself. Here we see a final point in which the recent rise of militant forms of atheists, usually described as the New Atheism, have resulted in an internal debate among atheists concerning whether their position does or does not entail a commitment to actively pursuing socially progressive views.

The most recent sociological evidence currently available largely dispels this negative stance toward atheism. There exists a large body of evidence that supports the view that a nonreligious lifestyle is not only a respectable one that does not undermine social justice but actually tends to support and promote progressive views on diversity and social justice. Not believing in God does not imply that one does not maintain strong beliefs on a number of different issues, including political and moral ones. Nonbelievers generally have a strong commitment to certain kinds of values. For example, numerous studies show that when compared with the values and beliefs of religious people, secular individuals tend to be less nationalistic, less prejudiced, less racist, less close-minded, and less authoritarian (Zuckerman, 2009, p. 953). More specifically, within the political realm, atheism is correlated with liberal, progressive views, and atheists themselves are found to be more politically tolerant than their religious peers, supporting the extension of civil liberties to minority groups. Atheists also tend to be supportive of gender equality and women's rights and are accepting of homosexuality and gay rights. Other studies find that atheists tend to adopt a more progressive viewpoint on a number of contemporary social issues. Atheists are less supportive of the death penalty than religious people and are the group least supportive of the government's use of torture. They are more likely to support doctor-assisted suicide, stem cell research, and the legalization of marijuana than their religious peers (Zuckerman, 2009, pp. 953–54). Atheists then exhibit a commitment to a set of beliefs and values on a number of moral, political, and social issues. The American sociologist Phil Zuckerman has even argued that this evidence supports the claim that atheists possess a more ethical sense of social justice than their religious counterparts.

The Rise of the "New Atheism"

Much of the recent discussion of the merits (or lack thereof) of a nonreligious, secularist view has been influenced by the rise of the New Atheism given expression in the widely read books of Dawkins, Hitchens, and others (2006; 2007; Kettell, 2013, p. 62). The general viewpoint of the New Atheism may be characterized in the following terms. It begins with a basic commitment to a naturalist worldview that cites the centrality of reason and science as the best means for understanding reality. Religion is further viewed as consisting of a set of beliefs about reality that should be treated like any other scientific hypothesis and measured against the best available evidence. The New Atheists conclude that, in the case of religion, no such evidence is available that lives up to such scientific standards, and so religious belief itself must be rejected. They further highlight the subjective and authoritative sources of religious belief, arguing that this reveals its irrational and dangerous nature. In their view, religious belief leads to an exclusionary and divisive type of mentality that fosters prejudice, discrimination, and violence. So construed, the New Atheism adopts an explicit critical perspective toward religion that attempts to prevent the increasing religious encroachment within public life by exposing the irrational and dangerous consequences of religious belief (Kettell, 2013, p. 62). The newness of the New Atheism stems less from its arguments that mostly repeat well-known points made against religious doctrines. Rather, its novelty is best located in its rather extreme, open, and public militancy against religion and its surprising public popularity and influence (Kettell, 2013, p. 64).

The aims of the New Atheism are not confined to the intellectual critique of religion found in its popular books, but also include a broader and significant political activism. This can be seen with some of the factors that help explain the rise of this new "movement." Importantly, the authority and prestige given to modern science has served to support and augment the perspective of the New Atheists and is used as a central platform from which they criticize religion. Two other more explicit political factors that help to explain the motives of the New Atheists involve the growing influence of religion in political matters and the importance of "identity politics" for the movement itself (Kettell, 2013, p. 63). Since the start of the current century, both the United Kingdom and the United States have seen a significant rise in the influence of religion in the public, political arena. The New Atheism has responded to this influence in a number of ways. Thought of as a larger movement that is best characterized as loosely organized, having little hierarchical structure, and no formal organization, its members nevertheless work within a set of existing secularist groups actively promoting atheism views and ideals. In America, this includes their participation in such groups as American Atheists, the Center for Inquiry, and the American Humanist Association among others (Kettell, 2013, p. 64).

They are also engaged in political activities found outside the formal public arena. Here they challenge religion in the private sphere and consider issues focusing on civil rights and group belonging. These issues involve the use of "identity politics" to widen the scope of the political where this is most prominent in the United States (Kettell, 2013, p. 65). Identity politics places special emphasis on groups as they promote shared interests that are based on a common set of concerns and issues. The success of identity politics relies on maintaining a strong sense of collective commitment, clear identity criteria, and a sense of group oppression, all of which are needed to help sustain group motivation. So construed, identity politics helps the New Atheists in their attempt to discredit religious belief by raising public awareness about atheism in order to counter its negative social stigma. This is furthered by, among other things, adopting a language of group rights and social justice and by attempting to establish a support network for atheists (Kettell, 2013, pp. 65–66).

While achieving some positive results, the use of identity politics has also fostered some conflicts within the atheist movement. The central problem here centers on questions of diversity, where general agreement that attempts be made to address the underrepresentation of ethnic minorities within secularism has been coupled with a somewhat divisive debate concerning gender equality (Kettell, 2013, p. 67). These discussions have even resulted in the attempt to forge a new identity for atheism known as "Atheism+." Introduced by Jen McCreight in a number of blog posts, Atheism+ has gained some popular traction with its proposal for a new "new atheism," claiming that the problems facing the atheist movement are the result of its overwhelming control by old, white, middle-class men. She presents Atheism+ as a call for more action where an atheist viewpoint is specifically connected to progressive political aims. This is further depicted as resulting in the need for a synthesis between atheism, secularism, and humanism in order to address questions of social justice, diversity, and provide a more uplifting, positive ethical vision for humanity (Kettell, 2013, p. 67). Reactions to Atheism+ have been mixed. While some see this suggestion as a positive step forward for the atheism movement, others view it as a potentially elitist and divisive viewpoint. They further note that a secular handling of social justice concerns is already conducted under the banner of secular humanism (Kettell, 2013, pp. 67–68).

Remaining Challenges

This recent upsurge of interest in atheism can then be understood as following from the general political motives of the New Atheism. While this trend began with an outspoken defense of the rational integrity and respectability of the atheist position, it has further focused on external political issues designed to curb the influence of religion in public life and internal issues concerned with establishing a community of purpose within the atheist movement. Recent data showing a decrease in religious commitment, coupled with a modest rise in those who openly declare their atheist commitment, suggest that the movement has been partially successful (Kettell, 2013, p. 68). However, the outspoken, militant nature of this call to action has served to partially reinforce skepticism concerning its ability to address social issues concerning justice. We saw that the lack of diversity within its existing ranks has led to a call for a renewed atheism that more explicitly addresses progressive issues of diversity and social justice. Moreover, aside from religious believers who find the New Atheist's arguments lacking, others more sympathetic to secular humanism place special emphasis on the shortcomings of the New Atheist's criticism of religious commitment. The philosopher Philip Kitcher (2011) argues that because of an exclusive focus on religious belief, militant forms of atheism remain unable to recognize the types of religious commitment that stem from a primacy of orientation rather than of belief. Focusing exclusively on belief seduces us into thinking that simply correcting false religious beliefs will automatically lead to a better view of what is significant and worth pursuing in human life (Kitcher, 2011, p. 10). It is not difficult to imagine circumstances in which the psychological and social conditions that support life, in terms of providing individuals with worthwhile goals to achieve, can only be sustained through their communal participation in religious practices and institutions. While arguably cogent in its attack on religious belief, the New Atheism fails to fully address the central psychological and social functions of religious commitment that are not specifically tied to the belief in religious doctrine or orthodoxy.

There then remains a general question concerning whether atheism can be seen as committed to addressing progressive social issues. In order to do so, the main suggestion has been that atheism be explicitly tied to a commitment to secular humanism. Carrying out this synthesis requires effectively addressing two main challenges. The first attempts to further demonstrate how an atheist position can be informed by a concern with issues of social justice. That is, noting that while an atheist position in the strictest sense does not imply any view on the question of social justice, neither should it be viewed as precluding any such commitment. In fact, as we have seen, while not explaining why secularism or atheism often involves a commitment to socially and politically progressive ideals, existing sociological data suggests a strong correlation between atheism and a commitment to such ideals. We have seen the introduction of Atheism+ as a recent attempt to meet this issue. The second challenge tries to show how atheism or secularism can both be recognized and offers ways for addressing the social and psychological functions found in religious commitment. In meeting this difficult challenge of locating shared values and ideals between secularism and those committed to religion, it has been suggested that we separate the religious from the supernatural (Dewey, 1934; Dworkin, 2013). Here we may find a shared interest in community and other values that are common to atheists, secularists, and those who in various ways are committed to religion. Further attempts to address these challenges when coupled with a deeper appreciation for the data that supports the social well-being that accompanies nonreligious attitudes could lead to a greater respect and cultural acceptance for atheism and secularism more generally.

Robert Sinclair

References

Dawkins, R. (2006). *The God delusion*. Boston: Houghton Mifflin.

Dewey, J. (1934). *A common faith*. New Haven: Yale University Press.

Dworkin, R. (2013). *Religion without God*. Cambridge: Harvard University Press.

Hitchens, C. (2007). *God is not great: How religion poisons everything*. New York: Twelve Books, Hachette Book Group.

Kettell, S. (2013). Faithless: The politics of the New Atheism. *Secularism and Nonreligion*, 2, 61–72.

Kitcher, P. (2011). Militant modern atheism. *Journal of Applied Philosophy*, 28, 1–13.

Locke, J. (1983). *A letter concerning toleration* (J. Tully, Ed.). Indianapolis: Hackett Publishing Company.

Zuckerman, P. (2009). Atheism, secularity and well-being. *Sociology Compass*, 3, 949–71.

Zuckerman, P. (2012). Contrasting irreligious orientations: Atheism and secularity in the USA and Scandinavia. *Approaching Religion*, 2, 8–20.

AUTOCRACY

There are many scholarly articles on autocracy. But in their studies, scholars do not often define what autocracy is. Their assumption is that "you will know it when you see it." Besides, it can be argued that there are as many different types of autocracies in the world as the number of autocratic regimes, which makes it difficult to define autocracy. Yet there are definitions of autocracy. If done, autocracy is often operationally defined as an ideal type of governance. According to Jaggers and Gurr (1995), autocracy is defined by the presence of a distinct set of characteristics. These characteristics include: (1) political participation that is sharply restricted or suppressed; (2) "executives are chosen in a regularized process of selection within the political elite"; and (3) "once in the office, the executive exercises power with few or no institutional constraints" (Jaggers & Gurr, 1995, p. 471). This is the mature form of autocracy. In its less mature form, "the personal authority of the chief executive is limited by the collective constraints of the authoritarian power bloc (e.g., the military or hegemonic party)" (Jaggers & Gurr, 1995, p. 472).

In autocracies, the state power is concentrated in the hands of a person or a group (i.e., a ruling minority in spite of the majority). But why should people let the power be concentrated in the hands of a minority? That is, where does autocracy come from? Olson (1993) offers a theoretical explanation for this paradox. In ancient China, there were peasants, roving bandits, and stationary bandits. Both roving and stationary bandits attacked peasant villages and sacked them. Roving bandits attacked randomly and took everything they could. On the other hand, stationary bandits attacked regularly but took only a part of the villagers' goods. They also protected the villages they regularly attacked (i.e., their turf) from roving bandits. Villagers were happier being attacked by stationary bandits than being attacked by roving bandits because life was more predictable in this way. They were more willing to produce because they knew that a part of their product would be left for them to consume. Otherwise, roving bandits would take their entire product, which made production pointless. In a sense, villagers exchanged predictability (or security) for goods. Stationary bandits exchanged part of their spoil for continuous income. According to Olson (1993), autocrats in the modern world are like the stationary bandits, and people are like the villagers in ancient China. Like the stationary bandits, autocrats, too, provide predictability and security in exchange for the people's taxes, but with an iron hand.

A lower form of governance than autocracy (i.e., stationary banditry) is anarchy, in which all bandits are roving. A higher form of governance is democracy, in which villagers rule together and protect themselves from roving bandits. However, no stationary bandit is likely to give up his power unless forced to do so. Then, where does democracy come from? According to Olson, when the leader of the stationary bandits dies, the power must be transferred to the new leader. The boldest in the band grasps the power, if there is one. If no one member (or a group of members) of the band can master the others, the power is shared/diffused within the band. Such a process leads to the diffusion of power to the villagers (or a representative portion of them), which eventually leads to democracy.

Autocracy is often conceptualized as the opposite of democracy. Thus, its various social, economic, and political outcomes are compared to the outcomes of democracy. These include, but are not limited to, individual rights, economic development (Olson, 1993), peacefulness (Bennett, 2006), formation of civil society (Bradley, 2002), electoral behavior (Gandhi & Lust-Okar, 2009), legitimacy, repression, co-optation (Gerschewski, 2013; Kailitz, 2013), durability (Kailitz, 2013), tax incentives (Li, 2006), violation of civil liberties (Møller & Skaaning, 2013), and terrorism (Wilson & Piazza, 2013).

Oftentimes, democracy is associated with more desirable outcomes than autocracy.

A major problem in autocracies is the succession of power from the previous ruler to the next. Many times this succession is not orderly, which makes the environment less predictable during successions. Moreover, the autocrat clings to power as long as he can, which makes the succession more painful. These affect many of the outcomes listed above. The autocrat and his possible successor(s) can resort to violence, which leads to the violation of individual rights and liberties. The autocrat is likely to repress his rivals, and the whole society, by different means, which also leads to the violation of individual rights and liberties. Since the environment is less predictable, economies do worse in autocracies. Foreigners are also not willing to invest in autocracies. If the succession is not successful, this can lead to a regime collapse or change. Autocrats can even start interstate wars to prolong their rule. This makes autocracies less peaceful than democracies. Autocracies are perceived as less legitimate than democracies. Therefore, again, autocrats need to resort to repression and co-optation. They need to repress the whole society to prevent rebellion and co-opt their possible rivals among the elite to prevent being toppled over. These techniques require the violation of civil liberties.

Initially, autocracy is perceived as only one type of governance. But recently, it has been argued that there is more than one type of autocracy, and the outcomes listed above vary between these types of autocracies. According to Geddes (1999), there are three types of autocracy. These are personalist, military, and single-party autocracies. In personalist autocracies, a single person rules the state. There is but a very limited circle of elites surrounding this person (e.g., the extended family, close friends). In military autocracies, a military officer by profession (current or retired) rules the state. The ruling elite in military autocracy are the high-ranked military cadres of the military. In single-party autocracies, a single party or a politburo rules the state (e.g., communist countries during the Cold War). Another form of autocracy is monarchy (Köllner & Kailitz, 2013). In monarchies, an aristocrat family rules the state. Personalist and military autocracies' reach to the society is narrower than monarchies.

Single-party autocracies are the ones that reach the widest portion of the society.

Autocracy is often conceived as a primitive form of governance, democracy being the developed one. Thus, it is (implicitly) assumed that autocracies will eventually become democracies. This might not be true (Levitsky & Loxton, 2013). At the individual level, autocratic behavior emerges when people have lower levels of tolerance for uncertainty or higher needs for closure (Pierro et al., 2003). That is, when people need to reach a decision soon, they tend to concentrate around boisterous people instead of voicing their preferences. At times of economic crises, social crises, and war, people need to reach a decision sooner. In such cases, populist leaders emerge—leaders who target the system or the status quo as a whole. People rally around them, which allow these leaders to overthrow the current institutions as a whole, and then they become autocratic leaders. Currently, about a third of the states in the world are autocracies.

Haci Duru

References

Bennett, D. S. (2006). Toward a continuous specification of the democracy-autocracy connection. *International Studies Quarterly*, *50*(2), 313–38.

Bradley, J. (2002). Subjects into citizens: Societies, civil society, and autocracy in tsarist Russia. *American Historical Review*, *107*(4), 1094–123.

Gandhi, J. & Lust-Okar, E. (2009). Elections under authoritarianism. *Annual Review of Political Science*, *12*, 403–22.

Geddes, B. (1999). What do we know about democratization after twenty years? *Annual Review of Political Science*, *2*, 115–44.

Gerschewski, J. (2013). The three pillars of stability: Legitimation, repression, and co-optation in autocratic regimes. *Democratization*, *20*(1), 13–38.

Jaggers, K. & Gurr, T. R. (1995). Tracking democracy's third wave with the polity III data. *Journal of Peace Research*, 32, 469–82.

Kailitz, S. (2013). Classifying political regimes revisited: Legitimation and durability. *Democratization*, *20*(1), 39–60.

Köllner, P. & Kailitz, S. (2013). Comparing autocracies: Theoretical issues and empirical analyses. *Democratization*, *20*(1), 1–12.

Levitsky, S. & Loxton, J. (2013). Populism and competitive authoritarianism in the Andes. *Democratization*, *20*(1), 107–36.

Li, Q. (2006). Democracy, autocracy, and tax incentives to foreign direct investors: A cross-national analysis. *Journal of Politics*, *68*(1), 62–74.

Møller, J. & Skaaning, S. E. (2013). Autocracies, democracies, and the violation of civil liberties. *Democratization*, *20*(1), 82–106.

Olson, M. (1993). Dictatorship, democracy, and development. *American Political Science Review*, *87*(3), 567–76.

Pierro, A., Mannetti, L., de Grada, E., Livi, S., & Kruglanski, A. W. (2003). Autocracy bias in the informal groups under need for closure. *Personality and Social Psychology Bulletin*, 29, 405–17.

Wilson, M. C. & Piazza, J. A. (2013). Autocracies and terrorism: Conditioning effects of authoritarian regime type on terrorist attacks. *American Journal of Political Science*, *57*(4), 941–55.

AVANT-GARDE

The phrase *avant-garde* derives from the French "advance guard," "vanguard," or, literally, "fore-guard," and is intended to refer to experimental and innovative people or works, such as works of art, and people involved in culture production, the arts, and political theory. There are avant-garde musicians and composers, artists and art movements, cultural producers, theorists, and critics in addition to social and political thinkers.

In general, the avant-garde is theorized as pushing the boundaries of what is usually accepted as the norm or status quo in a certain field or discipline by using unorthodox or experimental methods. In American music, the term *avant-garde* has been applied to saxophonist and composer John Coltrane (1926–1967), who was considered among the avant-garde in jazz, as is saxophonist and composer Ornette Coleman (1930–). Among classical musicians, John Cage (1912–1992) and Philip Glass (1937–), as well as Alban Berg (1885–1935), Anton Webern (1883–1945), Igor Stravinsky (1882–1971), Charles Ives (1874–1954), Arnold Schoenberg (1874–1951), Karlheinz Stockhausen (1928–2007), and Iannis Xenakis (1922–2001) are all considered avant-garde composers. Women avant-garde composers include Meredith Monk (1942–),

Laurie Anderson (1947–), Diamanda Galás (1955–
), and Pauline Oliveros (1932–), and are all active in
contemporary music.

In cultural criticism, one of the places the theory of the avant-garde was originally derived,
avant-garde theorists have included the Frankfurt
School's Theodor W. Adorno (1903–1969) and
Max Horkheimer (1895–1973), with their statement of the avant-garde contained in the 1944 text
"The Culture Industry: Enlightenment as Mass
Deception" from their coauthored book *Dialectic
of Enlightenment*. Frankfurt School associate Walter Benjamin (1892–1940), and his 1936 text "The
Work of Art in the Age of Mechanical Reproduction," is considered another key theoretical text of
the avant-garde in cultural criticism. The Frankfurt
School theorized of a Culture Industry that served as
the antithesis of the avant-garde. In 1939, art critic
Clement Greenberg (1909–1994) wrote the text
"Avant-Garde and Kitsch," which explained how the
avant-garde has historically been opposed to what is
considered "mass culture" while also serving as the
antithesis to both "mainstream" and "high" culture.
The art world was the other place that the theory
of the avant-garde was originally derived. Theorist
Guy Debord (1931–1994), in his text *The Society of
the Spectacle* (1967), conceptualized mainstream
and neoliberal economics as standing in opposition to avant-garde culture and art. In general, all
of the above cultural theorists and critics believed
avant-garde culture stood in stark contrast to capitalist culture and its works of art. Systematic studies
and full theories of the avant-garde were offered by
Peter Bürger in 1974 and Renato Poggioli in 1962.

Dustin B. Garlitz

References
Benjamin, W. (1968). The work of art in the age
of mechanical reproduction. In H. Arendt (Ed.),
Illuminations: Essays and reflections (H. Zohn,
Trans.) (pp. 217–51). New York: Schocken Books.
Bürger, P. (1984). *Theory of the avant-garde* (M. Shaw,
Trans.). Minneapolis, MN: University of Minnesota
Press.
Debord, G. (1983). *The society of the spectacle*. Detroit,
MI: Black & Red.
Greenberg, C. (1965). *Art and culture: Critical essays*.
Boston, MA: Beacon Press.
Horkheimer, M. & Adorno, T. W. (2002). The culture
industry: Enlightenment as mass deception. In G. S.
Noerr (Ed.), *Dialectic of enlightenment: Philosophi-
cal fragments* (E. Jephcott, Trans.) (pp. 94–136).
Stanford, CA: Stanford University Press, 2002.
Poggioli, R. (1981). *The theory of the avant-garde*
(G. Fitzgerald, Trans.). Cambridge, MA: The
Belknap Press of Harvard University Press.

Additional Reading
Cottington, D. (2013). *The avant-garde: A very
short introduction*. Oxford and New York: Oxford
University Press.
Foster, Hal. *The return of the real: The avant-garde at
the end of the century*. Cambridge, MA: The MIT
Press, 1996.

BABY BOOMER GENERATION

Each generation has its particular styles and peculiar attributes whether they are in music, fashion, taste, or political activism, just to name a few possible distinctions. Because of these instances of cultural idiosyncrasies, historians often frame individuals' contributions in the context of their generational titles. The boomers generational traits, titles, and tastes are many.

In the continental United States, the most recognizable generational title is the baby boomer generation. This generation lived through the post–World War II period between the years 1946 and 1964. As of 2011, there were about seventy-six million boomers in the United States representing about 29 percent of the population, making this generation the largest in U.S. history thus far (Bowman & Rugg, 2011).

The baby boomer generation is exceptional for several reasons. First, and most obviously, its members were born in the immediate aftermath of World War II and lived with a discomforting awareness of nuclear weaponry, which manifested itself in attitudes that made the Cold War abroad an ever present reality and fostered social unrest at home. The profound sense of unease that permeated the time period arguably inclined the baby boomers to engage in more rebellious and ambitious cultural movements compared to their predecessors. Boomers felt that it was their appointed duty to save the world and to make an indelible imprint on how society treats individuals. The carbon footprint of the boomers will forever be their social revolutionist views. Boomers lived in a generation that fought difficult wars in Korea and Vietnam, and at the same time, they adopted the nonviolent philosophies of Martin Luther King Jr. and the Flower Power movement. It was a generation that argued fiercely over civil rights, human rights, and women's liberation and danced wildly to the new sounds of rock 'n' roll and Motown, yet held its collective breath as Neil Armstrong and Buzz Aldrin carried mankind's imagination into the depths of space— boomers thought they found the good formula, and they tried to right wrongs and fix what seemed to be broken in the world. In short, the boomers can be seen as a culture of pioneers and trailblazers, and in the same instant, as a people grappling with frighteningly drastic shifts in influence, power, and human values.

Amid all the drama, and in some ways because of it, baby boomers cultivated a love affair with television. Due to the commercialization of TV in the 1950s and the widespread sale of televisions in American homes, most boomers have been exposed to television throughout their lives. They started with variety shows and nightly news and progressively gravitated toward a wide range of media that includes soap operas and cartoons, and now, they are obsessed with cable network channels. According to P. J. O'Rourke, the baby boomer generation was attached to television and pay-for-view entertainment. In the 1970s, a sitcom that received large ratings for its rare use of bigotry toward minorities and women was the CBS sitcom called *All in the Family*. This show was a hit among boomers; it aired until 1979, winning numerous Emmys and Golden Globe awards (Schumacher-Matos, 2012).

The need to be active and to avoid idleness was not exclusive to the living room; it also spurred baby boomers to earn and spend vast sums of money on vacations, homeownership, fancy cars, and electronic gadgets, hence their significant presence in the workforce and consumer markets. However, they have lost as much as they have gained in recent decades, especially during the financial crisis of 2007–2008. According to Steve Christ, the real estate market bust and stock market decline wiped out considerable portions of baby boomers' assets.

Using financial reports, economists estimate that baby boomers in the United States between forty-five and fifty-four lost 45 percent of their median net worth and those between fifty-five and sixty-four lost 38 percent of their net worth (Christ, 2009).

Throughout these tumultuous times, baby boomers have shifted from one political party affiliation to another, but nevertheless they have demonstrated their own brand of patriotism and loyalty to country. Compared to their older peers, young boomers tend to show more allegiance to the Democratic Party—an attachment that may be rooted in eyewitness accounts of the social and political upheavals of the 1960s and 1970s (Bowman & Rugg, 2011). Bowman and Rugg noted that as the baby boomers aged, they started to swing to the Republican Party, and they became more conservative in their views. Boomers that remained vigilant to social justice issues have criticized their fellow boomers for giving in to the comforts of the establishment. Some historians have recorded the baby boomer era as a generation that failed society and gave up on eliminating inequity and injustice in society between minority populations and majority populations. Researchers suggest that boomers became a functional part of the same system they had criticized when they were engaged in the civil rights movement, in many instances, because few gains were made to improve political and social conditions. This left the cherished movement for equity and social justice, abandoned by the majority of boomers, to a few die-hard activists while a tremendous number of boomers retreated to the comfort of their familiar middle class lifestyles.

Bowman and Rugg (2011) report that boomers' attitudes and ideological beliefs have changed since the 1960s and 1970s. Boomers are more conservative; they have a different set of religious views than their parents; and they are more liberal on racial issues, homosexuality, and women's roles. O'Rourke's (2013–2014) examination of this population found "boomers didn't exactly create a race-blind society, but the kids we've raised might" (p. 38).

O'Rourke (2013–2014) makes another great observation in his article "How the Boomers Saved Everything." He suggests that the boomers will take credit for social movements, but they fail to take responsibility. He states:

> But running the world means taking responsibility for it. The boomers have been good at taking things: Mom's car without permission, drugs, umbrage at the establishment, draft deferments, advantage of the sexual revolution, and credit for the civil rights and women's liberation movements that rightly belong to prior generations. The one thing that can be left in plain sight without us putting our [boomers] sticky mitts on it is responsibility. (p. 36)

Some activist boomers have called for their colleagues to leave their comfort zones and create something; to leave a legacy. Consequently, the grow-your-own, invent-something-now attitude is popular among this group; "rename it and claim it" is the clarion call. Many baby boomers thus feel pressure to grab hold of society's new challenges and extract new opportunities from their faded dreams. To that end, some die-hard boomers are starting nonprofit organizations to help inner-city youth, the elderly, and immigrants, and even pet rescue efforts are being headed by boomers. Other boomers are writing best-selling how-to books, and still others are on the speaking circuit discussing the virtues of spirituality. In sum, baby boomers are expected to create their route to success in order to fulfill their generational birthright.

Sherwood Thompson

References

Baby boom generation. (n.d.). United States History. com. Retrieved from http://www.u-s-history.com/pages/h2061.html.

Bowman, K. & Rugg, A. (2011). *As the baby boomers turn.* American Enterprise Institute. Retrieved from http://www.aei.org/article/politics-and-public-opinion/elections/as-the-baby-boomers-turn/.

Christ, S. (2009). Baby boomers meet the housing bubble: Trillions lost in run up to retirement. *Wealth Daily.* Retrieved from http://www.wealthdaily.com/articles/baby+boomers-housing-bubble/1718.

Gillon, S. (2004). Boomer nation: The largest and richest generation ever and how it changed America. New York: Free Press.

O'Rourke, P. J. (December 2013/January 2014). How the boomers saved everything. *AARP Magazine*, 36–64.

Schumacher-Matos, E. (2012). *Racism on fresh air? Lessons from Archie Bunker and Stephen Colbert*. NPR Ombusman. Retrieved from http://www.npr.org/blogs/ombudsman/2012/02/23/147294594/racism-on-fresh-air-lessons-from-archie-bunker-and-stephen-colbert.

Some historical events for baby boomer generation. (2013). BabyBoomer-Magazine.com. Retrieved from http://www.babyboomer-magazine.com/news/165/ARTICLE/1208/2013-06-16.html.

BICULTURALISM

The term *biculturalism* normally refers to the presence of two cultures in the same nation-state or region. The term may also refer to both an ontology—that is a way of being or existing in the widest sense—and the functional capacity to selectively appropriate from dual cultural backgrounds when navigating social spaces. If the term *culture* signifies, in part, a series of narratives that human beings construct to understand their world, biculturalism is invoked, in part, when human beings are able to access dual narratives and social identities. For example, using the modern notion of the nation-state, a group that maintains strong cultural, social, and political affiliation in a subculture (and perhaps dual citizenship) due to immigration might celebrate both the historical and culturally symbolic specificities of the nation of origin as well as the nation in which the group resides. It is important to note, however, that the specificities of "nation" are themselves a condition of social and cultural construct and therefore are perpetually undergoing change—particularly given the reality of biculturalism (Anderson, 1983). This condition is not solely restricted to immigrants since it is also often exhibited by children of immigrants who are born and raised in a receiving society and yet display degrees of affiliation with the heritage culture. The condition is also not always the result of movement between nation-states. There are groups that may have strong cultural affiliation but no specific nation-state of strong connection; such is the case of people who identify as Hmong in the United States.

Biculturalism should be viewed not as a state but a process, given that it is not conclusive. It is always a question of degree, and the determination of what counts as bicultural expressivity largely depends on the social context. Many Western societies are characterized by monocultural norms, which are normally defined and circulated by the ruling elite. Bicultural expression is, therefore, more marked; that is, it is more likely to be seen as unusual. In these contexts, families must make significant efforts to socialize children and youth in their heritage culture given that the institutions are structured and perpetually oriented toward the dominant culture. Western landlocked nation-states and those in the economic South are more likely to be marked by bicultural normativity. Although these societies may be dominated by a specific culturally identifiable group, biculturalism is not perceived as unnatural in most cases. Biculturalism emerges in social contexts in which individuals are exposed to two cultures and there is a social and often economic necessity to use elements of both cultures. Again, the manner in which the two cultures develop and are expressed largely depends on context.

Much of what has been written above, although important for the introduction of biculturalism, is misleading because it relies on a definition of culture and biculturalism as neutral categories. All cultural interactions are informed by and move through relations of power (Darder, 1991). The severity and nature of the power dynamics is largely determined by the social, political, economic, and historic context. Cultures compete, and one will often find the existence of a dominant culture and subordinate cultures in respective social spaces. Perhaps the most pronounced example is the existence of a standard language and policies of linguistic restriction, which serve as forces for the possibility of erasure of subordinated languages and biculturalism (Skutnabb-Kangas, 2000). Antonia Darder (1991) has theorized and documented how the language of bicultural youth in U.S. classrooms is "systematically silenced and stripped away through values and beliefs that support its inferiority to Standard English" and how bicultural youth are subjected to instrumental approaches that dissuade a critical and oppositional reading of negative relations of power (p. 36). The U.S. educational standardization movement (embodied in such policies as No Child Left Behind and Race to the Top) advanced since Darder's analysis has only regenerated the assault on bicultural youth.

Although language is a major marker of biculturalism, it is certainly not the only one. In the 1920s the Brazilian government pursued racial whitening policies that were effective not only in limiting nonwhites into the country but also in policing biculturalism writ large in social and institutional spaces. The policy was particularly harsh toward the Japanese and reached its most oppressive articulation following the Brazilian government's declaration of war on Japan in 1942. The mere identification with the nation-state of Japan and/or the exhibiting of desires to maintain subcultural spaces in the country was seen as taboo. Likewise, Christian missionaries and the Bureau of Indian Affairs (BIA) founded boarding schools in the United States whose immediate purpose was cultural erasure and assimilation. These efforts were not only linguistic in nature but also involved corporeal terrorism. The effort to socialize indigenous and bicultural identities out of existence was instantiated by a wider project of cultural and material imperialism.

The power dynamics at play, given the presence of biculturalism, need not always take a negative form. For example, Swiss cultural policy follows efforts to foster cultural diversity. In the realm of linguistic policy, Switzerland recognizes four official languages. Nation-states may also reverse policies that advance monoculturalism. There is some evidence that Māori resistance in New Zealand has led to renewed emphasis on biculturalism and the undermining of government policies favoring Pākehā culture (although some would claim minimal). Furthermore, in no power dynamic is any group totally powerless. Native American students in boarding schools, for example, were never passive recipients of Anglo- and Euro-centric culture (Adams, 1995).

Through much of the twentieth century, researchers and policymakers viewed biculturalism and bilingualism as a hindrance to intellectual development. Considerable current research exists on the cognitive benefits of biculturalism and bilingualism. In a 2004 study, psychologists Ellen Bialystok and Michelle Martin-Rhee found that bilingualism forced young children to resolve internal cognitive conflicts in the solving of puzzles much more efficiently than monolingual children. Some studies have also concluded that the higher the degree of bilingualism, the later the age of onset of conditions such as dementia and Alzheimer's disease.

Interesting areas of current research on biculturalism include examinations of the forces that both promote and serve as obstacles to its development. Current tensions in the use of the term exist as debates have surfaced regarding the use of biculturalism or multiculturalism. The former seeks formal recognition of two cultures, whereas the latter seeks the political and institutional legitimacy of more than one.

Ricardo D. Rosa

References

Adams, D. W. (1995). *Education for extinction: American Indians and the boarding school experience: 1875–1928.* Lawrence, KS: University Press of Kansas.

Anderson, Benedict. (1983). *Imagined communities: Reflections on the origin and spread of nationalism.* London: Verso Editions.

Bialystok, E. & Martin, M. M. (2004). Attention and inhibition in bilingual children: Evidence from the dimensional change card sort task. *Developmental Science, 7*(3), 325–39.

Darder, A. (1991). *Culture and power in the classroom: A critical foundation for bicultural education.* Westport, CT: Bergin and Garvey.

Skutnabb-Kangas, T. (2000). *Linguistic genocide in education or worldwide diversity and human rights.* Mahwah, NJ & London: Lawrence Erlbaum Associates.

BICULTURALISM
Bicultural Individuals

The U.S. Census Bureau (2013) reported that 21 percent of all married-couple households in America had at least one foreign-born spouse in 2011. Biculturalism is when individuals highly identify with two cultures, both home and host cultures, whether by being born in a country (i.e., home culture) and moving to another (i.e., host culture), or by being born into a setting (i.e., home culture) in which the primary caregivers do not identify with the mainstream culture (i.e., host culture). There are also many U.S.

(i.e., host culture)-born individuals who are born into ethnic and minority families (i.e., home culture), making them bicultural from their upbringing (Phinney, 1996). These individuals will likely have to balance the two identities within their surroundings, many times choosing which identity to display in different contexts. For example, Peter is Korean American. He was born in the United States, but his parents are Korean speaking and immigrated to the United States only a few years before he was born. Therefore, his home life is much different than his American peers whose parents speak English at home and know American culture. Peter has to decide how much he will identify with his Korean culture and how much he will try to fit into American culture. These choices are influenced by factors such as: mostly speaking English versus Korean, the general culture of his chosen peer group, his way of thinking, and his relationship with his parents.

Balancing Both Cultures

Bicultural individuals' constant need to switch between cultures may make them more aware to culture norms and understand the multidimensionality of multiple cultures (Gutierrez & Sameroff, 1990). Hong et al. (2000) described the notion of cultural frame switching, in which a bicultural individual needs to access and execute different parts of his or her culture at any given time, based on social cues. Social cues could include obvious symbols such as clothes, language, and food, or less obvious signs such as roles, tone, expectations, and facial expressions. Depending on the context, the bicultural individual quickly needs to decide and apply a socially acceptable behavior for that culture. For example, Peter's Korean culture requires him to speak and act extremely respectfully to adults, to use formal language specifically for addressing older people, and to engage in respectful behavior such as bowing. He is expected to show respect to his elders at his Korean church, with his parents' friends, and even with strangers at the Korean supermarket. However, although he is still expected to show respect at school, he can speak less formally with his older teachers and administrators. He is expected to address them with prefixes such as Mr. and Mrs. However, he is not expected to use a different language for adults, and he does not need to bow to

them when he greets them. Peter's inaccurate application to each culture could result in significant repercussions: Korean culture would classify him as extremely rude and disrespectful, and American culture may classify him as extremely strange.

Individuals' Biculturation Process

Acculturation is the process of cultural socialization or adapting to the norms of the dominant or mainstream culture. In contrast, enculturation is the retention of one's own culture or cultural socialization to one's culture of origin. Individuals will likely identify with one culture, and they will have a difficult time living in the dominant culture or will lose a large portion of their native culture.

Difficulties in the Biculturation Process

Bicultural individuals experience difficulties and challenging situations that are unique to their situation. Bicultural individuals do not adjust into either ethnicity, making it difficult for them to identify with either side. For example, Peter might naturally acculturate more with American culture because he spends most of his time interacting with Americans rather than Koreans, but his Asian appearance will automatically enforce stereotypes from others about his cultural identity. Even if Peter is fluent in English and was born and raised in the United States, strangers may assume that he cannot speak English or that he is new to the country. On the contrary, Peter may successfully preserve his Korean heritage because his parents are intentional about enforcing Korean traditions in the home. However, he will likely not be able to relate to native Korean people when he visits Korea because he was born and raised in America and grew up with a different lifestyle. Although Peter may have a new identity as a Korean American, he will never be able fully to identify as an American or a Korean.

Bicultural individuals also experience difficulty mastering both cultures in socially appropriate manners. Many times, their native ethnicity is compromised more than the culture in which they live. However, their native culture is what others assume they align with because of their appearance. Further, individuals in their native culture may also assume and expect them to identify fully with their culture just by looking at them. For example, Sarah is a Korean American female who grew up with

English-speaking parents. Therefore, she did not grow up learning Korean even in her home and does not understand Korean values. Her lack of exposure to Korean social norms is most problematic when she visits her relatives in Korea and does not show the proper respect they expect from her. She is expected to speak Korean in a formal language, bow, and not be completely comfortable around adults. However, her Americanized parents never expected these behaviors in her home, so she does not know how to interact with her Korean relatives. Because of Sarah's Korean ethnicity, she is held to the same standard as a Korean individual from Korea, even though she was raised in the United States with different expectations.

Recent Research Findings Related to Bicultural Individuals

BICULTURAL INDIVIDUALS' PSYCHOLOGICAL AND SOCIOCULTURAL ADJUSTMENT Although individuals experience many challenges in their biculturation processes, a high level of biculturalism is strongly and positively associated with both psychological and sociocultural adjustment. An extensive quantitative review (i.e., meta-analysis) study found this biculturalism-adjustment relationship is stronger than the relationship between monoculturalism (i.e., having only a single culture) and adjustment (Nguyen & Benet-Martínez, 2013). This study indicates that bicultural individuals acquire competencies and cognitive and social flexibility in the process of learning and accessing two cultures, which may lead them to be more adept at adjusting to various types of people and situations in their cultures and other cultures (Benet-Martínez, Lee, & Leu, 2006; Leung, Maddox, Galinsky, & Chiu, 2008; Nguyen & Benet-Martínez, 2013). Further, their social support networks in both cultures and their cognitive and social flexibility may protect them from the psychological maladjustment such as anxiety and loneliness, or sociocultural maladjustment such as interpersonal conflicts and intercultural miscommunication. They might have suffered from these kinds of maladjustment due to their challenging acculturation experiences if they were not bicultural (Nguyen & Benet-Martínez, 2013). The findings indicate that bicultural individuals' cognitive and social flexibility and competencies might increase their intercultural sensitivity and ethnorelativism, which may help them become excellent cultural mediators for intercultural conflicts or business negotiations (Nguyen & Benet-Martínez, 2013).

BICULTURAL INDIVIDUALS' COGNITIVE FLEXIBILITY AND COMPLEXITY Bicultural individuals are more creative and more professionally successful than monocultural individuals (Leung & Chiu, 2010; Leung, Maddux, Galinsky, & Chiu, 2008; Maddux, Adam, & Galinsky, 2010; Maddux & Galinsky, 2009; Tadmor, Galinsky, & Maddux, 2012). Tadmor, Galinsky, and Maddux (2012) found that bicultural individuals show (a) higher levels of creativity such as higher fluency, flexibility, and novelty; (b) higher innovation at work; (c) higher promotions; and (d) more positive professional reputations than monocultural individuals. More importantly, Tadmor et al. (2012) found that the relationship between biculturalism and creativity is due to bicultural individuals' high cognitive flexibility and complexity, which are the skills to process information through considering and combining multiple perspectives. Individuals' cognitive flexibility and complexity can explain why some bicultural individuals are more successful than others while living abroad (Tadmor et al., 2012). Therefore, just being exposed to new cultures and cultural knowledge(s) is insufficient to bring about creativity and other cognitive benefits associated with biculturalism. In fact, the number of years abroad is not a significant predictor of creativity (Tadmor et al., 2012). Bicultural individuals who experience the inconsistencies between the two cultures in a powerful way, resolve the inconsistencies between the two cultures in a complex way, and synthesize two cultural perspectives and achieve cognitive transformation are more creative and more professionally successful. This conclusion highlights the importance of a multicultural climate that allows acculturating individuals the freedom to adopt a bicultural strategy and thus develop the cognitive flexibility and complexity required to become more creative and successful (Tadmor et al., 2010).

Implications

As the United States is becoming more diverse and interracial marriages are becoming more prevalent, biculturalism is a growing phenomenon

(Coronado, Guevarra, Moniz, & Szanto, 2003). Biculturalism is an important social phenomenon, especially in a multicultural society and in today's increasingly interconnected and globalized world. If a society's climate insists on an assimilation mindset, which believes that minority members should be absorbed into mainstream culture, then the minority members cannot develop bicultural identities with cognitive flexibility and complexity. This chain of events could lead the society to reap fewer benefits from diversity and creativity (Tadmor et al., 2010). The relationship between biculturalism and adjustment indicates that if host countries adopt multicultural policies, they might achieve greater national success and well-being (Nguyen & Benet-Martínez, 2013). Further research specific to bicultural individuals may be helpful in making conclusions about cultural norms, societal expectations, and new norms related to the growing trend of diverse individuals. Bicultural individuals experience a unique set of advantages and disadvantages pertaining to education, career, and social interactions; more data on how to best cater to bicultural individuals may be beneficial. Even though there are more bicultural individuals now than ever before, issues such as racism, discrimination, and prejudice against bicultural individuals are existent and need to be eliminated.

Kyung-Hee Kim
Sharon Kim

References

Benet-Martínez, V., Lee, F., & Leu, J. (2006). Biculturalism and cognitive complexity: Expertise in cultural representations. *Journal of Cross-Cultural Psychology, 37*, 386–407. doi: 10.1177/0022022106288476

Coronado, M., Guevarra, R. P., Moniz, J., & Szanto, L. F. (Eds.). (2003). *Crossing lines: Race and mixed race across the geohistorical divide*. Santa Barbara, CA: Multiethnic Student Outreach, University of California.

Gutierrez, J. & Sameroff, A. (1990). Determinants of complexity in Mexican-American and Anglo-American mothers' conceptions of child development. *Child Development, 61*, 384–94.

Herskovits, M. J. (1948). *Man and his works: The science of cultural anthropology*. New York: Knopf.

Hong, Y. Y., Morris, M., Chiu, C. Y., & Benet-Martínez, V. (2000). Multicultural minds: A dynamic constructivist approach to culture and cognition. *American Psychologist, 55*, 709–20.

Leung, A. K.-Y. & Chiu, C.-Y. (2010). Multicultural experiences, idea receptiveness, and creativity. *Journal of Cross-Cultural Psychology, 41*, 723–41. doi: 10.1177/0022022110361707

Leung, A. K.-Y., Maddux, W. W., Galinsky, A. D., & Chiu, C.-Y. (2008). Multicultural experience enhances creativity: The when and how. *American Psychologist, 63*, 169–81. doi: 10.1037/0003-066X.63.3.169

Maddux, W. W., Adam, H., & Galinsky, A. D. (2010). When in Rome…learn why the Romans do what they do: How multicultural learning experiences facilitate creativity. *Personality and Social Psychology Bulletin, 36*, 731–41. doi: 10.1177/0146167210367786

Maddux, W. W. & Galinsky, A. D. (2009). Cultural borders and mental barriers: The relationship between living abroad and creativity. *Journal of Personality and Social Psychology, 96*, 1047–61. doi: 10.1037/a0014861

Nguyen, A-M. D. & Benet-Martínez, V. (2013). Biculturalism and adjustment: A meta-analysis. *Journal of Cross-Cultural Psychology, 44*(1), 122–59. doi: 10.1177/0022022111435097

Phinney, J. S. (1996). When we talk about American ethnic groups, what do we mean? *American Psychologist, 51*, 918–27.

Redfield, R., Linton, R., & Herskovits, M. (1936). Memorandum for the study of acculturation. *American Anthropologist, 37*, 149–52.

Tadmor, C. T., Galinsky, A. D., & Maddux, W. W. (2012). Getting the most out of living abroad: Biculturalism and integrative complexity as key drivers of creative and professional success. *Journal of Personality and Social Psychology, 103*, 520–42. doi: 10.1037/a0029360

U.S. Census. (2013, September 5). Census bureau reports 21 percent of married-couple households have at least one foreign-born spouse. U.S. Census Bureau. Retrieved from https://www.census.gov/newsroom/releases/archives/foreignborn_population/cb13-157.html.

BISEXUALITY

Bisexuality and Social Justice

Bisexuality has been defined in many ways. Although a common assumption is that bisexuality denotes sexual or romantic interest in only two sexes (i.e., male and female), this is often not the case for individuals who identify as bisexual. Instead, a more inclusive definition of bisexuality is often more appropriate—namely, that bisexuality is the possibility for sexual and/or romantic attraction or desire for more than one sex or gender (Ebin, 2012).

Indeed, individuals do not actually need to have engaged in sexual or romantic behavior with more than one sex or gender in order to identify as bisexual—just as individuals do not need to have had sex or a romantic relationship with someone of a different gender to identify as heterosexual. Rather, it is the capacity for attraction or desire (along with self-identification) that constitutes bisexuality. Additionally, there is a wide array of sexual and romantic attractions within bisexuality. Some individuals may indeed be romantically and/or sexually interested in only two genders (e.g., men and women), whereas other bisexual-identified individuals may be interested in more than two genders (e.g., men, women, and people who do not conform to a binary gender identity). In this context, bisexuality is used as an umbrella term for many different sexual identity labels that describe attractions and desires that are not limited to monosexual categories (i.e., heterosexuality or homosexuality). There are many other identity labels that could fall under the wider umbrella of bisexuality, such as pansexual, omnisexual, biromantic, or fluid (Eisner, 2013).

Finally, personal identification is an important part of any sexual identity label, including bisexuality. Many people exhibit bisexual behavior or desires, but they do not identify as bisexual.

Issues Facing the Bisexual Community

Social justice and political organizations are critical for the bisexual community. Two of the major social justice issues relevant to the bisexual community that are addressed here are the issue of *bisexual erasure* or *invisibility*, and the *health disparities* faced by bisexual people. Even though population-based studies have found the number of people who identify as bisexual to be at least the same as or larger than the number of those who identify as exclusively homosexual, bisexual people and issues that are important to the bisexual community are marginalized within the overall queer community—in addition to being marginalized within the larger heterosexual society. This process of minimization or lack of recognition refers to one of the frequently cited issues for the bisexual community—namely, bisexual erasure (Yoshino, 2000).

Bisexual erasure manifests in a multitude of ways ranging from incorrect assumptions about a bisexual person's identity, attractions, or behavior to the denial of the existence of bisexuality as a legitimate and stable sexual identity. Since people frequently identify others by the gender of their current sexual or romantic partner, and further, since people often are not simultaneously visibly involved with two or more partners of varying genders, bisexual people are usually miscategorized as being heterosexual or homosexual. Despite the growth in recognition of bisexuality as a legitimate and stable sexual identity in comparison to previous decades, bisexual people continue to encounter erasure and invisibility in their day-to-day experiences (e.g., via their encounters with individuals, systems, and contexts that refute the existence or legitimacy of bisexual identity; Ross, Dobinson, & Eady, 2010).

Bisexual erasure is a major issue for bisexual individuals because it can lead to difficulty in creating and maintaining a bisexual community and often results in the lack of attention for or recognition of bispecific needs. First, many people who identify as bisexual do not feel as though a bisexual community exists or see it as a part of their lives. The absence of a perceived community may exacerbate what is often already a lack of adequate social support for bisexual individuals. Many people who identify as bisexual do not always feel welcome in queer spaces, but they also may not feel at home within heterosexual communities. Social support has been found to be a protective buffer against minority stress for marginalized groups (Crockett, Iturbide, Torres Stone, McGinley, Raffaelli, & Carlo, 2007), and this has been found to be true for bisexual people as well (Ross, et al., 2010). Without community, bisexual people do not have the benefit of social support that other more easily identifiable groups enjoy.

Second, bisexual erasure leads to the lack of recognition and attention paid to bisexual needs. Currently, there is a scarcity of information and resources that specifically address the health needs of the bisexual community (Ebin, 2012). In research with sexual minorities, bisexual people are frequently either grouped together with gay men and lesbians, based on the assumption that they face identical challenges and have similar needs, or they are excluded all together from research due to low participant numbers. Kaestle and Holz Ivory (2012) conducted a content analysis of medical literature from 1987 to 2007 that exemplifies this issue. The researchers found, across the decades, that less than 20 percent of articles that mentioned bisexuality actually analyzed bisexual participants as a separate group from lesbians and gay men. In articles published in 2007, they found only 33 of the 162 articles discussing bisexuality analyzed the bisexual participant data as a separate group. In terms of being left out of research all together, another content analysis found that of all the research published on sexual minorities, only 16 percent included bisexuality within the title (Rosenthal, 2012).

This erasure becomes more malignant when one considers the health disparities observed when bisexual people are considered as a separate group from their heterosexual and homosexual counterparts. Researchers have found that people who identify as bisexual are more likely than non-bisexuals to report having worse access to health care services, to report fair or poor physical health resulting from a disability, to be diagnosed with heart disease, to currently smoke cigarettes, to report using alcohol and other drugs, and to experience sexual assault and violent victimization (Ebin, 2012). Bisexual people have also been found to report higher rates of anxiety and depression. In fact, Bostwick (2012) found that bisexual women reported a lifetime depression rate nearly double that of heterosexual women (59 percent compared to 30.5 percent, respectively), which was also significantly higher than the 44 percent lifetime rate reported by lesbian women. Bostwick (2012) also found that bisexual women reported experiencing higher rates of the seven out of nine mood and anxiety disorders classified in the *Diagnostic and Statistical Manual of Mental Disorders* (DSM). Similarly, Fredricksen-Goldsen, Kim, Barkan, Balsam, and Mincer (2010) found that in comparison to lesbian women, bisexual women report higher levels of mental distress and poorer general health. This disparity differed by geographic location, with bisexual women in urban areas reporting higher distress and lower overall health than bisexual women in rural areas.

In much of the research addressing health disparities observed with bisexual populations, researchers conclude that the disparities are likely caused and compounded in part by the systemic erasure of bisexuality and lack of supportive community (e.g., Ebin, 2012; Ross et al., 2010). As stated above, this erasure can lead to the neglect of the health experiences and needs of bisexual people, which can result in a lack of appropriate health services and resources.

Social Justice and Political Organizing

While these issues of erasure and health disparities are startling, it is important to highlight that they do not affect everyone equally within the bisexual community. Just as there are differences between bisexual people and monosexual people, there are differences among bisexual people themselves. This recognition is doubly important in the context of a call for social justice and political organization, as people with different lived experiences may need different resources or advocacy—an issue that has been silenced at the start of previous social movements in North America dominated by white, middle-class voices. Solutions for the issues outlined above should address people of varying social locations. For example, Ross et al. (2010) determined, through a community-based research project with bisexual people across Ontario, as well as other previous research, that pregnancy status, parental status, gender identity, race, and age intersect with bisexuality to shape their experiences. As Steinhouse (2001) writes, "No single aspect of her identity stands alone for identity is fluid and interconnected" (p. 8). Thus, one is not a parent separately from being a bisexual person, but is both at the same time. From an intersectional perspective, this means that we need to consider how different identities affect and influence one another, changing the lived experience of the people who embody these plural identities.

Taking first the issue of *parents who identify as bisexual*, it is important to note that these individuals' unique experiences have been largely ignored within parenting and LGBT research, as researchers have typically assumed that bisexual parents either experience parenthood as a heterosexual person would (when in a mixed-sex relationship) or as a homosexual person (when in a same-sex relationship). However, the limited research on parenting by bisexual individuals has found that bisexual people parent in a wide array of relationships and environments that include single parenting, coparenting with a same-sex partner or other-sex partner, coparenting with past romantic partners and current partners, and parenting with biological parents that they were never partnered with (Power et al., 2012). Power and colleagues found many of the parents in their study were not parenting in a "traditional" nuclear family context, and many had to continuously negotiate fluid relationships while also sometimes struggling with visibility of their own bisexual identity. While very few of the parents cited their bisexual identity as a negative factor within their parenting, research conducted by Ross and colleagues has found that women who identify as bisexual report poorer mental health and relationship satisfaction as well as higher levels of anxiety than do other sexual minority women (Ross, Siegel, Dobinson, Epstein, & Steele, 2012).

There are few examples of research that investigate experiences of bisexual parents, and more information is needed to know what types of support these individuals need to be supported in their identities both as bisexual and as parents. However, from this research we can see that visibility and health care needs may be different for bisexual parents compared to bisexuals who are not parents, as they may be more likely to be heterosexualized when viewed with their children. This is in part likely due to the incorrect assumption that only heterosexual couples have children. Further, bisexual women and women with sexual histories including both men and women may be at a higher risk for postpartum depression in comparison to lesbian-identified women (Ross, Gibson, & Goldberg, 2013). Thus, social justice and political organizations within the bisexual community need to address the different challenges of erasure and health needs faced by this particular group.

Trans individuals who identify as bisexual also face different challenges than cisgender bisexual people, in that they are perceived by some as being confused about not only their sexual identity but also their gender identity, thus ignoring the legitimacy and authenticity of both identities. In this sense, trans bisexual people may face double erasure of identity. Additionally, trans bisexual people can face obstacles in receiving competent health care, as some individuals report they have been told they cannot receive any care related to their trans identity until they have "sorted out" their sexual identity (meaning to endorse a monosexual identity) (Ross et al., 2010). In this case, bisexual social justice and political organizing means understanding how these two types of erasure influence each other and affect the people experiencing these identities as well as advocating for the access of competent health care for trans bisexual people.

When it comes to people of color and those who are racialized (i.e., people who are placed in a racial context by others, which can result in racism and discrimination), there may be complex layers to identity depending upon what community they are with in any given moment. There is both a history (and current existence) of racism within the queer community, and a history of homophobia or biphobia within some communities of color. First, within the queer community and the bisexual community, bisexual people of color may experience a lack of support from LGBT services or may be discriminated against within these communities on the basis of race. A qualitative study conducted by Goode-Crosse and Tager (2011), for example, found that black gay and bisexual men within predominantly white institutions found the support offered by an African American community was more important to them, and that they experienced discomfort in using the LGBT-specific resources. Conversely, men who have sex with men and women (who may or may not identify as bisexual) have been vilified by popular culture as being disease vectors within black communities and are blamed for the increase in HIV transmission to heterosexual black women (Allen, Myers, & Williams, 2014).

Racialized people and people of color who identify as bisexual are not only faced with the stressors of biphobia and heterosexism, but also those of racism. While we know bisexuals face disparities in health compared to monosexuals, people of color also are found to experience poorer physical and mental health due to race-based discrimination (Williams, Neighbors, & Jackson, 2003). Further, due to racism within bisexual communities and biphobia within heterosexual communities of color, they may not have the same visibility and access to social support in each community, thus removing a potential support strategy for maintaining well-being. Just as bisexual social justice and political organizing must be inclusive of parent status and gender identity, so too must it address social inequities based on racial inequality within the community and the visibility and health needs of members of the bisexual community who are racialized or of color.

A fourth marginalized group within the bisexual community is bisexual youth (Ross et al., 2010). Having less status within society, youth voices are often silenced within social movements. Bisexual youth, in particular, face the issue of erasure in that they may be perceived as just experimenting or that they will just be "gay/lesbian until graduation" (Diamond, 2003). Beyond the issue of identity erasure, bisexual youth also face health disparities even in comparison to bisexual adults. In a recent study conducted by Ross and colleagues, bisexual youth were found to have higher rates of depression and anxiety, as well as more frequent contemplation of suicide, than do bisexual adults (Ross et al., under review). Additionally, adolescent bisexual women in the United States have been found to experience higher sexual and reproductive health risks in comparison to heterosexual and lesbian young women (Tornello, Riskind, & Patterson, 2014). More work needs to be done to better understand the specific causes of elevated risk to mental and physical health of bisexual youth in comparison to bisexual adults since they too are important members of the overall bisexual community. Social justice and political organizing within the bisexual community that excludes bisexual youth is a disservice to the youth and to the future of the bisexual community overall.

Conclusion

There are many other social locations and identities within the bisexual community that are not addressed here, such as disability, socioeconomic status, and geographic location, for example.

The main point is to understand the bisexual community as a multifaceted group of people, and while overall bisexual individuals experience higher levels of mental health distress and lower functional health in comparison to monosexual people, it is important to keep in mind that social justice advocacy must not homogenize the bisexual community when attempting to find solutions to these disparities. Ignoring the diversity of experience within the bisexual community in social justice and political organizing would only reproduce the pattern of erasure and health disparity that the bisexual community faces within the queer community at large.

The challenge today is to find a balance between recognizing the diversity among people who identify as bisexual and the ability to create concrete goals to help advance the visibility and health status of the entire community. As Steinhouse (2001) writes, "We must grapple with how to reconcile individual agency, subjectivity, and difference with the need to create some uniformity of identity for organizing" (p. 18). The issue of bisexual social justice and political organizing is not merely an issue of recognizing bisexuality as a legitimate sexual identity and generating information and research about bisexuality separate from lesbian and gay people. Ensuring visibility of various identities that intersect with bisexuality within advocacy materials, community health resources and education, and mental and physical health research directed toward bisexual people is essential to working toward social justice for the bisexual community.

Corey Flanders
Abbie Goldberg

References

Allen, V. C., Myers, H. F., & Williams, J. K. (2014). Depression among black bisexual men with early and later life adversities. *Cultural Diversity and Ethnic Minority Psychology, 20*(1), 128–37.

Bostwick, W. (2012). Assessing bisexual stigma and mental health status: A brief report. *Journal of Bisexuality, 12,* 214–22.

Crockett, L. J., Iturbide, M. I., Torres Stone, R. A., McGinley, M., Raffaelli, M., & Carlo, G. (2007). Acculturative stress, social support, and coping: Relations to psychological adjustment among Mexican American college students. *Cultural Diversity and Ethnic Minority Psychology, 13*(4), 347–55.

Diamond, L. M. (2003). Was it a phase? Young women's relinquishment of lesbian/bisexual identities over a 5-year period. *Journal of Personality and Social Psychology, 84*(2), 352–64.

Ebin, J. (2012). Why bisexual health? *Journal of Bisexuality, 12,* 168–77.

Eisner, S. (2013). *Bi: Notes for a bisexual revolution.* Berkeley, CA: Seal Press.

Fredriksen-Goldsen, K. I., Kim, H., Barkan, S. E., Balsam, K. F., & Mincer, S. L. (2010). Disparities in health-related quality of life: A comparison of lesbians and bisexual women. *American Journal of Public Health, 100*(11), 2255–61.

Goode-Crosse, D. T. & Tager, D. (2011). Negotiating multiple identities: How African American gay and bisexual men persist at a predominantly white institution. *Journal of Homosexuality, 58,* 1235–54.

Kaestle, C. E. & Holz Ivory, A. (2012). A forgotten sexuality: Content analysis of bisexuality in the medical literature over two decades. *Journal of Bisexuality, 12,* 35–48.

Power, J. J., Perlesz, A., Brown, R., Schofield, M. J., Pitts, M. K., Mcnair, R., & Bickerdike, A. (2012). Bisexual parents and family diversity: Findings from the work, love, play study. *Journal of Bisexuality, 12,* 519–38.

Rosenthal, M. (2012). *Human sexuality: From cells to society.* Belmont, CA: Wadsworth, Cengage Learning.

Ross, L. E., Bauer, G. R., MacLeod, M. A., Robinson, M., MacKay, J., & Dobinson, C. (Under Review). Mental health and substance use among bisexual youth and non-youth in Ontario, Canada.

Ross, L. E., Dobinson, C., & Eady, A. (2010). Perceived determinants of mental health for bisexual people: A qualitative examination. *American Journal of Public Health, 100*(3), 496–502.

Ross, L. E., Gibson, M., & Goldberg, A. E. (August 2013). Perinatal mental health among sexual minority women. American Psychological Association 121st Convention, Honolulu, Hawaii.

Ross, L. E., Siegel, A., Dobinson, C., Epstein, R., & Steele, L. S. (2012). "I don't want to turn totally invisible": Mental health, stressors, and supports among bisexual women during the perinatal period. *Journal of GLBT Family Studies, 8,* 137–54.

Steinhouse, K. (2001). Bisexual women: Considerations of race, social justice and community building. *Journal of Progressive Human Services, 12*(2), 5–25.

Tornello, S. L., Riskind, R. G., & Patterson, C. J. (2014). Sexual orientation and sexual and reproductive health among adolescent young women in the United States. *Journal of Adolescent Health, 54*(2), 160–68.

Williams, D. R., Neighbors, H. W., & Jackson, J. S. (2003). Racial/ethnic discrimination and health: Findings from community studies. *American Journal of Public Health, 98*(Suppl 1), S29–S37.

Yoshino, K. (2000). The epistemic contract of bisexual erasure. *Stanford Law Review, 52*(2), 353–461.

BLACK DIALECT

According to sociolinguists, black dialect is a variation of general or mainstream English. General or mainstream English is the lingua franca (the most commonly used language) of the nation. A sociolinguistic perspective on language takes into account the social and political interactions among speakers that produce linguistic forms and norms (Wardhaugh, 2011).

Black dialect grows out of the African American speech community. A speech community is a group of individuals that have a shared identity and use the same language rules to interact. Members of the African American community are the primary users of black dialect. However, speakers from other racioethnic groups embedded in the community, or who have frequent interactions with African Americans, also use it.

Grammars from general American English and grammars from diverse African tribal languages inform the dialect (Smitherman, 2006). Africans brought here in bondage came from disparate tribes and even countries. Many who ended up on the same slave ship during the Middle Passage spoke different languages. The grammars undergirding those languages combined with southern English grammar evolved into black dialect. Speakers in all of the Confederate states, those states that seceded from the United States during the Civil War, use southern English. A southern dialect is also used in southern Missouri. People below St. Louis, and in the parts of Missouri below the Mason-Dixon line, seceded with the Confederacy. They also use a southern dialect of English.

Dialects in Relationship to Other Linguistic Forms
Language is a system of communication using an alphanumeric system, words, and behaviors to converse. Morphological, phonological, syntactical, semantic, and grammatical rules distinguish one language from another (Wardhaugh, 2011). Those language characteristics can also be used to differentiate black dialect from general English. People speaking the same language will be mutually intelligible. People speaking different languages will be unintelligible to each other. Speakers using various dialects of the same language will be able to understand each other. Americans from every dialect region in the country understand each other. However, Americans using disparate languages with each other, such as Italian, German, French, and/or Spanish, will not.

General American English language is the theme, and dialects are variations on the theme. Dialects can evolve from geographical, racioethnic, religious, and other speech communities. In addition, separate languages entwined with a dominant language can form dialects. In the United States, there are regional variations of English based on geographical locations such as Southern, Eastern seaboard, New England, Midwestern, Southwestern, Northwestern, and the West Coast of America. Linguists even separate these broad regions into smaller geographical units (Labov, 2012).

There are also linguistic variations on general English that are generated in bilingual communities, such as Spanish (Spanglish), Jamaican (Jamerican or JAmerican), and Hindi (Hinglish) (Wolfram & Schilling-Estes, 2005). Tex-Mex is a dialect of English occurring specifically in areas where Texas and Mexican communities interact.

To put the discussion of black dialect into focus, a metaphor would be useful. General English is like the melody of a song and dialects are variations on the melody. In the language of music, we call that jazz. What sounds like a cacophony of voices in America, when properly understood, might be interpreted as avant-garde jazz.

Pidgins are trade languages developed in communities where there is an inflow of transient and permanent dealers and merchants who do business together. The many groups that pass through the region often speak different languages but develop a truncated mutual language to communicate. They may borrow words and phrases from each language that identify objects, places, and processes integral to their functioning. Pidgins seldom develop into full-blown languages.

Jargon grows out of specialized word and phrase choices specific to an occupation. For instance, there are medical, legal, government, and even collegiate jargons. Every academic tradition has words used primarily in their community. Universities around the country use words such as *credits* or *units*, *matriculation*, *articulation*, *interdisciplinary*, and *class* (freshman, sophomore, junior, or senior standing). Class also refers to individual courses focused on rather narrow topics.

Words and phrases that come onto the language scene, usually from young people or countercultures, are considered slang or incorrect grammar. Words and phrases such as *whatever, yeah right, are you kidding me?, really, wannabe,* and *ain't* are originated in both youth and countercultures. *That's off the hook* or *that's tight* are adjectival phrases used to describe objects, people, places, or even experiences, and they are considered slang. The ubiquitous nature of the media often brings about the incorporation of slang words into the mainstream vocabulary. Slang tends to be short-lived.

Colloquialisms are local or regional variations of a language. Here are a few examples: *make groceries* rather than *get groceries* and *red soda* as a flavor rather than *strawberry* are both southern colloquialisms. The use of *soda pop, soda water,* or *soda* is regional, a distinction coming from the South and Midwest, and are chosen based on educational and Urban-Rural differences. Kansas and Missouri speakers use *katiwampus* to mean "askew or off center." *Hella* and *hyphae* are both slang words or phrases and colloquialisms from Northern California.

Idiolects are variations on a language that are specific to an individual person. Such as *they under arrested him* (they arrested him); She is my *friend girl* (my female friend that I am not romantically involved with); I brought it down to my *clear point* (here is the crux of the matter); *he is a Z* (idiot); *you look like Bozo's understudy* (you look terrible);

I look like dammit to hell I'll bite ch'a (I'm looking rough today); and *he looks like a wild Ubangi* (hair disheveled, clothes out of order, and he does not care). Idiolects include differences in word choices, pronunciations, syntax, and semantics.

Naming Language Variations of Black Americans

In the early years of the nation, 1600s, 1700s, 1800s, and 1900s, white scholars and grammarians deemed black dialect to be the result of intellectual deficits, a lazy tongue, incorrect English, or nongrammatical speaking. White literary authors, minstrel productions, and recorders of African American speeches exaggerated the differences between black dialect and general English to entertain audiences and reinforce the stereotypes of black speech. In an attempt to reflect the behavior of the oppressor, many African Americans also considered black dialect to be incorrect English. However, writers of the Harlem Renaissance questioned this interpretation of black dialect. An intense debate took place among the black intelligentsia to determine whether or not black authors should use black dialect. They questioned the legitimacy of black dialect as a tool of communication (Minnick, 2007). Eventually they decided that black dialect was a legitimate choice because: (1) both black and white audiences read the works, (2) dialects are indigenous to specific contexts, and (3) language usage is part of the identity of the character(s).

Black dialect was deemed right and reasonable in the 1970s as a result of the Black Power movement. The movement was a social and political push for African American self-empowerment through Afrocentric self-identity: who am I; self-definition: what am I; and to legitimize their own experiences: what do I know? Not only were blacks seeking to validate the beauty of their countenance but also the acceptance of all that was black, including natural hair, Afrocentric dress, and black dialect. The self-empowerment was a direct counter-oppressive tactic.

Dr. Robert Williams (1975) coined the term *Ebonics* in his book *Ebonics: The True Language of Black Folks*. Though he clearly stated that Ebonics was not a language, the Oakland Unified School District represented it as such to acquire funding

(1995). The funding was requested in an attempt to improve the educational experience of African American children by using Ebonics as a tool of instruction to facilitate the acquisition and mastery of (general) English language skills. One method of bilingual education uses the same model: teach the children formal Spanish to help them become fluent in mainstream English language. The school district was targeting the funding pot designated for bilingual education.

The proposal was to teach both students and teachers about the sociocultural origins of Ebonics in an attempt to raise the self-esteem of the students. The administrators also sought to increase the understanding of the teachers about the role of Ebonics in the identity of the African American speech community and the students themselves. Teaching the instructors and children to speak Ebonics would be the first step in developing general English proficiency (Bilingual Education Act, 2005). The Oakland Unified District's proposal used terms such as *African Language Systems* and *Pan African Communication Behaviors* along with *Ebonics*. *Black dialect*, *Black Vernacular*, *Black English*, and *Ebonics* are the words most frequently used to describe the communication system of African Americans.

The Role of Black Dialect in the African American Community

For those who use it, black dialect is a sign of membership in the African American community, part of their personal identity, and a cue to the level of formality in a communicative event.

COMMUNITY MEMBERSHIP All cultures tend to identify members by the language/dialect they use. If black dialect is used correctly, an African American will be accepted as part of that community. There are people of racioethnic designations that use black dialect. However, they may be seen as wannabes, fake, condescending, or patronizing even though they speak it well.

African American speakers who do not use black dialect at all may be marginalized in the black community. They may be marked as interlopers, wannabe whites, or arrogant. In other words, they are not members of the community. However, if the speaker is highly educated, the community will be more accepting of the fact that a black speaker does not use black dialect.

One excellent example of the role of language in community membership comes from the Native American experience. In the late nineteenth and early twentieth centuries, Indian boarding schools were established in the United States and Canada to educate Amerindian children and youths according to Euro-American standards. The children were not allowed to use their tribal tongues nor adhere to tribal traditions. The younger the child, the more difficult it was to maintain his or her native tongue. Once the children were "educated," they had nowhere to go. White communities did not accept them, and when they returned to the tribes they were no longer considered members of that community. This was so because most no longer knew their tribal language, and they had lost the knowledge of tribal culture, so they ended up in no-man's land. Tribal members refused to recognize them as members of the tribe. The forced separation of children from their parents and the eradication of tribal traditions and languages amounted to cultural genocide.

IDENTITY The language or dialect that one speaks is central to who he or she is. The manner in which one talks parallels who they think they are (Wardhaugh, 2011). There are dialect speakers who refuse to use mainstream English because it may lead to the loss of their personal identity: "If I don't sound black, then who am I?"

There are blacks from all walks of life and all socioeconomic levels who choose to use black dialect because it is part of their identity. As an African American professor, I have chosen to retain the basic phonology of my Southern Black dialect. In my classroom, the language of instruction is formal black dialect. At home, it is informal black dialect. This pays homage to the fact that higher education does not mean the lack of black identity.

LEVELS OF FORMALITY Regardless of class, black speakers who are upwardly mobile usually engage in code switching, moving through the various registers of black dialect to general English, depending on the setting. Registers of English is a concept put forth by Thomas Bertram Reid (1956), a sociolinguist. Register refers to the choice of a speaker's linguist behaviors based on the context in which

the communication occurs. Levels of formality are considered registers. For example, with black dialect there are urban, informal, and formal registers. Communication scholars might consider this phenomena "voice," the political, economic, and social factors shaping the choice of what linguistic behaviors to use in a setting.

Urban black dialect might be heard from the hip-hop generation or people who want to "keep it real." Steve Harvey, the actor, author, comedian, game show host, and radio DJ, always uses an urban black dialect no matter the public context.

Informal black dialect might be used among friends and family or to demonstrate familiarity or closeness. For example, while searching for my glasses in class one day, the students laughed at me because I had a pair hanging on my blouse. I said, "These are my computer glasses; I'm looking for my regular glasses." Then some female students my age just shook their heads and smiled. I responded with, "Don't be laughing at me, in a few years this gonna be you wearing glasses." I was showing an affinity with my mature female students who were also white.

Oprah Winfrey moves from formal to informal black dialect while on TV, but mainly she uses formal black dialect. Michelle Obama, the first lady, uses general American English in public settings. Dr. Martin Luther King Jr. used a very formal black dialect. While on air, Robin Roberts of *Good Morning America* uses formal English at all times. Phonology (sound) is the main difference between formal black dialect and general American English.

Black Dialect in the Classroom

Most educators are asking, "What do we do about it the use of black dialect among our students?" I would suggest that they start with an affirming attitude. Educators must have a sociolinguistic perspective about not only black dialect but also all dialects in the classroom. This includes the understanding that:

1. There is no correct English. The correctness of all language behavior depends on the context in which it is used. Each context has its own rules that depend on the who, what, when, where, and why of a situation. Those

questions dictate how the communicator should speak: the voice they use.

2. All language behavior is rule-governed. Dialects and languages grow out of rules generated in specific speech communities. Dialect speakers are using the morphological, phonological, syntactical, semantic, and grammatical rules set forth in their communities. They are using correct grammar for their social milieu—the teacher simply may not know what the rules are.

3. Dialects are not indicators of intelligence or class. Neither intelligence nor socioeconomic levels are bound by the dialect one speaks. Highly intelligent and moneyed people may use dialects different from mainstream English from situation to situation. Speakers using marginalized dialects may be as smart as the rest of the population.

4. Speakers should use general American English at all times. The manner in which one speaks is dictated by the individual's identity, speech community, and context in which the communication is taking place.

5. Language behavior is easily changed. Because language is integral to personal identity and group membership, it is not an easy thing to change. Language and dialects shape the way we see the world, the values we hold, what we deem important or insignificant, and who we think we are. Changing these things cannot be done without consequences (Labov, 1994; Labov, 2001).

6. Respecting one's own culture means disloyalty to the mainstream. Understanding one's own community, and the communal experience, enables one to make effective choices in the present and to maximize potential across the life span.

A sociolinguistic take on language behavior does not mean that we are to leave our children functionally unintelligible to the mainstream, bombarded with negative language attitudes, and blocked from upward mobility. All students must leave the educational system fluent in general or mainstream English.

Teachers should use an Additive, not Subtractive, model of language. The Additive model encourages the inclusion of multiple languages, dialects, and registers in our linguistic repertoire. Communicative competence is then increased because the speaker can choose from an expanded language reservoir, those language behaviors most appropriate in a situation. The Subtractive model assumes that people should speak the same way in all contexts. That teaching model means that students learn a second language at the expense of their first language (Cummins, 1994). Having access to only one linguistic code limits the effectiveness of a speaker.

Using the Additive model in teaching is not as daunting as it may sound. Never tell a student that the way he or she is speaking is wrong. That statement challenges their identity, community membership, and family linguistic system. Try, "That may not be the right way to say it at school." Start with a lesson on language and dialects. Second, help all students become aware of the various ways in which they communicate by using role-playing activities. Teach them about communication contexts: home, social, school, employment, and public. The public setting is the context in which we carry out our daily tasks: talking to the mail carrier, the bank teller, the butcher. Have them write scripts varying the way they might deliver the same message using different language variations in different contexts. Once the scripts are done, have them do a dramatic reading or group acting activity. Reinforce mainstream English by repeating, "This is how we say it in class or at school."

Lastly, help students to understand the market analogy of language. Language is a sort of "money" that we use in the marketplaces of life. If we want the best deal, we use the currency acceptable in that market. Use a comparison of Canadian money to the U.S. dollar. Occasionally one finds a Canadian penny or dime in our change. The buyer can go to an American store and present the Canadian change, but it will not be accepted; the buyer won't get what he or she came for. The change would have to be converted into American coins. The same would be true if one was in Canada attempting to use American coins. They may not be accepted, and the buyer leaves without what he or she came to purchase. Students can learn to "code switch" if they know what it is, are able to identify contexts, and grasp the notion of the marketplace analogy of language.

Summary

The sociolinguistics of black dialect is complex. There are many factors to take into account. The history and origins of the dialect are the results of social, economic, and political considerations. Southern English and tribal languages of Africans brought here in slavery inform the morphological, phonologic, syntactical, semantic, and grammatical rules. Black dialect is a valid linguistic tool, just like general or mainstream English, when used in the proper context. There is no "correct" way of speaking, only appropriateness for a particular setting. Those working with students to bring them to fluency in general English should use an Additive rather than a Reductionist model, which dictates that a speaker never be informed that their mode of communication is "wrong" but that it is inappropriate for a particular place and time.

America has always been a multilingual country. The Coalition on Language Diversity in Education supports the notion that dialects, be they informed by black dialect, Mexican, Hindi, Vietnamese, or even Jamaican linguistic forms, add richness to general American English (Macneil/Lehrer Productions, 2005).

Marquita L. Byrd

References

Bilingual Education Act, Title VII of the Elementary and Secondary Education Act of 1968. (2005). In J. D. Ramirez, T. G. Wiley, G. de Klerk, E. Lee, and W. E. Wright (Eds.), *Ebonics: The urban education debate* (2nd ed., p. 117). Clevedon, GBR: Multilingual Matters.

Cummins, J. (1994). The acquisition of English as a second language. In K. Spangenberg-Urbschat and R. Pritchard (Eds.), *Kids come in all languages: Reading instruction for ESL students* (pp. 33–62). Newark, DE: International Reading Association.

Labov, W. (1994). *Principles of linguistic change, vol. 1: Internal factors (language in society, No. 20)*. Hoboken, NJ: Blackwell Publishers.

Labov, W. (2001). *Principles of linguistic change, vol. 2: Social factors (language in society)*. Hoboken, NJ: Blackwell Publishers.

Labov, W. (2012). *Dialect diversity in America: The politics of language change (Page-Barbour lectures)*. Charlottesville, VA: University of Virginia Press.

Macneil/Lehrer Productions. (2005). American varieties: African American English: Language diversity. *From sea to shining sea*. Retrieved from http://www.pbs.org/speak/seatosea/americanvarieties/AAVE/coalition/

Minnick, L. (2007). *Dialect and dichotomy: Literary representations of African America speech*. Tuscaloosa, AL: University of Alabama Press.

Reid, T. B. (1956). Linguistics, structuralism, philology. *Archivum Linguisticum*, 8.

Smitherman, G. (2006). *Word from the Mother: Language and African Americans*. New York: Routledge.

Wardhaugh, R. (2011). *An introduction to sociolinguistics*. San Francisco, CA: Wiley.

Williams, R. (1975). *Ebonics: The true language of black folks*. Crawfordsville, IN: Malcolm X Institute of Black Studies.

Wolfram, W., & Schilling-Estes, N. (2005). *American English: Dialects and variation (Language in society,* vol. 25, 2nd ed.). Hoboken, NJ: Blackwell Publishers.

BLACK/AFRICAN AMERICAN ENGLISH

A variety of terms have been used to describe English as spoken by African Americans in the United States, Black English (BE) including Ebonics, and African American Vernacular English. African American English (AAE) and African American Language (AAL) are the most encompassing terms used by educators and linguists to refer to all varieties of English used by speakers where African Americans live or historically have lived. The terms *Urban English* and *Rural English* have been used across ethnic categorizations to refer to the English dialects that overlap with those of speakers of other races and ethnic groups who live there as well.

African American or Black English often has been used to refer to the language features of African Americans that are most unlike Standardized American English (SAE). The term *Ebonics* was coined during a conversation between Robert Williams and Ernie Smith as a combination of "ebony" and "phonics" (Williams, 1975). The term *Ebonics* was widely adopted by educators and the general public following a movement in Oakland, California, in 1996–1997 that was designed to help teachers use Black English as a way to help students acquire the language of school instruction and assessment. The efforts were widely misunderstood by the general public, as well as in the media, as an attempt to teach children to speak African American English in school, and thus the educators' efforts were thwarted (Perry & Delpit, 1997).

The U.S. government, particularly the U.S. Department of Education, funded seminal studies of Black English in the 1960s and 1970s in order to address academic inequality. Black English was examined in contrast to SAE. Large-scale research on speech communities in Detroit (Wolfram, 1969) and Harlem (Labov, 1972) provided seminal evidence for establishing Black English as a full linguistic system and not a result of language impoverishment or impairment.

As approaches to Black English have become more diasporic in nature, definitions of Black English have now been expanded to include varieties of African and Caribbean English in particular as well as individuals who come into contact with blacks of the diaspora and acquire some of their language patterns.

Research on African American English in the 1980s and 1990s centered on expanding the communities in which language was studied as well as understanding the social and cultural ramifications of AAE on its speakers (Smitherman, 1977; Stockman & Vaughn-Cooke, 1986). While much of the early work centered on the speech of men and boys, researchers added more information about the language of women and girls in the late 1980s and 1990s (Goodwin, 1990; Morgan, 1998). Current research on AAE continues to build on knowledge of specific social groups and African American communities as well as the educational implications for AAE use on language and literacy skill acquisition.

The linguistic construct of AAE is complex and variable. As such, scholars have operated on the premise that knowing more about the unique language patterns of students can help with the understanding of dialect versus difference in the acquisition of language and literacy as highlighted in Craig and Washington (2005).

Black English usage varies by the age, gender, region, and social class of the speaker. Most sociolinguistic studies do not examine every given feature of Black English, nor could they, and it is difficult to make cross-study comparisons of feature use over space, time, and demographic group. Many of the features and characteristics of Black English that have been reported, thus far, in the literature, however, have been measured or described for African Americans across the United States. Still, differences have been reported in the frequency of use of certain features by age, gender, region, and degree of segregation of the African American population in a given area (Rickford, 1999). Examinations of social class differences are limited, but the use of AAE features has been observed in the speech of middle SES African Americans (Horton-Ikard & Miller, 2004).

The AAE lexicon is perhaps the feature that is best known to the general American public. The lexicon is emphasized and frequently represented in popular culture. There are also other often-unnoticed lexical differences that may have an effect on a child's understanding and success in the classroom. Hart and Risley (1995) examined the speech of African American and white children of different socioeconomic (SES) backgrounds, and they suggested that the speech of low SES African American children is more linguistically impoverished than is the speech of white and middle-class children. Such research focuses on inequalities in the vocabulary and syntactic complexity of speech samples of children speaking with their caregiver; it does not, however, include an assessment of the linguistic structure of Black English or its lexical complexity (Green, 2002).

Many of the phonological features of AAE are shared by other varieties of American English, particularly Southern American English. Some features that are common to African American English also appear as features in the speech of younger Southern American English speakers; yet many listeners can determine if a speaker is African American after hearing just a short speech sample. One reason is that African Americans, for the most part, do not participate in the local vowel changes that characterize the speech of white speakers (Wolfram & Thomas, 2002).

Many listeners report that the melody and rhythm of a speaker's voice may mark a speaker as African American even if all other aspects of the speaker's language sound standardized. Rhythmic patterns are often preserved in speakers who do not use many of the more socially stigmatized lexical, phonological, and grammatical features of AAE.

The grammatical features of AAE are well studied because they are most unique to the language variety and thus of interest to linguists and most stigmatized by the general American public (Rickford, 1999). Grammatical features of AAE are often more noticeable and distinct than are the phonological features described previously. It is important to remember, however, that despite their uniqueness, the features are systematic and regular and thus not indicative of a degraded or defective form of School English (Green, 2013).

Black English is not an absolute construct but more of a linguistic continuum. Speakers vary in the frequency of appearance of features. The rate of use varies for most all of the linguistic features listed in this entry relating to both social and developmental sources of influence. Young male speakers use features of AAE, especially stigmatized features, more often than female speakers. For example, the acquisition of *the* does not occur until later in childhood (sometimes not until age six) but is also a feature of AAE, so the analysis of dialect versus deficit may be confounded overall, but it is especially likely to be misdiagnosed in African American males when it occurs more frequently. Some African American educators choose to switch linguistically and culturally, using standardized English and African American English to build rapport with their African American students (Foster, 1989). It is valuable to have educators who can discuss with students the social and cultural context of code switching and the significance of encountering multiple linguistic varieties at school.

The Ebonics controversy highlighted that language discrimination is one of the last acceptable forms of discrimination (Lippi-Green, 2011), and objection to African American English frequently has been used as a way to discriminate against African Americans without overtly judging their inherent being despite the fact that Title VII of the Civil Rights Act of 1964 prohibits workplace discrimination based on religion, national origin, race, color, or sex. Due to the history of racism and discrimination in the United States, the language patterns of African Americans often have been denigrated. African American English has been viewed as haphazard, substandard, undesirable, deviant, illogical, lazy, and broken. Yet there is

no truth in such opinions about African American English or any other variety of English. It is not the case that this variety of English is always informal. African Americans regularly use African American English in many formal situations: during political speeches, in church, and at funerals, to name a few. Listening to speeches by orators such as Martin Luther King Jr. quickly reveals how African American rhetorical style can be employed with great care to great effect in formal situations. Negative and incorrect ideas about African American English are found throughout society, including in the media. In books, on TV, in films, and in music, the public receives mixed messages about a variety of English that is often admired as being cool but is also often looked down on as being unprofessional, sloppy, or incorrect.

Language varieties hold inherent value as markers of culture and identity. As a result, some speakers of African American English, including students, may feel shame, insecurity, and embarrassment when they operate within a society that expects them to speak standardized English. Educators who teach African-American-English–speaking students have a special role to play in understanding these students' personal and cultural experiences and in helping them navigate comfortably between African American English and standardized English.

When students come to school speaking African American English, they are aware that many of their relatives, friends, and neighbors speak similarly to themselves. They may also be aware that many of their educators do not speak African American English. The message that African-American-English–speaking students may internalize from this situation is that educators expect them to learn a new way of communicating, which may be at odds with their home language and culture. Smitherman (2000) described this "push-pull" that many African American students face in classrooms and schools. Carter (2007) further notes that as some African American students push harder to assimilate to mainstream academic culture in order to succeed in school, they may feel forced to pull away from their home communities. Most people would find it difficult to accept a message, even an indirect message, that they have to suppress part of their linguistic identity to operate within mainstream culture.

African Americans, with their specific social and cultural history, often live this reality every day.

As educators may hold strong opinions about students' use of African American English, cultural and academic misunderstandings may arise between educators who speak Standardized English and students who speak African American English, particularly when each person assumes that the other understands them and is understood by them. African-American-English-speaking students may even receive differential treatment in the classroom due to lowered educational expectations and intolerance.

The goals of wanting to honor African-American-English-speaking students' cultural and linguistic heritage while also preparing them to live and work in a standardized-English-speaking society are complicated for educators and students. In other communities, including immigrant communities, students similarly face pressure to assimilate to English in order to do well in school and in careers. While there are many school and community programs in place to aid students who grow up speaking a foreign language in their quest to learn English, there are few programs in place to help speakers of nonstandardized varieties of English, including African American English. The general sentiment is that native English speakers should be able to produce standardized English forms no matter what their background. As Baldwin (1979) contended, however, succeeding at school should not require African American students to abandon their linguistic and cultural heritage. He stated, "A child cannot be taught by anyone whose demand, essentially, is that the child repudiate his experience, and all that gives him sustenance, and enter a limbo in which he will no longer be black, and in which he knows that he can never become white" (p. 652). It is, therefore, important to understand the language patterns that students bring with them into the classroom to best help all students attain academic success.

When students who speak nonstandardized varieties of English perceive that their language is devalued in school and that they are not receiving appropriate feedback from educators, they may feel discouraged from continuing their education. They may also perceive that their own culture, family, friends, and even they themselves are being devalued. In turn, they may lose confidence in school and in their educators. They may even resist feeling like their language and culture are devalued in academic settings by disengaging from the standardized-English-speaking school culture and climate altogether.

Some African-American-English–speaking students might go a different direction and accommodate as much as possible to the standardized-English-speaking culture. Much of educational literature has been devoted to understanding the concept that has come to be known as "sounding white" or "acting white," which refers to the academic bind felt by some African Americans who fear that any attempt to do well in school is seen by other individuals as trying to act white. The feeling of being pulled in two directions, linguistically and culturally, has been conceptualized as a "double consciousness" (Du Bois, 1903). The idea of sounding and acting white as a way of achieving educational success is complex. An African American student who mainly or exclusively uses the language of school assessment and resists using African American English may be stigmatized by other African Americans who see the student's linguistic choices as snubbing the local language variety and, as a result, their cultural background. At the same time, even if African American students who do sound and act in ways that are interpreted as being white, they may still not be accepted by white peers, whether due to prejudice or to a range of social factors.

Knowledge of how and why specific language variants appear in students' oral reading and writing is invaluable information when assessing students who speak African American English because features of this variety will often appear in students' speech, oral reading, and written work. When pointing out students' grammatical mistakes, it is important to consider whether potential errors might actually be characteristic of African American English. If so, it is important to explain the linguistic pattern to the student. This process entails teaching the student their African-American-English–influenced pattern, and while acknowledging and appreciating this language variation, showing the student how this pattern compares and contrasts with that of standardized English.

Above all, it is critical not to focus on identifying standardized English grammatical errors in students' speech, oral reading, and writing to the point that the quality of the content, organization, or style of the student's work is overlooked. Doing so without explicit instruction and support overpenalizes African-American-English-speaking students who use features of their home language variety, further creating a linguistic and structural inequality.

Educators' implicit and explicit reactions to African-American-English–speaking students' language sends an important message to these students about safety and acceptance, and positive messages help students view learning as an accessible and engaging process. Language differences can add to other school stressors. For these reasons, the classroom must be a safe place to take risks and speak up, if African-American-English–speaking students are to be willing to have their voices heard (Ball, 2000; Lee, 2006). Many complex linguistic and social issues must be taken into account to ensure African-American-English–speaking students' mental and emotional well-being in the classroom.

Linguistically informed, socially just educators are able to identify which features of students' speech and writing are related to African American English and which features may be evidence of reading comprehension, spelling, or writing mistakes, or even evidence of a language difference, delay, or disorder. As a result, educators feel more empowered to identify and address specific linguistic challenges that African-American-English–speaking students may face. Although forty years have passed since the original publication of the National Council of Teachers of English and Conference on College Composition and Communication's (NCTE/CCCC) Affirming Students' Right to Their Own Language: Bridging Language Policies and Pedagogical Practices (National Council of Teachers of English, 2003), the message of the text is still to be wholly fulfilled. It will be manifest when more students are able to use Black English in both community and academic contexts. Educators should work to create courses that teach Black English and design assignments in other courses that encourage all students to use Black English in written, spoken, and other forms. When such courses and assignments are engaged with the community, then the justice of the actual speakers of Black English is brought to bear.

With knowledge and understanding of African American English, educators have a greater appreciation for the communication patterns and rich linguistic heritages of their African American English–speaking students. Linguistically informed educators are also better equipped to instruct African-American-English–speaking students in ways that enable them to recognize and value the rules, norms, and conventions of standardized English while also recognizing and valuing the language patterns they bring with them from home. As such, the linguistic path to justice for African Americans begins.

Anne H. Charity Hudley

References

Baldwin, J. (1979, July 29). If Black English isn't a language, then tell me, what is? *New York Times*, E19.

Ball, A. F. (2000). Empowering pedagogies that enhance the learning of multicultural students. *Teachers College Record, 102*(6), 1006–34.

Carter, P. L. (2007). *Keepin' it real: School success beyond black and white*. New York: Oxford University Press.

Charity Hudley, A. H. (2008). African-American English: An overview. *Perspectives on Communication Disorders and Sciences in Culturally and Linguistically Diverse Populations, 15*(2), 33–42. doi:10.1044/cds15.2.33. 33-42

Charity Hudley, A. H. (2009). African American English. In H. Neville, B. Tynes, & S. Utsey (Eds.), *The handbook of African-American psychology* (pp. 199–22). Thousand Oaks, CA: Sage Publications.

Charity Hudley, A. H. & Mallinson, C. (2010). *Understanding English language variation in U.S. schools*. New York: Teachers College Press.

Charity Hudley, A. H. & Mallinson, C. (2013). *We do language: English language variation in secondary English classrooms*. New York: Teachers College Press.

Civil Rights Act. (1964). Retrieved from http://library.clerk.house.gov/reference-files/PPL_CivilRights-Act_1964.pdf.

Craig, H. K. & Washington, J. (2005). *Malik goes to school*. New York: Erlbaum.

Du Bois, W. E. B. (1903). *The souls of black folk.* Chicago: A. C. McClurg & Co., University Press John Wilson and Son.

Foster, M. (1989). "It's cookin' now": A performance analysis of the speech events of a Black teacher in an urban community college. *Language in Society, 18*(1), 1–29.

Goodwin, M. H. (1990). *He-said-she-said: Talk as social organization among black children.* Bloomington, IN: Indiana University Press.

Green, L. J. (2002). *African American English: A linguistic introduction.* Cambridge: Cambridge University Press.

Green, L. J. (2013). Beyond lists of differences to accurate descriptions. In C. Mallinson, B. Childs, and G. Van Herk (Eds.), *Data collection in sociolinguistics* (p. 281). New York: Routledge.

Hart, B. & Risley, T. R. (1995). *Meaningful differences in the everyday experience of young American children.* Baltimore, MD: Paul H. Brookes.

Horton-Ikard, R. & Miller, J. F. (2004). It is not just the poor kids: The use of AAE forms by African American school-aged children from middle SES communities. *Journal of Communication Disorders, 37*(6), 467–87.

Labov, W. (1972). *Language in the inner city: Studies in the Black English vernacular.* Philadelphia: University of Pennsylvania Press.

Lee, C. D. (2006). "Every good-bye ain't gone": Analyzing the cultural underpinnings of classroom talk. *International Journal of Qualitative Studies in Education, 19*(3), 305–27.

Lippi-Green, R. (2011). *English with an accent: Language, ideology and discrimination in the United States.* New York: Routledge.

Morgan, M. (1998). "More than a mood or an attitude": Discourse and verbal genres in African American culture. In S. Mufwene, J. Rickford, G. Bailey, & J. Baugh (Eds.), *African American English: Structure, history and use* (pp. 251–81). New York: Routledge.

National Council of Teachers of English. (2003). *Resolution on affirming the CCCC: "Students' right to their own language."* Retrieved from www.ncte.org/positions/statements/affirmingstudents.

Perry, T. & Delpit, L. (Eds.). (1997). *The real Ebonics debate: Power, language, and the education of African American children.* Boston: Beacon.

Rickford, J. (1999). *African American Vernacular English: Features, evolution, educational implications.* Malden, MA: Blackwell.

Smitherman, G. (1977). *Talkin and testifyin: The language of black America.* Boston: Houghton Mifflin.

Smitherman, G. (2000). *Talkin that talk: Language, culture, and education in African America.* New York: Routledge.

Stockman, I., & Vaughn-Cooke, F. (1986). Implications of semantic category research for the language assessment of nonstandard speakers. *Topics in Language Disorders, 6*(4), 15–25.

Williams, R. (Ed.). (1975). *Ebonics: The true language of black folks.* St. Louis, MO: Robert L. Williams & Associates.

Wolfram, W. (1969). *A sociolinguistic description of Detroit Negro speech.* Washington, DC: Center for Applied Linguistics.

Wolfram, W. & Thomas, E. (2002). *The development of African American English.* New York: Wiley.

BLACK SUBCULTURE

Womanist Theology

Founded in black theological and religious studies, womanist theology is most significantly characterized as a form of black liberation theology (Mitchem, 2002). Black liberation theology is a branch of the larger field of liberation theology, a Christian theological tradition that appropriates biblical teachings as primarily a vehicle for liberation and justice specifically as it relates to social, economic, and political conditions (Cannon, 1988).

Womanist theology also builds on womanism or the womanist tradition as initially articulated by Alice Walker (1983) in her book *In Search of Our Mother's Gardens*. While there has traditionally been both tension and harmony between the traditions, womanism (or womanist theology) should not be characterized as a subsidiary of feminism (Phillips, 2006). Instead, womanism and feminism should be understood as two distinct traditions rooted in disparate communal and epistemological groundings.

Lincoln and Mamiya (1990) note, when discussing the work of theologian and womanist theology scholar Jacqueline Grant, that womanist theology provides one of the broadest and most comprehensive critiques of social systems of oppression in multiple contexts, while couched in the particularities of liberation theology. In light of the fact that womanist theology, as a theoretical tradition, simultaneously takes up issues of sexism in religious and academic circles, while not neglecting the significance of white racism in feminist traditions and Christian churches, it is positioned to examine the nuances of privilege and oppression in thoughtful and complex ways. Further, the dimension of class is intricately interwoven into every analysis as poverty has been an ongoing struggle within black communities, particularly for black women. Consequently, many of the scholars that employ this particular theoretical frame are largely interested in continuing the pursuit for social justice and liberation within religious and theological studies, as well as the academy more broadly (Cannon, 1995).

Most significantly, womanist theology is a theoretical framework developed by black women scholars of faith, specifically interested in the ways black women in academe make meaning, struggle, and create. One of the most noteworthy aspects of womanist theology, as an epistemological tradition, is that it is not only a theory produced within the black female subjective but it also theorizes black female subjectivity. As Linda Thomas (1998) explains, "Womanist theology is critical reflection upon Black women's place in the world that God has created and takes seriously Black women's experience as human beings who are made in the image of God" (p. 1).

Although a theoretical tradition significantly influenced by the tenets of Christianity, womanist theology maintains a commitment to addressing issues of sexuality and sexual marginalization within multiple communities. Womanist theologians have embraced Walker's (1983) definition of a womanist as loving women both sexually and nonsexually. Hence, within black faith discussions, womanist theologians have been the most willing to engage in a serious dialogue about the evils of not only racism, sexism, and classism, but also heterosexism (Wilmore, 2004). "On the whole, womanist theology seems equally multidimensional (as male-centered Black liberation theology), but, in terms of larger theological and ideological building blocks, they have been willing to grapple with the *isms* that men neglected" (Wilmore, 2004, p. 67, emphasis in original). According to Wilmore (2004), as a consequence of multiple sources of marginalization, womanist theologians have been more willing to step outside the bounds of explicitly theological study and the institutional black church and ask more readily what is the role of God and faith in the everyday lives of *all* oppressed peoples. They have subsequently forged philosophical, progressive, and multidisciplinary exchanges within and outside of academia. The "privilege" of experiencing multiple and interlocking forms of oppression as religio-spiritual black women provides womanist theologians, as well as other marginalized communities, the insight needed to negotiate non-separatist methods of resistance (Walker, 1983).

The struggle for women of color, and specifically black women, to express the complications associated with the convergence of racism, sexism, and classism has been an ongoing conversation within the academy (Williams, 1991). However, within womanist theology, the additional complication of faith is interwoven into the texture of the conversation. This interweaving of complicated perspectives parallels much of the scholarship that critiques mainstream academic discourse for being overly positivist, rejecting discussions of faith and the supernatural as irrelevant to rigorous academic work, and ignoring spiritual understandings as a very real form of epistemological grounding (Mayuzumi & Shahjahan, 2008). Also, womanist theology's foundation within religio-spiritual tenets draws on and highlights a tradition of faith within marginalized communities, specifically black communities, as a cultural and communal source of strength and racial uplift under bleak circumstances. With its emphasis on oppression and liberation in manifold contexts, womanist theology as a theoretical tradition positions itself as an engine for equality and social justice in ever-increasing and transformative ways.

Kirsten T. Edwards

References

Cannon, K. G. (1988). *Black Womanist Ethics* (Vol. 60). Atlanta: Scholars Press.

Cannon, K. G. (1995). *Katie's canon: Womanism and the soul of the black community*. New York: The Continuum International Publishing Group, Inc.

Lincoln, C. E. & Mamiya, L. (1990). *The black church in the African American experience*. Durham and London: Duke University Press.

Mayuzumi, K. & Shahjahan, R. A. (2008). The sacred and resistance within the "prison": The narratives of racially minoritized women faculty. In A. Wagner, S. Acker, & K. Mayuzumi (Eds.), *Whose university is it, anyway? Power and privilege on gendered terrain* (pp. 187–202). Toronto: Sumach Press.

Mitchem, S. Y. (2002). *Introducing Womanist theology*. Maryknoll, NY: Orbis Books.

Phillips, L. (Ed.). (2006). *The Womanist reader*. New York & London: Routledge.

Thomas, L. E. (1998). Womanist theology, epistemology, and a new anthropological paradigm. *Cross Currents, 48*(4), n.p.

Walker, A. (1983). *In search of our mothers' gardens*. Orlando: Harcourt, Inc.

Williams, P. J. (1991). *The alchemy of race and rights: Diary of a law professor*. Cambridge & London: Harvard University Press.

Wilmore, G. S. (2004). *Pragmatic spirituality: The Christian faith through an Africentric lens*. New York and London: New York University Press.

BODY IMAGE

Body Images Issues in Asian American Men

A recent study, Ricciardelli et al. (2007), that systematically reviewed body image studies for Asian American men revealed variable results. For Asian American men's body image and their drive for muscularity, studies examining the desire to increase weight and muscles through the use of steroids revealed inconsistent findings; muscle-enhancing substance usage varied for these men from little to extreme levels. Whereas previous studies suggested that Asian American men hold similar muscularity ideals to Caucasian men (Mintz & Kashubeck, 1999), the inconsistency among recent research in Asian American men's drive for muscularity and body image ideals presented a lack of consensus in this regard, stemming from what the authors have indicated are due mainly to methodological limitations.

Despite the lack of consensus in outlining Asian men's body image concerns and preference for muscularity-oriented body image ideals, a growing number of studies have investigated the impact of cultural differences. In a qualitative study definiing masculinity definitions across ethnicities, Pompper (2010) highlighted an emerging theme among young Asian college men living in the United States capturing less emphasis on male muscularity. Interviewees expressed that muscularity ideals were rooted in the American culture and that Asian culture did not necessarily associate masculinity with muscularity. For these men, their ideal body image did not comform to a desire for a more muscular or larger body size but rather were more accepting of the thin or moderate types of body sizes. Some responses went on to suggest that the "muscle obsessed" and "macho" male Western media ideals had a detrimental effect on their host Asian culture. More interestingly, Watt and Ricciardelli (2012) qualitatively examined concurrent influences from both Asian and Western culture with fifteen Chinese men residing in Australia. The emerging themes conveyed that the majority of the men were not invested in achieving muscularity, while for those who were inclined, moderate muscularity was preferred. Overall, the results suggested less emphasis and a moderate drive for muscularity for Asian American men or Asian men immersed in Western culture with Caucasian men or when interpreting experiences from less acculturated international students and immigrants.

Brian Taehyuk Keum

References

Mintz, L. B. & Kashubeck, S. (1999). Body image and disordered eating among Asian American and Caucasian college students: An examination of race and gender differences. *Psychology of Women Quarterly, 23*(4), 781–96.

Pompper, D. (2010). Masculinities, the metrosexual, and media images: Across dimensions of age and ethnicity. *Sex Roles, 63*(9–10), 682–96.

Ricciardelli, L. A., McCabe, M. P., Williams, R. J., & Thompson, J. K. (2007). The role of ethnicity and culture in body image and disordered eating among males. *Clinical Psychology Review, 27*(5), 582–606.

Watt, M. & Ricciardelli, L. A. (2012). A qualitative study of body image and appearance among men of Chinese ancestry in Australia. *Body Image, 9*(1), 118–25.

BUDDHISM

Buddhism is one of the world's major religious or spiritual traditions. The Buddhist faith developed approximately 2,500 years ago in the northeastern regions of modern India. The founder of Buddhism is Siddhartha Gautama (c. 563–483 BCE), more commonly known by his honorific religious titles: Buddha, meaning the enlightened or awakened one, or Shakyamuni, or the Sage of the Shakya clan. The message of the Buddha shortly spread throughout India and into other neighboring regions. Today there are nearly five hundred million Buddhists around the globe, with the great majority of the worldwide population concentrated in East and Southeast Asia, especially China, Thailand, Japan, Burma/Myanmar, Sri Lanka, Vietnam, and Cambodia (Pew Forum, 2012, pp. 31–32). The attractiveness of Buddhism can be attributed to the lifestyle and teachings of its eponymous founder.

Siddhartha Gautama was born in Lumbini in modern Nepal. His family were members of the Hindu *kshatriyas*, or warrior class. The local mystics informed Siddhartha's father that his newborn son would become either a powerful emperor or an enlightened religious leader. Siddhartha's father did not want his son to become a wandering religious figure, so he ordered that all forms of suffering be concealed from his son. This attempt to protect his son from the harshness of reality proved futile, as the realities of the world would shortly present themselves to Siddhartha. In the turning point of Siddhartha's life, he ventured from the palace and visited the streets, only to encounter what has become known as the "four great visions" (Reat, 1994, p. 8). In his four visits to the streets, Siddhartha encountered an old man, a sick man, a dead man, and an ascetic. In response to these startling sights, Siddhartha decided to abandon his life of luxury and become like the ascetic from the streets. This decision to leave the benefits associated with his princely lifestyle is known as the "Great Renunciation" (Reat, 1994, p. 9) and marks the next phase of Siddhartha's life.

In the early years of his life of renunciation, Siddhartha practiced an extreme form of asceticism that changed his striking figure into an emaciated shadow of his former self. In time, Siddhartha stopped this intense asceticism, believing that it would not allow him to achieve enlightenment.

Consequently, Siddhartha resolved to meditate under a Bo tree, until he reached full enlightenment. During this period of meditation, he was tempted in several different ways by the infamous demon-god, Mara; however, these temptations did not stop Siddhartha from pursuing enlightenment, which he finally achieved, thus becoming the Buddha. In attaining enlightenment, the Buddha then decided to begin his teaching ministry. In this inaugural sermon, the Buddha highlighted the central concepts in Buddhism, such as the Middle Way, the Four Noble Truths, and the Eightfold Path. The Buddha did not cease his ministry after this first sermon, but rather continued teaching across northern India for another four and a half decades until his death at the age of eighty. The life of the Buddha lasted eighty years, but his effect on the future development of religious and spiritual thought continues to inspire countless generations.

There are several central concepts that were preached by the Buddha and remain important in Buddhist circles. In his first sermon, the Buddha preached the idea of the "Middle Way," whereby one should choose moderation over the extremes of excess and deficiency. The Buddha also explained the "Four Noble Truths" based on the four core precepts that life is suffering, suffering is caused by desire, desire can be overcome, and the way to overcome desire is by following the Eightfold Path. The Eightfold Path consists of eight characteristics, including Right Views, Right Intent, Right Speech, Right Conduct, Right Livelihood, Right Effort, Right Mindfulness, and Right Concentration. The purpose of the regimented lifestyle is not only to ensure the cessation of suffering but also to achieve nirvana. The term *nirvana* is often mistranslated as "bliss" when it actually means "blowing out" one's desires, which have brought about suffering. It is only in the achievement of nirvana that one can experience bliss on earth. In a later sermon, the Buddha discussed the three general features of life on earth—namely, the absence of self or *anatman*, impermanence or *anitya*, and suffering or *duhkha*. However, despite his pessimistic outlook on the nature of existence, the Buddha did identify "Three Jewels" or "Three Refuges" in which one could take comfort, including the Buddha, the *Dharma* or religious teachings, and the *Sangha* or community of initiated believers. These central teachings are complemented with others that are emphasized by the various different branches of Buddhism.

The Theravada branch, also known as "the Way of the Elders," is the only surviving branch to have reached the contemporary age. The prevalence of this branch can be attributed to the efforts of the missionary king, Ashoka (c. 304–232 BCE) of the Magadha Empire. The work of Ashoka can be witnessed today as the Theravada branch is prevalent is several Southeast Asian countries, including Sri Lanka, Burma/Myanmar, Cambodia, Laos, and Thailand. The Theravada branch accepts the oldest collection of scriptural texts, known as the Pali Canon. The Pali Canon, as its name suggests, was written in the ancient Indo-Aryan language of Pali likely around 100 BCE. The canon is comprised of three *pitakas* or collections including the *Vinaya Pitaka* describing hundreds of rules for Buddhist monks and nuns, the *Sutra Pitaka* containing the Buddha's sermons, and finally, the *Abhidhamma Pitaka*, comprising scholarly treatises. These key works were shortly accompanied by others put forward by an emerging branch of Buddhism.

The Mahayana, or "Great Vehicle," branch of Buddhism emerged around the first century of the Common Era. The Mahayana branch not only expanded the corpus of sacred literature by introducing new *sutras* or aphorisms to the Buddhist canon but also provided followers with countless *bodhisattvas* or individuals striving to become Buddhas to be revered. The more prominent collection of Mahayana *sutras* includes the *Perfection of Wisdom Sutra*, the *Vimalakirti Sutra*, the *Lankavatara Sutra*, and the celebrated *Lotus Sutra*. In addition to expanding the Buddhist canon, the Mahayana branch provides followers with several different schools to follow, such as the Zen or Chan School centering on mediation; the Pure Land School focusing on the celestial Buddha, Amitabha; and the Nichiren School and its devotion to the *Lotus Sutra*. Although the Mahayana branch remains popular in China, Japan, South Korea, and Vietnam, it would not be the last branch of Buddhism to develop.

Finally, the Vajrayana branch, referred to as the "Diamond Vehicle" or "Thunderbolt Vehicle," emerged about five hundred years after the Mahayana branch. In addition to these two names, the Vajrayana branch is also known as Tibetan Buddhism due to its popularity in the secluded mountain territory. This most recent branch of Buddhism studies the esoteric knowledge, complex practices, and elaborate rituals of the Tantras. These tantric practices are complex, but Tibetan Buddhism emphasizes concentrating one's mind and energies on *mantras* or chants, *mudras* or special movements, and *mandalas* or sacred icons (Smith & Novak, 2003, p. 109). This branch contends that it is through these tantric practices that one can achieve Buddhahood in the fastest possible manner. However, the most recognized component of Tibetan Buddhism is the institution of the Dalai Lama, the exiled political-religious leader of Tibet. In 1959, the fourteenth and current Dalai Lama, Tenzin Gyatso (b. 1935), was forced to leave his country due to the military threat posed by the presence of the Chinese army in Tibet. Following his exile, the Dalai Lama took up residence in Dharamsala, a city in northern India, where he remains today. The treatment of the Dalai Lama and the plight of Tibetans continue to attract international attention and sympathy.

The teachings of the Buddha have not only survived 2,500 years of history but also continued to influence countless generations of people. However, the religion still remains largely confined to one part of the globe, with nearly 99 percent of Buddhists living in the Asia-Pacific region of the world. There are small communities in North America and Europe, but together they only comprise just over 1 percent of the worldwide Buddhist population (Pew Forum, 2012, p. 31). This seems paradoxical considering the West's continued interest in Buddhism. Moreover, the acceptance of Buddhism by many prominent figures such as Richard Gere, Steven Seagal, Allen Ginsberg, Tina Turner, and Steve Jobs only serves to heighten the profile of the religion in the Western world. In the future, the enlightened system of beliefs enshrined in Buddhism will likely continue to attract followers in the West and perhaps other regions of the world.

John Cappucci

References

Pew Forum on Religion & Public Life. (2012). The global religious landscape: A report on the size and distribution of the world's major religious groups as of 2010. Washington, DC: Pew Forum on Religion & Public Life. Retrieved from http://www.pewforum.org/2012/12/18/global-religious-landscape-exec/.

Reat, N. R. (1994). *Buddhism: A history.* Berkeley, CA: Asian Humanities Press.

Smith, H. & Novak, P. (2003). *Buddhism: A concise introduction.* New York: Harper San Francisco.

Additional Reading

Amore, R. C. (2010). Buddhist traditions. In W. G. Oxtoby & R. C. Amore (Eds.), *World religions: Eastern traditions* (pp. 176–252). Don Mills, ON: Oxford University Press.

Humphreys, C. (1951). *Buddhism.* Harmondsworth, UK: Penguin Books.

Ikeda, D. (1976). *Living Buddha: An interpretive biography* (B. Watson, Trans.). New York: Weatherhill.

Keown, D. (2013). *Buddhism: A very short introduction* (2nd ed.). Oxford: Oxford University Press.

Lopez Jr., D. S. (2001). *The story of Buddhism: A concise guide to its history and teachings.* New York: Harper San Francisco.

Marshall, G. N. (1978). *Buddha, the quest for serenity: A biography.* Boston: Beacon Press.

Mitchell, D. W. (2008). *Buddhism: Introducing the Buddhist experience* (2nd ed.). Oxford: Oxford University Press.

Prebish, C. S. (1975). Doctrines of the early Buddhists. In C. S. Prebish (Ed.), *Buddhism: A modern perspective* (pp. 29–35). University Park, PA: Pennsylvania State University Press.

Rahula, W. S. (1974). *What the Buddha taught* (2nd ed.). New York: Grove Press.

Robinson, R. H. & Johnson, W. L. (1977). *The Buddhist religion: A historical introduction* (2nd ed.). Encino, CA: Dickenson Publishing Company.

Saddhatissa, H. (1976). *The life of the Buddha.* New York: Harper & Row Publishers.

Young, W. A. (2010). *The world's religions: Worldviews and contemporary issues* (3rd ed.). Upper Saddle River, NJ: Prentice Hall.

BULLYING

The *Oxford English Dictionary* (2012) noted that, as early as the mid-1500s, *bully* was actually a positive term referring to how gallant or good someone was, but by the late 1600s, the word *bully* was used as an indication of intimidation and violence. Today, bullying refers to the habitual abuse—be it emotional, verbal, and/or physical—an individual or group inflicts upon another person. The abuse can include aggressive behaviors directed at someone but can also be in the form of more passive-aggressive behavior whereby an individual is systematically and intentionally excluded from a group (Yamada, 2010). In today's technologically advanced world, bullying occurs not only face-to-face in real time but also online in cyberspace, where written posts in social media can perpetuate aggression indefinitely in the form of cyberbullying (Smokowski & Kopasz, 2005). Bullying is a learned behavior, and inequity of power, real or perceived, drives the act of bullying.

Participants

Scholars have noted four main types of participants who may be directly or indirectly involved in an act of bullying: pure bully, pure victim, bully/victim, and bystander. The role of pure bully or bully is fulfilled by the instigator of the abuse, and psychological literature discusses varying types of bullies (Olweus, 1978). Physical bullies, as indicated by the title, are involved in physical acts such as hitting or kicking and are most often male in gender. In contrast, verbal bullies use words to hurt their victims. Similarly, relational bullies, most often female in gender, use words but also have an added layer of complexity because their words are used to convince peers to exclude others. Reactive bullies can be difficult to discover, as they can pick fights with peers and later claim self-defense (Smokowski & Kopasz, 2005).

Pure victims, or victims, are those on the receiving end of these bullying acts, and scholars note that while the majority of them passively submit to their bullies, others can react with aggression. Often, they are quiet and/or anxious and lack sufficient communication and problem-solving strategies. As a result, victims can suffer from depression or other internalizing disorders such as eating disorders. For schoolchildren, claiming they have headaches or stomachaches can stem from fear of going to school, where they may have to confront a bully. The result is that victims are habitually absent from class (Smokowski & Kopasz, 2005).

Bully/victims are those who have been both victim and bully. Some scholars note the importance

of categorizing bully/victims differently than their pure bully or pure victim counterparts. In contrast, other academics claim that understanding pure bullies and pure victims is sufficient when considering practical treatment in counseling or educational settings. Most seem to agree on the fact that bully/victims are characterized by traits such as aggression or lack of social skills, which are significantly higher in severity when compared to their pure bully or pure victim counterparts (Sekol & Farrington, 2010).

The final category of participants, that of bystander, describes those who are neither bully nor victim but witness an act of bullying. Bystanders themselves have been identified to have varying typologies that range from those who are indirectly involved in the act of bullying to those who only see the bullying occur but take no action. At times, bystanders may be typified as relating more to the bully by assisting or encouraging a bully. At other times, bystanders relate more to the victim by either sympathizing with the victim or even becoming a victim (Smokowski & Kopasz, 2005).

While bullying is often thought of as an act done by schoolchildren against their peers, bullying has also been documented in situations with adult participants. Workplace bullying has become a topic of national interest as revealed by legislation passed by various states in an attempt to protect employees in their work environments. Additionally, research on those in prison systems and full-time care facilities seeks to find ways to eradicate acts of bullying within their instructions. Thus, bullying is an act that occurs not only among school-aged children but among adults as well (Yamada, 2010).

Causes of Bullying

Because bullying is an issue that arises from a real or perceived imbalance of power, the struggle for one person to control and/or appear superior to another is the underlying cause of bullying. However, these acts often occur within the confines of a variety of institutions, and cultural value placed on competition and acquirement of power in some corporations or organizations may perpetuate unhealthy environments that appear to encourage bullying. Other institutions appear to ignore that bullying even occurs within their walls as evidenced

by families who tell their stories via mass media and claim schools did nothing to shield their children from bullying.

In contrast, numerous researchers study bullying and its causes at an individual level, and the imbalance of power can come from any one or combination of demographic differences such as socioeconomic status, race or ethnicity, sexuality, and/or religious views (Percy & Flynn, 2012). A person's physical appearance such as body type or personal style and a person's ability or inability to perform tasks in a seemingly socially acceptable way can become a bully's justification for persecuting a victim. Why a bully desires such negative control and power is of special interest, and correlations to negative upbringings, histories of abuse, and family relationships have been noted (Smokowski & Kopasz, 2005).

Repercussions of and Responses to Bullying

Repercussions of bullying can include a myriad of problems for victims including emotional and physical issues that disrupt their quality of life. For instance, victims can report minor issues such as nausea, headaches, or mild cases of anxiety to more severe problems such as depression, chronic ulcers, and sleep disorders. Some researchers note consequences of bullying also may result in an increase in substance abuse or self-harm. Extreme cases that have been widely publicized in mass media in recent years include instances of suicide (Smokowski & Kopasz, 2005).

Society at large appears to be concerned about these issues, for a variety of responses to bullying do currently exist. Legislation in a number of countries worldwide and states within the United States attempts to protect employed persons from acts of bullying in the workplace. For children and adolescents, school districts are implementing zero-tolerance rules for bullying, but some scholars note that these polices mean nothing if school officials do not recognize bullying is occurring. With the modern advancement of technology, organizations from official governmental bodies to not-for-profit and profit businesses have launched websites addressing the widespread problem of bullying. Websites often discuss not only definitions of bullying but also describe what victims, parents of victims, educators, employers, and caretakers can do to respond to bullying. Thus, a myriad of trainings and programs that attempt to teach tolerance to both teachers and students are available.

Desiree R. Lindbom-Cho

References

Bully. (2012). In *Oxford English dictionary*. Retrieved from http://www.oed.com.

Olweus, D. (1978). *Aggression in the schools: Bullies and whipping boys*. Washington, DC: Hemsiphere.

Percy, M. S. & Flynn, K. (2012). Media representations of bullying toward queer youth: Gender, race, and age discrepancies. *Journal of LGBT Youth, 9*, 340–56.

Sekol, I. & Farrington, D. P. (2010). The overlap between bullying and victimization in adolescent residential care: Are bully/victims a special category? *Children and Youth Services Review, 32*, 1758–69.

Smokowski, P. R. & Kopasz, K. H. (2005). Bullying in school: An overview of types, effects, family characteristics, and intervention strategies. *Children & Schools, 27*, 101–10.

Yamada, D. C. (2010). Workplace bullying and American employment law: A ten-year progress report and assessment. *Comparative Labor Law & Policy Journal, 32*(1), 251–84.

CAJUN

Cajun is a term that refers to a French-speaking ethnic group located in Louisiana. Cajun peoples are thought to have had origins deriving from the Canadian Atlantic Maritime. In modern-day times, Cajun populations are most often found throughout South Louisiana, with Lafayette serving as a capital of sorts due to its location in the crossroads of the twenty-two parishes in Louisiana associated with Cajun ethnic groups (Dubois & Melançon, 1997).

Ethnic Group

Beginning in the early to mid-1600s, a group of French settlers, Acadians, moved to the Canadian Maritime (from Nova Scotia on the east through Quebec on the west and as far south as Main), creating a territory referred to as Acadia (Brasseaux, 1992). The territory of Acadia was understood to represent territories and lands north of what is today Virginia along the Atlantic Coast. As the territory moved northward toward the Atlantic Provinces in modern-day Canada, Samuel de Champlain is credited with the omission of the letter *r* in the spelling, leading to the name Acadia.

Acadians lived in this area until the mid-1700s when the British began to occupy the territory concurrent with the French and Indian Wars, eventually forcing Acadians away from the area in what was referred to as Le Grand Derangement (the Great Disturbance) in 1755. While Acadians distributed to many locations, a majority of Acadians moved to what was then the Louisiana Territory, settling in what is today south and south-central Louisiana. Acadians who moved to Louisiana became known as Cajuns.

In Louisiana, the newly transported Acadians began to establish themselves while mixing with other groups such as French and Spanish (see **Creole**) as well as Native American, German, Italian,

and other ethnic groups in the area. With the development of time, Cajun began to represent lower-economic strata white or mixed-race Louisianans located over a twenty-two-parish area of Louisiana commonly referred to as "Cajun Land USA" outside of Louisiana and "Acadiana" within Louisiana. This area ranges from east Texas until just west of New Orleans, with Lafayette, Louisiana, representing the cultural center of Cajun territory. The U.S. government recognized Cajun Acadians in 1980 as a result of the *Roach v. Dresser Industries Valve and Instrument Division* federal lawsuit. Cajuns were described in Judge Edwin Hunter's ruling as an ethnic group that is "alive and well" (Roach, 1980).

Cajuns of South Louisiana have developed a distinct dialectical version of French and English, which has been maintained in many South Louisiana communities (Bankston & Henry, 1998). In addition to language distinction, Cajuns have largely retained Catholicism. Many Louisianans who do not have an ethnic or heritage claim to Cajun still claim a Cajun cultural identity. While the majority of Cajun's are located in the twenty-two-parish area, Cajuns can be found all over the state of Louisiana, particularly in larger cities such as New Orleans and Baton Rouge.

Cajun Lifestyle

While *Cajun* refers to the group of people described above, Cajun is also a reference to particular cultural elements reflected in Louisiana. The Cajun lifestyle, as a cultural manifestation, has unique cuisine, religious celebrations, music, and linguistic constructs. Each area is explored in turn.

FOOD Cajun food is distinguished from Creole food based on elements of sophistication, with Cajun food seen as a spicier, less elaborate, and typically a one-pot meal. Because of the relationship in South Louisiana between Cajun and Creole groups, there is significant influence on the development of food from both groups. Cajun food draws significantly from locally available seafood (including crawfish and catfish), vegetables, meat (rabbit, duck, chicken), and rice. Cajun cooking is notable as Cajun cooks tend not to waste any part of an animal and are known, for example, to make boudin, which is ground-up, leftover meat mixed with rice and formed into sausage, and to fry pork skins to make cracklins.

RELIGIOUS ORIENTATIONS Because of the persecution of Acadians by Protestant groups prior to moving to Louisiana, many Cajun people are resistant to Protestant or other religious groups. Like Creoles, many Cajun's maintain an allegiance to Roman Catholicism. Many parishes in South Louisiana reflect names consistent with Roman Catholicism. Cajun celebratory events often center on the religious connection to Roman Catholicism, such as Mardi Gras, Lent, and Holy Week. Cajun celebration of Mardi Gras (Fat Tuesday) is notably different from the popularized celebration in New Orleans. Cajun Mardi Gras, historically, was a time to gather and use the foods that were to be refrained from during Lent so as to have a final celebration and use of the food (Lindahl, 1996). This Mardi Gras celebration is similar to Candlemas, celebrated by Acadian's in Nova Scotia where Cajuns originated.

SPEECH PATTERNS Cajun influence in Louisiana has led to a significant French influence in South Louisiana including schools with French-language instruction (Brasseaux, 2005). Two major dialects have developed through Cajun orientations, including Cajun-French and Cajun-English. Cajun-French is a French-influenced language dialect unique to South Louisiana. Similarly, Cajun-English is an English-influenced language dialect unique to South Louisiana. Together Cajun-French and Cajun-English have influenced many localized spellings of towns and cities, streets, products and objects, as well as family surnames (Dubois & Horvath, 1999). The Council for the Development of French in Louisiana was created in the late 1960s and served to help maintain the French cultural identity and influence of Cajuns. Cajun translators were used by the U.S. government, most notably during World War II.

MUSIC Cajun music is heavily influenced by both the fiddle and accordion. The musical style of Cajuns shares some similarity with Creole zydeco music (see **Creole**). Cajun music is heavily influenced by the French Catholic music brought from Acadia that is merged with the cultural influences of South Louisiana (Ancelet, 1989).

Kenneth J. Fasching-Varner
Margaret-Mary Sulentic Dowell

References
Ancelet, B. J. (1989). *Cajun music: Its origins and development.* Lafayette, LA: University of Southwestern Louisiana Press.

Bankston, C. L. & Henry, J. M. (1998). The silence of the Gators: Cajun ethnicity and intergenerational transmission of Louisiana French. *Journal of Multilingual and Multicultural Development, 19*(1), 1–23.

Brasseaux, C. A. (1992). *Acadian to Cajun: Transformation of a people, 1803–1877.* Jackson, MS: University Press of Mississippi.

Brasseaux, C. A. (2005). *French, Cajun, Creole, Houma: A primer on francophone Louisiana.* Baton Rouge, LA: Louisiana State University Press.

Dubois, S. & Horvath, B. (1999). When the music changes, you change too: Gender and language change in Cajun English. *Language Variation and Change, 11*(3), 287–313.

Dubois, S. & Melançon, C. (1997). Cajun is dead—long live Cajun: Shifting from a linguistic to a cultural community. *Journal of Sociolinguistics, 1*(1), 63–93.

Lindahl, C. (1996). Bakhtin's carnival laughter and the Cajun country Mardi Gras. *Folklore, 107*(2), 57–70.

Roach v. Dresser Industrial Valve and Instrument Division, 494 F. Supp. 215 (1980). Retrieved from http://www.ucs.louisiana.edu/~ras2777/civrights/roach.htm.

CAPACITY BUILDING

Capacity Building: Developing Teacher and Leader Capacity to Meet the Instructional Needs of Culturally and Linguistically Diverse Students
In the education field, the term *capacity building* for teachers and leaders refers to the development of skills, knowledge, and expertise that can contribute to the ability of these educators to more effectively meet the needs of their students, schools, and communities (Bransford, Brown, Cocking, Donovan, & Pellegrino, 2000). Developing teacher and leader

capacity can lead to improved academic and social outcomes for K–12 students and schools.

This entry focuses on the development of teacher and leader capacity with the goal of meeting the instructional needs of culturally and linguistically diverse students. In particular, this entry will discuss the connections between capacity building and how this is related to social justice, capacity building for preservice and in-service teachers and leaders, and the impact of capacity building on instruction for culturally and linguistically diverse K–12 students.

Connections between Capacity Building and Social Justice

The student population of the United States' K–12 schools is becoming increasingly more diverse, both culturally and linguistically (McGill, 2012). Most mainstream teachers and principals have little professional preparation for the instruction of second-language learners—those students that are learning English as a second language and speak a language other than English as their first language. This lack of preparation, knowledge, and expertise can lead to instruction and programs that are incongruous with the needs of this student population (Gold & Maxwell-Jolly, 2006). This gap in what teachers and leaders know about the instructional needs of linguistically diverse students and what the students need demonstrates this dearth of capacity.

Developing capacity of these educators is, therefore, a social justice issue. It is argued that by developing the capacity of these individuals, there is a greater likelihood that the instructional needs of culturally and linguistically diverse students will be taken into account in productive ways. Research on instructional and schooling practices that are most effective for second-language learners indicates that, when teachers and leaders work specifically from a framework that takes into account the specific needs of English-language learners, these students are better served (de Jong & Harper, 2005; Goldenberg & Coleman, 2010; Hakuta, 2011).

Meeting the needs of all learners, in particular students from language-minority backgrounds, is part of creating more socially just and equitable learning opportunities in K–12 schools. Creating

these beneficial instructional opportunities involves capacity building for teachers and leaders.

Capacity Building for Teachers and Leaders

Developing the capacity of teachers and leaders to more effectively meet the instructional needs of culturally and linguistically diverse students is accomplished either in preservice teacher or leadership preparation programs or through in-service professional learning experiences. Many preservice teacher education programs have begun to take into account the skills and knowledge needed to meet the needs of second-language learners in the mainstream classroom. Scholars argue that mainstream teachers need to become linguistically responsive (Athanases & de Oliveira, 2009; Lucas & Villegas, 2010). Once in the classroom, novice teacher attention must be directed toward meeting the needs of second-language learners in the mainstream classroom. Supporting novice teachers, as they negotiate their new roles as teachers, can contribute to their skill in meeting the needs of second-language speakers and their capacity in this area (Achinstein & Athanases, 2010). In addition, as experienced teachers with knowledge of language acquisition develop their capacity for supporting their colleagues, teachers that take on either informal or formal leadership responsibilities play a valuable role in developing the capacity of the teachers and principals in their schools. Specifically, English as a second language teachers are often called upon as the language experts and can be instrumental in the capacity of a school to meet the needs of second-language learners (Brooks, Adams, & Morita-Mullaney, 2010).

Leadership preparation programs are essential in developing the capacity of their graduates to lead from a social justice standpoint with a focus on meeting the needs of all students, including culturally and linguistically diverse students (Marshall & Oliva, 2006). Preparing principals who know how to draw on expertise and support their teachers and teacher leaders in their efforts to create equitable instructional practices and policies for culturally and linguistically diverse learners is part of developing this type of leadership capacity (Mangin, 2007). In-service programs and supports for instructional leaders contribute to capacity development as well, and, in particular, learning communities for principals that focus on issues of equity and instructional improvement (Knapp, Copland, Honig, Plecki, & Portin, 2010).

Impact of Capacity Building on Instruction

Building the capacity of teachers and leaders can have a positive impact on instruction for culturally and linguistically diverse K–12 students. Teachers and leaders that are focused on the specific needs of these students can be more culturally and linguistically responsive. Collaborative efforts of teachers and leaders can further contribute to responsive instruction as these educators work together to best meet the needs of their particular student population (Russell, 2012).

Instruction that is focused on developing both the English-language skills of students, as well as the required in-depth content knowledge through appropriate scaffolding, provides second-language learners in K–12 classrooms access to the curriculum, while at the same time facilitating language acquisition (Walqui, 2006). Teachers that have the capacity to develop the academic language of their linguistic minority students are well positioned to provide high-quality content-area instruction (Lucero, 2012). Developing teacher and leader capacity ultimately impacts what happens in classrooms and the educational opportunities that are made available to diverse K–12 students.

Felice Atesoglu Russell

References

Achinstein, B. & Athanases, S. Z. (2010). Mentoring for equity: Focusing new teachers on English language learners. In J. Wang, S. J. Odell, & R. T. Clift (Eds.), *Past, present, and future research on teacher induction: An anthology for researchers, policy makers, and practitioners* (pp. 187–204). New York: Commission on Teacher Induction and Mentoring, Association of Teacher Educators: Rowman & Littlefield Education.

Athanases, S. Z. & de Oliveira, L. C. (2009). Toward program-wide coherence in preparing teachers to teach and advocate for English language learners. In T. Lucas (Ed.), *Teacher preparation for linguistically diverse classrooms: A resource for teacher educators* (pp. 195–215). New York: Routledge.

Bransford, J. D., Brown, A. L., Cocking, R. R., Donovan. M. S., & Pellegrino, J. W. (Eds.) (2000). *How people learn: Brain, mind, experience, and school.* Washington: National Academy Press.

Brooks, K., Adams, S. R., & Morita-Mullaney, T. (2010). Creating inclusive learning communities for ELL students: Transforming school principals' perspectives. *Theory into Practice, 49*(2), 145–51.

de Jong, E. J. & Harper, C. (2005). Preparing mainstream teachers for English-language learners: Is being a good teacher good enough? *Teacher Education Quarterly, 32*(2), 101–24.

Gold, N. & Maxwell-Jolly, J. (2006). The high schools English learners need. Berkeley, CA: The University of California Linguistic Minority Research Institute.

Goldenberg, C. & Coleman, R. (2010). *Promoting academic achievement among English learners: A guide to the research.* Thousand Oaks, CA: Corwin.

Hakuta, K. (2011). Educating language minority students and affirming their equal rights: Research and practical perspectives. *Educational Researcher, 40*(4), 163–74.

Knapp, M. S., Copland, M. A., Honig, M. I., Plecki, M. L., & Portin, B. S. (2010). Learning-focused leadership and leadership support: Meaning and practice in urban systems. Seattle, WA: Center for the Study of Teaching and Policy, University of Washington.

Lucas, T. & Villegas, A. M. (2010). The missing piece in teacher education: The preparation of linguistically responsive teachers. *National Society for the Study of Education, 109*(2), 297–318.

Lucero, A. (2012). Demands and opportunities: Analyzing academic language in a first grade dual language program. *Linguistics and Education, 23*(3), 277–88.

Mangin, M. M. (2007). Facilitating elementary principals' support for instructional teacher leadership. *Educational Administration Quarterly, 43*(3), 319–57.

Marshall, C. & Oliva, M. (2006). Building the capacities of social justice leaders. In C. Marshall & M. Oliva (Eds.), *Leadership for social justice: Making revolutions in education* (pp. 1–15). Boston: Pearson.

McGill, B. (2012). Mapping language: Limited English proficiency in America. *National Journal.* Retrieved from http://www.nationaljournal.com/thenextamerica/demographics/mapping-language-limited-english-proficiency-in-america-20120730.

Russell, F. A. (2012). A culture of collaboration: Meeting the instructional needs of adolescent English language learners. *TESOL Journal, 3*(3), 445–68.

Walqui, A. (2006). Scaffolding instruction for English language learners: A conceptual framework. *International Journal of Bilingual Education and Bilingualism, 9*(2), 159–80.

CHICANO

Chicano refers to a person of Mexican descent living or born in the United States. However, Chicano's etymon is contested, and the term's meaning has continually changed over time. What is clear, though, is that the meaning of Chicano transformed during the 1960s and 1970s as Mexican Americans, especially the community's youth, called for social justice and formed their own civil rights organizations and ultimately the Chicano Movement. During this time, Mexican American high school and university students, as well as community activists, claimed Chicano as an identity ingrained with indigenous roots and political connotations, but Chicano still had diverse meanings to different individuals and social groups within the Mexican American community.

Although the etymology of Chicano is unclear, several possibilities of its origins have been presented. One possibility is the transformation of *Meshica*—the term the Aztecs (as modern Westerners have named them) of the Valley of Mexico used to identify themselves. When the Spanish invaded what is now Central Mexico, they learned the term but replaced the *sh* with an *x* to fit within Iberian pronunciation rules. Nevertheless, the original population continued to use *Meshica*, which evolved to *Meshicanos* and then to *Shicanos*. This last term later changed into *Chicanos* and *Chicano*. Another possibility is the Mexican linguistic tradition of replacing consonants, including *j*, *s*, and *x*, with *ch* (č) in speech between close friends and family in order to convey endearment. Although this linguistic practice is (usually) used in personal contexts, such as the consonants within the names of family or close friends, here the group name *Mexicano* (Mexican) was changed to the group name *Chicano* (Villanueva, 1978). Keeping in line with the linguistic practice from which the term derived, this possibility points to *Chicano* initially being a term of endearment. An additional possibility is the meshing of *Chihuahuense*, a person from the Mexican border state of Chihuahua, and *Mexicano* (Romo, 2005), or the meshing of *Chihuahuense* with *Texano* or *Tejano* (Texan) (Salazar, 1970). These last two possibilities originate with individuals from Chihuahua who migrated to Texas, specifically to the Far West Texas border region that includes El Paso. Just as the origins of the word *Chicano* are contested, the time frame from which the term arose is debatable as well (Villanueva, 1978).

As noted above, the use of the term has continuously been in flux. During the early twentieth century in Texas, *Chicano* was used as a derogatory term by U.S.-born Mexican Americans toward recently arrived poor Mexican immigrants (Gamio, 1930). Here, *Chicano* became a class-based slur. However, the term's use transformed during the mid-twentieth century. By the 1950s, *Chicano* became a positive term that signified solidarity and community among Mexican American youth, particularly for males (De León, 2013).

During the 1960s and 1970s, Mexican American civil rights activists claimed Chicano as an identity. This group preferred to think of the term emanating from the Meshica of the Valley of Mexico (Limón, 1981). Such self-identified Chicanos rejected Euro-American culture and claimed broad indigenous roots, including the Aztecs (or the Meshicas) and the Mayans of the Yucatan Peninsula and Southeastern Mexico. They also claimed the Southwest as their inherent homeland since many Mexican-origin individuals could trace their ancestry to the region before the 1948 Treaty of Guadalupe Hidalgo, which opened the Southwest for colonization by the United States after the Mexican American War (1846–1848) through both indigenous ancestry and Mexican ancestry. Additionally, many Chicanos rejected the English word *Mexican*, and thus at times also *Mexican American*, due to its negative implications rooted in Southwestern racism—where *Mexican* was often equated with inferiority by the region's Euro-American population. Therefore, *Chicano* was adopted as an empowering and politicized self-identifier (Salazar, 1970).

The self-identified Chicano youth had initiated a cultural renaissance throughout the Southwest by reclaiming their Mexican culture. This movement came out of Mexican American neighborhoods or *barrios*, high schools, as well as universities (Garcia, 1995). The Chicano youth rallied around César Chávez, who with Dolores Huerta cofounded the United Farm Workers (UFW) in California, and Reies López Tijerina, who founded the *Alianza Federal de Las Mercedes* (Federal Alliance of Land Grants) in Northern New Mexico. What emerged from this youth movement came to be known as the Chicano Movement or *el Movimiento Chicano*. The Chicano Movement demanded social justice for Mexican-origin people as well as other historically oppressed groups (Rosales, 2000).

From the Chicano Movement emerged student organizations such as the Mexican American Youth Organization (MAYO), whose members identified as Chicanos while keeping *Mexican American* in the organization's name, and the *Movimiento Estudiantil Chicano de Aztlán* or the Chicano Student Movement of Aztlán (MEChA). High school students participated in mass school walkouts, or blowouts. During walkouts in cities such as Albuquerque, Denver, and Los Angeles, students demanded a bettering of their education and opportunities to enter the university. Also established were Chicano-focused social justice publications. Such publications included the almost entirely female-produced newspaper *El Grito del Norte* (The Call of the North) in Española, New Mexico. A political party was also launched from the Chicano Movement: *La Raza Unida* Party. Chicano-identified activists established the short-lived political party during the first and only MAYO national meeting in Mission, Texas, held December of 1969 (Acuña, 2011). Chicano identity had helped galvanize an entire civil rights movement. Yet self-identifying as a Chicano and seeing the term as a positive group identifier did not become universal.

As the term became popular among politically active youth, it also faced rejection by a large segment of the Mexican American community. Some Euro-Americanized, economically mobile, and conservative Mexican Americans came to dislike the term *Chicano* for its historical, as previously mentioned, connotations of immigration, poverty, and thus the absence of middle-class and upper-class culture and mannerisms. For many, the term's use as a class-based slur often negated the term's relation with positive cultural camaraderie and identity. Others simply viewed *Chicano* with indifference or as the identity of politically active youth, not the identity of the general Mexican American population. Hence, the majority of Mexican Americans have not identified with the term *Chicano*. This is true for both middle-class and working-class individuals. Among other terms Mexican-origin people more commonly identify with are *Mexicano* and *Mexican*, *Mexican American*, *Latino*, and *Hispanic*. Yet after the 1960s and 1970s, *Chicano* continued to serve as a self-identifier and group identifier for a minority of Mexican-origin individuals in the United States. This was particularly true for college-educated social activists who still saw themselves as inherently connected with their indigenous ancestry and the Southwest (Limón, 1981).

Joel Zapata

References

Acuña, R. F. (2011). *Occupied America: A history of Chicanos* (7th ed.). New York: Longman.

De León, A. (2013). Chicano. *Handbook of Texas Online*. Retrieved from http://www.tshaonline.org/handbook/online/articles/pfc02.

Gamio, M. (1930). *Mexican immigrants to the United States: A study of human migration and adjustment*. Chicano: University of Chicago Press.

Garcia, R. A. (1995). The origins of Chicano cultural thought: Visions and paradigms—Romano's culturalism, Alurista's aesthetics, and Acuña's communalism. *California History, 74*(3), 290–305.

Limón, J. E. (1981). The folk performance of "Chicano" and the cultural limits of political ideology. In R. Bauman & D. Abrahams (Eds.), *"And other neighborly names": Social process and cultural image in Texas folklore* (pp. 197–225). Austin, TX: University of Texas Press.

Romo, D. D. (2005). *Ringside seat to a revolution: An underground cultural history of El Paso and Juárez, 1893–1923*. El Paso, TX: Cinco Puntos Press.

Rosales, F. A. (2000). *Testimonio: A documentary history of the Mexican American struggle for civil rights*. Houston, TX: Arte Público Press.

Salazar, R. (1970, February 6). Who is a Chicano? And what is it the Chicanos want? *Los Angeles Times*, p. B7.

Villanueva, T. (1978). Sobre el termino "Chicano." *Cuadernos Hispano-americanos, 336,* 387–410.

CHILD ABUSE AND NEGLECT

Child abuse and neglect are prevalent in every society, and both situations affect millions of children worldwide. Extensive attention has consequently been devoted by researchers and professionals to reviewing the underlying reasons for the prevalence of the problem and to seek contemporary remedies. The World Health Organization recognizes child maltreatment as any form of physical, psychological, sexual abuse, and neglect that result in actual or potential harm to the child's health, development, or dignity. The Child Abuse and Prevention and Treatment Act suggests:

> child abuse and neglect means, at a minimum, any recent act or failure to act on the part of a parent or caretaker, which results in death, serious physical or emotional harm, sexual abuse or exploitation, or an act or failure to act which presents an imminent risk of serious harm. (CAPTA, 2010, p. 6)

The term *child abuse and neglect* thus refers to different types of maltreatment including physical abuse, emotional abuse, sexual abuse, and fabrication as well as actions that result in the induction of illness in children. Among the various forms of child maltreatment, neglect is the most common form.

Root Causes of Child Abuse and Neglect and Attachment Behavior

Child abuse is a complex phenomenon with multiple causes. Examining these causes is important because social scientists and psychologists believe that the early life experiences of the infant might play a role in their growth and development as well as their emergent behaviors. Clinical experiences show that there is a meaningful relationship between children's experiences of early loss and trauma and the risk of later maladjustment, behavioral difficulties, and impaired mental health. Abusive parents who commonly have problems coping with any form of need, dependence, and vulnerability in themselves and others can impair the relationship between the child and the parent. That is, abusive parents and caregivers have commonly experienced some form of distress with respect to attachment behavior and the emotional dependency they experienced with those who cared for them in their childhood. In order to dispel these negative emotions from the unconscious mind, they handle these anxieties defensively. Whenever their emotionally painful memories about their caregivers are triggered, they deactivate from any attachment and caregiving-related concerns, and these can be seen to manifest as some form of maltreatment toward their children, such as ignoring their state of need, punishing displays of need, being dismissive, and controlling the child's mental states in a hostile manner.

During normal or low-stress conditions such caregivers may perform more responsibly toward the child, however. As a result of these anxiety-reducing strategies, caregivers can cope with their personal, abusive attitudes toward the children and may act in a relatively warm and accepting way when a child acts independently and does not show attachment behavior. However, in the presence of attachment needs and the care-seeking behavior of the child, along with factors such as poverty, domestic conflicts, being overwhelmed, and children who create anger situations, it is likely that the caregivers will become anxious, dismissive, and hostile. When these caregivers are dealing with the child's needs, feelings emerging from the unconscious mind of the individual are dealt with through the defensive exclusion of any attachment-related material, including protective and caregiving responses, thus causing the caregiver to become tense and anxious.

Those children who are faced with such a potentially dangerous situation can in turn develop various strategies to deal with the negative and hostile attitudes of their caregivers around avoidance, compliance, emotional inhibition, and aggression situations. However, abused children have to cope with these physical and emotional threats and survive in these hazardous environments. Abused and rejected children adjust their position and attitudes according to their disorganized relationship with the caregiver and try to mitigate their own needs. Abused children often conceal their fear and distress, which fails to signal their struggle with anxiety. They do not look for protection, help, and support (Howe, 2005, p. 67).

When frightened, such children deactivate their attachment to the behavioral figure, the person whom they feel mostly attached to when they are least available. Abused and rejected children may also view their personal self as being alone and isolated. When they are in a close relationship with others, they feel anxious and worthless. Abused, rejected, and avoidant children learn how to defend themselves from being hurt and from experiencing psychological pain by excluding attachment-related information. Psychologically stable caregivers pose no high risk to children for sustaining physical abuse during highly stressed states. Insecure caregivers, however, could present a risk for children who have intrinsic disabilities such as (ADHD) and other behavioral problems. This phenomenon could result in the likelihood of higher stress-management levels among those with the wealthier psychological resources. In families with large numbers of members and a low income, there may be a greater tendency for increased pressure and tension when there is a need to focus high attention on a newborn baby and fractious elder siblings. In such families, lack of temper control and violent actions may occur readily due to the nature of the prevailing conflict. Anger is the initial response of an abusive parent when faced with a problem. During a phase of anxiety and fear, the parent tries to regain order and control through the use of power and aggression.

Parents and caregivers with prior abuse involvement often conceal their emotional life and present themselves as tough and invulnerable. A child abuser often has a history of having parents with low education, low socioeconomic status, and high levels of social stress. Most abusive mothers report childhood experiences of abuse by parents of both genders. Mothers with an abusive past appear to have a heightened response to distressing situations, as in the case of a crying baby or ordinary attachment behavior compared to the low level of arousal of nonabusive mothers. Maternal rejection and abandonment among women who either killed their children or others have been recognized as noteworthy traits. They may even project their antisocial personalities upon their children by limiting their outdoor play time. These behaviors could be attributed to the psychological maltreatment of parents who feel anxious and agitated when dealing with the attachment behaviors of their children. At times, parents might find their children worthless, irritating, bothersome, flawed, unwanted, and inconvenient. They respond to these phases of anxiety by neglecting their caregiving. Alcohol and mental health problems of their parents often subjected them to physical abuse and neglect.

Physical Child Abuse

The physical abuse of children by their parents is a very widespread human rights issue. The term *physical child abuse* includes a wide range of harsh, punitive, controlling, and aggressive behaviors by the parents. Many parents attempt to control their unruly child with highly primitive and brutal techniques. Abused parents justify applying these techniques to discipline the wayward child.

Many cultures tolerate these brutal disciplinary practices in order to effectively control children. But while some types of disciplinary practices are not harmful to children and can be understandable, in abusive parental cases there is a consistently high level of danger because these practices can cause very brutal, frightening, and dangerous outcomes that can threaten the children's well-being. Physical maltreatment is a concept referring to behaviors by caregivers that make a child feel worthless, unloved, unwanted, and endangered. Rapp-Paglicci and Loeber (2007, p. 124) describe the term *physical abuse* as "the inflicting of a non-accidental physical injury upon a child." Physical abuse also refers to physical injuries a child may suffer caused by punches, smacks, kicks, shakes, burns, drowning, bites, or poisons. Physical abuse is an assault on both the body and the psychological integrity of a child (Howe, 2005, p. 69).

Physical abuse is the leading cause of half of all deaths of children who incur mistreatment. Many of the young children admitted to hospitals for physical injuries as severe as broken bones were not due to coincidences but due to being victims of parent abuse. Physical abuse is the main reason for about half of all deaths caused by child maltreatment. Death could be attributed to the accumulation of regular assaults or a single extremely violent attack. Head injuries, being the prime cause of death, are explained by parents as a child's fall from the sofa, stairs, or cot. Even though older children are subjected to physical abuse, they are less likely to be seriously injured or killed by abusive caregivers (Howe, 2005, p. 69).

Children, particularly disabled children, are the source of stress for their parents and caregivers. Physical disability attributions such as learning disabilities, visual and hearing impairments, low birth weights, and other physical health problems slightly increase the risk of children being physically abused. Disabled children and children with behavioral problems such as ADHD are more likely to be abused and neglected.

Although parents appear to be the main perpetrators of aggression, older sisters and brothers can also physically and sexually abuse younger children. In a study by Claussen and Crittenden (1991), victims of these violent attacks had higher mortality rates if they were under the age of five. Babies under twelve months of age were the third "most likely to die" as victims of physical abuse. Older children are comparably less likely to be critically injured or killed by the same forms of physical abuse. Some 90 percent of psychologically abused and neglected children have been subjected to physical maltreatment.

Characteristics of the Caregiving Environment

Many caregivers with a personal history of abuse and rejection suppress their emotions, they consider themselves as strong and invulnerable. Parents with a history of depression, a personality disorder, and abuse of either drugs or alcohol pose a higher risk of physical abuse for a child. Caregivers of physically abused children tend to have less sympathy for those they perceive to be in a vulnerable state due to dismissal of their attachment behavior (Reder & Duncan, 2000, p. 64).

According to results of many research studies, the childhoods of many physically abusive parents turn out to have been harsh and loveless. Their parents, many of whom had alcohol and mental health problems, had typically subjected them to prolonged physical abuse and neglect. The majority of abusive mothers report being severely assaulted in childhood by their own mothers, while about half say their fathers attacked them. Parents of large families on low incomes are likely to feel under considerable pressure and tension living in poor housing, who find themselves looking after a new baby and his/her fractious older siblings. Children in such families can find themselves in a world in which tempers rise sharply, violence erupts without warning, and conflict is never far away. The parents who have a lower educational level, low socioeconomic status, and high social stress are highly likely to have experienced physical abuse. Physical abusers of young children are more likely to be female. However, older children's abusers are more likely male. Most child deaths, whatever the age of the child, are the results of male violence (Howe, 2005, p. 72).

Children who have psychologically sick caregivers are at high risk for being physically abused during highly stressful states (Knutson, 1995, p. 412). In general, for the abusive parents, anger is the first response when faced with a problem. In response to the anxiety and fear triggered by such perceived challenges, the parent seeks to regain order and control by the use of power and aggression (Miller-Perrin & Perrin, 1999, p. 73). Compared with nonabusive mothers, physically abusive mothers show high levels of arousal when faced with a distressed, crying baby displaying ordinary attachment behaviors (Krugman, 1985).

Psychological Maltreatment: Emotional Abuse, Neglect, and Rejection

A more generic term, *psychological maltreatment*, covers emotional abuse, rejection, and neglect. Hart, Brassard, and Karlson (1996, p. 73) see psychological maltreatment as the absence of most, if not all, of a child's basic developmental needs. Iwaniec (2006, p. 14) defines emotional abuse as: hostile or indifferent behavior that damages a child's self-esteem, degrades a sense of achievement, diminishes a sense of belonging, prevents health and vigorous development, and takes away a child's well-being.

Bifulco et al. (1994) recognize two dimensions of emotional maltreatment: parental rejection and psychological abuse. According to Rapp-Paglicci and Loeber (2007, p. 124), psychological maltreatment is a form of caregiver behavior that involves extreme incidents that convey to children that they are worthless, unloved, unwanted, and endangered. Psychologically, maltreatment is recognized as a situation in which the majority of the child's developmental needs are neglected. According to Maslow's hierarchy, psychological maltreatment is highly contradictory to the fulfillment of basic needs such as psychological needs, safety needs, love and belonging needs, and self-esteem (Hart, Brassard, & Karlson, 1996, p. 73).

The complexity of psychological maltreatment is expressed in a wide variety of behaviors. The American Professional Society recognizes psychological maltreatment in children and adolescents in a *Guideline for Psychological Evaluation* publication as being categorized by major subtypes: spurning, degrading, and brutal rejection of children; threats as extensive as death or abandoning the child; and excluding the child from their social environment and activities. These forms of ill-treatment by abuser parents push children to develop antisocial, self-destructive, or criminal behaviors. These also include denying the child's emotional responsiveness and neglecting the child's medical needs. Not giving the child the opportunity to explore and understand their emotions is extremely dangerous and can lead to difficulty in them managing feelings in a socially competent environment (APSAC, 1995).

The outcome of failing to develop skills at managing the psychological consequences of emotional abuse and neglect that the authorities often fail to recognize increases with age, not because of their early occurrence but due to the accumulation of such events until a critical point is reached in which it is recognized by a schoolteacher, neighbor, or health worker. They inhibit oppositional and antisocial behavior, for example, and if they achieve making it to school, they tend to underachieve. They are socially removed, isolated, or aggressive. Their emotional fears and stresses lead to poor growth (Howe, 2005, p. 91).

Characteristics of the Caregiving Environment
Parents who maltreat their children were often subject to an emotionally brutal childhood themselves. Yet these painful memories are generally concealed from discussions with a professional. They represent themselves as polite and are wary and distant caregivers, and they may become disengaged from professional help. When they have problems with professionals they can react aggressively, and in a threatening way using intimidation. They keep away from doctors and health clinics even when they are pregnant (Howe, 2005, p. 92). These parents are socially separated, typically have a history of depression, and as a result, their contact with the outside world tends to be low (Reder, Duncan, & Gray, 1993, p. 99). Defensively, abusive parents deal with their anxiety by "deactivating" their caregiving. As a result, they fail to provide care and protection when their children need it. Deactivation of caregiving can be achieved using a number of strategies:

- Whenever the child calls his/her parent to provide his/her needs, the parent becomes emotionally occupied and unresponsive at the time of the child's problem.
- Parents may consider their child removed and unworthy of attention.
- A parent recognizes their previous attempts to help their child are futile.
- The parent feels outraged by the demands of the child, which eventually leads them to become subdued, fearful, and silent.
- A parent considers time dedicated toward a child as useless. (Howe, 2005, p. 93)

Children's Behavior and Development
Abuse and neglect can adversely affect both the physical and mental health and development of children. When the young child fails to explore and understand their emotions, this can damage their psychological development. According to Hart et al. (2002, p. 87), children who are exposed to parental rejection and lack of emotional responsiveness are more likely to commit juvenile crimes.

Compared to other children, emotionally abused children are more likely to feel scared, sad, anxious, and distressed. They show oppositional and antisocial behaviors. If they attend school, they generally fail. In situations of extreme emotional fear and stress, children can show poor development and a range of stress-related disorders. Extraordinary continuing stress such as chronic stress can affect children's development and physiological health (Howe, 2005, p. 99).

Child Neglect

Child neglect is a brutal element of maltreatment that prevents a child's developing mind from receiving stimulation. It also damages their spirit until they have little desire to connect and explore their environment. Neglect is forsaking a child's basic needs of physical, emotional, and educational needs (Erickson & Egeland, 2002, p. 3). Neglect is the failure to provide for the children's basic needs including physical, emotional, and educational needs (Rapp-Paglicci & Loeber, 2007, p. 124). Physical neglect involves failure to meet children's basic physical needs of good food, adequate housing, and proper clothing. Emotional neglect denies children psychological recognition and emotional understanding (Erickson & Egeland, 2002, p. 4). As a broad definition, child neglect can also be expressed as failing to provide for the physical, emotional, cognitive, educational, social, and cultural needs of children.

Many childcare practitioners are aware of the broad, familiar characteristics of physical neglect as follows: poverty, a general air of hopelessness, dirt, mess, and the ever-present smell of old food, greasy floors, and poor hygiene; parents leave children unsupervised and understimulated; parents fail to respond to their children's attachment needs and damage their social and emotional growth; and relationships and interaction between parties are very limited and perfunctory. As a consequence, neglected children tend to be passive. Their school attendance remains fairly poor, which is evidenced by their physical, educational, and emotional impairment.

Three types of neglect exist: (1) disorganized neglect: in which cognition, thought, and reflective reason are minimized; affect is dominant, and feelings drive behavior and social interactions; (2) emotional neglect and abuse: also referred to as psychological maltreatment, in which affect is omitted from mental processing; (3) depressed or passive neglect: in which both cognition and affect are discarded as meaningless sources of information about danger and protection (Crittenden, 1999, p. 51).

Conclusion

Having mentioned the underlying factors, we can conclude that child maltreatment extends as far as physical and psychological ill-treatment and sexual abuse and neglect that causes actual or potential harm to the child's health, development, or dignity. Even though child maltreatment is very prevalent and affects millions of children and adults in the world, very little can be done to protect children from this brutal threat. Several factors contribute to the generation of child abuse and neglect, and these early life experiences might affect the child's physical and emotional development. Child maltreatment is one early learning experience that can create trauma and emotional maladjustment in adulthood. Often, abusive parents were also victims of child maltreatment in their childhood. Today's victims of child maltreatments will become tomorrow's abusers if this cycle of violence is ignored. Professionally coordinated affective intervention policies and early child protection programs are needed to cope with this issue of child maltreatment.

Ilyas Ozgenturk

References

American Professional Society on the Abuse of Children (APSAC). (1995). *Guidelines for the psychosocial evaluation of suspected psychological maltreatment in children and adolescents.* Chicago, IL: APSAC.

Bifulco, A., Brown, G., Neubauer, A., Moran, P., & Harris, T. (1994). *Childhood experience of care and abuse (CECA) training manual.* London: Royal Holloway.

Child Abuse Prevention and Treatment Act (CAPTA). (2010). Section I, Definitions, p. 6. http://www.acf.hhs.gov/programs/cb/resource/capta2010.

Christoffersen, M. N. & DePanfilis, D. (2009). Prevention of child abuse and neglect and improvements in child development. *Child Abuse Review, 18*, 24–40.

Claussen, A. & Crittenden, P. (1991). Physical and psychological maltreatment: Relations among types of maltreatment. *Child Abuse and Neglect, 15*, 5–18.

Crittenden, P. (1999). Child neglect: causes and contributors. In H. Dubowitz (Ed.), *Neglected children: Research, practice and policy* (pp. 47–68). Thousand Oaks: Sage.

Erickson, M. & Egeland, B. (2002). Child neglect. In J. Myers, L. Berliner, J. Briere, C. T. Hendrix,

C. Jenny, & T. Reid (Eds.), *The APSAC handbook on child maltreatment* (2nd ed., pp. 3–20). Thousand Oaks, CA: Sage.

Fontaine, D. & Nolin, P. (2012). Personality disorders in a sample of parents accused of physical abuse or neglect. *Journal of Family Violence, 27*, 23–31.

Hart, S., Brassard, M., Binggeli, N., Rivelis, E., Diaz, V., & Davidson, H. (2002). Psychological maltreatment. In J. Myers (Ed.), *The APSAC handbook on child maltreatment* (2nd ed., pp. 79–103). Thousand Oaks: Sage.

Herrenkohl, T. I., Hong, S., Klika, J. B., & Herrenkohl, R. C. (2012). Developmental impacts of child abuse and neglect related to adult mental health, substance use, and physical health. *Journal of Family Violence, 28*(2), 191–99.

Howe, David. (2005). *Child abuse and neglect.* United Kingdom: Macmillan.

Iwaniec, Dorota. (2006). *The emotionally abused and neglected child.* Hoboken, NJ: John Wiley & Sons, Ltd.

Knutson, J. F. (1995). Psychological characteristics of maltreated children: Putative risk factors and consequences. *Annual Review of Psychology, 46*, pp. 401–31.

Krugman, R. (1985). Fatal child abuse: Analysis of 24 cases. *Pediatrician, 12*, 68–72.

McCabe, K. (2007). Child neglect. In N. A. Jackson (Ed.), *Encyclopedia of domestic violence* (pp. 142–46). New York: Routledge.

Miller-Perrin, C. & Perrin, R. (1999). *Child maltreatment: An introduction.* Thousand Oaks: Sage.

Polonko, K. (2006). Exploring assumptions about child neglect in relation to the broader field of child maltreatment. *JHHS Winter, 29*, 260–82.

Rapp-Paglicci, L. & Loeber, P. (2007). Child abuse and juvenile delinquency. In N. A. Jackson (Ed.), *Encyclopedia of domestic violence* (pp. 124–31). New York: Routledge.

Reder, P. & Duncan, S. (2000). Abuse then and now. In P. Peder, M. McClure, and A. Jolley (Eds.), *Family matters: Interfaces between child and adult mental health* (pp. 38–54). London: Routledge.

Reder, P. R., Duncan, S., & Gray, M. (1993). *Beyond blame: Child abuse tragedies revisited.* London: Routledge.

Schwartz, B. & McCauley, M. (2007). Child abuse: A global perpective. In N. A. Jackson (Ed.), *Encyclopedia of domestic violence* (pp. 119–23). New York: Routledge.

CHILDREN'S RIGHTS

International Convention on the Rights of the Child
In 1989, the General Assembly of the United Nations unanimously adopted the International Convention on the Rights of the Child (CRC). Initiated by the nation of Poland and developed by representatives from many countries and organizations, the CRC was negotiated through a series of laborious meetings spanning ten years. The United States played an important role in shaping the content of the CRC, and immediately after adoption, the U.S. ambassador to the United Nations, Madeleine Albright, signified the intent of her nation to ratify the CRC.

Part of a series of legally binding international agreements designed to define, guarantee, and protect human rights, the CRC was created to safeguard the rights of people under the age of eighteen throughout the world. (The text of the CRC states that a child is any human being below the age of eighteen years, unless under the law applicable to the child, majority is attained earlier.) Often labeled an "aspirational document" to signify its utility as a "tool, not a panacea," the CRC includes fifty-four ambitious and wide-ranging articles that establish important goals for nations to work toward improving the lives of children (Joint Committee on Human Rights, 2003, p. 13). The articles fall into three categories: protection rights, provision rights, and participation rights. "Protection rights" are intended to prevent harm from dangerous acts and practices, such as the right to be safe from discrimination (Article 2), physical and sexual abuse (Article 19), and conflict (Article 38). "Provision rights" address basic needs and include the rights to adequate health care (Article 24) and education (Article 28), along with rights to play, rest, and leisure (Article 31). "Participation rights" allow children to be a part of the decisions that affect their lives and to engage as rights-bearing members of society. Examples of such rights include freedom of speech (Article 13); freedom of thought, conscience, and religion (Article 14); and freedom of association (Article 15). The Committee on the Rights of the Child, an eighteen-person body of independent experts, is responsible for reviewing signatory nations' adherence to the articles of the CRC; the committee requires nations to submit treaty implementation reports within two years of ratification and every five years thereafter. Members of this committee, as stipulated by Article 43 of the commission, must be "experts of high moral standing" and are nominated by their country and elected by receiving a majority vote among ballots cast by at least two-thirds of all UN member states. In order to prepare these reports, signatories must develop a process to analyze the status of children's rights in their nation. Many advocates of the CRC argue that this analysis process and the resulting reports often draw important attention to rights issues within a given nation, along with policies and programs to address these issues.

Within three years after the CRC's adoption by the United Nations, 127 nations had ratified the agreement. Today, with formal adoption by 193 nations, the CRC is notable as one of the international human rights treaties with the greatest level of support from nations across the globe. None of the nations that ratified the treaty has since withdrawn its support, and remarkably, only two nations that are member states of the United Nations have not signed the CRC. One of the non-signatories, Somalia, is an extremely poor nation without a functioning government. The other nation is one of the world's wealthiest nations, with a venerable and thriving democracy: the United States. In light of the support that the United States gave to the CRC as it was being developed, many observers have expressed surprise that the United States has not yet ratified the treaty. To others, it is not only surprising but also blatantly shameful. During the presidential election campaign of 2008, Barack Obama stated: "It's embarrassing to find ourselves in the company of Somalia, a lawless land. I will review this and other treaties and ensure that the United States resumes its global leadership in human rights" (Walden University, 2008). To date, however, the treaty awaits ratification by the United States. This entry first describes the trajectory of the CRC in the United States and then offers three reasons why the agreement has yet to be ratified: a complex U.S. treaty ratification process; American unilateralism; and critiques from politically conservative organizations, legislators, and religious leaders that reflect concerns about parental rights, including the availability of abortion and contraception to minors.

The United States was heavily involved in the ten-year creation of the CRC, which took place during the Reagan and Bush administrations. Throughout this process, the United States expressed the need for provisions that included civil and political protections for children; these resulted in articles 12 through 17 of the treaty. The Clinton administration, amid broad international acceptance of the treaty, signed the CRC in February of 1995, but they did not submit it to the Senate to be voted on due to strong opposition to ratification. Some opponents charged that "more than other human rights treaties, the CRC addressed areas that are usually considered to be primarily or exclusively under the jurisdiction of state or local governments, including education, juvenile justice, and access to healthcare" (Blanchfield, 2009, summary section, para. 2). Typically, international treaties are intensively scrutinized before they are signed into law in the United States to ensure that all federal and state laws comply with the treaty guidelines prior to ratification; it is not at all unusual for this process to take decades. For example, the United States took more than thirty years to ratify the Convention on the Prevention and Punishment of the Crime of Genocide (Moravcsik, 2001).

The U.S. ratification process begins with the president signing a treaty if he judges it to be in the best interest of the nation. The president then submits the treaty to the Senate, which may include Reservations, Understandings, and Declarations, or RUDs. These statements allow the Senate Committee on Foreign Relations to "recommend that the Senate approve a treaty conditionally, granting its advice and consent subject to certain stipulations that the President must accept before proceeding to ratification" (Blanchfield, 2009, p. 8). Article II, Section 2, Clause 2 of the Constitution specifically states that the president "shall have Power, by and with the Advice and Consent of the Senate, to make Treaties, provided two thirds of the Senators present concur" (U.S. National Archives and Records Administration, n.d.). This stipulation complicates treaty ratification, as they require a strong senatorial supermajority, which is difficult to secure. As has been the case with the CRC, detractors of a treaty in the Senate can thwart its passage.

The power of the Senate is one element that enforces a larger sense of American unilateralism—that is, the tendency of the United States to approach foreign affairs in an individualistic manner and to regard international treaties with ambivalence. According to Andrew Moravcsik (2001), this worldview stems from four factors: geopolitical power, stable democratic governance, ideological conservatism, and political decentralization. The United States' status as a superpower allows it to weigh international treaties and multilateral decisions through a cost-benefit analysis lens. The guiding principle here is that "all other things being equal, the more isolated and powerful a state—that is, the more efficiently it can achieve its objectives by unilateral or bilateral means—the less it gains from multilateral cooperation" (Moravcsik, 2001, p. 348). This idea is not unique to superpowers, of course, but it becomes an even greater decision-making tool when faced with the reality that unilateral decision making may be more beneficial to the state as a whole. Additionally, international treaties allow for international judicial human rights enforcement; "to participate fully in such arrangements . . . countries sacrifice much of their bargaining power" (Moravcsik, 2001, p. 348). The judicial human rights "enforcer" of the CRC is the Committee on the Rights of the Child, which has the power to review and offer recommendations for policy to participating (and treaty-ratified) states.

The stability within the U.S. government structure can also encourage skepticism toward international governing institutions among the citizen body as a whole. Moravcsik (2001) argues that the United States operates almost exclusively within a system that is ideologically conservative and politically decentralized as present in the "relatively informal and underdeveloped (i.e., nonsolidaristic) conception of economic rights" (p. 354). A system that promotes ideological conservatism can, whether directly or indirectly, create a political environment of partisan conflict. This idea is present in the way party members approach and react to international treaties, including the CRC. Treaty signage is also affected by two important decentralizing elements of the U.S. political system involving the supermajoritarian Senate voting rules as they relate to treaty ratification, and "strong separation of powers" among the three branches of government (Moravcsik, 2001). Strong treaty skepticism can thwart passage, while domestic debate over human rights "has been bitterly partisan and intensely ideological, led by those who feel that international human rights norms [can pose] . . . a fundamental threat to the integrity of U.S. political institutions" (Moravcsik, 2001, p. 352).

Most early opposition to the CRC came from politically conservative organizations, legislators, and religious leaders, despite the deep U.S. involvement over the ten-year course of crafting the CRC throughout both the Republican Reagan and Bush administrations. Republican senator Jesse Helms, Chairman of the Foreign Relations Committee, refused to support the CRC, stating on the Senate floor in 1995 that "it is going to be very difficult for this treaty even to be given a hearing" (Gunn, 2006, p. 113). Senator Helms (1995) specifically objected to Article 12:

Article 12 of the Convention on the Rights of the Child requires that States Parties "shall assure to the child who is capable of forming his or her own views the right to express those views freely in all matters affecting the child, the views of the child being given due weight in accordance with the age and maturity of the child." What on earth does this mean? Will the U.S. be censured because a parent did not leave it to a child to choose which school to attend? Will the U.S. be censured because a parent did not allow a child to decide whether to accompany the family to church? Will the U.S. be censured because a parent did not consult a child before requiring that he or she complete family chores? (para. 10)

Following Senator Helms's denouncement of the CRC, others, including the Parental Rights Movement, cited issues with the CRC and the state of parental rights in the United States. Helms and others assert that the CRC will potentially undermine the rights of parents to rear their children in the way that they see fit. These concerns are echoed in the words of contemporary detractors, including the Parental Rights Movement spearheaded by creators of the website parentalrights.org, who describe their mission, in part, as seeking to "protect children by empowering parents . . . by preventing U.S.

ratification of the UN's Convention on the Rights of the Child CRC" (n.d.). Opponents specifically cite abortion and family planning as areas in which parents or guardians should have the right to decide what is in the best interest of their children. Article 16 in particular raises some concern, as it states: "No child shall be subjected to arbitrary or unlawful interference with his or her privacy, family, home, or correspondence."

Critics of the treaty believe that the "right to privacy" would allow children to decide independently and without parental input to have an abortion. The decade-long creation of the treaty saw much debate concerning abortion and "where life begins," with delegates ultimately deciding to ensure that the treaty was "abortion-neutral" and voided any specific language on abortion (Blanchfield, 2009). Additionally, Article 24(2)(f) states that states parties "take appropriate measures . . . to develop preventive health care, guidance for parents and family planning services." Opponents worry that this article would legally require the distribution of contraception and student participation in sex-education classes. Supporters of the treaty rebut this claim by maintaining that "the CRC was established not to circumvent the role of parents but to protect children against government intrusion and abuse" (Blanchfield, 2009, summary section, para. 3). The CRC, in fact, makes mention of parents as highlighted in Articles 3, 9, and 10, with Article 3 specifically "taking into account the rights and duties of his or her parents" and Article 10 maintaining the importance of the parent-child relationship (Blanchfield, 2009). All of these concerns raised by opponents of the CRC, however, can be addressed through the treaty process that allows for RUDs.

To date, the Obama administration has not forwarded the treaty to the Senate, but has ratified both of the CRC Optional Protocols on Children in Armed Conflict and the Sale of Children. The UN describes optional protocols as additional agreements, created after the initial treaty, that "either provide for procedures with regard to the treaty or address a substantive area related to the treaty" (2009). These are treaties in their own right and open for signature or "ratification by countries who are party to the main treaty." The signing of these protocols has provided a source of hope to supporters for the complete ratification of the CRC, but given the issues cited by opponents of the CRC, the United States must take the treaty into careful consideration, assuring that it can seamlessly integrate it into American law. In her remarks to UNICEF in June of 2009, Susan Rice, the U.S. ambassador to the United Nations, spoke of the Obama administration's continued support of the treaty and affirmed that the United States was currently reviewing the treaty and remains "committed to working with the international community to promote many of the principles embodied in it" (para. 9). What is apparent is that many confounding ideas have delayed the ratification of the treaty, including opposition by conservatives, a complex treaty process, and a government whose preference for unilateralism results in ambivalence toward multinational treaties.

Raymonda Reese
Diana Hess

References

Blanchfield, L. (2009). The United Nations Convention on the Rights of the Child: Background and policy issues. Washington, DC: Congressional Research Service.

Convention on the Rights of the Child, November 20, 1989, 1577 U.N.T.S. 3; 28 I.L.M. 1456 (1989).

Gunn, J. (2006). The religious right and the opposition to U.S. ratification on the Convention on the Rights of the Child. *Emory International Law Review, 20*(1), 111–28.

Helms, J. (1995, June 14). Comments of Senator Jesse Helms (R-SC) on Senate Resolution 133—relative to the United Nations Convention on the Rights of the Child. *Congressional record.* Retrieved from http://pangaea.org/street_children/world/helms.htm.

Joint Committee on Human Rights. (2003). *The UN Convention on the Rights of the Child: Tenth report of session 2002–2003.* Retrieved from the United Kingdom Parliament, http://www.publications.parliament.uk/pa/jt200203/jtselect/jtrights/117/117.pdf.

Moravcsik, A. (2001). Why is U.S. human rights policy so unilateralist? In S. Patrick & S. Forman (Eds.), *Multilateralism and U.S. foreign policy* (pp. 345–76). Boulder: Lynne Riener Publishers.

Parentalrights.org. (n.d.). *Our mission*. Retrieved from parentalrights.org.

Rice, S. (2009, June 8). Comments of Ambassador Susan E. Rice on U.S. mission to the United Nations. *United Nations*. Retrieved from http://usun.state.gov/briefing/statements/2009/125983.htm.

United Nations. (2009). *Convention on the elimination of all forms of discrimination against women: What is an optional protocol?* Retrieved from http://www.un.org/womenwatch/daw/cedaw/protocol/whatis.htm.

U.S. National Archives and Records Administration. (n.d.). Constitution of the United States. The Charters of Freedom. Retrieved from http://www.archives.gov/exhibits/charters/constitution.html.

Walden University (Producer). (2008). *The Walden University presidential youth debate: Question 12: Human rights* (video). Retrieved from http://www.youthdebate2008.org/video/question-12/.

CHURCH OF SOCIAL JUSTICE

The Catholic Church and Social Justice

Social justice is conceptualized as the right and obligation of individuals to be involved in determining the way in which larger social, economic, and political institutions of society are organized (U.S. Catholic Bishops, 1986). This justice in the Roman Catholic tradition refers to a preferential option for the poor and marginalized groups in society (Galilea, 1984; Hennelly, 1995; Tilley, 1995). The Catholic theological and biblical perspective emphasizes the responsibilities of all citizens to assist in creating patterns of societal organization and activity essential both for the "protection of minimal human rights and for the creation of mutuality and participation by all in social life" (Hollenbach, 1977, p. 220). Therefore, there are claims that every human being can make on others not because they are highly intelligent, gifted, wealthy, or wellborn, but because they are human and children of the same God; the notion that all people are created in the image of God, *imago Dei*.

A theological and biblical focus on social justice within the Catholic Church includes a vision of community, family, and the individual in relationship to the poor, marginalized, and vulnerable. Catholic social teaching requires individuals to practice their faith in community to bring about transformation for the common good. Social equity can only be achieved through sociopolitical involvement, a commitment to service, and advocacy on behalf of marginalized populations. "Without a clear option for justice, especially to the poor, the Church could not fulfill [its] responsibility" (Balasuriya, 2007, p. 59).

The responsibility to social justice within Catholicism is evident throughout history, especially with liberation theology. Liberation theology and its emphasis on social justice is directly connected to the social teachings of the Catholic Church and its preference for the plight of the poor "as the locus theologicus . . . of the manifestation of God" (Galilea, 1984, p. 11; Oliveros, 1993, p. 13). The theology of liberation is spiritually based on biblical narratives of justice in relationship to God and the Covenant, the Exodus, The Psalms (lamentations), the Beatitudes, and redemption (Galilea, 1984; Gutierrez, 1993). More precisely, liberation theology became a movement within the Catholic Church as a result of the Second Vatican Council, which called for "the church to act as a sacrament of salvation" (Oliveros, 1993, p. 4), and where Christian charity focused on the poor and their conversion to Catholicism. Pope John Paul II emphasized the poor as God's favorite children (Oliveros, 1993, p. 12). Pope Francis continues to emphasize the theme of social justice, the biblical teachings of the church, and the preference for the poor as espoused in liberation theology (Aponte & De La Torre, 2006; Groody, 2007; Hennelly, 1995; Maldonado, 2007; Rowland, 1999; West, 1999).

Liberation theology, "a postmodern theology of communal praxis," emerged with Latin American Roman Catholic priests such as Gustavo Gutierrez from Peru as well as other male and female theologians (Tilley, 1995, p. 128). During a 1968 conference in Medellin, Colombia, Latin American bishops debated the definition of evangelical poverty and resolved that liberating the poor was God's will. A subsequent conference in Puebla, Mexico, in 1979 produced the Puebla Document, which developed the concept of a preference for the poor, and emphasized that "t[o] be converted to Christ means becoming a brother or sister of the poor" (Oliveros, 1993, p. 5). Liberating the poor of Latin

America—peasants, natives, and blacks living in urban slums and rural areas—was a commitment to social justice for the Latin American Catholic Church that required communal praxis (Oliveros, 1993, p. 4). This Catholic theology became a critical reflection on the praxis of liberation for equity in society (Oliveros, 1993, p. 12).

Liberation theology is concerned with the rights or freedom of *all* marginalized groups in society across class, race, gender, and other cultural differences. Grounded on scripture illustrating God's preference for "the least of our brothers and sisters," leaders of the movement sought action from those committed to the belief (Gutierrez, 1993, pp. 247–48). "At the root of the theology of liberation is the nexus with concrete praxis. It is within this major dialect of theory (of faith) and practice (of charity) that liberation theology operates" (Boff, 1993, p. 73). According to Boff, "Liberation theology is the theology of the liberation of the oppressed; the liberation of their whole person, body, and soul; and all of the oppressed—the poor, the subjugated, those who suffer discrimination" (p. 77). Based on this ideology of freedom, the theology of liberation movement has also inspired Christian women in Latin America to advocate for the role of feminist perspectives in theological studies (Aquino & Rosado-Nunez, 2007; Tepedino & Brandao, 1993; Tilley, 1995). This is evident in the influence of Latin American Christian Catholic women who have found their voices by rereading the Bible and rediscovering themselves as *vessels* of social action and transformation in their communities (Aponte & De La Torre, 2006; Aquino, 2007; Aquino, Machado, & Rodriguez, 2002; Aquino & Rosado-Nunez, 2007; Isasi-Diaz, 2007).

The moral theory in liberation theology accentuates the church of the poor and can been interpreted as an ethical model, "ethics at the service of the human being . . . how to be good by making this society good . . . a lived spirituality and as theological discipline" (Rejon, 1993, pp. 215–16). The strong relationship between liberation theology and the social teachings of the Catholic Church is evident throughout the world in its traditions as well as the governing decisions: "The liberative pastoral praxis of the church must be nourished by the word of God [and the poor]" (Antoncich, 1993,

p. 107). The concerns for the poor and marginalized are Christian moral imperatives within the Catholic tradition of theoretical conceptualization and the social action for bringing about equity in society. Jesus lived the same preference by associating with those who were considered to be undesirable in society, such as the woman at the well. Since the Second Vatican Council, the Catholic Church has made a commitment to social justice or the *new evangelization* with the preference for the poor based on Matthew 20:16, "the last will be first" (Gutierrez, 1993). Catholicism's call to action is biblically evident: "But be doers of the word, and not merely hearers who deceive themselves" (James 1:22).

Maria A. Pacino
Susan Warren

References

Antoncich, R. (1993). Liberation theology and the social teaching of the church. In I. Ellacuria & J. Sobrino (Eds.), *Mysterium liberationis: Fundamental concepts of liberation theology* (pp. 103–22). New York: Orbis.

Aponte, D. E. & De La Torre, M. A. (2006). *Handbook of Latina/o theologies*. St. Louis, MO: Chalice Press.

Aquino, M. P. (2007). The feminist option for the poor and oppressed in the context of globalization. In D. G. Groody (Ed.), *The option for the poor in Christian theology* (pp. 191–215). Notre Dame, IN: University of Notre Dame Press.

Aquino, M. P., Machado, D. L., & Rodriguez, J. (2002). *A reader in Latina feminist theology: Religion and justice*. Austin, TX: University of Texas Press.

Aquino, M. P., & Rosado-Nunez, M. J. (2007). *Feminist intercultural theology: Latino explorations for a just world*. New York: Maryknoll.

Balasuriya, T. (2007). Benedict XVI's Deus caritas est and social action. In P. Cullen, B. Hoose, & G. Mannion (Eds.), *Catholic social justice: Theological and practical explorations* (pp. 41–62). New York: Continuum.

Boff, C. (1993). Epistemology and method of the theology of liberation. In I. Ellacuria & J. Sobrino (Eds.), *Mysterium liberationis: Fundamental concepts of liberation theology* (pp. 57–84). New York: Orbis.

Galilea, S. (1984). *Liberation theology and the Vatican document*. Quezon City, Philippines: Claretian.

Groody, D. G. (Ed.). (2007). *The option for the poor in Christian theology*. Notre Dame, IN: University of Notre Dame Press.

Gutierrez, G. (1993). Option for the poor. In I. Ellacuria & J. Sobrino (Eds.), *Mysterium liberationis: Fundamental concepts of liberation theology* (pp. 235–250). New York, NY: Orbis.

Hennelly, A. T. (1995). *Liberation theologies: The global pursuit of justice*. Eugene, OR: Wipf & Stock.

Hollenbach, D. (1977). Modern Catholic teachings concerning justice. In J. C. Haughey (Ed.), *The faith that does justice: Examining the Christian sources for social change* (pp. 207–31). New York: Paulist.

Isasi-Diaz, A. M. (2007). *Mujerista theology: A theology for the twenty-first century*. New York: Orbis.

Maldonado, L. (2007). Popular Catholicism and the poor. In D. G. Groody (Ed.), *The option for the poor in Christian theology* (pp. 259–68). Notre Dame, IN: University of Notre Dame Press.

Oliveros, R. (1993). History of the theology of liberation. In I. Ellacuria & J. Sobrino (Eds.), *Mysterium liberationis: Fundamental concepts of liberation theology* (pp. 3–32). New York: Orbis.

Rejon, F. M. (1993). Fundamental moral theory in the theology of liberation. In I. Ellacuria & J. Sobrino (Eds.), *Mysterium liberationis: Fundamental concepts of liberation theology* (pp. 210–21). New York: Orbis.

Rowland, C. (Ed.). (1999). *The Cambridge companion to liberation theology*. Cambridge, UK: Cambridge University Press.

Tepedino, A. M. & Brandao, M. L. R. (1993). Women and the theology of liberation. In I. Ellacuria & J. Sobrino (Eds.), *Mysterium liberationis: Fundamental concepts of liberation theology* (pp. 222–34). New York: Orbis.

Tilley, T. W. (1995). *Postmodern theologies: The challenge of religious diversity*. New York: Orbis.

U.S. Catholic Bishops. (1986). *Economic justice for all: Pastoral letter on Catholic social teaching and the U.S. economy*. St. Paul, MN: Office for Social Justice.

West, G. (1999). The Bible and the poor: A new way of doing theology. In C. Rowland (Ed.), *The Cambridge companion to liberation theology* (pp. 129–52). Cambridge, UK: Cambridge University Press.

CITIZENS' RIGHTS

Citizens' Rights in a Globalized World

GLOBALIZATION AND CITIZENSHIP Globalization challenges definitions and rights of citizenship.

A citizen is defined as a member of a state to whom one owes allegiance to and is entitled to its protection, and a noncitizen is an individual who is not a national of a state in which he or she is present (United Nations, Article 1, 1985). In a globalized world, individuals move across national boundaries to live and work, calling into question previous definitions of citizenship, national identity, and citizens' rights (Gans, 2005). Immigration challenges definitions of citizenship. Who can be a citizen? What are the characteristics of a citizen? Is citizenship based on shared values, shared heritage, and/or shared country of origin or residence? These challenging questions emerge as immigration rates increase and globalization continues.

UNIVERSAL DECLARATION OF HUMAN RIGHTS In 1948, forty-eight countries, including the United States, signed the Universal Declaration of Human Rights (UDHR), outlining the fundamental freedoms and inalienable protections for all citizens of signing nations. Thirty articles comprise the UDHR affirming the equality of humanity, equal protection under the law, fair wages, the right to participate in government, the right to education, the right to medical care, and freedom of religion. Each country signing the UDHR agreed to uphold the principles in the charter for its citizens (United Nations, 1948). Social justice movements commonly cite the UDHR in their fight to increase freedoms and protections for all individuals, regardless of citizenship status. In commemoration of the signing of the UDHR, December 10 is declared worldwide Human Rights Day.

RIGHTS AND RESPONSIBILITIES OF CITIZENS Specific rights granted to citizens of one nation are not necessarily the same rights granted to a citizen of another nation. Citizens' rights fall along a continuum, with the most rights granted to citizens of liberal democracies and the least amount of rights granted to citizens of dictatorships (Gans, 2005). In the United States, the government differentiates between the rights of citizens and the responsibilities of citizens. Citizens' rights include the rights to freedom of expression, worship, fair trial, fair voting in elections, ability to run for office, ability to apply for federal employment requiring U.S. citizenship, and the freedom to pursue "life, liberty and the pursuit of happiness." Responsibilities of U.S.

citizens include the responsibility to support and defend the Constitution, to participate in democracy, obey laws, participate in community, pay taxes, serve on a jury, and defend the country if the need arises (United States Citizenship and Immigration Services, n.d.). Rights and responsibilities are commonly confused, as both are required and are privileges only for citizens of the United States.

Ultimately, the rights of a citizen are defined by country of citizenship. Living in a globalized world means that individuals are increasingly aware of the rights that they may or may not have relative to other nations. Today, citizens and noncitizens of numerous nations are united to demand their rights in struggles from access to health care and immigration reform to the ability to freely vote for elected officials.

Meredith A. Katz

References

Gans, J. (2005). *Citizenship in the context of globalization*. Retrieved from Udall Center for Studies in Public Policy, The University of Arizona, http://udallcenter.arizona.edu/immigration/publications/Citizenship%20and%20Globalization.pdf.

United Nations General Assembly. (1985). *Declaration on the human rights of individuals who are not nationals of the countries in which they live*. Retrieved from http://www.un.org/documents/ga/res/40/a40r144.htm.

United Nations. (1948). Universal declaration of human rights. Retrieved February 1, 2013, from http://www.un.org/en/documents/udhr/index.shtml.

United States Citizenship and Immigration Services. (n.d.). *Citizenship rights and responsibilities*. Retrieved from http://www.uscis.gov/portal/site/uscis/menuitem.749cabd81f5ffc8fba713d10526e0aa0/?vgnextoid=39d2df6bdd42a210VgnVCM100000b92ca60aRCRD&vgnextchannel=39d2df6bdd42a210VgnVCM100000b92ca60aRCRD.

CLASSISM

Classism is the systematic discrimination of poor and working classes, and it operates both at individual and institutional levels. Although there are various definitions of class, class status in the United States is generally designated by the following macro categories: poor/working poor, working class, lower middle class, middle class, professional class, upper class, and owning and ruling class (Sensoy & DiAngelo, 2012). *Class* is defined as "a relative social ranking based on income, wealth, education, status, and/or power" (Leondar-Wright & Yeskel, 2007). Class categories are not natural categories but have been shaped through the emergence of the modern global capitalist system and the ensuing economy of production and consumption. Capitalism is historical and emerged as an economic process distinct from prior economic systems such as feudalism. Classism should, therefore, be understood as a specifically modern phenomenon related to capitalism. Under capitalist production, owners of enterprises and corporations profit on the labor of the working class and poor who sell their labor to the capitalist owners. At a most fundamental level, then, class distinctions are relational to one another and cannot be understood without studying the relations between the rich and the poor, the owning class and the working class.

Classism functions both through individual prejudiced language and discriminatory actions, and at a broader level, through institutions and ideologies, cultural norms, beliefs, values, and practices, thus spanning micro to macro levels of society (Barone, 2008). In the analysis of classism, it is difficult to separate the individual and institutional realm because they are closely intertwined. Classism includes elitist attitudes toward the working class, where members of higher classes believe themselves to be innately superior in terms of economic standing and culture. This means that higher classes are perceived as more intelligent, deserving, more worthy of personal and economic success, more popular and more qualified (Barone, 2008). The tastes and values of the upper class are legitimated and posited as the highest in a given national culture. As a result, classist discrimination includes and is precluded by educational ideologies in which forms of knowledge and culture represent and validate higher classes and come to form the pedagogy, curriculum, and structure of the institution of schooling. The emphasis on higher-class knowledge in school subtly discriminates against poor and working-class students. Classism also includes workplace relations, where lower and working classes are mistreated, prevented from forming unions, prevented from participating in democratic decision making in the enterprise, and where wages are not raised to sustainable and equitable levels (Barone, 2008). Members of the lower classes can experience internalized classism and can harbor negative self-images toward themselves and discriminate against other working-class people (Leondar-Wright & Yeskel, 2007; Barone, 2008).

There are several conceptualizations of the enactment of classism. Leistyna (2009) explains that class status is enacted through three related domains: economic, political, and cultural. Economic classism is the process through which the rich have designed social institutions and processes to solidify class hierarchies and wealth inequalities. Political class refers to the oligarchic networks of rich families and corporate webs of relations that concentrate political and financial power. Cultural class pertains to the value attached to the lifestyles, education levels, and other cultural attributes of various classes.

Although Bourdieu (1984; 1986) does not use the term *classism*, he theorizes the ways upper classes maintain their class domination in society through the ways various forms of capital (social, economic, cultural, and symbolic) are enacted in different spheres or "fields" of life. Capital, according to Bourdieu, refers to the resources, abilities, and knowledge that people have available as social currencies that allow them to exert influence. Economic capital refers to wealth (cash and assets); social capital is the access to and knowledge of networks and social resources; cultural capital pertains to forms of knowledge and credentials highly valued in society; and symbolic capital consists of prestige and honor. The dominant classes not only use economic capital but also various forms of cultural, symbolic, and social capital in different combinations as a way to maintain their class position. For Bourdieu and Passeron (1977), culture is, therefore, at the center of the ways societal inequities reproduce themselves, and education is one of its most important engines. Schools privilege the knowledge of the upper class who have different combinations of cultural, social, and symbolic capital to navigate the institution of schooling to their advantage.

The importance of culture to the understanding of the ways class status reproduces itself is captured through the concept of hegemony. Hegemony, in the sense employed by the Marxist thinker Gramsci, refers to the ways economic domination is maintained, not through coercion and violence, but through the "soft," invisible power of culture. For Gramsci, the dominant classes exert intellectual, cultural, and moral leadership over working classes. One example of the working of hegemony in the United States is in the ideology of meritocracy, or the idea that if an individual works hard enough, he or she can be successful. While this idea has been shown to be a myth, the popular belief allows the underlying institutional and structural factors of classism and vast inequalities in wealth to go unnoticed (Leondar-Wright & Yeskel, 2007).

To understand classism, it is crucial to analyze how it is intertwined with other forms of oppression and privilege, such as racism, sexism, and ableism. Individuals' social class intersects with other social identities to intensify or mitigate the consequences of class-based identities. For example, the experience of a white male who has inherited capital and property from his family, in addition to holding a high-paying job, will be significantly different from the experience of a black female who has the same level of income. Here, race and gender come to nuance what might be considered similar class statuses, as it is widely documented in the United States that great wealth disparities exist between African American and whites, and that women are typically paid less than men for the same job with the same credentials (Sensoy & DiAngelo, 2012).

Elsa Wiehe

References

Barone, C. (2008). Bringing classism into the race and gender picture. In A. L. Ferber, C. Herrerra, & D. Samuels (Eds.), *Matrix reader: Examining the dynamics of oppression and privilege* (pp. 77–93). New York, NY: McGrawHill.

Bourdieu, P. (1984). *Distinction: A social critique of the judgement of taste.* Cambridge, MA: Harvard University Press.

Bourdieu, P. (1986). The forms of capital. In J. Richardson (Ed.), *Handbook of theory and research* for the sociology of education (pp. 241–58). New York: Greenwood Press.

Bourdieu, P., & Passeron, J.-C. (1977). *Reproduction in education, society, and culture.* Thousand Oaks, CA: Sage.

Leistyna, P. (2009). Exposing the ruling class in the United States using television and documentary film. *Radical Teacher, 85*, 12–15.

Leondar-Wright, B., & Yeskel, F. (2007). Classism curriculum design. In M. Adams, L. A. Bell, & P. Griffin (Eds.), *Teaching for diversity and social justice* (pp. 309–34). New York: Routledge.

Sensoy, O., & DiAngelo, R. (2012). *Is everyone really equal? An introduction to key concepts in social justice education.* New York: Teachers College Press.

CODE SWITCHING (LANGUAGE)

From a Chicana/Mexicana feminist perspective, code switching is a hybrid form of communication based on a variation of two languages (codes)—a fluid language switch or a back and forth between English and Spanish, for example. To code switch means to speak at least two languages fluently and yet be able to control a range of styles/rules/variations of each language—demonstrating a versatile use of these codes in creative and fluid forms. For Mexican Americans, for example, the use of two languages, English and Spanish, and their need to interact with these codes in places like the Southwest United States allows for this interaction and code switching to create a fluid alteration between the languages through their daily use and linguistic currency. The code switching, then, is an affirmation of language knowledge of the Mexican American/Chicana/o/Latina/o identity. This creative maintenance of languages also affirms bilingualism and bicultural identity for many U.S. Americans who can trace their ancestry to other countries. Chicana feminist Gloria Anzaldúa (2000) writes that code switching, in fact, is an act of resistance.

> My use of both languages, my code switching, is my way to resist being made into something else. . . . This resistance is part of the anticolonial struggle against both the Spanish colonizers and the white colonizers. . . . Chicanas [Chicanos] are using a language that is true to our experience, that is true to the places where we grew up—

New Mexico, Arizona, Texas the Midwest. To me it is a political choice, as well as an aesthetic choice. (Anzaldúa, 2000, p. 248)

Code switching is an act of resistance against hegemony—a way of maintaining language and ancestral, cultural, familial, communal ways of being and speaking in the United States. To code switch means that I can write and speak *en ingles* and Spanish without any *problemas*.

Judith Flores Carmona

Reference
Anzaldúa, G. E. (2000). *Interviews/entrevistas*, Ana-Louise Keating (Ed.). New York: Routledge.

COLORISM

Colorism: A Global Prejudice

Colorism is a form of prejudice occurring primarily among populations of the same race or ethnic identification in which significant variations in skin tone exist. This prejudice is institutionally directed toward those who are darker-skinned, although at the individual level, negative reactions can be directed toward those who are lighter-skinned as well. More broadly, colorism encompasses preferences and practices related to hair texture, eye color, eyelid structure, and nose size and shape, nearly always in the direction of enhancing a more Westernized appearance (Aydin, 2007; Russell-Cole, Wilson, & Hall, 2013). While skin color and feature discrimination are primarily a within-race phenomenon affecting populations of color, the harmful effects of colorism can be observed between races as well. For example, white employers preferring to hire lighter-skinned African American applicants over equally qualified darker-skinned ones is an expression of colorism (Harrison & Thomas, 2009). However, at least on a conscious level, most whites are largely unaware of the phenomenon of colorism as they tend to see skin of *any* color as an indicator of racial difference. While racism (i.e., discrimination between races) and colorism are sometimes conflated by those of European descent, the specific effects of colorism are very real and life limiting for many populations of color around the world. To understand colorism's global hold on billions of people, it is important to recognize the origins of colorism and its relationship to social status.

Anthropologists posit that skin color prejudice likely first emerged when human populations became less nomadic and more agrarian. From small villages to huge empires, owning property took on increasing significance, with the inevitable result that some individuals, usually self-proclaimed leaders, would hold more fertile ground than others. Those with the greatest amount of resources began to pay, or more likely to enslave, others to cultivate crops, tend livestock, and do other necessary tasks. The privilege of being able to outsource labor spared wealthier landowners from having to spend much time outside, which in turn slowed the tendency of their skin to darken due to sun exposure and age. Before long, having light skin became a highly visible and reliable signifier of social status (Van den Berghe & Frost, 1986).

Centuries later during the Age of Discovery (fifteenth to seventeenth century), the arrival of White Europeans in many regions of the world only fueled a preexisting valuation of lighter skin color. Through a lens of self-defined racial superiority, White Europeans noticed that the relatively lighter-skinned members of indigenous populations were also the leaders, and thus they concluded that their positions of influence were due to the presence of some "white blood," instead of lighter skin being an incidental consequence of their greater wealth (Russell-Cole et al., 2013).

In the American colonies, colorism was similarly fueled by the English settlers' false assumption that having some "white blood" was beneficial to those of African descent. In the Antebellum South, slave owners allocated slave chores on the basis of skin color. Those with the lighter skin color—quite possibly descendants of the owner himself—were assigned the slightly more preferable tasks in the master's residence. As a consequence of being indoors most days, these slaves were not only more exposed to European customs, but also less exposed to the sun, thereby permitting their skin to maintain its relative lightness. In contrast, darker-skinned slaves were sent to farm the crops or perform other forms of grueling manual labor. As a result of being outdoors much of the time, their skin increasingly became darker. Before long, a preoccupation

with skin color developed in the slave cabins as the lighter-skinned slaves, some of whom also were taught to read, began socially segregating themselves from the field hands (Akbar, 1984).

Skin color took on even greater significance among populations of free "mulattoes," as their relative lightness signified not only their own proclaimed superiority among other "Negroes" but also when necessary as potential proof of their free status. Following emancipation, the lighter-skinned blacks or "mulatto elite" strived to make clear that they were different from the masses of generally darker-skinned and recently freed "Negroes." They established their own churches, social clubs, schools, and business organizations, all of which required the passing of certain tests related to skin color and/or hair texture. Before one could be admitted into this elite society, the applicant's skin color had to be lighter than a brown paper bag and their hair had to pass through a fine-tooth comb without snagging. To maintain their separate social status, the mulatto elite sought to marry only those with equally light skin, or preferably even lighter than their own color. This singular preoccupation with skin color across successive generations is largely responsible for much of the colorism still in existence in the black community today (Frazier, 1962; Williamson, 1980). It should be noted that the color preoccupation was further fueled by a law adopted by the English colonists, which defined a person's racial identity according to whether there existed even "one drop" of "black blood" in a person's ancestral background (Davis, 1991). This law had the effect of grouping together a large population of people with widely varying skin tones.

Colorism is surely a global phenomenon, but much of the empirical research on its insidious effects has been conducted in the United States. Thus, while certain findings can technically generalize only to a U.S. population, similar outcomes would no doubt be found elsewhere, as well. For example, in looking at income inequalities, data from the Multi-City Study of Urban Inequality Survey confirm that there is a gap in earning power that widens as skin color darkens, whether that be between light- and dark-skinned African Americans or between whites and African Americans (Bobo et al., 2000). Similarly, the 2003 New Immigrant

Survey found that even when a multitude of factors (e.g., country of origin, education level, English-language proficiency) are held constant, those with the lightest skin color will eventually earn an average of 17 percent more than those immigrants of a darker complexion. In short, research informs us that skin color matters in the same vein as other socioeconomic factors (Jasso, Massey, Rosenzweig, & Smith, 2003). Throughout Latin and Central America, Asia, the Middle East, and even parts of Africa, those with the lightest skin color have assumed positions of authority at the highest levels of government and grabbed the largest shares of land and wealth, while those with the darkest skin color have progressively sunk to the bottom of the social strata (Telles, 2009).

Alongside earning potential, electoral outcomes and the judicial system have also fallen prey to the effects of colorism. In campaigns, for instance, the lighter skinned of two African American candidates has a better chance of winning the election (Terkildsen, 1993). What's more, colorism also has the power to distort our perceptions of candidates. A 2009 study found that in the 2008 presidential election, those who were planning to vote for Obama saw him as lighter skinned than he actually is, while those intending to vote for McCain actually perceived Obama as darker skinned than he actually is (Caruso, Mead, & Balcetis, 2009). In the criminal justice system, lighter-skinned black male defendants have a better chance of winning a not-guilty verdict than those who are darker skinned for the same offenses. And if convicted, lighter-skinned defendants receive on average lighter sentencing than those who are darker skinned and have committed the exact same crime (Gyimah-Brempong & Price, 2006; Hochschild & Weaver, 2007; Levinson & Young, 2010).

The negative effects of colorism can extend beyond politics into domestic circles. Large variations in skin color among family relatives can occasionally cause strife (Boyd-Franklin, 1989). A relatively lighter-skinned daughter from a financially struggling family may find it easier than her darker-skinned sisters to raise her socioeconomic status (Hunter, 2002). It is not unheard of for relatively darker-skinned children to be warned by familial elders to marry someone light skinned or else they will be disinherited. And to stop the taunting, dark-skinned teenage girls, especially those with lighter-skinned mothers and sisters, have confessed to getting themselves pregnant by a light-skinned boy, perhaps one who is Latino, in the hope that a light-skinned baby will redeem them in the eyes of others (Russell, Wilson, & Hall, 1992).

In foreign orphanages where babies of varying skin color are available for adoption, the lighter-skinned ones are typically selected first by the local citizens who suffer from infertility. The relatively darker-skinned babies are left behind for other countries to have. And within the United States, when white couples transracially adopt, or when black couples, regardless of their own skin color, intraracially adopt, again it is the lighter-skinned babies who are nearly always chosen first (Birmingham, 1977). Even at fertility clinics catering to African American clientele, donors are advertised to be light skinned, and that particular pitch is irrationally emphasized even more so when discussing the egg versus sperm donors—as if the greater societal emphasis on a woman's light skin will somehow tilt the scales for a particular biological outcome (Pray, 2008).

Findings by social scientists reveal that light skin is viewed as a signifier of beauty, attractiveness, and success. Skin color is a commodity to be traded on the interpersonal marketplace. More than a few dark-skinned men who become financially successful will use their newfound wealth to pursue lighter-skinned women, sometimes even divorcing a darker-skinned wife to do so (Ross, 1997). It has been said that an African American woman with light skin and "good" hair is the racial equivalent of the "blond hair and blue eyes" ideal sought by many white men.

Colorism can be found in all forms of visual media (Russell-Cole, Wilson, & Hall, 2013). Lighter-skinned women are overwhelming preferred as the love interest or video vixens in music videos, especially those featuring black male hip-hop artists. Lighter-skinned black models are chosen at a higher rate for the bread-and-butter (i.e., everyday commercial products) modeling jobs compared to models who are darker skinned (Russell-Cole, Wilson, & Hall, 2013). And when a black female celebrity of any type is featured on the cover of just about any magazine, she is routinely Photoshopped© to appear lighter. Even in South America, it has been observed that lighter-skinned women, some of whom also have blond hair, are nearly always the ones featured as stars of TV soaps and anchors of broadcast news outlets.

The social and economic burdens of colorism have led many darker-skinned individuals, especially women who are always judged more on their appearance, to seek out costly and potentially harmful products and procedures that claim to lighten appearance. One popular means for achieving a lighter look is through the use of skin-bleaching products. Despite often containing harsh chemicals and carcinogens, bleaching creams are scooped off the shelves every day by billions of women, especially in Asian countries such as India, Indonesia, China, and South Korea (Pitman, 2009). In fact, just about any product or procedure (e.g., laser resurfacing) that promises to lighten skin color, or Westernize facial features (e.g., double-eyelid surgery, nose jobs, etc.), will be profitable wherever color classism is found (Russell-Cole et al., 2013). For example, rates of plastic surgery, much of it double eyelid, are soaring in East Asia (McCurdy & Lam, 2005), and there is growing use of skin lighteners in Africa, along with a burgeoning interest in hair-straightening products (Arthur, 2009). In Jamaica, male celebrities such as Sammy Sosa and reggae musician Vybz Kartel have touted the use of Cake Soap, a popular skin-bleaching product that invites male usage (Hope, 2011).

In conclusion, it is critical to improve our understanding of colorism, as this kind of prejudice can result in devastating effects. One indicator of growing awareness is the rising number of workplace color discrimination charges being filed under Title VII of the 1964 Civil Rights Act (EEOC, n.d.). However, the conversation is partly hindered by the fact that mainstream media rarely analyze news events, especially in the United States, through a lens of color independent of race. Consider, for instance, how most whites saw Barack Obama as an African American rather than a dark-skinned man. Or consider what caused George Zimmerman, a light-brown-skinned Latino man, to pursue and kill Trayvon Martin, an innocent, medium-brown-skinned African American teenager—would Zimmerman have reacted as violently as he did if he and Martin had possessed similar skin color? To be clear, colorism does shade into racism, and the two are often deeply intertwined, but colorism can, and often does, exert its own socioeconomic and affect-laden consequences that are uniquely challenging and often difficult to address and resolve.

Midge Wilson
Or'Shaundra Benson

References

Akbar, N. (1984). *Chains and images of psychological slavery*. Jersey City, NJ: New Mind Productions.

Arthur, S. (2009). Dying to be white. *JENdA: A Journal of Culture and African Women Studies*, 14.

Aydin, C. (2007). *The politics of anti-Westernism in Asia: Visions of world order in pan-Islamic and pan-Asian thought*. New York: Columbia University Press.

Birmingham, S. (1977). *Certain people*. Boston: Little Brown.

Bobo, L., Johnson, J., Oliver, M., Farley, R., Bluestone, B., Browne, I., . . . Tilly, C. (2000). Multi-city study of urban inequality, 1992–1994: Atlanta, Boston, Detroit, and Los Angeles. *Ann Arbor, MI: Inter-university Consortium for Political and Social Research*. doi:10.3886/ICPSR02535.v3

Boyd-Franklin, N. (1989). *Black families in therapy: A multisystems approach*. New York: Guilford Press.

Caruso, E. M., Mead, N. L., & Balcetis, E. (2009). Political partisanship influences perception of biracial candidates' skin tone. *Proceedings of the National Academy of Sciences, 106*(4), 20168–73.

Clayson, D. & Maughan, M. (1986). Redheads and blonds: Stereotypic images. *Psychological Reports, 59*, 811–16.

Davis, F. J. (1991). *Who is black? One nation's definition*. University Park: Pennsylvania State University Press.

Equal Employment Opportunity Commission (EEOC). (n.d.). *Data on skin color claims*. Retrieved from http://www.eeoc.gov/eeoc/initiatives/e-race/caselist.cfm#color.

Frazier, E. F. (1962). *Black bourgeoisie*. New York: Collier.

Gyimah-Brempong, K. & Price, G. N. (2006). Crime and punishment: And skin hue too? *American Economic Review, 96*(2), 246–50.

Harrison, M. S. & Thomas, K. M. (2009). The hidden prejudice in selection: A research investigation on skin color bias. *Journal of Applied Social Psychology*, *39*(1), 134–68.

Hochschild, J. L. & Weaver, V. (2007). The skin color paradox and the American racial order. *Social Forces*, *86*(2), 643–70.

Hope, D. P. (2011). From browning to Cake Soap: Popular debates on skin bleaching in the Jamaican dancehall. *Journal of Pan African Studies*, *4*, 165–94.

Hunter, M. (2002). "If you're light you're alright": Light skin color as social capital for women of color. *Gender and Society*, *16*, 175–93.

Jasso, G., Massey, D. S., Rosenzweig, M. R., & Smith, J. P. (2003). The new immigrant survey in the U.S.: The experience over time. *Migration Information Source*. Washington, DC: Migration Policy Institute.

Levinson, J. D. & Young, D. (2010). Different shades of bias: Skin tone, implicit racial bias, and judgments of ambiguous evidence. *West Virginia Law Review*, *112*, 307–50.

McCurdy, J. & Lam, S. (2005). *Cosmetic surgery of the Asian face* (2nd ed.). New York: Thieme.

Pitman, S. (2009). *In-Cosmetics Asia focuses on skin lightening trend*. Retrieved from http://www.cosmeticsdesign-asia.com/Market-Trends/In-Cosmetics-Asia-focuses-on-skin-lightening-trend.

Pray, L. A. (2008). Embryo screening and the ethics of human genetic engineering. *Nature Education*, *1*(1), 207.

Ross, L. (1997). Mate selection preferences among African American college students. *Journal of Black Studies*, *27*, 554–69.

Russell, K., Wilson, M., & Hall, R. (1992). *The color complex*. New York: Anchor Books.

Russell-Cole, K., Wilson, M., & Hall, R. (2013). *The color complex (revised): The politics of skin color in a new millennium*. New York: Random House Digital, Inc.

Telles, E. (2009). The social consequences of skin color in Brazil. In E. N. Glenn (Ed.), *Shades of difference: Why skin color matters* (pp. 9–24). Redwood, CA: Stanford University Press.

Terkildsen, N. (1993). When white voters evaluate black candidates: The processing implications of candidate skin color, prejudice, and self-monitoring. *American Journal of Political Science*, *37*, 1032–53.

Van den Berghe, P. L., & Frost, P. (1986). Skin color preference, sexual dimorphism and sexual selection: A case of gene culture co-evolution? *Ethnic and Racial Studies*, *9*(1), 87–113.

Williamson, J. (1980). *New people: Miscegenation and mulattoes in the United States*. New York: Free Press.

COMMUNITY CONTROL

Community control refers broadly to the ideological vision and struggle of black empowerment activists to control the economic, educational, and political institutions in black, inner-city communities. This was a precept of Malcolm X, which gained traction during the Black Power era, 1965 to 1976. A more focused definition of community control refers specifically to the black urban initiative for educational empowerment, which was implemented in 1967 in New York City school districts in Brooklyn and Harlem. Community control of schools involved the governance of local school districts by community school boards largely composed of parent representatives and community activists.

The movement for community control of schools in New York City was closely aligned with an experimental school decentralization program piloted in 1967. Decentralization involved a shift of decision-making powers, such as curriculum design, from the central administrative office of the New York Board of Education (BOE) to administrators at the district level. This experiment in local governance of education was initially sanctioned by the office of Mayor John V. Lindsay, funded by the Ford Foundation, and backed by the teacher's union, the United Federation of Teachers (UFT). The experiment was in response to agitation by a black teachers' caucus, the African-American Teachers Association (ATA), for the community control of schools in predominantly black neighborhoods such as Harlem and Ocean Hill-Brownsville in Brooklyn, schools that the ATA claimed failed to provide black children with an adequate education because they were deeply entrenched in racism. The ATA—spearheaded by the imposing 6′8″ Les Campbell, who was popularly known by his adopted Swahili name Jitu Weusi meaning "Big Black"—pressed for the right to design curricula that were oriented toward a system of "black values" (i.e., in contemporary parlance, Afrocentric curricula).

The uproar of the ATA and community activists pressured the New York state legislature to commission the Ford Foundation to design a way for parents to partner with educators. A committee headed by McGeorge Bundy, president of the Ford Foundation, issued the report proposing decentralization as a path to a solution of this urban school crisis.

The report, titled *Reconnection to Learning* but better known as the Bundy Report, had both its proponents and its critics from the very beginning. The critics blatantly stated, among other objections, that decentralization would stymie efforts at integration and balkanize the school system resulting in disparate curricula; that ghetto parents were incompetent to deal with educational issues; and that the schools would be turned over to the control of vigilantes and racists. However, the power of Albany (i.e., the seat of New York state government), the mayor's office, and the Ford Foundation pushed the decentralization experiment forward. The detractors were not placated and their wounds would fester, but for a while their voices were marginalized and muted. Proponents of the plan carried the day.

At the outset, decentralization was viewed as desirable by both the community control advocates and the UFT. The UFT members were on board because the BOE's central administration had become notorious for its ossified and cumbersome bureaucracy, a stony, impersonal labyrinth appropriately referred to by the address of the building that housed it, "110 Livingston Street." They were not only unresponsive to the needs of the communities, they were also unresponsive to the needs of rank-and-file teachers. Thus, the UFT initially gave support to an experiment designed to make schools accountable to communities, particularly communities of color. The experiment was launched in three trial districts with predominantly black and/or Latino populations: the Ocean Hill-Brownsville district in Brooklyn, the IS 201 district in East Harlem, and the Two Bridges district in Manhattan's Lower East Side. If the pilot program succeeded, a blueprint for more widespread decentralization—involving thirty to sixty school districts—was to be implemented by the start of the 1969 to 1970 school year.

Eventually, however, as the experiment progressed, tensions built up between these pilot black and Latino community school boards and the largely Jewish UFT, ultimately provoking a backlash of resistance against community control from the UFT that culminated in the infamous Ocean Hill-Brownsville Teachers' Strike of 1968—a strike that paralyzed the school system and polarized the city.

Inherent in the conflict that emerged between community school boards and the UFT were the differences between community control and decentralization. For community control advocates, community control was simply one of the possible variations of decentralization. Opponents of community control insisted that the community control and decentralization were so distinct that they should not be conflated or confused. In the standard model of school decentralization, governance is handed to professional educational administrators at the local level, such as superintendents, principals, or assistant principals. In the community control model of decentralization, governance is handed to nonprofessionals—community school boards largely composed of parents and community activists—although professional educators—teachers, not necessarily administrators—may also be involved. Community control also differs from the standard model of decentralization because the demand for community control was essentially rooted in the Black Power movement. Mass media–induced white fears of militant Black Power advocates formed the basis of the early critics' charge that the schools would be turned over to vigilantes and racists. Though vilified by the media, empowerment activists essentially argued justly and reasonably that America was not really a "melting pot" but a pluralistic society in which ethnic bloc politics were central in public affairs. In short, they contended that community control existed in fact, if not in name, in all ethnic enclaves in America except in black communities, where outsiders controlled all of the community institutions. Both Malcolm X and Martin Luther King Jr. had observed that the ghetto was like a colony: a community controlled by outsiders, rather than an ethnic enclave where the institutions are controlled by its own residents.

Despite these theoretical differences between decentralized school boards and community-controlled school boards, in practice the actual school board that was implemented in the Ocean Hill-Brownsville district was racially integrated and consisted of twenty-four members: eight parents and eight teachers elected from each of the district's eight schools, five community representatives chosen by the parents, two representatives of the school supervisors in the district, and one representative from academia chosen by the board as a whole (a balance of thirteen community members and eleven professional educators). The board was chaired by Reverend Herbert Oliver, a well-respected neighborhood pastor. Rhody McCoy, a former acting principal for a special school for boys, was chosen as the unit administrator for the Ocean Hill-Brownsville district, and he reported to this community school board.

The UFT embraced the community initiatives, such as the introduction of multicultural content (African, African American, and Latino), into the curricula. But they came to loggerheads with the community school board over the issue of involuntary teacher transfers. The community school board voted to transfer thirteen teachers and six principals out of the Ocean Hill-Brownsville district ostensibly because of poor performance, though their adamant opposition to community control was also a factor. They were viewed by the board members as recalcitrant troublemakers who were undermining and sabotaging the decentralization experiment, thereby threatening its viability.

The UFT charged that the nineteen individuals were being railroaded because of their vocal opposition to community control and contended that their freedom of speech was being abridged. Led by the UFT president Albert Shanker and field representative Sandra Feldman, the teacher's union challenged the transfers, demanding due process hearings for the teachers. It was not customary for the UFT to challenge transfers since transfers were merely reassignments to other schools that did not involve any financial or professional penalties and were routine across the school system. In challenging routine transfers, the UFT had challenged the community school board's right to govern.

Drawing a line in the sand, the community school board contended that they had full authority to transfer teachers and administrators and refused to readmit them as the UFT demanded. This action resulted in a walkout by 350 UFT members in the Ocean Hill-Brownsville district in support of the dismissed teachers and administrators. By September, the beginning of the 1969 school year, the UFT called a general teacher's strike in support of the nineteen dismissed educators, shutting down the entire New York City school system for two months and adversely affecting one million students.

However, many young, idealistic, and dedicated teachers, black and white, who were committed to quality education and had been drawn to the community control experiment, crossed picket lines in the Ocean Hill-Brownsville and East Harlem districts and held regular classes in defiance of the strike. They faced angry opposition from UFT members who charged that they were scabs. The very heavy police presence and barricades around the schools separating striking UFT members from procommunity control educators, parents, schoolchildren, and community members (including the vociferous Abubadika Sonny Carson, the executive director of Brooklyn CORE) created the atmosphere of an armed encampment. The pitched racial battles for community control in the North eerily resembled the battles for school desegregation in the South.

By October, the UFT strike, and charges of black community anti-Semitism, pressured Superintendent of Schools Bernard Donovan, the BOE's chief administrator, to suspend the Ocean Hill-Brownsville Community School Board and end the decentralization experiment for all three districts. Donovan also fired Rhody McCoy when McCoy insisted that he would follow the mandate of the community school board rather than 110 Livingston Street. These actions sparked citywide protests in black and Latino neighborhoods in support of community control, including a massive march to, and demonstration in front of, 110 Livingston Street.

Community control politics had been placed on trial and had been effectively defeated by the UFT. The aftermath of the failed community control experiment was a markedly changed political landscape in New York City. Relations between blacks and Jews, who had been allies in the civil rights movement, were now irreparably damaged. The black community, however, became more unified than ever, as a broad spectrum of civil rights and Black Power organizations had joined together in support of community control. Black and Latino coalitions were also forged as the two communities joined forces to fight for community control. The black educators in the ATA left the public school system to create alternative African-centered private schools.

The struggle for community control of public education was accompanied by a vision for community control of other significant institutions within inner-city communities (e.g., renewed struggles for a Civilian Complaint Review Board that would have oversight of police activity, and the creation of Community Development Corporations that would grant poor neighborhoods some measure of control over economic development and the development of affordable housing). The establishment of food cooperatives in the inner city was another example of community control—control of economics, nutrition, and consumer choice. Community control/black empowerment activists were also concerned with winning elected seats in local municipal governments. This resulted in the transformation of the racial and ethnic composition of the New York City Council, the legislative body of New York City, from a predominantly white membership to a membership predominately of people of color, thus representing the actual demographics of the city. Finally, when faced with a defeat in the struggle to control existing political, economic, or educational institutions in their communities, black empowerment activists were determined to exert community control by developing new and alternative institutions. These new alternative institutions (e.g., the Uhuru Sasa Shule—Swahili for "Freedom Now School") and a national organization to foster them, the Council of Independent Black Institutions (CIBI), both the brainchildren of the renowned Jitu Weusi, sprung up phoenix like from the ashes of the Ocean Hill-Brownsville experiment.

Yusuf Nuruddin

References

Fantini, M., Gittell, M., & Magat, R. (1970). *Community control and the urban school.* New York: Praeger Publishers.

Hampton, H. (Executive Producer). (1990). *Power!* (Video documentary episode). In H. Hampton (Executive Producer), *Eyes on the prize II: America at the racial crossroads.* United States: Public Broadcasting Service.

Nuruddin, Y. (2007). Ocean Hill-Brownsville teachers' strike. In G. L. Anderson & K. G. Herr (Eds.), *Encyclopedia of activism and social justice* (vol. 3, pp. 1051–53). Thousand Oaks, CA: SAGE Publications.

Nuruddin, Y. (2009). Black nationalists. In M. Ezra (Ed.), *Civil rights movement: People and perspectives* (pp. 99–120). Santa Barbara, CA: ABC-CLIO.

Van DeBurg, W. L. (1993). *New day in Babylon: The Black Power Movement and American culture, 1965–1975.* Chicago: University of Chicago Press.

CONCRETE CEILING

Most are relatively familiar with the sociopolitical phrase *glass ceiling* used to explain perceived barriers that prevent or limit women and persons of color from senior-level advancement within corporate contexts, regardless of their qualifications and achievements. However, for women of color, African American women in particular, the combination of sexism coupled with racism creates a more complex dynamic that can be understood as a *concrete ceiling* not experienced by white women or African American males (Eagly & Carli, 2007). While the glass ceiling and concrete ceiling are synonymous in that they both represent barriers for career advancement among women, they are markedly different in that the glass ceiling is transparent and can be shattered with enough force. Although limited, at the very least, white women can view opportunities, role models, and possibilities for advancement through this glass ceiling. In contrast, the concrete ceiling describes a perceived, impervious barrier ("concrete") through which qualified African American women are not provided access, opportunity, or consideration for advancement ("ceiling"). In essence, African American women cannot so much as "see" advancement opportunities, let alone attempt to shatter the ceiling with any reasonable amount of force. Therefore, African American women must act as their own advocate and supporter to obtain and garner insight on potential advancement opportunities. These experiences for African American women cultivate a need whereby they are compelled to work harder than their white counterparts in order to prove self-worth and value as well as maintain high personal and professional standards (Bloom & Erlandson, 2003).

The experiences resulting in both the glass ceiling and concrete ceiling are literally and figuratively debilitating. In contrast, with enough force or pressure, glass (glass ceiling) can shatter, resulting in wounds from the gashes. However, the extent of injuries would not be comparable to the crippling effects sustained while attempting to break through concrete (Love & Thomas, 2013). The double-blind syndrome of racism and sexism subjects African American women to a covert form of marginalization not experienced by white women or African American males (Stanley, 2006). Researchers have shown that African American women who perceive a "concrete ceiling" tend to experience not only a lack of advancement but also other adverse outcomes such as work dissatisfaction, loneliness, devaluation, and overall emotional distress (Love & Thomas, 2013). In one study, women executives of color were found to suffer from distrust, uncomfortable interactions, and were excluded from upper management networks, which are primarily composed of white males (Lott, 2006). Another study revealed this similar occurrence was a common practice among African American women in higher education (Love & Thomas, 2013). Of those who were in senior-level positions, many reported sacrificing valued family time as well as a "life" outside of their work, discrimination, and extreme stress. In fact, African American women hold less than 1 percent of corporate officer positions at the five hundred largest publicly traded companies in the United States (Lott, 2006). Likewise, reports indicate a bleaker picture when one examines African American women in higher-education, upper-level administrative positions. For example, women of color only made up 10.6 percent of professors in full-time administrative positions in 2007, which remains a serious underrepresentation compared with white women and males in presidential, chancellor, provosts, and other executive faculty positions (American Council on Education, 2010).

Career advancement for women of color, specifically African American women, remains a strong research agenda in both the private and public sectors of the workforce (King, 2003). Theoretical groundwork has been forged supporting the notion that inequality (e.g., gender inequality, feminism, and leadership theories) in advancement exists between genders, with the workforce as the primary perpetrator. Irby and Brown (1995) argued for a need for more profound theories that attend to the realities and experiences of women accounting for their unique identities, cultural context, and experiences in a variety of organizational and institutional settings. Grogan (1999) further pointed out gender inequities in traditional leadership theories, noting the lack of women's lived experiences, and proposed that new theoretical frameworks are necessary to explain the depth and understanding of social justice issues. Thus, findings examining the concrete ceiling maintain theoretical underpinnings within sociocultural perspectives (i.e., social dominance theory and critical race theory) that consider race, gender, and social class in analyzing power dynamics within bureaucratic and other systems, where power can be used to oppress (Merriam, Caffarella, & Baumgartner, 1999). For example, within social dominance theory (SDT), people support the inequalities to keep the majority group in positions of power while oppressing the marginalized group (Sidanius, Pratto, Van Laar, & Levin, 2004; Love & Thomas, 2013). In addition, critical race theory (CRT) (Bell, 1995; Delgado & Stefancic, 1993; Ladson-Billings & Tate, 1995) examines the inequities existing in organizations to promote social change within organizational contexts. Specifically, CRT speaks from critical race-gender orientations that embrace qualitative approaches to unveil the unique experiences of African American women (Bernal, 2002).

While in the budding stages of the concrete-ceiling view, Love and Thomas (2013) have distinguished the notion beyond corporate contexts with empirical findings and continue further investigation among African American women within all organizational contexts to support their psychological and overall wellness. Such research is necessary as overall health disparities show that health-related stressors including heart disease, diabetes, and hypertension remain most prevalent among African American women (U.S. Census Bureau, 2011). As such, psychological distress resulting from the concrete ceiling negatively exacerbates physical wellness, impacting overall wellness among African American women. Furthermore, lack of attention to the concrete ceiling thwarts institutional efforts toward equity and diversity in organizational institutions and the workforce (Love & Thomas, 2013).

Deneia M. Thomas
Keisha M. Love

References

American Council on Education. (2010). *Gender equity in higher education*. ACE Center for Policy Analysis. Washington, DC.

Bell, D. (1995). Who's afraid of critical race theory? *University of Illinois Law Review*, 1995(4), 893–910.

Bell, E. L. & Nkomo, S. (1992). *The glass ceiling vs. the concrete wall: Career perceptions of white and African American women managers*. In A. P. Sloan School of Management, Working Paper No. 3470-92:52.

Bernal, D. (2002). Critical race theory, Latino critical theory, and critical raced-gendered epistemologies: Recognizing students of color as holders and creators of knowledge. *Qualitative Inquiry*, 8(1), 105–26.

Bloom, C. M. and Erlandson, D. A. (2003). African American women principals in urban schools: Realities, (re)constructions, and resolutions. *Educational Administration Quarterly*, 39(3), 339–69.

Cook, S. G. (2012, April). For black women administrators, merit is not enough. *Women in Higher Education*, 21(4), 13–14.

Delgado, R. & Stefancic, J. (1993). Critical race theory: An annotated bibliography. *Virginia Law Review*, 79(2), 461–516.

Eagly, A. H. & Carli, L. L. (2007). Women and the labyrinth of leadership. *Harvard. Business Review*.

Grogan, M. (1999). Equity/equality issues of gender, race and class. *Educational Administration Quarterly*, 35(4), 518–36.

Irby, B. J. & Brown, G. (1995, April). *Constructing a feminist-inclusive theory of leadership*. Paper presented at the Annual Meeting of the American Educational Research Association, San Francisco, California.

King, K. R. (2003). Do you see what I see? Effects of group consciousness on African American women's attributions to prejudice. *Psychology of Women Quarterly*, 27(1), 17–30.

Ladson-Billings, G. & Tate, W. F. (1995). Toward a critical race theory of education. *Teachers College Record*, 97(1), 47–68.

Lott, J. (2006). Racial identity and black students' perceptions of civic skills. *Race, Gender & Class*, 13(3–4), 239–54.

Love, K. M. & Thomas, D. M. (2013). The concrete ceiling: An exploration of African American women in higher education. Submitted to the *Journal of Diversity in Higher Education*.

Merriam, S. B. & Caffarella, R. S., & Baumgartner, L. M. (1999). *Learning in adulthood*. San Francisco: Jossey-Bass.

Sidanius, J., Pratto, F., van Laar, C., & Levin, S. (2004). Social dominance theory: Its agenda and method. *Political Psychology*, 25(6), 845–80.

Stanley, C. A. (Ed.). (2006). *Faculty of color: Teaching in predominantly white organizations*. Boston, MA: Anker Publishing Co.

U.S. Census Bureau. (2011). Census briefs. *The Black Population 2010*.

U.S. Department of Labor, Bureau of Labor Statistics. (2011). *Highlights of women's earnings in 2010*.

CONFUCIANISM

Confucianism is a complex religious, philosophical, and ethical system that originated over 2,500 years ago during the long Zhou dynasty (c. 104–221 BCE) in China but has since spread to Taiwan, Korea, Japan, Singapore, and parts of North America. This multifaceted system of thought is based on the teachings of its founder, Confucius (c. 551–479 BCE), also known by his more reverential title of Kongfuzi or Master Kong and *xianshi*, meaning "the first teacher." Confucius was born in the ancient state of Lu in the northeastern region of modern China. In his early years, Confucius shared his time between working in low-ranking government positions and teaching students. In his later years, Confucius was appointed to the position of minister of crime of Lu, but he shortly resigned from this mid-ranking bureaucratic position. After his resignation, Confucius attempted to offer advice to political leaders, but when his attempts were rebuffed he resumed his teaching career until his death.

The principal sayings and teachings of Confucius are contained in the *Lunyu* or *Analects* compiled several years after his death. The *Analects* provide the image of the *Tao* or the Way in order to express the importance of living a proper life. One of the most important concepts expressed in the *Analects* and in Confucianism in general is the notion of *xiao*, or filial piety. The importance of filial piety is based on the idea that if one is respectful to one's parents, one will practice this virtuous behavior in society. The concept of filial piety can be expressed in what is known as the Five Relationships—namely, between parent and child, husband and wife, sibling and sibling, friend and friend, and ruler and subject. In addition to filial piety, Confucianism stresses the importance of virtuous behavior, with both *nei* or inner and *wai* or outer virtues. The inner virtue of *ren* or *jen*, loosely translated as *humaneness*, is one of the most prominent inner virtues. This central virtue could be exemplified by practicing various forms of *li* or rituals that range from proper manners and decorum to correct ritualistic and religious practices. The practice of both *ren* and *li* are necessary if one hopes to exemplify the most important virtue in Confucianism.

The virtue of harmony or *he* is not only the pre-eminent virtue in Confucianism but also a virtue that manages to exemplify the symbiotic relationship between the individual and the state. The individual citizen is required to cultivate harmony from within so as to ensure that the harmony exists within the state. The leaders of this ideal society, known as *junzi*, are expected to be exemplars of *te* or moral virtue in order to maintain harmony in the state. The teachings of Confucius were shortly expanded upon by other scholars that emerged years after Confucius's death, such as Mengzi or Mencius (c. 372–289 BCE), Xunzi (c. 310–220 BCE), and Dong Zhongshu (c. 179–104 BCE). However, a major development in Confucianism would not appear until the tenth common century with the birth of Neo-Confucianism.

The traditional teachings of Confucianism were soon complemented by the more metaphysical concerns of Neo-Confucianism. During the Song (c. 960–1279 CE) and Ming dynasties (c. 1368–1644), the two major schools of Neo-Confucianism emerged—namely, Zhu Xi's (c. 1130–1200 CE) School of Principle and Wang Yangming's (c. 1472–1529 CE) School of Mind. The School of Principle states that *qi* or matter is composed of an eternal life force known as the principle. The absolute principle is the Supreme Ultimate/Supreme Ultimate-less, a contradictory and complex abstraction. One of the major figures of the School of Mind, Wang Yangming, attempted to find the principle of an object, but achieved little success. Due to his failure, Wang's School of Mind stresses that it is only important to find the principle within one's own mind and heart. This task can be accomplished through a form of mediation or "quiet sitting." Despite the differentiation between the two schools, Confucianism remained a prominent feature of Chinese society.

Confucianism continued to play an important role throughout the Ming dynasty and into the subsequent Qing dynasty (c. 1644–1912 CE). Toward the end of the Qing dynasty, several imperial powers were successful in subjecting China to their demands. This subjugation produced a sense of bitterness among the Chinese population, resulting in the collapse of the Qing dynasty and the creation of a republic in 1911. The resentment toward Confucianism and its antiquated ideals and feudalistic outlook remained during the early republican period. In the aftermath of the Communist Revolution of 1949, Chairman Mao Zedong (1893–1976), along with his communist regime, condemned religion and officially embraced an atheistic outlook. This hostility toward religion reached a peak during the Cultural Revolution of 1966, which resulted in the destruction of countless religious temples and shrines throughout the country. In the past few decades, the People's Republic of China has become more accommodating toward Confucianism, particularly toward New Confucianism. In contrast to previous manifestations, New Confucianism attempts to reconcile modernity with the classical teachings of Confucius. This unification has not only attracted a host of scholars from within China and East Asia but has also led to the development of Confucianism in the West. In light of its ability to attract individuals from around the globe, it appears that Confucianism has managed to reassert itself even in the contemporary era.

John Cappucci

References

Chin, A. (2008). *Confucius: A life of thought and politics*. New Haven: Yale University Press.

Fingarette, H. (1972). *Confucius—The secular as sacred*. New York: Harper & Row Publishers.

Hart, M. H. (1978). *The 100: A ranking of the most influential persons in history*. New York: Galahad Books.

Littlejohn, R. L. (2011). *Confucianism: An introduction*. London: I. B. Tauris.

Oldstone-Moore, J. (2002). *Confucianism: Origins, beliefs, practices, holy texts, sacred places*. Oxford: Oxford University Press.

Rainey, L. D. (2010). *Confucius & Confucianism: The essentials*. Malden, MA: Wiley-Blackwell.

Simpkins, C. A. & Simpkins, A. (2000). *Simple Confucianism: A guide to living virtuously*. Boston: Tuttle Publishing.

Smith, D. H. (1973). *Confucius*. New York: Charles Scribner's Sons.

Sun, A. (2013). *Confucianism as a world religion: Contested histories and contemporary realities*. Princeton: Princeton University Press.

Thompson, L. G. (1989). *Chinese religion: An introduction* (4th ed.). Belmont, CA: Wadsworth Publishing Company.

Woo, T. T. (2010). Chinese and Korean traditions. In W. G. Oxtoby & R. C. Amore (Eds.), *World religions: Eastern traditions* (3rd ed., pp. 254–327). Don Mills, ON: Oxford University Press.

Yao, X. (2000). *An introduction to Confucianism*. Cambridge: Cambridge University Press.

Young, W. A. (2010). *The world's religions: Worldviews and contemporary issues* (3rd ed.). Upper Saddle River, NJ: Prentice Hall.

CONNECTIVE MARGINALITY

Connective Marginalities through Hip-Hop

Connective marginality is a theoretical construct that drives the global hip-hop underground movement linking loosely connected localized groups of street-oriented hip-hop practitioners (as opposed to mere consumers) and was first articulated in *The Africanist Aesthetic in Global Hip-Hop: Power Moves* (2007). Connective marginalities are geospatial resonances of social inequities across the globe that can manifest as four particular configurations internationally—youthful rebellion, class inequality, historical oppression, and culture—that often overlap in particular nations. Inherited social inequalities find fertile ground among today's youth, who often challenge their social and political contexts through popular culture rather than specific political movements. Hip-hop culture, as a youthful rebellious subculture in all nations throughout the globe through its very aesthetics developing from African American youth culture in the 1970s, instigates global connections between various peoples' local marginal status. For example, the Middle Eastern and North African uprisings starting in 2011, dubbed the Arab Spring, were largely generated through grassroots rappers articulating their class and youth marginal status in sites such as Tunisia, Libya, Bahrain, and Egypt.

Connective marginality, as a theoretical perspective beyond the obvious cultural hegemony of the American transnational pop culture industry, allows researchers to discern how hip-hop culture was initiated and then developed its various national styles among so many youth cultures in far-flung regions of the globe. In *The Africanist Aesthetic in Global Hip-Hop*, four global sites outside the United States—Russia, England, France, and Japan—and Hawaii within the United States, are compared and contrasted regarding their appropriation and adaptations of U.S. hip-hop culture, as well as their discrete perceptions about themselves in relation to blackness, which accompanies hip-hop's often commercialization as black thug culture. The global adoption of hip-hop culture over the last thirty years occurred in large part due to its adaptive connective marginality facilitated by youths' participation in international b-boy (breaking) conventions, sharing of rap lyrics and beats, connecting various crews through hip-hop e-zines, global social networking, and the bootlegging of hip-hop tracks via the Internet.

The global poor as the world's underclass is a uniting construct for hip-hop's protest voice, yet it is only one of four major connective marginalities that tend to bind the hip-hop generation internationally. Connections or resonances can take the form of culture (Jamaica, Brazil, and Cuba), class (North African Arabs in France), historical oppression (American Indians, Native Hawaiians, Palestinians on the West Bank), or simply the discursive construction of *youth* as a peripheral social status (Japan). Joe Austin and Michael Nevin Willard, editors of *Generation of Youth* (1998), remind us about the marginality of youth: the term *youth* can become "a metaphor for perceived social change and its projected consequences; as such it is an enduring locus for displaced social anxieties" (p. 1). Along these lines, black American rap *is* an in-your-face rebellious youth culture that challenges the adult status quo wherever it expresses itself on the globe. The generational youth dynamic of international hip-hop culture remains, even as its practitioners themselves grow older.

The conceptual geopolitical construct of connective marginalities, encompassing culture, class, historical oppression, and generation, can be understood more clearly through detailed critical analyses of specific international sites. The culture marginality is thoroughly explored in *The Hiplife in Ghana: West African Indigenization of Hip-Hop* (Palgrave Macmillan, 2012), in which African-based aesthetics within the world's high culture/low culture paradigm is investigated. These four marginalities of global hip-hop also offer insight into different ambivalent perspectives on the implications of race and how black American culture is perceived globally. The study of global links through hip-hop permits an overview of several approaches to the "glocalization" process, which mediates global and local exigencies resulting from the global (American hip-hop) colliding with particular local cultural priorities. Young people internationally, who often speak languages other than English and can't always understand American rap lyrics, decode and reinvent African American and Latino hip-hop culture emanating from urban United States. The adaptation phase of this process is facilitated by local artists' recognition of their social marginalities through the narrative of black Americans' historic marginal status in the United States.

Halifu Osumare

References

Austin, J. & Willard, M. N. (1998). Introduction: Angels of history, demons of culture. In J. Austin & M. N. Willard (Eds.), *Generations of youth: Youth cultures and history in twentieth-century America* (pp. 1–20). New York: New York University Press.

Osumare, H. (2007). *The Africanist aesthetic in global hip-hop: Power moves*. Basingstoke: Palgrave Macmillan.

Osumare, H. (2012). *The hiplife in Ghana: West African indigenization of hip-hop*. Basingstoke: Palgrave Macmillan.

CONSCIOUSNESS RAISING

Consciousness raising is a process by which one has their awareness of a particular issue increased, and thereby, the individual becomes more informed. It is not necessary for the one having their conscious raised to be aware of what is raising their consciousness and even the fact that their consciousness is being raised.

This process, as a form of social activism, has been widely used by grassroots organizations and special interest groups throughout the world. The logic behind consciousness-raising methodologies involves the theory that if the awareness of a critical mass of people is focused on a single issue, it will then draw the attention of institutions and larger organizations in order to influence policies, laws, and even societal norms. During the rise of the Nazi regime in Germany, Joseph Goebbels served as the Minister of Propaganda with the primary task of raising awareness of the German people about the cause of the Nazis and influencing them to acquiesce and support the injustices being dealt by the same.

Oftentimes, we see consciousness raising being attributed to special interest groups dealing with gender and sexuality issues (feminism and the LGBT community), or with animal rights organizations (PETA), health-related issues (breast cancer, addiction, AIDS), and groups advocating for ecological preservation causes (global warming, endangered species, pollution); however, rarely is this form of social activism equated to the actions of civil rights organizations and grassroots movements.

Many of the early civil rights organizations (SCLC, NAG, SNCC, NAACP, UNIA, Nation of Islam, Black Panther Party) all used a form of consciousness raising in order to spread their political ideology and to win supporters. The use of pamphlets, books, lectures, speeches, workshops, education programs, songs, public demonstrations, and protests are all examples of consciousness-raising tactics used by civil rights organizations in the 1960s and 1970s. The major issue being brought to light by the organizations via these tactics was that of racial justice, freedom and equality, and the abolishing of the system of racism and white supremacy.

In more modern times, technology, marketing, and media have increased and facilitated the efforts of consciousness raising. The ease that social media provides to today's activist has increased the extent of their efforts and magnified their local causes to the global stage. A properly placed consciousness-raising meme can become internationally viral in a matter of seconds, bringing attention from around the world to the local cause. This new technology helps to broaden the reach but may perhaps also spread it thin.

Jeff Menzise

COSMOPOLITAN
Community, People, and Boundaries
Originally derived from the Greek word *kosmopolitês* (the citizen of the world), the word *cosmopolitan* is a popular term used in moral, social, or political philosophy to signify that all people, regardless of differences of location, nationality, class, ethnicity, or gender, are members of a universal community. In such community, people are bounded by their ties as citizens of the world. Cosmopolitanism is the philosophy that envisages a type of world citizenry irrespective of political, cultural, economic, or legal boundaries. The source of the cosmopolitan goes back to the Roman Stoics. In ancient Greece, people were perceived as a citizen of the polis (Greek city-state). However, the Roman Stoics saw citizenship as a universal ideal of what human community should look like. They argued that all people share an element universally equalizing: reason. This bond bridging them together is not circumscribed by the borders of their political communities. In the eighteenth century, Immanuel Kant, the German Enlightenment philosopher, gave a moral foundation to the idea of the cosmopolitan. For Kant, the rational idea that everyone has a moral obligation toward his/her fellow and non-fellow citizens stems from the Stoic political philosophy. If all men are connected to each other via their reason, then they have a duty of reciprocal hospitality toward one another, Kant argued. In the eighteenth and nineteenth centuries, the cosmopolitan acquired a more economic definition. The three main versions of the cosmopolitan are the moral cosmopolitan, the political cosmopolitan, and the economic cosmopolitan. Cosmopolitan democracy, applying some of the principles and values of democracy globally, is also a debated issue in international politics.

The Moral Cosmopolitan
On moral cosmopolitan grounds, everyone has a moral obligation toward his/her fellow and non-fellow citizens to help each other and to alleviate suffering in times of war, conflict, and violence. Moral cosmopolitanism is concerned with respecting and promoting human rights and ensuring justice. It is based on the premise that all human beings are morally important and their interests must be considered. Peter Singer (1972), in his utilitarian approach to moral cosmopolitanism, famously debated that the affluent countries have a moral responsibility to partake in humanitarian assistance and famine relief up to a point where they would sacrifice something "morally significant."

The Political Cosmopolitan
Political cosmopolitanism is preoccupied with the principles of justice that apply to everyone in the world and the responsibility to follow them. It focuses on the needs and interests of people in the world, not as a citizen of a particular country, but as a world citizen. It is not concerned with the moral obligations of individuals or the politics that go on between and among countries. It emphasizes the need for global and political institutions to ensure global justice and prevent the violation of individual interests for the sake of state interests. Immanuel Kant argued that being a member of an international community assigns people the responsibility for governing their social and political institutions and settling public conflicts in a universal manner. He believed that world peace is only possible through respecting and ensuring human rights not only at home for citizens, but also abroad for noncitizen foreigners.

The Economic Cosmopolitan
Karl Marx and Friedrich Engels, fathers of the Marxist theory, provided an economic foundation for the understanding of the cosmopolitan in its relation to capitalism. Marx's proletarian cosmopolitanism created a political and economic movement, urging workers around the world to unite based on their shared grievances and universal class of exploitation.

On the other hand, economists such as Friedrich Hayek and Adam Smith advocated for a free global economic market open to all with minimal political involvement. Marx's socialist cosmopolitanism disputed that a global free market would widen the inequality gap between the wealthy and poor and would not ensure that there would be a sufficient number of jobs for all citizens in the world.

Elcin Haskollar

References

Bohman, J. & Lutz-Bachmann, M. (Eds.). (1997). *Perpetual peace: Essays on Kant's cosmopolitan ideal.* Cambridge, MA: The MIT Press.

Held, D. (2010). *Cosmopolitanism: Ideals and realities.* Malden, MA: Polity.

Kant, I. (2003). *Political writings* (H. S. Reiss, Ed.). Cambridge, MA: Cambridge University Press.

Marx, K. (2011). *Das capital, volume one: A critique of political economy* (S. Moore & E. Aveling, Trans., F. Engels, Ed.). New York: Dover Publications, Inc.

Singer, P. (1972). Famine, affluence, and morality. *Philosophy of Public Affairs, 1*(3), 229–43.

COSMOPOLITANISM

"Citizens of the World"

The term *cosmopolitanism* refers to the creation of a community inclusive of all demographic groups based on the belief that all humans are connected and responsible for each other. A person who lives according to this spirit is called a *cosmopolite* or *cosmopolitan*. Although similar ideas have been traced back to other ancient civilizations, such as pharaonic Egypt, the English word *cosmopolitanism* is derived from the ancient Greek word *cosmopolites* (κοσμοπολίτης), a composite of *cosmos* (world) and *polites* (citizen). It is widely believed that the term was first used when Diogenes the Cynic (c. 412–323 BCE) proclaimed himself a "citizen of the world," thus questioning traditional concepts of Hellenistic collective identity that had centered on a shared belonging to a *polis* (city) rather than to the *cosmos*. This idea became a major concern in the writings of the Stoics—both Greek and later Roman—who challenged the rigid distinction between local community and cosmopolis by arguing that the interconnectedness of all men renders each accountable

to both. Accordingly, each individual inhabits both a local community and the moral community of all humans. This school of thought was expressed most famously in Seneca the Younger's (4 BCE–65 CE) declaration that "the whole world is my country" (1882, p. 139). Likewise, Roman emperor Marcus Aurelius (121–180 CE) reflected in his *Meditations* that "[i]n so far as I am Antoninus [his adopted name], my city and country is Rome, but so far as I am a man, it is the world" (1894, p. 98). Likewise reconciling ostensibly conflicting notions of home and the world, Hierocles in the second century proposed a model of cosmopolitanism as a series of concentric circles, beginning with the self at the center and successively widening to encompass family, extended family, neighbors, fellow city citizens, countrymen, and ultimately humanity as a whole.

In modern Western philosophy, the concept is often traced back to Immanuel Kant's *Perpetual Peace* (1795, *Zum ewigen Frieden*), which calls for the establishment of a law of world citizenship to protect citizens of individual states from violations of certain rights that Kant deemed universal. In particular, Kant argued that such a cosmopolitan law had become imperative in a world in which violations of the law in one part were felt by all. Soon after Kant wrote these words, debates about cosmopolitanism began to have focus on the tensions, discontents, and overlaps that arose out of the concept's universal claims and the emerging principle of the nation-state, which gained appeal in the early decades of the nineteenth century. In 1809, Samuel Taylor Coleridge warned against what he called "the false philosophy or mistaken religion which would persuade him that cosmopolitanism is nobler than nationality, and the human race a sublimer object of love than a people" (1867, p. 189). In 1828, Thomas Carlyle lamented that "[a] certain attenuated cosmopolitanism had . . . taken place of the old home feeling [although it] was not nourished by the affections which spring from national soil" (1899, pp. 287–88). And writing in 1848, Karl Marx and Friedrich Engels identified cosmopolitanism in *The Communist Manifesto* (*Das Kommunistische Manifest*) as an expression of the growing power of the bourgeoisie and of the world market to exploit the working classes of European nation-states. Concomitant with the boom of nationalist sentiment at the turn of the twentieth century, the adjective *cosmopolitan* in many European countries took on almost exclusively negative connotations, conveying a lack of proper affiliation and identification. By contrast to these European thinkers, cosmopolitanism in the United States of the nineteenth century emerges primarily in the context of New England transcendentalism, before it, too, merges with burgeoning nationalist rhetoric during the Gilded Age. According to Jessica Berman, Ralph Waldo Emerson's cosmopolitan visions, for instance, grew out of his belief in the primacy of the individual and the wider context of American expansionism.

In the twentieth century, the debates regarding cosmopolitan societies were shaped by the Cold War's ideological partition of the world into three camps. In the so-called First World, comprised of capitalistic nations that were allied with the United States, cosmopolitan ideals found articulation in the creation of international institutions, laws, and norms that shaped international relations after World War II and the Jewish Holocaust. At its very best, cosmopolitan thought, inspiring the foundation of the United Nations, international courts, and an emerging human rights discourse, incited an expansion of solidarity across territorial borders. Yet because of their origin in the context of the Cold War, these principles and organizations have often been criticized by scholars such as Pheng Cheah for their implicit bias toward capitalist Western politics. In contrast to Europe and North America, where the term *cosmopolitanism* was mostly positively connoted, the Soviet Union during the early years of the Cold War launched campaigns against an allegedly parasitic "rootless cosmopolitanism," which targeted intellectuals, many of them Jewish, who were accused of lacking patriotism and harboring pro-Western loyalties. In the so-called Third World, consisting of nonaligned countries, the era of decolonization in Africa and Asia during the 1950s and 1960s saw alternative schools of cosmopolitan thought that focused on transnational solidarity movements of people struggling against imperialism and oppression. Inspired by Marxist/socialist and humanist worldviews, intellectuals in formerly colonized countries, the foremost, Frantz Fanon, envisioned the creation of cosmopolitan communities built on international solidarity and a shared opposition to Western imperialism. The collapse of the Soviet Union in the early 1990s and the rise of the United States to become the world's sole superpower have further strengthened the institutionalized cosmopolitanism exercised by the United Nations and its numerous aligned organizations. However, critics have lamented the subordination of individual states, accompanying weakening of democratic principles, and increasing exploitation of labor that underlies the rhetoric of free trade and liberal democracy that is eschewed by what Peter Gowan has labeled "neoliberal cosmopolitanism."

Today, questions of cosmopolitanism are central to debates about globalization—namely, the increasing interconnectedness of humanity in regard to the movements of ideas, people, and commodities. While globalization is often understood to result in a homogenization of planetary cultures, cosmopolitanism is often understood as the envisioning, rather than reflecting on existing, communities that respond to this development by extending notions of citizenship and belonging to diverse newcomers. The conflict between the universal and the local or national still informs recent treatises. In his essay "On Cosmopolitanism," the poststructuralist thinker Jacques Derrida (2001) concurs with Hannah Arendt's verdict that the proliferation of the sovereign nation-state as political entity has been accompanied by a progressive abolition of the right to asylum and has produced an increasing number of stateless people. Critiquing that Kant's cosmopolitan vision did reserve the power to grant the right of residence to particular treaties between states, Derrida calls for the establishment of a global network of autonomous "open cities" (*ville franches*) or "refuge cities" (*villes refuges*) that will offer a home to exiled, deported, or displaced persons. Similarly, Martha Nussbaum (2002) critiques the limitations that patriotism imposes upon our ability to imagine bonds with people outside of our national communities, calling nationalistic attachment morally irrelevant. By contrast, however, Kwame Anthony Appiah (1997) reconciles these two ideas by envisioning a world in which everybody can be both cosmopolitan and patriot, thus remaining rooted in his or her own cultural background while being open to creating multiple other affiliations. In this sense, then, cosmopolitanism celebrates local forms of difference and particularity, rather than working toward global sameness or uniformity, tendencies which Appiah ascribes to humanism. Others, such as Craig Calhoun (2007), have defended the nation-state against the criticism of cosmopolitan thinkers, asserting nationalism's democratic potential and integrative possibilities, including social solidarity and distributive justice, and suggesting that a cosmopolitan world order needs to accommodate these feelings of attachment and belonging.

Alongside this debate, however, a vast group of scholars have begun to mount a profound critique of the traditional genealogy that renders cosmopolitanism as a Stoic concept made available to us by Kant and his followers. As such, Walter Mignolo (2000) instead identifies the context of European colonial expansion and the triangular trade system of the Atlantic—which brought into contact European colonizers and missionaries, indigenous peoples of North America, and African slaves—as pivotal for the emergence of new intercultural relations and cosmopolitan modes of living. Cosmopolitan ideas—articulated by clergy and intellectuals in Renaissance Spain, Enlightenment thinkers, and in the nascent human rights discourse during the Cold War—always emerged in the context of Europe's colonial and capitalist ventures. Defying cosmopolitanism as a Eurocentric project, Mignolo guides our attention to what he terms *critical cosmopolitanism* that has been articulated from the perspective of coloniality. In the course of the past thirty years, numerous scholars have decentered this history and highlighted the existence of cosmopolitan communities in non-Western societies. Most famously, among many others, Jean Bernabe, Patrick Chamoiseau, and Raphael Confiant's "Éloge de la Créolité" (1989) evokes Caribbean modes of cultural fusion and hybridity as models for global conviviality, Amitav Ghosh's *In an Antique Land* (1992) reconstructs the Eastern Mediterranean and the Indian Ocean of the twelfth century as important sites of inclusive community building, Paul Gilroy's *The Black Atlantic* (1993) allows us to understand African diasporic identity formation and crucial to the articulation of modernity, Ammiel Alcalay's *After Jews and Arabs* (1993) reminds us of Levantine

cosmopolitan societies prior to the Cold War, and Nick Bromell's *The Time Is Always Now* (2013) sheds light on cosmopolitan thought in African American letters from Frederick Douglass to today. In this sense, Sheldon Pollock, Homi K. Bhabha, Carol A. Breckenridge, and Dipesh Chakrabarty define *cosmopolitanism* as a term that remains wide open, rather than clearly defined, and emphasize that, rather than speaking of one cosmopolitan doctrine with a clear trajectory from the Stoics to Kant, we are dealing with *cosmopolitanisms*; that is, decentralized and local forms of conviviality. This view replaces the philosopher at the center of the study of cosmopolitanism with that of the victim of modernity to examine how refugees, exiles, diasporic communities, and migrants practice new forms of cosmopolitan community building.

Balthazar Becker

References

Appiah, K. A. (1997). Cosmopolitan patriots. *Critical Inquiry, 23*(3), 617–39.

Aurelius, M. (1894). In A. Zimmern (Ed.), *The meditations of Marcus Aurelius* (J. Collier, Trans.). London: Routledge & Sons.

Berman, J. (2001). *Modern fiction, cosmopolitanism, and the politics of community*. New York: Cambridge University Press.

Calhoun, C. (2007). *Nations matter: Culture, history, and the cosmopolitan dream*. New York: Routledge.

Carlyle, T. (1899). *Critical and miscellaneous essays* (Vol. I). London: Chapman and Hall.

Cheah, P. (2006). *Inhuman conditions: On cosmopolitanism and human rights*. Cambridge, MA: Harvard University Press.

Coleridge, S. T. (1867). *The friend: A series of essays*. London: Bell & Daldy.

Derrida, J. (2001). *On cosmopolitanism and forgiveness* (M. Dooley & M. Hughes, Trans.). New York: Routledge.

Gowan, P. (2001). Neoliberal cosmopolitanism. *New Left Review, 11*, 79–93.

Kant, I. (1903). *Perpetual peace: A philosophical essay* (M. Campbell Smith, Trans.). London: Swan Sonnenschein.

Mignolo, W. D. (2000). The many faces of cosmopolis: Border thinking and critical cosmopolitanism. *Public Culture, 12*(3), 721–48.

Nussbaum, M. C. (2002). Introduction: Cosmopolitan emotions? In M. Nussbaum and J. Cohen (Eds.), *For love of country?* (pp. 3–20). Boston: Beacon Press.

Pollock, S., Bhabha, H. K., Breckenridge, C. A., & Chakrabarty, D. (2000). Cosmopolitanisms. *Public Culture, 12*(3), 577–89.

Seneca, L. A. (1882). *Seneca's morals: Of a happy life, benefits, anger and clemency* (R. L'Estrange, Trans.). Chicago: Belford, Clarke & Co.

COSMOPOLITANISM

Cosmopolitanism can be traced back to the Greek word *kosmopolitês, meaning "citizen of the world."* Cosmopolitanism, during this time, meant to reject the notion that all people belonged to a specific community, nestled within larger communities. Cosmopolitanism enjoys a long history in both Greek and Roman societies as well as in the work of Immanuel Kant, Christoph Martin Wieland, and Voltaire. In the eighteenth century, the term, along with *world citizenship*, came to mean someone who was open-minded and impartial, often citing the concept of the universal human community. Voltaire, however, spoke less of universalism and more of the obligation of human beings to understand those with whom we share our planet and not just those of our local communities or ethnicities.

In the early twenty-first century, we see efforts to shift the meaning of the term away from its often-negative interpretations focusing on ethnocentric, relativistic, superiority, or universalism. Appiah (2006) frames cosmopolitanism according to two strands: (a) understanding that people have obligations to each other; and (b) needing to value and learn from human differences (p. xv). Cosmopolitanism, outside the world of transnational capitalism, is used to describe people who seek a "global civil society" and is conceptualized as a "moral project to free the world's peoples from oppression and bigotry" (Merryfield, 2006, p. 1).

Cosmopolitanism encompasses concepts related to citizenship, such as border crossing, diaspora, curiosity, tolerance, localism, nationalism, interconnectedness, and global mindedness. Cosmopolitanism embraces the concept of multiple identities and affiliations, reaching outward from the focus on self and family, beyond ethnic group identification, beyond the narrow loyalties of imagined boundaries encompassing the nation-state to, finally, include all of humanity.

Cosmopolitanism informs discussions of place and identity development in that cosmopolitanism can be thought of as "placeless" in order to disrupt narratives of a shared history based on territory to instead foster a sense of transnational solidarity against injustice. The ongoing emergence of global citizenship and flexible identities increases the possibility of a cosmopolitan world. Either within physical communities or through twenty-first-century technologies, cosmopolitanism involves increased engagement in commercial, cultural, and political exchanges across space and time. Various groups may debate the place of cosmopolitan ideals within citizenship education, seeking a return to education that focuses on strictly national citizenship. More recently, however, we see a push toward inclusivity; a type of both/and citizenship education that teaches how to be citizens of the nation-state and citizens of the world (Mitchell & Parker, 2008). Many young people have already begun to function comfortably within a world of flexible and multiple allegiances. While some criticize it for its utopian ideals, cosmopolitanism offers a powerful and guiding concept in an ever-changing and shifting world and may point toward a future that, while not yet enacted, has been imagined.

Tami A. Augustine
Jason R. Harshman

References
Appiah, K. (2006). *Cosmopolitanism: Ethics in a world of strangers.* New York: Norton.

Merryfield, M. (2006, May–June). Citizens of the world? Thoughts about cosmopolitanism. Global TeachNet. Retrieved from www.globalteachnet.org.

Mitchell, K. & Parker, W. (2008). I pledge allegiance to . . . Flexible citizenship and shifting scales of belonging. *Teachers College Record, 110*(4), 775–804.

CREOLE

Creole is a frequently misused, misunderstood, and misapplied term that refers to both an ethnic group as well as a language in development. The word *Creole* originates from the Latin word *creare*, which translates as "to create or to beget," as well as from the words *criollo* from Spanish and *creole* from French, indicating a person indigenous to a particular locality (Bernard, 2012). In a more regional context, *Creole* can mean "native to Louisiana." Historically, the term *Creole* referred to any black, white, or mixed-raced person born in Louisiana with French or Spanish heritage.

Historical Meaning of Creole: Free Blacks Born in the Colonies

In the New World or Colonial America, Portuguese slave traders first used the term *crioulo* to differentiate between enslaved Africans who were born in the colonies and those who were born in Africa proper (Hall, 1995). By the 1600s, the Portuguese *crioulo* referred to anyone born in the New World irrespective of racial or ethnic background. In the Louisiana territory, *criollo* or *creole* also signified anyone born in the New World who was black, white, or of mixed-race descent; for many, *creole* denoted someone born a slave in the New World. In the eighteenth century, the term *Creoles of color* began to evolve, describing free persons of color living within New Orleans. By the early 1700s, Creoles, or free persons of color, constituted a large segment of New Orleans' population (Kein, 1977). In addition to having obtained free status, these Creoles also owned property, many "owned" slaves, and many were educated in Europe. The term *Creole* continued to mean an individual born in the New World or a native New World person as opposed to the increasing number of immigrants. Starting with the Louisiana Purchase and continuing through the Civil War, Creoles of color lost their free status, but not their ways of being (Mills, 1977). These Creoles maintained a group identify manifested in such practices as endogamy—marrying other Creoles as opposed to marrying someone black whose family had never been free.

Historical Meaning of Creole: Whites Born in the Colonies

From roughly 1812 to 1861, a time period referred to as antebellum, many individuals who were racially white also called themselves Creole. These Creoles were also native-born, upper-income Louisianans, who were of either French or Spanish descent (Valdman, 1998). Many of these Creoles were established in New Orleans but also in Avoyelles and Evangeline parishes, spoke French, and viewed themselves as aristocratic (Bernard, 2012). The Civil War marked a decline in many white Creoles' economic fortunes, and as a result, many began to marry the less wealthy Acadians who settled in parts of South Louisiana after being forced to leave Canada in 1755. White Creoles and the Acadians both began to be referred to as Cajuns. By the 1900s, poor Americans of French descent living in Louisiana, despite origins and former status, became known as simply Cajun (Bernard, 2007).

Contemporary Meaning of Creole

Some white, southern Louisianans still refer to themselves as Creole and refuse the descriptor "Cajun." These individuals self-identify as being descended from moneyed French or Spanish who were born in the New World and resided in or near New Orleans, Louisiana (Bernard, 2007). The term *Creole* has also evolved to mean any individual who claims either complete or partial African heritage, who speaks French, and is Catholic (Ioup, 2012). These cultural markers of speaking French and practicing Catholicism differentiated Creoles from other African-descended individuals who speak English and are Protestant. Significant Creole communities can be found in New Orleans in South Louisiana's Acadiana area; in the Cane River–Isle Revelle region near Natchitoches, Louisiana; in and around Pointe Coupee Parish, Louisiana; and in many East Texas communities extending as far as Houston (Mills, 1977). Other Creole communities exist in Oakland and San Francisco, California (Bernard, 2012). What sets this particular ethnic group apart from other African, African American, and Afro-Antillean groups is adherence to self-identity as either Black Creoles or Creoles descended from the original free blacks of color. Speaking French and being Catholic are tenets of Creole culture outside of racial identity.

Creole: Local Applications

While *Creole* first and foremost is an ethnic label, the term also applies to food, music, and language. Creole cooking is often associated with New Orleans fare and means a multicourse meal similar to French cooking involving numerous, varied courses. Creole tomatoes are a distinct variety of tomato locally grown and produced in Louisiana.

CREOLE MUSIC Creole music can range from Caribbean-originated folk music to the accordion-driven Creole Zydeco, which is related to blues. In the tradition, the Black Creole zydeco music of South Louisiana is sung in French. Geno Delafose, son of the famous zydeco accordion player John Delafose, and his French Rocking Boogie band is a prime example of such music. Born in Eunice, Louisiana, Delafose self-describes as one of the younger generations of the zydeco genre who has created the sound known as the nouveau zydeco. Stanley "Buckwheat Zydeco" Dural Jr. from Lafayette, Louisiana, is credited with bringing Black Creole culture to the mainstream with his music as he played at the closing of the 1996 Olympics games and was featured at both of former president Bill Clinton's inaugurations. Dural follows in the footsteps of Amédé Ardoin and Clifton Chenier, earlier Creole zydeco artists who forged the musical genre (Tisserand, 1999).

CREOLE LANGUAGE Language, derived from the Old French term *language* and the Latin *lingua*, can be defined as the systematic ways of communicating ideas through speaking, and the specific methods of combining them used and understood by a group of individuals (Webster's New Student's Dictionary, 1969). A *pidgin* is a language that has no native speakers, representing a first level of language development. A *creole* is a language that was first a pidgin in an early stage of development, but then became the capital language of a speech community (Dillard, 1972). Creole French, for example, is considered a separate, autonomous language, with documented existence, and governed by its own set of grammatical rules—not a dialect of French (Valdman, 1998; Valdman, Rottet, Ancelet, Klinger, LaFleur, Lindner, Picone, & Ryon, 2010). Historically, Creole French was spoken primarily by twenty thousand to thirty thousand African Louisianans and also spoken by some whites (Valdman, 1998). According to Valdman:

> Creole French remains as a spoken language today in four distinct areas of the state of Louisiana: 1) a central area in the Bayou Teche region located in the communities of St. Martinville, Parks, Cecelia, and Breaux Bridge, Louisiana; 2) the town of New Rhodes in Pointe Coupee Parish which is north of Baton Rouge, Louisiana; 3) an area referred to as the German Coast which is situated in St. John the Baptist and St. James Parishes along the Mississippi River between Baton Rouge and New Orleans, Louisiana; and in 4) Bayou Lacombe and Bayou Liberty in St. Tammany Parish situated north of New Orleans, Louisiana. (1998, p. 3)

Creole French has been referred to as a special language group of Atlantic Creoles that derived from French immigrant colonists and African immigrant slaves (Brasseaux, 2005; LaFleur, 1999; Marshall, 1997; Morgan, 1959; 1960; Neumann-Holzschuh & Schneider, 2001).

Margaret-Mary Sulentic Dowell
Kenneth J. Fasching-Varner

References

Bernard, S. (2007). *Cajuns and their Acadian ancestors: A young reader's history.* Jackson, MS: University of Mississippi Press.

Bernard, S. (2012). Creoles. *KnowLA Encyclopedia of Louisiana.* Retrieved from http://knowla.org/entry.php?rec=627.

Brasseaux, C. (2005). *French, Cajun, Creole, Houma: A primer on francophone Louisiana.* Baton Rouge, LA: Louisiana State University Press.

Dillard, J. (1972). *Black English.* New York: Random House.

Hall, G. M. (1995). *Africans in colonial Louisiana: The development of Afro-Creole culture in the eighteenth century.* Baton Rouge, LA: Louisiana State University Press.

Ioup, G. (2012). Creoles would reflect our history. Letter to the editor, *The Times Picayune*, p. 2C.

Kein, S. (1977). *Creole: The history and legacy of Louisiana's free people of color.* Baton Rouge, LA: Louisiana State University Press.

LaFleur, A. (1999). *Tonnerre mes chiens!: A glossary of Louisiana French figures of speech.* Montreal, Canada: Renouveau Publishing.

Marshall, M. (1997). The origin and development of Louisiana Creole French. In A. Valdman (Ed.), *French and Creole in Louisiana* (pp. 333–49). New York: Plenum Press.

Mills, G. B. (1977). *The forgotten people: Cane River's Creoles of color*. Baton Rouge, LA: Louisiana State University Press.

Morgan, R. (1959). Structural sketch of St. Martin Creole. *Anthropological Linguistics*, *1*(8), 20–24.

Morgan, R. (1960, January). The lexicon of St. Martin Creole. *Anthropological Linguistics*, *2*(1), 7–29.

Neumann-Holzschuh, I. & Schneider, E. (2001). *Degrees of restructuring in Creole languages (Creole language library)*. Amsterdam, The Netherlands: John Benjamins Publishing Company.

Tisserand, M. (1999). *The kingdom of zydeco*. New York: Arcade Publishing.

Valdman, A. (1998). *Dictionary of Louisiana Creole*. Bloomington, IN: University of Indiana Press.

Valdman, A., Rottet, K., Ancelet, B., Klinger, T., LaFleur, A., Lindner, T., Picone, M., & Ryon, D. (2010). (Eds.). Dictionary of Louisiana French: As spoken in Cajun, Creole, and American Indian communities. Jackson, MI: University of Mississippi Press.

Webster's New Student's Dictionary. (1969). New York: American Book Company.

CRITICAL PEDAGOGY

Critical pedagogy refers to both the theory and the practice of social transformation that links education to social justice. Theoretically, critical pedagogy sees cultural institutions (such as schools) as extensions of the state that reward complacency with social, political, and economic inequality. In practice, critical pedagogy is a joint engagement between teachers and students to bring about social justice by enacting change.

History

Critical pedagogy has evolved from the 1920s critical theory of the Frankfurt School. The critical theoretical tradition, greatly influenced by the work of Karl Marx, argues that schools are a vehicle for the reproduction of existing class structures needed to maintain capitalism. Critical pedagogy represents a response and seeks to expose the implicit and explicit capitalist functions of schooling. Critical pedagogy, as a pedagogical movement, grew out of the efforts of Brazilian liberatory education philosopher Paulo Freire and his literacy campaigns in rural areas of South America. Freire argued that education as a function should challenge existing social structures through an emancipatory practice of critique and social action.

North American scholars focused their attention on critical pedagogy in the late 1970s and 1980s, coupling the theory's criticality with Dewian principles of democratic education. Most notably, Henry Giroux, Peter McLaren, and Michael Apple examined schools as social, cultural, and political institutions that perpetuate dominant ideologies and maintain the status quo. They saw the potential of using critical pedagogy to cultivate critical capacities among teachers and students to transform schools into sites of resistance and change. Critical or feminist pedagogues, such as Ira Shor, Antonia Darder, Deborah Britzman, and bell hooks have extended the ideological foundations of critical pedagogy from a focus on class to that of race, gender, sexual orientation, disability, and their intersectionality.

Tenets

POWER A central tenet of critical pedagogy is the understanding that power operates in language, actions, and interactions associated with daily social life (Foucault, 1991). In schools, this further extends to an understanding of power as implicitly and explicitly operating through policies, curricula, and practices. Therefore, a starting point for teachers and students is to make evident how power operates through schooling to maintain asymmetry in the social order.

KNOWLEDGE CONSTRUCTION Another central tenet of critical pedagogy is that knowledge is not neutral but rather a social construction rooted in power. As such, knowledge must be interrogated to understand how it privileges particular voices, experiences, and perspectives. Rejecting the claim of "objective" knowledge, critical pedagogues recognize that traditional curricular programs work against the interests of students who are most vulnerable in society. Critical pedagogues see how all facets of schools, including curricula, reproduce dominant ideology that rationalizes social and economic hierarchy. The legitimacy of inequality is implicitly taught to students through the forms of knowledge valued in the curricula. For example, school curricula frequently position Western ideology, literature, and practices as central to economic advancement while simultaneously relegating non-Western traditions and intellectualism to the periphery. This act of the "Othering" of knowledge, practices, and literary traditions of non-Western communities demonstrates the institutional reproduction of dominant knowledge forms.

DIALOGIC LEARNING Another central tenet of critical pedagogy is for teachers and students to mutually engage in critical dialogue. In traditional pedagogies, the teacher is cast as "knower" and the student as "learner"; the teacher deposits knowledge into students who passively receive and memorize it. This tradition, what Freire (1972) terms the *banking model of education*, is fundamentally hierarchical and inequitable. In contrast, critical pedagogues understand that learning should involve teachers and students engaging in dialogue together. By learning to critically interrogate inequalities through dialogue, teachers and students are engaging in social reflection and action, what Freire called *conscientização* or critical consciousness. Developing critical consciousness is a significant undertaking that begins with a deceptively simple premise: dialogue lays the groundwork for consciousness-raising. This has two important and interrelated implications: (1) the hierarchical distinction between teacher and student is challenged; and (2) teachers and students engage in dialogue to reflect and act transformatively upon their world. For example, a teacher might begin a problem-posing dialogue by presenting school suspension and expulsion rates disaggregated by race and gender to students. The teacher might ask: "What do you notice?" This conversation, which focuses on taken-for-granted policies and practices, begins a dialogue that recasts the policies in terms of power, punishment, and marginalization.

LIBERATORY ACTION A central tenet of critical pedagogy is that it leads to some form of liberatory change. As a consequence of dialogic learning, teachers and students develop what Giroux (1988) calls a *language of critique* and a *language of possibility*. Unifying critique and possibility is akin to what Freire (1972) called *praxis*: the unification of reflection with action. Where developing a language of critique and possibility falls short is in the distance between imagining possibilities and taking action to create new social realities. For example, when students were presented with school disciplinary data, the intention may have been to reveal disproportionate punishment toward racial minorities. The dialogue must develop to a point of action if it is to reflect the tenets of critical pedagogy. This could mean, for example, a change in the school's disciplinary policies and practices.

Critiques

The theory and practice of critical pedagogy is ever advancing, in part, because of critiques that focus on issues of inclusivity and diversity. First, some charge that the discourse of critical pedagogy perpetuates marginalization because the language used is too abstract. Such esoteric language can serve as a form of oppression and exclusion. Rather than serving as an emancipatory tool, critical pedagogy only reinscribes power and privilege, thereby contradicting its inclusive aims. Grounding the discourse in the daily language and concrete struggles of practitioners, students, and civic activists, and not abstractions, might better mitigate this concern. Another critique is the extent to which teachers and students interrogate their social positions intersectionally.

Intersectionality, rooted fundamentally in feminist standpoint theory (Harding, 2004), recognizes how race, class, and gender together and apart differentiate one's social location, and, therefore, experiences of subjugation or privilege. Just as understandings of power suggest *all* are both subject to and reproducers of power (Foucault, 1991), an intersectional analysis would allow students to understand how they might benefit from racial privilege while being marginalized through social class hierarchies. Third and finally, critical pedagogy was designed to include the voices of cultural, ethnic, gender, and economic differences, but the recognized North American leaders of critical pedagogy are white, Western theorists. While there is a long tradition of women and men of color that have advanced the field, they have not received the same recognition and status as many white male critical pedagogues. A consequence of this trend, and its continued Marxian emphasis, is the perception among communities of color that critical pedagogy fails to explicitly treat race, culture, or indigeneity as central concerns.

Tesha Sengupta-Irving
Cathery Yeh

References

Foucault, M. (1991). *Discipline and punish: The birth of a prison*. London: Penguin.

Freire, P. (1972). *Pedagogy of the oppressed*. New York: Herder and Herder.

Giroux, H. (1988). *Teachers as intellectuals: Toward a critical pedagogy of learning*. South Hadley: Bergin Garvey.

Harding, S. G. (2004). The feminist standpoint theory reader: Intellectual and political controversies. New York: Routledge.

CRITICAL PEDAGOGY

Critical pedagogy is an approach through which "students and teachers are encouraged to view what they learn in a critical light" (Nieto, 2005, p. 409). In the 1970s, it sparked an educational movement whose goal was to encourage students and learners to develop the consciousness for freedom and power in order to transform and possibly balance opportunities in an unjust and unequal society. Critical pedagogy became popular with Paulo Freire's book *Pedagogy of the Oppressed* (1970). Some researchers and educators, however, have criticized critical pedagogy as being essentialist, populist, and unpatriotic (Chege, 2009). Essentialism rests on an assumption that there is an essential body of knowledge and human values that have stood the test of time. It argues that these should be identified and transmitted from generation to generation in the name of education. The essentialist view of learning conceptualizes students as empty vessels that need to be filled. Teachers are expected to be the transmitter of information and role models. Students are expected to retain, recall, and apply knowledge within and outside the classroom (Koppelman & Goodhart, 2005, pp. 295–96). The criticism against critical pedagogy argues that it assumes that all students are oppressed. Apart from the essentialist argument, there are some educators who argue that critical pedagogy is for marginalized groups such as workers, those who are racially and culturally discriminated against, and/or women. Lastly, some "right-wing" educators claim critical pedagogy is unpatriotic because critical pedagogy empowers students as catalysts of social dissent and change.

Critical pedagogy has three aspects to it—namely, pedagogy of praxis, reproduction theory, and radical multiculturalism. Pedagogy of praxis anchors on liberation principles, coming out of the Latin American Liberation Theology of the 1970s. Reproduction theory anchors on the assumption that schooling in capitalist systems has failed its real purpose. Critics argue that schooling in a capitalistic society exists for reproducing the current social system, with class divisions (Bowles & Gintis, 1976). Radical multiculturalism argues that schools have failed in empowering students from minority populations to actualize their potential in school settings. It seeks the social and political redistribution of power, with the primary goal of curriculum development for student social action and empowerment skills (Haddad, 1999, p. 218).

Chinaka Samuel DomNwachukwu

References

Bowles, S. & Gintis, H. (1976). *Schooling in capitalist America*. New York: Basic Books.

Chege, Mwangi. (2009). Literacy and hegemony: Critical pedagogy vis-à-vis contending paradigms. *International Journal of Teaching and Learning in Higher Education, 21*(2), 228–38.

Freire, P. (1970). *Pedagogy of the oppressed*. New York: Seabury.

Haddad, D. W. (1999). And who is my neighbor: Multicultural education challenges Christian educators. In D. C. Elliott & S. D. Holtrop (Eds.), *Nurturing and reflective teachers: A Christian approach for the 21st century* (pp. 217–27). Claremont, CA: Learning Light Educational Publishing.

Koppelman, K. L. & Goodhart, R. L. (2005). *Understanding human differences: Multicultural education for a diverse America*. New York: Pearson.

Nieto, S. (2005). School reform and student learning: A multicultural perspective. In J. A. Banks & C. A. M. Banks (Eds.), *Multicultural education issues and perspectives* (5th ed.) (pp. 401–20). Hobeken, NJ: John Wiley & Sons, Inc.

CRITICAL PERSPECTIVES

Critical Perspectives in Diversity and Social Justice Education

This entry provides definitions, a framework, and examples of critical diversity and social justice education. Additionally, strategies that teachers can use to achieve a critical approach to diversity and social justice education are explored, providing a deeper understanding of what it means to engage in a critical approach. Diversity and social justice have become important goals in education. Changing demographics and social realities in schools have increased calls for more diversity and social justice in teacher education in response to the increasing diversity of the student population (Cochran-Smith & Fries, 2008). There are more students in schools in North America from diverse ethnic, linguistic, racial, religious, and cultural backgrounds. This demands that schools and teachers respond by implementing more inclusive and culturally relevant curricula and socially just practices. In an increasingly diverse world, schools are expected to meet the needs of a population that is more racially, culturally, and linguistically diverse as well as to confront gender, racial, sexual, and economic discrimination.

Defining Critical Diversity and Social Justice Education

Research shows that there is no consensus on approaches to diversity and social justice education. Darling-Hammond (2011) suggests that dealing with diversity is one of the fundamental challenges of twenty-first-century education. Likewise, there is a lack of consensus among educational leaders on what defines social justice education (Lopez, 2013). Shoho, Merchant, and Lugg (2005) suggest that social justice is a politically loaded and elusive construct, while scholars such as Dantley and Tillman (2006) urge social justice educators to develop some shared understandings. Social justice, diversity, and equity are constructs oftentimes used interchangeably and contextualized. Diversity and social justice education, viewed from a critical perspective, challenge school practices that marginalize some students and are barriers to their academic success.

This discussion of critical diversity and social justice education draws from Burbules and Berk's (1999) notion of criticality as a practice that encourages educators to think outside a framework of conventional understanding and to engage in praxis that challenges power and privilege. Over the years we have seen some forms of multicultural, diversity, and equity education that have focused on "celebrating diversity" through festivals and foods. Critical approaches to diversity and social justice education that go beyond "celebrating diversity" include conversations about power and privilege and actions and behaviors that are transformative. Critical diversity and social justice education challenges, confronts, and disrupts structural inequities based on class, race, gender, and other social and human differences (Nieto & Bode, 2008). Grounded in Frieirean notions of critical pedagogy, critical approaches acknowledge that schooling is politically mediated and all knowledge is contested.

Envisioning Critical Diversity and Social Justice Education

Critical approaches to diversity and social justice education do not happen by chance but require focused attention, planning, and action to bring about change. Current school realities and contexts sometimes make it difficult for educators to embark on critical transformative practice, develop critical approaches, and implement these practices in their classrooms and schools. The following framework for critical action provides an avenue for consideration by educators that places students at the center of the teaching and learning process. This approach moves away from traditional approaches to teaching and embraces culturally relevant practices that encourage students and teachers to examine social, political, and economic contradictions in the world around them and to take action where there are injustices. It is represented as a continuous circle representing growth and a cyclical journey, as represented in Figure C.1.

1. *Examination of Self.* Starting from a position of self-examination, educators (administrators and teachers) can begin the journey by looking at their personal histories, values, and beliefs. Beliefs have an impact on the choices educators make in dealing with students, particularly from diverse backgrounds. Teachers

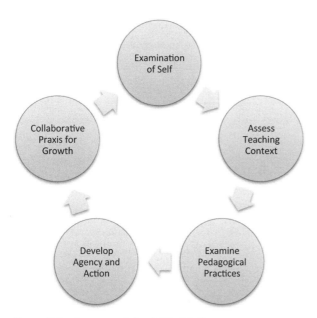

Figure C.1. Framework for Critical Action

and administrators could ask questions such as, What negative views do I hold about students? What do I think about communities that are different from mine? What do I need to learn about other groups? Beliefs guide a teacher's classroom practices and inform interactions with students. This is more relevant in an increasingly diverse world.

2. *Assess Teaching Context.* To be critical, diversity and social justice educators must have a sense of agency and take action to change the contexts for themselves and their students. Examples of this could be seeking out culturally relevant resources, engaging in collaborative praxis that involves engaging others in the community circles of growth, wrestling with tensions and contradictions in practice, and using research and theory to inform actions.

3. *Examine Pedagogical Practices.* The act of teaching and pedagogy must be problem posing and inquiry based, and knowledge must be deconstructed from various vantage points. It requires engagement with new and critical epistemologies. Also, the knowledge that students and communities bring must be embedded in the teaching and learning process for it to be critical. Educators are encouraged to think about their pedagogical choices and ask critical questions about their teaching, such as: Whose voices are included and excluded in texts? Does my pedagogy raise the

social consciousness of students? Are the texts representative of different communities?

4. *Develop Agency and Action.* It is not enough to ask deep and critical questions. Critical educators who believe in diversity and social justice must develop a sense of agency, be leaders, and take action to counteract acts of injustice and inequities. Agency requires a commitment to diversity and social justice even in contexts that do not highlight equity and social justice as goals. Agency demands a shift in thinking and acknowledgment that, for change to occur, action is an important ingredient.

5. *Collaborative Praxis for Growth.* Building a community of critical friends undergirded in dialogic inquiry is an essential ingredient for critical diversity and social justice education. It is a way to sustain a critical path. Teachers and administrators are encouraged to ask questions, such as: Where can I find support for the work I am doing? Engaging in diversity and social justice education that is critical is complex and tension filled, and for some, it can involve both professional and personal risks. It is important that critical educators find a community of support, find spaces to dialogue, and engage in courageous conversations and critical reflection.

Critical diversity and social justice education represents a paradigm shift in ways of thinking about education in an increasingly diverse world. It demands new epistemologies and theories of action beyond feel-good approaches to diversity and social justice symbolized by the celebration of festivals, cultural foods, and other token symbols of tolerance to one that embraces dialogic change. In many schools, the approach to diversity and social justice remains diversifying lunch in the cafeteria, multicultural days, multicultural clubs, and so on, while curriculum and pedagogy exclude the lived experiences and knowledge of students from diverse backgrounds. The framework that is proposed here enhances and supports culturally relevant and responsive teaching approaches that will improve the educational experience of students and communities that have traditionally been underserved by the school system. Ensuring that diversity and social justice education is practiced and envisioned from critical perspectives is essential in bringing about meaningful change in the lives of students instead of token symbols of tolerance.

Ann E. Lopez

References

Burbules, N. C. & Berk, R. (1999). Critical thinking and critical pedagogy: Relations, differences, and limits. In Thomas S. Popkewitz & Lynn Fendler (Eds.), *Critical theories in education: Changing terrains of knowledge and politics* (pp. 46–66). New York: Routledge.

Cochran-Smith, M. & Fries, K. (2008). Research on teacher education: Changing times, changing paradigms. In M. Cochran-Smith, S. Feiman-Nemser, J. McIntyre, & K. Demers (Eds.), *Handbook of research on teacher education: Enduring questions in changing contexts* (pp. 1050–93). New York: Routledge.

Dantley, M. & Tillman, L. (2006). Social justice and moral transformative leadership. In C. Marshall & M. Olivia (Eds.), *Leadership for social justice: Making revolutions in education* (pp. 16–30). Boston: Allyn and Bacon.

Darling–Hammond, L. (2011). Foreward. In A. Ball & C. Tyson (Eds.), *Studying diversity in teacher education* (pp. xi–1). Washington, DC: Rowman & Littlefield Publishers.

Lopez, A. E. (2013). Reconceptualizing teacher leadership through curriculum inquiry in pursuit of social justice: Case study from the Canadian context. In I. Bogotch & C. Shields (Eds.), *International handbook of educational leadership and social (in) justice* (pp. 465–84. New York: Springer Dordrecht Heidelberg.

Nieto, S. & Bode, P. (2008). *Affirming diversity: The sociopolitical context of multicultural education* (5th ed). Boston, MA: Allyn & Bacon.

Shoho, A.R., Merchant, B.M., & Lugg, C.A. (2005). "Social justice" A common language. In F.W. English (Ed.), The *Sage handbook of educational leadership: Advances in theory, research and practice* (pp. 47–66). Thousand Oaks, CA: Sage Publications.

CROSS-CULTURAL STUDIES

The term *cross-cultural studies* is a specialized branch of social sciences that includes cross-cultural comparisons of human behaviors, languages, social traits, and cases across cultures. In the past few years, cross-cultural studies has been widely studied in several disciplines including psychology, sociology, anthropology, economics, political science, history, literature, and business. In a broader perspective, cross-cultural studies include studies related to intercultural relationships, hybridity, transculturation, multiculturalism, cultural diversity, diaspora, and cultural interactivity.

A cross-cultural study is also used as a research design to conduct systematic comparisons of human behaviors in different cultural contexts. From the early 1930s, this approach has provided a methodological parameter that differentiates cross-cultural similarities. Across the social sciences, a cross-cultural study is a reference to compare large samples of human behaviors and their associations with other cultural groups through surveys and ethnographic data. The pioneers of modern cross-cultural research are George P. Murdock and Douglas R. White, who studied standard cross-cultural samples to explore human relationships and behaviors. In interdisciplinary studies, the general concept of the cross-cultural studies is used to refer to "a cross-cultural perspective," "cross-cultural difference," and "a cross-cultural study of" human norms, values, and perceptions. Cross-cultural research, according to White (2002), takes a comparative approach of understanding the forms and patterns of coherence in the practice of human beliefs, norms, and communities.

From the early 1990s, cross-cultural studies has been extensively and alternatively used in educational domains as cross-cultural pedagogies (to focus academic diversity, teaching pedagogy, and multiculturalism), intercultural communication (to stress cross-cultural awareness, stereotypes, etc.), and cross-cultural movements in arts, music, and literature (to exercise freedom, literary, and cultural hegemony of colonial/postcolonial societies and cultures). In recent years, we see the notion of cross-cultural studies in print media, social media, television, and films. For example, in literature, the seminal works of travel writers such as Rudyard Kipling, Jhumpa Lahiri, Anna Leonowens, and Victor Segalen have significantly illustrated the concepts of cultural variations through their fictional characters. Such writers have adopted different cross-cultural narratives (e.g., ethnographic description, travel writing, cultural shock, and social obstacles) to depict the human behaviors and contemporary societies in their fictional works.

Cross-Cultural Studies at Colleges and Universities

Cross-cultural studies has become an emerging program at the institutions of higher education in the last few years. Educators and policymakers have focused on cross-cultural experiences, knowledge, values, and skills gained from students and faculty who pursue overseas education; for instance, international students who study in English-speaking countries—the United States, the United Kingdom, Canada, and Australia. Through the cross-cultural studies programs, educators and faculty organize and offer cross-cultural experience exchanges in which international students and scholars and students from the United States participate in exploring regional and global issues in teaching, research, and seminars. The colleges and universities have designed such cross-cultural studies programs to offer a broader cross-cultural context for students who are studying a particular area of the world or discipline (e.g., history, geography, literature, psychology, etc.). In addition to research, seminars, and discussions on the topics of cross-cultural issues, some institutions offer a degree-oriented academic program in cross-cultural studies. For example, at the University of Houston at Clear Lake, students can pursue a master's degree in cross-cultural studies. This program is designed for students interested in developing knowledge and skill sets appropriate to working in cross-cultural environments. The focus of this program is in "understanding cultural dynamics, appreciating cultural diversity, and negotiating differences between cultures and societies with the goal of bridging these differences" (University of Houston at Clear Lake, 2012, para. 1).

Selected Colleges and Universities with Cross-Cultural Studies Programs

- *Carleton College*: Offers a minor in cross-cultural studies in undergraduate programs in psychology, history, economics, political science, and more.
- *The Center for Cross-Cultural Studies at the University of Alaska at Fairbanks*: Offers an MA and PhD in cross-cultural studies; supports faculty and students in research and instructional issues related to educational policies, programs, and practices in culturally diverse contexts.
- *The University of Houston at Clear Lake*: Offers a master's degree in cross-cultural studies and research related to culturally diverse issues of human societies.
- *Spring Arbor University's Cross-Cultural Program*: Offers a cross-cultural program to help students integrate their existence into the contemporary world with an international interest and understanding about people and cultures.
- *Palm Beach Atlantic University's Cross-Cultural Program*: Offers programs to equip students with the knowledge, skills, and character needed for effective transformational work in international and urban settings.
- *University College London's Cross-Cultural Program*: Offers a cross-cultural research experience to students in linguistics, psychology, sociology, and media in various parts of the world including Sweden, Namibia, Australia, and India.

Professional Cross-Cultural Journals

- *Cross-Cultural Research* quarterly publishes peer-reviewed articles related to societies, nations, and cultures by testing the theories of cross-cultural and comparative studies of human behaviors.
- *World Cultures* publishes articles, data, and comparative research materials dealing with all aspects of human behaviors.
- *Journal of International Students* biannually publishes peer-reviewed articles that focus on cross-cultural experiences and academic issues and concerns of international students in the United States and elsewhere.
- *Journal of Cross-Cultural Psychology* publishes interdisciplinary and cross-cultural issues related to individualism, self-enhancement, acculturation, changing family values, ethnic group comparisons, gender differences, and personality.

Cross-Cultural Films

The Namesake (2006), *The Man Who Would Be King* (1975), *Princess Tam Tam* (1935), *Jodhaa Akbar* (2008), *Outsourced* (2006), *The African Queen* (1951), *Anna and the King* (1999), *Babel* (2006), *The King and I* (1999), *The Last Samurai* (2003), *The Joy Luck Club* (1993), *Monsoon Wedding* (2001), *The Terminal* (2004).

Krishna Bista

References

University of Houston at Clear Lake. (2012). *Cross-cultural studies program*. Retrieved from http://www.uhcl.edu/portal/page/portal/HSH/HOME/HSH%20Programs/Cross%20Cultural%20Studies.

White, D. R. (2002). Cross-cultural research: An introduction for students. Retrieved from http://eclectic.ss.uci.edu/~drwhite/courses/Cross-Cultural_Research.pdf.

Additional Reading

Ember, C. R. & Melvin. E. (2001). *Cross-cultural research methods*. Lanham, MD: AltaMira Press.

Lynch, E. W. & Hanson, M. J. (2011). *Developing cross-cultural competence: A guide for working with children and their families* (4th ed.). Baltimore, MD: Paul H. Brookes Publishing Co., Inc.

Minkov, M. (2012). *Cross-cultural analysis: The science and art of comparing the world's modern societies and their cultures*. Thousand Oaks, CA: Sage.

Moore, C. C. & Mathews, H. F. (2001). *The psychology of cultural experience*. Cambridge, UK: Cambridge University Press.

Trimmer, J. F. & Warnock, T. (1992). *Understanding others: Cultures and cross-cultural studies and the teaching of literature*. Urban, IL: National Council of Teachers of English.

CROSS-CULTURAL, LANGUAGE, AND ACADEMIC DEVELOPMENT (CLAD)

California Assembly Bill AB 2987 was passed in 1992 to create a two-tiered teacher certification structure for teaching English Language Learners (ELLs). This law was known as the Bilingual, Cross-cultural, Language and Academic Development Examination and Certificate. This consisted of six test domains:

- Test 1: Language Structure and First-and Second-Language Development
- Test 2: Methodology of Bilingual Instruction, English Language Development, and Content Instruction
- Test 3: Culture and Cultural Diversity
- Test 4: Methodology for Primary-Language Instruction
- Test 5: The Culture of Emphasis
- Test 6: The Language of Emphasis (listening, reading, speaking, and writing) (State of California, 2006, p. 1)

The first tier of this certification was called the Crosscultural, Language, and Academic Development (CLAD) certificate. California Senate Bill 1969 (Chapter 1178, Statutes of 1994), added Section 44253.10 to the California Education Code, which became effective on January 1, 1995.

The law allows school districts, county offices of education, colleges, universities, and professional organizations to provide staff development programs for teachers of English learners. Districts and county offices issue certificates of completion to teachers who successfully complete staff development programs that are consistent with regulations adopted by the Commission. A certificate of completion authorizes the teachers to provide instruction for ELD in self-contained classrooms and/or SDAIE. (Swofford, 1997, pp. 1–2)

There were three major domains to the CLAD certification program:

Domain 1: Language structure and first- and second-language development, including

- language structure and use: universals and differences (including the structure of English), and
- theories and factors in first-and second-language development.

Domain 2: Methodology of bilingual instruction, English language development, and specially designed academic instruction delivered in English, including

- theories and methods of bilingual education,
- theories and methods of instruction for English language development,

- theories and methods of specially designed academic instruction delivered in English, and
- language and content area assessment.

Domain 3: Culture and cultural diversity, including

- nature and content of culture,
- cross-cultural contact and interactions,
- cultural diversity in the United States and California, and
- providing culturally responsive instruction. (Swofford, 1997, pp. 2–3; Yee-Sakamoto, 2007, p. ix)

While the certificate has remained Crosscultural, Language, and Academic Development (CLAD), the examination and coursework process leading to this certificate was renamed California Teachers of English Learners (CTEL) in 2005. Under this new structure, new standards and structure for obtaining the CLAD certificate were redesigned along the following general principles:

- that the primary purpose of examination and program standards is to determine whether California public school teachers seeking certification have the knowledge and skills to provide instruction to English learners;
- that the examination and program routes require candidates to demonstrate the knowledge and skills necessary for California public school teachers to provide effective instruction to English learners; and
- that the examination and the program standards are aligned with the Reading/Language Arts Framework adopted by the California State Board of Education, English Language Development Standards for California Public Schools, the Standards of Quality and Effectiveness for Teacher Preparation Programs, the Standards of Quality and Effectiveness for Teacher Induction Programs, and the TPEs. (Commission on Teacher Credentialing, 2006, p. 5)

Diaz-Rico and Weed (2006), articulated a theoretical model for CLAD learning that includes three aspects: Learning about the Learner, Learning about Language Structure, and Learning about Second Language Acquisition (p. 1). Other issues covered under the CLAD certification process include the following:

I. Instruction
   a. Oracy and Literacy for English Language Development
   b. Content and Instruction
   c. Bilingual Education
II. Assessment
   a. Language Assessment
   b. Content Area Assessment
III. Culture
   a. Cultural diversity in the United States
   b. The Intercultural Educator
   c. Culturally Responsive Schooling
IV. Policy
V. Language Planning and Policy
VI. Special Populations of English Learners (Diaz-Rico & Weed, 2006, pp. 1, 174).

The CLAD certification aims at giving teachers in the P–12 setting the skills and competencies they need to be able to support students who are nonnative speakers of the English language in the United States to develop skills in reading, conversational, discrete language skills, and academic language proficiencies in English (Cummins, 2003, pp. 3–5).

Among other things, the CTEL program and the resulting CLAD certificate provides candidates with opportunities to develop research-based conceptual understanding of language systems, structures, forms, functions, and variation. It provides candidates with in-depth knowledge of current research and research-based theories in the specialized instruction of English Language Development (ELD). It also shows teacher candidates how to help English learners access grade-level content instruction and prepares them on how to provide benchmarks of English learners' progress toward California's Reading and Language Arts Framework (Standards of Quality and Effectiveness for California Teachers of English Learners (CTEL) Programs Leading to CLAD Certification).

Chinaka Samuel DomNwachukwu

References

Cummins, J. (2003). Reading and the bilingual student: Fact and fiction. In G. G. Garcia (Ed.), *English learners: Reaching the highest level of English literacy* (pp. 2–33). Newark, DE: International Reading Association.

Diaz-Rico, L. T. & Weed, K. Z. (2006). *The cross-cultural language and academic development handbook: A complete K–12 reference guide.* New York: Pearson.

State of California Commission on Teacher Credentialing. (1997). *Proposed amendments to sections 80015, 80015.2, and 80015.3 of Title 5, California code of regulations, pertaining to the CLAD and BCLAD certificates.* Retrieved from http://www.ctc.ca.gov/notices/coded/1997/979716.pdf.

State of California Commission on Teacher Credentialing. (2006). *Standards of quality and effectiveness for California teachers of English learners (CTEL) programs leading to CLAD certification: A handbook for teacher educators and program reviewers.* Sacramento: Commission on Teacher Credentialing.

Swofford, S. W. (1997). *Proposed amendments to sections 90015, 80015.2, and 80015.3 of title 5 California code of regulations, pertaining to the CLAD and BCLAD certificates. A Notice of Public Hearing, August 14, 1997.* Retrieved from http://www.ctc.ca.gov/notices/coded/1997/979716.pdf.

Yee-Sakamoto, I. (2007). Introduction. In *English language learner and diversity manual* (p. ix). New York: Pearson.

CROWD MANAGEMENT

Crowds are the groups that have the common ideas and excitements. They are not organized and everlasting within themselves. The remarkable characteristics include: being at the same environment physically; being together for a certain period of time; and not having collaboration, hierarchical order, and an audited interaction among people forming the crowd. Crowds are divided into two categories: planned and unplanned. Both categories have also two subcategories: active and inactive. Demonstrations are planned, active crowds. Crowd management is important for preventing the gathering of a crowd without permission and preventing a peaceful demonstration from turning into a violent one (Akyol, 2010; Cerrah, 1998; Reicher et al., 2004; Waddington, 2011; Göksu, 2000).

Although some may occur spontaneously, most demonstrations are planned. There is a preparatory phase for many demonstrations, and they come into existence as a result of a systematical work. It is important for the law enforcement agencies to follow the mentioned phase in order to manage the gathered crowd and not to let it turn into a violent one (Douglas, 2004; Cerrah, 1998; Cerrah, 1997; Reicher et al., 2004; Göktepe, n.d).

In demonstrations, people in groups have different motivations, and they are not monotype. For example, while some people are provocateurs and show provocative attitudes, some others are just in a supporting position. Some of the latter are dignified people who do not want to be a cause for a violent demonstration, and some are just bystanders. This issue must be kept in mind by organizers of a demonstration in order not to get out of the objective of the demonstration. This issue must be considered also by the law enforcement agencies to manage the crowd in a successful way (Zengin & Gözübenli, n.d; Ünal, n.d.; Waddington, 2011; Van & Walgrave, 2001; Sharp & Paulson, 2005; King & Brearley, 1996; Douglas, 2004).

Power of the group and its potential to be effective cannot be measured in some cases by the number of people forming the crowd in demonstrations. When a demonstration turns into a violent one, depending on the motivation of people or their anger level, destructive power can be higher than estimated. People in demonstrations cannot be expected to be conscious in their actions. Responsibility notion is lost among these people. Their actions are rather emotional. Suppressed feelings are released and put into practice. Self-control is seen to be weak in people, and they get affected quickly. They are open to infusions and imitate people around them without considerations of right or wrong (Meyer & Tarrow, 1998; Cerrah, 1998; Chenoweth & Stephan, 2012; King, 2011; Reicher et al., 2004; Ünal, n.d.; Göksu, 2000).

Detecting the ones directing the group, and separating them from the group if there is a risk of getting out of the aim for the demonstration, is crucial. In such cases, the group must be divided into as small as possible subgroups in order to end the communication and interaction between them. In cases in which the group must be dispersed, the way to do it is through distracting the crowd or diverting its attention. There may be occasions, such as a violent demonstration, in which law enforcement agencies are forced to use batons, tear gas, and/or plastic bullets in order to intervene (Akyol, 2010; Cerrah, 1997; Göksu, 2000; Göktepe, n.d.; Waddington, 2011; Toliver et al., 2006; King & Brearley, 1996; Douglas, 2004).

The rules and limits of demonstrations are specified in the legislation of every country. Intervention of security forces and limits for these interventions also take place within those legislations. These legislations are similar in basis despite some differences from one country to another. The overall accepted idea is that demonstrations are considered a democratic right if they are approved, not violent, and not violating others' rights (Meyer & Tarrow, 1998; Sharp & Paulson, 2005; Roberts & Ash, 2009; Chenoweth & Stephan, 2012; Van & Walgrave, 2001; Karakuş & Ünal, 2010; Göksu, 2000).

Aykut Töngür
Hasan Hüseyin Çali

References

Akyol, Z. (2010). Kalabalık Yönetimi. in O. Karakuş & B. Ünal (Eds.), *Özel Güvenlik Eğitimleri Ders kitabı*. Ankara: Dörtbay Yayın Dağıtım.

Cerrah, İ. (1997). Toplumsal Olaylar ve Çevik Kuvvet Eğitimi. *Amme İdaresi Dergisi*, 30(3), 135–49.

Cerrah, İ. (1998). *Crowds and public order policing: An analysis of crowds and interpretations of their behavior based on observational studies in Turkey, England and Wales*. Aldershot: Ashgate.

Chenoweth, E. & Stephan, M. (2012). *Why civil resistance works: The strategic logic of nonviolent conflict*. New York: Columbia University Press.

Douglas, R. N. (2004). *Dealing with demonstrations: The law of public protest and its enforcement*. Sydney: Federation Press.

Göksu, T. (2000). *Toplumsal psikoloji, toplumsal olaylar ve müdahale esasları*. Ankara: Özen yayıncılık.

Göktepe, F. (n.d.) Toplumsal olayların yönetimi ve müdahale esasları. Retrieved from Ataturk University, http://lms.atauni.edu.tr/FileUploads/Src/5f4a429e-3069-4f6b-a03b-88cffe4b2b8c/10.%C3%9Cnite-%20Toplumsal%20Olaylar%C4%B1n%20Y%C3%B6netimi%20ve%20M%C3%BCdahale%20Esaslar%C4%B1.pdf.

Karakuş, O. & Ünal, B. (Eds.). (2010). *Özel güvenlik eğitimleri ders kitabı*. Ankara: Dörtbay Yayın Dağıtım.

King, B. G. (2011). The tactical disruptiveness of social movements: Sources of market and mediated disruption in corporate boycotts. *Social Problems*, 58(4), 491–517.

King, M. & Brearley, N. (1996). *Public order policing: Contemporary perspectives on strategy and tactics*. Leicester: Perpetuity Press.

Meyer, D. S. & Tarrow, S. G. (1998). *The social movement society: Contentious politics for a new century*. Lanham, MD: Rowman & Littlefield.

Reicher, S., Stott, C., Cronin, P., & Adang, O. (2004). An integrated approach to crowd psychology and public order policing. *Policing: An International Journal of Police Strategies & Management*, 27(4), 558–72.

Roberts, A. & Ash, T. G. (Eds.). (2009). *Civil resistance and power politics: The experience of non-violent action from Gandhi to the present*. New York: Oxford University Press.

Sharp, G., & Paulson, J. (2005). *Waging nonviolent struggle: 20th century practice and 21st century potential*. New Hampshire: Extending Horizons Books.

Toliver, J., Murphy, J., McFarland, M., & Ederheimer, J. (2006). Police management of mass demonstrations: Identifying issues and successful approaches. *Police Executive Research Forum*. Washington DC: Police Executive Research Forum.

Ünal, M. (n.d.) Toplumsal Olaylar ve Özellikleri. Retrieved from Ataturk University, http://lms.atauni.edu.tr/FileUploads/Src/76881882-d526-4811-9301-88cfdfaeab18/3..%20%C3%9Cnite-%20Toplumsal%20Olaylar%20ve%20%C3%96zellikleri.pdf.

Van Aelst, P. & Walgrave, S. (2001). Who is that (wo)man in the street? From the normalisation of protest to the normalisation of the protester. *European Journal of Political Research*, 39, 461–86.

Waddington, D. P. (2011). Public order policing in South Yorkshire, 1984–2011: The case for a permissive approach to crowd control. *Contemporary Social Science*, 6(3), 309–24.

Zengin, S. & Gözübenli, M. (n.d.) Toplumsal Olaylarda Müzakere, Müzakereci Ve Müzakere Teknikleri. Retrieved from Ataturk University, http://lms.atauni.edu.tr/FileUploads/Src/d9dd9590-07cb-4218-8fea-88cffe4b9375/13.%20%C3%9Cnite%20Toplumsal%20Olaylarda%20M%C3%BCzakere,%20M%C3%BCzakereci%20ve%20M%C3%BCzakere%20Teknikleri.pdf.

CULTURAL BACKGROUND

Culture refers to patterns of thoughts, beliefs, and values that distinguish members of a particular social group and that are acquired through social interaction rather than being based in biology (i.e., inherited). Anthropologists have studied culture since the origins of that field of study, and over recent decades their findings and interpretations of cultural differences and similarities have become influential in interpreting human behaviors in other fields ranging from education to medicine.

Cultural background thus refers in broad terms to the combination of one's ethnic, geographic, and linguistic origins, with varying weights assigned to these and to related but less central areas (e.g., socioeconomic, religious, or political affiliation), depending on beliefs about the relative importance of each area. Though it may be identified ethnically by researchers or by others—for example, as someone having an Asian, versus American, versus Asian American cultural background—when considered at a more fine-grained or emic level, cultural background becomes primarily a self-identified construct.

Cultural background is important in education because research indicates that a mismatch between the cultural background of teachers and of their students can lead to decreased achievement and other undesirable outcomes (such as increased disciplinary referrals for these students; Gregory, Skiba, & Noguera, 2010). This mismatch, and corresponding achievement issues, hold true not only in the United States where teachers tend to be predominantly (>80 percent) white and female, but also in other settings across the globe.

Fortunately, there are some strategies that appear to be effective in helping teachers address this mismatch (e.g., Beyer, 2010). Thoughtful exploration by teachers of their own cultural background, specifically as it informs their status in society (i.e., by examining white identity and corresponding white privilege, as well as examining one's own cultural background in depth) offers an effective strategy set (cf. Kaufman & Hines, 2010). The use of these strategies leads to the development of increased cultural competence (i.e., the ability to interact effectively with individuals from cultural backgrounds different from one's own). Participation in professional development training that focuses on developing teachers' ability to infuse multicultural content into the curriculum is another strategy that may be effective in reducing the effects of differing cultural background on student achievement and related outcomes of interest.

Research Findings Related to Cultural Backgrounds

Researchers have used cultural background to explain individual and group differences in a variety of areas. Some cultural backgrounds are more conforming and submissive than others. Bond and Smith, in a 1996 extensive quantitative review (i.e., meta-analysis) study, found that conformity was higher in collectivist cultures than in individualist cultures, and that cultural values had a stronger impact on conformity than any other variables.

CULTURAL BACKGROUND AND THE SELF Individuals' reasons for happiness vary depending on their cultural backgrounds. In Western cultures, individuals' happiness is dependent on their pleasure and positive feelings, whereas in Eastern cultures, it is dependent on actualizing their potential (Joshanloo, 2014). In Western cultures, the self is based on the ideals of individualism, enhancing autonomy, independence, self-esteem, and a strong ego, which are viewed as essential ingredients of individuals' happiness. In contrast, in Eastern cultures, individuals' self is seen as a small part of the collective and the cosmos; the self alone is de-emphasized, and its relational aspects are emphasized, transcending personal desires for the sake of family and group (Joshanloo, 2014). In Eastern cultures, the Western concept of happiness is criticized for being too self-focused and temporary, and it is thought eventually to lead to individual and collective unhappiness. In Eastern cultures, filial piety is considered as an important sign of maturity, whereas in Western cultures, family obligations and social expectations may be viewed as constraints preventing the full expression of unique selfhood (Christopher & Hickinbottom, 2008).

HUMANITY'S PLACE IN THE WORLD In Western cultures, humankind is seen as privileged, attempting to master, manipulate, or control the world in various aspects that include one's life, relationships, and raw nature; autonomy and independence are core values. In Eastern cultures, in contrast, humankind is but a small part of the cosmos; adjustment to the environment and achieving harmony with others and the cosmos are valued, and thus mastery, manipulation, or control over nature are devalued (Joshanloo, 2014).

CULTURAL BACKGROUND, HAPPINESS, AND CONTENTMENT In Western cultures, it is difficult to accept hardship, negative experiences and feelings, and unhappiness as integral parts of a good life, whereas in Eastern cultures, happiness includes the wisdom to embrace unhappiness as part of life. Negative feelings are to be accepted as parts of a truly happy life, given that hardship, suffering, and pain are unavoidable. An emphasis on self-cultivation and self-discipline renders Eastern concepts of happiness more tolerant toward negative experiences and feelings. Despair and failure are expected in the process of self-actualization and self-development (Joshanloo, 2014).

In Eastern cultures, *contentment* should be preserved in both happy and sad times (Kwee, 2012). Contentment is a balance between joy and sorrow, and it involves satisfaction and a sense of being at peace with oneself, others, and the whole cosmos, which is achieved through spiritual practice. Individuals' goal achievement, social comparison, and even the amount of suffering should not affect the sense of contentment, as it is accompanied by a sense of fulfillment and abundance (Joshanloo, 2014).

LOCUS OF CONTROL Culture shapes the way individuals appraise their emotions by informing individuals' subjective appraisal in the form of locus of control. Individuals characterized by an *internal* locus of control consider the outcomes of events to be contingent upon their own actions, whereas those characterized by an *external* locus of control view event outcomes as largely influenced by outside forces, such as other people and chance. In general, an internal locus of control is beneficial in motivating people to gratify their need for competence by actively engaging in strategic coping behavior. In a meta-analytic study, Cheng, Cheung, Chio, and Chan (2013) found moderately strong relationships between external locus of control, depression symptoms, and anxiety symptoms, and showed that the link between external locus of control and anxiety symptoms was weaker within collectivist cultures compared with individualist cultures. Autonomy,

which is felt more strongly in individualist cultures, is related to psychological well-being; the willingness of individuals in these cultures to confront and change the environment rather than staying inert fosters attainment of agentic goals (Cheng et al., 2013). By contrast, collectivist cultures promote interpersonal harmony and alignment with the environment, and their members are encouraged to change themselves, rather than their surroundings, which may foster calmness or contentedness (Cheng et al., 2013).

Cultural background explains not only differences in coping outcomes but also in strategies for handling stress. Members of collectivist cultures report more frequent deployment of *acceptance* for handling stressful events whose outcomes are beyond their control, resulting in lower levels of anxiety (Gan, Shang, & Zhang, 2007). In Eastern cultures, individuals have to accept the influence of the environment by following the flow of nature. Thus, acceptance of external control is also a form of personal control (Cheng et al., 2013). The term *fate control* refers to the belief that although events in life are predetermined by impersonal outside forces, there are ways in which individuals can shape the degree of such forces via specific culturally endorsed strategies. Fate control is endorsed more by collectivist cultures than their counterparts from individualist cultures (Leung & Bond, 2004). Although members of collectivist cultures tend to believe that events are predetermined by fate, they continue to strive to achieve better outcomes (Leung, Chen, & Lam, 2010), which is referred to as *negotiable fate*. Asians and Asian Americans believe in negotiable fate more than Caucasian Americans (Au et al., 2011).

Cultural backgrounds shape individuals' psychological, emotional, and cognitive tendencies, and at the same time, individuals also shape cultures. Lamoreaux and Morling, in a 2012 meta-analysis study, found that individuals shape cultural products through shared, tangible representations such as advertising, television, texts, laws, public behavior norms, Internet content, language, architecture, and the like. Thus, individuals are shaped by participating in the meanings, opportunities, and norms of specific cultures, and in turn, these culturally shaped individuals reinforce, recreate, and maintain those cultural contexts (Lamoreaux & Morling, 2012). For example, U.S. cultural products manifest: power distance more than Korean cultural products; feminine characteristics less than Mexican, Korean, or Hong Kong cultural products; and masculinity more than non-U.S. cultural products. In an earlier meta-analysis, Morling and Lamoreaux (2008) also reported that North American cultural products such as psychology, communication, and business literatures are more individualistic and less collectivistic than those from East Asia.

Conclusions

Understanding the role cultural background may play in relations among and between individuals and groups can strengthen efforts to achieve social goals, particularly in educational settings but also in other spheres of interaction. An understanding of the cultural background's role is also helpful in examining general trends related to individuals' perceptions of happiness, locus of control, and agency. As with other aspects of culture, while some generalization is possible, there also may be variation among individuals who outwardly may appear to share similar backgrounds. Thus, caution is advised in making broad explanatory statements, and individuals' self-perceptions must be taken into account.

Kyung-Hee Kim
Michael S. Matthews

References

Au, E. W. M., Chiu, C., Zhang, Z., Mallorie, L., Chaturvedi, A., Viswanathan, M., & Savani, K. (2011). Negotiable fate: Social ecological foundation and psychological functions. *Journal of Cross-Cultural Psychology*. doi: 10.1177/0022022111421632

Beyer, C. (2010). Innovative strategies that work with nondiverse teachers for diverse classrooms. *Journal of Research in Innovative Teaching, 3*(1), 119–29.

Bond, R. & Smith, P. B. (1996). Culture and conformity: A meta-analysis of studies using Asch's (1952b, 1956) line judgment task. *Psychological Bulletin, 119*, 111–37. doi: 10.1037/0033-2909.119.1.111

Cheng, C., Cheung, S-F., Chio, J. H-M., & Chan, M-P. S. (2013). Cultural meaning of perceived control: A meta-analysis of locus of control and psychological symptoms across 18 cultural regions. *Psychological Bulletin, 139*, 152–88. doi: 10.1037/a0028596

Christopher, J. C. & Hickinbottom, S. (2008). Positive psychology, ethnocentrism, and the disguised ideology of individualism. *Theory & Psychology, 18*, 563–89.

Gan, Y., Shang, J., & Zhang, Y. (2007). Coping flexibility and locus of control as predictors of burnout among Chinese college students. *Social Behavior and Personality, 35*, 1087–98. doi: 10.2224/sbp.2007.35.8.1087

Gregory, A., Skiba, R. J., & Noguera, P. A. (2010). The achievement gap and the discipline gap: Two sides of the same coin? *Educational Researcher, 39*(1), 59–68. doi: 10.3102/0013189x09357621

Joshanloo, M. (2014). Eastern conceptualizations of happiness: Fundamental differences with Western views. *Journal of Happiness Studies, 15*, 475–93. doi: 10.1007/s10902-013-9431-1

Kaufman, J. S. & Hines, S. M. (2010). Cultivating an understanding of privilege among teacher candidates. *Race, Gender & Class, 17*(1–2), 135–47.

Kwee, M. G. (2012). Relational Buddhism: A psychological quest for meaning and sustainable happiness. In P. T. P. Wong (Ed.), *The human quest for meaning: A handbook of psychological research and clinical applications* (2nd ed., pp. 249–73). New York: Routledge.

Lamoreaux, M. & Morling, B. (2012). Outside the head and outside individualism-collectivism: Further meta-analyses of cultural products. *Journal of Cross-Cultural Psychology, 43*, 299–327. doi: 10.1177/0022022110385234

Leung, C. H. Y., Chen, S. X., & Lam, B. C. P. (2010). Where there's a will, there's a way: The mediating effect of academic aspiration between beliefs and academic outcomes. *Journal of Psychology in Chinese Societies, 11*, 53–72. doi: 10.1111/1467-8624.00273

Leung, K. & Bond, M. H. (2004). Social axioms: A model for social beliefs in multicultural perspective. *Advances in Experimental Social Psychology, 36*, 119–97. doi: 10.1016/S0065-2601(04)36003-X

Morling, B. & Lamoreaux, M. (2008). Measuring culture outside the head: A meta-analysis of individualism-collectivism in cultural products. *Personality and Social Psychology Review, 12*(3), 199–221.

CULTURAL CAPITAL

As the word *capital* suggests, *cultural capital* describes the "return on investment" (or lack thereof) that culture can pay in the context of human social interaction. Like other forms of capital, individuals and/or groups can exchange cultural capital for access to exclusive interpersonal, academic, and professional goods and services—though often more intangible in nature—in the social realm. However, whereas other forms of capital are typically more proactively cultivated and, therefore, operate more consciously, cultural capital can be acquired more passively, often during early childhood, consequently often manifesting and proliferating more subconsciously. For that reason, cultural capital is more often unrecognized, or at least unacknowledged.

Origins

From the 1970s into the turn of the twenty-first century, French sociologist Pierre Bourdieu (1977, 1984, 1986) recognized that economic differences alone could not explain differences in educational outcomes; accordingly, he sought out alternative explanations for this phenomenon. Specifically, Bourdieu theorized a cultural form of capital, that in concert with economic capital, works as social currency to make "it possible to explain the unequal scholastic achievement of children originating from the different social classes by relating academic success . . . to the distribution of cultural capital between the classes and class fractions" (1986, p. 243). By expanding the definition of *capital* to include *culture*, Bourdieu opens new ways of explaining social inequality, specifically as it is related to the role of education in maintaining the existing social order.

Transparency

Bourdieu (1977) argues that cultural capital operates invisibly on three distinct levels: embodied, objectified, and institutionalized. *Embodied* cultural capital refers to the investments (of time, resources, experiences) an individual receives from the people, places, and things that surround her or him (most notably family) while growing up in an elite environment (Bourdieu, 1977). These investments make the person adept at traversing this environment in a manner that becomes uniquely fixed upon her or him such that this adeptness is carried for the rest of the individual's life. For example, by visiting museums as a child, an individual has the opportunity to develop knowledge about art that enables her or him to participate with acumen in exclusive circles later in life.

Objectified cultural capital describes the material objects with which an individual interacts in the development of embodied cultural capital (Bourdieu, 1977). The function of these objects is to convey the criteria for what the society defines as "cultured"—for example, learning to distinguish "good," and, therefore, rare and valuable art, from other creative forms of expression.

Institutionalized cultural capital refers to the institutions that are granted the authority by elite society to delineate what investments have value and who is deemed to possess them (Bourdieu, 1977). Private preparatory school education serves as an example of this kind of cultural capital.

It is important to note that cultivation of all three of these forms of cultural capital is predicated upon the understanding that the individual does not first need to possess economic capital. In other words, if an individual must work to gain the economic capital necessary to access cultural capital, then possession of cultural capital is considered inauthentic and generally prohibited.

Habitus and Distinction

Because a minimum level of individual effort is necessary to accumulate cultural capital (e.g., a recalcitrant child must still go to the museum for its effect), Bourdieu (1977, 1984) suggests that environments of the dominant class imbue individuals with the values and, thus, dispositions that facilitate the accumulation of cultural capital. Accordingly, members of this class pass these values and dispositions from one generation to the next. Bourdieu (1977) describes the intergenerational inclination to develop these values and dispositions as a system that he terms *habitus*: "the laws that determine the tendency of structures to reproduce themselves by producing agents endowed with the system of predispositions which is capable of engendering practices adapted to the structures and thereby contributing to the reproduction of the structures" (p. 258). Accordingly, the drive to accumulate cultural capital is derived through habitus, precisely because habitus deems this accumulation to be a cross-generationally worthy pursuit.

Operating as a reciprocal cycle in which individual cultural capital supports and reinforces societal cultural capital and vice versa, an intergenerational return on investment is made manifest (Bourdieu, 1977). For example, "By conferring institutional recognition on the cultural capital possessed by any given agent, the academic qualification also makes it possible to compare qualification holders and even to change them" (1986, p. 247). It is this credentialing process that Bourdieu (1984) calls *distinction*: the cultural equivalent of deeming things scarce or rare and, therefore, valuable. Distinction can even occur when things deemed uncommon are not in actuality, but are made to be by the use of power to limit access to them (e.g., the diamond market). Distinction has the added benefit of providing a minimum guarantee of access to elite social spaces in which "educational capital" is construed as "guaranteed cultural capital" (1984, p. 80).

Distinction enables some individuals to be seen as more valuable than others in social settings in two ways (Bourdieu, 1984). The first is the inherent value of the embodied cultural capital that only some individuals have. The second is the value ascribed to the set of dispositions that only some individuals possess, by virtue of habitus, that mark them as agents dedicated to the reproduction of the dominant social system. When an array of distinct individuals are deployed in a society, the effects of habitus are attributed to them as individuals, rather than as members of a group, a function of social class, or a byproduct of an embedded societal structure. Ostensibly hidden within the dispositions of individuals, habitus is easily produced and reproduced in social systems. At a meta level, however, these dispositions are carefully vetted and policed.

Habitus is further solidified through so-called equal access to public education, which claims to level the social and economic "playing field" in society (Bourdieu, 1977). As Bourdieu asserts, the educational system dually contributes "to the reproduction of the structure of class relations . . . by concealing, by an apparently neutral attitude, the fact that it fills this function" (p. 258). In disguising its own effect in this regard, education "reproduces all the more perfectly the structure of the distribution of cultural capital among classes," further

perpetuating the falsehood that such capital only serves individual interests (p. 267).

Capital, Funds, and Wealth

Some academics have attempted to reframe Bourdieu's (1977) notion of cultural capital in order to extend worth to nondominant cultural expressions and attributes by arguing that all cultures have capital (González, Moll, & Amanti, 2005; González, Moll, Floyd Tennery, Rivera, Rendon, & Amanti, 1993; Moll, Amanti, Neff, & González, 1992). Other scholars have argued that because Bourdieu's (1986) notion of capital is predicated upon capitalism, it is inextricably linked to competition, and competition is often at odds with the perceived capital of many nondominant cultures (Yosso, 2005; Yosso & García, 2007). Consequently, the question of whose culture has capital has been amended to consider whose culture has worth as capital in the context of capitalism. Literacy scholar Luís Moll (Moll, Amanti, Neff, & González, 1992) describes nondominant groups' *funds of knowledge* in arguing that the knowledge that all students bring with them into the classroom has worth, though these funds are often unrecognized or, worse, unacknowledged by teachers, the educational establishment, and society at large. Building on Moll's work, critical race theorist Tara Yosso (2005) articulates that nondominant groups hold *community cultural wealth* characterized by six forms of capital: resistant, navigational, social, linguistic, familial, and aspirational. These forms of capital enable nondominant groups to cope with the oppression they experience as a consequence of the manifestations of cultural capital that Bourdieu (1977) delineates. Resistant capital is used to challenge inequality and subordination; navigational capital is employed to maneuver in indifferent and hostile social institutions; social capital provides access to kinship networks and related resources; linguistic capital affords the ability to communicate in different linguistic styles and languages; familial capital speaks to family histories and related bodies of knowledge; and aspirational capital promotes hope in the face of continuing challenges (Yosso & García, 2007). These forms of capital do serve nondominant groups in the context of capitalism, but in manners that attempt to compensate for their lack of cultural capital rather than to undergird their exclusive access to it.

Coda

Fundamentally, cultural capital exists as a mechanism to keep distinct social classes separate in a way that is not possible with economic capital alone. Because cultural capital operates invisibly, is carefully constructed as an individual attribute (not the function of a hierarchical social order), and is attained through an ostensibly neutral educational system, it serves to justify social inequality, especially in societies that describe themselves as egalitarian and individually meritocratic. Public education is pivotal in the proliferation and perpetuation of cultural capital because it enables the conversion of

> social hierarchies into academic hierarchies . . . which is more and more necessary to the perpetuation of the "social order" as the evolution of the power relationship between classes tends more completely to exclude the imposition of a hierarchy based upon the crude and ruthless affirmation of the power relationship. (Bourdieu, 1977, p. 271)

For this reason, many social justice educators argue that the persistent educational "achievement gap" between white and/or at least middle-class students, and students of color and/or working-class students, is, in actuality, evidence that the education system is operating exactly as is intended.

Mark Brimhall-Vargas
Christine Clark

References

Bourdieu, P. (1977). Cultural reproduction and social reproduction. In J. Karabel and A. Halsey (Eds.), *Power and ideology in education* (pp. 487–511). New York: Oxford University Press.

Bourdieu, P. (1984). *Distinction: A social critique of the judgement of taste* (R. Nice, Trans.). Cambridge, MA: Harvard University Press.

Bourdieu, P. (1986). The forms of capital. In J. G. Richardson (Ed.), *Handbook of theory and research for the sociology of education* (pp. 241–58). New York: Greenwood Press.

González, N., Moll, L. C., & Amanti, C. (2005). *Funds of knowledge: Theorizing practices in households and classrooms.* Mahwah, NJ: Lawrence Erlbaum Associates.

González, N., Moll, L., Floyd Tennery, M., Rivera, A., Rendon, P., & Amanti, C. (1993). Funds of knowledge for teaching in Latino households. *Urban Education*, *29*(4), 443–70.

Moll, L., Amanti, C., Neff, D., & González, N. (1992). Funds of knowledge for teaching: Using a qualitative approach to connect homes and classrooms. *Theory into Practice*, *31*(2), 132–41.

Yosso, T. (2005). Whose culture has capital? A critical race theory discussion of community cultural wealth. *Race, Ethnicity and Education*, *8*(1), 69–91.

Yosso, T. & García, D. (2007). "This is no slum!" A critical race theory analysis of community cultural wealth in Culture Clash's *Chávez Ravine*. *Aztlan: A Journal of Chicano Studies*, *32*(1), 145–79.

CULTURAL CHAUVINISM

Cultural Chauvinism: The Art of Masking Abuse of Power

> There are too many idiots in this world. And having said it, I have the burden of proving it.
>
> —Frantz Fanon, *Black Skin, White Masks*

According to Webster's dictionary, the term *chauvinism* derived from the French word *chauvinisme* after Nicolas Chauvin, who served as a soldier under Napoleon I and who was infamous for his fondness to the royal cause (Webster, 2010). In the United States, many equate chauvinism with gender discrimination, and it is often a trait ascribed to Hispanic men. Historically, it is those of the dominant group who have employed this type of discrimination, and Hispanic men have tailored it to serve their needs. Having said that, it would stand to reason that cultural chauvinism is perhaps ethnic discrimination whereas one group may feel superior to another group or even a sense of entitlement over another group.

While there is a dearth of information on this topic, there seems to be a need for clarification. Cultural chauvinism has often been synonymous with xenophobia. It is here where it becomes complicated. The question then becomes; Who is determining who is foreign? For example, most refer to the United States as America and not North America. When we use the term *America* in reference to the United States, we chauvinistically omit all Latin American countries. We also refer to United States citizens as "American." However, the undertone is that American citizens are of European descent. To further amplify the argument, in 2013, an American child of Mexican descent was selected to sing the National Anthem at a sporting event. The young man was wearing a mariachi costume, which is the traditional street music ensemble in the Mexican culture. There was immediate outpour of disdain by "Americans" who were outraged that a non-American was singing the anthem. Mark Anthony, a famous Puerto Rican singer, also sang the anthem elsewhere, and many "Americans" reacted with the same outrage.

Cultural chauvinism can manifest itself in many different forms and take on new meaning. Garcia (1982) (in Pahnos & Butt, 1992) asserts that "when cultures are determined to be inadequate, backward, or inferior to one's own, it is referred to as cultural chauvism" (p. 118). Taylor-Brown, Garcia, and Kingson (2001) argue that cultural chauvinism occurs when members of a particular group promote that "only members of the same ethnic, racial, or cultural group are qualified to serve individuals from the particular group" (p. 185). This type of construct serves a particular purpose dependent on desired outcomes. There are times when only members of a particular group who share similar experiences based on treatment are the only ones who can adequately address issues that may arise as a result of said treatment, or even just offer moral support.

Cultural chauvinism may have a bad connotation. However, it may also serve as a coping mechanism for those who are recipients of institutional racism and other "isms" that discriminate. There are times when the very systems that are in place to protect individuals are the gatekeepers to resolve. Aside from the typical discriminatory "isms," there is also nepotism that occurs in various forms and that is frequently overlooked. One has to wonder if nepotism isn't the real culprit in the world of abuse of power. Perhaps cultural chauvinism is just an innocent bystander, and we should be promoting "cultural intelligence."

Sylvia Fuentes

References

Fowers, B. & Davidov, B. (2006). The virtue of multiculturalism: Personal transformation, character, and openness to the other. *American Psychologist*, 61(6), 581–94.

Garcia, R. I. (1982). Teaching in a pluralistic society: Concepts, models, strategies. New York: Harper and Row.

Pahnos, M. & Butt, K. (1992). Ethnocentrism—a universal pride in one's ethnic background: Its impact on teaching and learning. *Education*, 113(1), 118.

Taylor-Brown, S., Garcia, A., & Kingson, E. (2001). Cultural competence versus cultural chauvinism: Implications for social work. *Health & Social Work*, 26(3), 185–87.

Webster's New World College Dictionary. (2010). Cleveland, OH: Wiley Publishing, Inc.

CULTURAL COMPETENCY

Cultural Competency in Open Source Systems

Cultural competency in open source systems (OSS) is a complex process involving the way in which individuals use OSS and how they apply this technology to individuals, communities, and nation-states who have limited access to technology for educational purposes. It regards how code is designed and how open source resources are used and distributed (Choi, Kim, & Yu, 2009). There are four key elements necessary to achieve open source cultural competence. First, individuals must have a conscious awareness of sociocultural, sociopolitical, and socio-racial issues that impact OSS (Carroll, 2013). Second, individuals must have specific cultural content knowledge and show the ability to apply cultural content to the resolution of open source challenges. Third, individuals must demonstrate culturally appropriate open source practices (Cockerill & Knols, 2008). Fourth, individuals must use advocacy to alter the systemic influences and cultural biases to OSS or their distribution to developing groups and nation-states. Advocacy requires a proactive engagement that involves a user's affirmation and commitment to share culture-specific elements of code design with others in the open source community (Carroll, 2013, p. 8).

Open source cultural competency challenges male-gendered privilege in writing open source code and recognizes that OSS can perpetuate systemic colonialism and technological imperialism. Moreover, it recognizes and deconstructs coding biases, especially those based on race, gender, country of origin, nationalism, or linguistic differences.

The foundation for open source cultural competency originates within the core features of the Open Source Definition (OSD), a set of operating or practice guidelines for open source users and consumers under one of several open source licenses (http://opensource.org/docs/osd). They are presented below in Table C.1. Standards 5 and 6 are relevant to cultural competency practice. Standard 5 states that there is no discrimination against persons or groups, while standard 6 notes that there is no discrimination against a field of endeavor or a research activity.

Cultural competency in OSS represents a set of deliberate and intentional actions and practices, each of which is designed to promote culturally responsive usage of OSS across the globe. As an operating premise, it is designed to ensure equitable access to OSS by all users, regardless of academic preparation, economics, or country of origin. It creates an open academic cultural environment around which educational activities are shared and promoted with honesty, integrity, and fairness for all who use it.

Doris Wright Carroll

References

Carroll, D. (2013). A model of cultural competence in open source systems. In S. Hai-Jew (Ed.), *Open-source technologies for maximizing the creation, deployment, and use of digital resources and information.* Hershey, PA: IGI-Global.

Choi, C. J., Kim, S. W., & Yu, S. (2009). Global ethics of collective Internet governance: Intrinsic motivation and open source software. *Journal of Business Ethics, 90*(4), 523–31. doi: 10.1007/s10551-009-0057-5

Cockerill, M. J. & Knols, B. G. J. (2008). Open access to research for the developing world. *Issues in Science and Technology, 24*(2), 65–69.

Table C.1 The Open Source Definition

1. Free Redistribution. The license shall not restrict any party from selling or giving away the software as a component of an aggregate software distribution containing programs from several different sources. The license shall not require a royalty or other fee for such sale.
2. Source Code. The program must include source code, and must allow distribution in source code as well as compiled form. Where some form of a product is not distributed with source code, there must be a well-publicized means of obtaining the source code for no more than a reasonable reproduction cost preferably, downloading via the Internet without charge. The source code must be the preferred form in which a programmer would modify the program. Deliberately obfuscated source code is not allowed. Intermediate forms such as the output of a preprocessor or translator are not allowed.
3. Derived Works. The license must allow modifications and derived works, and must allow them to be distributed under the same terms as the license of the original software.
4. Integrity of the Author's Source Code. The license may restrict source code from being distributed in modified form *only* if the license allows the distribution of "patch files" with the source code for the purpose of modifying the program at build time. The license must explicitly permit distribution of software built from modified source code. The license may require derived works to carry a different name or version number from the original software.
5. No Discrimination Against Persons or Groups. The license must not discriminate against any person or group of persons.
6. No Discrimination Against Fields of Endeavor. The license must not restrict anyone from making use of the program in a specific field of endeavor. For example, it may not restrict the program from being used in a business, or from being used for genetic research.
7. Distribution of License. The rights attached to the program must apply to all to whom the program is redistributed without the need for execution of an additional license by those parties.
8. License Must Not Be Specific to a Product. The rights attached to the program must not depend on the program's being part of a particular software distribution. If the program is extracted from that distribution and used or distributed within the terms of the program's license, all parties to whom the program is redistributed should have the same rights as those that are granted in conjunction with the original software distribution.
9. License Must Not Restrict Other Software. The license must not place restrictions on other software that is distributed along with the licensed software. For example, the license must not insist that all other programs distributed on the same medium must be open source software.
10. License Must Be Technology Neutral. No provision of the license may be predicated on any individual technology or style of interface.

Source: Open Source Initiative, http://opensource.org/docs/osd

Open Source Initiative. (n.d.) Retrieved from http://opensource.org/docs/osd.

CULTURAL DIFFERENCES

Understanding Cultural Differences

Cultural differences may be defined as variations in the way of life among people and society in regard to cultural beliefs and traditions, including religious observance and educational practices. The emergence of a global society, resulting from technological innovations during the end of the twentieth century and into the twenty-first century, has put different patterns of family, work, and education into contact with each other. Globalism of education is happening within a cultural world that encompasses variations in traditions, norms, values, and shared history. Also, emphasis on globalization focuses less on distinguishing societies from one another and more on viewing cultural differences as an advantage in the world as well as a means to strengthen one another's worldview. This entry examines why understanding cultural differences is essential to educating the next generation of learners.

An Ideological Perspective of Cultural Differences

In light of the proliferation of technologies, such as text messaging, Twitter, Facebook, and the Internet, understanding cultural differences has become imperative for applicable learning experiences. Some groups share social norms and traditions, including how they approach learning and how they construct their identity, while other groups have extremely contradictory norms and traditions. This is where cultural differences come into the picture. Therefore, a useful way to understand cultural differences is through the principles of collectivist and individualist cultures. According to Wagner (1995),

> Individualists look after themselves and tend to ignore group interests if they conflict with personal desires . . . and collectivists look out for the well-being of the groups to which they belong, even if such actions sometimes require that personal interests be disregarded. (p. 153)

This suggests that collectivists are more likely to believe that they are more similar to others, and they are more likely to be more attentive to the views of others as well.

If one takes a closer look into this generalization, it is apparent that this universal characterization of collectivists is incomplete. In work preceding Wagner's research, other researchers suggested that the global representation of collectivist cultures is imprecise, especially when considering college students. Triandis, Bontempo, Villareal, Asai, and Lucca (1988) concluded that conformity is context specific, meaning individuals may be collectivists relative to their in-group (e.g., family and friends) but may not be for other groups (e.g., cultures that are generally different from their own). "Paying attention to the views of others and conforming to them are techniques for gaining acceptance by others. Such techniques are more important in an individualist society where one's in-groups are formed by the individual" (p. 333). Greenfield and Quiroz (2013) argue that for some cultural groups, such as Latino immigrant children, the individualism-collectivism ideologies are more context bound. Emerging from their research, is the suggestion that Latino immigrant children acquire a collectivistic message in the home (e.g., competing as a family, or group of friends) and an individualistic one in school (e.g., competing as individuals in a classroom setting). For Latino immigrant children, this characteristic seems to be an essential cultural difference, and it is contrary to the competitive orientation of autonomy or self-confidence.

Distinguishing between individualist and collectivist cultures on the basis of context is only part of the story; the other essential part concerns the role of competition in education. The most recognizable aspect of the U.S. culture is the country's educational purpose for its students (Greenfield & Quiroz, 2013). The idea is to develop students who will function as autonomous thinkers; they are unique, confident individuals who embrace freedom of expression and display cultural beliefs and customs of individualism with respect to their education. The expectation is that students will mature into individuals who are accountable for their achievements, or lack thereof, in life (Fryberg et al., 2013). This paradigm goes beyond the explicit functions of individuality and confidence in promoting self-determination and academic achievement in conventional scholastic contexts. Students will implicitly have social support, community connections, and sustained interactions with teachers and mentors who promote self-determination and academic achievement. Developing from this point of view, then, is that either the individual or the group contextualizes achievement, and individuals are the achievers or doers in individualistic cultures (Triandis et al. 1988). The opposite is the case in collectivist cultures, where it is the group that achieves. In general, regardless of context—the individual or group—people of both cultures are proud of their accomplishments and cultural differences are critical for identity development.

Application of Cultural Differences in Education

A fundamental characteristic of student identity is their culture as it stipulates the foundation for group membership and consistency. The existence of diverse groups and the cultural differences among students in the classroom presents unique challenges for educators. Students enter our classrooms with a set of beliefs and a code of behavior and values; they share a common history and traditions with a particular group. Being aware of students' beliefs and values may help educators promote understanding of cultural differences. Equally important, educators must be careful not to make broad generalizations about cultural differences in any particular group. A starting point for educators for promoting the appreciation of cultural differences is to understand the cultural assumptions held by students. To prevent confusion, educators must first acknowledge cultural differences, and then address them by providing students with experiences in which they, too, can learn about and develop an appreciation of diverse cultures.

To actualize the concept of appreciating culture differences in classrooms, educators can begin with being conscious of their own cultural standing. The assumption is that once educators acknowledge their own cultural standing, they may go about the business of promoting understanding of cultural differences through three interrelated modules recurring in the literature. These three modules are, creating learning environments that are challenging yet encouraging, offering an intellectually rigorous curriculum, and promoting respect across cultural groups. As culture and cultural differences are not static formations, the construction of learning environments that are challenging will be a dynamic process for the educator. Students must be encouraged to participate in activities and tasks that challenge them, yet they also need to be prepared to take on intellectually rigorous assignments. For instance, it is important that teachers do not associate language difficulty with low intelligent for second-language learners, which might result in teachers providing work that is below the students' intellectual level, or they might avoid calling on the students because they may not want to expose these students' low language proficiency, which might result in silencing these students. A supporting aspect of the learning environment should provide explicit explanations, instructions, and expectations, which might include modeling skills, encouraging students to represent concepts in multiple ways in order to make sense of them, and giving sufficient chances to practice skills to improve performance. Therefore, regardless of the students' cultural orientations, expectations for academic performance must be high; therefore, the support structures for mastery must be in place for all learners.

To expose students to different cultural norms and practices, classroom environments should encourage collaborative discourse (e.g., interaction and working in small groups), which facilitate the exchange of ideas, beliefs, and assumptions. Not only is collaborative discourse suitable for all types of learners, but it is also an appropriate pedagogical strategy for teaching varying degrees of complexity in critical thinking and understanding of cultural differences. To understand collaborative discourse as it relates to cultural differences in regard to language, worldview, and geography, it is important to focus the interplay that exists between the level of intragroup interaction on the required task and the task's level of complexity. The degree of complex critical thinking is developed or enhanced in collaborative discourse, especially when the group consists of members who are culturally different (e.g., language, social class, worldview), which may have an effect on the level of group collaboration needed to complete tasks. This in turn relates to the effectiveness of collaborative discourse. Wagner (1995) reminds us that students who think of themselves as independent, self-reliant individuals may be less apt to engage in collaborative work, and those students who view themselves as interdependent group members are more likely to engage in collaborative work. Promoting a feeling of interdependence among students with different cultural orientations is not always an easy charge because it takes time for students to develop a cohesive bond with their peers, but doing so is one of the most essential aspects of effective collaborative discourse that promotes practices that foster an understanding of cultural differences.

The intensification of globalization, and especially the rise in global communication through various social networks, make promoting respect across cultural groups an essential component of developing an understanding of cultural differences and "identifying the multidimensional aspects of those differences" (Kwong, 2012, p. 854). Furthermore, understanding cultural differences is an important benefit to bring about educational insights about the wider world as we become less concerned about distinguishing societies from one another and more interested in the greater similarity across societies.

Lillie R. Albert

References

Fryberg, S. A., Troop-Gordon, W., D'Arrisso, A., Flores, H., Ponizovskiy, V., Ranney, J. D., Mandour, T., . . . Burack, J. A. (2013). Cultural mismatch and the education of aboriginal youths: The interplay of cultural identities and teacher ratings. *Developmental Psychology*, 49(1), 72–79.

Greenfield, P. M. & Quiroz, B. (2013). Context and culture in the socialization and development of personal achievement values: Comparing Latino immigrant families, European American families and elementary school teachers. *Journal of Applied Developmental Psychology*, 34(2), 108–18.

Kwong, M. H. (2012). Incorporating multicultural learning in clinically-based education in the United States. *Social Work Education: The International Journal*, 31(7), 848–65.

Triandis, H. C., Bontempo, R., Villareal, M. J., Asai, M., & Lucca, N. (1988). Individualism and collectivism: Cross-cultural perspectives on self-ingroup relationships. *Journal of Personality and Social Psychology*, 54(2), 323–38.

Wagner, J. A. III. (1995). Studies of individualism-collectivism: Effects on cooperation in groups. *Academy of Management Journal*, 38(1), 152–72.

Additional Reading

Eberly Center for Teaching Excellence & Intercultural Communication Center. (2013). *Recognizing and addressing cultural variations in the classroom.* Retrieved from http://www.cmu.edu/teaching/resources/PublicationsArchives/InternalReports/culturalvariations.pdf.

CULTURAL EDUCATION

The concept of culturally appropriate education has been in the forefront as a result of an increase in diversity around the world. Cultural education promotes cultural knowledge, creativity, and intercultural understanding through education. It is an education that teaches learners about culture and provides the opportunity for learners to open their minds about others who are culturally different and to understand who people are in regard to their identities. Cultural education helps teach learners to respect differences among various groups of people and involves teaching for a diverse society so learners are able to live in an inclusive and multicultural world.

Culture

Sonia Nieto (2010) defines *culture* as "dynamic, active, changing, always on the move" (p. 79.). It is "multifaceted, meaning our identities are multiple, eclectic, mixed, and heterogeneous" (p. 80), and that we cannot use race and ethnicity as a term to define culture. Culture does not exist in isolation because it is "embedded in context and influenced by its environment in which it exists" (p. 82), as well as by social, economic, and political conditions defined by various levels of power. Culture is created and socially constructed as a result of what people do on a daily basis and the decisions they make about their lives. Culture is dialectical and full of contradictories and is learned through interactions between people and entire communities.

The Roles of Cultural Education

Helping learners explore, appreciate, and value what makes other people such as neighbors, classmates, community, and people around the world unique is important in the multicultural society we live in today. Understanding what people have in common, and what makes them tick, helps build knowledge of various cultures around the world. The foundation of one's culture is comprised of a variety of factors such as norms, knowledge, beliefs, behaviors, experiences, and language. Understanding that these factors vary among cultures is an important aspect of cultural education. Ignoring the reality of a culturally diverse world has its consequences. Learners who view the world through a limited lens that paints a picture of one culture being the norm may struggle to recognize that other norms exist when they become working adults and come into contact with someone who is culturally different for the first time.

Today's classrooms are filled with learners who come from various cultural backgrounds with differing languages and abilities. Therefore, it is important for teachers to include cultural education in relation to students' various cultural backgrounds in the curriculum (Gay, 2010). Helping learners understand their own cultural identity is critical before they are able to understand others' cultures.

People belong to a variety of cultural groups and communities, which impacts the development of their cultural identity and the values and assumptions they adopt as part of their behavior. Cultural education enables learners to deconstruct their paradigms and understand their own cultural identity, assumptions, and values. By understanding who they are, why they behave in certain ways, and why they believe what they believe, they are able to transfer this new knowledge into understanding others.

Despite the fact that society continues to increase in diversity, there are people who do not have any experience interacting with others who are culturally different from them. Cultural education is a vehicle that helps learners understand diversity among various cultures by providing them with opportunities to interact with others who are culturally different. By providing opportunities to interact and explore, in environments that are culturally different from their own, learners are able to learn about new cultures, ultimately resulting in respect for people who are culturally different from them.

People's values, patterns of behavior, and sense of cultural identity are a result of many factors that have changed over time. Cultural education helps learners understand the processes that influence culture and how culture is influenced by change. Forces that exist outside of the learner, such as forces within a society, contact between societies, and changes in the environment, all influence change in cultures (National Advisory Committee on Creative and Cultural Education, 1999). For example, technological advances have impacted change in many cultures, with cultures adopting technological tools for more efficient means of transportation, commerce, and communication. Another example is related to language. Many cultures have adopted the English language as a result of pressure to adapt the language at the cost of losing the language of their ancestors. By providing learners with examples, they are able to understand the evolution of culture as a result of outside forces.

In order to understand the present, learners must also understand the past. Cultural education encourages learners to examine the historical context of cultural behavior and patterns and to make connections to current behavioral patterns that have played a part in the development of their culture, other cultures, and the intersectionalities of their own cultural identity. Cultural education teaches learners to understand why things are the way they are and what could lead to possible cultural change at the local, national, and global level as a result of their roles in shaping these changes (NACCCE, 1999).

Cultural education is a tool that can help promote respect and understanding for different cultures, practices, values, and perspectives. Additionally, cultural education is the key to a better understanding of people, their cultures, and the world in which we live (Banks, 2010).

Sandra Foster

References

Banks, J. A. & Banks, C. A. M. (2010). *Multicultural education: Issues and perspectives* (7th ed.). Danvers, MA: John Wiley & Sons, Inc.

Gay, G. (2010). *Culturally responsive teaching: Theory, research, & practice* (2nd ed.). New York: Teachers College Press.

National Advisory Committee on Creative and Cultural Education. (1999). *All our futures: Creativity, culture and education.* London: DFEE.

Nieto, S. (2010). *The light in their eyes: Creating multicultural learning communities.* New York: Teachers College Press.

CULTURAL HEGEMONY

Our examination of *cultural hegemony*, often pronounced (hi-**jem**-*uh*-nee or **hej**-*uh*-moh-nee), or avoided altogether for academic fear of mispronunciation, begins by tracing the word's origin, then takes up the scholar, Antonio Gramsci, whose conceptualization has persisted through academic discourse, and finally applies the concept to a specific cultural construct—hegemonic masculinity.

Hegemon to Cultural Hegemony

From ancient Greek, a *hegemon* is a domineering leader; yet taken up in world system theory, it is articulated as a government or state that predominates over the world economy to such an extent that the rest of the world is dependent on its sustainability, growth, and success (Wallerstein, 1983). Hegemons create "universal" rules (read norms) that apply to everyone equally, but serve to influence the state's own interests (Boswell, 2004). Examples of hegemons include the U.S. presence in Iraq and Afghanistan, the reich's of Germany, and the Spanish and British empires.

In the early twentieth century, Antonio Gramsci, a philosopher, politician, and later a founder and leader of the Communist Party, took up and translated hegemons into a greater application of the theorization of cultural hegemony and its conjugation, hegemonic. While he offered no precise definition, what is most often quoted and characterized as his starting point is that hegemony moved from the geopolitical to the cultural as the "spontaneous" consent given by masses of the culture to the general direction imposed on social life by the dominating group. Gramsci, who was concerned mostly with issues of economics, indicated that this consent is "historically offered by the prestige, power, and eventually unquestioned confidence the dominant group enjoys because of its position and function in the world of economic production" (1971, p. 3). Put another way, the rich impose their vision of social life, and the poor/working/middle class are implicitly and manipulatively persuaded to adopt the dominant groups' vision (Gramsci, 1971; Lears, 1985).

Taking up the writings of Karl Marx, Gramsci explained how the dependence of economic growth on profitability gave capitalist elites a "hegemonic position" over government and cultural institutions even when they had little or no direct control. Rather than focusing specifically on economics, cultural hegemony can be understood in more varied historical and theoretical contexts. Gramsci argued that hegemony manifests in the relationships between dominant and nondominant social groups and requires no force, instead operating through the use of indirect coercion and unconscious consent.

No Force

The first condition of hegemony is that force is not required for domination. For example, the tsarist regime ruled primarily by monopolizing the instruments of coercion. Among parliamentary regimes, only the weakest are forced to rely on force; instead they rule through hegemony, and if force is even a part of the equation, it is usually only understood as an implicit threat. Dominant groups do not maintain the hegemonic order merely by giving their domination an aura of moral authority, but they also maintain it through the creation and perpetuation of legitimating symbols that seek to win the consent of subordinate groups to the existing social order (Lears, 1985).

Indirect Coercion

The ideas, values, beliefs, and practices that are hegemonic in a society legitimize existing arrangements as natural, reasonable, and inevitable, while rendering alternative conceptions of how good the world might be as naïve, impractical, or foolish. In this way, the cultural hegemony that sustains elite rule greatly inhibits the appearance and proliferation of potent opposition forces (McGovern, 1997). Hegemony functions not through coercion "from the top down" but rather through social institutions that legitimize domination through the creation of a normative and ideological consensus of the dominated. Hegemony establishes a taken-for-granted reality that is rarely questioned (Smyth, 2006).

Unconscious Consent

Gramsci argued that elites in Western industrial nations maintained control not just through coercion but also primarily by securing the consent of the masses to the prevailing distribution of wealth and power. Gramsci recognized that the consciousness of most people is conflicted, a mixture of a worldview formed by how one actually experiences life on a daily basis and a worldview transmitted through the multiple institutions of civil society that rationalizes the status quo. The effect of this contradictory consciousness, Gramsci contended, was to immobilize subordinate groups from acting on the very real grievances that they feel. The result is a kind of political passivity that is often assumed to be a general consent to economic and political conditions (McGovern, 1997).

Although force is not present, indirect coercion and unconscious consent must be present. Any analysis of cultural hegemony has to begin with a precise analysis of social formation, and this, according to Wolf (1983), has to begin at those historical moments when people enter processes of primary accumulation, when the definitions, negotiations, and structurally determined applications of terms of ownership, rights, alienation, and appropriation change. This is where modes of cultural production are born and die, where they begin and terminate their articulations, where cultural hegemonies struggle for dominance, and where they collapse and reform (Rebel, 1989). One example that illuminates the process of hegemony is one seemingly stable yet fragile notion of gender—hegemonic masculinity.

An Applied Example of Cultural Hegemony: Hegemonic Masculinity

Connell (1995) described "masculinity" as those practices in which men (and sometimes women) engage male social gender roles with the effects being expressed through the body, personality, and culture. Culture, then, serves as both a cause and effect of masculine behavior, and in our Western society, masculinity has taken shape in relation to securing and maintaining dominance. The masculine power is balanced by the general symbolism of difference, whereby the masculine is valued over the feminine. While masculinity is grounded in difference, it is not a static characteristic or personal identity trait. Instead, masculinity is a fluid construct that is organized within social relations and, ultimately, changes those social relations. According to Connell, masculinity is not just an object of knowledge but the interplay between the agency of the individual and the structure of the social institution.

Hegemonic masculinity, then, can be defined as the configuration of gender practices that embody the currently accepted answer to the problem of legitimacy of patriarchy, which guarantees the dominant position of men and subordination of women. Connell (1995) described how "terms such as 'hegemonic masculinity' name not fixed character types but configurations of practice generated in particular situations" (p. 196). Thus, hegemonic masculinity is enacted in individual social interactions as well as conveyed through institutional practices (Connell, 1998).

Although hegemonic masculinity is not itself fixed, it is possible to identify some of its critical components in a specific culture and time period, such as postindustrial America. Elucidating the features of hegemonic masculinity is a necessary starting point for any cultural analysis. This is not to say that these are the only features of postindustrial hegemonic masculinity; rather, it merely serves as a point of departure for later arguments. Hegemonic masculinity, in this context, manifests itself in a variety of social practices. A central feature of hegemonic masculinity is its definition of masculinity as being "not-female" (Bird, 1996, p. 125). This concern with avoiding femininity manifests in practices that objectify, control, and abuse women (Bird, 1996; McCreary, 1994; Schultz, 2001), a reluctance to express emotions (Bird, 1996), and a privileging of rationality.

Hegemonic masculinity is also constructed corporeally (Gerschick & Miller, 2001). Body performances associated with hegemonic masculinity include the exercise of physical violence and heterosexual sexual activity (Connell, 1995). These practices associated with the body, particularly for young men, are often socially constructed as markers of "true manhood." For example, competitive sports represent a major arena in which masculinity is performed (Kimmel, 1996; Messner, 1992; Whitson, 1990). Analyses of masculinity, and critical analyses of hegemonic masculinity located in the sports sociology in the United States and United Kingdom, have devoted extensive attention to examining sports as a context for the construction and maintenance of hegemonic masculinity (Anderson, 2005; Bryson, 1987; Messner, 1998). These researchers have articulated connections between sports contexts, episodes of aggression, socialization processes, and the ways in which sporting contexts serve as a fertile training ground for the construction of masculinity and the construction of violent masculinity (Bryson, 1987). In addition to analyses that examine the ways in which representations of male athletes normalize violent masculinity, sports sociologists have also attended to the ways in which media representations of males and females contribute to gendered binaries and oppressive ideologies (Anderson & Dill, 2000). Hegemonic masculinity, by its very nature, has social authority, and is not easy to challenge openly. Those men who choose separation, or otherwise find themselves separated from hegemonic masculinity, face negative consequences that result from defying social norms (McCreary, 1994). Given that hegemonic masculinity is constructed in individual and institutional practices, it is important to consider the cultural (con)texts through which the gender order is constructed, reified, and negotiated.

Corey W. Johnson
Joshua Trey Barnett
Anthony Hansen

References

Anderson, C. A. & Dill, K. E. (2000). Video games and aggressive thoughts, feelings and behavior in the laboratory and in life. *Journal of Personality and Social Psychology, 78*(4), 772–90.

Anderson, E. (2005). *Suny series on sport, culture, and social relations: In the game: Gay athletes and the cult of masculinity.* SUNY Press.

Bird, S. R. (1996). Welcome to the men's club: Homosociality and the maintenance of hegemonic masculinity. *Gender & Society, 10*(2), 120–32.

Boswell, T. (2004). American world empire or declining hegemony? *Journal of World-Systems Research, 11*(1), 516–24.

Bryson, L. (1987). Sport and the maintenance of masculine hegemony. *Women's Studies International Forum, 10*(4), 349–60.

Connell, R. W. (1995). *Masculinities.* Los Angeles, CA: University of California Press.

Connell, R. W. (1998). Masculinities and globalization. *Men and Masculinities, 1*(1), 3–23.

Gerschick, T. J. & Miller, A. S. (2001). Coming to terms: Masculinity and physical disability. In M. S. Kimmel & M. A. Messner (Eds.), *Men's lives* (5th ed.) (pp. 313–26). Boston: Allyn and Bacon.

Gramsci, A. (1971). *Selections from the prison notebooks.* London: Lawrence & Wishert.

Kimmel, M. (1996). Baseball and the reconstitution of American masculinity. In M. A. Messner & D. F. Sabo (Eds.), *Sport, men, and the gender order: Critical feminist perspectives* (pp. 55–66). Champaign, IL: Human Kinetics Books.

Lears, T. (1985). The concept of cultural hegemony: Problems and possibilities. *American Historical Review, 90*(3), 567.

McCreary, D. R. (1994). The male role and avoiding femininity. *Sex Roles, 31*(9/10), 517–31.

McGovern, S. J. (1997). Cultural hegemony as an impediment to urban protest movements: Grassroots activism and downtown. *Journal of Urban Affairs, 19*(4), 419.

Messner, M. A. (1992). *Power at play: Sports and the problem of masculinity.* Boston: Beacon Press.

Messner, M. A. (1998). Masculinities and athletic careers: Bonding and status differences. In M. Messner & D. F. Sabo (Eds.), *Sport, men, and the gender order: Critical feminist perspectives* (pp. 97–108). Champaign, Ill.: Human Kinetics Books.

Rebel, H. (1989). Cultural hegemony and class experience: A critical reading of recent ethnological-historical approaches (Part two). *American Ethnologist, 2,* 350.

Schultz, J. (2001). Getting off on feminism. In M. S. Kimmel & M. A. Messner (Eds.), *Men's lives* (5th ed.) (pp. 390–98). Boston: Allyn and Bacon.

Smyth, M. A. (2006). Queers and provocateurs: Hegemony, ideology, and the "homosexual advance" defense. *Law & Society Review, 40*(4), 903–30.

Wallerstein, I. (1983). The three instances of hegemony in the history of the capitalist world-economy. *International Journal of Comparative Sociology*, 24(1–2), 100–8.

Whitson, D. (1990). Sport in the social construction of masculinity. In M. A. Messner & D. F. (Eds.), *Sport, men, and the gender order: Critical feminist perspectives*. Champaign, IL: Human Kinetics Books.

Wolf, E. (1983). *Europe and the people without history*. Berkeley: University of California Press.

CULTURAL INFLUENCES

Cultural influences in the early history of anthropology as a discipline (approximately the late nineteenth to early twentieth century) referred to the widespread supposition that ideas, technology, and artistic styles had diffused from one central, originating cultural context to other peripheral cultures, rather than having been independently invented in different locations. While some cultural innovations do appear to have been transmitted in this manner, it has since become clear through improved dating of archaeological finds and other refinements to methods of study that independent invention is likely an equally or more important mechanism. Interrelationships between the concepts of cultural diffusion, unsupported early generalizations based on racial differences, and the now-discredited view of the general superiority of some cultures over others also have led to a decline in support for ideas about diffusion via cultural influences.

Cultural influences came to be considered in education through the adaptation of anthropological theories into educational thought. In education these ideas have been conceptualized using a variety of theories and terms, among which may be counted culturally relevant pedagogy (Ladson-Billings, 1995), critical race theory, and multicultural education. These viewpoints commonly focus on the role of cultural influences on learning, including components such as how family and community culture influence students' academic identity, or on learning style preferences (e.g., culture's role in fostering an individualist versus collectivist orientation toward learning). In addition, these approaches tend to foreground the role of differential access to power across cultural actors and to privilege the understanding of how such power relationships may institutionalize inequity in educational outcomes.

Ideas about cultural influence ultimately have led to a position that espouses the need for teachers to be nonjudgmental and inclusive of the cultural backgrounds of their students in order to be effective in promoting learning in diverse classroom settings (e.g., Brown-Jeffy & Cooper, 2011). To develop a nuanced understanding of cultural influence is viewed as a difficult but achievable task, and one that is seen as vital to addressing inequity in the context of the larger, culturally pluralistic and democratic society.

Research Findings Related to Cultural Influences
Cultures influence individuals' values, personalities, cognitive styles, and psychological orientations to the world (Chang et al., 2011). At the broadest level, cultures may be considered collectivist or individualist in orientation based on how their members perceive relationships between individuals and society. Individualist cultures value (a) individualism, (b) change over tradition, and (c) gender equality, and individualism in turn is inversely correlated with cultural perceptions of power distance (i.e., accepting an unequal distribution of power). Collectivist-oriented cultures value stability and agreement across groups within the culture, and devalue individual freedom if it conflicts with these goals.

Examining these differences in slightly different terms, Fischer, Hanke, and Sibley (2012) in an extensive quantitative review (i.e., meta-analysis) study found that some cultures foster high social dominance orientation or group-based hierarchy. Lee, Pratto, and Johnson (2011) found that a higher social dominance orientation was associated with higher hierarchy-enhancing ideology in individualist cultures, and thus in these cultures subordinates (i.e., members of lower power ethnic groups) and females disagreed more with dominants (i.e., members of a more powerful group) in their views of group-based hierarchy, whereas in collectivist cultures subordinates are more similar to dominants in their approval of group-based hierarchy (Lee et al., 2011). Collectivist cultures, such as those in Albania, China, Colombia, India, Israel, Lebanon,

Pakistan, Palestine, Taiwan, the Tunisian Republic, Russia, and others also maintain or create political consensus by preventing calls from subordinates for greater equality, which helps preserve hierarchical social order (Lee et al., 2011). Thus, hierarchy and constraint mutually reinforce one another, so that inequality and social stability are maintained and that the existing hierarchical arrangements appear relatively beneficial, fixed, and inevitable (Lee et al., 2011).

Eastern and Western cultural differences can broadly be viewed in terms of social hierarchy versus equality, with Eastern cultures valuing hierarchy, conservatism, and harmony, whereas Western cultures value intellectual and affective autonomy and egalitarianism (Chang et al., 2011). Easterners focus on collectivism and an interdependent self—that is, seeing the self as part of an encompassing social relationship within which everyone's behavior is determined by and contingent on the thoughts, feelings, and actions of others in the relationship. Individuals may copy or learn from others either by directly interacting with them or by studying their ideas. In contrast, Westerners focus on individualism and independent self, valuing the inner feelings, thoughts, and actions of the self rather than comparing these to the feelings, thoughts, and actions of others. So Easterners focus on interpersonal relatedness, social hierarchy, and authority, whereas Westerners focus on independence, autonomy, and equality (Chang et al., 2011).

Individualist cultures eschew power distance between individuals and allow for greater intergroup dissension. Subordinates differentiate themselves from dominants more in individualist cultures than in collectivist cultures. Individualist cultures offer individuals more freedom to think and feel for themselves; thus subordinates may compare themselves to dominants, become more aware of how unequal their groups are, and reject group-based hierarchy. Thus, social mobility and freedom are associated with greater intergroup dissent, whereas security concerns and stability lead to less intergroup differentiation. Greater group dissension in individualist cultures suggests that greater freedom may give rise to greater demands for equality, especially among subordinates, leading

eventually to cultures with greater equality (Lee et al., 2011).

Culture not only influences how individuals understand their world but also influences their emotional, attitudinal, and behavioral responses to the events in their world, including their perceptions of justice or injustice. Shao, Rupp, Skarlicki, and Jones (2013) in a meta-analysis study found that culture influences employees' perceptions of how fairly they are treated at work. Justice effects are strongest among countries characterized by (a) individualism, (b) femininity (i.e., valuing interpersonal relationships and concerns for others; vs. masculinity [i.e., valuing personal assertiveness and personal gains]), (c) management certainty/predictability, and (d) low power distance (i.e., rejecting an unequal distribution of power). Although collectivist cultures also focus on interpersonal relationships, they value in-group goals over personal goals and norms rather than diversity of attitudes; individualist cultures focus not only on personal gains but also on personal feelings and rights.

Culture also influences expressions of individuals' emotions. In a meta-analysis study, Matsumoto (1989) found that high-power-distance (i.e., accepting an unequal distribution of power) collectivist cultures (a) valued hierarchy and group cohesion, while (b) devaluing individuality, and thus (c) the communication of negative emotions such as anger, fear, and sadness threatened group solidarity and interpersonal social structures, and therefore were discouraged. In contrast, low-power-distance individualist cultures valued the communication of negative emotions, viewing these as related to individual freedom to perceive and express one's self rather than as something threatening to social structures.

Cultures also influence individuals' learning styles. Collectivist Eastern cultures emphasize conservatism, harmony, and hierarchy, leading to learning behaviors that are oriented toward copying, memorizing, and attending to details. These also depend on conformity, compliance, and relatively low self-concept, all of which facilitate getting along with and copying others. These learning styles are based on cultural attitudes about conformity and compliance. In contrast, in individualist Western cultures, independence, autonomy, self-confidence, equality, lack of compliance and conformity, and individual detachment from groups characterize learning styles. These are based in drawing reference internally to one's own attributes rather than externally by comparison to group norms. Associated learning styles in these cultures are supportive of critical thinking and innovative problem solving (Chang et al., 2011).

Effectiveness of teaching approaches are also influenced by culture, as learning preferences vary across cultures (Rodrigues, Bu, & Min, 2000). Individuals in low-power-distance individualist cultures tend to be low on measures of uncertainty avoidance and prefer a hands-on approach, whereas individuals in high-power-distance collectivist cultures tend to score higher on measures of uncertainty avoidance and prefer a teacher-centered approach (Rodrigues et al., 2000).

Culture influences individuals' ideological attitudes, which in turn are related to their measured cognitive ability. In a meta-analysis, Van Hiel, Onraet, and De Pauw (2010) found that authoritarianism, ethnocentrism, conservatism, and dogmatism were associated with (a) lower cognitive flexibility and complexity; (b) lower tolerance for ambiguity; and (c) lower cognitive ability: individuals with higher cognitive ability tend to adhere to left-wing social attitudes (social progressivism), whereas those with lower cognitive ability tend to adhere to right-wing social attitudes (social conservatism; Van Hiel et al., 2010). This might indicate that individuals in traditional, conservative, dogmatic, authoritarian, and ethnocentric cultures use fewer cognitive resources than other cultures.

Conclusions

Having an understanding of cultural influences and how their history and operation inform roles and relationships in contemporary society is vital to the success of efforts to promote tolerance, equity, and excellence in education and other social endeavors. Research provides one way to develop such understanding, but thoughtful discussion and reflection also are vital components. Broad conceptions of individualist versus collectivist perspectives and the corresponding influences of these conceptions provides a foundation upon which to build a more

nuanced understanding of specific cultures and the individuals who constitute them.

Kyung-Hee Kim
Michael S. Matthews

References

Boer, D. & Fischer, R. (2013). How and when do personal values guide our attitudes and sociality? Explaining cross-cultural variability in attitude-value linkages. *Psychological Bulletin, 139,* 1113–47. doi: 10.1037/a0031347

Brown-Jeffy, S. & Cooper, J. E. (2011). Toward a conceptual framework of culturally relevant pedagogy: An overview of the conceptual and theoretical literature. *Teacher Education Quarterly, 38*(1), 65–84.

Chang, L., Mak, M. C. K., Li, T., Wu, B. P., Chen, B. B., & Lu, H. J. (2011). Cultural adaptations to environmental variability: An evolutionary account of east-west differences. *Educational Psychology Review, 23*(1), 99–129. doi: 10.1007/s10648-010-9149-0

Fischer, R., Hanke, K., & Sibley, C. G. (2012). Cultural and institutional determinants of social dominance orientation: A cross-cultural meta-analysis of 27 societies. *Political Psychology, 33,* 437–67. doi: 10.1111/j.1467-9221.2012.00884.x

Ladson-Billings, G. (1995). But that's just good teaching! The case for culturally relevant pedagogy. *Theory into Practice, 34*(3), 159–65.

Lee, I.-C., Pratto, F., & Johnson, B. T. (2011). Intergroup consensus/disagreement in support of group-based hierarchy: An examination of socio-structural and psycho-cultural factors. *Psychological Bulletin, 137,* 1029–64. doi: 10.1037/a0025410

Matsumoto, D. (1989). Cultural influences on the perception of emotion. *Journal of Cross-Cultural Psychology, 20,* 92–105. doi: 10.1177/0022022189201006

Rodrigues, C. A., Bu, N., & Min, B. (2000). Learners' training approach preference: National culture as a determinant. *Cross Cultural Management, 7*(1), 23–32. doi: 10.1108/13527600010797048

Shao, R., Rupp, D. E., Skarlicki, D. P., & Jones, K. S. (2013). Employee justice across cultures: A meta-analytic review. *Journal of Management, 39,* 263–301. doi: 10.1177/0149206311422447

Van Hiel, A., Onraet, E., & De Pauw, S. (2010). The relationship between social-cultural attitudes and behavioral measures of cognitive style: A meta-analytic integration of studies. *Journal of Personality, 78,* 1765–99. doi: 10.1111/j.1467-6494.2010.00669.x

CULTURAL MAINTENANCE

Cultural maintenance refers to the ability to choose to continue adhering to selected tenets of the culture in which one was raised, while living within the context of a different mainstream culture. These tenets may involve areas such as religion, family structure, and especially one's language (cf. Baker, 2011). In the context of education, cultural maintenance has been the subject of extensive debate because of its close relationship to issues raised by demographic change.

The extent to which cultural maintenance is tolerated within a given society can be expressed by the degree to which the society adheres to an assimilationist rather than a pluralist ideology. In essence, in the assimilationist view (often referred to as the "melting pot" view, especially with regard to the United States) the dominant group asserts that its language and culture are essential to national cohesiveness and, therefore, that these aspects of the dominant group must be adopted by immigrants as replacements for their home culture and language.

On the other end of the spectrum, the so-called salad bowl metaphor (or pluralist view) envisions the presence of diverse cultures and languages as strengthening rather than as being divisive to national unity. In this view, the freedom to maintain one's culture and to use multiple languages is viewed as a decision that should be left to the individual, rather than being prescribed by the government.

Cultures that have more power (often conceptualized in the forms known as "social capital" or "cultural capital") may be more likely to be maintained by their members in the face of an assimilationist society than cultures that have less power are. The idea of "cultural capital" (cf. Bourdieu, 1977) has provided a powerful analytical framework within which to examine cultural maintenance, differential achievement, and numerous other educationally related issues. This theoretical lens offers a cogent explanation of why, for example, Canadian schools and society have been far more successful in promoting bilingual education than the United States has.

Outcomes Associated with Cultural Maintenance

Maintaining cultural identity is associated with individuals' psychosocial and academic adjustment.

A recent extensive quantitative review (i.e., meta-analysis) study (Rivas-Drake et al., 2014) found that adolescents' good, happy, and proud feelings about their cultural identity were associated with more favorable psychosocial and academic adjustment. Adjustment outcomes included aspects of positive social functioning such as social competencies, peer acceptance, and self-esteem; positive academic dispositions toward school and academic attitudes about achievement; reduced depressive symptoms; and reduced health risks such as sexual and substance use outcomes, which held true across age, gender, and ethnicity (Rivas-Drake et al., 2014).

Outcomes for Black Americans

Maintaining cultural identity through affiliations with their own cultural groups is associated with individuals' psychological well-being. A meta-analysis by Lee and Ahn (2013) found that those who were more closely affiliated with members of their own cultural group tended to report experiencing less distress, even though they perceived more experiences of racial discrimination. The authors suggest this indicates that in-group affiliation may serve to protect individuals from internalizing negative self-concepts that result from racial discrimination, as well as offering them significant others with whom they can process their experiences and feel a sense of belonging. For example, black Americans who adopted positive views about their race had stronger ties with others in the black community, and individuals at advanced stages of racial identity development tended to report less discrimination-related distress, particularly among adolescents (Lee & Ahn, 2013). Though perceptions of increased racial discrimination also may increase distress indirectly, this indicates that it is helpful to promote black individuals' connections with their community and facilitate racial identity development (Lee & Ahn, 2013). Black individuals' association with individuals from other races who hold favorable views of black Americans also was associated with decreased discrimination-related distress (Lee & Ahn, 2013).

Outcomes for Asian Americans

Another meta-analysis by Lee and Ahn (2011) found that racial discrimination was associated with greater overall distress and that Asian Americans suffered from discrimination-related depression and anxiety at the same rates as, or higher rates than, other ethnic groups. Further, individualistic forms of resources such as strengths and coping strategies showed equal or stronger protective effects against discrimination-related depression and anxiety than collectivistic forms such as social support and cultural identity did. This finding held despite Asian cultures' association with collectivism, or placing the needs of a family before individual needs; being relation-oriented, or defining themselves in relation to their family instead of focusing on themselves as individuals (Yee, Su, Kim, & Yancura, 2009); and focusing on filial piety, or abiding by family elder members and conforming to parents' expectations and cultural traditions (Iwamoto & Liu, 2009).

Conclusion

In the context of public education in the United States, schools often fall toward the assimilationist end of the spectrum. Because U.S. public school teachers tend to be a homogeneous group and from culturally mainstream, monolingual backgrounds, they tend (if only unconsciously) to support the assimilationist ideology of U.S. society at large. This means that educational institutions and practices tend to do little to support cultural maintenance, and often actively discourage it. Again, this is particularly the case for the linguistic aspects of culture; other aspects that may be less evident to the observer, such as traditions and beliefs, may be more easily maintained by practices within the family. This also may be in part because these other aspects of culture, while not actively supported in the schools, are neither actively discouraged. Understanding cultural maintenance can help support achievement of learners from all backgrounds, especially among those students who may find themselves struggling to thrive in an environment that differs from their own background.

Kyung-Hee Kim
Michael S. Matthews

References

Baker, C. (2011). *Foundations of bilingual education and bilingualism* (5th ed.). Tonawanda, NY: Multilingual Matters.

Bourdieu, P. (1977). Cultural reproduction and social reproduction. In J. Karabel & A. H. Halsey (Eds.), *Power and ideology in education.* Oxford, UK: Oxford University Press.

Iwamoto, D. K. & Liu, W. M. (2009). Asian American men and Asianized attribution: Intersections of masculinity, race, and sexuality. In N. Tewari & A. N. Alvarez (Eds.), *Asian American psychology: Current perspectives* (pp. 211–32). New York: Routledge.

Lee, D. L. & Ahn, S. (2011). Racial discrimination and Asian mental health: A meta-analysis. *Counseling Psychologist, 39,* 463–89. doi: 10.1177/0011000010381791

Lee, D. L. & Ahn, S. (2013). The relation of racial identity, ethnic identity, and racial socialization to discrimination-distress: A meta-analysis of Black Americans. *Journal of Counseling Psychology, 60,* 1–14. doi: 10.1037/a0031275

Rivas-Drake, D., Syed, M., Umaña-Taylor, A., Markstrom, C., French, S., Schwartz, S. J., Lee, R., & Ethnic and Racial Identity in the 21st Century Study Group. (2014). Feeling good, happy, and proud: A meta-analysis of positive ethnic–racial affect and adjustment. *Child Development, 85*(1), 77–102. doi: 10.1111/cdev.12175

Tewari, N. & Alvarez, A. N. (Eds.), *Asian American psychology: Current perspectives* (pp. 211–32). New York: Psychology Press.

Yee, B. W. K., Su, J., Kim, S. Y., & Yancura, L. (2009). Asian American and Pacific Islander families. In N. Tewari & A. N. Alvarez (Eds.), *Asian American psychology: Current perspectives* (pp. 295–316). New York: Psychology Press.

CULTURAL PLURALISM

Definition

Cultural pluralism exists when minority cultures are present within a context of a larger dominant culture. In a culturally plural environment, minority or enclave cultures are permitted to exist provided that they do not violate the major culture of the dominant group. The relationship between the minority culture and the dominant culture can be one largely, though not entirely, of mutual exclusivity—such as the Amish who reside in Pennsylvania. At the same time, the relationship could also be one in which the minority culture retains high authenticity to their culture of origin yet interacts within the broader culture, such as the Hasidic Jews in metropolitan New York. Further, the minority or enclave culture can become symbiotic with the dominant culture, both being influenced by it and influencing it. Such an example is the case of Italian Americans, who have an extraordinary influence in American culture, from the arts to cuisine.

A feature of a culturally pluralistic society is that diversity represented by the minority culture is valued and respected both by its own members and by the dominant culture. Today the United States is culturally pluralistic, but that has not always been the case.

During the eighteenth and nineteenth centuries, the basic assumption of Americans and immigrants into the United States was that all ethnic groups would merge into one American identity, which schools then sought to Anglicize with a largely English-Puritan cultural coding. Immigrants themselves, and especially children, sought to shed much of their Old World cultural identity by Anglicizing names, refusing to speak their parents' language outside the home, and modeling themselves on the dominant culture. In this context, children were more likely to marry outside of their ethnic groups, further weakening the Old World cultural attributes.

During and after the great wave of Southern and Eastern European immigrants in the late nineteenth and early twentieth centuries, attitudes toward cultural difference began to change. Reasons for this shift included the sheer numbers of immigrants, their high concentration in the northeastern United States, especially in New York City, and the cultural distance between these immigrants, which included large numbers of Eastern European Jews and large numbers of Italians and the dominant American culture. For Jews, a high degree of cultural maintenance and isolation was seen as necessary to preserve their faith. Though Italians were not as isolated as Jews, their poverty, lack of modern middle-class skills and values, and prejudice against them encouraged a degree of cultural maintenance different than other immigrant groups, such as Germans, typically experienced. Over time, the dominant culture of the United States began to recognize the merits of cultural pluralism. This shift was partially driven by historical experiences, especially that of World War II. The war effort was a homogenizing force, bringing large numbers of Americans of different cultural backgrounds together. At the same time, Americans began to learn more about those who were culturally different and often came to value those differences. The war effort itself was well served by American cultural pluralism: many Americans, knowing the language of their parents, could read, write, and speak Albanian, German, Italian, Japanese, Korean, Navajo, Tagala, and many other languages needed to fight the war.

Recognition of the merits of cultural pluralism also stemmed from the intellectual, artistic, and cultural developments that, together, are referred to as postmodernity. Postmodern thinkers rejected the confidence and hubris of the Enlightenment and Positivism, both of which presumed that truth could be known and discovered and that truth was universal and constant. Postmodernists are much more skeptical about truth. For them, no direct, necessary correspondence exists between *reality* and ideas about it—because there is no unitary, unified reality. A center does not exist, ontologically, epistemologically, or culturally (Beck, 1993). As a result, postmodern thinkers reject the idea of a dominant voice or metanarrative with claims to authority. This rejection of a dominant voice legitimized different voices rather than strengthened the dominant culture (Eagleton, 1987). An outgrowth of this intellectual turn is that cultural minorities or enclaves began to be and are valued as different voices, each voice with its own claim to partial, provisional truth.

Taken to its logical limits, postmodernity would value multiculturalism over cultural pluralism. Cultural pluralism assumes a dominant culture exists, such as the largely Anglo-Puritan identity dominated the American imagination for much of American history. If current demographic trends continue, however, within the twenty-first century, the United States will no longer have a European-descended, Caucasian majority. Every ethnic group will be a minority, which could conceivably lead to no dominant culture. Such a situation would indicate a shift from cultural pluralism to multiculturalism.

Recent Trends in Cross-Cultural and Ethnic Minority Publications

In local contexts, some degree of multiculturalism already exists in the United States, though the

United States still has a dominant culture derived from European perspectives. Although the proportion of ethnic minority in the United States and thus cultural diversity has been continuously increasing, psychology has historically been dependent on theories derived from Eurocentrism (Hartmann et al., 2013). Hartmann et al. (2013) conducted a ten-year follow-up on Hall and Maramba's (2001) report of cross-cultural and ethnic minority publications in order to compare data trends in publications and psychology organizations between 1993–1999 and 2003–2009. They found that, despite numerous awareness-raising efforts, research on cross-cultural and ethnic minority issues continues to be underrepresented. The absence of top cross-cultural and ethnic minority authors on their editorial boards of psychology's two flagship organizations' (i.e., the American Psychological Association and Association for Psychological Science) journals indicates a barrier to broader cultural diversity research. However, Hartmann et al. (2013) also found promising developments; representations of ethnic minority psychology in medical and health journals, as well as in marketing and business management journals, have been increased.

Recent Research Findings
Related to Cultural Pluralism

INTEGRATED MULTICULTURAL IDENTITIES FOR WELL-BEING Multicultural individuals are required to navigate the different norms and values related to their multiple cultural identities. How they manage these different identities within the self predicts their well-being, and individuals with integrated multicultural identity tend to show greater well-being than others (Carpentier & de la Sablonnière, 2013; Yampolsky, Amiot, & de la Sablonnière, 2013). According to Amiot et al. (2007)'s cognitive-developmental model of social identity integration, compartmentalization is where individuals maintain multiple and separate identities within themselves; and integration, the coherence within the self, is where individuals link their multiple cultural identities. Yampolsky et al. (2013) found that individuals with integrated cultural identities report greater narrative coherence than individuals who compartmentalized their cultural identities, showing that integrating one's multiple cultural identities within the self predicts greater well-being than compartmentalizing one's identities. This indicates that individuals with integrated multicultural identity tend to be able to frame the context of their narrative better, to convey their story in a logical order better, to have a clear emotional evaluation of the events better, and to derive a sense of meaning and resolution in their narratives better than compartmentalized individuals who have a fragmented view of the self in relation to their cultures (Yampolsky et al., 2013).

MULTICULTURAL SENSITIVITY REQUIRED FOR CULTURAL PLURALISM If we want to develop multicultural sensitivity to understand individuals from diverse backgrounds and help them adjust to new cultures, we must recognize individuals' different cultural backgrounds regarding their unique expectations and interpretation of positive coping strategies that influence their subjective well-being. For example, individuals' active confrontation of stressful events mitigates their fear and uncertainty in individualist cultures, but in collectivist cultures, these strategies are not always desirable, and individuals who use these strategies tend to report higher levels of anxiety than those in individualistic cultures (Cheng, Cheung, Chio, & Chan, 2013). Further, we need to be also aware that cultural backgrounds also influence the way individuals see themselves. For example, for individuals in individualist cultures, their self is independent from others, but individuals' construal of the self in collectivist cultures exists in *relation* to their social network members, which also influences their well-being (Cheng et al., 2013).

MULTICULTURAL COUNSELING COMPETENCY REQUIRED FOR CULTURAL PLURALISM Counselors who exhibit multicultural counseling competencies show improved counseling outcome with clients across cultures. An extensive qualitative review (i.e., content analysis) study (Worthington, Soth-McNett, & Moreno, 2007) consistently found that counselors who exhibit multicultural counseling competencies tend to show improved counseling processes and positive outcomes with clients across racial and ethnic differences. When counselors exhibit multicultural counseling competencies, clients tend to (a) perceive their counselors positively; (b) show positive counseling outcomes; (c) show less attrition and more self-disclosure; and (d) show no negative outcomes (Worthington et al., 2007).

Counselors or other mental health professionals who modify their interventions, such as psychotherapy or counseling, to better match their clients' cultural values and contexts tend to have better intervention outcomes. Another meta-analysis study (Griner & Smith, 2006) found that interventions targeted to a specific racial, ethnic, or cultural group are four times more effective than interventions provided to groups consisting of clients from a variety of cultural backgrounds. Further, interventions conducted in clients' preferred, native language, if other than English, are twice as effective as interventions conducted in English (Griner & Smith, 2006).

MULTICULTURAL EDUCATION IN MENTAL HEALTH PROFESSIONALS FOR CULTURAL PLURALISM The American Psychological Association and many other professional mental health organizations have developed multicultural education initiatives in psychology, and they require, as compliance with accreditation standards, graduate programs to provide education in multicultural issues to enhance mental health professionals' abilities to effectively serve an increasingly diverse society (Smith, Constantine, Dunn, Dinehart, & Montoya, 2006). Mental health professionals who have had education in multicultural issues tend to show positive outcomes. An extensive quantitative review (i.e., meta-analysis) study (Smith et al., 2006) found an overall positive effect of multicultural education across a wide variety of participant and study characteristics. Further, they found that multicultural education interventions that are explicitly based on theory and research report almost twice as effective outcomes as those that are not. This indicates that when instructors develop multicultural education courses, they need to design all research- and theory-based curriculum, instructional strategies, competency-based objectives, multicultural competence principles, counseling skills, education and training resources, educational interventions, and assessments, which increase the effectiveness of multicultural education interventions (Smith et al., 2006).

Conclusions
Cultural difference falls on a spectrum, from monoethnic (ethnocentric), to cultural pluralism, to multiculturalism. The United States has never been monoethnic; and starting in the late nineteenth century, the United States increasingly became more culturally pluralistic. Since World War II, the United States has been shifting further along the multicultural spectrum, although Eurocentrism yet remains dominant.

Because cultural difference falls on a spectrum and varies according to context, it is not always clear whether research agendas relate to different cultural pluralism or multiculturalism. The findings reported above indicate that in the United States, appreciation of cultural diversity is improving, although cultural minorities still function in relationship to a dominant culture. As a means to improve the lives of cultural minorities, with an aim of social justice, researchers have reached some important conclusions, mainly that individuals such as teachers, counselors, and researchers need to develop multicultural competencies, which can enhance their ability to work with culturally diverse people and groups.

Kyung-Hee Kim
Robert A. Pierce

References
Amiot, C. E., de la Sablonnière, R., Terry, D. J., & Smith, J. R. (2007). Integration of social identities in the self: toward a cognitive developmental model. *Personality and Social Psychology Review*, 11, 364–88.
Beck, C. (1993). Postmodernism, pedagogy, and philosophy of education. *Philosophy of Education*. Retrieved from http://www.ed.uiuc.edu/EPS/PES-Yearbook/93_docs/BECK.HTM.
Carpentier, J. & de la Sablonnière, R. (2013). Identity profiles and wellbeing of multicultural immigrants: The case of Canadian immigrants living in Quebec. *Frontiers in Psychology*, 4, Article 80. doi: 10.3389/fpsyg.2013.00080
Cheng, C., Cheung, S-F., Chio, J. H-m., & Chan, M-p. S. (2013). Cultural meaning of perceived control: A meta-analysis of locus of control and psychological symptoms across 18 cultural regions. *Psychological Bulletin*, 139, 152-188. doi: 10.1037/a0028596
Eagleton, T. (1987). Awakening from modernity. *Times Literary Supplement* (20 February), 194.
Griner, D. & Smith, T. B. (2006). Culturally adapted mental health intervention: A meta-analytic review.

Psychotherapy: Theory, Research, Practice, Training, 43, 531–48. doi: 10.1037/0033-3204.43.4.531

Hall, G. C. N. & Maramba, G. G. (2001). In search of cultural diversity: Recent literature in cross-cultural and ethnic minority psychology. *Cultural Diversity and Ethnic Minority Psychology, 7,* 12–26. doi: 10.1037/1099-9809.7.1.12

Hartmann, W. E., Kim, E. S., Kim, J. H. J., Nguyen, T. U., Wendt, D. C., Nagata, D. K., & Gone, J. P. (2013). In search of cultural diversity, revisited: Recent publication trends in cross-cultural and ethnic minority psychology. *Review of General Psychology, 17,* 243–54. doi: 10.1037/a0032260

Hodge, D. R., Jackson, K. F., & Vaughn, M. G. (2010). Culturally sensitive interventions for health related behaviors among Latino youth: A meta-analytic review. *Children and Youth Services Review, 32,* 1331–37. doi: 10.1016/j.childyouth.2010.05.002

Smith, T. B., Constantine, M. G., Dunn, T. W., Dinehart, J. M., & Montoya, J. A. (2006). Multicultural education in the mental health professions: A meta-analytic review. *Journal of Counseling Psychology, 53*(1), 132–45. doi: 10.1037/0022-0167.53.1.132

Wilson, J., Ward, C., & Fischer, R. (2013). Beyond culture learning theory: What can personality tell us about cultural competence? *Journal of Cross-Cultural Psychology, 44,* 900–27. doi: 10.1177/0022022113492889

Worthington, R. L., Soth-McNett, A. M., & Moreno, M. V. (2007). Multicultural counseling competencies research: A 20-year content analysis. *Journal of Counseling Psychology, 54,* 351–61. doi: 10.1037/0022-0167.54.4.351

Yampolsky, M. A., Amiot, C. E., & de la Sablonnière, R. (2013). Multicultural identity integration and well-being: A qualitative exploration of variations in narrative coherence and multicultural identification. *Frontiers in Psychology, 4,* Article 126.

CULTURAL RELEVANCE

Cultural relevance is a concept that emphasizes the importance of individuals learning about, and developing relationships with, those outside their own culture and using that familiarity to improve cross-cultural interactions, engender effective communication, and empower others. Originally identified as a way to provide for the academic success of African American and other children underserved by America's public schools, the concept was introduced to the field of education in 1992 by Dr. Gloria Ladson-Billings as culturally relevant teaching. However, anthropologists, sociologists, and teacher educators have also used terms such as *culturally appropriate, culturally congruent, culturally responsive,* and *culturally compatible* to describe this type of pedagogy. Ladson-Billings (2009) defines this pedagogy as one that "empowers students intellectually, socially, emotionally, and politically by using cultural referents to impart knowledge, skills, and attitudes" (p. 18).

There are many communities and cultures represented in the United States. Nevertheless, most individuals know little about those outside their cultural group. In the United States at this time, over 89 percent of teachers are European American; many of this number are also middle class and female. Meanwhile, an overwhelming number of U.S. students are children of the global majority, which is largely of color and lower socioeconomic status; at this time, this population of students surpasses 60 percent in larger urban areas and is only slated to grow larger in the coming years. Thus, there continues to be a clear and pressing need for U.S. teachers to become familiar, and develop relationships, with those outside their culture for the betterment of student outcomes. Teachers must accept the reality that most students are coming to their classrooms with cultural, ethnic, linguistic, racial, and social class backgrounds that are different from their own and, when faced with the heterogeneous mixture of students in their classrooms, teachers must be prepared to effectively work with, and thus empower, all students.

In defining cultural relevance, it is important to remember that this type of pedagogy is about more than cultural knowledge or familiarity due to its emphasis on encouraging the academic success of students through empowerment and elevation of student cultural perspectives. Ladson-Billings contends that pedagogy demonstrating cultural relevance is an aspect of the curriculum in its own right and should have three outcomes: (1) students must experience academic success, (2) students must maintain or develop cultural competence, and (3) students must develop a critical consciousness through which they challenge the status quo of the current social order. These pedagogical requirements are supported by the work of many scholars and practioners of education, of which, Irvine (2003), Gay (2000), and Howard (2003) are only a few.

Academic Success

To attain academic success for students through cultural relevance, teachers must consciously maintain or develop knowledge of the cultural components of their students' lives, and then demonstrate respect for the culture that students bring to the classroom by making this knowledge a key component of instruction. In doing so, teachers make the classroom a familiar place where students feel affirmed, supported, and accepted. Irvine (2003), explains that this type of culturally congruent behavior creates seamlessness between home and school—a supportive classroom environment where, regardless of social inequities, all students are provided with the tools to achieve positive academic outcomes (p. 7).

Further, Ladson-Billings (1995) maintains that culturally relevant teaching requires teachers to attend to students' academic needs, not "merely make them 'feel good'" and emphasizes that culturally relevant teachers foster a desire for intellectual achievement in which they *make* students choose academic excellence (p. 160). Gay (2000) adds to the discussion by indicating that an essential element of culturally relevant teaching involves caring and indicates that, without such, students may have a difficult time experiencing academic success.

Cultural Competence

Students frequently bring culture to the classroom that is incongruent with mainstream norms and worldviews, and as previously mentioned, teachers are frequently unfamiliar with the student's cultural experiences. Thus, here again, teachers must consciously maintain or develop knowledge of the cultural components of their students' lives and use this to inform their pedagogy. A primary way cultural knowledge may be gained is through active engagement and immersion in another culture. Earnestly participating in cultural engagement and immersion enables teachers to blend important aspects of student lives with curricular content, thus increasing the possibility of student comprehension

of and relation to the curriculum. Howard (2003) suggests that teachers must "construct pedagogical practices in ways that are culturally relevant, racially affirming, and socially meaningful for their students" (p. 197). However, self-development is not a teacher's only responsibility in this area.

To engage in effective, culturally relevant instruction, teachers must also assist students' development of their own cultural consciousness and competence. This involves encouraging students to maintain their cultural integrity while also providing opportunities for students to experience, analyze, and accept multiple mores, worldviews, and perspectives.

Critical Consciousness

Schools make a difference in the life of students and are key in the establishment and maintenance of a democratic society. Ladson-Billings (1995) contends that culturally relevant teachers "should engage in the world and others critically," and, in doing so, will help students "develop a broader sociopolitical consciousness that allows them to critique the cultural norms, values, mores, and institutions that produce and maintain social inequities" (p. 162). Ladson-Billings suggests that providing opportunities for students to critique society may not only make them informed participants in a democratic society but will also encourage them to *change* oppressive structures such as institutional racism. In many proposed or attempted implementations of culturally relevant pedagogy, the aspect of critical consciousness is often overlooked; yet, without it, such an attempt is greatly weakened at best and totally ineffective at worst.

Social Justice, Education Policy, and Culturally Relevant Pedagogy

Although cultural relevance embodies the ideals of a socially just society, present changes in education policy and practices, catalyzed by the No Child Left Behind legislation of 2001 (the Elementary and Secondary Schools Act), have threatened the very application of its tenants. Current curricular changes encouraged by a dramatic increase in standardized testing as required by the Act and the application of test and punish methodologies have created an atmosphere of standardization never before present in U.S. public schools (Kohn, 2000a, 2000b; Robertson, 2012; Wellstone, 2002/2003). As a result of the aforementioned changes, an educator's curricular autonomy to dedicate class time to the application of culturally relevant pedagogy has been co-opted by education policymakers and regulated to a required, unilateral, homogeneous approach to pedagogy that leaves little time for student-centered foci. As of this date, this approach to education has only been strengthened through governmental interventions to educational policy such as Race to the Top, a federal grant incentive program that encourages increased standardized testing and requires the implementation of a Common Core Curriculum, who's stated purpose is to "provide a consistent [homogeneous], clear understanding of what students are expected to learn" (Common Core State Standards, 2012). Currently, Race to the Top grant money has been applied for and accepted by multiple U.S. states, and its requirements are diligently being met; thus, further narrowing the existence of student-centered, culturally relevant instruction across much of the United States.

In an ironic twist of fate, while U.S. public education seems to be rejecting the elements of individualized education and cultural relevance, the importance of cultural relevance has emerged as a key focus in a number other fields that interact with or wish to market to U.S. citizenry. Multiple fields such as marketing, medicine, and technology have begun to acknowledge the importance of studying and addressing the cultural needs and desires of the multicultural communities with which they are connected (i.e., Jankowski, 2011; Coolen, 2012; Nias, 2014).

In the current educational policy climate, far too many students have given up on waiting for a chance to demonstrate their creativity and intellect, have their individual self-worth affirmed, or have their cultural needs met by their schools or teachers. An ever-present deficit in culturally relevant pedagogy and curriculum in U.S. public schools has resulted in the continued presence of an education debt owed by the United States to its students in marginalized populations and, tragically, this debt most frequently manifests in inequitable educational outcomes for students of the global majority (Ladson-Billings, 2006).

A commitment to cultural relevance in U.S. public schools would begin to address the education debt owed to so many students, yet, to do so would require an education informed by the content of the discipline, the lives of students, the inclusion of multicultural perspectives, and an active effort from U.S. educators, administrators, and public officials to learn, grow, and evolve beyond their own understandings. As stated by Irvine in Milner (2010), a courageous vision is necessary to establish excellence and equity in the United States. Cultural relevance is a key part of that vision and must include an equitable interplay between culture, curriculum, and identity. Only then will social justice in education become an attainable goal.

Mari Roberts

References

Au, K. & Jordan, C. (1981). Teaching reading to Hawaiian children: Finding a culturally appropriate solution. In H. Trueba, G. Guthrie, & K. Au (Eds.), *Culture and bilingual classroom: Studies in classroom ethnography* (pp. 69–86). Rowley, MA: Newbury House.

Common Core State Standards Initiative. (2012). *Mission statement.* Retrieved from www.corestandards.org.

Coolen, P. R. (2012). Cultural relevance in end-of-life care. *Ethno-Med.* Retrieved from http://ethnomed.org/clinical/end-of-life/cultural-relevance-in-end-of-life-care.

Gay, G. (2000). *Culturally responsive teaching: Theory, research and practice.* New York: Teachers College Press.

Howard, T. (2003). Culturally relevant pedagogy: Ingredients for critical teacher reflection. *Theory into Practice, 42*(3), 195–202.

Irvine, J. J. (2003). *Educating teachers for diversity: Seeing with a cultural eye.* New York: Teachers College Press.

Irvine, J. J. (2010). Forward. In R. Milner (Ed.), *Culture, curriculum, and identity in education.* New York: Palgrave Macmillan.

Jankowski, P. (2011). Ways to make your brand culturally relevant. Retrieved from http://www.forbes.com/sites/pauljankowski/2011/11/17/5-ways-to-make-your-brand-culturally-relevant/.

Jordan, C. (1985). Translating culture: From ethnographic information to educational program. *Anthropology and Education Quarterly, 16,* 105–23.

Kohn, A. (2000a). Standardized testing and its victims. *Education Week.* Retrieved from http://www.alfiekohn.org/teaching/edweek/staiv.htm.

Kohn, A. (2000b). *The case against standardized testing: Raising the scores, ruining the schools.* Portsmouth, NH: Heinemann.

Ladson-Billings, G. (1992). Culturally relevant teaching: The key to making multicultural education work. In C. A. Grant (Ed.), *Research and multicultural education* (pp. 106–21). London: Falmer Press.

Ladson-Billings, G. (1995). But that's just good teaching! The case for culturally relevant pedagogy. *Theory into Practice, 34*(3), 159–65.

Ladson-Billings, G. (2006). From the achievement gap to the education debt: Understanding achievement in U.S. schools. (Presidential address). *Educational Researcher, 35*(7), 3–12.

Ladson-Billings, G. (2009). *The dreamkeepers: Successful teaching for African-American students (2nd ed.).* San Francisco: Jossey-Bass.

Nias, J. (2014). *Cultural relevance and social impacts of user-defined gestures for touchscreen user interfaces.* Retrieved from http://tapiaconference.org/schedule/saturday-february-8-2014/800am-500pm/doctoral-consortium/cultural-relevance-and-social-impacts-of-user-defined-gestures-for-touchscreen-user-interfaces/.

Robertson, P. (2012). Opting out and speaking up. In W. Au & M. B. Tempel (Eds.), *Pencils down: Rethinking high-stakes testing and accountability in public schools* (p. 210). Milwaukee, WI: Rethinking Schools.

Vogt, L., Jordan, C., & Tharp, R. (1987). Explaining school failure, producing school success: Two cases. *Anthropology and Education Quarterly, 18,* 276–86.

Wellstone, P. (2002/2003). Wellstone on testing: A harsh agenda. *Rethinking Schools, 17*(2). Retrieved from http://www.rethinkingschools.org/archive/17_02/Hars172.shtml.

CULTURAL SENSITIVITY

While there are many perspectives on, and definitions of, culture, it is generally agreed upon that culture is "a set of beliefs, values, attitudes, role perceptions, and customs shared among a group of people" (Triandis, 1972, as cited in Corneille, Ashcroft, & Belgrave, 2005, p. 39), wherein group can be a cultural, societal, or ethnic group. Thus, cultural sensitivity may be defined as a skill set of acceptance and awareness of the ways in which cultural difference manifests in values, traditions, behaviors, and social interactions across cultural, societal, or ethnic groups, augmented by a willingness to accommodate difference. Given that social interactions are complex within a cultural group, cultural sensitivity requires equally complex negotiations to adapt one's communication style and behavior to be compatible with another's cultural norms, taking into account one's own culturally based beliefs about how to behave in certain situations (Corneille, Ashcraft, & Belgrave, 2005; Robinson, Bowman, Ewing, Hanna, & Lopez-De Fede, 1997). One's capacity to adapt, however, is largely predicated on knowledge of self.

Knowledge of self, as the basis for negotiating complex social interactions with the cultural other, requires exploring, confirming, and confronting one's own cultural values and prejudices. As Locke and Bailey (2013) assert, "[k]nowing one's own personal biases, values, interests, and worldview—which stem from culture—as well as knowing one's own culture will greatly enhance one's sensitivity toward other cultures" (p. 2). Congruently, relationships with people from different cultures provide an authentic context for learning about difference and the opportunity to practice intricate, social negotiations over cultural differences. Therefore, fostering genuine, healthy relationships with people from differing cultural backgrounds can pose a synergistic opportunity for the individuals involved in the form of a positive feedback loop of growth and experience for developing cultural sensitivity.

Resnicow, Baranowski, Ahluwahlia, and Braithwaite (1999) describe cultural sensitivity as aligning one's modes of interaction with the cultural other in ways that respect the surface, or observable, and deep, aesthetically indistinguishable, structural levels of culture. Observable cultural characteristics include, but are not limited to, geographical places of origin, common language, musical expression, foodstuffs and ways in which those foodstuffs are prepared for consumption, and clothing style.

Deep culture knowledge involves, but is not limited to, understanding characteristics adopted by a cultural, societal, or ethnic group to self-identify or self-describe, and the ways in which members of that group weave social and historical experiences into their group-determined, agreed-upon identity.

It stands to reason that cultural sensitivity, as a skill set, requires acceptance of cultural difference, willingness and intentional knowing of one's self and the cultural other, and a culturally diverse context in which to hone one's skill at navigating and negotiating within culturally complex social situations.

Lisa E. Wills

References

Corneille, M. A., Ashcroft, A. M., & Belgrave, F. Z. (2005). What's culture got to do with it? Prevention programs for African American adolescent girls. *Journal of Health Care for the Poor and Underserved, 16*(4), 38–47.

Locke, D. C. & Bailey, D. F. (2013). *Increasing multicultural understanding* (3rd ed.). Thousand Oaks, CA: Sage Publications.

Resnicow, K., Baranowski, T., Ahluwalia J. S., & Braithwaite, R. L. (1999). Cultural sensitivity in public health: Defined and demystified. *Ethnicity & Disease, 9*(1), 10–21.

Robinson, J. S., Bowman, R., Ewing, T., Hanna, J., & Lopez-De Fede, A. (1997). *Building cultural bridges*. Bloomington, IN: National Educational Service.

Triandis, H. C. (1972). *The analysis of subjective culture: An approach to cross-cultural social psychology*. New York: Wiley-Interscience.

CULTURAL TAXATION

The Other Burden: Cultural Taxation in Higher Education

Within predominantly white institutions (PWIs), faculty of color are often disproportionately represented within their colleges. Not only must this population shoulder the responsibilities of their position, they are often responsible for additional workload opportunities that can impede tenure processes, productivity, and overall value of being a respected faculty member. Cultural taxation is a concept adopted by Amado Padilla in 1994 to describe additional workload issues experienced by minority faculty on PWIs (Samano, 2007, pp. 13, 21). This tax often pressures faculty of color to take upon diversity-related opportunities and other workload responsibilities that they cannot manage without sacrificing other works in the process. Pivotal pieces of literature in understanding cultural taxation, and its impact on faculty of color, have been written by prominent scholars. This entry describes the research and the implications of cultural taxation expressed by scholars Amado Padilla, Joanne E. Cooper and Dannelle D. Stevens, and Michael Samano.

Amado Padilla's (1994) "Ethnic Minority Scholars, Research, and Mentoring: Current and Future Issues" in *Educational Researcher* highlights the challenges that scholars of color face in research, finding a mentor, and publishing. In this landmark article, Padilla (1994) describes cultural taxation in great detail. He explains that ethnic scholars are often asked to complete certain tasks by administration due in part to their cultural background. Some of these workload issues include but are not limited to:

- acting as the expert advisor on diversity
- educating the majority group on diversity
- serving on committees that are related to diversity
- being the "diversity-liaison" for a department
- translating for non-English speakers (p. 26)

All of these tasks can be admirable roles; however, when administration assumes that this is the primary role for faculty of color, this burden can be detrimental to their advancement and professional development. In short, this form of cultural taxation has undue consequences that administration may not consider. Further, when faculty of color undertakes a workload due to "cultural obligation," they often neglect their responsibility to publish and research (Padilla, 1994). These obligations may garner special recognition but have very limited impact on tenure and promotion (Padilla, 1994).

In Joanne E. Cooper and Dannelle D. Stevens's (2002) book, *Tenure in the Sacred Grove: Issues and*

Strategies for Women and Minority Faculty, they shed light on the challenges women and faculty of color encounter in academia. The book reveals various factors that ethnic and women faculty members face in their quest for tenure and promotion. The authors assert that

> minority faculty continue to be underrepresented in the academe holding a higher percentage of part-time and non-tenure track positions. Minority faculty remain disproportionately located in less prestigious community colleges and four-year schools. When minorities are hired, they may face disproportionate advising and service loads because they are often the only minorities in a department. Minority faculty tend to spend more time on teaching and service, leaving them vulnerable to attack at the point of tenure and promotion. (Cooper & Stevens, 2002, pp. 7–8)

Although Cooper and Stevens do not use the term *cultural taxation* based on Padilla's (1994) definition, the aforementioned commentary describes factors that tax women and faculty of color, which ultimately serve as obstacles to tenure and promotion.

Michael Samano's (2007) "Respecting One's Abilities, or (Post)Colonial Tokenism? Narrative Testimonios of Faculty of Color Working in Predominantly White Community Colleges" is a comprehensive body of work that explains "cultural taxation" from faculty and historical points of view. Samano explains that one challenge that faculty of color experience is not always the overt racism, but microaggressions that consist of nonverbal and verbal communication. He believes this hostile work environment is a stumbling block that causes a hindrance in job performance, productivity, job satisfaction, and tenure and promotion. Further, he explains that the low representation of minorities in faculty membership, coupled with mistreatment, can cause a sense of "minority burden" within faculty of color. This minority burden is not limited to faculty of color and women, but also exists within any marginalized and underrepresented group (e.g., LGBTQ faculty). Samano offers several suggestions for institutions to address "minority burden." These suggestions

include contractual work that describes teaching and service loads, expectations, and roles; compensation for degree of cultural competency; campus diversity initiatives; recruitment and hiring process, mentorship, and retention; tenure/promotion of faculty; and the quality of work environment (pp. 53–55).

Faculty of color and other minority groups can experience an overcommitment due to the feeling that they are the representatives of their culture, which is defined by Padilla (2004) as "cultural taxation." This cultural burden can cause this population to feel as if they are obligated to take on additional roles in committees, to be representatives of diversity, and to educate others about diversity issues. When the commitment is being suggested by an administrator, there is even more pressure to complete designated tasks (even at the expense of one's own productivity). To many faculty of color, saying "no" is risking reputation and job security. The three pieces of literature discussed all highlight the issues that faculty of color and of other marginalized populations face in their process of tenure and promotion. Though Samano provided several recommendations, more research is needed to find a solution for cultural taxation within PWIs.

Roger Cleveland
JaDora Sailes
Jillian Watts
A. Dexter Samuels

References

Cooper, J. E. & Stevens, D. D. (2002). The journey toward tenure. In J. E. Cooper & D. D. Stevens (Eds.), *Tenure in the sacred grove: Issues and strategies for women and minority faculty*. New York: State University Press.

Padilla, A. M. (1994). Ethnic minority scholars, research, and mentoring: Current and future issues. *Educational Researcher, 23*(4), 24–27.

Samano, M. (2007). Respecting one's abilities, or (post)colonial tokenism?: Narrative testimonios of faculty of color working in predominantly white community colleges. (Doctoral Dissertation). Retrieved from http://ir.library.oregonstate.edu/xmlui/handle/1957/5011.

CULTURAL TRANSFORMATION

Cultural transformation is a process by which changes in cultural perspective, worldview, and action are achieved. Critical cultural incidents, cultural immersions, and critical guided reflection are among the learning experiences that promote cultural transformation by fostering a deeper understanding of contextual and systemic processes within a political and sociocultural context. Cultural perspectives are transformed as the practices and policies that promote social inequities in marginalized communities are critically explored. Cultural transformation results in increased professional and cultural competence at the individual, organizational, and societal levels. Cultural transformation is aimed at social justice and equity for all members of society.

Transformative learning theory (Mezirow, 2006) provides the conceptual framework for cultural transformation. Transformative learning encourages critical examination of concepts, issues, themes, and problems from various viewpoints (Banks, 1997). Learning experiences that promote critical reflection and higher-order thinking challenge and assist learners in developing a deeper understanding of experience. Recognition of discriminatory practices and social polices that serve to oppress marginalized communities facilitates a shift in thoughts, feelings, and actions (Lemley, 2014). Specific to cultural transformation, the shift changes the cultural perspectives of the individual and cultural practices within organizations or within societies. Knowledge acquired, and the social and cultural changes that occur, have meaning and purpose. Cultural transformation demonstrates what was learned and how the learner has changed in light of new knowledge.

A social justice agenda provides a comprehensive framework for examining institutional and structural polices, social and economic conditions, and the intersectionality of multiple identities in exploring multicultural and diversity issues (Ortiz & Jani, 2010). With a social justice paradigm as the foundation, cultural transformation results in transformative leadership for social change. Cultural transformation creates social change agents empowered to act in society in support of social justice advocacy. Transformative leaders have developed cultural competencies and social justice advocacy skills needed for personal, social, and civic action. Transformative leaders possess a heightened social consciousness and increased awareness of oppression, power and privilege, and act in support of social equity and social justice.

Saundra M. Tomlinson-Clarke

References

Banks, J. A. (1997). Approaches to multicultural curriculum reform. In J. A. Banks & C. A. M. Banks, *Multicultural education: Issues and perspectives* (3rd ed., pp. 229–50). Boston, MA: Allyn and Bacon.

Lemley, C. (2014). Social justice in teacher education: Naming discrimination to promote transformative action. *Critical Questions in Education, 5*, 26–51.

Mezirow, J. (2006). An overview of transformative learning. In P. Sutherland & J. Crowther (Eds.), *Lifelong learning: Concepts and contexts* (pp. 24–38). New York: Routledge.

Ortiz, L. & Jani, J. (2010). Critical race theory: A transformative model for teaching diversity. *Journal of Social Work Education, 46*, 175–93.

CULTURALLY AND LINGUISTICALLY DIVERSE

The term *culturally and linguistically diverse* (CLD) is used to describe persons whose home culture and language usage are different than that of the dominant mainstream culture. The term rose to popularity in the 1990s in reference to the increasing diversity in K–12 classrooms in the United States. It is commonly used in schools and educational research to refer to students with limited or no English proficiency who also participate in customs, traditions, social norms, and expectations not common in dominant culture (Gonzales, Pagan, Wendell, & Love, 2011).

Dominant culture in the United States refers to traditions, norms, and values based on Western European histories and British language traditions; that is to say, white, middle-class, Protestant, English-speaking norms. This definition is not limited to race and ethnicity, but also includes European students who may indeed participate in nondominant linguistic and cultural expressions. Cultural representations and ways of knowing include, but are not limited to, language, style of dress, diet, religion, gender roles, and nonverbal expressions. Variations in socioeconomic status

(SES) are also included as poverty and/or the availability of resources can influence classroom instruction and participation.

Linguistic diversity itself not only includes language differences but also the use of nondominant dialects and indigenous languages. As cultural and linguistic diversity often occur simultaneously, the term is often used interchangeably with English-Language Learners (ELLs), but this latter term does not encompass the needs of students beyond that of language acquisition (Stritikus & Varghese, 2007; Terry & Irving, 2010).

Culturally and linguistically diverse students often face challenges in the classroom due to perceptions of deficiencies in their intellectual capability linked to the existence of these sociocultural differences. Some educators may make instructional decisions based on personal or dominant social norms and expectations, resulting in inappropriate or unnecessary labeling. These perceptions have led to a disproportionate number of CLD students being incorrectly labeled as having learning disabilities or as being difficult to teach (Sharma, 2007; Terry & Irving, 2010). Educators who link cultural and linguistic diversity to limited intellectual capability may have low expectations for students and provide less challenging assignments, thus inhibiting their cognitive development.

To overcome these challenges and work effectively with CLD students, educators are encouraged to develop an understanding of their student's cultural and linguistic backgrounds and their relevance in classroom instruction and practice. The literature on instructional strategies is extensive, and suggestions of scaffolding, modeling, and guided practice are highly prevalent (Gonzales, Pagan, Wendell, & Love, 2011; Sharma, 2007; Stritikus & Varghese, 2007, Terry & Irving, 2010). Many educators advocate for a culturally relevant pedagogy in acknowledgment that students come to the classroom with prior knowledge and understandings about the world around them. Rather than viewing this background knowledge as a deficiency, educators can use it to enhance the educational experiences of all students in the classroom. Classroom assignments and assessments can be adjusted to alter culturally specific questions or methods of evaluation that place CLD students at a disadvantage. The challenge

of working effectively with CLD students continues to emphasize ways to balance students' personal and academic needs within the larger framework of standardized testing.

Dyanis Popova

References

Gonzales, R. J., Pagan, M., Wendell, L. & Love, C. (2011). *Supporting ELL/culturally and linguistically diverse students for academic achievement.* Rexford, NY: International Center for Leadership in Education.

Sharma, S. (2007). The education of culturally and linguistically diverse students. *Journal of College Teaching & Learning, 4*(11), 20–30.

Stritikus, T. T. & Varghese, M. M. (2007). Language diversity and schooling. In J. A. Banks & C. A. M. Banks (Eds.), *Multicultural education: Issues and perspectives* (6th ed., pp. 297–325). Hoboken, NJ: John Wiley & Sons.

Terry, N. P. & Irving, M. A. (2010). Cultural and linguistic diversity: Issues in education. In R. P. Colarusso & C. M. O'Rourke (Eds.), *Special education for all teachers* (5th ed.) (pp. 109–32). Dubuque, IA: Kendall Hunt Publishing.

CULTURALLY RELEVANT EDUCATION

Culturally Relevant Teaching, also known as Culturally Responsive Teaching (CRT) or Culturally Relevant Pedagogy (CRP) in education, is a philosophically grounded approach to pedagogy. CRP is a tradition that gained popularity within the U.S. educational context in the early to mid-1990s. It has established connections with black feminist thought, multiculturalism, and race studies in education, yet it stands on its own as a pedagogical tradition. While at times reduced to be a series of prescribed teaching strategies or approaches to teaching, CRP is centered on empowering students to be intellectual, political, and socioeconomic leaders, reflecting teacher disposition over pedagogical strategy (Ladson-Billings, 1994).

Theoretical Foundations

Since the early 1980s, cultural and educational anthropologists began to use the constructs of "culturally congruent" and "culturally responsive" as mechanisms to examine the extent to which school-based practices did or did not align with home-based practices rooted in the cultural backgrounds and dispositions of families (Mohatt & Erickson, 1981; Shulman, 1987). Literacy educators, during this same time frame, became interested in understanding the lived realities of student home life as a means of understanding potential disconnects in teachers' understandings of language and literacy practices (Casden & Leggett, 1981). While educational scholarship from the 1970s through the mid- to late 1980s focused on critical orientations and approaches to teaching, it was not until 1990 that Jackie Jordan Irvine began to highlight the cultural disconnect that occurs between a predominantly white and female teaching force and a public school student body, particularly in urban settings, that is representative of historically underrepresented groups.

Gloria Ladson-Billings (1990) first conceptualized CRP in a groundbreaking article titled "Like Lightning in a Bottle: Attempting to Capture the Pedagogical Excellence of Successful Teachers," and she followed it with the seminal work *The Dreamkeepers: Successful Teachers of African American Children* (1994). Ladson-Billings' work in CRP is similar to other critical approaches in education insofar as it is concerned with power dynamics between teachers and students. CRP, however, is centered on group empowerment through three interrelated tenets that include high expectations for student academic success, students' and teachers' ability to develop and sustain culturally competent understandings, and a level of sociopolitical engagement that demonstrates critical consciousness.

Other predominant scholars in the field have expanded upon the ways in which CRP creates living/learning environments whereby students are not forced to exchange cultural identity for academic achievement (Gay, 2000). Consequently, it is believed that a culturally relevant approach draws richly from students' experiences outside of school to engage students in the act of being sociopolitical leaders within the landscapes of their communities. Therefore, CRP validates cultural knowledge, is complex and multidimensional in nature, and is emancipatory in scope (Ladson-Billings, 1994; Gay, 2000).

Practice and Engagement

Given the complexities of teacher-student demographics, and the rhetoric concerning student achievement that intensified with the passage of the No Child Left Behind Act, many practitioners began to evoke the language of CRP to describe teaching strategies and approaches that are not actually consistent with culturally relevant teaching. Professional development approaches that claim to draw from CRP often ignore the practices of exemplary experienced urban educators and instead have focused on short-term professional development that still positions students from historically underrepresented groups as deficient (Foster, Lewis, & Onafowora, 2005). In practice, culturally relevant teachers believe that they are teaching for social justice and create intellectually stimulating environments with high expectations for student academic achievement. In these classrooms, furthermore, teachers see their own futures reflected in the eyes of their students and build on students' strengths and cultural competencies to drive instruction. It is believed by culturally relevant scholars that a teacher's belief in the fundamental humanity of her/his students is pivotal toward understanding the extent to which a teacher is culturally relevant (Dixson & Fasching-Varner, 2009).

Kenneth J. Fasching-Varner
Desiree R. Lindbom-Cho

References

Cazden, C. & Leggett, E. (1981). Culturally responsive education: Recommendations for achieving Lau remedies II. In H. Trueba, G. Guthrie, & K. Au (Eds.), *Culture and the bilingual classroom: Studies in classroom ethnography* (pp. 69–86). Rowley, MA: Newbury House.

Dixson, A. D. & Fasching-Varner, K. J. (2009). This is how we do it: Helping teachers understand culturally relevant pedagogy in diverse classrooms. In C. Compton-Lilly (Ed.), *Breaking the silence: Recognizing the social and cultural resources students bring to the classroom* (pp. 109–24). Newark, DE: International Reading Association.

Foster, M., Lewis, J., & Onafowora, L. (2005). Grooming great urban teachers. *Educational Leadership*, *62*(6), 28–32.

Gay, G. (2000). *Culturally responsive teaching: Theory, research, and practice.* New York: Teachers College Press.

Irvine, J. J. (1990). *Black students and school failure.* Westport, CT: Greenwood Press.

Ladson-Billings, G. J. (1990). Like lightning in a bottle: Attempting to capture the pedagogical excellence of successful teachers of black students. *Qualitative Studies in Education, 3*(4), 335–44.

Ladson-Billings, G. J. (1994). *The dreamkeepers: Successful teachers of African American children.* San Francisco, CA: Jossey-Bass.

Mohatt, G. & Erickson, F. (1981). Cultural differences in teaching styles in an Odawa school: A sociolinguistic approach. In G. Spindler (Ed.), *Doing the ethnography of schooling* (pp. 105–19). New York: Holt, Rienhart & Winston.

Shulman, L. (1987). Knowledge and teaching: Foundations of the new reform. *Harvard Educational Review, 57*(1), 1–22.

CULTURALLY RESPONSIVE TEACHING

The last two decades have seen a rising interest in culturally responsive teaching, largely due to concerns over the lack of success experienced by many ethnic/racial minority students despite years of education reform. Critics of traditional schooling suggest that the curriculum taught in classrooms is devoid of multicultural content. The serious achievement gap between certain student populations has prompted educational researchers to consider the degree to which the failure to include multicultural content into instruction has dissuaded nonwhite students from wanting to learn.

Educational critics and researchers have claimed that schools in the United States seem to take a one-size-fits-all approach to teaching students (Lee, Lamotey, & Shujaa, 1990). As such, the students' individual cultural differences often go unrecognized in the traditional classroom setting in the United States. This proves to be evident when looking at the education of African American students and students living in poverty: there appears to be little regard for cultural or stylistic differences among school-age students (Williams, 2003). In short, this approach to teaching reportedly ignores the complexities of how individuals from different backgrounds (e.g., racial, ethnic, and socioeconomic) learn. In response, scholars have examined ways that teaching can better match the home and community cultures of students who have been unable to find academic success.

Teachers' perceptions, approaches, and expectations of students are shaped by the teachers' own culture and upbringing. Thus, parents, educators, and scholars believe that teachers should be trained to address cultural styles and multicultural differences among their students. Therefore, all teachers should be engaged in culturally mediated instruction that recognizes the unique cultural base that each student brings to the classroom (Durodoye & Hildreth, 1995).

Teachers should affirm, appreciate, embrace, recognize, respect, and celebrate the human difference and the cultural integrity of their students by creating culturally derived educational settings that are consistent with the cultural contexts with which the students are familiar. The educational experience is enhanced when it is complementary to the home environment and cultural background of the student (Madhere, 1999). This concept is referred to as culturally responsive teaching (Eggen & Kauchak, 2003), which occurs when teachers understand the cultures of the students they teach, communicate positive attitudes about cultural diversity, and employ a variety of instructional approaches that build upon students' cultural diversity (p. 37).

Culturally responsive teaching is based on the idea that culture is central to student learning. Ladson-Billings (1992) created the term *culturally relevant teaching* to describe a pedagogy that empowers students intellectually, socially, emotionally, and politically by using cultural referents to impart knowledge, skills, and attitudes. Ladson-Billings (1994) identified three components of culturally relevant teaching: (a) the teachers' conceptions of themselves and others, (b) the manner in which classroom social interactions are structured, and (c) teachers' conception of knowledge.

Culturally relevant teachers must be observant and alert to the classroom behaviors and communications, verbal and nonverbal, of students. Culturally relevant teaching occurs when teachers are sensitive to cultural differences and when culture is naturally integrated into the curriculum, into instructional and assessment practices, and into classroom management. This integration should include textbooks, aesthetics, classroom themes, holidays, rituals, and other multicultural relevant themes. Villegas and Lucas (2002, p. 121) described culturally responsive teachers as those who:

1. are socioculturally conscious
2. are favorably disposed to diversity
3. see themselves as cultural brokers in educational institutions
4. understand and embrace constructivist views of knowledge, teaching, and learning
5. know about the lives of their students
6. design instruction to draw on students' strengths and to address their needs

Educational researchers agree that culturally responsive teachers who draw on students' cultural heritage in the classroom affect students' dispositions, attitudes, and approaches to learning as well as students' self-concept. Jordan (1985) stated that educational practices must match with the children's culture in ways that ensure the generation of academically important behaviors. In essence, students' diverse cultural experiences should be used as a guide in the selection of educational program elements so that academically desired behaviors are produced and undesired behaviors are avoided. Gay (2002) defined culturally responsive teaching as using the cultural knowledge, prior experiences, and performance styles of diverse students to make learning more appropriate and effective for them. Gay suggests that there are five important areas that need to be addressed when educating culturally responsive preservice teachers to work effectively with cultural and linguistically diverse (CLD) backgrounds: (a) develop a culturally diverse knowledge base, (b) design culturally relevant curricula, (c) demonstrate cultural caring and establish a learning community, and (d) build effective cross-cultural communications and deliver culturally responsive instruction.

Culturally responsive teaching must incorporate the daily experiences and culture of students into the overall context of the learning environment. This teaching method may have a powerful impact on the way some students learn and how they see themselves among their majority peers. Based on the research and the ongoing discussion about school improvement and student achievement, it seems obvious that classroom teachers would want to incorporate this teaching method. By using this teaching method, the classroom teacher can become active in researching this new pedagogy and reaching all students regardless of their cultural background. Employing culturally responsive teaching will convince students and parents that teachers have a vested interest in the knowledge and skills that are most important to all students.

Doris L. Crawford

References

Durodoye, B. & Hildreth, B. (1995). Learning styles and the African American student. *Education, 116,* 241–47.

Eggen, P. D. & Kauchak, D. P. (2003). *Learning and teaching: Research-based methods.* Boston, MA: Pearson Education.

Gay, G. (2002). Preparing for culturally responsive teaching. *Journal of Teacher Education, 53*(2), 106–16.

Gay, G. (2010). *Culturally responsive teaching: Theory, research, & practice* (2nd ed.). New York: Teachers College Press.

Jordan, C. (1985). Translating culture: From ethnographic information to educational program. *Anthropology and Education Quarterly, 16,* 105–23.

Ladson-Billings, G. (1992). Reading between the lines and beyond the pages: A culturally relevant approach to literacy teaching. *Theory into Practice, 31*(4), 312–20.

Ladson-Billings, G. (1994). *The dreamkeepers: Successful teachers for African-American children.* San Francisco, CA: Jossey-Bass.

Lee, C. D., Lomotey, K., & Shujaa, M. (1990). How shall we sing our sacred song in a strange land? The dilemma of double consciousness and the complexities of an African centered pedagogy. *Journal of Education, 172,* 45–61.

Madhere, S. (1999, February). *Psychology, pedagogy, and talent cultivation.* Presented at the Conference on Psychology and Caribbean Development, University of the West Indies at Mona.

Villegas, A. M. & Lucas, T. (2002). *Educating culturally responsive teachers: A coherent approach.* Albany, NY: State University of New York Press.

Williams, B. (2003). *Closing the achievement gap*. Alexandria, VA: Association for Supervision and Curriculum Development.

CULTURE

Discussions about culture—especially those occurring in the United States—tend to center around culture as being a living, breathing relationship among individuals with mutual interests. The National Center for Culturally Responsive Educational Systems (2007) defines *culture* as "a system of shared beliefs, values, customs, behavior, and artifacts with which the members of society use to understand their world and one another." This definition mirrors what other social scientists describe as culture.

Researchers from anthropology to sociology have a conception and definition of the term *culture*, which differs somewhat from the vernacular, but generally speaking the definition includes items such as traditions, influences, beliefs, customs, expectations, values, norms, celebrations, and shared meanings. In other words, culture can be summarized as the way of life for an individual or group of people that is shared by a national, ethnic/racial, or religious population.

One metaphor for culture is that of a big tent: it includes everything that a population of people believe is their unique identity—their conceptions, behaviors, heritage, and symbols. Culture can and often does encompass arts, beliefs, and institutions of a population that are passed down from generation to generation. Culture is also a group's oneness—its rituals, rites of passage, celebrations, and behavioral patterns that acknowledge what is important to them. In short, culture is the way in which people understand themselves and establish their personhood.

Because all people and cultures differ in meaningful ways, we need to create a society in which different cultures can coexist side by side without major conflicts, and all cultures are encouraged to uphold their customs as they see fit. In doing that, people need to recognize the dimensions of culture that are very important to cultural groups. Language is one such dimension, which includes written and spoken language. In the United States, English is the predominant language, but people speak languages other than English in the United States, and these languages must be respected. According to the U.S. Census (2011), 55.4 million people (20 percent of the U.S. population) spoke a language other than English at home. Other dimensions of culture include: attitude toward time, space, and proximity; gender roles; family roles; status of age; and taboos.

Culture is not static, but ever changing. Ethnic origins and ancestry create the background and profile of many cultures, but those cultures continue to evolve over generations, leaving a record of historical information that weaves a chronological mosaic of cultural narratives and rituals. Culture brings with it a certain political and economic philosophy, social structure, spirituality, language, and education, all of which confirms that culture matters.

Even though culture is the passport for most people's self-concept and indigenous nature, it should not create boundaries restricting and preventing multicultural relationships. Being culturally responsive and sensitive provides a new horizon for appreciating multicultural awareness. Being open to other cultures will help people discover the items in cultures that reaffirm that we are alike in many ways. Individuals are responsible for stretching beyond their limited worldview and accepting the existence of different cultural practices. This practice will broaden our shared traditions and allow us to learn from each other.

Sherwood Thompson

References

National Center for Culturally Responsive Educational Systems. (2007). Retrieved from www.NCCRESt. org.

U.S. Census Bureau. (2011). *Native North American language spoken at home in the United States and Puerto Rico: 2006–2010*. Retrieved from http://www. census.gov/prod/2011pubs/acsbr10-10.pdf.

CULTURE FAIR TEST

Definition

A test would be considered a culture fair test or a culture free test if it predicts future academic and test performance equally well for all groups of individuals. A culture fair test is one that assesses content, knowledge, skills, or aptitudes and could be used in any cultural context without the culture of the examinee being assessed influencing the outcome or results. Unfairness of a test is found when the test or testing process interacts with examinees' internalized cultural experiences or their environmental socialization. The test shows unfair scores if examinees' test scores are affected by cultural and other factors that are not intended to be assessed by the test (Helms, 2006). Identifying test unfairness requires that test developers and test scores determine why one group of examinees tends to do better or worse than another group on a particular test. If the content of a test is comparatively more difficult for one group of individuals than for others, the test is unfair. The key assessment concept underpinning the idea of a culture fair test is that of validity. A valid assessment is one that measures what the assessor intends. If a test or other assessment instrument favors one culture over another, the validity of the test is compromised. A particularly famous and often-cited example of a cultural bias or unfairness in assessment was when the Scholastic Aptitude Test (SAT) had an analogy using the word *regatta*, which many white students knew but far fewer African Americans knew. A test is also considered *unfair* if a test design or the way results are interpreted and used systematically advantages or disadvantages certain groups of examinees, such as individuals of color, individuals who are not proficient in the English language, individuals who are not fluent in certain cultural customs and traditions, or individuals from lower-income backgrounds.

In general, hands-on performance assessments are considered more culture fair than pencil and paper tests; nonverbal contents are considered more culture fair than verbal contents; power tests, which measure how much the examinees know, are considered more culture fair than speed tests, which measure how many questions per hour the examinees can answer correctly; oral instructions are more culture fair than written instructions; and familiar-item contents to the examinees are considered more culture fair than unfamiliar-item contents. Developing culture fair tests should not be the only answer to testing the disadvantaged (Arvey, 1972). In addition to fair test construction, for the disadvantaged, other accommodations should be made to minimize the distortions in testing that stem from their specific disadvantage.

Is a Truly Culture Fair Test Possible?

Producing a truly culture fair test may be impossible given that communication is involved between the examiner and the examinee. When formal languages are used, such as in tests like the SATs, Advanced Placement exams, or International Baccalaureate exams, people who speak as a first language the language of the assessment have some advantage over those who do not speak the language of assessment as their first language. When the academic subject of the assessment is not language, examining boards generally stress that exam takers should not be penalized for their language skills. For example, in written responses on a biology exam, students should be assessed on their knowledge of biology, not their eloquence or skill in the language of the assessment. However, given that the examinee must read questions in the language of assessment and produce answers in the language, native speakers of the language have greater ease in understanding questions and producing responses that reflect their thoughts. The compromise to validity may be minor—with subtle nuances of reading or writing preventing strong students from earning the high-range marks they would if the test were in their first language, to major—students literally being unable to read the questions asked. Validity can be compromised in ways beyond linguistic skill. Students working in a language other than their mother tongue may experience more stress than other students, and test anxiety can compromise a test's results.

Some assessments do not rely on formal language but rather on informal languages of hand actions, signs, markers, and other nonlinguistic representations. However, for the assessment instructions and questions to have meaning, the examinees must understand and know the meaning of the various forms of nonlinguistic representations. However, as Europeans quickly discovered when they came to the New World in the fifteenth century, Amerindians, who had had no contact with Eurasians for possibly thousands of years, had different meanings for even the most basic hand signals, which Europeans considered natural and normal and which all humans would understand (Greenblatt, 1992). In light of the fact that some communication must occur between the examiner and the examinee, a truly culture fair test is virtually impossible.

The issue of culture fair tests has grown in importance in the last seventy years, as societies increasingly value diversity and cultural pluralism (see **Cultural Pluralism**). Educators, institutions, and other stakeholders have come to recognize that culture can have a significant bearing on how individuals perform. To honor diversity, ideally assessments would be crafted and administered in a fashion that would not disadvantage individuals because of their cultural background. Having culture fair tests would represent a form of social justice, as no one would be discriminated against based upon their culture. However, most assessments have to be given in a language. Since language is the central element of culture, to be culturally fair would mean to offer exams in test takers' first language, which is often a nonstandard or dialect version of a language. Not only would this not be possible, powerful forces would work against it. For example, one of the most important bases for assessment is to advance educationally, through K–12 education and on to higher education. The results of various educational assessments ultimately have the power to determine how societies allocate important rewards. As is the case with institutional assessment across cultural borders (see **Fair Assessment**), many stakeholders in educational assessment want national and even international benchmarks using standardized assessments and uniform scales of measurements so that these rewards are fairly allocated to those who aspire to them. However, to do so requires using the major languages of common use, especially standard American or British English. Thus, in the name of one type of fairness (a common measurement), another type of fairness (eliminating or reducing the force of culture) is compromised.

Research Findings Related to Culture Fair Test

SEARCH FOR CULTURE FAIR TESTS Despite the conclusion above that a truly culture fair test is probably impossible, researchers should try, and do try, to identify specific cognitive abilities that are *strongly* impacted by examinees' sociocultural and/or ethnic factors that may characterize a particular sociocultural group, such as sociocultural beliefs and behaviors, environment demands, language, and level and quality of education, and to identify or develop a *relatively* culture fair test (e.g., Shuttleworth-Edwards, Donnelly, Reid, & Radloff, 2004). For example, researchers (Shuttleworth-Edwards et al., 2004) found no significant test performance difference on the Wechsler Adult Intelligence Scale-III (WAIS-III) Digit Symbol-Incidental Learning Pairing and Free Recall between black African first-language and white English first-language examinees with various levels and qualities of education, indicating that these memory tasks are *relatively* culture fair to disadvantageous influences of examinees' ethnic and sociocultural backgrounds, including at least twelve years of education, and that Digit Symbol-Incidental Learning Pairing and Free Recall of the WAIS-III is a relatively culture fair test (Shuttleworth-Edwards et al., 2004).

CROSS-CULTURAL DIFFERENCES IN TEST PERFORMANCE Differences in test performance stem from factors outside a test as well as inside a test. An extensive quantitative review (i.e., meta-analysis) study (Van der Vijver, 1997) found that cross-cultural differences in test performance tend to increase (a) as wealth differences such as Gross National Product (GNP) and educational expenditure (i.e., amount of money spend on education per capita per year) of nations increase; and (b) as age and years of schooling increase (Van der Vijver, 1997), which indicates differences in test performance due to factors outside a test.

Factors inside a test could also influence test performance differences. Cross-cultural differences in test performance increase as stimuli complexity of tasks increase, and the differences are also related to types of tasks, because Western tasks show the biggest performance differences and locally developed non-Western tasks show the smallest differences across diverse cultural groups (Van der Vijver, 1997).

CULTURE FAIR TEST AND CULTURAL CHANGES OVER TIME A culture fair test would be fair not only in terms of existing cultures but also in terms of cultures over time, indicating the vastness of human diversity. The well-known Flynn effect (1984, 1987) indicates that intelligence test scores increased in developed countries during the twentieth century and continue to increase in other parts of the world. These findings confuse researchers because the increases are the largest on abstract reasoning (e.g., fluid intelligence, which is related to creativity, which has decreased since 1990 [Kim, 2011]) and culture-free tests, which in fact are *not* supposed to measure cultural changes (Fox & Mitchum, 2013). In contrast, the tests that are supposed to measure cultural changes (e.g., crystallized intelligence) did not increase significantly, even though culture in the world has clearly changed since the early twentieth century. Many hypotheses have been advanced to explain this confusion. Recent research has shown that the increases are due to examinees' know-how (e.g., test-taking skill) or approach to the test item, which is more common among examinees in modern cultures, as individuals take tests more often than people in the 1940s. Test-taking skill is not a real part of intelligence. A study (Fox & Mitchum, 2013) looked into item-specific predictions about differences between cohorts in pass rates and item-response patterns on the Raven's matrices (Flynn, 1987), a seemingly culture-free test that showed the largest Flynn effect. Fox and Mitchum (2013) found that Raven's matrices scores violated measurement invariance between cohorts by underestimating the number of rules inferred by 1940 cohort examinees compared to 1990 cohort examinees. This finding indicates the vast and irregular human diversity that needs to be addressed by culture fair tests. Culture fair tests must try to be fair in terms of diversity and change, which requires "looking beneath the surface features of human variation for principles that transcend both culture and time" (Fox & Mitchum, 2013, p. 995).

Suggestions for Increasing Cultural Fairness
Businesses and educational institutions use tests extensively for the screening of applicants for jobs or training programs. Therefore, ensuring cultural fairness of these tests is critical (Petersen & Novick, 1976). Suggestions to reduce cultural unfairness and to increase fairness include (Gregory, 2004):

- Base major decisions about or characterization of examinees on at least two different test scores.
- Ensure diversity in test developers and test scorers.
- Train test developers and test scorers to be aware of the potential for cultural bias, linguistic bias, and socioeconomic bias.
- Have test materials reviewed by experts in identifying cultural bias, linguistical bias, and socioeconomical bias.
- Have test materials reviewed by representatives of culturally, linguistically, and socioeconomically diverse groups.
- Ensure that norming processes used to develop norm-referenced tests include culturally, linguistically, and socioeconomically diverse groups.
- Ensure sample sizes used to develop norm-referenced tests are large enough to constitute a representative sample for each culturally, linguistically, and socioeconomically diverse group.
- Be aware that although diverse groups can be proportionately represented in the standardization sample, their actual numbers may still be too small to be representative.
- Eliminate any test item on which certain groups perform differently.
- Eliminate items, references, and terms offensive to certain groups.
- Translate tests into the examinees' native language.
- Use interpreters to translate test items for the examinees.
- For determining academic achievement and progress, use multiple assessment measures, such as performance assessments, besides the use of test scores.
- Interpret test scores in the context of collecting multiple sources and use this comprehensive method to make decisions.
- Consider the examinee's background experience when interpreting test scores.
- Be aware that groups have different backgrounds and experiences that affect their test performance and that not all groups have equal opportunity to learn.
- Be aware that a test may be inappropriate or unfair when an individual or a group scores low.

- Be aware that despite the best intentions to develop tests that are culture fair, individuals' stereotypes and prejudice still undermine test administration, interpretation, and use.

Kyung-Hee Kim
Robert A. Pierce

References

Arvey, R. D. (1972). Some comments on culture fair tests. *Personnel Psychology, 2,* 433–48. doi: 10.1111/j.1744-6570.1972.tb00828.x

Born, M. P., Bleichrodt, N., & Van der Flier, H. (1987). Cross-cultural comparison of sex-related differences on intelligence tests: A meta-analysis. *Journal of Cross-Cultural Psychology, 18,* 283–314. doi: 10.1177/0022002187018003002

Flynn, J. R. (1984). The mean IQ of Americans: Massive gains 1932 to 1978. *Psychological Bulletin, 95,* 29–51. doi: 10.1037/0033-2909.95.1.29

Flynn, J. R. (1987). Massive IQ gains in 14 nations: What IQ tests really measure. *Psychological Bulletin, 101,* 171–91. doi: 10.1037/0033-2909.101.2.171

Fox, M. C. & Mitchum, A. L. (2013). A knowledge-based theory of rising scores on "culture-free" tests. *Journal of Experimental Psychology: General, 142,* 979–1000. doi: 10.1037/a0030155

Greenblatt, S. (1992). *Marvelous possessions: The wonder of the new world.* Chicago: University of Chicago Press.

Gregory, R. J. (2004). *Psychological testing: History, principles, and applications.* Boston: Allyn & Bacon.

Helms, J. E. (2006). Fairness is not validity or cultural bias in racial-group assessment: A quantitative perspective. *American Psychologist, 61,* 845–59.

Kim, K. H. (2011). The creativity crisis: The decrease in creative thinking scores on the Torrance Tests of Creative Thinking. *Creativity Research Journal, 23,* 285–95. doi: 10.1080/10400419.2011.627805

Petersen, N. S. & Novick, M. R. (1976). An evaluation of some models for culture-fair selection. *Journal of Educational Measurement, 13,* 3–29. doi: 10.1111/j.1745-3984.1976.tb00178.x

Shuttleworth-Edwards, A. B., Donnelly, M. J. R., Reid, I., & Radloff, S. E. (2004). A cross-cultural study with culture fair normative indications on WAIS-III Digit Symbol-Incidental Learning. *Journal of Clinical and Experimental Neuropsychology, 26,* 921–32.

Van de Vijver, F. (1997). Meta-analysis of cross-cultural comparisons of cognitive test performance. *Journal of Cross-Cultural Psychology, 28,* 678–709. doi: 10.1177/0022022197286003.

CYBER RACISM

Les Back, a professor of sociology at the University of London, coined the term *cyber racism* in the early 2000s. His definition describes how digital technology is being used to promote racism: "The Net has provided a means for people to sense, listen, feel and be involved intimately in racist culture from a distance" (Back, 2002, p. 629). According to Back, cyber racism encompasses a range of subcultural movements in Europe, North America, and beyond. However, despite the diversity of these movements, they exhibit the following common features:

- A rhetoric of racial and/or national uniqueness and common destiny
- Ideas of racial supremacy, superiority, and separation
- A repertoire of conceptions of racial Otherness
- A utopian revolutionary worldview that aims to overthrow the existing order (Back, 2002, p. 632)

The Internet offers a new medium for the expression of racism due in large part to its nearly autonomous environment. The perpetrators use simulation games, cartoons, online books, digital newsletters, photos, white power music, and video feeds of racial activities. These sites, of which there are hundreds, promote a vast amount of conspiracy theories including the denial of the Holocaust and the justification of slavery. Not surprisingly, the net of hate cast by cyber racists reaches far and wide; as Back (2002) says, they "define a gallery of 'Others' as their enemies" (p. 639). The enemy list often includes blacks, Jews, and whites who are in blended relationships and marriages—race mixers, gays, lesbians, and immigrants. As an aside, it appears that cyber racists also constitute one of the largest groups in favor of gun ownership. While gun ownership obviously does not equate with being a supporter of the cyber racist movement, there are some close ties and convincing correlations among gun ownership advocates—especially the strong emotional appeal made by people in the cyber racist movement for not banning assault weapons.

Of course, the proliferation of cyber racism on the Internet belies the movement's origins in print media (Gilligan, 2011), but recent controversial events such as Barack Obama's presidential election have spurred the culture to grow in both size and volume. The relative affordability and accessibility of digital media has allowed individuals to reach out, from the comfort of their homes, and discover others who are willing to engage in violent rhetoric. For many people who are involved in this culture, the Internet provides an effective and autonomous means of communicating hate messages, as opposed to the obvious personal confrontations of the past. The old robe-and-hood wardrobe of groups like the Ku Klux Klan (KKK) have now given way to the more fashionable attire of laptop computers and iPads. These digital devices serve as the new tools of persuasion and propaganda for the racial hate movement.

In addition to promoting racial intimidation, cyber racism has created a unique form of cyber bullying. According to the Racism No Way (2014) project, "Cyber bullying is commonly defined as the use of information and communication technologies to support repeated and deliberate hostile behavior intended to harm others." Obviously, these activities carry a racist intent when enacted by cyber racists, who often rely on racially offensive materials or campaigns to support familiar themes: white nationalism, common destiny, racial supremacy, superiority, and genocide. In some regions of the United States and Europe, these bullying efforts have garnered a substantial following of white female and youth, but regardless of the perpetrator, there is always a frightening potential for violent rhetoric to manifest into real-life violence.

Attention must be given to these acts of violence, especially among law enforcement agencies that must practice more vigilance in actively investigating individuals and organizations engaged in this type of terrorism. More often than not, the position of some law enforcement agencies is that cyber racist media is protected as free speech.

However, there are increasingly more cases being brought before courts challenging the free speech claims of cyber racists. One such case involved a former city of Denver employee who worked at the city of Denver's planning department. He was arrested after authorities traced a racist, hate-filled email to a computer in his home. The former employee, who is white, allegedly sent an email to an African American woman, who works as a human resources manager, on the same day that he was notified of his termination. In the email, this employee repeatedly called the HR manager a "n***" and suggested that she was now being targeted by the KKK (Daniels, 2009). According to Daniels (2009), the reason that this former employee's email was not considered "free speech" is that both the state of Colorado and the city of Denver have laws against "ethnic intimidation/threats," and it was under those laws that the former employee's email was prosecuted.

Online hate is not going away any time soon; however, individuals who are victims of this type of racism should not be left to fight off these attacks alone. Law enforcement agencies should become more active in investigating the cyber racist movement. Perhaps more states and cities should consider enacting an ethnic intimidation/threats law in order to prosecute offenders. Just as neighborhoods become aware of child sex offenders through the Sex Offender Registry, cyber racism attackers should also be listed in a type of government-sponsored registry. Neighborhoods could develop a service for their residents in which the names and locations of individuals and Internet servers posting cyber racist content would be made known, thereby helping to identify these reprobate individuals in local communities. This service could build on the neighborhood watch group model by posting information of racist cyber sites that are discovered in communities across the United States. By taking such action, individual residents would have the information they need to make informed decisions about whether or not they want to live in a community that houses a cyber-racist element.

Sherwood Thompson

References

Back, L. (2002). Aryans reading Adorno: Cyber-culture and twenty-first century racism. *Ethnic & Racial Studies*, 25(4), 628–51. doi: 10.1080/01419870220136664

Daniels, J. (2009). *Cyber racism: White supremacy online and the new attack on civil rights.* Lanham, MD: Rowman & Littlefield.

Gilligan, C. (2011). Cyber racism: White supremacy online and the new attack on civil rights.

Visual Studies, 26(1), 79. doi:10.1080/1472586X.2010.502689

Racism No Way. (2014). *Cyber racism.* Retrieved from http://www.racismnoway.com.au/about-racism/cyber-racism/index.html.

D

DAOISM/TAOISM

Definition of Daoism/Taoism (道教)

Daoism, based on the standard Mandarin spelling, or *Taoism*, as it is traditionally known in English, is a comprehensive Chinese philosophy and spiritual practice. It is an all-encompassing belief system that integrates metaphysics, epistemology, axiology, aesthetics, natural sciences, social sciences, literature, medicine, and daily lives, theoretically and practically. It has had a strong influence on Chinese culture since prehistoric times, in a variety of ways, from religious practices to scientific discoveries to medicine and politics. Its calendar is currently in its 4,710th year. Due to the very inclusive nature of Daoism/Taoism, it has been an intellectually challenging and scholarly daunting task to narrow down to one clear, concise, and authoritative definition of this term. Often, it is considered one of the three pillars in connection with Confucianism and Buddhism as the impetus and foundations that provide enduring value to Chinese culture. Saso (1995), a Taoist scholar, states, "Taoism furthers a sense of well-being and harmony with nature that fosters long life and good health," while Confucianism "provides guidelines for perspective human relations" and Buddhism "teaches a sense of compassion for the living and care for the afterlife" (p. 1).

Webster's Universal Encyclopedic Dictionary defines Daoism/Taoism as both a "mystical philosophical tradition that teaches conformity to the Tao by unassertive action and practice" and a "religion" that is "concerned with obtaining a long life and good fortune by mystical means" (2002, p. 1887). It might be mystical and intriguing to many who are unfamiliar with Eastern cultures, philosophy, and practices, but in reality, Daoism is a very simple and profound holistic spiritual teaching and practice that emphasizes the Oneness of human and all other natural elements in the universes and strives for making the right choices by following nature's way for the perfect balance and thence obtaining long life, wellness, and peace to benefit and enhance all elements as a whole. Daoism (道教), in Chinese, means "the teaching of Dao," and later in its expansion and practice, some deem it as a form of religion (Robinet, 1997).

Origin

The origin of Daoism can be traced to Lao Zi (老子), who is considered the founder of this philosophical and spiritual tradition. While most Chinese and international scholars seem to reach the consensus of Lao Zi's birth in the sixth century BCE, there are not exact dates that clearly and authoritatively document his entire life span (Fung, 1983). Recent archaeological findings revealed a carved stone memorial tablet in Shan Xi Province, China, honoring Lao Zi dating back to 1122 BCE, approximately Xi Zhou dynasty (西周, c. 1066 to 771 BCE).

"Lao Zi" is an honorific title, which means "Venerable/Old Master and Teacher" in Chinese. Based on the Chinese historians, Lao Zi's real name is Li Er (李耳), and he served as an imperial official in archives during the fifth and sixth century BCE, Chun Qiu (春秋, Spring and Fall Period) in ancient China, and he was a contemporary of Confucius (孔子). His other name is Li Dan (李聃). Historically, there is a well-accepted record that Confucius consulted Lao Zi regarding spiritual reality, since Confucius primarily focused on the social and human context of life and their governance while Lao Zi studied the realms of social, physical, and spiritual realities and their balances. Confucius was reported as saying, "I have finally met the Dragon of China!" (Lau, 1963, p. 150). During the meeting, Lao Zi interpreted death as the birth of life's beginning, while Confucius focused on the living.

Some historians put Lao Zi as Lao Lai Zi (老莱子 "Venerable/Old Lai Master") during the Han dynasty, while others put him as the grand historian and astrologer Lao Dan (老聃) during Duke Xian pre–Qin dynasty, 384 to 362 BCE (Fowler, 2005; Robinet, 1997). The legends of Lao Zi have posted a challenge for historians and scholars for over two thousand years. Confronted by incomplete and conflicting historical records, some scholars and historians even went so far as to deem Lao Zi as a fabricated legend entirely, stating, "We have no reason to believe Lao Tsu as a real person" (Lau, 1963, p. xi). Daoist disciples and practitioners, on the other hand, often are not overly concerned or troubled about pinpointing the exact physical dates of his physical existence, for it is commonly believed that Lao Zi, the master of the cosmos and universes, obtained the ability of longevity and had eighty-one Hua (化, incarnations or transformations) through various lifetimes, similar to the eighty-seven manifestations of Guan Yin, the Goddess of Compassion (Avalokitesvara), as in Buddhist tradition. It is his teaching and practice that have profound spiritual, philosophical, and practical meanings that influence and shape all aspects of human existence that received the most and foremost attention.

Lao Zi's work, *Dao De Jing* (道德經, or *Tao De Jing*, or *Tao Te Ching*), dated between the fourth and sixth centuries BCE, was the cornerstone and most important classics of Daoism. According to the legend, as Lao Zi was traveling west, the Official Keeper of the West Pass recognized him and would not allow him passage to leave the country until Lao Zi penned down all his wisdom so that people would be able to study and benefit from his teaching (Lau, 1963, p. vii). *Dao De Jing* has five thousand Chinese characters and eighty-one chapters, which is viewed by his disciples and spiritual practitioners as the teaching and insights Lao Zi received directly through his spiritual communication from the Void, or Nature and Cosmos. For the first time in history, he described and advocated Dao (the Way) as the natural principles that governed all, transcending time, geographic, social, and cultural boundaries and spaces. He revealed the cosmic paths and cycles of the natural state of being and the essential components for peaceful and lasting existence, in accordance with nature, such as virtue, selflessness, oneness, nonaction, equality, and tranquility, both in theories and practices.

Since Lao Zi, the Daoist philosophers and practitioners that have significantly influenced the development of Daoism include Lao Zi's students Zhuang Zi (庄子), Wen Zi (文子, or Wen Tsu), and later Lie Zi (列子, fifth century BCE).

Daoist philosophy and practices have developed through history. During the Eastern Han dynasty (23–230 CE), Zhang Dao Ling (张道陵) established the Dao of Heavenly Master (Tian Shi Dao, 天师道), and his eighth-generation descendant Zhang Liang (张良) became its master and reformed it to "Zheng Yi Dao (正一道)" (c. 500 CE), which has been passed on till today (now the sixty-fourth lineage). Throughout Chinese history, Daoism has been viewed as a philosophy that is naturalistically oriented, nonpolitical, and nonparticipatory in imperial ruling and administration in accordance with Lao Zi's belief of "Wu Wei (无为, nonaction)." Unlike Confucianism, it rarely received endorsements from the emperors or empress, except in the Tang dynasty. Emperor Xuanzong of Tang (唐玄宗, 李隆基, 685–762 CE) claimed his ancestral lineage from Lao Zi. As Lao Zi's descendant, he glorified Lao Zi with the title "Supreme Mysterious and Primordial Emperor" and designated the works of Lao Zi, Zhuang Zi, Wen Zi, and Lie Zi as the Four Daoist Classics. In the Yuan dynasty, c. 1000 CE, Wang Chong Yang (王重阳) established the Quan Zheng Taoist School (全真道). Zheng Yi (two thousand years) and Quan Zhen (one thousand years) are deemed the most important Daoist schools in the history of China up to the present day. Both schools practice the Daoist art of healing and enlightenment under the same Master, Lao Zi, or "Tai Shang Lao Jun (太上老君)," and study *Dao De Jing* as their core text. The Purist Three (三清, Sanqing) are their supreme masters: Tai Qing (太清, or Dao De Tian Zun—道德天尊), Yu Qing (玉清, or Yuan Shi Tian Zun—元始天尊), and Shang Qing (上清, or Lin Bao Tian Zun—靈寶天尊). They focus on achieving the same goals as specified by Lao Zi via various methods.

Essence of Daoism

The essence of Daoist teaching and practice is the Oneness with nature and the cosmic principles, embedded and named as the Dao, through life-long cultivation and virtuous deeds so as to reach purity, longevity, sagehood, and enlightenment. Based on the direct spiritual connections with the universe and nature, as well as the wisdom accumulated through thousands of years of human effort in search for truth, Daoism has adopted, created, and developed a rich and complex system of knowledge. While the earliest sources and practices left no written and documentable records, the existing Daoist teaching can be traced back to thousands of years ago. The primary contents of Daoist teaching and practice, the Six Taoist Arts, to date, have amazingly remained the same as in the Zhou dynasty, and they include:

- Li (礼, Ritual)—Reverent observation of laws of Heaven, Earth, and Man in the universe through respectful and ceremonial spiritual practices
- Yue (乐, Music)—Study of the harmonious sound of nature (healing harmonies, frequencies, rhythm, and tones)
- She (射, Archery)—Practice of energy movement and power to focus and concentrate energy by storing and releasing as appropriate
- Yu (御, Charioteering)—Abilities to harness, discipline, control, and direct energy through loyal persistence and faithful practice in accordance with one's beliefs, aspiration, and talents
- Shu (書, Writing)—The discipline and cultivation of energy flow (chi) for refinement, expression, focus, and clarity as manifested through calligraphy or writing
- Shu (数, Numerology)—Mystical calculation and divination to influence, interpret, and predict any occurrence in the universe

The Sixth Art, Shu, uses divine numbers 0 to 9 (9 is the highest number) for astrological and cosmic forecasts, and thus the most mysterious and challenging Daoist art is divination. The ten numbers include all there is, the beginning and ending of a cycle as well as the rebirth, reconstruction, and the new cycle that will come forth infinitely.

Daoist classic texts include ancient works of *I Ching* (易經, or *Yi Jing*, Wilhelm, 1997), *Huang Di Nei Jing* (黄帝内經, *Yellow Emperor's Cannon*, 1995), and *Dao De Jing* (道德經) by Lao Zi (1891, 1989, and 1999), the Founder of Daoism, as well as *Zhang Zi* (*Nan Hua Zhen Jing*, 南華眞經, Watson, 1968), *Wen Zi* (*Tong Xuan Zhen Jing*, 通玄真經,

1991), *Lie Zi* (*Chong Xu Zhen Jing*, 沖虛真經), and *Dao Zang* (Treasure of Dao, 道藏), as mentioned before. In addition, they include *The Art of War* (*Sun Zi Bin Fa*, 孙子兵法), *The Secret of the Golden Flower* (*Tai Yi Jin Hua Zong Zhi*, 太乙金華宗旨, 1962), and *The Seal of the Unity of the Three* (丹, or *The Golden Elixir*, 2012).

Lao Zi's *Dao De Jing* lays down the solid foundation and uniqueness of Daoism and establishes the spiritual, philosophical, and practical system and focus of this school of thought. While the content of the book is all encompassing and inclusive of the heaven, earth, and humanity, and all species in the past, present, and future, its key focus is to show the way or path to enlightenment by observing the spiritual and natural principles, following them via peaceful coexistence with all elements, thus reaching the highest virtue, longevity, and even immortality in accordance with the cosmos. As the most important ancient philosopher of the East, Lao Zi's *Dao De Jing* has had many English versions since James Legge's first translation (1891) and has immense influence worldwide. As the title indicated, the essence of *Dao De Jing* is all about Dao (the Way), De (Virtue), and related concepts such as equality, diversity, and wu wei (nonaction).

DAO Daoist philosophy is based on the concept of the "Dao" or "the way," which is in line with nature. However, no words can sufficiently describe its essence, as Lao Zi opened his entire book by stating, "The Tao that can be told is not the eternal Tao" (Lao Tzu, 1989b, chapter 1). *Dao De Jing* explains humanity's place in relation to the Dao as "Man follows earth. Earth follows heaven. Heaven follows the Tao. Tao follows what is natural" (Lao Tzu, 1989b, chapter 25). Since Daoists follow "earth" on their path to the *Dao*, natural surroundings are vital to their practice as they harmonize with and observe the cycles of nature. For them, keeping one's natural surroundings healthy and keeping one's body healthy go hand in hand, and any disruption of nature leads to disruption in one's health. *The Yellow Emperor's Classic of Medicine* (the *Huang Di Nei Jing*, 1995) states:

There is an intimate relationship between the activity and life of human beings and their natural environment . . . [there] are the six atmospheric influences that govern the weather patterns that reflect in changes in our planetary ecology. If people violate or disrupt this natural order, then pathogenic forces will have an opportunity to cause damage to the body. (p. 5)

For Daoists, it is therefore of utmost importance to preserve natural environments, such as forests and streams, and to prevent artificial chemicals from damaging food and water sources, not only for a healthy environment but also as a security measure for public health.

The Dao is the ultimate and original source of all universes, past, present, and future, in all forms or formless, in all beings or being-less. The Dao is the primal origination, and it is the omnipresent living force that rules all things with its natural laws and principles. The Dao existed even before the religious understanding and interpretations of the world by human beings. Thus, the Dao is the true meaning and purpose of all life and death, and heaven and earth. To Lao Zi, following the Dao is to "submerge," by being part of, or melting into, or becoming the Dao.

VIRTUE When the world and humanity need to return to the Dao, where they come from, virtue comes into being and becomes extremely important. "When the Way is lost, only then do we have virtue" (Lao Tzu, 1989a, p. 7). In order to follow the Dao, and become the Dao, one has to observe virtue. Lao describes virtue as:

Highest virtue is not virtuous; therefore it truly has virtue.

The lowest virtue never loses sight of its virtue; therefore it has no true virtue. (Lao Tzu, 1989a, p. 7)

Virtue is the product of losing the Dao, and it is the means to regain the Dao. While virtue is not distinguished by the high and low, it can be cultivated, developed, and preserved. At the same time, there is a distinction of what Lao Zi calls "Profound Virtue," which matures people without making them dependent, and "gives birth to them but does not try to own them" (Lao Tzu, 1989a, p. 51). What he means is that people with profound virtue are

virtuous voluntarily and naturally without thinking of personal benefits and gains in any form or shape, in the present or future.

The contents of virtue or virtues are many according to *Dao De Jing*. Lao Zi has forty-four chapters dedicated to virtue, describing and discussing various virtues, their rationales, and their impacts. The themes occur repetitively and strongly throughout the text, and they are faith, selflessness, love and compassion, and sincerity and tranquility.

The first and foremost for Lao Zi is to have strong faith in the Dao and to "obtain the One" (Lao Tzu, 1989a, p. 8), "following the Constant" (p. 21). Such following requires "submission," which provides "deep roots and a firm base" for "long life and long lasting vision" (p. 28). He strongly urges diligence in practicing the Dao (p. 9). A true spiritual faith in the Dao will make it possible for total submission and diligence. Or, looking from another perspective, one can view the latter two as the manifests of the sincere belief and faith in, and the passageway to, the Dao.

An essential virtue for practicing the Dao is self-lessness: "He takes the mind of the common people as his mind" (Lao Tzu, 1989a, p. 18). Human beings should "desire no desire" (p. 26), become one "who do[es] not act for the purpose of living" (p. 46), and who has contentment (p. 13). In this way the personal motivation and drive are aligned with the Dao, and for the Dao, instead of for personal interests or interests of certain groups or factions.

Lao Zi highly values love of all humanity, good and bad. For the sage, "Those who are good he regards as good; Those who are not good he also regards as good. In this way he attains goodness" (Lao Tzu, 1989a, p. 18). Of the three treasures that Lao Zi possesses, the foremost and most powerful is "compassion," and the other two treasures are "frugality" and "not presuming to be at the forefront in the world" (p. 38). "Compassion" is the "protective wall of heaven" and man, and it is the true foundation of "courage" (p. 38). Love and compassion unite humanities as well as universes, and they are the most powerful and effective forces for transformation and transcendence.

Equality and Social Justice

For Lao Zi and Daoists, equality of humanity and all elements are embedded in the fact that we all come from the same source and return to the same source, a profound shared destiny—"Dao (道)." Nature is the Oneness that unites all without competition and superiority. As chapter 42 indicates, "Dao gives birth to one; one produces two; two creates three; and three manifested into ten thousands of things. All elements carry yin and embrace yang. Through the integration and balancing of the elements the state of harmony is created" (Lao Tzu, 1989b).

In nature's creation, there is no difference between the polished "jade" and the "stone" (Lao Tzu, 1989b, chapter 39). The humbleness is the virtuous manifestation of the cosmic force that each and all are a part of without exception. The highest goodness is "like water, quietly benefiting all while residing at the lowest place where all try to avoid" (chapter 8). All are equally responsible for his or her journey through one's choices regarding whether or how to follow nature's way. Those whose actions affect others, according to Lao Zi, can live and lead by "unselfishness" and nonconflict with all others (chapter 7). Thus, they nurture and enrich all naturally and possess the "highest virtue" (chapter 51).

Social justice is not a term that appeared in Lao Zi's text, and for him, it is the recognition of the natural "Dao" that balances all elements regardless. Those with virtue in alignment the Dao will live long and peacefully, and those without will perish. "The Tao of heaven is impartial. It stays with good men all the time" (Lao Tzu, 1989b, chapter 78). Lao Zi does not advocate fighting in any form, especially violence in the name of justice. He uses the metaphor of "water" to teach the development of the "highest virtue" and understanding of the cosmos to influencing and shaping all those who lack virtue, or more accurately, those who are on the way of developing virtue (chapter 80).

DIVERSITY Just as Daoists believe that every human should have the opportunity to contribute to his or her community, they also see the diversity of each person's unique contribution as a virtue for society. This nondiscriminatory philosophy presents as follows: "Under heaven all can see beauty as beauty only because there is ugliness. All can know good as good only because there is evil. Therefore having and not having arise together" (Lao Tzu, 1989b, chapter 2).

Likewise, chapter 27 reads: "What is a good man? A teacher of a bad man. What is a bad man? A good man's charge" (Lao Tzu, 1989b). These interdependent dualities are central to the idea of acceptance and harboring a place for everything in Taoist philosophy. In fact, one of the core principles of Taoism is the concept of yin and yang, or feminine and masculine energies, which are simultaneously opposite and dependent on each other. In effect, Taoists embrace the multiplicity of natural expressions of humanity without preference toward any race, gender, religion, sexual orientation, or political stance. In effect, they often are strong supporters of women's rights, civil rights, and human rights issues, such as gay marriage.

WU WEI (NONACTION OR NONVIOLENCE) A unique and signature concept of Lao Zi is "Wu Wei." Daoists value the art of "nonaction" in order that "the ten thousand things would develop naturally" (Lao Tzu, 1989b, chapter 37). To embrace a state of "nonaction," Daoists follow the natural flow of life, the "Dao," or "the way." Anything that seems forced or resisting of this organic flow would be considered as parting from this path. Therefore, forcing someone or something to act contrary to its nature would be considered as unjust.

One of the prominent themes, as well as a significant virtue of Lao Zi, is his insistence on noncompeting, and noncontentious approaches, which is climaxed in his statement of "wu wei (无为)" (Lao Tzu, 1989a, p. 35). Unlike most of the philosophers, before and after him, who encourage competing, striving, and winning for success, Lao Zi (1989a) says, "I don't advance an inch, but rather retreat a foot" (p. 40), and he prefers that "no one summons it, yet it comes on its own" (p. 44). The Dao is nonviolent, for "the strong and violent do not come to a natural end" (p. 11).

These unique approaches of Lao Zi's, however, cannot be mistaken as a "laissez-faire" or "passive-aggressive" strategy. While his fruitfulness seemingly comes with ease, it takes the efforts of careful planning to follow the natural way. Together with these approaches is the quality of humbleness, which echoes the ancient Chinese saying "zhen ren bu lu xiang" (真人不露相, The real sage never shows himself). In Lao Zi's words, "the Sage wears coarse woolen cloth, but inside it he holds on to jade" (Lao Tzu, 1989a, p. 41), "knows himself but does not show himself" (p. 43), and "is his desire not to make a display of his worthiness" (p. 48). It is this nonforwardness that positions the person as an effective servant for humanity and the Dao.

War is an example of force, violence, and conflict that Daoists seek to avoid. They therefore embrace a very modest war policy in that it should only occur when it is absolutely unavoidable. For them, these occasions are a time of mourning, and even "a victory must be observed like a funeral" (Lao Tzu, 1989b, chapter 31). Observing nonaction by preventing violence and casualties for both allies and enemies is the highest aim in Taoist philosophy on warfare. Though Sun Tzu (孙子) wrote a whole book about war strategies in his *Art of War* (孙子兵法), he reminds his readers that "supreme excellence consists in breaking the enemy's resistance without fighting" (Sun Tzu, 1910, chapter 3, para. 2) and that "there is no instance of a country having benefited from prolonged warfare" (Sun Tzu, 1910, chapter 2, para. 6). The greatest war hero of all, for Daoists, is he or she who prevents war while, as Sun Zi states, "the worst policy of all is to besiege walled cities" (Sun Tzu, 1910, chapter 3, para. 3).

Daoists' respect for nonviolence extends to their interactions with other countries as well. If a country wants to partake in another country's resources by letting down its guards to let others in, it will gain them in a peaceful manner. Lao Zi explains this concept: "A great country is like low land. It is the meeting ground of the universe . . . Therefore, it is fitting for a great nation to yield" (Lao Tzu, 1989b, chapter 61).

Instead of actively and forcefully seeking out the resources of other countries, by remaining still and acting as a fertile meeting ground, a country will draw others in in a peaceful manner. In this way, exhibiting the feminine characteristics of stillness and submission makes a country wealthy and strong. By yielding, a country conquers the trust and the resources of another. However, just as in their art of war, they are able to do so without using force or violence.

ZHUANG ZI Zhuang Zi viewed himself as a disciple of Lao Zi and has been considered one that fiercely taught, and his work, *Zhuang Zi*, reflected and continued Daoist philosophy and practices (Ames, 1998; Palmer, 1996). The Dao is at the core of *Zhuangzi*, and nature is the center of valued existence. Zhuang Zi is famed for his unique and highly literary style in his writing and his use of parables and humor to convey the meaning of the profound Daoist teaching.

Zhuang Zi's belief of relativism and equality of all elements is expressed in his experience in passing a skull as he traveled; when he pitied the dead skull, the latter responded "How do you know it's bad to be dead?" (Zhuang Zi, chapter 18, sec. 4)

The famous Chinese saying "Zhuang Zhou Dreamed of Butterfly" (莊周夢蝶, Zhuang Zhou meng die) refers to his chapter 2, in which he expresses his Daoist metaphysics that all elements are related and transformable with the equal value of existence, meaning, and relevance. Watson (1968) translated the passage as the following:

Once Zhuangzi dreamt he was a butterfly, a butterfly flitting and fluttering around, happy with himself and doing as he pleased. He didn't know he was Zhuangzi. Suddenly he woke up and there he was, solid and unmistakable Zhuangzi. But he didn't know if he was Zhuangzi who had dreamt he was a butterfly, or a butterfly dreaming he was Zhuangzi. Between Zhuangzi and a butterfly there must be *some* distinction! This is called the Transformation of Things. (p. 49)

To the Daoist disciples after Zhuang Zi, he is greatly admired for someone who not only taught and shared Lao Zi's teaching and Daoism, but also lived it as a role model and sage. He resided in nature and developed a systematic way to cultivate his physical and spiritual body, fasting in Daoist method, and manifesting with the Daoist special abilities.

THE DAOIST PRACTICES Indeed, Daoism is not only a theoretic belief or value text; more importantly, it has actually developed a rich system of spiritual and practical means for its followers and believers to use and benefit from still today. There are corresponding Daoist practices and methods for each chapter of Lao Zi's *Dao De Ching*. For instance, the Daoist Cosmo Chart, developed from Ba Gua, integrate all directions, Chinese zodiac signs, all natural forces and elements (water—水, fire—火, metal—金, earth—土, and wood—木), primal numbers, their reflection and connections with the

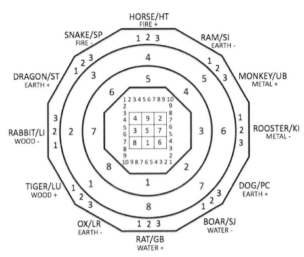

Figure D.1   The Daoist Cosmo Chart

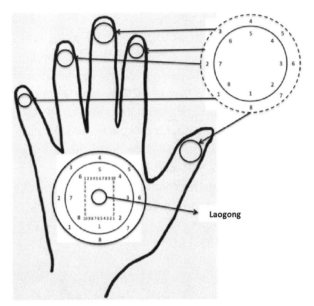

Figure D.3   Daoist Cosmo Chart Reflected in the Hand

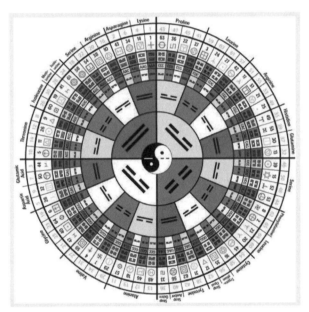

Figure D.2   Sixty-Four Hexagrams of the *I Ching* and Sixty-Four Cordons of DNA

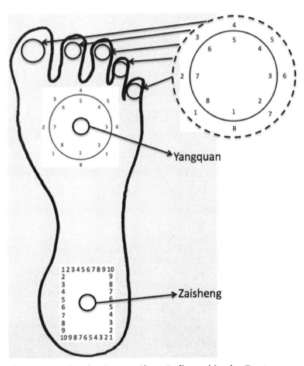

Figure D.4   Daoist Cosmo Chart Reflected in the Foot

human body (physical, emotion, mental, and spiritual) in one to illustrate the encompassing Oneness. The recently updated chart even includes its connection with the new sciences of human DNA. These charts illustrate the profound connection between all elements in heaven and earth, and they guide the Daoists' daily living, meditation practices, medicine, understanding, and learning.

The Daoist training and practices focus on the essence of humanity, which is the very mirroring reflection of that in nature, water, metal, fire, wood, and earth. Water is "Jing (精)," the highest and purest essence of all; Metal corresponds with "Po (魄),"

the soul; Fire connects with "Shen (神)"; Wood links with "Huen (魂)"; and Earth is "Hua (化)." The same Daoist Cosmo Chart is also reflected in various components of the human body, such as hands or feet. "The Palace of Nine (Jiu Gong, 九宫)," is a symbol to illustrate the representation of the entire Cosmos inside each person in his or her energy centers, organs, and systems.

All the Daoist practices are embedded in this holistic, inclusive, and virtuous orientation. They consist of numerous means including, but not limited to, mudra, chanting, qi gong, meditation, wu shu or martial arts, acupuncture, herb medicine, divination, spiritual charms, palmistry, and more. The current Daoist practice, "One Palm Gold Light Shines," is taught to generations of Daoists, based on chapters 1, 3, 6, 8, and 10 in *Dao De Ching*. The practice aims at the connection of Oneness with nature to overcome illness and achieve mental peace and spiritual enlightenment.

Impact of Daoism

Throughout history, Daoist temples have been established in many regions of China. Some are dualist with both components of Daoism and Buddhism, and some even integrate with multiple Chinese folklores. The most famous Daoist temples and sites are Qingyang Taoist Temple (青羊寺, Green Goat Temple) in Chengdu, where Lao Zi taught his Dao de Jing to his disciple Ying Xi, who urged him to write the book; Mount Longhu (龙虎山) in Jiangxi, China, famous for being one of the birthplaces of Taoism (UNESCO World Heritage site); Tai Temple (泰山寺) at the southern foot of Mount Tai, Tai An, Shang Dong, the shrine of Taoism and a place for emperors to hold worship ceremonies and to offer sacrifices to the God of Mount Tai.

Daoist Temples
Important and Famous Daoist Temples

1. Qingyang Taoist Temple (青羊寺, Green Goat Temple)—Located in the western part of Chengdu, it is the largest and oldest Taoist temple in the city, and the largest Taoist temple in Southeast China. The temple houses the only existing copy of Daozang Jiyao, a collection of classic Taoist scriptures. According to history, Qingyang Temple was the place where Lao Zi taught his famous Dao De Jing to his disciple, Ying Xi, the Official Keeper of the Pass, who was instrumental in Lao Zi's writing of the book (estimated fourth to sixth century BCE). http://www.absolutechinatours.com/Chengdu-attractions/Qingyang-Temple.html

2. Mt Longhu (龙虎山)—Located in Jiangxi, China, it is famous for being one of the birthplaces of Taoism, with many Taoist temples built upon the mountainside. It is particularly important to the Zhengyi Dao, as the Shangqing Temple and the Mansion of the Taoist Master are located here. In August 2010, UNESCO inscribed Mount Longhu on the World Heritage List as part of the complex of six sites that make up the China Danxia: http://whc.unesco.org/en/list/1335. On the site are the temples of Immortal City (仙岩) and Zheng Yi (正一), founded by Zhang Dao Lin (张道陵) in East Han dynasty (23–230 CE). http://www.cultural-china.com/chinaWH/html/en/19Scenery909.html

3. Tai Temple (泰山寺)—Located at the southern foot of Mount Tai, Tai An, Shangdong, the Tai Temple is the largest and the most complete ancient building complex in Mount Tai. It covers an area of ninety-six thousand square meters and adopts the architectural style of an imperial palace. It is the shrine of Taoism and a place for emperors to hold worship ceremonies and to offer sacrifices to the God of Mount Tai. http://www.billirwinphotography.com/taishan.htm

4. Yuquan Temple (玉泉寺, Jade Spring Temple)—Situated against Tianjin Mountain in Tianshui, Gansu, it receives its name after jade spring (yuquan in Chinese). The water here is clear and sweet, and the spring has long been a scenic spot in the area. The temple was first built in the early Tang dynasty, has collapsed, and has been destroyed and rebuilt several times. It blends with the surroundings harmoniously, which is a signature component of Taoism. http://history.cultural-china.com/en/169H3522H9830.html

5. Temple of the City God (平遥城隍庙)—Situated in the southeast of the ancient city, in Pingyao, Shanxi, the temple covers an area of 7,302 square meters (around 8,733 square yards). It has a long history and is a well-preserved UNESCO World Heritage site. The structures embody the combined culture of Buddhism, Daoism, and folk culture. The wonderful woodcarvings and mural paintings inside the temple reflect excellent

craftsmanship. http://www.travelchinaguide.com/attraction/shanxi/pingyao/city_god.htm

6. Bai Yun Guan (白云观)—Located in Beijing, it was build in the fourteenth century, and it houses the Chinese Taoist College and plays an important role in Daoism and its education and continuation in contemporary China due to its location in the capital. http://hua.umf.maine.edu/China/HistoricBeijing/History/pages/123_WhiteCloudTemple.html

7. World Medicine Institute—Nestled in the mountain range, facing the ocean, in Honolulu, Hawaii, it is both a Daoist temple and school. The current Daoist Lineage holder, Dr. Chang Yi Xia, founded it in 1973 during her travel and teaching around the world. Currently it is the biggest and only school that offers master and doctorate degrees in the Daoist Philosophy outside China. http://worldmedicineinstitute.com/

Daoism, as one of the prominent existing philosophies and religions originating in China, has remained one of the primary sources for learning and living in Chinese communities inside and outside China. Lao Zi's *Dao De Jing* is one of the most translated and studied Chinese texts in the world. It not only presents a philosophical framework of theory; more importantly, it is also lived and practiced in real human lives for thousands of years.

As a philosophy, its influence touches every aspect of human existence, especially the relation between humanity and cosmos. It has shaped spirituality, state affairs, education, medicine, and individual lives, even politics and military strategies (when it is the least political philosophy by intent in the world and totally against violence). The original and vigorous Daoist teaching can be found today in Daoist temples and institutes in China and the world such as Chinese Daoist College in Beijing, China, and the World Medicine Institute in Honolulu, Hawaii, United States. Daoism has become a standard study in the fields of philosophy, religion, and alternative medicine.

Lillian Chang
Xu Di

References

Ames, R. T. (Ed.). (1998). *Wandering at ease in the Zhuangzi.* Albany: State University of New York Press.

Fowler, J. (2005). *An introduction to the philosophy and religion of Taoism: Pathways to immortality.* Brighton: Sussex Academic Press.

Fung, You-lan. (1983). *A history of Chinese philosophy: Volume 1: The period of the philosophers (from the beginnings to Circa 100 B.C.)* (D. Bodde, Trans.). Princeton, NJ: Princeton University Press.

Huang, D. (1995). *The yellow emperor's classic of medicine: A new translation of the Neijing Suwen with commentary* (M. Ni, Trans.). Boston: Shambhala Publications, Inc.

Lao Tzu. (1989a). *Lao Tzu: Te-Tao Ching—A new translation based on the recently discovered Ma-wang-tui texts (Classics of Ancient China)* (R. G. Henricks, Trans.). New York: Ballantine Books.

Lao Tzu. (1989b). *The Tao Te Ching* (G. Feng & J. English, Trans.). New York: Vintage Books. Also available online at http://terebess.hu/english/tao/gia.html.

Lau, D. C. (1963). Introduction. *Lao Tzu: Tao Te Ching* (D. C. Lau, Trans.). New York: Penguin Books.

Legge, J. (1891). *The sacred books of China: The texts of Taoism, part I.* Oxford: Oxford University Press. Reprint: 1962. New York: Dover Publications.

Lu, Y. (1962). *The secret of the golden flower: A Chinese book of life* (R. Wilhelm, Trans. German, first, 1931; C. F. Baynes, Trans. English). Orlando, FL: Harcourt, Brace & Co.

Merriam-Webster. (2002). *Webster's universal encyclopedic dictionary.* New York: Barnes & Noble Books.

Palmer, M. (1996). *The book of Chuang Tzu.* London: Penguin Books.

Robinet, I. (1997). *Taoism: Growth of a religion.* Stanford: Stanford University Press.

Saso, M. (1995). *The gold pavilion: Taoist ways to peace, healing, and long life.* Boston: Charles E. Tuttle Co., Inc.

Sun Tsu. (1910). *The art of war* (Lionel Giles, Trans.). Retrieved from http://suntzusaid.com/artofwar.pdf.

Watson, B. (1968). *The complete works of Chuang Tzu.* New York: Columbia University Press.

Wei, B. Y. *The seal of the unity of the three: A study and translation of the Cantong qi, the source of the Taoist way of the golden elixir* (F. Pregadio, Trans.). (2011).

Retrieved from http://www.goldenelixir.com/gold-enelixir_press.html.

Wen Zi. (1991). *Wen-Tzu* (T. Cleary, Trans.). Boston: Shambhala Books.

Wilhelm, R. (1997). *The I Ching or book of changes* (C. F. Baynes, Trans.). New York: Princeton University Press.

Zhuang Zi. (1964 [1966]). How do you know it's bad to be dead? In *Chuang Tzu basic writings*, B. Watson (ed.). New York: Columbia University Press.

Additional Resources

Chinese Digital Resources of Traditional Chinese Taoism (Daoism) Culture for Free Download @ Homeland Shrouded in Mists. http://www.byscrj.com/jmm/

Lao Zi. (1989). *Dao De Ching* (G. F. Feng & J. English, Trans.). http://terebess.hu/english/tao/gia.html

The Complete Chuang Tsu based on James Legge's Translation. http://oaks.nvg.org/ys1ra5.html

Taoism from Wikipedia, the free encyclopedia. http://en.wikipedia.org/wiki/Taoism

Taoism, *Standford Encyclopedia of Philosophy*. http://plato.stanford.edu/entries/taoism/

DE FACTO SEGREGATION

De facto is Latin, meaning "of fact, in deed," and when paired with segregation, it refers to segregation that occurs as a matter of fact and not as a result of intentional government action. *De facto segregation* is segregation based on custom, tradition, or social norms. De facto segregation has a long history in the United States like *de jure segregation*.

Courts were often reluctant to acknowledge or remedy de facto segregation like de jure segregation. A number of de facto segregation cases arose from challenges to public school conditions. Although many states had laws that prohibited racial discrimination in public schools, many cities, both in the North and in the South, maintained separate educational systems decades after the initial *Brown* case. In the South, school administrators faced scrutiny from African American parents and the federal courts. Increasingly, northern African American parents began to challenge the status of the education their children received. Such was the case in the 1960s and 1970s when, after years of

protests and complaints, African American parents in Boston, via the local NAACP chapter, sued the Boston School Committee. The lawsuit, *Morgan v. Hennigan*, 379 F Supp 410 (D. Mass 1974) alleged that the school committee's administration of the Boston public schools violated the Thirteenth and Fourteenth Amendments and the Civil Rights Act of 1964.

The Supreme Court had given the federal courts authority to address de facto segregation in *Swann v. Charlotte-Mecklenburg*, 402 U.S. 1 (1971). The facts in *Swann* were common in spite of a desegregation plan ordered in 1965. In the 1968–1969 school year, fourteen thousand of the twenty-one thousand African American students in the greater Charlotte school system attended schools that were 99 or 100 percent African American. The federal district court had ordered the Charlotte school board to plan for both student and faculty desegregation. Once the defendants failed to produce a plan that remedied the segregation, the district court sought to do so. The district court hired an expert to review the board's plan. The expert's plan mirrored the board plan in many respects but differed sharply in the treatment of elementary schools. The school board sought further judicial review, challenging the Court's authority to craft a plan. Justice Burger, writing for a unanimous Court, held "If school authorities fail in their affirmative obligations under these holdings, judicial authority may be invoked. Once a right and a violation have been shown, the scope of a district court's equitable powers to remedy past wrongs is broad, for breadth and flexibility are inherent in equitable remedies" (*Swann*, 1971, p. 15).

Although the school committee alleged that the composition of the schools was due to housing patterns and the placement of schools in distinct neighborhoods, the committee records provided documentation that the committee had intentionally maintained racial segregation, choosing to overcrowd some "white" schools and to build new schools in locations that would ensure their composition would be nearly 100 percent African American. In the *Morgan* case, Judge Garrity found in favor of the plaintiffs on June 21, 1974, in a decision that would divide the city and lead to violence. Based on the *Swann* case, he crafted a desegregation plan for Boston. Unfortunately, over forty years after the decisions in *Swann* and *Morgan*, de facto segregation remains an issue of concern for African Americans and Latinos. A 2012 study conducted by the Civil Rights Project and the University of California Los Angeles found segregation in public schools is increasing for both groups.

Pamela Nolan Young

References

Abrams, R. I. (1975). Not one judge's opinion: *Morgan v. Hennigan* and the Boston schools. *Harvard Educational Review, 45*(1), 5–16.

Black, H. C., Nolan, J. R., & Nolan-Haley, J. M. (1983). *Black's law dictionary* (6th ed.). St Paul, MN: West Group.

Goodman, F. I. (1972). De facto school segregation: A constitutional and empirical analysis. *California Law Review, 60*(2), 275–437. Retrieved from http://scholarship.law.berkeley.edu/californialawreview/vol60/iss2/1.

McCall, H. (1975). Viewpoint: To bus or not to bus. *Christianity and Crisis, 34*(23), 302–4.

Orfield, G., Kucsera, J., & Hawley, G. S. (2012). E Pluribus . . . separation: Deepening double segregation for more students. *The Civil Rights Project*. Retrieved from http://civilrightsproject.ucla.edu/news/press-releases/crp-press-releases-2012/civil-rights-project-reports-deepening-segregation-and-challenges-educators-and-political-leaders-to-develop-positive-policies.

The Oyez Project at IIT Chicago-Kent College of Law. *Plessy v. Ferguson*. Retrieved from http://www.oyez.org/cases/1851-1900/1895/1895_210.

Smith, J. (1978). Boston: Cradle of liberty or separate but equal? *Theory into Practice, 17*(1), 54.

Sugrue, T. J. (2012). Northern lights: The black freedom struggle outside of the south. *OAH Magazine of History, 26*(1), 9–15.

Tushnet, M. V. (2003). Segregation. In S. I. Kutler (Ed.), *Dictionary of American history* (3rd ed., vol. 7, pp. 301–4). New York: Charles Scribner's Sons.

Williams, P. N. & Lovin, R. W. (1978). Rights and remedies: A study of desegregation in Boston. *Journal of Religious Ethics, 6*(2), 137.

Cases

Brown v. the Board of Education, 347 U.S. 483(1954).

Morgan v. Hennigan, 379 F. Supp. 410 (D.C. Mass., June 21, 1974).

Swann v. Charlotte-Mecklenburg, 402 U.S. 1 (1971).

DE JURE SEGREGATION

De jure is Latin, meaning "lawful, legitimate, or by right," and when paired with segregation, it refers to state authorized or mandated segregation. *De jure segregation* occurs when a government—local, state, or national—by its actions or laws, establishes and enforces segregation. Throughout the history of the United States, there have been many examples of racial de jure segregation: these include the forced removal of Native Americans from their ancestral lands and their segregation on reservations, the internment of Japanese Americans during World War II, and the Jim Crow laws of the South that began to regulate and restrict the rights of the newly freed slaves after the Civil War.

For African Americans, "Jim Crow" is synonymous with de jure segregation. Jim Crow laws were enacted in the Southern states as early as the 1880s, and they continued to plague African Americans into the 1900s. In fact, it was not until 1950s that the U.S. judicial system started the systematic dismantling of these laws in the South in areas of voting rights, housing, and education. Although history places an emphasis on de jure segregation in the South where it was most egregious, one should not think that segregation was limited to the Southern states alone. De jure segregation was practiced in many Northern cities both in the 1800s and the century that followed.

One of the first challenges to de jure segregation occurred in Boston, Massachusetts, in the case of *Sarah Roberts v. the City of Boston*, 49 Mass. (5 Cush.) 198 (1850). Benjamin Roberts sued the City of Boston on behalf of his daughter, five-year-old Sarah. At the time, Boston had a small "colored" population. The city's school committee had established two schools to serve the colored residents. The Roberts lived a long distance from both schools. The closest school, located on Belknap Street, was some 2,100 feet from the Roberts' home. The other school on Sun Court Street was even farther. Mr. Roberts sued the city so that Sarah could attend a neighborhood school that was both physically closer to their home and, in his opinion, superior to the "colored" schools. In court, Roberts was represented by one of the first African American attorneys, Robert Morris, and abolitionist Charles Sumner. They argued the policy of the school committee was unconstitutional, and that it would cause undue psychological trauma and create a caste system. "The separation of schools so far from being for the benefit to the races is an injury to both. It lends to create a feeling of degradation in blacks and of prejudice and un-charitableness in whites" (*Roberts*, 1850, p. 204).

The case was tried before Justice Shaw. He said in his opinion, "It is argued that this maintenance of separate schools tends to deepen and perpetuate the odious distinction of caste founded in a deep rooted prejudice in public opinion. This prejudice, if it exists, is not created by law, and probably cannot be changed by law" (*Roberts*, 1850, p. 210). Roberts lost the court case. Nonetheless, Roberts's pursuit of justice did not end at the court. With the help of Charles Sumner, he was able to persuade the state legislature to take action. In 1855, the Massachusetts legislature banned segregated schools in Massachusetts.

Following the end of the Civil War, and the enactment of the Thirteenth Amendment that abolished slavery, white Southerners looked for methods to maintain their dominance and power over newly freed slaves. Often they turned to legislatures to create systemic divisions. These laws, which mandated the separation of the races in education, housing, and public facilities, came to be known as Jim Crow laws. In *Plessy v. Ferguson*, 163 U.S. 537 (1896), the Supreme Court addressed a challenge to de jure segregation in the state of Louisiana. Homer Adolph Plessy, a seven-eighths Caucasian, boarded the whites only section of a passenger train. Plessy refused to leave the section and was arrested. He sued, challenging the law as unconstitutional under the Thirteenth and Fourteenth amendments. In the Supreme Court's opinion, Justice Brown noted the earlier *Roberts v. The City of Boston* decision, in which the Massachusetts court had ruled separate facilities were constitutional. The *Plessy* decision established the doctrine of "separate but equal,"

which remained the law of the land until 1954. In 1954 the U.S. Supreme Court struck down the notion of "separate but equal" de jure segregation in the landmark case of *Brown v. the Board of Education*, 347 U.S. 483 (1954).

The *Brown* case was similar in facts to the *Roberts* case. In *Brown*, Oliver Brown and others in Topeka, Kansas, sued to gain access to a white-only public school that denied admission to their children. They argued that separate schools were not equal and the policy was unconstitutional. The plaintiffs in *Brown* were represented by the National Association for the Advancement of Colored People's Thurgood Marshall. Marshall would later be the first African American to join the U.S. Supreme Court.

Justice Warren, writing for a unanimous Court, wrote:

Today, education is perhaps the most important function of state and local governments.... Today it is a principal instrument in awakening the child to cultural values, in preparing him for later professional training, and in helping him to adjust normally to his environment. In these days, it is doubtful that any child may reasonably be expected to succeed in life if he is denied the opportunity of an education. Such an opportunity, where the state has undertaken to provide it, is a right which must be made available to all on equal terms....

To separate them [children in grade and high schools] from others of similar age and qualifications solely because of their race generates a feeling of inferiority as to their status in the community that may affect their hearts and minds in a way unlikely to ever be undone.... Whatever may have been the extent of psychological knowledge at the time of *Plessy v. Ferguson*, this finding is amply supported by modern authority....

We conclude that in the field of public education the doctrine of "separate but equal" has no place. Separate educational facilities are inherently unequal. Therefore, we hold that the plaintiffs and other similarly situated ... are ... deprived of the equal protection of the laws guaranteed by the Fourteenth Amendment. (*Brown*, 1954, pp. 493–95)

After the first decision in *Brown*, the Court rendered a second decision known as *Brown II, Brown v. The Board of Education*, 349 U.S. 294 (1955). In *Brown II*, the Board of Education sought guidance on how to implement the prior decision. Again, writing for a unanimous Court, Justice Warren wrote that local authorities should craft remedies to meet the particularities of local needs at "all deliberate speed" (*Brown II*, 1955, p. 301). Local officials would use the vagueness of the language to delay implementation, and many schools remained segregated a decade later.

Pamela Nolan Young

References

Abrams, R. I. (1975). Not one judge's opinion: *Morgan v. Hennigan* and the Boston schools. *Harvard Educational Review*, 45(1), 5–16.

Black, H. C., Nolan, J. R., & Nolan-Haley, J. M. (1983). *Black's law dictionary* (6th ed.). St Paul, MN: West Group.

Goodman, F. I. (1972). De facto school segregation: A constitutional and empirical analysis. *California Law Review*, 60(2), 275–437. Retrieved from http://scholarship.law.berkeley.edu/californialawreview/vol60/iss2/1.

McCall, H. (1975). Viewpoint: To bus or not to bus. *Christianity and Crisis*, 34(23), 302–4.

Orfield, G., Kucsera, J., & Hawley, G. S. (2012). E Pluribus . . . separation: Deepening double segregation for more students. *The Civil Rights Project*. Retrieved from http://civilrightsproject.ucla.edu/news/press-releases/crp-press-releases-2012/civil-rights-project-reports-deepening-segregation-and-challenges-educators-and-political-leaders-to-develop-positive-policies.

The Oyez Project at IIT Chicago-Kent College of Law. *Plessy v. Ferguson*. Retrieved from http://www.oyez.org/cases/1851-1900/1895/1895_210.

Smith, J. (1978). Boston: Cradle of liberty or separate but equal? *Theory into Practice*, 17(1), 54.

Sugrue, T. J. (2012). Northern lights: The black freedom struggle outside of the south. *OAH Magazine of History*, 26(1), 9–15.

Tushnet, M. V. (2003). Segregation. In S. I. Kutler (Ed.), *Dictionary of American history* (3rd ed., vol. 7, pp. 301–4). New York: Charles Scribner's Sons.

Williams, P. N. & Lovin, R. W. (1978). Rights and remedies: A study of desegregation in Boston. *Journal of Religious Ethics*, 6(2), 137.

Cases

Brown v. Board of Education, 347 U.S. 483 (1954).

Sarah Roberts v. the City of Boston, 49 Mass. (5 Cush.) 198 (1850).

Plessy v. Ferguson, 163 U.S. 537 (1896).

DEMOGRAPHIC DIVERSITY

Demographic categorizations are dedicated to illuminating distinctions among groups based on shared characteristics including race, gender, socioeconomic status, schooling attainment, professional credentials, disability, language facility, citizenship status, geographic location, and other features. Classifications are used to set forth broad social overviews as well as tightly focused profiles of groups within groups such as portraits of Latinos in the United States and African American women, respectively. Data on demographic diversity is also useful in contextualizing an individual's experiences against overarching historical and sociopolitical backdrops.

From an educational standpoint, measures and reports that center on demographic diversity are a critical means of assessing the degree to which institutions and societies are socially just. Researchers, for example, commonly use statistics that are disaggregated by subgroup to focus attention on unsettling trends in school discipline, such as the regular overrepresentation of minority males in institutional suspension rates (Skiba, Michael, Nardo, & Peterson, 2000). Equity advocates, thus, heavily rely on clear conceptualizations of demographic diversity to clarify trends that run counter to fair principles and outcomes. Organizations such as the Children's Defense Fund (CDF) and the Schott Foundation provide strong examples for how examinations of demographic diversity may inform reform initiatives.

What has emerged, in part, from regular analyses of demographic diversity in the social justice conversation is a multifaceted effort to promote educational and civic ideals. On one level, individuals have complicated and deepened their understanding of human experiences and how various identities intersect with specific measures such as educational access and forms of marginalization. Such insights help move the field of education away from uncritical falsehoods that perpetuate inequality. On a second level, practitioners, policymakers, researchers, theorists, and other stakeholders are furnished with compelling evidence that documents whether (or the degree to which) just aims are realized—information that may be used to redress wrongs through legislation, litigation, professional development, and teacher education, among other avenues.

Carla R. Monroe

Reference

Skiba, R. J., Michael, R. S., Nardo, A. C., & Peterson, R. (2000). *The color of discipline: Sources of racial and gender disproportionality in school punishment* (Report #SRS1). Bloomington, Indiana: Indiana Education Policy Center. Indiana Education Policy Center Research Report #SRS1.

DEMONSTRATIONS

Demonstration linguistically has the meanings *show, exhibit, explain, proof*, and *opinions*, and *reactions shown by the public* (Walter, Woodford, & Good, 2008; Sinclair, 1998). In terms of social sciences and security sciences, demonstrations are collective activities performed by groups of people in the form of crowds in order to support, criticize, react, sound their voices, express themselves, and explain their complaints and displeasure on any issue related to politics, social, or economics (Blumberg, 1968; Cerrah, 1997; Göktepe, n.d.; Akyol, 2010; Douglas, 2004). The main goal here is to draw the attention of the media, and thus, society, to a desired point. There is an aimed population at demonstrations, and the goal is to produce an awareness among the mentioned population and to effect and direct their ideas or behaviors (Chenoweth & Stephan 2012; Sharp & Paulson, 2005; Göktepe, n.d., Ünal, n.d.; Van & Walgrave, 2001).

Demonstrations generally occur with people in crowded groups walking from one point to another, chanting slogans, singing songs, and/or holding signs; a gathering of crowded groups of people to listen to a speech; or sit-ins. Acting out a drama, singing a song, and acting out a comedy show on the streets are also among the methods used. In this way, people attract other's attention and demonstrate their opinions, ideas, and reactions. Demonstrations may be violent or nonviolent. It is generally accepted that peaceful demonstrations have the potential to turn into violent demonstrations. In some cases, such as in an unauthorized demonstration, law enforcement agencies may intervene in order to prevent the gathering of the crowd, or to get them to give up and go home, or to prevent a peaceful demonstration from turning into a violent one (Douglas, 2004; King, 2011; Waddington, 2011; Ünal, n.d.; Akyol, 2010; Karakuş & Ünal, 2010; Cerrah, 1997; Toliver, Murphy, McFarland, & Ederheimer, 2006).

It is accepted that the more crowded a demonstration is the more successful it is. The reason for this is the potential of a crowded demonstration to attract more attention and to provide much more visibility and awareness. Place and time of demonstrations are decided according to the subject that will be supported or protested (Meyer & Tarrow 1998; Cerrah, 1998; Chenoweth & Stephan, 2012; Roberts & Ash, 2009; Zengin & Gözübenli, n.d.; Blumberg, 1968).

Common forms of demonstrations are:

- picket lines—surrounding a building or area and chanting and holding signs
- marches—walking on a set route and holding signs and shouting chants
- meetings and rallies—people in a huge crowd gathered to listen a speech
- sit-ins—occupying a certain area by sitting with a crowd
- vigils—peaceful demonstration for a specific reason
- dramaturgical demonstrations—concerts, dance, street performances
- motorcade/autocade—a huge convoy of automobiles or any vehicles

While some demonstrations are planned and tactical, others occur spontaneously. In demonstrations, people come together physically, but in some cases, people plan demonstrations in virtual environments via the Internet (Akyol, 2010; Cerrah, 1998; King & Brearley, 1996; Göktepe, n.d.; Reicher, Stott, Cronin, & Adang, 2004; Ünal, n.d.).

Aykut Töngür
Hasan Hüseyin Çali

References

Akyol, Z. (2010). Kalabalık Yönetimi. Karakuş. B. Ünal (Ed.), Özel *Güvenlik Eğitimleri Ders kitabı.* Ankara: Dörtbay Yayın Dağıtım.

Blumberg, H. H. (1968). Accounting for a nonviolent mass demonstration. *Sociological Inquiry, 38*(1), 43–50.

Cerrah, İ. (1997). Toplumsal Olaylar ve Çevik Kuvvet Eğitimi. *Amme İdaresi Dergisi, 30*(3), 135–49.

Cerrah, İ. (1998). *Crowds and public order policing: An analysis of crowds and interpretations of their behavior based on observational studies in Turkey, England and Wales.* Aldershot: Ashgate.

Chenoweth, E. & Stephan, M. (2012). *Why civil resistance works: The strategic logic of nonviolent conflict.* New York: Columbia University Press.

Douglas, R. N. (2004). *Dealing with demonstrations: The law of public protest and its enforcement.* Sydney: Federation Press.

Göktepe, F. (n.d.). Toplumsal olayların yönetimi ve müdahale esasları. Retrieved from Ataturk University, http://lms.atauni.edu.tr/FileUploads/Src/5f4a429e-3069-4f6b-a03b-88cffe4b2b8c/10.%C3%9Cnite-%20Toplumsal%20Olaylar%C4%B1n%20Y%C3%B6netimi%20ve%20M%C3%BCdahale%20Esaslar%C4%B1.pdf.

Karakuş, O. & Ünal, B. (Eds.). (2010). Özel *güvenlik eğitimleri ders kitabı.* Ankara: Dörtbay Yayın Dağıtım.

King, B. G. (2011). The tactical disruptiveness of social movements: Sources of market and mediated disruption in corporate boycotts. *Social Problems, 58*(4), 491–517.

King, M. & Brearley, N. (1996). *Public order policing: Contemporary perspectives on strategy and tactics.* Leicester: Perpetuity Press.

Meyer, D. S. & Tarrow, S. G. (1998). *The social movement society: Contentious politics for a new century.* Lanham, MD: Rowman & Littlefield.

Reicher, S., Stott, C., Cronin, P., & Adang, O. (2004). An integrated approach to crowd psychology and public order policing. *Policing: An International Journal of Police Strategies & Management, 27*(4), 558–72.

Roberts, A. & Ash, T. G. (Eds.). (2009). *Civil resistance and power politics: The experience of non-violent action from Gandhi to the present.* New York: Oxford University Press.

Sharp, G. & Paulson, J. (2005). *Waging nonviolent struggle: 20th century practice and 21st century potential.* New Hampshire: Extending Horizons Books.

Sinclair, J. (Ed.). (1998). *Collins cobuild essential English dictionary.* London: HarperCollins Publishers Ltd.

Toliver, J., Murphy, J., McFarland, M., & Ederheimer, J. (2006). Police management of mass demonstrations: Identifying issues and successful approaches. *Police Executive Research Forum.* Washington, DC: Police Executive Research Forum.

Ünal, M. (n.d.) Toplumsal Olaylar ve Özellikleri. Retrieved from Ataturk University, http://lms.atauni.edu.tr/FileUploads/Src/76881882-d526-4811-9301-88cfdfaeab18/3..%20%C3%9Cnite-%20Toplumsal%20Olaylar%20ve%20%C3%96zellikleri.pdf.

Van Aelst, P. & Walgrave, S. (2001). Who is that (wo)man in the street? From the normalisation of protest to the normalisation of the protester. *European Journal of Political Research, 39*, 461–86.

Waddington, D. P. (2011). Public order policing in South Yorkshire, 1984–2011: The case for a permissive approach to crowd control. *Contemporary Social Science, 6*(3), 309–24.

Walter E., Woodford, K., & Good, M. (Eds.). (2008). *Cambridge advanced learner's dictionary.* Cambridge: Cambridge University Press.

Zengin, S. & Gözübenli, M. (n.d.) Toplumsal Olaylarda Müzakere, Müzakereci Ve Müzakere Teknikleri. Retrieved from Ataturk University, http://lms.atauni.edu.tr/FileUploads/Src/d9dd9590-07cb-4218-8fea-88cffe4b9375/13.%20%C3%9Cnite%20Toplumsal%20Olaylarda%20M%C3%BCzakere,%20M%C3%BCzakereci%20ve%20M%C3%BCzakere%20Teknikleri.pdf.

DESEGREGATION

The Supreme Court decision in *Brown v. Board of Education*, which struck down public school racial segregation in 1954, was, for a segment of black and white citizens, a hopeful legislation (Anderson & Byrne, 2004). Many believed that desegregating public schools would increase educational and economic opportunities for marginalized youth and attune the more privileged to issues of social justice (Eick, 2010; Wells, Holme, Revilla, & Atanda, 2004). The hope was that, if students met across racial divides during their formative years, generations of students would grow up to be adults who more easily crossed racial divides and more equitably shared in the political, economic, and social life of their democracy. Unfortunately, resistance to school desegregation in the South *and* the North (Lukas, 1985) by whites *and* blacks (Dougherty, 1999) before *and* after *Brown* (Dittmer, 1995) challenged what some historians have identified as the power of an educational legislation to serve as a "catalyst for substantial changes in social relations and policies outside of school" (Urban & Wagoner, 2000, p. 288).

Resistance, notwithstanding struggles for ever-greater inclusion of all constituents within public schools, found impetus and momentum in the civil rights movement. Thus, a series of legislations would be drafted to include students with disabilities (Education for All Handicapped Children of 1975, renamed and amended in 1997 as the Individuals with Disabilities Education Act), to increase participation of women (Title IX law of 1972), and to address the needs of immigrant and first-generation immigrant youth (The Bilingual Education Act of 1974).

However, the political and judicial changes that ensued during the civil rights movement cannot be easily or primarily attributed to *Brown v. Board of Education*. The story of school desegregation in the United States precedes *Brown* and goes beyond the black and white divide. Throughout our nation's history, Mexican Americans and Asian Americans also fought for their children's rights to attend school along with their white counterparts (Anderson & Byrne, 2004; Banks, 2009; MacDonald, 2004).

At the turn of the twenty-first century, the story of school desegregation would be further complicated by the second largest wave of immigration within a century in U.S. history (Portes & Rumbaut, 1996). By the 1990s, the meanings attached to categories of racial identity had gained considerable complexity as more diverse peoples entered a country sensitized to issues of civil rights and multiculturalism/interculturalism (Banks, 2009). Yet too many immigrant children of color continued to be funneled into the lower academic tracks, were often misdiagnosed as needing special education, and were too often trapped in English-language-learner classes out of which they never graduated (Eick & Valli, 2010).

A decade into the twenty-first century, the expectations that might have been attached to *Brown v. Board* by some remain unrealized. Thus, while officially desegregated according to racial quota, too many schools continue to be segregated within their walls, overwhelmingly placing African American, Latina/o, and other youth of color, particularly of lower socioeconomic status, in lower academic tracks (Eick, 2010). But just as disturbing is the accelerated resegregation of schools at the turn of the twenty-first century (Orfield, 2006). While "white flight" from urban centers following *Brown v. Board* de facto segregated or resegregated city schools, the increasing privatization of schools at the turn of the twenty-first century has exacerbated school segregation. Saporito and Sohoni (2006) report that "public schools would be less racially segregated if all children living in a school district attended their neighborhood schools" (p. 81). In addition, private, magnet, and charter schools contribute to overall racial segregation within many school districts. The effects are particularly striking for segregation between white and Hispanic children.

The concept of desegregation should not be confused with integration. Authentic integration of children and youth across racial, ethnic, class, religious, and other social markers within school boundaries should be understood as the "intellectual and social engagement across . . . groups" (Fine, Weiss, & Powell, 1997, p. 248). The task remains not only to ensure that our public schools and any and all schools publicly funded be lawfully desegregated, but also that within desegregated schools, true integration of students across social markers of difference be a reality.

Thus, research on school desegregation must go beyond examining the effects of desegregation on a single minority group treated monolithically, and must go beyond assessing the consequences of policy in easily measurable terms, such as student body composition or aggregate test scores. Processes of integration within desegregated school spaces over time must become the task of educational researchers interested in identifying the barriers to authentic integration in order to propose viable solutions to within-school segregation of students, whether the segregation is institutionally generated or student self-generated. For example,

Eick's work examines the evolving social relationships of students within a comprehensive high school from 1950 to 2000. Miller High desegregated as early as 1956 and underwent considerable demographic changes over the fifty-year period, transforming from predominantly white, middle class, and Christian to multiracial, multiethnic, and religiously and economically diverse by the turn of the twenty-first century. Eick identifies a highly nuanced account of patterns of inclusion and exclusion, continuity and change in peer group relations, as well as the factors that inhibited or facilitated the formation of relationships across differences (Eick, 2010). She brings to light the multiple markers of difference in the experience of youth; for example, between girls and boys of the same social class but different races, or among boys of different social classes within the same race. Investigating the relational consequences of desegregation is the next frontier in the growing understanding of the role of desegregated schools in the making of a democratic citizenry.

Caroline Eick

References

Anderson, J. & Byrne, D. (Eds.) (2004). *The unfinished agenda of* Brown v. Board of Education. Hoboken, NJ: John Wiley & Sons.

Banks, J. (2009). *The Routledge international companion to multicultural education.* London & New York: Routledge.

Dittmer, J. (1995). *Local people: The struggle for civil rights in Mississippi.* Champaign, IL: University of Illinois Press.

Dougherty, J. (1999). From anecdote to analysis: Oral interviews and new scholarship in educational history. *Journal of American History, 86*(2), 712–23.

Eick, C. (2010). *Race-class relations and integration in secondary education: The case of Miller High.* New York: Palgrave and Macmillan.

Eick, C. & Valli, L. (2010). Teachers as cultural mediators: A comparison of the accountability era to the assimilation era. *Critical Inquiry in Language Studies, 7*(1), 54–77.

Fine, M., Weis, L., & Powell, L. (1997). Communities of difference: A critical look at desegregated spaces created by and for youth. *Harvard Educational Review, 67*(2), 247–85.

Lukas, A. (1985). *Common ground: A turbulent decade in the lives of three American families.* New York: Vintage Books.

MacDonald, V. M. (2004). *Latino education in the United States: A narrated history from 1513–2000.* New York: Palgrave and Macmillan.

Orfield, G. (2006). Schools more separate: Consequences of a decade of resegregation. Harvard University. The Civil Rights Project, http://www.civilrightsproject.harvard.

Portes, A. & Rumbaut, R. (1996). *Immigrant America: A portrait.* Berkeley & Los Angeles: The University of California Press.

Saporito, S. & Sohoni, D. (2006). Coloring outside the lines: Racial segregation in public schools and their attendance boundaries. *Sociology of Education, 79*(2), 81–102.

Urban, W. & Wagoner, J. (2000). *American education.* New York: McGraw Hill Companies, Inc.

Wells, A. S., Holme, J. J., Revilla, A. T., & Atanda, A. K. (2004). How society failed school desegregation policy: Looking past the schools to understand them. *Review of Research in Education, 28,* 47–100.

DIASPORA

Historically, diaspora has referred to dispersed individuals and communities who reside outside of a country of origin and either relocated voluntarily or through force. Diasporic communities have been thought to maintain a sense of connection to their country and/or culture of origin, either through visits to the country of origin or symbolically in psychological experience. For example, the term *diaspora* has referred to individuals of Jewish descent who have experienced displacement from their ancestral home due to ethnic, religious, and political persecution, representing a "victim diaspora" (Brenick et al., 2012; Tsuda, 2009). Another example of this type of diaspora involves the forced migration of Africans to the United States for the purpose of slavery.

While historical definitions of diaspora focused on individuals' idealized or romanticized fantasies of the country of origin, recent definitions of diaspora are more complex. Scholars have expanded diaspora to encompass not only geographical shifts but also a sense of history, experience, and understanding (Daniel & Johnson, 2010). Recent definitions have challenged previous assumptions that individuals born and raised in the new country, and their descendants, are more culturally similar to individuals in their parents' or grandparents' country of origin than individuals in their birth countries. For example, many second- and third-generation Asian Americans are perceived as "perpetual foreigners" (Liang, Li, & Kim, 2004), even though they identify as Americans. In other cases, immigrants with shared physical features, such as skin color, are assumed to be of the same country or culture of origin. For example, Afro-Caribbean immigrants are often assumed to be African Americans, and Bangladeshi immigrants are often assumed to be Indian Americans in the United States.

Diaspora has increasingly become a core area of inquiry in the social sciences and humanities. Some social science research has focused on the contrast between diaspora and transnationalism, and other research has focused on diaspora experiences in the immigrant and refugee contexts across generations. Some scholars have conceptualized diaspora as "an open system, a dialectic sphere that uses the image of crossroads" (Lam, 2011, p. 311), emphasizing the hybrid nature of identity among diaspora individuals and communities. Hybridity is evident in language, culture, religion, and feelings of belonging. Scholars have noted that identity in the diaspora relies on context, and that diasporic individuals' relationships with their countries and cultures of origin are complex, contradictory, and dynamic (Morawska, 2011). For example, men and women may have qualitatively distinct relationships with their countries of origin, as some women may experience an increased sense of freedom and opportunity in the new country and may have less nostalgia for the country of origin in contrast to men who may experience a loss of status or power in the new country.

The connection with one's country of origin is also influenced by the reason for migration (e.g., refugee, voluntary immigration). Some individuals maintain a transnational identity through which they meet psychological needs of attachment to two or more countries and/or cultures. Diasporic identity is further complicated with relocations across multiple countries. For example, individuals may have spent their childhood in their ancestral country, moved to a different country during their adolescence, and still to another country in their adulthood. The nature of these shifts across developmental stages contributes to a layered, complex identity, at times as a source of conflict and other times as a source of flexibility and creativity. Identity among diaspora individuals may also vary across generations. There is mounting evidence for the "immigrant paradox" (Garcia-Coll & Marks, 2012), a phenomenon in which second-generation or U.S.-born individuals report worse educational and mental health outcomes compared with first-generation or foreign-born individuals. Diaspora studies have been concerned with acculturation and immigrant identity. Specifically, in contrast with classic acculturation theories that assume universality of psychological processes and acculturation strategies (e.g., assimilation, integration) across cultural groups, scholars have suggested that sociopolitical context defines diaspora communities. In fact, diasporas are thought to be created when immigrant communities are not represented or silenced in mainstream culture (Bhatia & Ram, 2009). Further, with increasing globalization, migration, and communication via the Internet, identity is thought to be situated in culture, history, and power (Bhatia & Ram, 2009). For example, disparities in access to social, economic, and political power influence acculturation and identity formation in distinct ways.

Scholars have debated the utility of the term *diaspora* in recent years. For example, Nesbitt-Larking (2008) has argued that diaspora is no longer a useful term for "highly functional multicultural societies" (e.g., Canada) (p. 351), as the term promotes an outsider status to individuals considered to be in a diaspora. From this perspective, genuine and open dialogue is critical to avoid the isolation of cultural groups. Other scholars (Garner, 2008) have criticized this view, noting the problem of assuming homogeneity among minorities and instead emphasizing the importance of intergroup differences and related power differences based on social class and race. Brah (2008) further argued that the term *diaspora* does not necessarily imply a devalued status and that diaspora does not negate full participation of all individuals in a nation. The value of using the term *diaspora* continues to be debated in the social sciences, with a movement toward researchers and scholars from diasporic backgrounds writing with a sense of agency that is critical for a perspective that is indigenous, rather than imposed by authors from only mainstream backgrounds.

Pratyusha Tummala-Narra

References

Bhatia, S. & Ram, A. (2009). Theorizing identity in transnational and diaspora cultures: A critical approach to acculturation. *International Journal of Intercultural Relations, 33*(2), 140–49. doi: http://dx.doi.org/10.1016/j.ijintrel.2008.12.009

Brah, A. (2008). Commentary: Dissolving diasporic identities? *Journal of Community & Applied Social Psychology, 18*(4), 387–89.

Brenick, A., Titzmann, P. F., Michel, A., & Silbereisen, R. K. (2012). Perceptions of discrimination by young diaspora migrants: Individual- and school-level associations among adolescent ethnic German immigrants. *European Psychologist, 17*(2), 105–19. doi: http://dx.doi.org/10.1027/1016-9040/a000118

Daniel, B. & Johnson, L. (2010). Conversations on the African diaspora(s) and leadership: Introduction to the Special Issue. *Urban Education, 45*(6), 767–76.

Garcia Coll, C. & Marks, A. K. (2012). *The immigrant paradox in children and adolescents: Is becoming American a developmental risk?* Washington, DC: American Psychological Association.

Garner, S. (2008). Dissolving the diaspora. *Journal of Community & Applied Social Psychology, 18*(4), 382–86. doi: http://dx.doi.org/10.1002/casp.953

Lam, M. (2011). Diasporic literature: The politics of identity and language. *Journal of Asian Pacific Communication, 21*(2), 309–18. doi: http://dx.doi.org/10.1075/japc.21.2.08lam

Liang, C. T. H., Li, L. C., & Kim, B. S. K. (2004). The Asian American racism-related stress inventory: Development, factor analysis, reliability, and validity. *Journal of Counseling Psychology, 51*(1), 103–14.

Morawska, E. (2011). "Diaspora" diasporas' representations of their homelands: Exploring the polymorphs. *Ethnic and Racial Studies, 34*(6), 1029–48. doi: http://dx.doi.org/10.1080/01419870.2010.533783

Nesbitt-Larking, P. (2008). Dissolving the diaspora: Dialogical practice in the development of deep multiculturalism. *Journal of Community & Applied Social Psychology, 18*(4), 351–62. doi: http://dx.doi.org/10.1002/casp.956

Tsuda, T. (Ed.). (2009). *Diasporic homecomings: Ethnic return migration in comparative perspective.* Palo Alto, CA: Stanford University Press.

DIFFEREND

Differend has a lot to do with how reality differs from the pictures of the world we create inside our heads (Lippman, 1922). The language we use interacts with those pictures so that even though different groups may use the same words, the meanings clash and erupt.

The word *differend* itself comes from the postmodern philosopher Jean Francois Lyotard (1983, 1989) and began as a legal concept. Two parties have differing views on the meaning of a term, but only one interpretation is used to pass judgment. Both have merit, but one view is ignored, and by ignoring that other view, a type of violence occurs. The ignored person becomes silenced. The basic rules of discourse, language, and debate create injustice. In court, a plaintiff is someone who can rely on the idioms of existing law to explain his or her experience. A victim simply does not have the same tools available, Lyotard explained.

Breaking free requires creating new idioms, in essence a new language, to address the silence where words fail to describe truth. A feeling without a name needs definition in order to be understood. Lyotard classified these feelings as important sentiments.

Words such as *justice* became a source of differend after the 2013 George Zimmerman/Trayvon Martin manslaughter trial in Jacksonville, Florida. Zimmerman was a neighborhood watch volunteer who spotted Martin as he walked home from a convenience store. He followed first in his car, then on foot, pulled his gun, and demanded the African American teenager stop. Martin fought Zimmerman and was shot. Florida law allows someone who feels threatened to defend himself or herself with a weapon. In this case, Zimmerman's actions were called self-defense because Martin fought the man, even though Zimmerman was the one who brandished a gun. Both were in essence on trial based on the term *self-defense*. Whose *self-defense* became the focus of a yearlong, highly publicized spectacle.

At the close, it was just as natural to call the trial the "Martin verdict" as it was the Zimmerman trial. *Washington Post* columnist Eugene Robinson (2013) argued that society had already dictated that young black men are dangerous, interchangeable, and expendable. The determination of who was really in danger seemed to defy logic and ignore who ended up dead on the sidewalk, but the legal definitions went to Zimmerman.

Differend extends beyond trial courts and into the court of public opinion. Lyotard pointed to Holocaust survivors as particularly encountering differend. Nazis and history revisionists want to deny genocide occurred. If a survivor explains his or her personal story, then the experience is dismissed as an exaggerated anecdote. In fact, survivors often do not want to talk about their trauma, and when they do, they speak in halting terms. Their silence itself becomes a testimony asserting that the Holocaust must be a fabrication. In contrast, if the survivor provides statistics and data, that evidence is also called fabricated. One Holocaust denier insisted that he would only believe Auschwitz had gas chambers if he could talk with someone who had seen people die in one. Of course, the only way to see someone die in the Auschwitz gas chamber was to die there (Faigley, 1992). Lyotard likened the Holocaust to an earthquake that destroyed the equipment designed to measure it.

Women encounter differend on entering a host of arenas because of the traditional supposition that to be a woman is to be passive. Women's voices are reduced to silence, because silence is supposed to be what defines them (Walker, 1998). Workers might speak of being exploited while a manager/owner describes the worker as a resource to raise capital. In essence, both are correct, but until the one in power understands the language of those without power, the conflict will lead to silencing. If the differend could be easily resolved, then it would not exist in the first place (Sim, 2011).

Differend itself follows a series of stages. First, a conflict occurs that creates strong sentiment. Then, violence and silencing occurs. Those who bear witness can break the paralysis. Those who have been silenced may speak, and those who observe the injustice may cry out against it. Lyotard did not believe differend could be resolved, but it could

be felt. The anomaly of language differences can become visible even if by their very nature they are invisible.

The South African Truth and Reconciliation Commission (TRC) offered a model for bearing witness and breaking silence following apartheid. Those who suffered under the political system, and those who profited from it, were asked to listen to each in a spirit of compassion that began with recognizing each other's humanity, rather than building a new country on vengeance. The TRC was able to become "the narrator for the nation," thus building the new language needed (Praeg, 2000).

Ginny Whitehouse

References

Faigley, L. (1992). *Fragments of rationality: Postmodernity and the subject of composition.* Pittsburg: University of Pittsburg Press.

Lippmann, W. (1922). *Public opinion.* New York: Harcourt Brace.

Lyotard, J. F. (1983). *Le différend.* Paris: Minuit).

Lyotard, J. F. (1989). *Differend: Phrases in dispute.* Minneapolis: University of Minnesota Press.

Praeg, L. (2000). *African philosophy and the quest for autonomy: A philosophical investigation.* Amsterdam: Rodopi.

Robinson, E. (2013, July 15). Black boys denied the right to be young. *Washington Post,* A14.

Sim, S. (2011). *The Lyotard dictionary.* Edinburgh: Edinburgh University Press.

Walker, M. B. (1998). *Philosophy and the maternal body: Reading silence.* New York: Routledge.

DIGITAL DIVIDE

The *digital divide* is a phrase popularized in the 1990s to explain the socioeconomic, sociopolitical, and technology gaps between communities that have access to computers, the Internet, and those who do not. While it was first used to characterize the computer and Internet gaps, in the 2000s, the phrase was expanded to discuss gaps between broadband technology and dial-up access, and the time and ease of access using smartphones and other mobile technology. The argument in 2000 was explained simplistically as the "haves" and "have-nots" in the technology revolution (National

Telecommunication and Information Administration, 2000). However, the digital divide is more complex and technologically sophisticated than simply a matter of Internet access in today's world.

Multicultural educator Paul Gorski (2001) noted that the term *digital divide* has traditionally described inequalities in access to computers and the Internet between groups of people based on one or more social or cultural identifiers. Under this conceptualization, researchers tend to compare rates of access to these technologies across individuals or schools based on race, sex, disability status, and other identity dimensions. The *divide* refers to the difference in Internet access rates among groups. The racial digital divide, for example, describes the difference in rates of access to computers and the Internet, at home and school, between those racial groups with high rates of access (white people and Asian and Asian American people) and those with lower rates of access (black people and Latina(o) people). Similarly, the gender digital divide refers to the gap in access rates between men and women.

The Pew Research Center (2013) reported there are five factors associated with nonuse of technology: (1) age, (2) income and educational attainment, (3) community type, (4) disability status, and (5) Spanish-speaking preference. These factors may play a role in whether or not a digital divide exists. Future research should address how these sociocultural and socio-racial issues impact the digital divide.

In that same year, the Pew Center reported on technology use by African Americans and wrote, "the black/white 'digital divide'" continues to persist, but is not consistent across technology platforms or demographic groups (2013, p. 1). African Americans have long been less likely than whites/Caucasians to use the Internet and to have high-speed broadband access at home, and that continues to be the case. Today, African Americans trail whites/Caucasians by seven percentage points when it comes to overall Internet use (87 percent of whites and 80 percent of blacks are Internet users), and by twelve percentage points when it comes to home broadband adoption (74 percent of whites and 62 percent of blacks have some sort of broadband connection at home). At the same time, blacks and whites are on more equal footing when it comes

to other types of access, especially on mobile platforms (p. 1).

When speaking about traditional measures of Internet and broadband adoption, the gap between whites and blacks is more pronounced among certain demographic subgroups than among others. The black/white "digital divide" continues to persist, but it is not consistent across technology platforms or demographic groups. Specifically, older African Americans, as well as those who have not attended college, are significantly less likely to go online or to have broadband service at home compared to whites with a similar demographic profile (Pew, 2014, pp. 1–2).

Overall, 73 percent of African American Internet users and 96 percent of those ages eighteen to twenty-nine use a social networking site of some kind. African Americans have exhibited relatively high levels of Twitter use since researchers began to track the service as a stand-alone platform. Younger African Americans, in particular, have especially high rates of Twitter use. Fully 40 percent of eighteen-to-twenty-nine-year-old African Americans who use the Internet say that they use Twitter. That is twelve percentage points higher than the comparable figure for young whites (28 percent of whom are Twitter users). This utilization pattern continues. Some 22 percent of online blacks are Twitter users, compared with 16 percent of online whites.

The digital divide between Hispanics/Latinos and whites is smaller now than it was just a few years ago, according to a report from the Pew Hispanic Research Center (2012). Between 2009 and 2012, the share of Latinos who said they went online occasionally increased from 64 percent to 78 percent when compared to whites, whose Internet use increased from 80 to 88 percent during that same time period. It is noteworthy that the percentage of increase of whites was half that of Latinos.

Similarly, the cell phone ownership gap between Latinos and other groups was either diminished or had disappeared entirely (Pew Hispanic Center, 2012, p. 5). With regard to Internet usage, nearly eight of ten Latino adults (78 percent) go online occasionally when compared to 87 percent of whites and 78 percent of African Americans. Furthermore, approximately 72 percent of Latinos report they own either a computer or desktop.

The digital divide has changed dramatically since its introduction in the 1990s due to technological enhancements coupled with societal demographic changes. The digital divide must be reframed for the twenty-first century to examine its intersection with sociodemographics, including income, gender, education, language spoken in the home, and career aspirations, to best understand its implications for multicultural and multiracial communities. It is hoped that by the end of this century, the digital divide will have disappeared.

Doris Wright Carroll

References

Gorski, P. C. (2001). *Multicultural education and the digital divide.* Hamline University and EdChange. Retrieved from http://www.edchange.org/multicultural/papers/edchange_divide.html.

National Telecommunications and Information Administration. (2000). Falling through the Net: Toward digital inclusion. A report on American's access to technology tools. (October). Retrieved from http://www.ntia.doc.gov/files/ntia/publications/fttn00.pdf.

Pew Research Center. (2013). *African Americans and technology use: A demographic portrait.* Retrieved from http://pewinternet.org/Reports/2014/African-American-Tech-Use.aspx.

Pew Hispanic Research Center. (2012). *Closing the digital divide: Latinos and technology adoption.* Retrieved from http://www.pewhispanic.org.

Pew Research Center. (2014). *Digital life in 2025.* Retrieved from http://www.pewinternet.org/2014/03/11/digital-life-in-2025/.

DIPLOMA RECOVERY

With the advent of advanced technology, acquiring an education today in the United States is more valuable than at any other time in history. However, a large number of adolescents cannot take advantage of these opportunities due to their difficulty in completing high school. While a report by the Child Trends Data Bank (2013) indicates that the overall high school dropout rate has been declining since 1967, the actual number of dropouts is still too high, particularly among certain populations.

As more people succeed in graduating from high school, the high school diploma (or its equivalencies) becomes ever more a basic standard, leaving those without one to be burdened with many negative effects. Such effects, according to contemporary research, include higher rates of unemployment, negative health effects, greater risk of incarceration, increased use of drugs and alcohol, and lower overall lifetime earnings and life expectancy (Rumberger & Lim, 2008; Lever et al., 2004). Males are at a generally higher risk than females, as are blacks, Hispanics, and Native Americans compared to Caucasians and Asians. In fairness, factors such as family structure, socioeconomic status, peer support, extraneous responsibilities, and personal self-esteem are more relevant to the decision to drop out than simply one's race or gender (Rumberger & Lim, 2008; Child Trends Data Bank, 2013).

Whatever the reason for dropping out, the lack of a high school diploma restricts students from better income sources and rewarding professional careers. According to the U.S. Bureau of Labor Statistics, the unemployment rate for persons without a high school diploma was 12.4 percent, compared to 4.5 percent for college graduates. For those able to obtain employment, the typical occupations for persons with less than a high school diploma are janitors, cleaners, cashiers, and carpet installers, just to name a few. These occupations provide high school dropouts a median weekly income of $471, compared to the median weekly income of $1,066 for bachelor's degree holders (U.S. Department of Labor, 2013).

Several programs exist to help high school dropouts bolster their education and find better work opportunities. The Diploma Recovery Program is one such effort intended to encourage students who dropped out of school to return and complete their high school diploma. The Diploma Recovery Program offers students who have dropped out of one of the two local high schools an opportunity to return to school after hours as to earn credits toward graduation online. In order to accommodate people's busy schedules, students are oftentimes allowed to participate in online courses, as well as weekend and night classes. The program promotes student success by motivating students to persist to graduation and to improve their life skills training.

Through the Diploma Recovery model, school districts develop plans to help dropouts acquire a high school diploma. First, the district identifies those former students who ended their high school career prematurely at one of the school district's high schools. Afterward, each student receives a letter from the district inviting him or her to enroll in the Diploma Recovery Program. The invitation is the first attempt at providing appropriate intervention to this population of students. It is the intention of the district to combine the program's efforts and resources with students' change in attitude in order to increase students' chances of graduating. In order for this program to succeed, school districts must have a strong commitment to changing the academic trajectory of dropout students and accelerating their level of achievement.

Classes are provided at no cost for any students who may have dropped out of high school within the past three years. The program adopts a flexible schedule that allows students to work during the day and study for their diploma in the evening. This personal involvement on the students' part requires a commitment of two hours (or four nights) a week.

The program is computer based and can be accessed from any Internet-connected location. A computer-based curriculum called Compass Learning was incorporated to allow students to work at their own paces. Compass Learning assesses the students in the beginning of the program and details the courses that students need in order to earn the remaining credits to graduate. The Compass Learning Odyssey model, designed for secondary students, focuses on differentiation and personalized instruction. It is a computer-based program designed to facilitate diploma recovery, credit recovery, summer schooling, and individualized instruction. The web-based program is built to core standards and meshes with MAP (Measure of Academic Progress), which is a national assessment tool. The Compass Learning Odyssey software is also used for credit recovery in a way that would give a student credit for lifelong learning while providing coursework so that students are prepared to learn as they complete course credits. Certified instructors and facilitators are on hand during class time to work with each student. By using both the Compass Learning Odyssey and the nighttime Diploma Recovery Program, students can meet their graduation goal at their own pace.

The teachers in the Diploma Recovery program developed a checklist so that students only focused on the remaining courses needed to meet graduation requirements. Students at one school district in the Midwest are required to have a health and physical education credit, along with math, English, social studies, science, arts and humanities, practical living/career studies, and electives (e.g., personal finance and work-based learning). In this same district, students were expected to work a job in the community during the day to fulfill the work-based learning hours as elective credits. If students did not have a job, the program organizers would help them find one. If students had less than 25 percent of elective credits, they would be enrolled in the personal finance elective through Compass Odyssey in addition to working a job. The job assignment was a key component of the program because it helped the students gain confidence and personal responsibility. Compass Odyssey made the process run smoothly for each student by identifying the knowledge level of each student in a course and moving that student forward toward his/her goal.

The Diploma Recovery Program set goals to exhaust all possible ways of providing students with the greatest opportunity for success; however, much of the students' success is directly related to the level of effort, self-motivation, and persistence that students put into this program. Students are required to attend the classes regularly and work on assignments without falling behind. Students are required to take a pretest, which allows for the computer software program to credit them for what they have already learned from previous classes. Students then take the next step of completing the lessons/modules for each class. Upon completion of each class, students are required to take a posttest to demonstrate that they have mastered the material in that class. In doing so, they receive credit toward graduation. Teachers help students with an Individual Learning Plan, which is a plan that aids students in identifying their professional interests and outlines steps to help them achieve their professional goal(s).

The differences in the Diploma Recovery program and other intervention programs are the following advantages:

- Students can earn a high school diploma instead of a GED.
- They can take coursework online, at school, at home, or wherever Internet services are available.
- Students have appropriate levels of assistance in the lab to intervene on difficult learning problems (software-embedded learning instruction and teachers on staff for face-to-face guidance).

In summary, the mechanics of the Diploma Recovery Program are quite simple. A number of teachers sign on to teach evening classes in the required courses such as mathematics, English, and science. In some cases, the program offers students career advisors, special education assistance, and individual coaching. The classes are usually held in an off-campus location, and in some cases, the program provides students with transport and infant children care while in class. Students only work on the remaining nonelective course requirements they need to graduate. When the students have successfully completed the courses and passed the examinations to qualify for graduation, they are then invited to attend a special graduation ceremony in their honor. Family and friends are invited along with teachers and employers to celebrate their success.

The success of the Diploma Recovery Program has its roots in the literature that suggests that when students are seriously engaged, they will perform better. In order to keep them engaged, it is important to provide improved instructions, better teachers, smaller classes, more individualized help, more tutoring, and extra time on assignments. These elements, along with the students' own sense of motivation, are necessary to sustain students' determination to complete their high school diploma (Azzam, 2007).

Education pays big dividends, and not simply in higher salaries. Educational training helps individuals, and especially the youth of society, to gain a broader and richer appreciation of the world around them. Additionally, educational experience stimulates students to be innovative and creative in their endeavors. Education not only opens up a new world filled with meaning and understanding, but educated individuals are able to participate more fully in democratic activities, knowing that their civic roles help to enhance society and provide quality lifestyles for others. The Diploma Recovery Program has rescued a number of students across the United States and helped them to become active and productive members of society.

Doris L. Crawford

References

Azzam, A. M. (2007). Why students drop out. *Educational Leadership, 64*(7), 91–93.

Child Trends Data Bank. (2013). High school dropout rates. Retrieved from http://www.childtrends.org/?indicators=high-school-dropout-rates.

Lever, N., Sander, M. A., Lombardo, S., Randall, C., Axelrod, J., Rubenstein, M., & Weist, M. D. (2004). A drop-out prevention program for high-risk inner city youth. *Behavior Modification, 28*(4), 513–27. doi: 10.1177/014544550325920

Rumberger, R. & Lim, S. A. (2008). Why students drop out of school: A review of 25 years of research. The California Dropout Research Project is an affiliated project of the University of California Linguistic Minority Research Institute and the UC Santa Barbara Gevirtz Graduate School of Education. Policy Brief 15.

U.S. Department of Labor. (2013). Employment projections. Retrieved from http://www.bls.gov/emp/ep_chart_001.htm.

DISABILITY

Disable the Label: Communicating with and about People with Disabilities

Words have power! The words we use to describe people can either be uplifting and encouraging or degrading and dehumanizing. Words shape the attitudes and beliefs of society and influence our world. Brault (2008) reported that more than fifty million people in the United States have a disability. That translates to one out of every five people having a disability. People with disabilities constitute the largest minority group in the United States. It is the only minority group comprised of all genders, races, age groups, socioeconomic levels, and religions. This minority group is not exclusive; anyone can join this group at any time.

Historically, individuals with disabilities have been portrayed as weak individuals who are to be feared, ignored, pitied, assisted, or institutionalized. Society has had two distinct responses to individuals with disabilities: to protect and contain or to be charitable (Smart, 2009). These responses to individuals with disabilities have determined the language used to describe this group of people.

Similarly, the words used to describe individuals with disabilities have not been accurate or representative of the person. Previously, words such as *retard*, *disabled*, *handicapped*, *schizophrenic*, and *crazy* were acceptable terms used to depict individuals with disabilities. These old, inaccurate, and inappropriate descriptions perpetuate the negative stereotypes and attitudinal barriers toward individuals with disabilities. When described by medical diagnoses, we devalue and disrespect people as individuals. These outdated terms have led to beliefs that have been reinforced by legislative policy, society's language and treatment, and environmental and attitudinal barriers. In recent years, there has been a push to create legislative policy to protect the rights of and to provide more access for individuals with disabilities. While this has been a great move in the right direction, progress to address attitudinal barriers has been slow.

What Is Person First Language?

One approach to modifying the negative attitudes and beliefs commonly held about individuals with disabilities is to use person-first language. Person-first language communicates respect and is an objective way of acknowledging, communicating, and reporting on individuals with disabilities. It eliminates generalizations, assumptions, and stereotypes by focusing on the person rather than the disability.

Person-first language simply puts the individual first. Whether referring to the individual orally or in writing, this language focuses on the individual and not the disability. Person-first language empowers the person with a disability by removing inappropriate terms. For example, an appropriate person-first statement would be "a person uses a wheelchair" instead of "wheelchair bound," or "a child with Down syndrome" instead of "a retarded child."

Person-first language can be accomplished by acknowledging the individuals' strengths rather than focusing solely on deficits. For example, a wheelchair is valued for mobility as opposed to devalued for walking or running. Quadriplegic is associated with limitations, while quadriplegia is one of many aspects of the individual, such as ethnicity, religion, marital status, occupation, and role, that are less likely to dominate or fully describe the individual. By putting the person first, the effect of the asset value (strength) is to appreciate the value of something that falls short (deficit) of a higher comparative standard.

The Importance of Person-First Language

The quest for appropriate language used to describe individuals with disabilities is long overdue. However, the solution to this complex issue still remains unclear as it relates to individuals with disabilities. Kendrick (1998) chronicled the experiences of a woman whose daughter was diagnosed with Down syndrome. The mother walked out of a store and saw volunteers collecting donations to benefit persons with mental retardation. She recalled being offended by the vest the workers were wearing that read "Help Retarded Children." Perhaps a more appropriate use of language would have been "help children with mental retardation." Alternatively, a descriptor such as Down syndrome might have been an appropriate choice of terminology. It is important to choose terminology that reflects that the individual is more than Down syndrome.

The problem still exists some fourteen years later in how we describe individuals with disabilities. The use of person-first language has made progress, but until media descriptions and depictions change, embracing person-first language will not occur. Some recent changes that have occurred resulted in Boards of Developmental Disabilities dropping the word *mental retardation* from their agency titles. This act symbolized the understanding that words reflect attitudes and may have been contributing to the negative connotations associated with mental retardation, such as *retard*.

Labels, such as *schizophrenic*, categorize the individual and dismiss everything else about them. Labels such as this should be replaced with words that clearly describe and accurately reflect the disability but don't leave one guessing. Shame may be conveyed when vague references, such as challenged or special needs, are used to describe individuals with disabilities.

Media influences and attitudes toward individuals with disabilities play a large role in the containment of the spread of negative attitudes toward those individuals. Negative worldviews of individuals with disabilities can be contained if the disability can be seen as one characteristic of the individual rather than their entire being (Dell Orto & Powers, 2007).

Conclusion

Whether an individual has a congenital, gradual, or traumatic disability, it exerts a major influence on his or her own values and worldviews. Physical disabilities are often globally debilitating and can affect emotional and intellectual arenas. Recognizing that there is more to the individual with a disability is essential, as it will assist in disengaging the attitudinal barriers they face and will empower them to be viewed as the person they really are.

DeAnna Henderson
Denise Y. Lewis
Mona Robinson

References
Brault, M. (2008). *Americans with disabilities: 2005, current population reports, P70–117.* Washington, DC: U.S. Census Bureau.
Dell Orto, A. & Powers, P. (Eds.). (2007). *The psychological and social impact of illness and disability* (5th ed.). New York: Springer.
Kendrick, D. (1998, June 14). People with disabilities are, first and foremost, people. *Cincinnati Enquirer.* Retrieved from http://enquirer.com/columns/kendrick/1998/06/061498dk.html.
Smart, Julie. (2009). *Disability, society, and the individual* (2nd ed.). Austin, TX: Pro Ed.

DISCRIMINATION

Discrimination is a concept that encompasses treating a person or group of people unfairly and differently from others. Discrimination is closely related to prejudice, social bias, or perception based on race, ethnicity, age, disability, or gender. It involves unfair treatment or denial of normal privileges to persons because of their race, age, nationality, or religion (Bayer, n.d.). Discrimination is a stressor that may affect the self-esteem and mental health status of individuals (Dulin-Keita, 2011; Nadimpalli, 2012). Two examples of discrimination are racial discrimination and sexual discrimination.

Racial discrimination is conceptualized as unfair treatment based on one's race resulting from interpersonal interactions. It has been described as the prevention or exclusion of blacks and other racial and ethnic minority groups from access to ordinary or equal involvement in society (Henner, 2006). Sexual discrimination is criterion or practices which, when applied, would apply equally to a man, but would put women at a particular disadvantage when compared with men (Atkinson, 2010). One example of sexual or gender discrimination is differences in the pay rate, scale, and how often an employee is paid or given raises, based on gender.

John W. Miller Jr.

References
Atkinson, J. (2010). Does the Sex Discrimination Act provide a right to work part-time for mothers? *Journal of Social Welfare & Family Law, 32*(1), 47–57.
Bayer, P. B. (n.d.). Mutable characteristics and the definition of discrimination under Title VII. *20 U.C. Davis L. Rev. 769,* 769–882.
Dulin-Keita, A. H. (2011). The defining moment: Children's conceptualization of race and experiences with racial discrimination. *Ethnic and Racial Studies, 34*(4), 662–82.
Henner, M. (2006). Why definitions of racial discrimination under U.S. domestic law are woefully inadequate. *International Journal of Diversity in Organizations, Communities and Nations, 5*(6), 167–87.
Nadimpalli, S. B. (2012). An integrative review of relationships between discrimination and Asian American health. *Journal of Nursing Scholarship, 44*(2), 127–35.

DISCRIMINATORY ATTITUDES

Examining Discriminatory Attitudes
toward Latino Immigrants

Discriminatory attitudes toward immigrants work to inform and produce a particular image of the nation that individuals carry with them and reflect back on. Immigration has always played a significant role in the formation of America's national identity: who we are, and who we imagine ourselves to be. Unfortunately, race has also been inextricably linked to immigration, thus further informing our national identity. Take, for example, the 1882 Chinese Exclusion Act, the 1907 Gentleman's Agreement, and the 1924 Johnson-Reed Act. These sought to restrict, or outright exclude, potential immigrants based upon ethnicity and race (Gray & Raza, 2012). The long history of exclusionary immigration policies is thought to have ended with the 1965 Immigration and Nationality Act (aka Hart-Celler Act), which overturned the national quota system found in the Johnson-Reed Act. Interestingly, the 1965 Immigration and Nationality Act coincided with the Civil Rights Act of 1964, which effectively ended discrimination at the national level.

These pieces of legislation made it seem that when taken as a whole, the United States was becoming a post-racial nation. This sentiment was reflected in both the nondiscriminatory policies taken up at the domestic level and within a deracialized immigration system. Yet if this was the case, how can we account for the fact that today racial inequalities are among their highest since the Jim Crow era, and discriminatory attitudes and hostilities are targeted toward poor working immigrants of color (Haney-Lopez, 2010; Johnson, 2010)? To examine this issue, the relationship between color-blind racism and national identity formation must be explored as they continue to inform discriminatory attitudes specifically toward immigrant populations.

Color-Blind Racism and Anti-Immigrant Attitudes

According to Bonilla-Silva (2003), color-blind racism reproduces inequality and perpetuates white privilege because its practices are subtle, institutional, and overtly nonracial. Importantly, color-blind ideology is a political tool that is used by the dominant group consciously or unconsciously to maintain the racial order and to preserve white privilege (Gray & Raza, 2012). Therefore, color-blind ideology is a pervasive belief system that rationalizes and gives power to the existing social structure, or rather, the racialized social system (Bonilla-Silva, 2003). Bonilla-Silva contends that this new racism is difficult to detect because color-blind ideology camouflages racist practices. In fact, color-blind racism reproduces inequality and perpetuates white privilege because its practices are subtle and embedded in the operational functions of institutions.

Related to immigration issues, since anti-immigration legislation disparately impacts Latin populations, any deflection of hostility away from them is hard to accept as nonracially motivated. As Johnson (2010) explains, hostility toward Latin immigrants has been increasing and harsh measures have been directed toward them for punitive reasons. Further, by referring to undocumented populations as illegal and/or alien minimizes the effects of racism. This level of immigrant discourse is inherently racialized because mediated uses of these terms are directed toward migrants hailing from Latin countries.

Discriminatory Attitudes in Media

The media has played a significant role in how immigrant populations, especially undocumented populations, are portrayed and depicted. As Fryberg et al. (2012) suggest, the media "contributes to the ways in which the debate over illegal immigration is processed and understood" (p. 3). The media regularly labels news about immigration as a "problem," constructing a particular image of an unwanted person coming to America (Cisneros, 2008). Much of the coverage on the problem of immigration surrounds the use of metaphors, which is an easy way to narrate a story for an audience to absorb. As Cisneros (2008) explains, using metaphors helps create a visual "other" to dehumanize immigrants and confirms punitive measures enacted upon them. Deconstructing the metaphors commonly used to describe immigrants as toxic, as aliens, and as a disruption to community life could help unmask and demystify dominant assumptions held about immigrants (Cisneros, 2008). Researchers have also found that the terms *illegal alien* and *illegal immigrant* are often used to exclusively describe Latin immigrants, both documented and undocumented (Stewart, Pitts, & Osborne, 2011). Media representations of immigrants feed into the fears and hostilities between Latinos and other racial groups in the United States (Stewart, Pitts, & Osborne, 2011). Dominant themes disseminated by the press suggest that immigrants take away jobs, commit crimes, spread disease, take advantage of social and economic services, and fail to conform to American norms, among others (Stewart, Pitts, & Osborne, 2011). These mediated themes have become a part of the larger conversation about immigrant populations, specifically those from Latin countries.

Mediated representations of immigrant populations help inform public opinion about migrants, especially those from Latin countries. Identifying the subtle racism inherent in public perceptions of immigrants requires an assessment of prejudice in a covert, nonreactive manner. Unlike overt, blatant racism and prejudice, the subtle form incorporates a defense of traditional values, a denial of positive emotions, and an exaggeration of cultural differences. The defense of traditional values assumes that the out-group (immigrant) has violated values of the in-group (native population) while denial of positive emotions involves systematic bias when interpreting positive attributes of the out-group (Gray & Raza, 2012). The exaggeration of cultural differences entails maximizing groups' actual differences and minimizing or ignoring similarities, thus viewing the in-group as the complete opposite of the out-group (Pettigrew & Meertens, 1995).

Related to immigrant populations, especially the undocumented segment, the modern or subtle racist would suggest that the immigrant has done something to warrant the discrimination experienced (i.e., crossing the border). As Simmons & Lecouteur (2008) suggest, discrimination can be articulated via a premise that the minority has done something to warrant the discrimination experienced. Specifically looking at media representations, Liu & Mills (2006) identified two ways that racism was achieved in print media in relation to two race-related events: "(1) minorities were typically criticized for violating traditional mainstream values, and (2) nationalist discourse was repeatedly deployed to affirm the values and wellbeing of the majority and to defend against threat from outsiders" (Simmons & Lecouteur, 2008, p. 669). Race-based discrimination and practices have taken on new forms as a result of legal and social pressures to eradicate these overt, discriminatory behaviors. This new racism presents even more of a problem than overt racism ever did. In the research conducted by Dovidio and Gaertner

(1986), they found that a large portion of the white population expressed no prejudiced views, but at the same time, expressed racial biases. This type of aversive racist endorses egalitarian values and wants to be fair toward people. They do not discriminate in situations in which discrimination would be the obvious choice for overt racists. However, the aversive racist is still left with negative feelings and may express negative behavior when they can justify their actions by some factor other than race. Aversive racists will avoid interracial interaction due to discomfort rather than hostility or hatred. A problematic characteristic of the aversive racist is that he or she is not aware of the racist feelings and actions.

This tenet of color-blind ideology relies on linking contemporary race issues on the racialized other (Bonilla-Silva, 2003). Therefore, color-blind racism manifests in narrative statements like "I'm not racist if they are in fact illegal." As Bonilla-Silva contends, these narratives are indicative of the collective ideological practices that reinforce the contemporary racial order. Color-blindness renders cultural and racial difference irrelevant and blames people of color for their underprivileged position by attributing their failures to the individual. Within this color-blind framework, inequality is not explained as a structural problem that is maintained by persistent racism; rather, it is explained away as a result of individual- or group-level deficiencies (Doane, 2003). Bonilla-Silva (2003) argues that this new ideology is a way to individualize the ills of racism, and dismisses racism as a structural component within the larger social system (Carr, 1997).

Adopting a color-blind stance and negating the importance of race in understanding immigration is dangerous and unfair—dangerous in the sense that such a stance leads to the passage of racist policy such as Arizona's Senate Bill 1070 and Kentucky's proposed Senate Bill 6, among other copycat laws. It is also dangerous considering the resulting actions lead to racial profiling, as has been historically seen. As Johnson (2010) posits, supporters of strict immigration reform contend that their aim is to enforce the law and secure the borders. What occurs no matter the intention is a disparate impact on Latin and Asian migrants. He furthers states that "ignoring those impacts and attempting to obscure, marginalize, and discredit them through the invocation of catchy slogans, will not make them go away" (p. 41). This negation of race only perpetuates the continuance of disparities, discrimination, and structural and institutional racism. A larger point to highlight is that immigration has been historically tied to racial and civil rights issues and cannot be separated in rhetoric as a means of shifting the focus solely to issues of borders, law, order, and geography. We must seek humane solutions to immigration reform and not just reinforce racial injustice (Johnson, 2010).

Kishonna L. Gray

References

Bonilla-Silva, E. (2003). *Racism without racists: Color-blind racism and the persistence of racial inequality in the United States.* Lanham, MA: Rowman & Littlefield Publishing, Inc.

Carr, L. G. (1997). *"Color-blind" racism.* Thousand Oaks, CA: Sage Publications, Inc.

Cisneros, J. D. (2008). Contaminated communities: The metaphor of "immigrant as pollutant" in media representations of immigration. *Rhetoric & Public Affairs, 11*(4), 569–601.

Doane, A. W. (2003). Rethinking whiteness studies. In A. W. Doane and E. Bonilla-Silva, *White out: The continuing significance of racism*, 3–18. London: Routledge.

Dovidio, J. F. & Gaertner, S. L. (1986) *Prejudice, discrimination, and racism.* Waltham: Academic Press.

Fryberg, S. A., Stephens, N. M., Covarrubias, R., Markus, H. R., Carter, E. D., Laiduc, G. A, & Salido, A. J. (2012). How the media frames the immigration debate: The critical role of location and politics. *Analyses of Social issues and Public Policy, 12*(1), 96–112.

Gray, K. L. and Raza, A. E. (2012). Racism in the colorblind era: Examining the mediated responses to Arizona SB1070. *Border-Lines: Journal of the Latino Research Center, 1*, 7–27.

Haney-López, I. F. (2010). Post-racial racism: Racial stratification and mass incarceration in the age of Obama. *California Law Review, 98*, 1023.

Johnson, K. (2010). A case study of color-blindness: The racially disparate impacts of Arizona's SB 1070 and the failure of comprehensive immigration reform. *Arizona State Law Journal for Social Justice*; UC Davis Legal Studies Research Paper No. 229, 1–43. Retrieved from http://papers.ssrn.com/sol3/papers.cfm?abstract_id=1695236

Liu, J. H. and Mills, D. (2006). Modern racism and neo-liberal globalization: The discourses of plausible deniability and their multiple functions. *Journal of Community & Applied Social Psychology, 16*(2), 83–99.

Pettigrew, T. F. and Meertens, R. W. (1995). Subtle and blatant prejudice in Western Europe. *European Journal of Social Psychology, 25*(1), 57–75.

Simmons, K. & Lecouteur, A. (2008). Modern racism in the media: Constructions of the "possibility of change" in accounts of two Australian "riots." *Discourse & Society, 19*(5), 667–87.

Stewart, C. O., Pitts, M. J., & Osborne, H. (2011). Mediated intergroup conflict: The discursive construction of "illegal immigrants" in a regional U.S. newspaper. *Journal of Language and Social Psychology, 30*(1), 8–27.

DISPROPORTIONATE MINORITY CONTACT

Disproportionate Minority Contact (DMC) is a core requirement of the Juvenile Justice and Delinquency Prevention Act (JJDP). Amended in 2002, the JJDP Act requires that U.S. states address the disparate representation of minority youth in the juvenile and adult criminal justice system. Minority youth are black or African Americans, Hispanic or Latinos, Asians, American Indian or Alaska Natives, and Native Hawaiian or other Pacific Islanders and are between ten and seventeen years old. DMC is assessed based on contact points, which are decision points in the system. Minority youth have been disproportionally represented where the rate of arrest through the rate of transfer to the adult system has been higher than nonminority youth.

The relative rate index (RRI) is the formula used to confirm whether a jurisdiction has a DMC problem. The RRI is calculated via a comparison of intragroup and intergroup rates of contact. The number of contacts in the system for a particular minority group is divided by the population totals for that group. DMC is then measured where the rate of contact for minority youth is divided by the rate of contact for nonminority youth. DMC is evident when the RRI is greater than one. DMC exists in the following example of a pseudo jurisdiction. A nonminority arrest rate of 75 percent, and a black or

African American rate of 200 percent, equates to an RRI of 2.67 (200/75 = 2.67). Where the RRI is greater than one, the jurisdiction has a DMC problem.

Natasha C. Pratt-Harris

References

Office of Juvenile Justice and Delinquency Prevention. (2009). *Disproportionate minority contact technical assistance manual* (4th ed.). Washington, DC: U.S. Department of Justice, Office of Justice Programs, Office of Juvenile Justice and Delinquency Prevention.

Parsons-Pollard, Nicolle. (2011). *Disproportionate minority contact: Current issues and policies.* Durham, NC: Carolina Academic Press.

DISPROPORTIONATE REPRESENTATION

Disproportionate Representation of Culturally and Linguistically Diverse Students in Special Education

In this entry, the term *culturally and linguistically diverse* allows for the varying cultural elements that exist within larger "geographic" contexts among certain populations (i.e., Hispanic populations). As a result of the separate and distinct cultures that may exist within populations, it is important to remain sensitive to the nuances of their language (for example, between Mexican and Puerto Rican populations), their attitudes toward teachers and education, and the roles that their families play. As Arnold and Lassman (2003) pointed out, ignoring these factors can lead to disproportionate representation.

Disproportionate representation of cultural and linguistically diverse (CLD) children has plagued special education for almost four decades, almost since it became a discipline in the mid-1970s (Arnold & Lassman, 2003; Skiba et al., 2008). When referring to disproportionate representation (over- and underrepresentation), we typically discuss it in the context of African American, American (Native) Indian, Latino, and Asian, but not Caucasian, students. Generally speaking, disproportionate representation is "the extent to which membership in a given group affects the probability of being placed in a specific disability category" (Oswald, Coutinho, Best, & Singh, 1999, p. 198). Most commonly, there is an overrepresentation of specific groups (e.g., African American, Latino, and Native Indian) in high-incidence categories (i.e., intellectual disabilities, specific learning disabilities, emotional and behavioral disabilities). Additionally, there is underrepresentation for some groups (African American, Latino, and Native American) in gifted and talented programs (Gentry, 2009; Skiba et al., 2008).

Smith (2003) and the U.S. Department of Commerce (2000) have indicated that the nation's school-age population is becoming culturally and linguistically diverse at an unprecedented rate. This diversity makes the phenomenon of disproportionate representation even more problematic for schools. It is critical now more than ever that schools address the three interrelated domains (e.g., policies, practices, and people) that affect the placement of CLD students into special education at disproportionate rates (Klinger et al., 2005). This entry thus discusses the potential causes of disproportionate representation and its long-term impact on CLD students.

Potential Causes of Disproportionate Representation

Disproportionate representation is not easily explained nor understood. While it is a complex phenomenon, the literature has offered a variety of factors that are thought to be at the root of disproportionate representation. According to Harry and Klinger (2006, 2007), some of the factors that contribute to the misidentification of CLD students for special education often include: (1) inadequate classroom instruction prior to referral to special education; (2) inconsistent or arbitrary placement policies and processes; and (3) a lack of effective schooling options due to living in low-income communities. Additionally, Harry and Klinger (2006, 2007), Ford et al. (2004), and Skiba et al. (2008) asserted that the over-identification of low-income and CLD students for special education and other remedial classes, alongside the underrepresentation of CLD students in gifted and talented programs, is often reinforced by cross-cultural misunderstanding, assessment bias, and/or teacher referral processes.

According to Klinger et al. (2005) and others (see Artiles et al., 2010), there are several significant issues that should be considered regarding disproportionate representation. First, we have to reject the notion of *intrinsic deficit*. That is, CLD students are not disproportionately represented in special education because they are more likely to have true disabilities. Instead, Artiles (2003) argued that more attention should be paid to the contextual, historical, and/or institutional issues that exacerbate disproportionality.

Researchers such as Artiles et al. (2004), Losen and Orfield (2002), and others have suggested that *contextual issues* wield a significant influence on higher disproportional representation. Specifically, factors such as (1) decision-making processes that determine eligibility; (2) placement in special education programs with uneven levels of restrictiveness; (3) administrative decisions regarding hiring practices and resource allocations that result in disparities; (4) interactions among school location, disability, ethnicity, poverty, and numbers of CLD students; (5) lack of availability of alternative programs (e.g., bilingual education, Title I); (6) presence of subtle forms of bias at various stages of the referral process; (7) an uneven quality of instruction and management in general education classrooms; and (8) the effects of various discipline policies (e.g., discipline referrals, suspensions, expulsions) all contribute to increased numbers of CLD students in special education programs.

Donovan and Cross (2002) looked at classroom context in terms of teacher effectiveness. They and others noted how children perform based on the effectiveness of the teachers. They pointed out that determining the difference between a child who requires ongoing support for special education services due to some internal trait and a child who receives inadequate opportunity or contextual support for learning and behavior is almost impossible to do.

A second area of concern regarding the disproportionate representation of CLD students in special education is the *power and hegemony in the education of these students* (Klinger et al., 2005). Klinger and colleagues examined the impact of oppression and hegemony in CLD students' opportunities for learning in general education and in the special education referral process. Additionally, they noted that because CLD students' performance does not align with the white, middle-class normative of competence, they are often regarded

as deficient. Hence their referral to and placement in special education.

A third area contributing to the disproportionate representation of CLD students in special education is the *assumptions regarding their intelligence*. Despite the untrue nature of these assumptions, these beliefs have been institutionalized in the policies and practices of U.S. public schools (Steele, Perry, & Hilliard, 2004). The fact that eligibility is tied to IQ measurement means that CLD students continue to be more likely found deficit, especially since the measures reflect cultural, social, and linguistic knowledge that is counter to CLD students' knowledge (Klinger et al., 2005).

A fourth area contributing to the disproportionate representation of CLD students in special education is the *assumption about behavior*. Obiakor (2002) emphasized that personal and cultural norms are inseparable from decisions about which behaviors are acceptable, to whom, and under what circumstances. Yet school personnel tend to judge students' actions through a narrow, white, mainstream lens. When behavior is viewed this way, coupled with tests that exclude subjectivity in judgment, what results is a "punishment paradigm" (Maag, 2001) that includes zero-tolerance policies, corporal punishment, suspension, and expulsion. All of these strategies target CLD students at disproportionately high rates (Fenning & Rose, 2007; Gregory, Skiba, & Noguera, 2010; Skiba, 2002).

The next area of concern is the *wait to fail model*. The President's Commission on Excellence in Special Education (2002) noted that students must have a documented history of failure prior to receiving assistance. In fact, even those who are struggling in kindergarten and first grade do not receive early intervention in reading and behavior, even if intervention might allow them to catch up with their peers. According to Donovan and Cross (2002), there are no mechanisms in place to guarantee that students receive opportunities to learn from the best reading instruction or classroom management before they are identified as children with a "problem."

Finally, the *research to practice gap* has been attributed to the disproportionate representation of CLD students in special education. It has been suggested that one of the challenges to addressing disproportionate representation lies between what is known to work by researchers and what is actually implemented by teachers in the classrooms. We have to do a better job of addressing the issues of culture and language and the context in which they take place (Artiles, Trent, & Huan, 1997). When we can do this, the gap will begin to close. If we do not do this, then the long-term damage experienced by CLD students will continue.

Long-Term Impact of Disproportionate Representation

Although most would agree that disproportionate representation is problematic, there are still some who dispute this. The main argument is that special education placement results in the provision of additional resources and supports (that would not be otherwise received) and should thus be considered a benefit. Although special education, in the right instances, can be beneficial, the drawbacks to misplacement and overrepresentation outweigh the benefits for many children.

For instance, there is evidence in three key areas that highlight that special education has not delivered on its promises from the 1970s. Namely, the literature (see Artiles et al., 2010) has pointed to *academic performance*, *placement restrictiveness*, and other *equity* indices (e.g., dropouts) as evidence of long-term harm being inflicted on CLD students.

In terms of *academic performance*, it is clear that:

1. Students with disabilities (SWDs) are slowly improving their educational outcomes since they were mandated to participate in state assessments (Cortiella, 2007).
2. There is a considerable achievement gap between SWDs and their peers without disabilities in language arts, mathematics, science, and social studies (Wagner, Newman, Cameto, Levine, & Garza, 2006).
3. Data from the National Assessment of Education Progress (NAEP) indicated that SWDs are performing about thirty-two points below their general education peers. These numbers are even higher across state-level aggregated data.

In terms of *placement restrictiveness*, Cartledge, Singh, and Gibson (2008) noted that CLD students placed in special education are more likely to be placed in more segregated settings than their Caucasian peers. Additionally, Urban School Improvement (2008) and Fierros and Conroy (2002) found that African American students get placed in general education settings half as often as their Caucasian peers. This is, of course, troubling because we know that students who spend more time in general education classrooms fare better (e.g., in terms of absences, grade-level performance, and achievement test scores) (Blackorby et al., 2005) than those who are segregated out.

Moreover, in terms of *equity*, researchers have noted:

1. The dropout rate is considerably higher for SWDs and even higher in specific disability categories (i.e., emotional and behavior disorders) (Kemp, 2006).
2. SWDs are less likely to attend college.
3. Quinn, Rutherford, Leone, Osher, and Poirier (2005) reported that 30 to 70 percent of youth with disabilities were in detention, private, and public correctional facilities.
4. Employment rates are lower for out-of-school youth compared to their peers without disabilities. (Wagner et al., 2006)

It is obvious from the data that special education placement (and subsequently its outcomes) is problematic for certain student groups. Therefore, overidentifying CLD students for special education is not in their best interest. It places them at a clear disadvantage while in school, and that disadvantage continues as they transition out of the school environment.

Conclusion

As indicated by Donovan and Cross (2002), key aspects of the school context itself, including administrative, curricular/instructional, and interpersonal factors, may contribute to CLD students' identification as having a disability, which may further add to the disproportionately high or low placements in special education. If special education is to be fully realized as promised in the mid-1970s, the goal should be to assist people (i.e., administrators, teacher educators, educators, students, families, etc.) to unite around culturally responsive, evidence-based interventions and strategic improvements in policy and practices to help close the achievement gap between CLD students and their peers. If we can do this, then we will be successful in reducing the numbers of CLD students who are disproportionately referred to and placed in special education.

Monica R. Brown

References

Arnold, M. & Lassman, M. E. (2003). Overrepresentation of minority students in special education. *Education, 124*(2), 230–36.

Artiles, A. J. (2003). Special education's changing identity: Paradoxes and dilemmas in views of culture and space. *Harvard Educational Review, 73*, 164–202.

Artiles, A. J., Kozleski, E. B., Trent, S. C., Osher, D., & Ortiz, A. (2010). Justifying and explaining disproportionality, 1968–2008: A critique of underlying views of culture. *Exceptional Children, 76*(3), 279–99.

Artiles, A. J., Trent, S. C., & Kuan, L. A. (1997). Learning disabilities empirical research on ethnic minority students: An analysis of 22 years of studies published in selected refereed journals. *Learning Disabilities Research & Practice, 12*, 82–91.

Artiles, A. J., Trent, S. C., & Palmer, J. (2004). Culturally diverse students in special education: Legacies and prospects. In J. A. Banks & C. M. Banks (Eds.), *Handbook of research on multicultural education* (2nd ed., pp. 716–35). San Francisco, CA: Jossey-Bass.

Blackorby, J., Wagner, M., Cameto, R., Davies, E., Levine, P., Newman, L. . . . Sumi, C. (2005). *Engagement, academics, social adjustment, and independence.* Palo Alto, CA: SRI.

Cartledge, G., Singh, A., & Gibson, L. (2008). Practical behavior-management techniques to close the accessibility gap for students who are culturally and linguistically diverse. *Preventing School Failure, 52*, 29–38.

Cortiella, C. (2007). *Rewards and roadblocks: How special education students are faring under No Child Left Behind.* New York: Center for Learning Disabilities.

Donovan, S. & Cross, C. (2002). *Minority students in special and gifted education.* Washington, DC: National Academy Press.

Fenning, P. & Rose, J. (2007). Overrepresentation of African American students in exclusionary discipline: The role of school policy. *Urban Education, 42*(6), 536–59.

Fierros, E. G. & Conroy, J. (2002). Double jeopardy: An exploration of overrepresentation of minority children in special education. In D. J. Losen & G. Orfield (Eds.), *Racial inequity in special education.* (pp. 39–70). Cambridge, MA: The Civil Rights Project, Harvard Education Press.

Ford, D. Y. & Moore III, James L. (2004). Creating culturally responsive gifted education classrooms: Understanding "culture" is the first step. *Gifted Child Today, 27*(4), 34–39.

Gentry, R. (2009). Disproportionate representation of minorities in special education—How bad? Presentation at the Third Annual Jane H. Leblanc Symposium in Communication Disorders. Arkansas State University, June 4–5, 2009. Retrieved from http://files.eric.ed.gov/fulltext/ED505997.pdf

Gregory, A., Skiba, R. J., & Noguera, P. A. (2010). The achievement gap and the discipline gap: Two sides of the same coin? *Educational Researcher, 39*(1), 59–68.

Harry, B. & Klinger, J. (2006). *Why are so many minority students in special education?* New York: Teacher College Press.

Harry, B. & Klinger, J. (2007). Discarding the deficit model: Improving instruction for students with learning needs. *Educational Leadership, 64*(5), 16–21.

Kemp, S. (2006). Dropout policies and trends for students with and without disabilities. *Adolescence, 41*, 235–50.

Klinger, J. K., Artiles, A. J., Kozleski, E., Harry, B., Zion, S., Tate, W., Durán, G. Z., & Riley, D. (2005). Addressing the disproportionate representation of culturally and linguistically diverse students in special education through culturally responsive educational systems. *Education Policy Analysis Archives, 13*(38), 1–40. Retrieved from http://epaa.asu.edu.

Losen, D. J. & Orfield, G. (Eds.) (2002). *Racial inequity in special education.* Cambridge, MA: Harvard University Press.

Maag, J. W. (2001). Rewarded by punishment: Reflections on the disuse of positive reinforcement in education. *Exceptional Children, 67*(2), 173–86.

Obiakor, F. (2002). Multicultural education: Powerful tool for preparing future general and special educators. *Teacher Education and Special Education, 24,* 241–55.

Oswald, D. P., Coutinho, M. J., Best, A. M., & Singh, N. N. (1999). Ethnic representation in special education: The influence of school-related economic and demographic variables. *Journal of Special Education, 32*(1), 194–206.

President's Commission on Excellence in Special Education. (2002). *A new era: Revitalizing special education for children and their families.* Jessup, MD: U.S. Department of Education.

Quinn, M. M., Rutherford, R. B., Leone, P., Osher, D., & Poirier, J. (2005). Youth with disabilities in juvenile corrections: A national survey. *Exceptional Children, 71*(3), 339–45.

Skiba, R. J. (2002). Special education and school discipline: A precarious balance. *Behavioral Disorders, 27*(2), 81–97.

Skiba, R. J., Simmons, A. B., Ritter, S., Gibb, A. C., Rausch, M. K., Cuadrado, J., & Chung, C. (2008). Achieving equity in special education: History, status, and current challenges. *Exceptional Children, 74*(3), 264–88.

Smith, D. D. (2003). *Introduction to special education: Teaching in an age of opportunity* (4th ed.). Boston: Allyn & Bacon.

Steele, C., Perry, T., & Hilliard, A., III. (2004). *Young, gifted, and Black: Promoting high achievement among African American students.* Boston: Beacon Press.

U.S. Department of Commerce, Bureau of the Census. (2000). Overview of race and Hispanic origin 2000. Retrieved December 10, 2013, from http://www.census.gov/prod/2001pubs/c2kbr01-1.pdf.

Wagner, M., Newman, L., Cameto, R., Levine, P., & Garza, N. (2006). An overview of findings from wave 2 of the National Longitudinal Transition Study-2 (NLTS-2). Retrieved December 17, 2013, from www.nlts2.org/reports/2006_08/nlts2_report_2006_08_complete.pdf.

DIVERSITY MANAGEMENT

In North America, Western Europe, and South Africa, to name a few geographic areas, concerns about a multicultural workforce have been reformulated into an affirmative agenda for diversity. Diversity discourse came into full force in the late 1980s and left an imprint on the (global) business (and educational) world. For instance, in the United States, inclusion strategies on narrowly defined multicultural (i.e., racial/ethnic) and gender grounds were considered inadequate such that the broader category of diversity emerged (Nagel & Asumah, 2014). Calls for racial justice and women's rights in all walks of life were followed by a lavender revolution (recognition for LGBT rights), and equity for people with disabilities. Thus, diversity emerged as a fitting umbrella term in terms of diversity education and diversity management. However, diversity management may devolve into "managing" diversity.

It is laudable and good practice when a diverse management team calls for hiring a diverse workforce in all its areas and sets the tone for an inclusive, accepting, and equitable workplace atmosphere. It is another matter entirely when a homogenous, white (male) management presides over a workforce that may have a few persons of color in decision-making roles, but otherwise relegates LGBT persons, as well as ethnic and culturally diverse individuals, to backroom, low-paying, and invisible, glass-ceiling, and sticky-floor jobs such as janitorial staff (Cox, 1991). Another pitfall is when managing diversity looks like managing culture, in which employees are told to fit into the hegemonic national or cultural ethos; different cultural expressions are deemed deviant and therefore are proscribed (Human, 1996). Within the United States, this management model thrives on a post–civil rights business ideology of nominal inclusion and provides lip service to fostering respect for an increasingly diverse population and workforce. What is lost in these management strategies is the crucial awareness of power differentials among workers of different ranks and responsibilities. Take, for instance, discussions on "difficult dialogues" (Nagel & Asumah, 2014). If a training module on difficult dialogues between an employer and an employee teaches about the different dimensions of "intent" and "impact," the trainers are often silent on the power differential between both persons. In reality, if the employee were to point out the psychological impact of her boss's statement, she may not fare so well in her next performance review. Her assertiveness may be taken as a sign of disrespecting the culture of hierarchy within that organization, and she may be disqualified as a "good fit."

Lacking a commitment toward a culture of diversity has its own drawbacks. We may perhaps know more about the disastrous impact of a multi-national business failing to appeal to the local customer and employer base than about the successes of those businesses and institutions that create a diverse and inclusive work environment. One such remarkable example of failure is Wal-Mart, which had to pull out of Germany's retail market due to "their profound lack of intercultural competence and management skills" (Knorr & Arndt, 2003, p. 20). Wal-Mart's rigid corporate climate proved to be completely alienating to a German workforce and consumers.

Thus, an inclusive diversity philosophy is critical to the success of a corporation or other institution; it should be pursued as an intrinsic good rather than as a means to increasing profit margins. The latter approach is perhaps showcased in the socially conscious "United Colors of Benetton" ad campaign, which is designed to eclipse the sweatshop conditions of Global South workers producing the multinational corporation's apparel (Bhasin, 2013). Thus, a diversity business motto or mission statement is a necessary, but not sufficient, condition to creating a social justice paradigm within an organization.

Mechthild Nagel

References

Bhasin, K. (2013, May 8). In first interview since Bangladesh factory collapse, Benetton CEO confirms company's tie to tragedy. *The Huffington Post.* Retrieved from http://www.huffingtonpost.com/2013/05/08/benetton-bangladesh-factory-collapse_n_3237991.html?utm_hp_ref=business.

Cox, T. (1991). The multicultural organization. *Academy of Management Executive, 5*(2), 34–47.

Human, L. (1996). Managing workforce diversity: A critique and example from South Africa. *International Journal of Manpower, 17*(4/5), 46–64.

Knorr, A. & Arndt, A. (2003). Why did Wal-Mart fail in Germany? *Institute of World Economics and International Management.* Retrieved from http://www.iwim.uni-bremen.de/publikationen/pdf/w025.pdf.

Nagel, M. & Asumah, S. N. (2014). Diversity studies and managing differences: Unpacking SUNY Cortland's case and national trends. In G. Hentges, K. Nottbohm, M. M. Jansen, & J. Adamou (Eds.), *Sprache–Macht–Rassismus* (Language–power–racism) (pp. 349–466). Berlin: Metropol Verlag.

DIVERSITY STATEMENT

A Diversity Statement within institutions of higher education is text that recognizes the responsibility of creating an environment that affirms the diversity of people and ideas and assists its members in developing the knowledge, skills, and dispositions of intercultural competence and effective appreciation for diversity on university campuses and communities at-large.

In pursuit of these ends, institutions develop Diversity Statements in striving to attract its students, develop curriculum, recruit and retain faculty and staff, and revise and develop processes as well as implement institutional practices that respect diversity. In part, its approach is quantitative, in that Diversity Statements pursue demographic, programmatic, and funding targets designed to enhance inclusiveness and intercultural and international exposure. Recognizing, however, that numeric goals are only a part of the challenge, Diversity Statements establish qualitative goals with which to gauge, enhance, and reward competency in facilitating diversity in interpersonal, intercultural, and international relationships. Diversity Statements in higher education are designed as aspirational commitments to the community (OMara & Morrish, 2010) and are not necessarily institutional realities.

Diversity Statements may be developed with at least three areas of focus. Each area recognizes continuous institutional change and active learning on the part of all members of the academic community (students, faculty, administrators, and staff) in the pursuit of cultural awareness, sensitivity, and social justice.

At the interpersonal area: Diversity Statements strive to enhance the development of attitudes, dispositions, and communication skills that are required to have active, thoughtful, and respectful dialogues including courtesy, respect, professionalism, and dedication. This area of focus acknowledges individual differences, whether they are political ideology, gender, age, ethnicity, sexual orientation, lifestyle, disability, and other differences.

At the intercultural area: Diversity Statements recognize that societies comprise cultural groups that significantly shape the worldview and social attributes of their members and that they often stand in historic relations of power and disparity to each other. Therefore, commitment is to the promotion of equity, access, and inclusion in matters of collective difference such as customs, traditions, ethnicity, race, language, religion, military service, geographical origin, and more.

At the international area: Diversity Statements promote awareness of the increasing complexity of the world community and commits to education that recognizes the increasing impact of global and transnational movement and developments. Therefore, Diversity Statements aim to attract, retain, and reward those who incorporate the complex skills, insights, and attitudes to effectively and inclusively prepare students for the present and future world.

Each area of a Diversity Statement calls for institutions to examine their mission, external relationships, organizational structures and processes, and institutional climate when addressing its commitment to diversity. This text should accurately reflect the institutional values (Wilson, Meyer, & McNeal, 2012) in an effort to purposefully confront prejudicial, discriminatory, or racist behaviors and policies.

Joya Carter-Hicks

References

OMara, K. & Morrish, E. (2010). A glass half full or half empty?: A comparison of diversity statements among Russell Group v. US Research Universities. *International Journal of Diversity in Organisations, Communities and Nations, 10*(3), 243–59.

Wilson, J., Meyer, K., & McNeal, L. (2012). Mission and diversity statements: What they do and do not say. *Innovative Higher Education, 37*(2), 125–39.

DOMESTIC VIOLENCE PREVENTION

At the beginning of the domestic violence or battered women's movement, most efforts were focused on enacting legislation, providing services to victims, and holding batterers accountable. The field was focused on responding to, not necessarily preventing, abuse. The 1990s saw increased attention to the importance of prevention and ushered in a variety of groups, institutions, and funding streams devoted to multiple levels of prevention.

The Centers for Disease Control and Prevention (CDC) and World Health Organization (WHO) see domestic violence as a public health concern and have supported research and funding for prevention programs. They emphasize systemic data gathering to fully document the scope and magnitude of the problem, and then more advanced research that identifies the causes of abuse as well as risk and protective factors. This data is then used to craft and implement a prevention strategy.

The CDC and other groups articulate three levels or tiers of prevention. Primary prevention involves efforts to prevent abuse from ever occurring. This is done by changing the social norms and the societal conditions that allow abuse to happen. Most primary prevention programs focus on educational initiatives, often school-based programs. Examples of primary prevention programs include the Safe Dates curriculum for eighth- and ninth-grade students and ExpectRespect, a school-based program developed by SafePlace: Domestic Violence and Sexual Assault Survival Center (NRCDV). Different from intervention, secondary prevention involves identifying a problem as soon as it begins so as to stop it before it escalates. Secondary prevention efforts include such things as medical professionals screening patients for abuse and home visitations to families who might be at risk, such as low-income women, based on statistical evidence. Tertiary prevention is intervening after an incident occurs. Efforts are taken to minimize the impact of the abuse and to restore the victim, his or her family, and the community to health and well-being.

Prevention efforts can also be universal, selected, and indicated. Universal efforts may target the general public, or at least a wide demographic group; for instance, adolescent boys. One example of such a program is Coaching Boys into Men, a male-focused initiative developed by Futures without Violence (then the Family Violence Prevention Fund). Selective prevention efforts target particularly vulnerable groups. Research has shown that women and girls ages sixteen to twenty-four are particularly at risk, as are homeless and runaway youth. Indicated prevention is aimed at those who are uniquely at risk and who have already experienced at least minimal signs of the problem. For instance, indicated prevention efforts might focus on immigrants. Further, given that abuse takes many forms, from extreme violence to emotional, verbal, financial, spiritual abuse, and more, prevention programs must go beyond simply addressing just physical incidents. Domestic violence scholars have provided a Spectrum of Prevention to provide a framework for comprehensive prevention programs. Level One involves strengthening skills and knowledge; Level Two focuses on promoting community education; Level Three is designed to educate those who provide important services, such as daycare centers; Level Four is to foster coalitions and networks; Level Five involves changing organizational practices; and Level Six focuses on influencing policy and legislation.

Primary Prevention

It is important that prevention programs draw on the literature regarding best practices but that they also incorporate local data so as to ensure that efforts target the most vulnerable in a particular community and are also applicable to the wider population of residents.

The DELTA Program emerged from the Family Violence Prevention Services Act (FVPSA), which authorized the CDC to distribute federal funds to support coordinated community responses (CCRs) that address domestic and dating violence. DELTA Programs also receive funding from The National Center for Injury Prevention and Control (NCIPC). In 2002, the DELTA Program began focusing on primary prevention.

A CCR is an organized, community collective that is intended to both respond to and prevent domestic violence in a particular community. Each community selects their own members, attempting to involve key organizations, educators, faith leaders, politicians, criminal justice practitioners, and health professionals.

There are fourteen state-level domestic violence coalitions that receive DELTA funds. Funder coalitions are in Alaska, California, Delaware, Florida, Kansas, Michigan, Montana, North Carolina, North Dakota, New York, Ohio, Rhode Island, Virginia, and Wisconsin. These coalitions then provide financial support to CCRs as well as provide training and technical support. DELTA practitioners receive training from an NCIPC program called PREVENT (Preventing Violence through Education, Networks, and Technical Assistance).

Many primary prevention programs are aimed at informing and empowering bystanders. In most acts of violence, there are other people around. Many people either witness incidents of abuse or see the aftereffects, such as scratches, bruises, and the signs of emotional trauma. This is particularly true of dating violence, which is much more likely to occur in front of peer witnesses. These bystanders may be passive or active. Passive bystanders are those who watch or witness an incident or its effects but do not get involved or attempt to disrupt it. Active bystanders tend to be vocal or involved in some way. That does not mean, however, that active bystanders help the situation. Instead, they may egg it on by cheering or otherwise encouraging the behavior.

Bystander approaches emphasize that individuals can be trained to actively interrupt incidents of domestic or dating violence. Bystander intervention programs emerged from social norms theory. Social norms theory says that people behave according to the way they perceive others behave. Individuals may misperceive others' attitudes or behavior, or misunderstand their approval or disapproval of behavior. In general, people, especially youth, overestimate the amount of risk-taking behavior occurring and underestimate the amount of prosocial behavior. This may lead individuals to feel as though they should conform to the risk-taking behavior they believe to be common or to reject the more healthy behaviors they perceive to occur less frequently.

Many bystander intervention programs are directed at males. Research has found that men and boys are less likely to intervene than are women, so bystander intervention programs seek to empower men to resist a hypermasculine gender identity and to discourage peers from acting aggressively. Evaluations of bystander intervention programs have generally supported their effectiveness. One example of a Bystander Intervention Program is Mentors in Violence Prevention (MVP), which was founded by feminist scholar Jackson Katz. MVP uses former college and professional athletes as trainers. Evaluations have found MVP to result in significant changes in knowledge about domestic abuse.

Laura Finley

Additional Reading

Chamberlain, L. & Rivers Cochran, J.-A. (2008, March). *A prevention primer for domestic violence: Terminology, tools, and the public health approach.* Harrisburg, PA: VAWnet, a project of the National Resource Center on Domestic Violence/Pennsylvania Coalition against Domestic Violence. Available at http://www.vawnet.org.

Foshee, V., Bauman, K., Ennett, S., Linder, G. F., Benefield, T., & Suchindran, C. (2004). Assessing the long-term effects of the safe dates program and a booster in preventing and reducing adolescent dating violence victimization and perpetration. *American Journal of Public Health, 94,* 619–24.

Graffunder, C., Noonan, R., Cox, P., & Wheaton, J. (2004). Through a public health lens: Preventing violence against women: An update from the U.S. centers for disease control and prevention. *Journal of Women's Health, 13,* 5–14.

Katz, J. *The macho paradox: Why some men hurt women and how all men can help.* New York: Sourcebooks.

Ricardo, C., Eads, M., & Barker, G. (2011). Engaging boys and young men in the prevention of sexual violence: A systemic and global review of evaluated interventions. Washington, DC: Promundo-US. Available at http://www.scribd.com/doc/80282147/Engaging-Boys-and-Young-Men-in-the-Prevention-of-Sexual-Violence.

DOMESTIC VIOLENCE SERVICES

Given that an estimated one-third of the world's women will endure an abusive relationship in her lifetime, it is essential that communities provide services to victims of domestic violence. More than just shelter for those fleeing abusers, victims may need legal and medical help, therapy and counseling, workforce training, transportation, childcare, and more. Many domestic violence shelters or centers either provide these services or make referrals to community organizations that can provide them.

Prior to the Battered Women's Movement of the 1970s, no organized services were available for victims of domestic violence. Victims had to rely on their family and friends for shelter and support. Women's Advocates, established in 1974 in St. Paul, Minnesota, is considered to be the first emergency shelter for domestic violence victims. By 1982, the United States had more than three hundred shelters.

These shelters were generally organized around radical feminist principles, as they were modeled after homes and operated with an egalitarian, communal structure.

As the number of women seeking shelter continued to grow, advocates realized that they needed to collaborate with other agencies in order to meet the demand for assistance. Shelters reached out to form alliances with other groups and organizations, including local, state, and federal government entities. These coalitions helped fund the work, but according to numerous scholars, it resulted in a gradual shift away from the founding feminist principles. Some have criticized domestic violence shelters because of this change in philosophy.

Today many shelters or centers operate under a philosophy that seeks to empower victims to take control of their lives. This philosophy is enacted through services and support that are intended to put the victim in charge of his or her life. This might include emergency shelter as well as assistance with safety planning, therapy, support groups, referrals to and collaborations with area agencies, efforts to help children who have witnessed abuse, legal assistance, and more. Since most domestic violence victims never stay in a shelter, these outreach services are critical forms of support. Most domestic violence shelters operate twenty-four-hour crisis lines to counsel victims. Increasingly, domestic violence services also include an educational component.

While domestic violence shelters offer an important lifeline for victims, they struggle to meet the demand for help. Each year since 2005, the National Network to End Domestic Violence (NNEDV) has coordinated a one-day census of domestic violence centers in order to assess the scope of services provided and to identify areas in need of improvement. In 2012, 86 percent of the 1,924 certified centers participated in the twenty-four-hour census. The survey found that 64,324 victims were served in one day. Three-quarters of the responding centers provide emergency shelter, and some 35,323 victims stayed in shelters or transitional housing during the twenty-four-hour census. Of these, 24,783 were children. Additionally, 29,001 adults and children received nonresidential assistance and services, including counseling, legal advocacy, and children's support groups. More than 50 percent of the responding centers provided court accompaniment and/or advocacy for survivors, half provided transportation, 45 percent provided some form of group support, and 44 percent offered advocacy related to public benefits. Local and state hotlines answered 20,119 calls, and the National Domestic Violence Hotline answered 702 calls, averaging more than fourteen hotline calls every minute. Additionally, 25,182 individuals in communities across the United States and territories attended 1,162 training sessions provided by local domestic violence programs.

More than ten thousand requests for help went unmet during the twenty-four-hour census. Some 65 percent of the unmet requests, or 6,818, were for emergency shelter or transitional housing. Often, all shelter beds are full, thus victims in need must be referred to other services. Only 41 percent of responding centers have transitional housing for victims. Counseling and legal assistance were the second and third most unmet requests. While more than half of the centers were able to provide advocates to support victims in court, only 11 percent could offer actual legal assistance. Centers cited numerous reasons for their inability to meet all of the requests. These include: not enough funding for needed programs and services (42 percent); not enough staff (30 percent); lack of available beds and/or funding for hotels (26 percent); too few specialized services (23 percent); and limited funding for translators, staff who are bilingual, or accessible equipment (10 percent).

Most shelters are designed for women and may not be open to male victims. Although women make up the majority of domestic violence victims, it is imperative that males who fear for their lives have access to safe spaces. Across the United States there are only a few shelters specifically for men, and thus men must remain in dangerous situations, seek help from family or friends, or end up at homeless shelters where abusers can find them. Teen victims may find it difficult to access the support of domestic violence centers, as many are not knowledgeable about where to go, do not have the support of an adult to help them get there, or believe that the services are only for adults. Domestic violence centers

can also improve on their capacity to serve elder victims.

Similarly, many shelters are not well equipped to serve victims with unique culture, physical, or mental needs. Immigrants from other cultures may not be familiar with the laws and type of assistance offered to victims in the United States, and they may not know how to contact service providers. Language barriers may also leave some immigrant victims without help. Domestic violence centers must work to offer culturally competent services.

Additionally, domestic violence centers must work to ensure that services are accessible to those with physical or mental disabilities. This includes, but is not limited to, phone services that can work for those with hearing challenges; braille or sign language interpreters for persons with visual impairments; and ramps, modified bathrooms, and other accommodations for those with physical disabilities. Center staff should be trained on how to deal with specific mental or emotional disabilities, including when it is appropriate to refer a victim elsewhere for more extensive assistance. Further, crisis line and shelter staff must understand how to work with victims who may express suicidal tendencies.

Domestic violence centers can also assist victims by referring them to other community agencies. That is, centers can and should partner with housing authorities, workforce training programs, local legal aid entities, medical doctors, and others to ensure that victims receive the help that the center cannot provide. Domestic violence centers can provide these referrals and help train professionals in these fields to understand domestic violence and to support victims.

Medical professionals are encouraged to screen patients using specific questions or surveys. Well-trained medical professionals can help victims once abuse is disclosed or identified by taking careful documentation that can be used in legal proceedings or to access other services and by providing support and information about other services. Although not all victims call police, some do. Many police agencies now have victim advocates who assist in cases of domestic and sexual violence.

Laura Finley

Additional Reading

National Network to End Domestic Violence. (2012). Domestic violence counts 2012: A 24-hour census of domestic violence shelters and services. Retrieved from http://www.nnedv.org/downloads/Census/DVCounts2012/DVCounts12_NatlReport_Color.pdf.

Sokoloff, N. & Dupont, I. (2005). Domestic violence at the intersections of race, class and gender: Challenges and contributions to understanding violence against marginalized women in diverse communities. *Violence against Women, 11*(1), 38–64.

Sullivan, C. (2012). *Advocacy services for women with abusive partners: A review of the empirical evidence.* Harrisburg, PA: National Resource Center on Domestic Violence. Retrieved from http://www.dvevidenceproject.org/wp-content/themes/DVE-Project/files/research/DVAdvocacyResearchSummary10-2102.pdf.

DOMINANT CULTURE

The Impact of Dominant Culture on Black Education

Dominant culture represents the socially dominant Anglo-American male cultural group in American society. The dynamics of power, control, racial subservience, and class impacted American culture during the pre–Civil War era. Views of racial inferiority toward African Americans had developed among American society, giving way to the power of the dominant culture. The dominant culture was embraced by society as the superior race, while blacks were described as inferior and ignorant. Societal order dictated that the dominant culture could not be interrupted by lower racial groups. It was the dominant culture's belief that the long enslavement of African Americans was evidence that African Americans were intellectually inferior. This societal concept, based on the historical context of scientific racism, impacted the foundation of black education.

African Americans had to learn their place in the new industrial order that the dominant culture had created for them. The theory of structural pluralism dictated that the socially subordinate culture (African Americans) unilaterally accommodated the dominant white culture. The dominant culture insisted upon cultural assimilation as a prerequisite to social integration. Social values were implemented through the dominant culture mind-set. The accommodation theory framed the legacy of racism and its role in the history and founding of minority-serving institutions. This theory also influenced the labor market and the establishment of black education.

During the post–Civil War era, the majority of African Americans were freed but uneducated. African Americans were initially given minimal access to education. The lack of access to education given to African Americans demonstrated the control by the dominant culture. The view of education being a path to equality for African Americans troubled the dominant culture. While they believed in providing African Americans the opportunity to receive an education, the dominant culture was successful in keeping the societal order that had been established. Segregation laws, such as the Black Codes and Jim Crow, kept the races separated. African Americans were met with resistance while trying to obtain an education by white Southerners who were opponents of the idea. Some African Americans were fired from their jobs if it was found that their children attended school. Others faced harassment by whites if they were attending school. The connection of the establishment of black education to the labor market explained why the dominant culture allowed blacks only minimal access to education. Politics interjected itself into the education of blacks. The dominant culture was interested in the industrialization and reunification of the United States.

Missionary societies were formed by powerful white Northern industrialists to provide the foundation for a system of black education while addressing the growing issue of educating blacks. Race philanthropy became the vehicle to address this issue. These new missionary societies sought to work toward their own political and policy agendas. Missionary societies, such as the American Missionary Association and Methodist Episcopal Freedman's Aid Society, were the force behind some of the most well-known minority-serving institutions. Early black institutions such as Spelman, Morehouse, and Fisk enrolled over 60 percent of black students attending colleges at that time.

The goal of missionary societies was to support a reordering of society and redistribution of wealth. The establishment of a system of black education supported the view that missionaries wanted the modernization and industrialization of the North to reign over the agricultural, old South. The building and support of schools to educate blacks was a key component in creating policy without lawmakers slowing down the process for the Northern white philanthropists. The dominant culture promoted industrial education over liberal arts education for African Americans because they believed industrial education was intellectually easier for African Americans to manage. Industrial education also supported Northern philanthropists' goal of industrialization.

The industrial curriculum offered a new model of education that incorporated social progress for African Americans. Samuel Chapman Armstrong, a strong advocate of industrial education, founded the Hampton Normal and Agriculture Institute. With the help of Booker T. Washington, Armstrong pushed the ideology of the dominant culture to create a curriculum that did not challenge the inequality of race and power. As the power and wealth of these foundations grew, industrial philanthropists became the leading influence in black education. Washington went on to help found Tuskegee Normal and Industrial Institute, later known as Tuskegee University. This form of education was thought to be appropriate in assisting with racial peace, political stability, and material prosperity for the dominant culture in both the North and the South.

Charmaine Troy

References

Anderson, J. D. (1988). *The education of blacks in the south: 1860–1935*. Chapel Hill: The University of North Carolina Press.

Bennett, M. (1998). *Basic concepts of intercultural communication*. Boston: Intercultural Press.

Drewry, H. A. (2001). *Stand and prosper: Private black colleges and their students*. Princeton: Princeton University Press.

Kochman, T. (1981). *Black and white styles in conflict*. Chicago: The University of Chicago Press.

DROPOUT FACTORIES

Dropout factories are high schools "where 60% or less of the students who enter the school as freshman graduate" (Balfanz & Legters, 2014). Dr. Robert Balfanz, a John Hopkins University researcher, coined the term to encapsulate those schools who fit certain profiles: they are in mostly urban communities (although some are in small towns and rural communities); in communities that have lost their industrial and employment base; in low-income neighborhoods; in areas with large ethnic minority populations, and in areas where the parents of students who attend these schools have low educational attainment. While half of dropout factories are located in urban areas, the other half are primarily found in the Southern and Southwestern regions of the United States (Balfanz & Legters, 2006). Researchers such as Balfanz and Legters (2006) have found that poverty plays a profound role in dropout rates. Further complicating this situation is a racial correlation—namely, that almost half of the nation's African American and Latino students attend high schools with high poverty and low graduation rates (Balfanz & Legters, 2006).

Many of the students who attend dropout factories enter school poorly prepared to be successful (Balfanz & Legters, 2006). Hindered by inadequate knowledge and/or personal difficulties, they routinely fail classes and lose motivation, which eventually leads to them dropping out of school. Researchers highlight that teachers and administrators, in collaboration with community organizations, parents, faith-based organizations, and government agencies, must band together to provide these students with the resources and encouragement needed to succeed. It is also recommended that intervention programs be developed in order to reach out to the majority of potential students who might drop out by letting them know that adults care about them and their future. Such resources are badly needed in these schools, according to Balfanz and Legters (2006):

A central feature of these dropout factories is that they serve an overwhelming concentration of needy students. Thus, it is essential that the federal government, states, districts, and foundations bring to bear human and financial resources that are equal to the challenge. These schools' resources vary considerably. Some struggling high schools can implement proven reforms by reallocating existing resources; others need additional support, and a quarter or more need a 25 percent to 33 percent increase in resources. (p. 43)

School reform is needed in order to turn dropout factories around, but this reform must include stakeholders from all sectors of society. State and federal officials, businesses, civic groups, faith-based organizations, and community colleges and universities can lend their resources and personnel to help improve or rebuild dropout factories. Major cities should take a leading role—for example, by developing and carrying out systemic plans for transforming or replacing these high schools and accounting for graduation and dropout rates (Almeida, Balfanz, & Steinberg, 2009, p. 21). Other reform strategies suggested by Almeida et al. (2009) include the following:

- Develop and carry out systemic plans for transforming or replacing dropout factories.
- Develop innovative schools and programs tailored to helping students recover lost credits and get back on track to graduation.
- Assemble powerful public-private partnerships to redesign low-performing high schools.
- Implement portfolios of new small schools that accelerate students toward graduation and postsecondary success.
- Attract top-notch teachers to more challenging schools.
- Engage key community leaders who have the credibility and skill to rally residents around the need for change.
- Find innovative means, such as partnerships with nearby community colleges, to create viable pathways to college and career training for all students.
- Implement a flexible federal-state-local system for improving high schools in which different levels of government play either lead or supporting roles, depending on the circumstances. (pp. 20–22)

Solving the problems of dropout factories will not happen overnight, as evidenced by the tremendous efforts that have been ongoing for the last decade. Fortunately, those efforts are not in vain: the National Center for Education Statistics (2014) indicated in the Condition of Education report that the status dropout rates decreased from 12 percent in 1990 to 7 percent in 2012. The *status dropout rate*, according to the report, represents the percentage of sixteen-to-twenty-four-year-olds who are not enrolled in school and have not earned a high school credential (either a diploma or an equivalency credential such as a General Educational Development [GED] certificate) (NCES, 2014). While such improvements are commendable, these efforts must continue in order to defeat a culture of failure in some of the lowest-performing schools in the United States. In order to reform dropout factories and improve student achievement, educators need the resources and support structures necessary for bolstering students' confidence in developing their skills and ultimately helping them cultivate a positive self-concept.

Sherwood Thompson

References

Almeida, C., Balfanz, R., & Steinberg, A. (2009). Dropout factories: New strategies states can use. *Education Week*, *29*(15), 20–22.
Balfanz, R. & Legters, N. (2006). Closing "dropout factories." *Education Week*, *25*(42), 42–43.
National Center for Education Statistics. (2014). Status dropout rates. In *The condition of education*. Retrieved from http://nces.ed.gov/programs/coe/indicator_coj.asp.
What is a dropout factory? (2014). *WiseGEEK*. Retrieved from http://www.wisegeek.com/what-is-a-dropout-factory.htm.

DUE PROCESS
Originating from the Anglo-Saxon legal tradition, the term *due process* initially emerged to ensure procedural rights. However, the meaning of the concept today also comprises substantive rights that pave the way for supervision of both state and federal government actions.

The word *due* means "fair, or someone has a right," as indicated in the statement, "Give someone his due." As the name implies, due process is determined in terms of the process rather than the outcome. The main and feasible goal is to ensure a fair process.

As a rule in English Common Law, due process requires that individuals shall not be deprived of life, liberty, or property without notice and an opportunity to defend themselves, which predates written constitutions. The phrase *due process* appears in the U.S. Constitution in the Fifth and Fourteenth Amendments, in which the expression is modified by the term *of law*. The phrase *due process of law* refers to the constitutional guarantees that all legal proceedings will be fair and that one will be given notice of the proceedings and an opportunity to be heard before the government acts to take away one's life, liberty, or property. Furthermore, a law shall not be unreasonable, arbitrary, or capricious.

Legal scholars and judges have used the phrases *due process of law* and *by the law of the land* as equivalent words. The phrase *by the law of the land* was first established in 1215 in the Magna Carta: "No freemen shall be taken or imprisoned or disseized or exiled or in any way destroyed, nor will we go upon him nor send upon him, except by the lawful judgment of his peers or by the law of the land."

This was rendered into statute in 1354: "No man of what state or condition he be, shall be put out of his lands or tenements nor taken, nor disinherited, nor put to death, without he brought to answer by due process of law." This was reaffirmed in 1628 in the Petition of Right: "no freeman may be taken or imprisoned or be disseized of his freehold or liberties, or his free customs, or be outlawed or exiled, or in any manner destroyed, but by the lawful judgment of his peers, or by the law of the land."

Enacted in 1791, the due process clause of the Fifth Amendment affirms that no person shall "be deprived of life, liberty, or property, without due process of law." This emendation restrains the powers of the federal government and applies only to actions by it. The Due Process Clause of the Fourteenth Amendment, passed in 1868, declares, "[N]or shall any State deprive any person of life, liberty, or property, without due process of law." This clause restricts the powers of the states rather than those of the federal government.

As legal tradition applied, constitutional due process can be categorized as *substantive due process* and *procedural due process*. These categories stem from an analysis that is made between two types of law. While substantive law defines and regulates rights, procedural law enforces those rights or seeks redress for their violation. Therefore, the issues, such as privacy and freedom of speech, are dealt with under substantive due process, whereas the issues, such as the right to an attorney and right to be present during testimony, are dealt with under the procedural due process.

The main tenets of procedural due process are the notion that government action that deprives the individual of life, liberty, or property must be congenial with the rule of law. Furthermore, government action must be nonarbitrary; hence, individuals must be put on notice of the reasons for an impending deprivation of life, liberty, or property, and they must be given a fair opportunity to respond to the official written accusations made. In addition to constitutional mandates, the requirements of due process are also observed in civil court procedures (e.g., schools, social security, public employment, and civil suits). Thus, for instance, the court held that the federal government must hold hearings before terminating welfare (*Goldberg v. Kelly*, 397 U.S. 254, 90 S. Ct. 1011, 25 L. Ed. 2d 287 [1970]).

Substantive due process allows the procedures that are established to be challenged based on their effects (this doctrine in the United States was first applied in *Griswold v. Connecticut*, 1965). Procedures will generally fail the substantive due process test in the courts if they are arbitrary, violate constitutional rights, or are unrelated to a legitimate state interest. The substantive due process doctrine has been used by the U.S. Supreme Court to support several rights not specifically guaranteed in the Constitution (e.g., rights to privacy and freedom of choice regarding sexual practices and health).

In special education, the term *due process* refers to the procedures and policies that were established to ensure equal educational opportunities for all children, including children with disabilities. Parents can use these procedures to disagree with the decisions of school district officials concerning special education. Due process in special education requires school officials to inform parents of their rights by written notice, which describes the options of a pre-hearing conference, a formal hearing, and appeals.

Zeki Pamuk

Additional Reading

Hyman, A. T. (2005). The little word "due." *Akron Law Review, 38*(1), 1–51.

Karnes, F. A., Troxclair, D. A., & Marquardt, R. G. (1998). Due process in gifted education. *Roeper Review, 20*(4), 297–301.

Richardson, A. J. (2008). Due process and standard-setting: An analysis of due process in three Canadian accounting and auditing standard-setting bodies. *Journal of Business Ethics, 81*(3), 679–96.

Sandefur, T. (2012). In defense of substantive due process, or the promise of lawful rule. *Harvard Journal of Law and Public Policy, 35*(1), 284–326.

EBONICS

Origin

Ebonics first appears as a scholarly concept when Williams (1975) combined two terms—*ebony* ("black") and *phonics* ("language"). The term was officially defined by Williams (1975) in *Ebonics: The True Language of Black Folks* as the "linguistic and paralinguistic features which on a concentric continuum represent the communicative competence of the West African, Caribbean, and United States slave descendant of African origin" (p. 5). Synonyms for *Ebonics* include African American English, African American Vernacular English (AAVE), Black English, and Black English Vernacular (BEV). Ebonics, however, is the only term that links its origin directly to Africa through the African diaspora. Yancy (2011) notes, "Ebonics is the African American's retention of African languages just as we have retained vestiges of African culture in our literature, food, music, etc." (p. 44).

Language Structure

The structure of Ebonics, when reviewed by linguists, contained the general principles needed to be classified as a true language, including the principles that all languages have dialects, and that languages and dialects are systematic and rule-governed (Rickford, 1997). Examining the verb tenses of Ebonics, one sees that the rules of the language are quite different from Standard English, as illustrated by Rickford (1997):

1. He runnin. (He is running.)
2. He be runnin. (He is usually running.)
3. He be steady runnin. (He is usually running in an intensive, sustained manner.)
4. He bin runnin. (He has been running.)
5. He bin runnin. (He has been running for a long time and still is.) (p. 2)

The difference between example four and example five is the stressing of the word *bin*. In example four, *bin* is not stressed, where it is stressed in example five. Ebonics is also known for its tendency to omit consonants at the ends of words, specifically when the consonant comes after another consonant; however, this does not apply when the consonants are voiceless, as with *st*, or voiced as with *nd* (Rickford, 1997).

Ebonics in Schools

On December 18, 1996, the Oakland Unified School District (OUSD) unanimously resolved that Ebonics was more than the language of Oakland's African American students; it was also a language that was genetically based and more than a simple dialect of Standard English (OUSD, 1996). The resolution caused a firestorm of controversy across the United States. Much of the controversy arose from the concern that Ebonics would be taught in classrooms, which was not the primary intent of the Oakland Unified School District. Their purpose in passing this resolution was to provide a basis for recognizing that African American students in their school district did not speak Standard English as their first language, and therefore, they should be taught Standard English in the same manner and with the same federal funds as other English Language Learners (ELL) in the district. In response to public outcry and negative publicity, the Oakland Unified School District passed a second resolution in January 1997 nullifying the idea that Ebonics was genetically based yet retained that it was not a simple dialect of Standard English, but a language derived from African languages (OUSD, 1997).

The Oakland Unified School District's resolutions brought national attention to Ebonics. As a result, educators across the country began to acknowledge that many of the nation's students spoke Ebonics at home and needed to be taught to speak Standard English at school. This acknowledgment allowed educators to unofficially apply techniques used in teaching ELL students when teaching African American students.

Benterah C. Morton
Kenneth J. Fasching-Varner

References

Oakland Unified School District. (1996). *Synopsis of the adopted policy on standard American English language development.*

Oakland Unified School District. (1997, January 15). *Amended resolution.*

Rickford, J. R. (1997). Suite for ebony and phonics. *Discover, 18*(12), 82–87.

Williams, R. L. (1975). *Ebonics: The true language of black folks.* St. Louis, MO: Robert Williams and Associates.

Yancy, G. (2011). The scholar who coined the term *Ebonics*: A conversation with Dr. Robert L. Williams. *Journal of Language, Identity, & Education, 10*(1), 41–51. doi: 10.1080/15348458.2011.539967

THE ECONOMIC AND SOCIAL COUNCIL OF THE UNITED NATIONS (ECOSOC)

ECOSOC and Social Justice

Social justice has been defined as a form of justice with social dimensions: "inspiring, working with, and organizing others" and "primarily involv(ing) the good of others" (Novak, 2000). Implying as it does the work of civil society rather than that of government, social justice is a prominent agendum of the world's largest nongovernmental organization (NGO), the United Nations (UN), as well as its Economic and Social Council (ECOSOC), one of the five suborganizations (or "organs") of the UN System (the others being the General Assembly (GA), the Security Council, the Secretariat, and the International Court of Justice).

The "International Covenant on Economic, Social and Cultural Rights," adopted by a resolution of the GA in 1966, went into force in 1976 (OHCHR, n.d.). Although the term *social justice* is not contained in this document, many of the social dimensions associated with social justice are explicitly stated, among them: equal rights of women and men, the right to work and to form trade unions, and the rights to social security, food, clothing, housing, physical and mental health, and education. The covenant assigns ECOSOC responsibilities for receiving reports relating to human rights from States Parties (the signatories of the covenant) as well as from UN agencies and for making reports and recommendations to the GA and the other three UN suborganizations. Beyond that, this international covenant gives ECOSOC the central role in monitoring its implementation, a task ECOSOC delegated by resolution in 1985 to the UN Committee on Economic, Social and Cultural Rights (CESCR, n.d.).

In 2007, the GA adopted Resolution 62/10, "World Day of Social Justice," calling for a symbolic observance of social justice on the twentieth day of every February, recognizing "that broad-based and sustained economic growth in the context of sustainable development is necessary to sustain social development and social justice" and "the need to consolidate further the efforts of the international community in poverty eradication and in promoting full employment and decent work, gender equality and access to social well-being and justice for all" (United Nations General Assembly, 2007). The first observance of the World Day of Social Justice was in 2009. In his message, the Secretary-General (SG) of the UN said, "We advance social justice when we remove barriers that people face because of gender, age, race, ethnicity, religion, culture or disability," and went on to say, "The observance is meant to underscore the importance of social justice as an ethical imperative that should guide all our work" (SG/SM/12106 OBV/764 SOC/4755). The following year, the message of the SG included reference to the Millennium Development Goals (MDGs) as a "key means of bringing social justice and development together to benefit the poorest and most vulnerable" (SG/SM/12749 OBV852 SOC 4764).

The 2011 message included reference to a report from the UN International Labor Organization (ILO, a Specialized Agency of ECOSOC, like, e.g., the World Health Organization [WHO], the UN Educational, Scientific, and Cultural Organization [UNESCO], and the International Monetary Fund [IMF] of the World Bank) and the UN Development Program (UNDP, a joint Program of ECOSOC and the GA) about social protection policies "to reduce inequality and social exclusion for achievement of the MDGs" as well as the observation that "the pursuit of social justice is crucial to maximizing the potential for growth with equity and minimizing the risks of social unrest" (SG/SM 13403 OBV/962 SOC/4775).

The 2012 message for the World Day of Social Justice says, "For the UN, the pursuit of social justice for all is at the core of our global mission to promote development and human dignity" and gives the ILO's "Declaration on Social Justice for a Fair Globalization" as "just one recent example of the UN system's commitment to social justice" (SG/SM/14111 OBV/1071 SOC/4795).

The 2008 ILO Declaration acknowledged the

> universal aspiration for social justice, to reach full employment, to ensure the sustainability of open societies and the global economy, to achieve social cohesion and to combat poverty and rising inequalities; Convinced that the International Labor Organization has a key role to play in helping to promote and achieve progress and social justice, in a constantly changing environment: . . . provides the ILO with the responsibility to examine and consider all international economic and financial policies in the light of the fundamental objective of social justice. (ILO, 2008, p. 6)

The MDGs, initiated by the UN Millennium Declaration adopted by the GA in 2000 (United Nations, 2000), delineate eight goals and quantified targets for their achievement by 2015: *eradicate extreme poverty and hunger* by reducing by half between 1990 and 2015 both the proportion of people with income less than $1 per day and the proportion of people suffering from hunger; *achieve universal primary education* by insuring that boys and girls everywhere complete primary school; *promote gender equality and empower women* by eliminating the gender-based disparity in primary and secondary education by 2005 and at all levels by 2015; *reduce child mortality* by reducing the mortality rate of children under five by two-thirds between 1990 and 2015; *improve maternal health* by reducing the maternal mortality ratio by three-quarters between 1990 and 2015 and achieving universal access to reproductive health by 2015; *combat HIV/AIDS, malaria, and other diseases* by halting

and reversing their spread and achieving by 2010 universal access to treatment for HIV/AIDS for everyone that needs it; *ensure environmental sustainability* by achieving a significant reduction in the rate of loss of biodiversity by 2010, integrating sustainable development principles into country policies and programs, and reverse environmental resource losses, reducing by half the proportion of the population without sustainable access to safe drinking water and basic sanitation, and achieving significant improvement in the lives of at least one hundred million slum dwellers by 2020; *develop a global partnership for development* through an open, rule-based, predictable, nondiscriminatory trading and financial system, addressing the special needs of least developed, landlocked, and small island countries and developing states, dealing comprehensively with developing countries' debt, providing access to affordable, essential drugs in developing countries in cooperation with pharmaceutical companies, and making Internet and communication technologies available in cooperation with the private sector. New commitments from governments, the private sector, and NGOs to meet the MDGs totaled $56 billion by 2010 (United Nations, 2000).

The concern of ECOSOC for social justice occurs within this historical and organizational context. ECOSOC is endowed with approximately 70 percent of the financial and human resources of the UN System (ECOSOC, n.d.). Its fifty-four member governments are elected for three-year terms by the GA (fourteen from African States, eleven from Asian States, six to Eastern European States, ten from Latin American and Caribbean States, and thirteen from Western European and other States). Each year ECOSOC convenes a month-long session in July, alternating between New York Headquarters and Geneva. This session is preceded by preparatory meetings and discussions with civil society members throughout the year, which include the annual sessions of the ECOSOC Commission on Social Development (CSocD) and the ECOSOC Commission on the Status of Women (CSW).

Although the functions of ECOSOC were stated in the UN Charter, two new functions were added at the 2005 World Summit, endorsed by the GA in 2006 and implemented in 2008. These functions, which are intended to make ECOSOC a stronger UN organ, are the biennial Development Cooperation Forum (DCF) and the Annual Ministerial Review (AMR). The DCF was established to increase coherence in international development policies. The AMR was established to monitor progress toward achieving internationally agreed development goals (IADGs), including the MDGs (ECOSOC, n.d.).

Themes of the annual ECOSOC substantive sessions correspond to the titles of the AMR for that year. The theme of the 2012 ECOSOC substantive session of the High-Level Segment (with the participation of national cabinet ministers and heads of international agencies) was "promoting productive capacity, employment and decent work to eradicate poverty in the context of inclusive, sustainable and equitable growth at all levels for achieving the MDGs."

The Humanitarian Affairs Segment of the 2012 ECOSOC session included panel discussions on humanitarian coordination and assistance. Among the resolutions passed at the end of the 2012 ECOSOC session are: "United Nations system-wide coherence on tobacco control," "Science and technology for development," "Mainstreaming disability in the development agenda," "Standard Minimum Rules for the Treatment of Prisoners," "Strengthening the rule of law and the reform of criminal justice institutions, particularly in the areas related to the UN system-wide approach to fighting transnational organized crime and drug trafficking," "United Nations Principles and Guidelines on Access to Legal Aid in Criminal Justice Systems," "Promoting efforts to eliminate violence against migrants, migrant workers and their families," "Improving the quality and availability of statistics on crime and criminal justice for policy development," "Genetic privacy and non-discrimination," "Economic and social repercussions of the Israeli occupation on the living conditions of the Palestinian people in the Occupied Palestinian territory, including East Jerusalem, and the Arab population in the occupied Syrian Golan," "Mainstreaming a gender perspective into all policies and programs in the UN system" (ECOSOC, n.d.).

The theme of the 2013 Ministerial Review is "science, technology and innovation (STI) and culture for sustainable development and the MDGs." This theme emphasizes the place of STI in relation to the MDGs, which includes increasing productivity and the creation of decent work, promoting health, achieving food security, promoting renewable energy to address energy-related poverty and climate change, and considering effects on countries, especially the Least Developed Countries (LDCs), of intellectual property policies. ECOSOC will coordinate the participation of the UN programs, funds, and specialized agencies (ECOSOC, n.d.).

Other recent annual ECOSOC substantive sessions also have had themes directly related to the MDGs as well as to IADGs resulting from UN conferences and summits, for example, "Implementing the internationally agreed goals and commitments in regard to education" (2011), "Implementing the internationally agreed goals and commitments in regard to gender equality and empowerment of women" (2010), "Implementing the internationally agreed goals and commitments in regard to global public health" (2009), and "Implementing the internationally agreed goals and commitments in regard to sustainable development" (2008) (ECOSOC, n.d.). Each theme reflects one or more dimensions of social justice as implied by the MDGs.

Civil society organizations seeking ECOSOC accreditation are screened by the NGO Branch of the Department of Economic and Social Affairs (DESA) of the UN Secretariat. NGOs seeking ECOSOC accreditation for consultative status apply to the ECOSOC Committee on NGOs, which makes a recommendation to ECOSOC. The 3,536 NGOs in consultative status with ECOSOC can participate in the annual sessions of ECOSOC as well as its regional commissions and functional commissions on Population and Development, Social Development, Status of Women, Narcotic Drugs, Crime Prevention and Criminal Justice, Science and Technology for Development, Sustainable Development, and the Statistical Commission. NGOs participate actively by making oral or written interventions at meetings, by organizing or attending parallel side events that occur during the annual sessions of ECOSOC and its commissions, by attending official meetings as Observers, and by participating in panel discussions. NGOs in consultative status with ECOSOC are understood to be of potential value to ECOSOC through their expertise in their region or field of knowledge or practice. They also are of assistance to ECOSOC in the monitoring and implementation of international agreements. NGOs have opportunities to advocate on behalf of their own agendas in ways that can influence the work of ECOSOC and its commissions (UN, 2011).

Through its mandate and thematic agenda; through its existence and activities with Member States, functional and regional UN commissions, and specialized agencies; through its work with the other UN organs and their subsidiaries, programs, funds, departments, and offices; through its involvement with the NGOs in consultative status with ECOSOC; and through its major role in monitoring targets of the MDGs, ECOSOC is both implicitly and explicitly in pursuit of a form of justice with social dimensions. Through its presence and example in the world, ECOSOC helps define social justice.

Brent Mack Shea

References

International Labor Organization (ILO). (2008). *ILO declaration on social justice for a fair globalization.* Retrieved from http://www.ilo.org/global/topics/economic-and-social-development/globalization/WCMS_099766/lang--en/index.htm.

Novak, M. (2000). Defining social justice. *First Things, 108,* 11–13. Retrieved from http://www.calculemus.org/lect/FilozGosp04-05/novak.html.

Office of the United Nations High Commissioner for Human Rights (OHCHR). (n.d.). *International covenant on economic, social and cultural rights.* Retrieved from http://www.ohchr.org/EN/ProfessionalInterest/Pages/CESCR.aspx.

United Nations (UN). (2000). *Millennium development goals.* Retrieved from http://www.un.org/millenniumgoals/bkgd.shtml.

United Nations (UN). (2011). *Working with ECOSOC: An NGOs guide to consultative status.* Retrieved from http://www.csonet.org/content/documents/Brochure.pdf.

United Nations Committee on Economic, Social and Cultural Rights (CESCR). (n.d.). *Monitoring the economic, social and cultural rights.* Retrieved from http://www2.ohchr.org/english/bodies/cescr/.

United Nations Department of Economic and Social Affairs. (n.d.). *NGO branch.* Retrieved from http://csonet.org/.

United Nations Economic and Social Council (ECOSOC). (n.d.). *About ECOSOC.* Retrieved from http://www.un.org/en/ecosoc/about/index.shtml.

United Nations Economic and Social Council (ECOSOC). (n.d.). *Mandate.* Retrieved from http://www.un.org/en/ecosoc/newfunct/.

United Nations Economic and Social Council (ECOSOC). (n.d.). *2012 ECOSOC resolutions.* Retrieved from http://www.un.org/en/ecosoc/docs/res2012.asp.

United Nations Economic and Social Council (ECOSOC). (n.d.). *2013 annual ministerial review.* Retrieved from http://www.un.org/en/ecosoc/newfunct/amr2013/shtml.

United Nations Economic and Social Council (ECOSOC). (n.d.). *Substantive sessions.* Retrieved from http://www.un.org/en/ecosoc/about/substantive.shtml.

United Nations General Assembly. (2007). *Resolution 62/10 world day of justice.* Retrieved from http://www.un.org/ga/search/view_doc.asp?symbol=A/RES/62/10&Lang=E.

ECONOMIC JUSTICE

Economic Justice: Who Gets Paid and Who Pays?
"To be poor in the United States today is to be always at risk, the object of scorn and shame" (hooks, 2000, p. 45). The upper classes in America have established a set of cultural guidelines that the rest of society follows. In order to avoid being shamed, or treated as if they are poor, Americans engage in conspicuous consumption and a race to have it all—money, toys, cars, and vacations. But control over the economy and cultural values should not be in the hands of the richest members of society (Brouwer, 2000). Economic justice asks us to examine our cultural values in relation to access to resources and attempts to provide equity in resources for all members of society.

In order to be successful, a capitalistic system needs excess laborers who are willing to work at competitive wages and who can compete for jobs. Capitalism requires a class system that includes the poor working to aid the rich in becoming richer. "Wages have been falling even though labor productivity continues to rise and the workforce is much better educated than it was in the past" (Brouwer, 2000, p. 387). Even in the face of increased access to education and job training, economic justice is not realized. When excess laborers compete for the available jobs, wages fall as employers attempt to pay as little as possible to their workforce. Economic justice requires not only that there be enough jobs that pay a living wage for all who wish to work, but that access and education is available for all members of society. Creating equality in pay across race, class, and sex lines is important, but more important is equitable access to resources in order to achieve economic freedom.

The myth of meritocracy, reinforced by the mass media and popular culture, espouses the capitalistic values of America. If one works hard, one will be rewarded with riches. Yet we know this to be untrue. Hard work and effort does not necessarily result in wealth. We also know that one does not succeed alone—often the life situation one was born into is the most powerful indicator of future economic success. Identifiable, categorical differences exist among people, and these differences strongly influence one's future income and class status (Lareau, 2003). In order to begin to have economic justice, we must first recognize the role that social structure and social class positioning plays in shaping individual and collective lives that, in turn, shapes the ability of individuals to transition across class and economic lines. Similar to social justice, in order for economic justice to be realized, the environmental conditions in which one is born must be changed to be as equitable as possible (Barry, 2005). The cultural practices of families and social class positioning provide children with a starting point for long-term financial success. When the cultural practices that are taught at home are not valued by society at large, it makes it more difficult for individuals to navigate government and employer institutions. The result is a permanent class system based on economic power and freedom that permeates American society.

Poverty and class positioning is not controlled by the individual and is not reflective of individual morals and effort (Langston, 2000). In an effort to increase the common good for all, and the individual life situations of future generations, economic justice addresses a variety of aspects related to access to resources. Availability of jobs, paying a living wage, and equal wages for equal work are cornerstones of the economic justice movement. Sweat equity, work for trade, and bartering systems also work to increase one's purchasing power and access to resources. Economics is often discussed as earnings from income, but unearned incomes, taxes paid, welfare benefits received, assets held, education, and access all combine to form one's "bank" of assets (Barry, 2005). The efforts made by economic justice work, to close the gap between rich and poor and to reduce the influence of class, benefits economic success (Adams, 2000). A recognition and celebration of a variety of cultural norms across class lines and providing access to education, jobs, and social power is the social responsibility of those who work toward economic justice. A nation's economy should not be based on the lower classes fighting for low-paying jobs but on the intellectual capabilities of a nation to succeed for the common good of all members of society. The poor should not be working to increase the wealth of the rich; they should be working to provide a better future for themselves and their children. In that way, we all can achieve the American Dream.

Laurel P. Richmond

References

Adams, M. (2000). Classism. In M. Adams, W. J. Blumenfled, C. R. Castaneda, H. W. Hackman, M. L. Peters, & X. Zuniga (Eds.), *Readings for diversity and social justice: An anthology on racism, heterosexism, ableisim, and classism* (pp. 379–82). New York: Routledge.

Barry, B. (2005). *Why social justice matters.* Malden, MA: Polity Press.

Brouwer, S. (2000). Sharing the pie. In M. Adams, W. J. Blumenfled, C. R. Castaneda, H. W. Hackman, M. L. Peters, & X. Zuniga (Eds.), *Readings for diversity and social justice: An anthology on racism, heterosexism, ableism, and classism* (pp. 382–96). New York: Routledge.

hooks, b. (2000). *Where we stand: Class matters.* New York: Routledge.

Langston, D. (2000). Tired of playing Monopoly? In M. Adams, W. J. Blumenfled, C. R. Castaneda, H. W. Hackman, M. L. Peters, & X. Zuniga (Eds.), *Readings for diversity and social justice: An anthology on racism, heterosexism, ableisim, and classism* (pp. 397–402). New York: Routledge.

Lareau, A. (2003). *Unequal childhoods: Class, race and family life.* Berkeley, CA: University of California Press.

ECONOMIC REDISTRIBUTION

Economic Redistribution: The Ignored Legacy of the 1960s Civil Rights Movement

Racial inequality is promulgated as the main focus of the civil rights movement of the 1960s. American civic culture provides continuous substantiation of the movement by referring to it as black people's courage to resist often violent oppression and decades of racial discrimination. Missing from much of the analysis is a discussion regarding the movement's focus on economic justice (Wright, 2013). Upon further examination, even those rare discussions regarding economic justice seem to be relegated to demands for businesses to employ black workers who had systematically been locked out of the labor market (Wright, 2013). However, in many ways, the struggle of the 1960s eventually became a conquest for economic redistribution.

Dr. Martin Luther King Jr., in his pursuit of a beloved society, strongly advocated for wealth redistribution. In the post–"I Have a Dream" era, King moved further to the left on issues of political, social, and economic justice. He would eventually shift his focus to the Poor People's Campaign, which he saw as a means of gaining genuine equality for people from diverse, economically depressed backgrounds (Franklin, 1968). It was his belief that full citizenship would never be acquired if economic security was not a main focus of the struggle and a priority for the society.

In one of his later speeches, King proclaimed, "We are dealing with issues that cannot be solved without the nation spending billions of dollars and undergoing a radical redistribution of economic power" (King, 1967). The idea of redistributive economic power, with the announcement of the Poor People's Campaign, was met with both reception and critique. On one level it mobilized poor and working-class people from varied backgrounds to engage in mass resistance regarding economic disparities, which had never been done in the twentieth century. However, this mobilization threatened America's economic and political status quo. Demanding a sweeping restructuring of America's political economy posed a tremendous threat to the capitalist elite.

Andre P. Stevenson

References

Franklin, B. (1968, May 13). 5,000 open poor people's campaign in Washington. *New York Times.*

King, M. (1967, November 29). Address to workshop on civil disobedience at SCLC staff retreat. Speech.

Wright, G. (2006). The economics of the civil rights revolution. Retrieved from http://economics.yale.edu/sites/default/files/files/Workshops-Seminars/Economic-History/wright-061206.pdf.

Wright, G. (2013). The stunning economic impact of the civil rights movement. *Bloomberg Review.* Editorial.

EDUCATION IN APPALACHIA

The Primary inequality in Appalachia lies in the ownership and control of its vast resources. Appalachia and her people are at once wealthy and impoverished; independent and dominated. No single theme permeates, as this does, all other issues.

—John Gaventa (1978)

Throughout history, a chasm has existed between the Appalachian region and the rest of the country with respect to the provision of and appreciation for quality education. Many factors contribute to this phenomenon. As John Gaventa (1978) noted, much of academic literature addresses either the "culture or the sociology of the grassroots of the region" or the "perspective of the dominant corporate and government institutions about the region" (p. 322). Historically, there has been little emphasis on the interrelationship of these factors and how the population is affected as a result. This lack of analysis of the systems underlying and supporting the cultural status quo of the region has contributed to its continued economic, educational, and social stagnation.

Conversely, throughout most of the country, the relationship between economic opportunity and education has been an intrinsic philosophy supporting political decision making, economic development, and the allocation of resources for quality education. Hence, "the concern with educational attainment is also in part a concern for markets and local quality of life" (Haaga, 2004, p. 3). The complex problems facing Appalachia are nothing new to civic leaders, educators, and policymakers who have been working to address these issues for decades.

Throughout the twentieth century, missionaries from the north came to the region to establish settlement schools to provide educational opportunities to the geographically isolated people of Southeastern Kentucky. Local settlement schools were often the only place remote mountain people could obtain a quality education. The Hindman Settlement School, established in 1902, became a model for rural settlement schools throughout the country as a means for creating regional social change through education, health care, and social services (Hindman Settlement School, 2013).

The founders of the settlement schools were part of a national political and social movement called Progressivism that began in the 1890s and continued until World War I. According to Kiffmeyer (2008):

> Katherine Pettit and May Stone founded settlement schools [in the region]. Modeled after their urban counterparts, including Hull House in Chicago, these turn-of-the-century mountain schools instructed students in proper living as well as academic subjects. Like their 1960s descendants, reformers designed these efforts to lift Appalachians out of their depressed conditions. (p. 7)

Other notable members of the Progressive movement who came into the Appalachian region of Southeast Kentucky were Alice Spencer Geddes Lloyd and June Buchanan. Upon her arrival, Alice Spencer Geddes Lloyd recognized that "Eastern Kentucky was sorely lacking in educational opportunities" (Alice Lloyd College, 2012).

This movement resulted in the establishment of Alice Lloyd College in 1923 with the focus of creating social change and educating the leaders that Alice Spencer Geddes Lloyd believed were already there (Alice Lloyd College, 2012). In addition, many federal, state, and local school districts have developed collaborative partnerships to address the issue. Grants, directed specifically at promoting education

in Appalachia, were established to help alleviate the problem. These efforts may have been slightly more successful, but only marginally so. According to Starnes (2006):

> These schools focused on educating children and creating strong communities within the isolated hollows where they were located, and—at least according to my mother, who sent my four oldest siblings to school at Caney Creek and regarded the outsiders with great Skepticism— on "'civilizing'" the inhabitants. (p. 330)

The resistance of mountain people, to outside influence such as this, ignited the myth that mountain people are inherently ignorant, stubborn, and lazy—a belief that they are either willfully resistant or genetically incapable of learning. Such views are not only inaccurate but are also counterproductive. Further, they fail to recognize the strength and dedication that mountain people have toward their families and homeland. "Moonshiners had been so interested in educating their children that they donated the land and cut the logs and pounded the nails that built the first school building" (Starnes, 2006, p. 331). When one understands that the Appalachians' relationship to the land is utterly sanguine, one begins to understand the significance of this gift. Further reports from the period illustrate the level of dedication the mountain people have toward the education of their children. An anecdotal record of the Kingdom Come School further chronicled:

> Frank Cornett transformed his old pickup truck into a school bus and drove along creekbeds into the narrow slits in the mountains to bring the children to school. When it rained, the creekbeds filled with water, and the children had to stay with families near the school. Miss Anne Parrish, one of the school's first teachers, reports, "Some . . . students left before daybreak and returned home after dark . . . [walking] . . . through rain, snow, and mud . . . [often without] adequate clothing to protect them." (Starnes, 2006, p. 331)

There have also been various movements from nonprofit organizations with the mission of promoting the importance of quality education in the Appalachian region. Despite these efforts, the region is still lacking in educational achievement.

According to Williams (2002),

Most of the experts and bureaucrats who came from Washington and elsewhere to fix the region's problems beginning in the 1960s . . . were perceived as outsiders who didn't know what they were talking about but were more than willing to tell people from the mountains what to do and how they should do it. (p. 14)

Despite the efforts of reformers, conditions remain out of step with mainstream America. This is apparent on common measures of educational achievement. Appalachia has consistently been significantly below state and national averages when it comes to the percentage of high school and college graduates. A study conducted by the Appalachian Regional Commission (ARC) showed that 37.5 percent of Kentuckians living in the Appalachian Region, as defined by the ARC, did not have a high school diploma. By comparison, only 21.3 percent of Kentuckians living outside the Appalachian region did not have a high school diploma (Haaga, 2004, p. 10). Further, only 10.5 percent of Kentuckians living in Appalachia had college degrees, compared to 19.8 percent of citizens living outside the region (p. 10).

With the exception of New York and Pennsylvania, this is a consistent pattern in all states with Appalachian counties. The Appalachian Region 2014–2015 Kentucky County Profile reports that graduate and professional degrees are also less prevalent in Kentucky, with only 5.7 percent of the population holding these degrees (Kentucky Center for Education & Workforce Statistics, 2014). This is compared to 8.5 percent that have graduate and have professional degrees in the state of Kentucky and 10.6 percent in the United States (Kentucky Center for Education & Workforce Statistics, 2014).

Although education is a problem throughout Appalachia, it is not a reflection of the entire region as a whole. Haaga (2004) states that counties with "high levels of educational attainment are scattered around the region, with concentrations around metropolitan Atlanta and along a belt leading from eastern Tennessee and Western North Carolina up Interstate 81" (p. 6).

The ARC divides the region into three different subregions: northern, central, and southern Appalachian. The Central Appalachian region, which contains the southeastern counties of Kentucky, can be described as having some of the more distressed counties, which continually lag behind in educational achievement. According to Haaga (2004), "The increase in Appalachia in the percentage of college graduates was somewhat greater in Southern Appalachia than in Central or Northern Appalachia. In 2000, Central Appalachia had less than half the national proportion of college graduates" (p. 4). These numbers are especially high in the coalfield region of Southeastern Kentucky. This region, historically plagued by poverty and isolation, is an area where the majority of citizens simply do not see the need for an education. The few jobs that are available to the area are mostly blue-collar, manual-labor jobs that rely more on training and hard work than formal higher education. Furthermore, the isolation of the area has made it hard to establish quality, financially stable educational institutions. Though progress has been made throughout the decades to help heighten the educational standards in Eastern Kentucky, they are still behind the national trends.

Southeastern Kentucky trails a majority of the state and nation in test scores. In 2008, Kentucky juniors' average composite score on the ACT was 18.3 compared with a national average test score of 21.1 (Kentucky Department of Education, 2008). Furthermore, average school attendance in the Appalachian region is consistently four percentage points lower than county averages statewide. Despite an influx of state and federal grants to assist the region, the trends in education achievement persist. Although some positive measurable outcomes have been observed recently, the region is far from the national average in almost every statistical category. According to the literature, these trends continue to follow a social norm that has been prevalent in Appalachia for centuries. According to Haaga (2004), "Family environment, limited expectations for educational success, not counteracted by encouragement from teachers and other early mentors can be as great an impediment as the direct and opportunity costs of college attendance" (pp. 5–6). A predominant theory of explanation is that education is not viewed as a necessary condition to be successful in the region. As a result, this viewpoint contends, the trends in education have led to a cultural mind-set that is widely accepted across the region. This viewpoint, however, does not fully explain the reasons for the disparity.

Given the magnitude and longevity of the effort to reform Appalachia, particularly in the area of education, deeper analysis of the reasons for its failure is needed. An understanding of the political, social, and cultural factors affecting reform efforts is essential. Initial efforts toward reform espoused a paternalistic philosophy that viewed Appalachian people and their culture as comparatively inferior to mainstream America. Kiffmeyer (2008) states, "Using labels such as *contemporary ancestors* and *a strange land and peculiar people*, reformers, from William Goodell Frost, the president of Berea College at the turn into the twentieth century, to the settlement schools' teachers, described a 'culture of poverty' that existed in the mountains" (p. 7). Such viewpoints focused on what were viewed as inherently flawed differences and failed to recognize and respect the cultural values, norms, and strengths of Appalachians. Kiffmeyer continues:

> According to this explanation, mountaineer lifestyles more closely resembled those of generations past, typified as they were by sparsely settled communities, subsistence farming, a Calvinistic sense of fatalism, and, most important, a value system that was incongruent with modern, urban standards. (p. 7)

While most mainstream Americans would likely reject attempts to change their own social systems, the country as a whole has not recognized why Appalachians, quite naturally, would do the same. Instead, mountain people are exploited in the media, are viewed as inferior, and are blamed for their own demise. Kiffmeyer (2008) points out that the belief has been that "the mountaineers were poor because they had no education, and, if they failed to get an education, it was their own fault that they remained poor. Questions concerning the economic or political environment do not enter into this simplified analysis" (p. 209).

When federal and state reform began to defund smaller rural schools in favor of the more economically viable consolidated schools, again, mountain people resisted. Starnes (2006) gives an example:

"'The teachers in the consolidated schools don't know our kids or our community,' a young mother [from Linefork] said, remembering her own experience as a student in a consolidated high school. 'And when they closed our high school, most of the kids dropped out'" (p. 331) The mountain people feel disconnected from consolidated schools because they are often farther away from their homes than smaller community schools and they do not know the teachers and administrators. They do not feel that their values and culture are reflected in the curriculum or are appreciated by teachers and administrators in the consolidated schools. They doubt the effectiveness, and there is some research to support their concerns. According to Starnes (2006), "When WestEd, one of the six federally funded regional educational labs, analyzed 'gold-standard' data on school size, their findings were almost identical to the points made by the Linefork citizens that day" (p. 331).

While it is likely that efforts to reform education in Appalachia will continue, the efficacy of those initiatives will most likely depend upon efforts to truly understand, value, and infuse culturally responsive ideology and inclusive practices into decision making at all levels.

Roger Cleveland
Corlia Logsdon

References

Alice Lloyd College. (2012). *Our history*. Retrieved from http://www.alc.edu/about-us/our-history/.

Gaventa, J. (1978). Inequality and the Appalachian studies industry. *Appalachian Journal*, 5(3), 322–29.

Haaga, J. (2004). Educational attainment in Appalachia. *Demographic and Socioeconomic Change in Appalachia*, 1, 3–14.

Hindman Settlement School. (2013). *About us*. Retrieved from http://www.hindmansettlement.org/about-us.

Kentucky Center for Education & Workforce Statistics. (2014). Appalachian region: 2014–2015 Kentucky county profile. Retrieved from http://kcews.ky.gov/(X(1)A(u6gWA3FEzwEkAAAANjA2NjQxNjYtNz-YwZC00N2ZiLTlhNDUtYWRlOTE2Yjc2ODI1n6jTuq7YytDMd2YrTqeXXivru-cl55LltRyRjZ8JmXg1))/Reports/CountyProfile/CPG_201415_ARprofile.pdf.

Kentucky Department of Education. (2008). *School report cards*. Retrieved from www.education.ky.gov.

Kiffmeyer, T. (2008). *Reformers to radicals: The Appalachian volunteers and the war on poverty*. Lexington, KY: University Press of Kentucky.

Starnes, B. (2006). On a trip to Kingdom Come. *Phi Delta Kappan, 88*(4), 330–31.

Williams, J. A. (2002). *Appalachia: A history*. Chapel Hill, NC: University of North Carolina Press.

EDUCATIONAL ATTAINMENT

Still Separate, Still Unequal: Discussions of Racial Composition, School Funding, and Educational Attainment

May 17, 2014, marks the sixtieth anniversary of the historically significant U.S. Supreme Court (USSC) case decision of *Brown v. the Board of Education* (1954). The ruling of *Brown v. the Board of Education* deemed racially segregated schools unequal and thus segregation within schools unconstitutional. Evidence suggests that gains achieved via court-mandated desegregation policies have regressed (Orfield & Lee, 2004). To illustrate, Thompson Dorsey (2013) states, "In other words, Black and Latino students are more segregated today in the 21st century than they were in the late 1960s during the Civil Rights Movement and prior to the implementation of desegregation plans in school districts across the country" (p. 534). Even though the United States is becoming increasingly racially diverse, today's minority students are less exposed to whites and are increasingly isolated relative to several decades ago (Fiel, 2013).

Residential Segregation: A Cause for Concern

While de jure segregation has ended, residential segregation, specifically along racial and class lines, perpetuates inequalities within the educational system. Income and socioeconomic status are significant indicators of where families live, a factor that directly relates to—and often dictates—the school district their children will attend. Neighborhoods affect the amount of funding for school districts through financial systems that rely on property taxes for district resources. Consequently, schools within lower-income communities receive less funding and fewer resources (Condron & Roscigno, 2003). To demonstrate, Condron and Roscigno (2003) state

that "because American schools are funded primarily by local property taxes, the wealthiest districts spend as much as three times the per-pupil amount of the most economically disadvantaged districts" (p. 18). The Census Bureau reports that almost 40 percent of school-district funding derives from local sources, such as property taxes (Dixon, 2013).

School funding is directly associated with school resources; indeed, researchers have concluded that academic performance improves for students in school districts that spend more on resources (Condron & Roscigno, 2003). Schools with more funding are able to provide more resources that aid in the students' experiences and opportunities in school. Resources include, but are not limited to, teacher salaries, curriculum materials, textbooks, building expenses, transportation, and extracurricular activities. These resources are imperative to learning and the overall educational environment. Research has shown that districts in lower-income communities and schools with disproportionate amounts of minority students lack imperative resources in comparison to wealthier school districts (Condron & Roscigno 2003; Roscigno, Tomaskovic-Devey, & Crowley, 2006).

The Impact of Disproportionate Funding on Educational Attainment

Thus far we have established that local sources provide a significant portion of school funding. Consequently, an unequal distribution of funding results in disparate funding and, by extension, offers inadequate resources for some students, even those within the same district. This problem warrants attention because evidence suggests that school resources are positively related to improved student achievement and attainment (Archibald, 2006).

A closer look at recent educational attainment statistics reveals stark differences between white and black students. Figure E.1 illustrates that whites (at a rate of 18.9 percent) are more than twice as likely to obtain a bachelor's degree as blacks (at a rate of 8.9 percent). Similarly, whites are significantly more likely (10.5 percent) than blacks (4.6 percent) to complete a graduate level or professional degree. This figure uses data from the 2008 General Social Survey (GSS). The GSS is a national, random sample survey conducted in the United States.

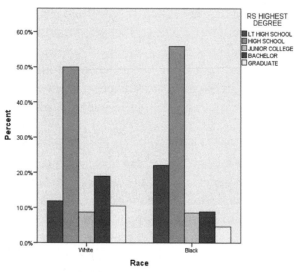

Figure E.1 Educational Attainment by Race

In other words, this analysis illustrates that blacks are less likely to finish high school and thus less likely to attain a bachelor's or graduate degree when compared to white students.

Implications

Public school districts in the United States are partially funded by neighborhood property taxes. Communities that house disproportionate amounts of renters and/or lower-valued homes result in funding inequality within school districts. Children that attend schools in resource-deprived districts are more likely to lack essential resources that may help them complete high school and college.

The early successes of a good education can anticipate the job type and salary an individual can obtain in adulthood. This is problematic because research concludes that educational attainment is one of the most significant social factors in predicting lifetime earnings. According to the U.S. Census Bureau, a person who has earned a bachelor's degree can expect to earn approximately $1 million more than a high school graduate over the course of a lifetime (Julian, 2012).

A good education benefits students well beyond the classroom. While education can lead to individual success, existing inequalities in public education can be detrimental to students in disadvantaged school districts.

Jacqueline Coffey
Kamesha Spates

References

Archibald, S. (2006). Narrowing in on educational resources that do affect student achievement. *Peabody Journal of Education, 81*(4), 23–42.

Condron, D. J. & Roscigno, V. J. (2003). Disparities within: Unequal spending and achievement in an urban school district. *Sociology of Education, 76*(1), 18–36.

Dixon, M. (2013, May). *Public education finances: 2011.* Retrieved from http://www.census.gov/govs/school/.

Fiel, J. E. (2013). Decomposing school resegregation: Social closure, racial imbalance, and racial isolation. *American Sociological Review, 78*(5), 828–48. doi: 10.1177/0003122413496252

Julian, T. (2012). Work-life earnings by field of degree and occupation for people with a bachelor's degree: 2011 (pp. 1–4). *American Community Survey Briefs.* U.S. Census Bureau.

National Opinion Research Center. (2008). *General social survey (GSS).* The National Data Program for the Sciences.

Orfield, G. & Lee, C. (2004). Brown at 50: King's dream or Plessy's nightmare? *Civil Rights Project.* Los Angeles, CA: Havard University.

Roscigno, V. J., Tomaskovic-Devey, D., & Crowley, M. (2006). Education and the inequalities of place. *Social Forces, 84*(4), 2121–45.

Thompson Dorsey, D. N. (2013). Segregation 2.0: The new generation of school segregation in the 21st century. *Education and Urban Society, 45*(5), 533–47. doi: 10.1177/0013124513486287

EGOCENTRISM

Egocentrism in Self and Society

While the term *ego* originates from psychoanalysis, it is typically used to refer to a person's sense of self-importance—for example, "He has a big ego; he cares only about himself." Similarly, *egocentrism* refers to a state of thinking of oneself, only without regard to the feelings or desires of others. People who are egocentric consider themselves and their beliefs or interests to be the most important or valid and have difficulty experiencing empathy.

Egocentrism has a direct impact on diversity and social justice when leaders of a community make decisions based on ego or self-interest rather than for the common good or collective interests of community members, concentrating power and exacerbating inequalities. When combined with inequitable campaign finance structures, competitive economic systems such as capitalism or neo-liberalism, and a lack of accountability measures to prevent decisions with known conflicts of interest, leadership or governance that is egocentric can have particularly deleterious effects on community members, especially those from already marginalized groups. Entire discourses have been contrived (e.g., meritocracy, equal opportunity) to mask these harmful effects and create a false sense of democracy and equality.

One form of critique of egocentrism is on its narrow focus on the individual human psyche. Placing the individual psyche as the unit of analysis rather than larger social units reifies meritocratic arguments that rest on comparing individual human beings rather than examining why a society or societies privilege(s) certain social groups while subjugating others. This hyperfocus on individuals obscures systemic and structural aspects of social issues such as racism, sexism, classism, heterosexism, able-ism, and other forms of oppression.

There have been recent efforts to thwart egocentrism and move toward the common good. For example, teaching elementary and secondary school students about a range of perspectives allows them to develop empathy and look for commonalities across multiple points of view. Occupy movements, workers' solidarity actions, and other forms of justice-oriented coalitional work serve as models for collectively reinserting missing voices left out by the ego-based decisions of those in power.

Scott Ritchie

EMERGING TECHNOLOGIES
Emerging Technologies That Support Culturally Responsive Instructional Strategies in the Classroom
Today's school classroom is more diverse than ever. To promote the achievement of students from culturally diverse backgrounds, teachers must provide an instructional environment in which student strengths are identified, nurtured, and used in classroom instructional activities. Teaching to the wide range of diversities in the classroom is one of the

hardest yet most important aspects of a teacher's job. The emergence of technologies now makes it easier than ever for teachers to provide cultural responsive instruction (CRI). This entry will briefly describe some culturally responsive strategies and emerging technologies that facilitate their delivery in the classroom instruction.

CRI include acknowledging student differences and commonalities, validating students' cultural identity in classroom practices and instructional activities, educating the students about the diversity of the world around them, and motivating students to become active participants in their own learning (Richards, Brown, & Forde, 2007).

As the cost of technologies continues to decline, the economic feasibility of providing CRI has increased. Thus, teachers have at their disposal a myriad of technological tools to facilitate effective instruction. Among the many technologies on the landscape, there are a few that are especially suited to support teachers' attempts to provide CRI in the classroom. Additionally, these technologies require very little or no capital for additional computers and network devices.

Three Emerging Technologies That Support Culturally Responsive Instruction (CRI)
OPEN SOURCE CONTENT Given the plethora of information available via the Internet, educators now have access to authentic data sources that allow students to acquire knowledge about different cultures and history facts by researching authentic documents and primary data sources. Students also can learn higher-order thinking skills as they learn to classify, compare and contrast, and formulate conclusions about the data they find as a result of their research. Textbooks that used to be the authoritative source on information presented in the classroom can now be supplanted with technological concepts such as open content, open data, and easy access to data and information. This technological change allows teachers to tailor culturally responsive instruction to fit the background of each student.

CLOUD COMPUTING Cloud computing refers to a kind of computing that is scalable and has virtual resources that can be shared by anyone with an Internet connection. Today's cloud platforms are offering free services to students such as email, contact lists, calendars, document storage, and the creation and sharing of documents. These features allow students to explore authentic problems of their own design, develop cognitive mentoring relationships with mentors across the world, collaborate with peers and students, and gain a greater appreciation of the differences that exist among their peers. Students can now research information, compare multiple perspectives on any given topic, and ask others to review and share their comments. As the students become active participants in their own learning, they are also learning to collaborate, communicate, and be reflective of their ideas.

BRING YOUR OWN DEVICES (BYOD) Smartphone ownership has experienced explosive growth over the past five years. According to a Ball State University study (Hanley, 2013), 99.5 percent of the students reported having a mobile phone and 74 percent of the students have a smartphone. Additionally, 98 percent of smartphone users can access the Internet. The advent of affordable smartphones makes it possible for all students to instantly interact, and the smartphone's simplicity and touchscreen interface enables easy usage. Smartphones are gateways to collaborative exchanges and authentic problem-solving environments, and they provide channels of communication to others outside of the school walls. Students can now easily create oral histories by interviewing family members and others by recording digitally the conversations, and others can view this information. Further, as school districts continue to revise and open up their access policies, technology costs will be positively affected as schools will spend less money on technology overall and can focus their efforts on providing technological tools to the students who cannot afford their own devices.

Conclusion

The potential of the latest emerging technologies to support CRI is exciting. Through these emerging technologies—open content, cloud computing, and BYOD—CRI can now be used by more teachers to accommodate the diversity in today's classroom. Further, with the lowering cost of these technologies, students can truly be the subject of the learning environment not an object in the learning environment.

Timothy Forde

References

Hanley, M. (2013). College student smartphone usage hits 74%; tablet ownership at 30%. Retrieved November 9, 2013, from http://th-ebooks. s3.amazonaws.com/Hanley_Ball_State_College_ Student_Cell_Phone_Study_Summary_Febru- ary%202013.pdf.

Johnson, L., Adams Becker, S., Cummins, M., Estrada V., Freeman, A., & Ludgate, J. (2013). *NMC Horizon Report: 2013 K–12 Edition.* Austin, TX: The New Media Consortium.

Richards, H., Brown, A. F., & Forde, T. B. (2007). Addressing diversity in schools: Culturally Responsive Pedagogy. *Teaching Exceptional Children, 39*(3), 64–68.

EMPATHY

Empathy and the Quest for Socially Just Interpersonal Interactions

Scholarship examining the nature, utility, function, development, and operation of empathy in social relationships is voluminous. This literature cuts across multiple disciplines and disciplinary subfields from evolutionary biology to political science, folk psychology to linguistics, and social neuroscience to education. The purpose of this entry is to spotlight the benefits of empathy's application as a tool for improving the individual outcomes of cross-cultural interpersonal interactions. Minimizing instances of oppression, while at the same time affirming the cultural expertise and perspectives of individuals from historically marginalized groups, serves as the platform for empathy's significance. Thus, empathy, in this context, is viewed as a tool most useful for helping individuals imagine the needs and circumstances of diverse counterparts from culturally appropriate viewpoints, which, in turn, increases the likelihood of socially just institutional practices, policymaking, individual responses, and solutions to everyday problems.

Empathy: A Social Psychological Approach

Decades of debate among scholars led Mark H. Davis (1994) to conclude that empathy must be understood as multidimensional, including both an emotional or affective domain and a more intellectual or cognitive domain. The emotional domain of empathy is referred to as *empathic concern* in the literature. It is generally likened to the familiar concept of sympathy. The intellectual domain of empathy is referred to as perspective taking. Perspective taking, simply put, is the adoption or acquisition of someone else's point of view. In other words, it is the act of *seeing* the helping circumstance through the eyes or frames of reference of someone else. The observer is the individual applying empathy, while the target is the intended beneficiary of empathy's application. Imagining the target's experience or attempting to internalize his or her point of view becomes more sophisticated over time with age, familiarity to the target, social context, and the goal/intention of the observer for broaching the helping situation in the first place. Davis's (1994) work, and the development of his *Interpersonal Interactivity Index* (Davis, 1980, 1983), an instrument intended to measure the two aforementioned dimensions of empathy, is most useful for understanding the pragmatic adoption of empathy in social interaction. This bird's-eye view of empathy's anatomy provides the theoretical framework needed to conceptualize empathy's relevance for improving the quality and frequency of socially just interpersonal interactions.

Empathy and the Quest for Socially Just Interpersonal Interactions

While many have written about empathy and diversity as stand-alone concepts, very little work has been done to look squarely at their overlap, especially in regard to matters of social justice. A simple Google scholar search of "empathy social justice" literature written since 2010 will populate a short range of articles and books across several helping professions such as a nursing, counseling, social work, and education. Some of the earliest mentions of empathy in these fields date back to the late 1950s/early 1960s. However, there has been a growing empirical knowledge base of empathy's importance in client-practitioner relationships for improving client outcomes in recent years, particularly when cultural differences exist.

Socially Just Interpersonal Interactions (SJII) are human exchanges that minimize, to the extent possible, any form of oppression or subordination of individuals based on the difference (e.g., racial, religious, sexual orientation, etc.) they bring to the interaction. SJIIs are interactions in which all participating parties are aware of any existing disproportionality in power. That disproportionality is dealt with proactively through open dialogue and commitment to understanding one another's point of view. It is at this point that empathy is of greatest consequence. Working from the assumption that empathy closes gaps in perception and minimizes divergence in social and cultural perspectives, its application is viewed as central to socially just interpersonal interactions. Likewise, differences in race, language, religious affiliation, age, physical ability, sexual orientation, and more can cause rifts between how individuals interpret one another's actions and/or intentions in the range of social interactions. Empathy is a mechanism for responding to others in such a way that they feel heard, seen, and cared for.

An Empirical Example

A recent example of research seeking to understand empathy as a component of socially just interactions can be found through the study of white female teachers and their interpersonal interactions with black male students. Warren's (2013) work examines the utility of empathy for bolstering culturally responsive teaching across racial and cultural difference. Interrogating the affective, intellectual, and behavioral dimensions of empathy's application by white female teachers with their black male students has helped develop a language and approach for understanding empathy's intersection with one's pedagogy. Empathy—namely, perspective taking—was found to improve the likelihood that these women would be risk takers and flexible to the diverse needs of their black male students. This means that the teachers in these studies make personal and professional adaptions to ensure the most favorable student outcomes for the black male students under their care. Evidence of empathy's application also helped these women to establish affirming classroom communities and trusting relationships with youth. Finally, the teachers in this study use what they know about students to intervene proactively in the academic affairs of their students.

SJIIs were not the explicit goal for the four white female teacher participants in the study. Nevertheless, they allowed themselves to become vulnerable by surrendering aspects of their own privilege and authority to make decisions that may be uncomfortable but favorable for students. This is evident in the range of personal and professional adaptations necessary to maximize student outcomes (Warren, 2013). The teachers diligently pursued student-centered interactions that affirmed the unique social and cultural perspectives of the black male students who they taught. The conscious effort to both understand students' points of view (perspective taking) and reproducing or recycling deficit perspectives of these young men offers some evidence of empathy's utility for cultivating socially just interpersonal interactions with youth of color.

At the core of these teachers' interactions with students was their commitment to partner with each young man on every aspect of their academic, behavioral, and social/relational interactions. The teachers maintained high behavioral and academic expectations while at the same time differentiating the processes employed by the young men to help them meet those expectations. The women negotiated the boundaries of their professional relationships with the young men by making their voices, experiences, and realities central to the teachers' instructional decision making. Their interactions were messy and imperfect, some days good, some days bad, and always fluid—a work in progress. Trial and error and the teachers' capacity to respond to student feedback were found to be significant for improving the quality of each interaction over time. The key point is that SJIIs must consider the multiple social and cultural perspectives of the persons involved to ensure that all decisions made in such interactions do not advantage one set of cultural norms while at the same time systematically disadvantaging someone else's.

Conclusion

Empathy is a robust, complex, slippery concept. It is the centerpiece of debate among intellectuals across multiple academic traditions. Still, empathy represents the essence of what it means to be human. Research in social cognitive neuroscience and developmental psychology confirms that every human has the ability to empathize (Decety & Ickes, 2009). Alternatively, with whom empathy is applied, when, and how it is applied is a different story altogether. The quest for SJIIs represents the pursuit all human beings must engage in to ensure no one person feels devalued, beleaguered, or ostracized. Twenty-first-century endeavors to improve diversity and social justice must incorporate discussions of empathy. The quality of life for those on the margins of our society depends on it.

Chezare Warren

References

Davis, M. H. (1980). A multidimensional approach to individual differences in empathy. *JSAS Catalog of Selected Documents in Psychology, 10*, 85.

Davis, M. H. (1983). Measuring individual differences in empathy: Evidence for a multidimensional approach. *Journal of Personality and Social Psychology, 44*, 113–26.

Davis, M. H. (1994). *Empathy: A social psychological approach*. Boulder, CO: Westview Press.

Decety, J. & Ickes, W. (2009). *The social neuroscience of empathy*. Cambridge, MA: The Massachusetts Institute of Technology Press.

Warren, C. A. (2013). The utility of empathy for white female teachers' culturally responsive interactions with black male students. *Interdisciplinary Journal of Teaching and Learning, 3*(3), 175–200.

EMPATHY

Definition

Empathy is the ability to take another's perspective and share the feelings of that person. A person with empathy can understand the other person's perspective without experiencing the same situation. For example, Peter could have empathy for Sarah when she shares about her pregnancy. Even though Peter does not know what it feels like to be pregnant, he can imagine Sarah's struggles, understand that she must be going through a difficult time, and therefore empathize with her. Low levels of empathy prohibit healthy interactions due to the difficulty of recognizing others' emotions, sharing perspectives, and adapting behavior appropriately to others' needs. High levels of empathy are associated with increased social interaction and higher levels of maturity, and can lead to more successful relationships and more life satisfaction overall (Vachon, Lynam, & Johnson, 2014).

Differences with Similar Terms

The true notion of empathy lies in the ability to remain in the feelings or perspective of another without needing to agree with the emotion. Sympathy, on the other hand, is when a person acknowledges someone else's situation but doesn't feel the same emotions as that person in the situation. A person with sympathy merely feels sorry for the other individual but doesn't take the time to share that individual's emotions. For example, Peter may be able to understand that pregnancy is difficult, but knowing that pregnancy is difficult would be the extent of his concern for Sarah. With sympathy, he would tell her that he was sorry she was having a difficult time and move on with his own life. With empathy, on the other hand, he would be able to experience her struggle by thinking and feeling it as his own. Sympathy limits the connection between two individuals because the concern only extends to the well-being of the other. Any further emotion, feeling, or thought may be disregarded.

Types of Empathy

There are generally more terms within empathy. *Affective empathy* refers to a person's *emotional* response to another person's emotions. For example, Peter may feel Sarah's anxiety when Sarah tells him that sometimes she doesn't feel fit to be a mother. His affective empathy allows him to mirror what Sarah is feeling without being pregnant himself. *Cognitive empathy* refers to the ability to *think* about someone else's emotions and understand why he or she might be feeling that way. For example, Sarah may share with Peter that she doesn't feel as if her body is made for pregnancy because of all the health issues she's experiencing. Peter may be a physician and know that most women experience Sarah's health struggles during pregnancy, and he would be able to think about and understand how Sarah was feeling.

Although having both types is ideal for maximum empathy, one does not need to possess both to have empathy; however, experiencing one type of empathy will likely result in the experience of the other, as they tend to coexist. Individuals with more levels of emotion will likely experience affective empathy before cognitive empathy, as they are able to easily identify with another's emotions without understanding why. For example, Sarah may share with Peter that she is terrified of becoming a mother, and Peter may immediately feel her anxiety. Individuals with higher levels of thought processes may identify more with cognitive empathy because they need to understand someone else's emotions before experiencing it on their own. For example, Peter may not be able to understand Sarah's concern of becoming a mother until she explains all of the reasons why she might be anxious about her upcoming role. Regardless of what type of empathy one experiences, affective or cognitive empathy is sufficient to share in another's emotion.

Gender Differences in Empathy

Research has shown that girls are traditionally more inclined to show empathy for others than boys, and they are also more inclined to receive empathy from others than boys (Hastings, Zahn-Waxler, Robinson, Usher, & Bridges, 2000; Olweus & Endresen, 1998). More research has indicated higher levels of empathy in women than men from multiple angles: self-report questionnaires, more activity in emotional areas of the brain when prompted with empathy-related emotional judgment tasks, and an increased measure of relatable emotion with statements such as "it makes me sad to see a lonely stranger in a group" (Ruekcert, Branch, & Doan, 2011). However, further research has shown that women are in fact more empathic and helpful when it comes to personal relationships or friendships (Ruekcert et al., 2011). Although motives are not certain, Eagly and Crowley (1986) found that men are less likely to feel threatened and therefore more likely to help strangers than women.

Benefits of Empathy

Increasing empathy has many benefits. High levels of empathy are associated with positive outcomes such as greater life satisfaction, better relationships, and increased opportunities for social and financial success (Gottman, 1998). High levels of empathy within families could lead to lower separation and divorce rates, improved parent-child relationships, and overall increased familial satisfaction. Further, higher rates of empathy within couple relationships may lead to lower conflict and increased conflict resolution as each individual would more likely be able to understand the other's perspective (O'Brien, DeLongis, Pomaki, Puterman, & Zwicker, 2009). Each individual would not simply understand the other's perspective, but would go as far as to feel what the other is feeling, resulting in a genuine apology, discussion, or other means of healthy conflict resolution. In a professional context, workers, colleagues, and superiors would be able to communicate more effectively with empathy, resulting in increased work performance among all individuals and better camaraderie between team members and coworkers. Increased empathy would lead to better communication because individuals would be able to imagine someone else's anxiety, curiosity, or need for information and deliver that information in a more appropriate manner. Also, empathy may lead to better communication because workers may be able to understand others' circumstances and adjust expectations accordingly.

Engaging in an empathic conversation may strongly lead to both physical and emotional healing in hurting individuals. For example, the quality of health care is impacted by the quality of the relationship between the physician and patient. A large component of this relationship is empathy, where the physician develops a relationship of trust with the patient, which leads to better care and treatment outcomes (Bayne, Neukrug, Hays, & Britton, 2013). This relationship is not exclusive in a medical context—empathy within relationships between couples, family members, coworkers, friends, and other relationships would all benefit from two individuals showing each other empathy.

Recent Needs for More Empathy

Growing trends in multiculturalism require individuals to be culturally sensitive to individuals in other races, ethnicities, and backgrounds. More educational institutions, workplaces, organizations, and social arenas are becoming increasingly diverse than before, resulting in a hodgepodge of upbringings, experiences, and perspectives among individuals

(Brouwer & Boros, 2010). Therefore, cross-cultural empathy is necessary for people to coexist in a harmonious manner. Ethnocultural empathy refers to the ability to take the perspective of another whose racial/ethnic background is different than one's own (Mallinckrodt et al., 2014). Ethnocultural empathy allows individuals to work together and thrive within multicultural contexts. Although all individuals are not from the same background, they are able to successfully communicate, share, and even experience thoughts and feelings despite their differences. As factors like technology increase globalization and internalization in all fields, ethnocultural empathy is essential in allowing diverse individuals to vicariously understand one another for productive relationships, work experiences, and task completion.

Recent Research Syntheses Related to Empathy

EMPATHY AND AGGRESSION An extensive quantitative review (i.e., meta-analysis) study (Vachon, Lynam, & Johnson, 2014) found that empathy has a weak relationship with aggression in general ($r = 0.11$) and also weak relationships with verbal aggression, physical aggression, and sexual aggression. Vachon, Lynam, and Johnson (2014) explained that the true relationship between empathy and aggression is diminished by measurement problems and by a narrow conceptualization of affective empathy that fails to capture the full range of the construct. For example, those who enjoy seeing others in pain are afflicted with more than a mere lack of empathy, and this dissonant emotion, pleasure at another's pain, is not included in the current measures of empathy. Based on a long history of clinical observation and data from multiple levels of analysis, empathy is deficient in aggressive behavior. Thus, Vachon et al. (2014) suggested that broadening the affective empathy construct beyond resonant responses to include callous and dissonant responses will unify basic research on empathy with clinical research on callousness, which will reveal a stronger relationship between empathy and aggression.

EMPATHY AND VIOLENT VIDEO GAMES Exposures to violent video games are related to more aggression, less empathy, and less prosocial behavior among children and adults. A meta-analysis study found that exposure to violent video games is positively associated with aggressive behavior, aggressive cognition, and aggressive affect (Anderson et al., 2010). Exposure to violent video games was negatively associated with empathy and prosocial behavior. Further, exposure to violent video games was a *causal* risk factor for increased aggressive behavior, aggressive cognition, and aggressive affect as well as decreased empathy and prosocial behavior. There was no difference in susceptibility to aggression across Eastern and Western cultures or across gender, indicating that people in general were susceptible to the harmful effects of violent video games (Anderson et al., 2010). Recent longitudinal studies also confirmed long-term harmful outcomes of playing violent video games. Exposure to violent video games had more long-term effects on aggressive cognition and aggressive behavior than aggressive affect, indicating longer-lasting aggressive knowledge and behavior than aggressive emotions (Anderson et al., 2010).

Public policy debate is necessary regarding how to best deal with the risk factors of playing violent video games. Some of these techniques include: public education about the risks of playing violent video games; how parents, schools, and society at large can deal with the risks; and suggestions on healthy amounts of video game usage or alternatives to playing violent video games (Anderson et al., 2010).

Greitemeyer and Osswald (2009), however, found that playing *prosocial* video games *decreased* aggressive cognition, such as hostile expectations of others; aggressive responses in behavior, thoughts, and feelings; and hasty access to antisocial thoughts. These findings indicated that, although video games may not be positive or negative, the content of the video games was relevant (Greitemeyer & Osswald, 2009).

EMPATHY AND ONLINE CHILD PORNOGRAPHY OFFENDERS Online child pornography offenders and offline sexual offenders against children differ in levels of empathy. A meta-analysis study (Babchishin, Hanson, & VanZuylen, 2014) found that that offenders who restricted their offending behavior to online child pornography offenses showed greater victim empathy and lower antisociality than offline sexual offenders or mixed offenders (with both

contact and noncontact offenses). Compared to online child pornography offenders, offline sexual offenders tended to have more access to children and less access to the Internet, indicating that motivated offenders took advantage of the opportunities available to them (Babchishin et al., 2014). Compared to offline sexual offenders and mixed sexual offenders, online offenders (a) identified more with homosexual or bisexual orientations; (b) had more lifestyle and psychological barriers that prevented them from acting directly on their interests, such as lower victim access, fewer cognitive distortions, lower antisociality, and greater victim empathy; (c) had more identified sexual interest only in children; and (d) showed lower rates of contact sexual offenses, even according to their confidential self-report (Babchishin et al., 2014).

Mixed offenders showed similar Internet access tendencies as online child pornography offenders and access to children in between the online-only offender group and offline-only offender group. Among the three offender groups, mixed offenders were a particularly high-risk group in terms of sexual deviancy as they (a) were the most pedophilic (i.e., greatest sexual interest in children); (b) had greater access to children than the online sexual offender group; and (c) had the fewest psychological barriers to acting on their deviant impulses, such as antisocial behaviors (Babchishin et al., 2014).

EMPATHY AND FORGIVENESS Empathy is a major factor in the forgiveness process and has the largest impact on forgiveness. Empathy has a stronger relationship with forgiveness (i.e., a prosocial change toward the transgressor) than any other non-social-cognitive antecedent except for trait agreeableness (Riek & Mania, 2012). All outcomes are significantly related to forgiveness, demonstrating that choosing not to forgive may lead to a number of negative results. With the exception of agreeableness, state empathy was more strongly correlated with forgiveness than all assessed non-social-cognitive antecedents (Riek & Mania, 2012).

The relationships for forgiveness with religiosity, attributions, and negative emotions are stronger when a hypothetical, rather than actual, incident of forgiveness is used. This scenario indicates that religion increases the tendency to say individuals would hypothetically forgive rather than actually forgive, and that forgiving in real-life situations may be more difficult when confronted with a real offense. Stronger correlations are generally found when hypothetical, rather than real offenses, are used to study forgiveness (Riek & Mania, 2012).

Conceptualizations and requirements of forgiveness change throughout development. Age is a moderator of some personality-level effects, suggesting that one's personality may have a larger impact on the forgiveness process as a person develops. Also, the impact of forgiveness on depression (i.e., forgiving people are generally less depressed) seems weaker in older adults. It is unclear why this would happen, although perhaps as a person ages, there are other factors introduced (e.g., family and workplace issues) that may impact depression more strongly than forgiveness-related issues (Riek & Mania, 2012).

PSYCHOTHERAPY WITH EMPATHY Higher empathy in therapists is associated with better psychotherapy outcomes. A meta-analysis study found that therapists' empathy is strongly related to a positive psychotherapy outcome (Elliott, Bohart, Watson, & Greenberg, 2011). This relationship is stronger for less experienced therapists, indicating that empathy may not be effective unless the client perceives it is grounded in authentic and genuine care for the client. Clients' perceptions of therapists' empathy is more strongly associated with positive therapy outcomes than therapists' perceptions of empathy (Elliott et al., 2011). Empathy is more associated with positive outcomes (a) in group therapy rather than in individual therapy; (b) with more severely distressed clients rather than with less distressed clients; and (c) in outpatient settings rather than in inpatient settings (Elliott et al., 2011).

MULTICULTURAL EMPATHY AND TRAINING Multicultural empathy can be increased with intervention programs. A meta-analysis study found that standardized intervention programs designed to prevent and reduce prejudice or improve positive intergroup attitudes in children and adolescents were effective, indicating that improved intergroup attitudes led to less discrimination or prevented violent behavior toward out-group members (Beelmann & Heinemann, 2014). The positive effects were not only sustained but also sometimes even higher than short-term changes. Interventions

based on direct contact experiences along with social-cognitive training programs designed to promote empathy and perspective taking were the most effective, above other interventions involving vicarious, extended, or indirect contact. Successful outcomes of empathy training interventions depended on whether the programs succeeded in initiating personal relationships and friendships between members of different ethnic groups. The importance of personal friendships made programs surrounding indirect contact impossible or very difficult. Promoting moral development was also effective for prejudice and intergroup attitude development. Interactive, structured, well-planned, and well-implemented programs were the most effective (Beelmann & Heinemann, 2014).

Almost all emotional indicators tapped positive aspects of intergroup attitudes (e.g., liking and sympathy and not disliking, anger, fear, or intergroup threat), which was not sensitive to intended changes. This outcome was because contact-based interventions promoted intergroup attitudes by changing negative emotions such as fear or intergroup threat, indicating that negative emotions played an important role in the development of serious prejudice and discrimination (Beelmann & Heinemann, 2014).

When the target out-group consisted of persons who were handicapped, empathy training programs were more effective when the target out-group consisted of ethnic groups, indicating that attitudes toward individuals who were disabled were easier to improve than ethnic out-groups. Interventions for minority groups who identified with the in-group were not effective when the interventions addressed majority group issues (e.g., prejudice against majority children). Further, these interventions were far less effective than interventions for majority groups that addressed minority group issues (e.g., prejudice against minority children). Despite the assumption that implementing interventions earlier was more effective (e.g., prevention is more effective in younger age groups), there were no differences in effectiveness of programs according to the age group treated (Beelmann & Heinemann, 2014).

DECREASE IN EMPATHY AMONG COLLEGE STUDENTS Empathy has been declining among college students in the United States. A meta-analysis study found that *empathic concern* (i.e., others-oriented feelings of sympathy for the misfortunes of others; emotional aspect of empathy) is decreasing the most, followed by *perspective taking* (i.e., tendencies to imagine other people's points of view; cognitive aspect of empathy) among college students in the United States between 1979 and 2009 (Konrath, O'Brien, & Hsing, 2011). However, *fantasy* (i.e., tendencies to identify imaginatively with fictional characters in books or movies) and *personal distress* (i.e., self-oriented feelings of distress during others' misfortunes) showed no changes over time. The declines in empathic concern and perspective taking are more recent phenomena, occurring mostly after 2000. Today's college students tend to agree less with statements such as "I often have tender, concerned feelings for people less fortunate than me" and "I sometimes try to understand my friends better by imagining how things look from their perspective," compared to college students in the late 1970s and early 1980s in America (Konrath et al., 2011).

On the contrary, narcissism has been increasing among college students in America over a similar time period. Narcissism is negatively associated with empathy. Although empathy has been decreasing at a higher rate than the rate at which narcissism is increasing, the data indicates that today's college students, or young adults in general, are more self-concerned, competitive, confident, and individualistic than before (Twenge & Foster, 2008). One factor for this outcome may be the consistent advancement of technology, which may lead young people to care more about themselves than others or interacting face-to-face with others. For example, a 2006 survey found that 64 percent of young American adults between the ages of eighteen and twenty-five believed getting *rich* was the most important goal in life, and another 17 percent chose it as the second most important goal; moreover, only 30 percent chose helping others as their ultimate goal (Pew Research Center, 2007), indicating that today's young adults are far more self-centered in comparison with thinking of others.

Increasing Empathy

Depending on personality, way of thinking, and upbringing, the average individual may or may not have a natural inclination to empathy. However, anyone can increase empathy by engaging in the following techniques:

1. *Active listening.* Individuals may increase empathy by tracking their conversational partner's words through paraphrasing, reflecting emotion and meaning, and summarizing. These techniques entail repeating back to the other person what they just heard without echoing the words verbatim. Individuals should use their own words and express their understanding of the other's previous statement. Examples for all three techniques will be derived from the following scenario.

Peter and Sarah are friends. They meet at a coffee shop to catch up after a long week.

Sarah: My day was horrible. I walked in four minutes late because there was an accident on the freeway so my bus was running behind. I am never late to work, but my boss yelled at me the moment I walked in for always being late. It's so unfair! I am a good worker and my boss usually loves me. I don't even know why she was so upset today. Maybe she was in a bad mood. Then, I had the longest day at work because I argued with my team and then spilled food all over myself during lunch. Not only that, I am feeling really inadequate on this new project because it's really out of my comfort zone. I don't know if I can do a good job with it.

Paraphrasing includes repeating back what one just heard without using the other person's exact words. For this example, Peter might paraphrase back to Sarah by saying, "You had a hard day at work because your boss was angry even though you're usually on time." Reflecting emotion and meaning includes adding an emotion or meaning word that the other person might be experiencing through the situation. For example, Peter might tell Sarah, "You felt really misunderstood when your boss said you were late" or "You felt like it was really unfair for him to say that you were always late." Lastly, summarizing includes synthesizing all, or a large part, of the conversation and reporting the general understanding of what was just said. For example, Peter might summarize the above scenario by saying, "So today you got yelled at, fought with co-workers, ruined your lunch, and you're not too comfortable with this new project. What a rough day!" Each technique includes an accurate portrayal of the other person's words. Therefore, active listening includes intently following the other person's narrative and leaving room for correction of one's own interpretation.

2. *Remaining nonjudgmental.* One of the biggest barriers to empathy is when one imposes his or her judgments on another's situation or feelings. Engaging in empathy includes seeing the view of another, meaning, figuratively placing oneself in the other's situation and attempting to encapsulate everything that person is experiencing: circumstance; emotions; future implications of the situation; impact on relationships; disruption of dreams, goals, and values; and more. Whether one can agree or relate with the individual is irrelevant. One way to remain nonjudgmental is to practice components of motivational interviewing, a counseling technique used to facilitate *change talk* without being judgmental or aggressively directive (Miller & Rose, 2009). Rather than correcting behavior or imposing one's own suggestions onto the other, the individual wishing to practice empathy should allow the other person to process his or her own thoughts pertaining to the situation by merely asking guiding questions and affirming thoughts and feelings along the way. Through this nonjudgmental dialogue, the conversationalist is able to listen to the other person without imposing his or her values and thus create a warm environment for the other person to decide how to proceed with the presented issue.

3. *Increased conflict resolution.* Individuals in any relationship can exhibit empathy by engaging in healthy conflict resolution. When a conflict erupts, both sides can benefit from wondering about the other's perspective before initiating a premature, rash conversation. In these circumstances, taking at least one hour to reduce primary emotions can be beneficial. Empathy is more likely to be achieved through a clearer perspective without intense emotions. Therefore, empathy can be increased by forcing oneself to calm intense, negative emotions before dialoguing with the other party in order to allow

for the ability to think more rationally. Once a calmer state is achieved, considering the other's reasoning, perspective, and purpose for his or her behavior may increase empathy and result in better conflict resolution.

Implications

Current individuals spend so much time interacting with technology rather than human beings or with others through a screen rather than in real life. As a result, interpersonal dynamics such as empathy may continue to decrease dramatically in the next several years or decades (Twenge & Foster, 2008). Further, the convenience of technology may lead them to become more easily bored or frustrated when interacting with others, which may result in less empathic interactions. They may not have enough time to reach out to others and show empathy in a fast-paced world with highly accessible technology. Constant exposure to media and technology may desensitize people to the pain of others if people are continuously flooded by reports of crime, violence, and others that may also decrease empathy (Twenge & Foster, 2008).

Empathy began as a basic, animalistic need for social beings to interact with one another by adapting to, and relating with, the emotional expressions of others, resulting in an ability to coexist in a relatively harmonious manner (Vachon et al., 2014). Increased empathy could lead to many positive outcomes, including but not limited to prosocial behavior, increased life satisfaction, better work outcomes, improved relationships, and more altruistic behavior overall. In order to increase empathy everywhere, empathy training can be implemented in fundamental social learning contexts, such as schools, in order to prevent negative social behaviors such as bullying (Frey, Hirschstein, Edstrom, & Snell, 2009).

Continued research studying the effect of empathy on common interactions (e.g., marital relationships) is being conducted because of the positive factors associated with empathy. Empathy is being studied in a variety of contexts: couple relationships, parent-child relationships, in athletics, with learning disorders, in multicultural contexts, gender differences, and more (Conway, 2014; Mallinckrodt et al., 2014; Miller, Johnston, & Pasalich, 2014;

O'Brien et al., 2009; Ruekcert, Branch, & Doan, 2011; Sevdalis & Raab, 2013). Although empathy may be decreasing, and factors such as technology are reducing empathic tendencies, consistent research, programs, and implementation may continue to promote empathic behavior and continue developing more empathy in society.

Kyung-Hee Kim, PhD
Sharon Kim, MS

References

Anderson, C. A., Shibuya, A., Ihori, N., Swing, E. L., Bushman, B. J., Sakamoto, A., Rothstein, H. R., & Saleem, M. (2010). Violent video game effects on aggression, empathy, and prosocial behavior in Eastern and Western countries: A meta-analytic review. *Psychological Bulletin, 136*, 151–73. doi: 10.1037/a0018251

Babchishin, K. M., Hanson, R. K., & VanZuylen, H. (2014). Online child pornography offenders are different: A meta-analysis of the characteristics of online and offline sex offenders against children. *Archives of Sexual Behavior.* doi: 10.1007/s10508-014-0270-x

Bayne, H., Neukrug, E., Hays, D., & Britton, B. (2013). A comprehensive model of optimizing empathy in person-centered care. *Patient Education and Counseling, 93*, 209–15.

Beelmann, A. & Heinemann, K. S. (2014). Preventing prejudice and improving intergroup attitudes: A meta-analysis of child and adolescent training programs. *Journal of Applied Developmental Psychology, 35*(1), 10–24. doi: 10.1016/j.appdev.2013.11.002

Brouwer, M. A. R. & Boros, S. (2010). The influence of intergroup contact and ethnocultural empathy on employees' attitudes toward diversity. *Cognition, Brain, Behavior, 14*, 243–60.

Conway, F. (2014). The use of empathy and transference as interventions in psychotherapy with attention deficit hyperactive disorder latency-aged boys. *Psychotherapy, 51*(1), 104–9. doi: 10.1037/a0032596

Eagly, A. H. & Crowley, M. (1986). Gender and helping behavior: A meta-analytic review of the social psychological literature. *Psychological Bulletin, 100*, 283–308. doi:10.1037/0033-2909.100.3.283

Elliott, R., Bohart, A. C., Watson, J. C., & Greenberg, L. S. (2011). Empathy. *Psychotherapy, 48*(1), 43–49. doi: 10.1037/a0022187

Frey, K. S., Hirschstein, M., Edstrom, L., & Snell, J. (2009). Observed reductions in school bullying, nonbullying aggression, and destructive bystander behavior: A longitudinal evaluation. *Journal of Educational Psychology, 101*, 466–81. doi: 10.1037/a0013839

Gottman, J. M. (1998). Psychology and the study of marital processes. *Annual Review of Psychology, 49*, 169–97.

Greitemeyer, T. & Osswald, S. (2009). Prosocial video games reduce aggressive cognitions. *Journal of Experimental Social Psychology, 45*, 896–900. doi: 10.1016/j.jesp.2009.04.005

Hastings, P. D., Zahn-Waxler, C., Robinson, J., Usher, B., & Bridges, D. (2000). The development of concern for others in children with behavior problems. *Developmental Psychology, 36*, 531–46. doi: 10.1037/0012-1649.36.5.531

Konrath, S. H., O'Brien, E. H., & Hsing, C. (2011). Changes in dispositional empathy in American college students over time: A meta-analysis. *Personality and Social Psychology Review, 15*, 180–98. doi: 10.1177/1088868310377395

Mallinckrodt, B., Miles, J., Bhaskar, T., Chery, N., Choi, G., & Sung, M. (2014). Developing a comprehensive scale to assess college multicultural programming. *Journal of Counseling Psychology, 61*(1), 133–45. doi: 10.1037/a0035214

Miller, N., Johnston, C., & Pasalich, D. (2014). Parenting and conduct problems: Moderation by child empathy. *Journal of Psychopathology and Behavioral Assessment, 36*, 74–83. doi: 10.1007/s10862-013-9366-1

Miller, W. R. & Rose, G. S. (2009). Toward a theory of motivational interviewing. *American Psychologist, 64*, 527–37.

O'Brien, T., DeLongis, A., Pomaki, G., Puterman, E., & Zwicker, A. (2009). Couples coping with stress. *European Psychologist, 14*(1), 18–28. doi: 10.1027/1016-9040.14.1.18

Olweus, D. & Endresen, I. M. (1998). The importance of sex-of-stimulus object: Age trends and sex differences in empathetic responsiveness. *Social Development, 7*, 370–88. doi: 10.1111/1467-9507.00073

Pew Research Center. (2007). A portrait of "generation next": How young people view their lives, futures and politics. Retrieved from http://www.people-press.org/2007/01/09/a-portrait-of-generation-next/.

Riek, B. M. & Mania, E. W. (2012). The antecedents and consequences of interpersonal forgiveness: A meta-analytic review. *Personal Relationships, 19,* 304–25. doi: 10.1111/j.1475-6811.2011.01363.x

Rueckert, L., Branch, B., & Doan, T. (2011). Are gender differences in empathy due to differences in emotional reactivity? *Psychology, 2,* 574–78. doi: 10.4236/psych.2011.26088

Sevdalis, V. & Raab, M. (2013). Empathy in sports, exercise, and the performing arts. *Psychology of Sport and Exercise, 15,* 173–79.

Twenge, J. & Foster, J. D. (2008). Mapping the scale of the narcissism epidemic: Increases in narcissism 2002–2007 within ethnic groups. *Journal of Research in Personality, 42*(6), 1619–22. doi: 10.1016/j.jrp.2008.06.014

Vachon, D. D., Lynam, D. R., & Johnson, J. A. (2014). The (non)relation between empathy and aggression: Surprising results from a meta-analysis. *Psychological Bulletin, 140,* 751–73. doi: 10.1037/a0035236

EMPOWERMENT

Definition of Empowerment

The word *empower* arose in the mid-seventeenth century with the legalistic meaning "to invest with authority, authorize." Shortly thereafter, it began to be used in a more general way, meaning "to enable or permit." Following from this conception, World Bank (n.d.) defines empowerment as the process of increasing the assets and capabilities of individuals or groups to make purposeful choices and to transform them into desired actions and outcomes. Scholars such as Frendendall and Robbins (1995) define empowerment as the ability to enact, equip, or enable positive personal and professional change. Other scholars define empowerment as "a progression that helps people gain control over their own lives and increases the capacity of people to act on issues that they themselves define as important" (Luttrell, Quiroz, Scrutton, & Bird, 2009, p. 16). The Merriam-Webster Dictionary defines empowerment in both legal and general ways: 1) "to give official authority or legal power to," and 2) "to promote the self-actualization or influence of." Today, the word *empowerment* has itself been extended by its use in politics and psychology. Although definitions differ, they all address one or more of five common degrees of empowerment:

1. *Safety.* Safety is a prerequisite of empowerment. It means that individuals or groups feel secure in displaying their true identity and are provided with the necessary food, shelter, property, income, medical care, and companionship. When these basic needs are instead a constant concern (e.g., worrying about receiving tenure), people will feel afraid to express their true selves and thus be unable to fully realize their potentials (Boyanton, in press). This aspect of empowerment is similar to Longwe's (1991) definition of "welfare degree" empowerment.

2. *Belief.* Belief means that individuals or groups believe that they have the necessary capabilities—including potential, talent, ability, skill, or intelligence—to make a contribution to themselves, others, or society. This belief is a result of the individual's own perception (Holden, Barker, Meenaghan, & Rosenberg, 1999). This perception can be influenced by 1) their own self-efficacy (Klecker & Loadman, 1996); 2) the work environment (Short, 1994); 3) professional or personal efficacy (Frans, 1993); and 4) interpersonal strengths or strategies (Frans, 1993).

3. *Resources/opportunities.* This criterion means that individuals or groups are provided with the necessary resources or assistance to exercise their talents and potentials. Examples of resources/opportunities include access to education, training, technology, funding, status, language programs, books, teachers, knowledge, and skills (Huff & Johnson, 1998). This degree of empowerment is similar to the "access degree" empowerment by Longwe (1991) as well as the concept of "economic empowerment" (Luttrell, Quiroz, Scrutton, & Bird, 2009).

4. *Autonomy/participation.* Autonomy/participation means that individuals or groups are given substantial freedom and control during participation in deciding how to use resources and equipment. Such decisions are based on their own needs, interests, preferences, and goals (Klecker & Loadman, 1996). This internal locus of control is believed to be essential to empowerment (Koeske & Kirk, 1995). In fact, Page and Czuba (1999) defined empowerment as the process of gaining control over one's life. This degree of empowerment is

similar to the "control degree" empowerment as defined by Longwe (1991), as well as the concept of "human and social empowerment" by Page and Czuba (1999).

5. *Outcome.* Outcome means that individuals or groups feel that their participation brings positive change to someone's life, which, as a result, gives them a sense of self-worth or self-actualization (Maslow, 1987). Positive outcome occurs when one feels that their participation matters either to self or to others.

Since few people are privileged enough to fulfill all of these conditions, the above five empowerment degrees have to be understood through the lens of "power." Our society is often divided into two groups: the empowered group and the disempowered. Empowerment is used specifically to address the disempowered group, such as helping them gain more control over their lives by obtaining food, shelter, recognition, resources, or autonomy from the empowered group. Depending on the types of power, the empowered and disempowered groups can be categorized into different subgroups, as shown in Table E.1.

History of Empowerment

Empowerment has existed since humans invented the first tool to improve their living conditions. Although empowerment itself developed as early as the beginning of human civilization, the term *empowerment* did not develop its contemporary meanings until the 1900s when people became more aware of and resistant to the broken communal systems that unequally distributed power and supplies. The empowerment movement began as a means of addressing these inequalities and helping the disempowered.

Early empowerment movements in the United States mostly focused on the racial inequalities between Caucasians and African Americans. The abolition movement, one of the better known, dates back to at least the eighteenth century. One of the earliest successes for empowerment movements can be traced back to 1863, when President Abraham Lincoln executed the Emancipation Proclamation and freed the slaves. However, African Americans struggled for nearly another century to gain empowerment alongside freedom—a struggle that materialized finally in the civil rights

Table E.1 Groups of the Empowered and Disempowered

Types of Power	The Empowered	The Disempowered	Examples of Redress
Race	White	Colored	Civil rights movement, affirmative action, ethnic minority empowerment (Devore & Schlesinger, 1999); African American empowerment (Calhoun-Brown, 1998)
Gender	Man	Woman	Feminist movement, girl empowerment (Hyde et al., 1990; O'Brien & Crandall, 2003)
Sexual Orientation	Heterosexual	Homosexual	LGBT empowerment (D'Augelli, 1991)
SES	Upper class	Lower class	Empowerment of poor and homeless (Martin & Nayowith, 1988; Parsons, 1988); Economic empowerment (Luttrell, Quiroz, Scrutton, & Bird, 2009)
Language	Native/standard English speaker	Second-language speakers, Nonstandard English speaker	ESL programs; Minority language; Black English normalization
Age	Middle-aged	Elderly Youth Children	Youth empowerment (Wolin & Wolin, 1993); Elderly people empowerment (Parsons & Cox, 1994; Perlmutter & Hall, 1985)
Status/ Structure	Officials Officers Jury judge	Lay people	Paulo Freire (1970), *Pedagogy of the Oppressed*; Social structure and empowerment (Bartle, Couchonnal, Canda, & Staker, 2002; Carson, Carson, Roe, Birkenmeier, & Phillips, 1999)
Professional Role	Employer	Employee Consumer	Employee empowerment, patient empowerment (Kruger, 2000); Medical professional empowerment (Fisher, 1994); Consumer empowerment (Frese & Davis, 1997)
Household Role	Husband	Wife	Family empowerment (Wolin & Wolin, 1993)
Education	Intellectual	Illiterate	No Child Left Behind (2003)

movement of the 1960s. The main aim of the civil rights movement was to ensure the legal rights of African American people (Calhoun-Brown, 1998). Empowerment in the context of the civil rights movement can be understood as racial empowerment through the growing influence of African Americans in politics and society (Calhoun-Brown, 1998). Following the civil rights movement, the government officially endorsed affirmative action programs, which required policymakers to consider factors such as race, color, religion, sex, or national origin (National Archives, 2010). The justification for affirmative action was to benefit underrepresented groups "in areas of employment, education, and business" (Affirmative Action, 2013) as a compensation for their past discrimination, persecution, or exploitation by the dominant social group (Sowell, 2004).

Later, under the influence of social constructionism, empowerment became the major practice model in the social welfare field (Berger & Luckmann, 1967). Influenced by Paulo Freire and his famous work *Pedagogy of the Oppressed*, scholars and activists formally introduced the term *empowerment* in order to raise a critical awareness of oppressed people in society (Freire, 1970). The feminist movements started at the same time and further expanded the empowerment discussion. In the 1980s and 1990s, empowerment was mostly seen as social action and social reform (Bogo, Michalski, Raphael, & Roberts, 1995; Falck, 1984; Rubin & Johnson, 1984; Specht & Courtney, 1994). In the 1990s, with increasing democratization in Latin America and the retreat of the state, notions of participation and empowerment, previously the reserve of social movements and nongovernmental organizations (NGOs), were reformulated and became a central part of the mainstream development discourse (Van Dam et al., 1992).

In the field of education, the concept of empowerment has also gone through several changes. John Dewey, one of the pioneers of empowerment in education, made two significant contributions in this area: democratic education and pragmatics education (Dewey, 1916). Democratic education emphasized the importance of treating students as active learning agents who should take charge of their own learning and be given a choice in deciding what and

how to learn. The pragmatics education movement emphasized the creation of meaningful and practical learning using real-life experiences such as learning in real factories, farms, and hospitals rather than in isolated classrooms from old textbooks.

Although Dewey raised the awareness of student empowerment in the early 1900s, the first learning theory of the twentieth century, behaviorism (Skinner, 1963), still took students as passive learners who needed knowledge to be spoon-fed by teachers. This theory disempowered students as learners by ignoring individual voices, interests, and opinions in the process of learning. Bandura's (1986) self-efficacy theory, however, recognized the importance of individual factors such as confidence, motivation, goals, and personal relationships in the process of learning. According to Zimmerman's self-regulated learning theory (1990, 2008), when students have the necessary self-efficacy and motivation, they feel empowered to initiate learning on their own.

Constructivism is another approach that strongly emphasizes the individual's role in the process of learning by validating individual opinions, understandings, and interpretations in the learning process. Constructivists not only conceptualized students as active agents in the learning process, but they believed that learning is individually constructed through personal interpretation and creation based on personal and social factors (e.g., Piaget, 1952a, 1952b; Vygotsky, 1967). This new definition of learning sought to empower learners because it validated individual students' points of view. Influenced by constructivism, a series of education movements developed, including reflective learning, inquiry-based learning, problem-based learning, independent learning, and discovery learning (Bruner, 1973).

Humanistic education took the concept of empowerment even further than constructivism. Rather than focusing on what to teach and how to teach, this theory viewed students as human beings with various needs that teachers should understand, such as physiological, social, relational, psychological, and self-actualization needs (Maslow, 1968). According to this approach, when students feel they are being heard, understood, recognized, and respected, they will feel empowered (Roger, 1980;

Roger & Freiberg, 1994). The humanistic approach shifted educational focus from gaining knowledge and building skills to discovering talents and actualizing potentials.

The alternative education movement, begun in the late 1990s, emphasized democracy in learning. This movement stressed the importance of empowering students as active, independent learning agents who take full control of their own learning. Scholars of this approach promote the concept of "free learning" with no schools, homework, teachers, rules, tests, homework, or exams (Mintz, 2000). Students have absolute say in what they learn or even whether they want to learn. If students do not want to learn, then that is their recognized right (Mintz, 2000).

Lastly, the mutual value theory (Boyanton, in press) contributed to student empowerment in two ways. First, it classified student empowerment into two types: noncognitive and cognitive. Noncognitive empowerment focuses on the essential feelings of self-worth (self-value), self-worth as viewed by others (perceived self-value), and value assessment of others (other-value), which are prerequisites to cognitive empowerment and learning. Cognitive empowerment focuses on whether the learners are fully engaged in the process of learning and performing to their highest potential. Cognitive empowerment results in powerful learning outcomes such as gaining understanding, skills, and knowledge. Second, mutual value theory argues that empowerment is a two-way process. Unlike the traditional definition of empowerment that sees empowerment as always moving from the empowered to the disempowered, mutual value theory points out that the actions and views of the disempowered party in a relationship can affect the empowered party as well.

In addition to studies of student empowerment, research has also explored the empowerment of teachers (Vavrus, 1989). Literature on teacher empowerment began to appear in the late 1980s with the advent of school site-based decision making. Lightfoot (1986) defined teacher empowerment as providing teachers with autonomy, choice, responsibility, and participation in decision making. Bredeson (1989, p. 3) added that teachers should be empowered by taking greater responsibility in their professional work life in the areas of participatory decision making, professional development, and job enrichment as well as in the areas of professional autonomy and teacher efficacy.

Several trends can be generalized from this overview of empowerment within the field of education as well as the broader society. First, the battle for empowerment takes continuing effort and constant negotiation among different groups involved (Gaventa, 2003). Second, great progress has been made in this area, although we are still faced with many challenges and limitations. Third, the focus of empowerment has shifted from meeting basic survival needs to fulfilling the highest human potentials (e.g., Maslow's concept of self-actualization). Fourth, the targets of empowerment have moved from the macro level (e.g., race, gender) to the micro level (e.g., belief, self-esteem, relationships). Lastly, empowerment approaches have changed from being one way (from the empowered group to the disempowered) to two way (a mutual empowerment among different groups).

Approaches to Empowerment
Similar to the definition of empowerment, approaches to empowerment can be classified into different categories depending on their scale, purpose, and process. First of all, according to the scale, empowerment can be divided into four types: (1) personal empowerment, (2) interpersonal empowerment, (3) organizational empowerment, and (4) national empowerment. Personal empowerment refers to any effort that an individual takes to empower himself or herself (Bailey, 1994; Hasenfeld, 1987). According to Bandura's (1977) self-efficacy theory, "people guide their lives by their beliefs of personal efficacy" (p. 2). Interpersonal empowerment refers to how people interact and perceive each other on a daily basis (e.g., a child wants to tie his own shoes and whether the mother allows him to). Organizational empowerment refers to how an organization such as an institute or a company makes policies about a given group (e.g., whether to hire homosexual people). Organizational policies have a great impact on individual empowerment (Zimmerman, Israel, Schulz, & Checkoway, 1992). National empowerment refers to how a country makes laws and policies, including laws on

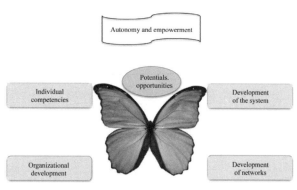

Figure E.2 CapDev Butterfly (modified from Arthur Zimmerman, SDC [2008])

immigration, affirmative action, abortion, or gay marriage that serve to empower the underprivileged group. National empowerment is similar to Piron and Watkins's (2004) concept of "political empowerment," which is to empower citizens to claim their rights and entitlements. According to SDC (2006), these four scales of empowerment interact with one another, as illustrated in Figure E.2.

Second, depending on how the empowered and disempowered interact with and relate to each other, Rowlands (1997) divides empowerment into four approaches: (1) power over, (2) power with, (3) power to, and (4) power within. The "power over" approach assumes that there is finite power ("zero sum") in society, and the only way for the disempowered to gain power is to take it from the empowered group. Power is seen as something that is wielded by the dominant and can be bestowed by one person on another (Luttrell, Quiroz, Scrutton, & Bird, 2009). Many scholars believe that empowerment means to reduce the power of the empowered group and to eliminate social structural barriers in order to empower the disempowered (Barker, 1991; Breton, 1994; Cowger, 1994; Gutierrez, Parsons, & Cox, 1998; Parsons & Cox, 1994; Pinderhughes, 1983, 1994; Rose, 1994; Rose & Black, 1985; Saleebey, 2002; Simon, 1994; Simon, 1990; Solomon, 1976; Staples, 1990; Washington & Moxley, 2003). The "power with" approach, however, does not agree with the "zero sum" power theory. Rather, it proposes that when the empowered bolster the opportunities of the disempowered, both groups can be empowered (Kabeer, 1999; Knack, 2005). This approach stresses that empowering others can actually strengthen the power of self rather than diminish it. The "power to" approach tries

to organize and change existing hierarchies with the purpose of increasing individual capacity and opportunities for access (Alsop & Norton, 2004; Mosse, 2005). The "power within" approach is similar to personal empowerment discussed earlier, in that it strives to increase people's awareness of and desire for change, as well as to empower them from within.

Thirdly, empowerment can be classified into two types depending on its nature: instrumental empowerment and transformative empowerment (Luttrell, Quiroz, Scrutton, & Bird, 2009). The instrumental empowerment approach focuses more narrowly on the importance of process with little attention to outcome, assuming that participation alone can be empowering. It focuses more on organizational capacity building or increasing the participation of previously excluded groups in the design, management, and evaluation of development activities. Transformational empowerment, however, emphasizes outcomes such as economic enhancement and increased access to economic resources.

Lastly, empowerment approaches can be divided into centralized approaches and decentralized approaches depending on the source of driving forces. The centralized approach is similar to the "power over" approach in that all the driving empowerment forces come from the empowered group and all the actions are taken by them. With the decentralized approach, however, all people act as transformative agents participating in the empowerment process. Figure E.3 summarizes the concept of empowerment.

Dengting Boyanton

References

Affirmative action. (2013). *Stanford Encyclopedia of Philosophy*. Retrieved from http://plato.stanford.edu/entries/affirmative-action/.

Alsop, R. & Norton, A. (2004). Power, rights and poverty reduction. In R. Alsop, *Power, rights and poverty: Concepts and connections*. Washington, DC: World Bank.

Bailey, D. (1994). Organizational empowerment: From self to interbeing. In L. Gutierrez and P. Nurius (Eds.), *Education and research for empowerment practice* (pp. 37–42). Seattle: Center for Policy and Practice Research.

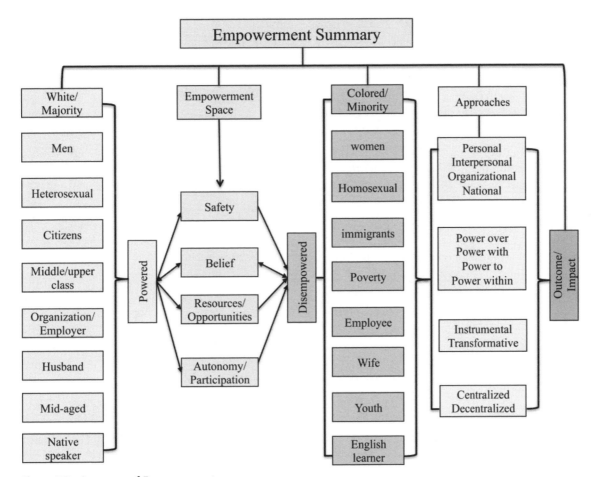

Figure E.3   Summary of Empowerment

Bandura, A. (1977). Self-efficacy: Toward a unifying theory of behavioral change. *Psychological Review*, *84*(2), 191–215.

Bandura, A. (1986). The explanatory and predictive scope of self-efficacy theory. *Journal of Social & Clinical Psychology*, *4*(3), 359–73.

Barker, R. L. (1991). *The social work dictionary* (2nd ed.). Washington, DC: NASW Press.

Bartle, E. E., Couchonnal, G., Canda, E. R., & Staker, M. D. (2002). Empowerment as a dynamically developing concept for practice: Lessons learned from organizational ethnography. *Social Work*, *47*(1), 32–43.

Berger, P. & Luckmann, T. (1967). *The social construction of reality*. Garden City, NY: Anchor Books.

Bogo, M., Michalski, J. H., Raphael, D., & Roberts, R. (1995). Practice interests and self-identification among social work students: Changes over the course of graduate social work education. *Journal of Social Work Education*, *31*(2), 228–46.

Boyanton, D. (In Press). *Students and teachers as co-learners: Toward a mutual value theory*. New York: Peter Lang Publishers.

Bredeson, P. V. (1989). *Empowered teachers-empowered principals: Principals' perceptions of leadership in schools*. Paper presented at the Annual Meeting of the University Council for Educational Administration, Scottsdale, AZ.

Breton, M. (1994). On the meaning of empowerment and empowerment-oriented social work practice. *Social Work with Groups*, *17*(3), 23–27.

Bruner, J. S. (1973). *Beyond the information given*. New York: Norton.

Calhoun-Brown, A. (1998). While marching to Zion: Otherworldliness and racial empowerment in the Black community. *Journal for the Scientific Study of Religion*, *37*(3), 427–39.

Capacity development: A process for change. (2006). Working Paper. Retrieved from http://www.deza.admin.ch/en/Home/About_SDC/Strategy/Implementation_channels_and_instruments/Learning_and_Networking/Capacity_Development.

Carson, K. D., Carson, P. P., Roe, C. W., Birkenmeier, B. J., & Phillips, J. S. (1999). Four commitment profiles and their relationships to empowerment, service recovery and work attitudes. *Public Personnel Management, 28*(1), 1–13.

Cowger, C. D. (1994). Assessing client strengths: Clinical assessment for client empowerment. *Social Work, 39*(3), 262–69.

D'Augelli, A. R. (1991). Teaching lesbian/gay development: From oppression to exceptionality. *Journal of Homosexually, 22*(3/4), 213–27.

Devore, W. & Schlesinger, E. G. (1999). *Ethnic sensitive social work practice* (5th rev. ed.). Needham Heights, MA: Allyn & Bacon.

Dewey, J. (1916). *Democracy and education.* Toronto: Macmillan.

Falck, H. S. (1984). A loud and shrill protest. *Journal of Education for Social Work, 20*(1), 3–4.

Fisher, D. B. (1994). Health care reform based on an empowerment model of recovery by people with psychiatric disabilities. *Hospital and Community Psychiatry, 45*, 913–15.

Frans, D. J. (1993). A scale for measuring social worker empowerment. *Research on Social Work Practice, 3*, 312–28.

Fredendall, L. D. & Robbins, T. L. (1995). Modeling the role of total quality management in the customer focused organization. *Journal of Managerial Issues, 7*, 403.

Freire, P. (1970). *Pedagogy of the oppressed.* New York: Continuum.

Frese, F. J. & Davis, W. W. (1997). The consumer-survivor movement, recovery, and consumer professionals. *Professional Psychology: Research and Practice, 28*, 243–45.

Gaventa, J. (2003). *Towards participatory local governance: Assessing the transformative possibilities.* Paper presented at Conference on Participation: From Tyranny to Transformation, Manchester.

Gaventa, J. (2005). Reflections of the uses of the "power cube" approach for analyzing the spaces, places and dynamics of civil society participation and engagement. *CFP Evaluation Series, 4.* The Hague, Netherlands: MBN Secretariat.

Gutierrez, L., Parsons, R. J., & Cox, E. O. (1998). *Empowerment in social work practice.* Pacific Grove, CA: Brooks/Cole.

Hasenfeld, Y. (1987). Power in social work practice. *Social Service Review, 61*, 469–83.

Holden, G., Barker, K., Meenaghan, T., & Rosenberg, G. (1999). Research self-efficacy: A new possibility for educational outcomes assessment. *Journal of Social Work Education, 35*, 463–476.

Holden, G., Anastas, J., Meenaghan, T., & Metrey, G. (2002). Outcomes of social work education: The case for social work self-efficacy. *Journal of Social Work Education, 38*(1), 115–33.

Huff, M. T. & Johnson, M. M. (1998). Empowering students in a graduate-level social work course. *Journal of Social Work Education, 34*(3), 375–85.

Hyde, J. S., Fennema, E., & Lamon, S. J. (1990). Gender differences in mathematics performance: A meta-analysis. *Psychological Bulletin, 107*(2), 139–55.

Kabeer, N. (1999). Resources, agency, achievements: Reflections on the measurement of women's empowerment. *Development and Change, 30*, 435–64.

Klecker, B. & Loadman, W. E. (1996). *Dimensions of teacher empowerment: Identifying new roles for classroom teachers in restructuring schools.* Paper presented at the annual meeting of the Mid-South Educational Research Association, Tuscaloosa, AL.

Knack, S. (2005). Empowerment as a zero-sum game. In D. Narayan (Ed.), *Measuring empowerment: Cross disciplinary perspectives.* Washington, DC: IBRD, World Bank.

Koeske, G. R. & Kirk, S. A. (1995). Direct and buffering effects of internal locus of control among mental health professionals. *Journal of Social Service Research, 20*(3/4), 1–28.

Kruger, A. (2000). Empowerment in social work practice with the psychiatrically disabled: Model and method. *Smith College Studies in Social Work, 70*, 427–40.

Lightfoot, S. L. (1986). On goodness of schools: Themes of empowerment. *Peabody Journal of Education, 63*(3), 9–28.

Longwe, S. (1991). Gender awareness: The missing element in the Third World Development Project. In T. Wallace & C. March, *Changing perceptions: Writings on gender and development.* Oxford, UK: Oxfam.

Luttrell, C., Quiroz, S., Scrutton, C., & Bird, K. (2009). *Understanding and operationalising empowerment.* London: Overseas Development Institute.

Martin, M. A. & Nayowith, S. A. (1988). Creating community: Groupwork to develop social support networks with homeless mentally ill. *Social Work with Groups, 11*(4), 79–93.

Maslow, A. H. (1968). *Toward a psychology of being* (2nd ed.). Princeton, NJ: Van Nostrand.

Maslow, A. H. (1987). *Motivation and personality* (3rd ed.). New York: Harper & Row.

Mintz, J. (2000). *No homework and recess all day: How to have freedom and democracy in education*. Bravura Books.

Mosse, D. (2005). Power relations and poverty reduction. In R. Alsop, *Power, rights and poverty: Concepts and connections*. Washington, DC: World Bank.

National Archives. (2010). *Executive Order 11246—Equal employment opportunity*. Retrieved from http://www.archives.gov/federal-register/codification/executive-order/11246.html.

O'Brien, L. T. & Crandall, C. S. (2003). Stereotype threat and arousal: Effects on women's math performance. *Personality and Social Psychology Bulletin*, *29*, 782–89.

Page, N. & Czuba, C. (1999). Empowerment: What is it? *Journal of Extension*, *37*(5), 1–6.

Parsons, R. J. (1988). Empowerment for role alternatives for low-income minority girls: A group work approach. *Social Work with Groups*, *11*(4), 27–45.

Parsons, R. J. & Cox, E. O. (1994). *Empowerment-oriented social work practice with the elderly*. Pacific Grove, CA: Brooks/Cole.

Perlmutter, M. & Hall, E. (1985). *Adult development and aging*. New York: John Wiley & Sons.

Piaget, J. (1952a). *The language and thought of the child*. London: Routledge & Kegan Paul.

Piaget, J. (1952b). *The origins of intelligence in children*. New York: International Universities Press.

Pinderhughes, E. (1983). Empowerment for our clients and ourselves. *Social Casework*, *64*, 331–38.

Pinderhughes, E. (1994). Empowerment as an intervention goal: Early ideas. In L. Gutierrez & P. Nurius (Eds.), *Education and research for empowerment practice* (pp. 17–30). Seattle: Center for Policy and Practice Research.

Piron, L. H. & Watkins, F. (2004). *DFID human rights review: A review of how DFID has integrated human rights into its work*. Report for DFID.

Roger, C. R. (1980). *A way of being*. Boston: Houghton Mifflin.

Roger, C. R. & Freiberg, H. J. (1994). *Freedom to learn* (3rd ed.). New York: Merrill.

Rose, S. M. (1994). Reclaiming empowerment: A paradigm for social work. In L. Gutierrez & P. Nurius (Eds.), *Education and research for empowerment practice* (pp. 31–36). Seattle: Center for Policy and Practice Research.

Rose, S. M. & Black, B. L. (1985). *Advocacy and empowerment: Mental health care in the community*. Boston: Routledge/Kegan Paul.

Rowlands, J. (1997). *Questioning empowerment: Working with women in Honduras*. Oxford, UK: Oxfam.

Rubin, A. & Johnson, P. J. (1984). Direct practice interests of entering MSW students. *Journal of Education for Social Work*, *20*(2), 5–16.

Saleebey, D. (2002). *The strengths perspective in social work practice* (3rd ed.). Boston: Allyn & Bacon.

Short, P. M. (1994). School empowerment through self-managing teams: Leader behavior in developing self-managing work groups in schools. *Education*, *114*(4), 493–503.

Simon, B. L. (1994). *The empowerment tradition in American social work: A history*. New York: Columbia University Press.

Simon, G. (1990). Rethinking empowerment. *Journal of Progressive Human Services*, *1*(1), 27–37.

Skinner, B. F. (1963). Behaviorism at fifty. *Science*, *140*, 951–58.

Solomon, B. (1976). *Black empowerment: Social work in oppressed communities*. New York: Columbia University Press.

Sowell, T. (2004). *Affirmative action around the world: An empirical study*. New Haven, CT: Yale University Press.

Specht, H. & Courtney, M. E. (1994). *Unfaithful angels: How social work has abandoned its mission*. New York: Free Press.

Staples, L. (1990). Powerful ideas about empowerment. *Administration in Social Work*, *14*, 29–42.

Swiss Agency for Development and Cooperation (SDC). (2006). *Capacity development in SDC*. Working Paper. Berne, Switzerland: SDC.

Van Dam, A., Ooijens, J., & Peter, G. (1992). *Popular education in Latin America. Synthesis of the discussion themes. Verhandelingen 50*. The Hague, Netherlands: CEIC.

Vavrus, M. (1989). *Alienation as the conceptual foundation for incorporating teacher empowerment into the teacher education knowledge base*. Proceedings of the National Forum of the Association of Independent Liberal Arts Colleges for Teacher Education, Indianapolis, IN.

Vygotsky, L. S. (1967). *Thought and language* (E. Hanfmann & G. Vakar, Trans.). Cambridge, MA: MIT Press.

Vygotsky, L. S. (1978). *Mind in society: The development of higher psychological processes* (M. Cole, V. John-Steiner, S. Scribner, & E. Souberman, Eds.). Cambridge, MA: Harvard University Press.

Washington, O. G. M. & Moxley, D. P. (2003). Group interventions with low-income African American women recovering from chemical dependency. *Health & Social Work, 28,* 146–56.

Wolin, S. J. & Wolin, S. (1993). *The resilient self: How survivors of troubled families rise above adversity.* New York: Villard.

World Bank. (n.d.). *Empowerment.* Retrieved from http://go.worldbank.org/V45HD4P100.

Zimmerman, B. J. (1990). Self-regulating academic learning and achievement: The emergence of a social cognitive perspective. *Educational Psychology Review, 2*(2), 173–200.

Zimmerman, B. J. (2008). Investigating self-regulation and motivation: Historical background, methodological developing and future prospects. *American Educational Research Journal, 45*(1), 166–83.

Zimmerman, M. A., Israel, B. A., Schulz, A., & Checkoway, B. (1992). Further explorations in empowerment theory: An empirical analysis of psychological empowerment. *American Journal of Community Psychology, 20,* 707–27.

EMPOWERMENT

When Power Moves from You to Me,
Even If I Don't Want It

First and foremost, empowerment is a process in which power moves from one person to another person or group. Most commonly, *empowerment* is defined as increasing capacity or helping an individual or group to make choices that improve their life. Empowerment is often part of the process that people go through as they become full and active citizens. In this context, empowerment is often used by development organizations such as the World Bank. Community organizing groups and nonprofits also use the term frequently. Empowerment as a concept and a goal has gained popularity since the 1970s and with the growth of the self-reliant neoliberal and neoconservative citizens.

While many only focus on the good that appears to come from empowerment, others have pointed to the importance of examining the movement of power that is inherent in the process. Empowerment can only exist alongside disempowerment and the assumption that those who require empowerment are somehow currently disempowered. The real question is, of course, who is measuring empowerment here? And by whose standards? If the goal of state and international organizations is to "empower" individuals, how do we measure this, and which aspects of their lives are we empowering? Too often those being "empowered" are not asked how they would like to transform their own lives.

Richa Nagar and Saraswati Raju (2003) discuss the complexity of the relationships between grassroots NGOs and empowerment programs in the lives of women in India. They found empowerment projects to be "nonlinear" and often producing contradictory effects. When women were empowered in one area of their life, the consequence could be disempowering in another. This is often true when marginalized groups gain power and there is a backlash.

Political scientist and critical theorist Wendy Brown (1995) questioned empowerment discourses in her book, *States of Injury,* noting that many located their goals in the "register of individual feelings" implicitly outside of political and social power relations. Her point being that often talk of empowerment with its focus on the individual, so common to liberal discourse, allows for the possibility that one can "feel empowered" but not actually be able to improve one's life. In this case, the real issue is the detachment of individual empowerment from power relations in society that must be affected in order for individuals to improve their situations. When empowerment is presented as a solely individual process or detached from greater social processes, individuals and communities cannot see how they fit into the very power relations that disempower them.

Barbara Cruikshank (1999) in *The Will to Empower* examines empowerment as a relationship established by expertise. In particular, she examines the war on poverty in the United States and its attempt to empower the poor as part of the very process that creates the poor as subjects. Those with the knowledge and expertise to "empower" the poor often do so whether the poor want to be empowered or not. These relations are both voluntary and coercive according to Cruikshank. This is the less sunny side of empowerment.

The dilemma of empowerment is finding a balance in which those who are empowered do so of their free will and in a manner that provides them with "power" to change their circumstances on many scales.

Rebecca Dolhinow

References

Brown, W. (1995). *States of injury: Power and freedom in late modernity.* Princeton, NJ: Princeton University Press.

Cruikshank, B. (1999). *The will to empower: Democratic citizens and other subjects.* Ithaca: Cornell University Press.

Nagar, R. & Raju, S. (2003). Women, NGOs and the contradictions of empowerment and disempowerment: A conversation. *Antipode, 35,* 1–13.

ENCULTURAL

En-cultural (en kul / char al) n., v., adj., or adv.
En-cultural is an operationally constructed learning that can take shape in or out of the classroom. Operational is demonstrated conformity to the way specific environments act and think. It can include one or more of an individual's ten biopsycho-social identities recognized by psychologist and/or educational researchers: age, religion, gender, ethnicity, race, socioeconomic status, cognitive abilities, sexual preference, class status, and physical appearance. It can be a reflective consciousness or unconsciousness that can be filtered out of a personality and/or behavior. Such examples are alluded to in history and defined by multiple situations. According to Sue and Sue (2003; 2013), personal choices of selection affiliation are attributed to and driven by one's exposure (internal or external).

For example, cultural consciousness legacy is stimulated by the assimilation of an individual's elected government and/or community choice and exposure for operations (Banks, 2001). The stimulus for public policy (social justice) and its relationship to communities are perpetuated by diversity of complex populations that have multiple needs and platforms. There are numerous domains that touch on advocacy and perceived cultural proficiencies. Being a bridge builder, and a connector for cultural acceptance and understanding of difference, is an ongoing societal quest. Examples range from the presence of possible overarching diversification outcomes for enhancement or derailing of national

worldwide credibility and legitimacy in dealing with global, political, and/or developmental issues, especially in Third World nations (Bullard, 2000). *This is a form of en-cultural-ism (noun). It is a movement to secure activities for a diverse population or a monopopulation.*

Subsequently, holistic, individual, and cultural identity clarification tenets often involve attitudes, feelings, leadership, knowledge, tactual skills, and high levels of cultural communication networks. The effectiveness of en-cultural is sustained by the ability to galvanize men from a point of "bondage of myths and half-truths" to a platform of "creative analysis and objective personal appraisal" (King, 1963, p. 291). Often, these components are aligned with some type of social justice movement or organization. *This is a form of en-cultural-ment (noun). It demonstrates great growth of public sentiment to become advocates for cultural acceptance. This can also be a form of en-cultural-lized (verb). It employs empathy from individuals, groups, and/or communities for some kind of action or stance.*

Martin Luther King spoke of social justice time periods and events in his letter from the Birmingham city jail (King, 1963). In another example, Hitler's time called for the elimination of Jewish brothers. King boldly articulated that if he had been living during that time, he might have been against that population. Culture has a way of dictating issues and behavior to man. The humanistic manipulation of thought can be attributed to *en-cultural-ism—the promotion for a culture. It contains the elements of speech, dress, and cognitive acquisition.*

School is an example of an organization with a culture aligned to promoting socialization of various subgroups with outcomes that produce student learners that value accountability, work ethics, and the acquisition of positive self-direction (Martinez & McGrath, 2013). Responsible communication networks are the underpinnings for perpetuating cultural consciousness. *This is a form of en-cultural (adjective). It addresses the system of elected ethnics for the promoting of an establishment for individual, group, and/or community behavior.*

It becomes the schools' responsibility to incorporate policies, regulations, and professional staff development that will have the academic tentacles to engage students. Thus, personal beliefs and values of society are rooted or contained in organizational legacy policy (Gladding, 2000). Legacy policy is the way people think, act, and function within their realm for "cultural" cognitive operations (Joplin, 2006). It is the manifestation of ethnic and/or racial groups with majority interests that become dominant mirrors for acceptance and practical operation of daily living. Analytical and sometimes relational processes that are ongoing generational legacy policies become nurtured by subcultural group interactions (Joplin, 2006, pp. 279–83). *This is a form of en-cultural-ly (adv.). It narrows the degree and depth for some of the bio-psycho-social identities that tie individuals together. It highlights power elites and political patterns for operation.*

Such principles of social justice can easily be woven into creative core diversity curriculum using teacher lesson delivery of situations via short stories, movies, textbooks, and virtual scenarios through technology. Lens for legacy policies are often altered or slightly manipulated by implemented academic materials depending on sought desired content outcome(s). However, real-life philosophies of individuals embrace transcendent generational perceptions. It alludes to the important question, "What is important and/or what is best for me" (King, 1963, pp. 295–96). King's famous letter spoke to the concept of Transcendent Law; *en-cultural* is a political tool for all people to live together and respect the presence of each other by touching in a philosophical, cultural manner. As in the blues, emphasis asserts dignity and individuality of each; it allows us to see inside and listen to another's world (West, 2004). Strong emphasis is on crossing cultural boundaries and experiencing different social networks.

Claudia Phillips Joplin
Kathy D. Evans

References

Banks, J. A. (2001). *Cultural diversity and education: Foundations, curriculum, and teaching.* Needham Heights, MA: Allyn & Bacon.

Bullard, R. D. (2000). *Dumping in Dixie: Race, class and environmental quality* (3rd ed.). Boulder, CO: Westview Press.

Gladding, S. T. (2000). *Counseling: A comprehensive profession* (4th ed.). Upper Saddle River, NJ: Prentice Hall.

Joplin, C. P. (2006). "Cultural roots": A possible systemic educational lens for mentoring African American students for academic acquisition of knowledge. In H. R. Milner & W. Ross (Eds.), *Race, ethnicity, and education: Racial identity in education* (vol. 3, 278–92). Westport, CT: Praeger Publishers.

King, M. L. (1963). *Essential writings and speeches of Martin Luther King Jr.* New York: Harper Collins Publishers.

Martinez, M. R. & McGrath, D. (2013). How can schools develop self-direct learners? *Phi Delta Kappan, 95*(2), 23–27.

Sue, D. W., & Sue, D. (2003). *Counseling the culturally diverse: Theory and practice* (4th ed.). New York: John Wiley & Sons, Inc.

Sue, D. W., & Sue, D. (2013). *Counseling the culturally diverse: Theory and practice* (6th ed.). Hoboken, NJ: John Wiley & Sons, Inc.

West, C. (2004). *Democracy matters: Winning the fight against imperialism.* New York: The Penguin Press.

ENGLISH AS A SECOND LANGUAGE (ESL)

ESL, or English as a Second Language, is a field of study designed to serve the needs of school-aged or adult learners of English. That is, ESL classes teach English in countries in which English is the majority language to new immigrants, or to their immigrant or native-born children. ESL classes combine good teaching practices and a focus on the needs of second-language learners to teach academic language—including grammar, writing, vocabulary, phonology or pronunciation, and the critical life skills the learners will need in their new home.

The discipline is a relatively young one, having grown out of foreign language education. A still burgeoning field, ESL began to come to fruition in the latter half of the twentieth century when researchers and educational linguists started studying the best ways to teach English Language Learners, or ELLs (see entry on ELLs in this volume), to discover what and how students learn. Early on, much of the pedagogy used in ESL classes was borrowed from foreign language teaching relying on methods such as grammar translation, or GT, where students learn through translation and grammar exercises; the Direct Method, in which all language taught is in the target language; Audiolingualism, in which long dialogues are presented and memorized; and even some more esoteric methods such as Lozanov's Suggestopedia, in which the learner is put in a relaxed state through music and other methods so they can absorb language; or Gattegno's Silent Way, in which learners are not mandated to speak and teachers communicate with few words and Cuisenaire rods (Hall, 2011). Since the 1980s, the field of ESL has moved toward communication and content learning as the preferred pedagogical approach. At the K–12 levels, students of ESL learn academic language and literacy through the assistance of well-trained ESL teachers, but also through content-area specialists knowledgeable in math, science, social studies, and the like. In adult ESL, academic language and literacy are also promoted, but life skills, citizenship, and even GED or high school equivalence content are primary curricular foci.

ESL has a number of names. In elementary and secondary schools, it can be termed *ESL* or *ESOL*—that is, *English for Speakers of Other Languages*. In countries in which English is not the majority language, the discipline is referred to as *English as a Foreign Language*, or *EFL*. As a field of study for teachers, ESL can be called *TESL* or *TESOL*, or *Teaching English as a Second Language/Teaching English to Speakers of Other Languages*.

Countries in which English is the majority language, such as the United States, United Kingdom, Canada, Australia, and others, commonly include ESL classes in their K–12 and postsecondary education. Similarly, these countries promote the teaching of ESL methodology to preservice and in-service teachers of ELLs in order to provide a just and equitable education that will give new English speakers the tools they need to be successful in their lives.

ESL education came about due to the influx of immigrants to English-speaking countries like the United States. In the United States, as in many other nations, new citizens are responsible for knowing English in order to not only be successful in work and school and their daily lives but also to become citizens. ESL classes are often designed to help new immigrants to learn English for citizenship. Assistance is also provided in ESL classes that help

learners adjust to and transition to their new situation, education, and environment.

ESL is similar to other kinds of language education such as bilingual education or foreign language immersion, but the primary goal in ESL is proficiency in the majority language, English. That said, English, rather than say, Spanish or another home language, is used as the medium to teach. Certainly, models in which the home language is also taught and maintained are preferable, but it is not always possible to teach through the mother tongue due to antibilingual laws or the lack of a critical mass of one particular language group (Wright, 2010). In these cases, English-medium models of ESL are used. Teachers of ESL do not need to speak other languages, but it is certainly helpful when an ESL teacher of primarily Spanish, Russian, German, or Vietnamese students speaks the language of their learners in order to communicate with them and teach them in the best way possible.

ESL is sometimes considered to be problematic because of the fact that ELLs are kept together in classes for many years and there can be a plethora of students called long-term ELLs (L-TELLs) who do not pass the high-stakes tests necessary to exit from ESL services. Some secondary students end up in what some have called the "ESL ghetto" (Valdes, 1998), unable to join regular classes. However, the new and pervasive ideology of ESL education is that ELLs should and will be mainstreamed by attending content classes with content experts as well as by working with expert ESL educators who can bring the students up to a high level of academic English.

With regard to the qualifications needed for ESL certification, each English-speaking country has its own criteria. In the United States, individual states have teaching certification qualifications for K–12 teachers of ESL, while adult teachers often get master's degrees in TESOL or adult education and specialize in ESL teaching. The international ESL teaching organization, TESOL (tesol.org), does not endorse specific certifications, but it is a good resource for non K–12 U.S. certification information. In the United Kingdom, Australia, and other nations using British varieties of English, Cambridge and similar organizations have multiweek certification courses in ELT or English Language

Teaching. While all of these certification programs differ in terms of length and to some degree, content, they all include a focus on appropriate language pedagogy and English-language content.

Overall, the main purpose of ESL is to provide ELLs with the tools they need to communicate, interact, become educated, work, and negotiate their daily lives in an English-speaking country. It is designed to support and shelter language learners while they navigate new systems, experiences, cultures, bureaucracies, and knowledge. ESL classes come in a wide variety of forms, but all have the primary goal of English-language acquisition.

Holly Hansen-Thomas

References

Hall, G. (2011). *Exploring English language teaching: Language in action.* London: Routledge.

Valdes, G. (1998). The world outside and inside schools: Language and immigrant children. *Educational Researcher, 27*(6), 4–18.

Wright, W. (2010). *Foundations for teaching English language learners: Research, theory, policy, and practice.* Philadelphia: Caslon.

ENGLISH LANGUAGE LEARNERS (ELLs)

English Language Learners or ELLs are students who need specific linguistic support to achieve academic success in instructional settings. In some, but not all cases, these students do not speak English as their native or home language, and they are in the process of acquiring English for educational purposes. In recent decades, literature related to ELLs referred to this group as *Limited English Proficient,* or *LEP.* Widespread disapproval of this term has grown as critics insist that the use of *limited* proposes a deficit perspective of learners by highlighting their areas of challenge rather than their areas of ability. As a result, some teachers, researchers, and immigrant advocates have adopted the term *ELL.* This appellation avoids negative connotations related to a focus on linguistic shortcomings that can result in stigmas toward or biases against ELLs. Instead, the term *ELL* is an attribution that highlights the ongoing process of developing English-language proficiency. Though most current social-justice-focused literature uses the term *ELL,* it should be noted that

the terms *LEP* and *ELL* are often considered synonymous and are used interchangeably. Importantly, as an example, the U.S. Department of Education uses a designation of Limited English Proficient to determine whether a student is eligible for bilingual language services resulting from Title VII of the Elementary and Secondary Education Act (ESEA), also known as the Bilingual Education Act of 1968.

ELLs and Colonial North America

Modern ideas have characterized the colonial period as a monolingual society dominated by Anglo traditions and values. A closer examination of this era reveals a cultural and linguistic reality featuring a broad spectrum of diversity and a complex makeup of the population (Zinn, 2005). As such, the Americas have been culturally and linguistically diverse since its inception—notably with an estimated 250 to 1,000 languages spoken in the region at the time of European contact at the end of the fifteenth century (Scherzer, 1992; Grosjean, 1982). Though diverse multilingual children were not allowed to attend early U.S. schools, English-language learning was certainly underway at the genesis of the nation.

Continuing from the colonial period until today, the United States has experienced numerous waves of elective and forced immigration. Voluntary immigrants initially arrived from Western Europe. These early immigrants were relatively similar to the European settlers who dominated the political landscape of the country in terms of appearance, culture, and religion. As a result, legal immigrant status for nonenslaved Westerners was relatively easy to obtain. Though migrants enjoyed relative equity with settlers and early generations of native-born citizens, in terms of social status and the right to own property, they were barred from receiving instruction in their native language in schools. Classroom instruction in the burgeoning public school system in any language other than English was shunned.

Demographics Shifts and Linguistic Implications for ELLs

Demographers predict that the racial composition of the United States will continue to shift over the next several decades. Referred to by some as the Browning of America, this phenomenon is due in large part to the rapid growth of the Latino population in conjunction with a decline in birthrates among Americans of European descent (Sundstrom, 2008). For example, from 2000 to 2010 the growth rate of Latino youth (those eighteen and younger) in the United States increased by 39 percent (NCLR, 2011). This growth translates to sizable populations of students who need language support to achieve academic success in U.S. schools. More ELLs in public schools also increase the demand for qualified teachers to provide them with linguistically appropriate and culturally relevant instruction.

Challenges to Success in Schools

There is a complex array of factors that influence ELLs' ability to succeed in U.S. schools. These factors ensure that ELLs are not a homogeneous group of students and therefore the types of services they need can vary widely. Foreign-born students arrive in the United States due to many different circumstances ranging from voluntary immigration to forced migration to flee war, famine, or natural disasters. Some situations faced by immigrants, refugees, and especially asylum seekers entail long periods of interrupted schooling, such as war or other forced migration. These factors, and the means by which these students are resettled in the United States, have a tremendous influence on learners' linguistic and affective characteristics and their ability to succeed in school.

Similarly, native-born ELLs are heterogeneous. Some learners live in homes where English is not spoken, while others live in homes where a mix of English and the native language is used. Additionally, a wide range of socioeconomic factors, such as poverty and a family's legal status, influence ELLs' academic achievement. Low English proficiency and fear of harassment can prevent parental involvement with homework assistance, school activities, and parent-teacher conferences. In some cases, ELLs as young as kindergarten age shoulder the responsibility to serve as liaisons between the school and their parents.

As ELLs are a diverse group of learners with differing needs and abilities, educators, researchers, and policymakers cannot portray them as a monolithic group with a singular profile. Similarly, there is no one pedagogical approach that will meet the needs of all ELLs. Debates among researchers and teachers continue about the most effective means of instruction for this population. Another challenge that receives significant public attention is how the growing number of ELLs in U.S. schools places a strain on urban and low-income schools already struggling to meet the needs of their students.

Current Language Policy Landscape

As the numbers of immigrants swell, and there is more and more competition for access to resources, debates about the presence of ELLs and how they should best be served in U.S. schools are underway at the state and federal level and in the popular press. The English Only movement with constituent support groups such as English First, English for Children, the American Ethnic Coalition, and U.S. English is a vocal component in a debate that proposes that English should be declared the official language of the United States in order to preserve national unity and stability via passage of a constitutional amendment. Numerous attempts to amend the Constitution to restrict the use of non-English languages have failed; however, the cumulative effect of these efforts on public attitudes is notable. These groups have shifted their efforts from amending the Constitution to lobbying individual states to adopt English as their official language. Notably, Proposition 227, California's antibilingual education initiative, was strongly supported by the English Only movement. The passage of this legislation in 1998 was a significant blow to proponents of multilingual classroom instruction. Critics of the English Only movement propose that some organizations and individuals who support this philosophy have dubious, anti-immigrant ties.

Standardized Testing and ELLs

ELLs face unique, and some say burdensome, challenges with respect to standardized testing. Title I of the No Child Left Behind Act requires that ELLs meet the same standards for reading and mathematics as native English-speaking students after being in the United States for three years. Often ELLs do not have sufficient linguistic proficiency to meet these requirements. Empirical research indicates that ELLs may need between two and ten years of intensive instruction in English to reach readiness for norm-referenced tests (Ovando, Combs, & Collier, 2006). Title I requires that ELLs are tested sooner than the lowest threshold of this range of readiness. Although some accommodations for ELLs can be made, such as use of bilingual dictionaries, additional time for testing, and testing in learners' native language, funding and the multiplicity of native languages of ELLs make some accommodations impractical. As a result, the availability of accommodations varies widely at the school level and may be nonexistent in many states.

ELLs and the Future

The presence of ELLs in U.S. schools enriches the educational experience for teachers and students. For example, foreign-born ELLs offer unique and diverse perspectives based on their international experiences. Similarly, multilingual ELLs have mastery of language acquisition skills and techniques that are assets to native-born American students seeking to study a foreign language. Possibilities for the exchange of ideas, as well as peer tutoring, are plentiful in schools and classrooms that value all learners' capabilities.

Due to the growing size and significance of ELLs as future voters, workers, policymakers, and professionals, thoughtful investment in the quality of their educational experiences is important. The increase in ELLs, whether foreign or native born, is a source of growth, vitality, and creativity in the United States. These youth will provide needed labor to bolster the shrinking pool of workers in the retirement era of baby boomers. They also provide linguistic variety and sophistication to a largely monolingual U.S. population.

Erica K. Dotson

References

Grosjean, F. (1982). *Life with two languages: An introduction to bilingualism.* Claremont, CA: Tomás Riveria Policy Center.

NCLR. (2011). *Toward a more vibrant and youthful nation: Latino children in the 2010 Census.* Retrieved from http://www.nclr.org/index.php/publications/ toward_a_more_vibrant_and_youthful_nation_ latino_children_in_the_2010_census/.

Ovando, C., Combs, M. C., & Collier, V. P. (2006). Bilingual & ESL classrooms. *Teaching in multicultural contexts* (4th ed.). New York: McGraw-Hill.

Scherzer, J. (1992). A richness of voices. In A. M. Josephy Jr. (Ed.), *America in 1492: The world of the Indian peoples before the arrival of Columbus* (pp. 251–57). New York: Alfred A. Knopf.

Sundstrom, R. R. (2008). *The browning of America and the evasion of social justice.* New York: SUNY Press.

Zinn, H. (2005). *A people's history of the United States: 1492 to present.* New York: Harper Perennial Modern Classics.

ENGLISH LANGUAGE LEARNERS (ELLs)

ELLs, or English Language Learners, are those students learning English as a second or additional language in a country in which English is the majority language. While adults can also be ELLs, the term is most commonly used to describe children in public schools. In the United States, there are a great number of ELLs, making up over 10 percent in K–12 schools (NCES, 2013). While some school-aged ELLs in the United States are immigrants, the majority of them are native born. In order to be classified as an ELL, parents of schoolchildren complete a home language survey that indicates if a language other than English is spoken at home when the child first enrolls in public school.

The nomenclature for ELLs is wide and varied, having changed considerably throughout the years and often leaning toward popular political or philosophical slants. For example, when George W. Bush was president, the term *bilingual* fell out of favor in political discourse, while it has become more acceptable in recent years. Today, some prefer the term *bilinguals*, while others use *emergent bilinguals* (Garcia, 2009), focusing on the positive characteristics of the learner. In contrast, the long-used acronym *LEP* or *limited English proficient* has for the most part fallen out of use, with the exception of government documents, as a result of its deficit perspective. Other acronyms such as *CLD* or *culturally and linguistically diverse*, *LM* or *language minority*, *ESL* or *English as a Second Language*, or even *ELs* or *English Learners* are used to describe ELLs in schools.

In the United States, the most commonly spoken first language (L1) by ELLs is Spanish, with Vietnamese coming in a far second. ELLs are a very diverse group with varied language, cultural, religious, and educational backgrounds. As a result, there are a number of programs that serve their educational needs. In some parts of the United States, bilingual education provides ELLs with support to learn English and, to varying degrees, their home language. Bilingual education comes in a variety of forms including transitional bilingual education, where the goal is to transition ELLs to all English classes; maintenance bilingual, in which students learn in both their L1 and English throughout their schooling; and two-way immersion, where students of two different home languages learn both languages together, just to name a few. ESL is another support program designed to help ELLs learn language, academic content, and transition to life in English as the dominant language (see entry on ESL in this volume). The difference between these kinds of programs has to do with the language learning goals (Wright, 2010). In all of these cases, however, the learners can be called ELLs.

Holly Hansen-Thomas

References

Garcia, O. (2009). Emergent bilinguals and TESOL: What's in a name? *TESOL Quarterly*, 43(2), 322–26.

U.S. Department of Education, National Center for Education Statistics (NCES). (2013). *The condition of education 2013 (NCES 2013-037) English Language Learners.*

Wright, W. (2010). *Foundations for teaching English language learners: Research, theory, policy, and practice.* Philadelphia: Caslon.

ENGLISH-ONLY MOVEMENT

The English-only movement refers to a political movement advanced mainly by U.S. English and English First—two national groups in the 1980s. The movement advocates for the exclusive use of the English language in official government operations as well as key institutions such as schools. Proponents have often advocated the ratification of a constitutional amendment to declare English the official language and to repeal the bilingual requirement under the Voting Rights Act. Proponents have also been sharply critical of bilingual education. Although several rationales have been advanced for the movement, they can ultimately be encapsulated in Theodore Roosevelt's well-known 1907 quote: "We have room for but one language in this country, and that is the English language, for we intend to see that the crucible turns our people out as Americans, of American nationality, and not as dwellers in a polyglot boarding house" (Roosevelt, 1926, p. 554). The date of Roosevelt's quote suggests that the roots of the English-only movement predate the 1980s. In fact, linguistic restrictions in the form of English literacy requirements were used in the late 1800s and early 1900s for public employment, immigration, suffrage, and naturalization, and the rationale for their use was quite similar to discourse mobilized by current day English-only advocates. At the time, linguistic restrictions were used as a tool to discriminate against African Americans, the poor, and "new" immigrants from Russia, Hungary, and Italy. World War I was also marked by extreme anti-German sentiment, which fueled English-only laws in a number of states.

Scholars often point to the 1980s when writing of the movement, given that it was the epoch that evidenced a stronger formation of organizations. The movement was specifically oriented toward the advocacy of English as the official national and state language as well as key institutional services. Leaders of the movement have advocated several initiatives: "elimination of 911 bilingual operators, health services, drivers' tests, and voting rights; endorsed English-only rules in the workplace; petitioned the Federal Communications Commission to limit foreign-language broadcasting; protested Spanish language menus at McDonald's; opposed Pacific Bell's *Páginas Amarillas en Español* and customer assistance in Chinese; and complained about federal tax forms in Spanish" (Crawford, 1999, p. 65). The foundations of the English-only movement often intersect with anti-immigrant movements. The current manifestation is anchored to the process of racialization and anxieties over racialized transitions.

California's Proposition 63, accelerated by the political advocacy group U.S. English, which was established by Senator S. I. Hayakawa and Dr. John

Tanton (Dr. John Tanton is a retired ophthalmologist, environmentalist, and population-control activist as well as a founder of the Federation for American Immigration Reform (FAIR), a nonprofit organization that advocates for a reduction in the level of immigration into the United States) in 1983, is considered an important achievement in launching English-only advocacy across the United States. The ballot initiative, passed in 1986, sought to ensure English as the common language of the state of California and included a provision to interrupt services in languages other than English in California's schools through lawsuit inducements (Crawford, 1999).

The major organizations that fuel the English-only movement position themselves as grassroots and populist and seductively use appeals to social justice and discourses anchored in "helping" immigrants. Several scholars have claimed that, although such appeals may appear innocent, English-only policies are discriminatory in practice. They limit access to education, government, and employment. Indeed, James Crawford (1999) has indicated that in some respects it may violate the Constitution by way of halting key services, such as due process, through the elimination of court interpreters.

The English-only movement must be understood within a larger discourse and critique of multiculturalism, which has been articulated and seen by some as leading to social tension and the downward spiral of quality education. Through this discourse, one finds an appeal to return to the romantic past and forms of curricula centered on Eurocentricism.

A number of the arguments that serve as the basis of the movement have largely been discredited. Three main arguments consistently surface. First, advocates of English-only consistently argue that the bilingual education movement has been a failure. They point to the lack of academic success of emergent bilingual youth as proof. Yet as Donaldo Macedo has observed, this argument evades the well-documented failure of foreign-language programs and fails to situate the wider failure of public education in major urban areas (Macedo, Dendrinos, & Gounari, 2003). Macedo also argues that the English-only movement seeks to impose English because advocates believe it is the most effective educational language and that it guarantees linguistic minorities a better future. He points out that illiteracy is widespread among monolingual Americans (that is, speakers of English), and that despite the ability of African Americans to speak English, economic success and mobility have been marginal. A number of critical scholars of education have claimed that the underlying impetus for the movement's attack on bilingual education is racist sentiment and seductive processes of racialization. Macedo is, perhaps, the most vocal opponent of English-only educational policy in claiming that it amounts to a form of colonialism.

Second, the movement often claims that current immigrants are refusing to learn English and instead opt to live in "linguistic ghettos." Very rarely do proponents of English-only claim that so-called linguistic ghettos are the result of wider structural inequalities and not simply a matter of option on the part of immigrants. The claim of refusal to learn English or slow rates of acquisition are also faulty. Waggoner (1995) has concluded through extensive research that the rate of acquisition of English is actually very high. Thus far, the research's methodology and conclusion has yet to be significantly challenged. Scholars have also documented the overenrollment and the extensive waiting lists for English programs throughout the nation and the documented rates of native language loss among immigrant schoolchildren, even in highly diverse areas such as San Diego and Miami (Veltman, 1988). Third, the movement claims that bilingual services threaten the unity of the nation. The historical record suggests that there has never existed a period of unity in the United States. Social conflict is endemic to the nation's historical narrative. Yet the existence of linguistic diversity since the colonial era has rarely been a source of political divisiveness. In fact, a number of states authorized the use of bilingual instruction in the nineteenth century without social tension (Crawford, 1997). Many political figures and elites were against the establishment of English as the official language prior to nationhood because, in their view, it ran counter to principles of democracy.

Ricardo D. Rosa

References

Crawford, J. (1997). *Best evidence: Research foundations of the Bilingual Education Act*. Washington, DC: National Clearinghouse for Bilingual Education.

Crawford, J. (1999). *Bilingual education: History, politics, theory and practice* (4th ed.). Los Angeles, CA: Bilingual Education Services, Inc.

Macedo, D., Dendrinos, B., & Gounari, P. (2003). *The hegemony of English*. Boulder, CO: Paradigm Publishers.

Roosevelt, T. (1926). *The memorial edition, 1923–1926* (Vol. XXIV). New York: Charles Scribner & Sons.

Veltman, C. (1988). *The future of the Spanish language in the United States*. Washington, DC: Hispanic Policy Development Project.

Waggoner, D. (1995, November). Are current home speakers of non-English languages learning English? *Numbers and Needs, 5*(6), 1, 3.

ENRICHMENT PROGRAM

Most understand the use of the word *enrichment* to mean the development, fortification, furthering, improvement, or enhancement of an idea, attribute, object, or person (Merriam-Webster, 2013). The term *enrichment program*, more specifically, refers to a curriculum, plan, training course, system, event, or mechanism with the goal of providing support, attention, and development to a specific group or demographic in categories such as education, culture, and vocation. Each of these three categories will be examined in detail.

Educational enrichment is typically geared toward enhancing the academic performance and college readiness of students or narrowing achievement gaps between specific groups of students (Bailey & Bradbury-Bailey, 2010). The U.S. Department of Education administers many programs with the goal of ameliorating low-educational attainment and achievement gaps as well as providing opportunities for adult learners to enter postsecondary education and develop increased vocational skills (U.S. Department of Education, 2012). The entire family of TRiO programs, developed as a result of Lyndon B. Johnson's Economic Opportunity Act of 1964 and Higher Education Act of 1965, focus on assisting students from disadvantaged, low-income, and/or potential first-generation undergraduate college student families. These programs have a history of increasing student undergraduate enrollment and educational attainment in their target populations (Bowling & Thompson, 2013; Graham, 2011; Mahoney, 1998; Trivette, Wilson-Kearse, Dunst, & Hamby, 2012; Pitre & Pitre, 2009). Many of these academic programs also assist in providing at-risk youth with productive after-school activities to help them avoid the temptations of negative activities such as drugs, gang violence, or premature sexual activity (Vinluan, 2005). Some programs, such as the Academic Cultural Enrichment (ACE) Mentorship program (Shinew, Hibbler, & Anderson, 2000), seek to instill strong cultural identities, values, and academic motivation in its participants.

The various goals of *cultural enrichment* include introducing or reinforcing culturally relevant values or identities, enhancing and expanding the perspective and worldview of participants, and improving relationships between disparate groups of individuals. Many cultural enrichment programs have a focus on minority group identity development and support (Ovink & Veazey, 2011) or on building stronger ties with an individual's community to promote increased health and social engagement (Johansson, Konlaan, & Bygren, 2001). The form and content of cultural enrichment can vary as much as the cultures they represent. For many individuals in the Western world, cultural enrichment comes not from specific programs or curricula but from activities such as museum trips; county, state, or regional festivals or fairs; and traditional holiday celebrations such as Thanksgiving, Christmas, and Halloween. Despite not always being viewed or presented as an organized program or plan of study, these events still serve the purpose of introducing or reinforcing relevant cultural values, mores, and oral history. Often these events can have underlying religious value for the community or for the entire country. Christmas in particular is a holiday that is celebrated in over 160 countries worldwide as both a national holiday and an observance of cultural and religious values such as the Christian belief in the divine birth of Jesus Christ (Meacham, 2004). A 2010 Gallup poll conducted by *USA Today* determined that 95 percent of Americans participated or celebrated the Christmas holiday, and of these individuals, 51 percent stated that it has deeply religious undertones. Other significant cultural events (and their respective cultures) that influence and strengthen cultural ties include Ramadan (Islam), Kwanzaa (African), Yom Kippur (Judaism), Hanukkah (Judaism), and Easter (Christianity).

Vocational enrichment typically takes the form of training, technical education, or rehabilitation with the goal of enhancing the skills of the participant or assisting the individual with joining the workforce (U.S. Department of Education, 2012), or in the case of individuals with disabilities, providing the participant with the training and assistance necessary to flourish as an individual in modern society (Mudd, 1980; Wave, 2013). The National Center for Education Statistics (2013) reports that during the 2004–2005 academic year as many as 47.9 percent of American adults participated in some form of career or technical education; many such opportunities for vocational enrichment come from nonprofit institutions such as academic universities and independent grant-funded programs or individual state agencies (within the United States). Vocational enrichment and training is also typically offered in the United States as an optional part of the traditional high school curriculum for those students who are interested in a more technical or "hands-on" field. The advent of modern technology has allowed for individuals without direct access to "brick and mortar" educational institutions to participate in career and vocational skill training through online programming at institutions throughout the United States, such as the University of Phoenix, Kaplan University, and ITT technical institute (Campus Explorer, 2013). To summarize, enrichment programs and activities provide the opportunity for individuals from all walks of life to further their education, cultural awareness, and vocational aptitude. Although these programs take various forms and delivery methods, depending on their content and context, their underlying goal is the same: personal development.

Will Bowling

References

Bailey, D. F. & Bradbury-Bailey, M. E. (2010). Empowered youth programs: Partnerships for enhancing postsecondary outcomes of African American adolescents. *Professional School Counseling, 14*(1), 64–74.

Bowling, W. D. & Thompson, S. (2013). Are we helping? A discussion of the effects of TRiO program intervention on K-12 Appalachian seniors. *Kentucky Journal of Excellence in College Teaching and Learning, 11*, 104–11.

Campus Explorer. (2013). *List of online vocational programs.* Retrieved from http://www.campusexplorer.com/colleges/search/?online=1&schooltype=17&page=2.

Graham, L. (2011). Learning a new world: Reflections on being a first-generation college student and the influence of TRIO programs. *New Directions for Teaching and Learning, 127*, 33–38.

Johansson, S., Konlaan, B., & Bygren, L. (2001). Sustaining habits of attending cultural events and maintenance of health: A longitudinal study. *Health Promotion International, 16*(3), 229–34.

Mahoney, R. G. (1998). Components of TRIO's success: How one student support services program achieved success. *Journal of Negro Education, 67*(4), 381.

Meacham, J. (2004). The birth of Jesus. (Cover story). *Newsweek, 144*(24), 48–58.

Merriam-Webster. (2013). Enrichment. Retrieved from http://www.merriam-webster.com/dictionary/enrichment.

Mudd, T. M. (1980). The life enrichment program. *Journal of Rehabilitation, 46*(4), 50.

National Center for Educational Statistics. (2013). *Career/technical education statistics.* Nces.ed.gov. Retrieved from http://nces.ed.gov/surveys/ctes/tables/A05.asp.

Ovink, S. & Veazey, B. (2011). More than "getting us through": A case study in cultural capital enrichment of underrepresented minority undergraduates. *Research in Higher Education, 52*(4), 370–94. doi: 10.1007/s11162-010-9198-8

Pitre, C. & Pitre, P. (2009). Increasing underrepresented high school students' college transitions and achievements. *NASSP Bulletin, 93*(2), 96–110.

Shinew, K. J., Hibbler, D. K., & Anderson, D. M. (2000). The academic cultural enrichment mentorship program: An innovative approach to serving African American youth. *Journal of Park & Recreation Administration, 18*(3), 103–21.

Trivette, C. M., Wilson-Kearse, J., Dunst, C. J., & Hamby, D. W. (2012). Access to higher education among high school students: Challenges and solutions. *Journal of Social Sciences, 8*(2), 252–57.

United States Department of Education. (2012). *Guide to U.S. Department of Education programs*. Retrieved from http://www2.ed.gov/programs/gtep/gtep.pdf.

USA Today. (2010). *Christmas strongly religious for half in U.S. who celebrate it*. Retrieved from http://www.gallup.com/poll/145367/christmas-strongly-religious-half-celebrate.aspx.

Vinluan, M. (2005). After-school programs alter lives of at-risk youth. *Parks & Recreation, 40*(8), 12–184.

WAVE. (2013). *Life skills program*. Retrieved from http://waveonline.org/.

ENVIRONMENTAL JUSTICE

The term *environmental justice* is defined by the U.S. Environmental Protection Agency (EPA) as the fair treatment and meaningful involvement of all people regardless of race, ethnicity, income, national origin, or educational level with respect to the development, implementation, and enforcement of environmental laws, regulations, and policies (IOM, 1999). The premise of environmental justice (EJ) is that African Americans and other racial or ethnic communities bear a disproportionate amount of exposure to a variety of environmental burdens and hazards. This exposure causes adverse environmental health effects that often result in lower life expectancies and other health disparities among U.S. racial and ethnic groups. Significant health disparities exist between U.S. racial and ethnic groups in terms of key health indicators such as low birth weight, infant mortality, death rates, and cancer. Although communities such as Love Canal and Times Beach, Missouri, received national press coverage for their environmental insults, the many incidents of environmental insults in minority communities are not often shared in the same way.

The EJ movement was ignited in 1982 when a rural, poor, and mostly African American county in North Carolina was selected as the location for a polychlorinated biphenyls (PCBs) landfill. PCBs are a mixture of individual chlorinated chemicals used as coolants and lubricants in transformers and other electrical equipment. The production of PCBs was stopped in the United States in 1977 because of evidence that showed harmful human effects, but they are still found in the environment (HHS, 2001). In fact, the EPA and the International Agency for Research on Cancer have determined that PCBs are probably carcinogenic, or cancer causing to humans (HHS, 2001). Warren County, North Carolina, was chosen as a PCB landfill site because developers saw it as an easy target with the least amount of resistance. The builders of the landfill assumed that rural, poor, black residents would not be able to fight such a development. The residents of Afton, North Carolina, formed the Warren County Citizens Concerned about PCBs and gathered over four hundred protesters and voiced their disapproval of the landfill (Bullard, 1994). It was during these demonstrations that the term *environmental racism* was born. Environmental racism is racial discrimination in environmental policymaking. This term was used frequently in the beginning, and at the height, of the EJ movement; however, the EPA later coined other terms such as *environmental equity* and *environmental justice* to reflect its efforts in addressing environmental racism.

In 1972, before the incidents in Afton, the United Church of Christ Commission for Racial Justice, a faith-based organization, voiced its disapproval of the Warren County PCB landfill and other sites like it in the nation. With the Commission's voice, the Congressional Black Caucus, and many other civic and political supporters pushing for justice, the U.S. Government Accounting Office (GAO) conducted a study in 1983 to determine where hazardous waste landfill sites were located. The GAO study revealed a strong relationship between the citing of hazardous waste landfills and the race and socioeconomic status of surrounding communities. The states in this study included North Carolina, South Carolina, and Alabama. Emelle, Alabama, in Sumter County is another well-known example of environmental injustice. The population of Emelle is mostly African American, and the majority of the residents live below the poverty line. Emelle is often described as the economically impoverished black belt of western Alabama. In 1978, the citizens of Emelle were told that a safe, new industry, which would provide jobs to replace the diminishing agricultural economy of the area, was coming to their town. However, only a small portion of local residents were offered jobs at the site, and ChemWaste (a subsidiary of Waste Management) proceeded to run its hazardous waste treatment, storage, and disposal facility in Sumter County. Emelle became the home for the nation's largest hazardous waste landfill.

In 1987, the United Church of Christ Commission for Racial Justice released its groundbreaking study titled *Toxic Wastes and Race in the United States*. The findings of this study showed that communities with greater minority percentages were more likely to be the sites of commercial hazardous waste facilities. This study was another spark in the EJ movement, and it spurred conversations and questions among academicians, politicians, and other grassroots organizations. In 1992, the EPA followed with its final release on a report titled *Environmental Equity: Reducing Risks for All Communities*. This report showed that there were clear differences between racial groups in terms of disease and death rates. The report also showed that racial minority and low-income populations experience higher-than-average exposures to pollutants and hazardous waste facilities. In 1994, the leaders of the EJ movement and six government agencies convened the first federal symposium on environmental justice. At this symposium, President Clinton signed Executive Order 12898: Federal Actions to Address Environmental Justice in Minority Populations and Low-Income Populations.

The primary intent of Executive Order 12898 was threefold. First, it was to assist federal agencies in recognizing EJ as an issue, thereby leading to the formation of EJ workgroups and the formation of the Office of Environmental Justice at EPA headquarters. Second, it required EPA and the other federal agencies to have a written plan to address EJ issues germane to their organizations. Third, and most importantly, the executive order gave impacted communities a chance to gain awareness and be educated about environmental health issues. Through the executive order, communities can apply for small grants and be a part of solving and preventing environmental injustice in their communities. A federal bill labeled as HR1103—the Environmental Justice Act—was proposed in 2007, but it never became a law and the last action by Congress on the bill was on October 4, 2007, when the House Energy and Commerce Committee held a hearing. The legislation introduced by Congresswoman Hilda Solis (D-Calif.) and others would have been used to codify the executive order on EJ. Moving forward with EJ will require more enforcement from the EPA and the Department of Justice in order for communities to see relief from disproportionate and cumulative pollution burdens.

After two decades, the detoxification of the PCB landfill in Warren County, North Carolina, began in 2001. The cleanup activity ended in 2003, and a park was constructed on the site of the old landfill. Despite numerous regulatory violations, worker exposure, offsite water contamination, local opposition, and the involvement of grassroots organizations, the landfill in Emelle remains open. Cases like those of Afton and Emelle are plentiful, and the fight continues.

Many of the communities labeled as EJ communities are located in small southern towns or neighborhoods like Afton and Emelle with very little political power and even fewer financial and educational resources. There is an enormous need for research related to the health disparities and the environmental impacts of residents in these areas. There are many untold stories and facts attached to EJ. The United Church of Christ Commission for Racial Justice conducted its own study and sought EJ for everyone, but other communities around the nation and internationally can be empowered to do the same.

Sheila Davidson Pressley

References

Bullard, R. D. (1994). *Dumping in Dixie: Race, class, and environmental quality*. Boulder: Westview Press.

Institute of Medicine (IOM). (1999). *Toward environmental justice: Research education and health policy needs*. Washington, DC: National Academy Press.

U.S. Department of Health and Human Services (HHS). (2001). *ToxFAQs for Polychlorinated Biphenyls (PCBs)*. Retrieved from the Agency for Toxic Substances and Disease Registry (ATSDR), http://www.atsdr.cdc.gov/tfacts17.html.

EQUAL PROTECTION

Equal protection is the notion that all people are equal before the law. In the context of the United States, the concept typically refers to the Equal Protection Clause of the Fourteenth Amendment, which reads: "no state shall . . . deny to any person within its jurisdiction the equal protection of the laws." The application of this concept has resulted in many important gains for marginalized groups. Yet at the same time, commitment to this principle has not necessarily produced equality in practice, and in some instances, its evocation has served to justify unequal social arrangements.

The notion of equal protection first took root in U.S. law after the Civil War, with the passage of the Fourteenth Amendment and the Civil Rights Act of 1868. Coming in response to the differential legal treatment of blacks and whites following the abolition of slavery, such legislative action in many respects foreshadowed the double-edged nature of equal protection that would follow. On the one hand, the law now afforded former slaves important legal protections, providing some with the ability to engage in civic life in ways that theretofore had been impossible. On the other hand, legalized segregation, and the racism that fueled it, persisted.

Looking back on the use of the concept of equal protection in the nineteenth century, one is also confronted with instances in which the concept was used to justify *in*equality. The case of *Plessy v. Ferguson* (1896) is exemplary here. In using the infamous phrase *separate but equal* to uphold a Louisiana law requiring blacks and whites to ride on separate railroad cars, the Supreme Court used the notion of equal protection to justify segregation while at the same time turning its back on the reality that racism and its consequences remained real.

It was not until almost a full century later that the U.S. government would give serious consideration to the thought of dismantling the legal and social barriers that became known as Jim Crow segregation. *Plessy* was overturned by the landmark school desegregation case, *Brown v. Board of Education* (1954), and amid the civil rights movement, Congress passed what is widely regarded as the most important piece of equal protection legislation in U.S. history: the Civil Rights Act of 1964. This landmark legislation prohibited, among other things,

employers from discriminating on the basis of race, religion, and national origin, and it made illegal unequal application of voter registration requirements and barred discrimination at public accommodation sites, such as restaurants and hotels. The bill also assured that laws were treating everyone equally by encouraging the desegregation of public schools and by prohibiting local governments from denying people access to public facilities.

Other historically marginalized groups have likewise made important gains pertaining to equal protection in recent decades. In 1971, the Supreme Court acknowledged for the first time in *Reed v. Reed* (1971) that the Equal Protection Clause should in fact apply to women. The Supreme Court also relied on the concept of equal protection in the case of *Romer v. Evans* (1996) when it notably struck down

---

A List of Some Key Supreme Court Decisions Dealing with Equal Protection

Plessy v. Ferguson (1896)—The Court upholds a Louisiana law requiring blacks and whites to ride on separate railroad cars, infamously declaring such arrangements were "separate but equal."

Brown Board of Education (1954)—The Court overturns Plessy, declaring the legally sanctioned segregation of schools unconstitutional.

Reed v. Reed (1971)—Dealing with the issue of the administration of estates, the Court declared for the first time that the Equal Protection Clause of the Fourteenth Amendment does indeed apply to sex discrimination.

Richmond v. J. A. Croson Co. (1989)—The Court struck down a Richmond bill designed to increase the amount of minority-owned businesses that would receive government contracts on the grounds that it amounted to a mistreatment of whites. This ruling came despite the fact that, without such a bill in place, African Americans received less than 1 percent of city contracts in a city where the population was 50 percent African American.

Romer v. Evans (1996)—A decision that struck down an amendment to the Colorado Constitution prohibiting any state laws that bar discrimination on the basis of sexuality.

an amendment to the Colorado Constitution prohibiting any state laws that bar discrimination on the basis of sexuality, thus providing lesbians, gays, bisexuals, and transsexuals (LGBT) with the assurance of equal protection under the law. And more recently, in *Olmstead v. L. C.* (1999), the Supreme Court affirmed that people who are mentally ill are deserving of equal protection under the landmark Americans with Disabilities Act (ADA) (1999).

Yet even amid such progress, inequality in practice persists into the present day and is often sanctioned by law. Women continue to make less money, on average, than men for working the same jobs (American Association of University Women, 2012); people of color find themselves facing institutional barriers in education, employment, health care, and the criminal justice system (Feagin, 2000); the LGBT community is legally barred from marrying and thus deprived of the several legal benefits that married couples receive; and people with disabilities continue to be treated as second-class citizens (Silvers & Stein, 2001).

What is more, in many recent legal decisions involving the notion of equal protection, the Supreme Court has been unwilling to apply the Equal Protection Clause absent clear evidence of discriminatory intent. While seemingly reasonable on the surface, many have raised questions about this standard, especially as it is applied in cases pertaining to race, considering that discriminatory intent is increasingly difficult to prove in an era where overt racism has, for the most part, been replaced with subconscious and covert racism (Haney López, 2006).

The case of *McClesky v. Kemp* (1987) provides a poignant example. In challenging a death sentence their client received for murdering a white Georgia police officer, attorneys for Warren McClesky, an African American, presented the court with a comprehensive study that revealed the stark tendency of the Georgia criminal justice system to disproportionately sentence blacks to death, especially when the victim was white. Indeed, such trends mirror a large body of social science research that reveals similar disparities in all stages of the administration of criminal justice (Tonry, 2011). People of color are more likely to be targeted, arrested, and more harshly sentenced than their white counterparts.

Despite this compelling evidence, however, the court upheld McClesky's conviction absent the defendant's ability to prove that criminal justice actors deliberately discriminated against him.

Similar trends are evident in recent affirmative action decisions. Many recent policies that were intended to achieve equality have been struck down on equal protection grounds. The argument here is that majority groups (e.g., whites, men) have been discriminated against by policies aimed at fostering the inclusion of historically marginalized groups. Again, this is despite the fact that social arrangements in the United States tend to be such that, absent these policies, widespread disparities and white privileges persist. In *Richmond v. J. A. Croson Co.* (1989), the Supreme Court struck down a bill designed to increase the amount of minority-owned businesses that would receive government contracts from the city of Richmond, arguing essentially that the bill amounted to the mistreatment of whites. Yet such a ruling overlooked the fact that, without the policy in place, less than 1 percent of city contracts went to African Americans in a city where the population is 50 percent African American.

Many have thus argued that modern equal protection jurisprudence is not unlike *Plessy* (Ross, 1990). The Court, somewhat ironically, has evoked the concept in a way that avoids confrontation with the glaring reality that people *are not* protected equally by the law. In this respect, the legacy of equal protection endures: as a central legal concept, it has helped move us toward a more inclusive society, but by no means has it been a panacea. Even after we reaffirmed our commitment to this principle during the civil rights movement, there remains a gulf between equal protection as an abstract ideal and equal protection as it plays out on the ground.

Jamie Longazel

References

American Association of University Women. (2012). *The simple truth about the gender pay gap*. Retrieved from http://www.aauw.org/research/the-simple-truth-about-the-gender-pay-gap/.

Feagin, J. R. (2000). *Racist America: Roots, current realities, and future reparations*. New York: Routledge.

Haney López, I. (2006). *White by law: The legal construction of race* (10th anniversary ed.). New York: New York University Press.

Ross, T. (1990). The rhetorical tapestry of race: White innocence and black abstraction. *William & Mary Law Review, 32*(1), 1–40.

Silvers, A. & Stein, M. A. (2001). Disability, equal protection, and the Supreme Court: Standing at the crossroads of progressive and retrogressive logic in constitutional classification. *University of Michigan Journal of Law Reform, 35*(1&2), 81–136.

Tonry, M. (2011). *Punishing race: A continuing American dilemma.* New York: Oxford University Press.

EQUITY

What Is Equity?

Equity is a term that is often conflated with other terms, such as *equality, diversity, fairness,* and more. Within social science, equity is viewed and understood in terms of one's relations and interactions with others, particularly where disconnects in opportunity, identity, and privilege occur. According to Unterhalter (2009), "Academic literature which uses the term equity in education does not stress . . . separating equity from equality, but concentrates primarily on fairness in distribution, collapsing equity into aspects of equality" (p. 416). However, equity and equality are not synonymous. While equity is characterized by fairness and justice, equality is characterized by all things being equal, the same. Using the term *equality* implies that all things are equal in quantity, degree, and value, whereas using the term *equity* implies that things are in the best interest of the other to assure that interactions are just—guided by truth, reason, fairness, and justice. As an example, if a shoe salesperson has a store full of customers that need shoes, exemplifying equality means that s/he gives size 6 shoes to all of the customers regardless of their foot size so as to be consistent and equal. On the other hand, exemplifying equity, s/he would ensure that each customer is able to obtain the shoe that is appropriate for each customer based on style, size, and purpose.

Types of Equity

The definition of *equity* varies in different fields of study and professions. In the profession of law, the term relates to the principles of natural justice to the settlement of controversies. When a judge rules on a case that does not have a set precedence by seeking a fair and just ruling based on the natural course of events to follow the incident, s/he is engaging in equity.

Equity in finance is much more straightforward than that of equity in law. Financial equity is the monetary value of a property or business after considering what is owed. For example, the homeowner of a $200,000 home that has paid the mortgage down to $125,000 has $75,000 equity in their home. The equity is the difference between the value of the home and the amount owed.

Identity equality and equity are different considerations all together. Identity equality relates to the conditions that would be achieved if identity was not a factor and all things were equal. Racial equity, on the other hand, would consider the role of race, and other intersections of identity, in determining equity when factoring in an identity feature can be used to help better distribute opportunities to those from underrepresented groups. The intention of affirmative action is to account for inequitable distribution of opportunities based on identity features.

Potential Drawback of Equity

Because equity is characterized by being equal and fair to others, challenges arise with the concern of what is fair to whom and determined by whom. Unterhalter explains that "diversity complicates the idea of fairness; without specifying how diversity intersects equity the term risks becoming either merely rhetorical or impossibly difficult to implement" (2009). When oppressive groups attempt to implement equity-based approaches, they may often be blinded consciously or subconsciously to their own privilege and work to create outcomes that may appear to be more equitable but may in fact be similarly troubling to underrepresented and oppressed groups.

Benterah C. Morton
Kenneth J. Fasching-Varner

References

Freire, P. (2000). *Pedagogy of the oppressed.* New York: Continuum International Publishing Group.

Unterhalter, E. (2009). What is equity in education? Reflections from the capability approach. *Studies in Philosophy and Education*, 28, 415–24.

ETHICAL DECISION MAKING

People have always confronted many different ethical problems and dilemmas in their daily life. However, the rapidly changing social environment brings up ethical issues that are more complicated than ever. In the past, people developed and tested ethical principles and values that were validated to be employed as a guide for most situations and circumstances. However, the steady guides are inadequate to provide guidance for every type of ethical issue people experience today. Ethical decisions need to be made by relying on a varied set of sophisticated principles that are applicable to many different ethical issues. There is no simple decision-making practice that is applicable to all ethical situations. Therefore, it is important to have ethical principles in place that allow judgments informed by ethical approaches. In this regard, before the ethical decision process, the main ethical approaches are reviewed.

Ethical Approaches

Individuals feel instinctively that a certain solution to an ethical problem is proper or improper. It is important to determine which ethical approach and criteria are used to make such judgments. Ethical decision making can be investigated based on various ethical perspectives. Here, the major ethical approaches of consequentialism, deontology, and virtue ethics will be handled in the decision-making context.

The first ethical decision-making approach is consequentialism, which mainly focuses on the consequences of action rather than means or intentions. In the consequentialist perspective, whether an action is morally acceptable or not depends on its consequences. The morally acceptable action is the one that creates the greatest happiness for the greatest number of people. Utilitarianism, one major branch of consequentialism, seeks the ultimate happiness for everyone. This approach emphasizes the ends of specific actions so that what a person achieves is more important than how that person achieves it. In other words, ends justify means. In this context, when an ethical decision is made, calculating and estimating the consequences of actions

is essential. In ethical decision making according to the utilitarian approach, the right alternative among various courses of actions is the one that maximizes happiness and minimizes pain for the greatest number of people.

Deontological ethics suggest that moral acceptability of an action depends on the action's compliance with the rules. Deontology emphasizes the intentions and motives of a person rather than the consequences of actions. Deontology requires adherence to obligations, rules, and duties. Morally right action needs to be motivated by universal principles that might be respected by everyone. Some of the duties, rules, and obligations are universal, such as "do not kill, steal and lie," while some others are specific to people depending on their role within the society. According to this approach, individuals who make decisions based on their duties and obligations are expected to behave consistently, since the same rules and obligations constitute a basis for their decision-making process.

A deontologist ethical approach suggests that results do not always justify the means. Adherence to rules with a good intention or motivation will produce consistent ethical behaviors. Therefore, deontologists suggest that any ethical action should not violate ethical rules and obligations. Since one cannot easily predict the consequences of any action, he/she is expected to behave in accordance to rules, obligations, and duties but not to the estimated consequences.

Virtue ethics refers to a normative ethical approach that emphasizes being an ethical person with a strong character rather than doing the right thing in given individual situations. In other words, virtue ethics argues that morality stems from the character of a person rather than an action of the person. Ethical behavior or actions of the individual are evaluated by his/her character in virtue ethics. Virtue ethics takes an individual's moral values and his/her reputation and motivation behind the action into account when evaluating his/her behavior. Virtue ethics argues that a human being is to live for a purpose, which is human flourishing.

Ethical Decision-Making Process

RECOGNIZING AN ETHICAL ISSUE Being sensitive to ethical issues and identifying the ethical problems constitutes the first step in ethical decision making. An ethical issue refers to a problem or dilemma that is either beyond being a legal and professional problem or combination of the two. The key point at this stage is having enough information to make a decision. At this stage, gathering specific and objective information on the issue under consideration will clarify the situation and ease the decision-making process. It requires more than one option toward a solution, each of which will have its own advantages and disadvantages.

DETERMINING ALTERNATIVE COURSES OF ACTION Ethical problems are usually complex, and solutions to those problems are not apparent and simple. Therefore, determining various aspects of the ethical issue is very essential in the ethical decision-making process. In addition, the stakeholders of the issue, and their role in this context, should be determined to be able to assess who will benefit and come to harm from a specific action. After determining all parties and the aspects of the ethical issue under consideration, possible courses of action are to be identified precisely. Ensuring that all alternatives are taken into account is essential to make an effective ethical decision.

MAKING A DECISION Decision making requires selecting one of the alternatives. In other words, decision makers need to make a judgment on which option is the right way to act. Sometimes a choice is not available between a right and wrong action; instead, it would need to be made between two right alternatives.

At this point, the different ethical approaches reviewed above might suggest a different way of acting in a given situation. Consequentialists, for instance, place emphasis on the consequences of the decision. They would ask which alternative will create the most good and do the least harm for the greatest number of people. Based on the answer to this question, they are expected to decide which option to choose. Deontologists, on the other hand, are expected to focus on the duties, obligations, and rules that bind individuals involved in the case, regardless of the consequences of their choice. According to this approach, the course of action that requires parties to behave in compliance with their immediate duty is preferred. Finally, virtue ethics emphasizes the character of individuals rather than

their actions. In this case, one must select the option that will probably lead an individual to act as the type of person he/she wants to be.

The appropriateness of the decision is usually assessed in two ways. First, the decision maker would be comfortable if his/her decision is publicized on the television or the front page of the newspaper. Second, the decision maker should ensure that the ethical code of someone that decision maker cares about (usually the decision maker's mother) is being respected. If at least one of these criteria is violated, the decision needs to be reconsidered by the decision maker.

IMPLEMENTING AND MONITORING THE DECISION After making the decision, an implementation plan needs to be made. The plan is to be implemented by taking into account the concerns of parties. Monitoring how the decision turns out and what the effects of the decision are offers valuable information for future decisions in similar situations. In this regard, each situation and related decisions made are an important source of learning.

In sum, making ethical decisions requires the capacity to choose between competing alternatives. The ethical decision-making model above can be taken as a guide to make better decisions. However, it is important to note that decisions are not free from social and professional pressures.

Hidayet Tasdoven

References

Cottone, R. R. & Claus, R. E. (2000). Ethical decision-making models: A review of the literature. *Journal of Counseling & Development, 78*, 275–83.

Forester-Miller, H. & Davis, T. (1996). *A practitioner's guide to ethical decision-making*. Alexandria, VA: American Counseling Association.

Johnson, C. (2001). *Meeting the ethical challenges of leadership*. Thousand Oaks, CA: Sage.

Josephson, M. (2002). *Making ethical decisions*. Marina del Rey, CA: Josephson Institute of Ethics.

ETHNIC CLEANSING

Ethnic cleansing (EC) has manifested itself among various ethnic groups over the past few centuries, and regrettably, it has taken place numerous times during the course of human history. Although there is no universal definition of the term, it commonly refers to the forcible geographic removal of a group of people primarily based on their race, ethnicity, and/or religious affiliation using violence, terror, and fear tactics. This systematic expulsion need not always take the form of mass murder but may also involve verbal and physical assault, rape, sterilization, intimidation, imprisonment, and forced relocation (i.e., ghettoization). EC is often rooted in dominant racial ideologies and stereotypes that assert that certain groups are inferior in some way and need to be removed in order to "purify" a particular society from social ills.

The term became popularized during the Bosnian Wars between 1992 and 1995 and was used by Western media outlets to garner public support for a United Nations–led intervention in the region.

Unfortunately, many groups have been the recipients of ethnic cleansing; most notably, the Hutus in Rwanda (ethnicity), Bosnian Muslims in Kosovo (religion), Rohingya Muslims in Burma (religion), Armenian Christians in Turkey (ethnicity/religion), Jews and Afro-Germans in Germany (race/ethnicity/religion), Palestinian Arabs in Israel (ethnicity/religion), non-Arabs in Darfur (religion), and countless other examples. Of particular concern is the fact that many incidents of ethnic cleansing are state sanctioned, which make them even more severe since they tend to be backed by those in political power. In order to fully understand the roots and complexities of ethnic cleansing, one must attempt to understand the historical context by which EC has arisen.

In order for a society affected by EC to properly heal, perpetrators at every level must be held accountable, and the political leadership must move beyond lip service by stating that the atrocities were merely wrong. Furthermore, mutual respect and tolerance must be fostered among the affected groups. After the mass killing of over one million Hutus in Rwanda, Truth and Reconciliation panels were set up in order to have dialogues surrounding forgiveness, empathy, and understanding between survivors, families of victims, and perpetrators and to potentially heal the physical and emotional wounds that were prevalent. They were largely successful.

However, this occurrence is rare. After ethnic cleansing, animosity and hatred may still be widespread and further cause emotional anguish for the surviving victims and their families, potentially fueling further ethnic conflict and political and economic instability.

Tariqah Nuriddin

References

Kamaroopi. (1993). Ethnic cleansing. *Economic and Political Weekly, 28*(41), 2172–73.

Pappe, I. (2006). *The ethnic cleansing of Palestine.* Oxford: One World Publications Limited.

Washington, H. (2006). *Medical apartheid: The dark history of medical experimentation on black Americans from colonial times to present.* Doubleday: New York.

World Affairs Institute. (1993). Bosnia and the future of ethnic cleansing. *World Affairs, 156*(2), 104–6.

ETHNIC GROUP

An ethnic group refers to a socially recognized set of people who have a common heritage or background who may share the same country of origin, cultural practices (e.g., religious beliefs, primary language, socially transmitted customs), or racial characteristics (e.g., skin color, facial structure, hair color). The interconnection between ethnic groups and other socially distinguished groups, such as cultural and racial groups, introduces sociocultural complexity when defining and classifying ethnic groups. Cultural groups are socially differentiated based on shared practices, beliefs, and values held by a collection of people. Racial groups are socially differentiated based on observable physical characteristics, such as skin color and hair texture. Ethnic groups may be interconnected with cultural and racial groups because people within the same ethnic group often engage in similar cultural activities and often display similar racial characteristics.

Theorists suggest that an ethnic group can be broadly or narrowly defined based on the primary characteristics considered (Yang, 2000). Ethnic groups can be narrowly defined if a collective body of individuals shares the same country of origin and/or cultural practices. Broadly defined ethnic groups are identified by a collective body of individuals who share the same country of origin, cultural practices, and/or racial characteristics. In either case, at least one of the corresponding facets must be met for each of the respective definitions. Ethnic groups, and membership within an ethnic group, may be self-defined (i.e., socially distinguished by members of the group itself) or objectively defined (i.e., socially distinguished by people outside of the group and usually based on external, observable ethnic features such as skin color and facial structure).

The shared practices, beliefs, and values of an ethnic group contribute to a sense of cohesion. In addition, the characteristics that differ from one ethnic group to another often further distinguish these groups and contribute to views among group members that their ethnic group is unique from other ethnic groups. The differences between ethnic groups, real or perceived, may sometimes contribute to tension and hostility between members of different ethnic groups. These hostile perceptions or interactions are more likely to occur when group differences are viewed in a negative light, or when there is a lack of understanding of the nature of the differences between ethnic groups. However, the differences between ethnic groups generally pale in comparison to the commonalities that can be found across members of certain ethnic groups, and the differences that do exist do not play a fundamental role in defining human nature.

Classification of Ethnic Groups

Ethnic groups are generally classified through the use of labels that represent some aspect of their shared characteristics or heritage. The label used varies based on how the term *ethnic group* is defined. For example, when "ethnic group" is linked to racial characteristics, names such as *white* or *black* may be used to identify specific ethnic groups. In other cases, when the conceptualization of an ethnic group is linked to country of origin or nationality, labels such as *European* or *African American* may be used.

There are several benefits to classifying ethnic groups. Ethnic group membership contributes to a social connection that is subjectively meaningful to many individuals. Members often base part of their identity on their ethnic group affiliation. This identification often has strong implications on an individual's psychological adjustment and social well-being. The classification of ethnic groups is also intended to provide information on the characteristics of a population. Information on the ethnic group representation within a population may be used to identify the social, political, and health needs of the groups and to ensure the provision of equal opportunities (e.g., employment, education) and appropriate services (e.g., health care) (Sandefur, Campbell, & Eggerling-Boeck, 2004). At times, the classification of ethnic groups may be disadvantageous when the categories used are too limited, heterogeneous, or nonrepresentative. Other issues that may arise from classifying ethnic groups for the purpose of identifying needs of specific groups is that, for certain aspects (e.g., education and employment), there may be more similarities between members of different groups than there are similarities among individuals within an ethnic group. In addition, some of the differences that are attributed to ethnic group status may actually be due to other socioeconomic influences.

Self-defined identification has become the more prevalent option for classifying ethnic groups due to the subjectivity of ethnic group membership. However, although this approach supports the saliency of personal affiliation with one's ethnic group(s), it may adversely affect the ability to adequately ensure equal opportunities and service provision. As noted by Waters (1990), while ethnic identity (i.e., how much an individual feels that he/she is a part of an ethnic group) is generally purely based on self-definition, being viewed by society as a member of an ethnic group is usually not solely based on self-defined classification. Many individuals have certain features or characteristics that associate them with a particular ethnic group. As a result, these individuals are often viewed by society as belonging to that ethnic group, which in turn influences the possible social implications (e.g., unequal treatment) associated with being perceived as belonging to the ethnic group. Thus, objectively defined identification of group members may be more useful in situations that concern the social consequences of ethnic group membership (Aspinall, 1997).

Defining and Classifying Ethnic Groups across Time

In industrialized Western nations, such as the United States, approaches to describing ethnic groups have varied across time (Sandefur et al., 2004). During the nineteenth and early twentieth centuries, ethnic and racial groups were essentially considered identical and predominantly biologically based, suggesting that individuals were born into a specific ethnic group, and ethnic group membership was permanent. Classification of ethnic group members was generally based on observable ethnic features.

During the second half of the twentieth century, the characteristics considered when defining ethnic groups became predominantly socially distinguished (e.g., based on heritage and cultural practices), rather than biologically determined. Choices about ethnic group membership also reflected a dynamic process that involved an interconnection between one's heritage, country of origin, racial characteristics, and cultural practices. Previously, when ethnic group information was gathered through most data collection systems (e.g., census data collection, social science and health research), ethnic enumeration generally relied on observer-selection. Toward the turn of the century, most Western nations began to shift to systems that allowed individuals to choose the ethnic group with which they felt most affiliated.

There is now a growing movement toward using the terms *ethnic* and *racial* interchangeably due to a converging conceptualization of the terms (American Anthropological Association, 1997). There is also an emergent trend toward deemphasizing the use of the words *race* or *racial*, and using classifications based on ethnic groups instead. As suggested by the American Anthropological Association, ethnic enumeration allows for the classification of more specific social categories, is more relevant for empirical purposes (e.g., is a better predictor of health and social outcomes), and generally holds less negative connotations than the concept of race. In addition, there is a need to better account for the increasing representation of individuals with multiple ethnic backgrounds. In response to this, many ethnic group data collection systems have begun to include opportunities for individuals to select more than one ethnic background.

Defining and Classifying Ethnic Groups across Countries

Using global data on the "2000 round" (1995–2004) of government census data collected by the United Nations Statistical Division, Morning (2008) documented variability in categories used for ethnic enumeration in over 140 countries. The overview revealed that over 60 percent of the countries used some form of ethnic enumeration in their government census. Of these countries, some used question-and-answer formats that better reflected ethnic characteristics based on country of origin or racial characteristics, whereas other countries used formats that defined and classified ethnic groups based on the different languages or dialects spoken by the inhabitants. In comparison to the other countries that did include some form of ethnic enumeration, the United States was the only one that categorized ethnic and racial group membership separately. The United States was also the only country that included just one ethnic affiliation (Hispanic or non-Hispanic) in the single question pertaining to ethnic group membership. The other nations that incorporated some type of ethnic enumeration used the terms *ethnic* and *racial* interchangeably, refrained from using the terms *race* or *racial* altogether, and/or included a wider range of possible affiliations in their questions directed at ethnic enumeration. Despite these differences, the approach to ethnic enumeration used by other nations with comparable demographic composition to the United States was conceptually similar to the approach to racial enumeration used by the United States (e.g., both approaches included similar response categories such as white, black, Chinese, and Korean). Similar to the 2000 census, the overall ethnic enumeration format used by the United States in the 2010 census still separates the categorization of ethnic and racial groups and includes only one option for ethnic affiliation (i.e., Hispanic or non-Hispanic) (Humes, Jones, & Ramirez, 2011).

The social-cultural complexities involved in the process of defining and classifying ethnic groups has led to variability in the conceptualization of the construct. Current understanding suggests that ethnic groups are primarily socially distinguished and are defined based on an interconnection between a variety of sociocultural factors, such as nationality, cultural practices, and racial characteristics. Existing lines of inquiry call for better representation of the term *ethnic group*, especially when used for ethnic enumeration, so that information gained through the use of the term will have empirical value and personal significance for members of identified ethnic groups.

Ayanda Chakawa
Steven K. Shapiro

References

American Anthropological Association. (1997). *AAA response to OMB Directive: Race and ethnic standards for federal statistics and administrative reporting.* Arlington, VA: American Anthropological Association.

Aspinall, P. J. (1997). The conceptual basis of ethnic group terminology and classifications. *Social Science & Medicine, 45*(5), 689–98.

Humes, K. R., Jones, N. A., & Ramirez, R. R. (2011). Overview of race and Hispanic origin: 2010 (Report No. C2010BR-02). *2010 Census Briefs.* Washington, DC: U.S. Census Bureau, U.S. Department of Commerce.

Morning, A. (2008). Ethnic classification in global perspective: A cross-national survey of the 2000 census round. *Population Research and Policy Review, 27*(2): 239–72.

Sandefur, G. D., Campbell, M., & Eggerling-Boeck, J. (2004). Racial and ethnic identification, official classifications, and health disparities. In N. B. Anderson, E. A. Bulatao, & B. Cohen (Eds.), *Critical perspectives on racial and ethnic differences in health in late life* (pp. 25–52). Washington, DC: National Academy Press.

Waters, M. (1990). *Ethnic options: Choosing identities in America.* Berkeley: University of California Press.

Yang, P. Q. (2000). *Ethnic studies: Issues and approaches.* Albany: State University of New York Press.

ETHNIC AND RACIAL STEREOTYPES

Ethnic and racial stereotypes are simplistic, often negative, generalizations ascribed to ethnic/racial/national groups and members based on perceived cultural deficiencies and characteristics. According to Madon et al. (2001), "Stereotypes can bias impressions of individuals, produce self-fulfilling prophecies, and lead to discrimination and harassment" (p. 997). Ethnic and racial stereotypes operate and are applied at various levels of social strata (e.g., racial groups, nation-states, ethnic communities, individuals) and are circulated through various forms of media (e.g., Internet, film, television, newspapers) and cultural practices (e.g., stories, games, jokes) (Feagin, 2014; Omi & Winant, 1994; Ramirez-Berg, 2002; Weaver, 2011). The continued persistence and power of ethnic and racial stereotypes to stigmatize and marginalize nonwhites, in particular, is evident in the historical absorption of previously stereotyped white ethnic groups into "whiteness" (Brodkin, 1998; Ignatiev, 2008; Roediger, 1999).

A cognitive psychological approach to stereotypes suggests stereotyping is an essential cognitive function that allows us to categorize and organize our experiences to make sense of the world around us (Lippman, 1932; Tajfel, 1982). However, a critical approach to ethnic and racial stereotyping suggests ethnic and racial stereotypes are also political and ideological constructions that allow dominant groups to categorize and inferiorize minority groups to the point where stereotypes become "common sense" (Feagin, 2014; Omi & Winant, 1994). The U.S. mass media contributes to shaping and reproducing ethnic and racial stereotypes that help preserve systemic racism in the United States and around the world. According to Ramirez-Berg (2002), while an individual's cognitive constructs, or stereotypes, may or may not be pernicious and may or may not remain a "private image," they are unlikely to travel far beyond an individual's in-group. Ramirez-Berg contrasts this "private image" with a "mediated public image," such as the stereotypical portrayal of ethnic and racial minorities in Hollywood cinema as criminal, dangerous, and/or buffoonish, which is "always public" and has the potential to circulate ethnic and racial stereotypes to a global audience (Ramirez-Berg, 2002, p. 38). Similarly, Feagin (2014) suggests U.S. media corporations and elites, which today comprise roughly eight out of nine multinational media conglomerates, have long contributed to the initiation and reproduction of stereotypical depictions of ethnic and racial minorities across media platforms and are a major force that circulates ethnic and racial stereotypes around the world from a "white racial frame" (pp. 140–42).

Ethnic and racial stereotypes are also commonly circulated as jokes (Davies, 1990; Feagin, 2014). Berger (1998) suggests ethnic and racial humor reinforces stereotypes and tends to rely on techniques such as "ridicule, insult, use of dialect, [and] revelation of ignorance," which work to depict the stereotyped target as inferior (pp. 67–68). However, ethnic and racial stereotypes have not gone uncontested. Because ethnic and racial stereotypes are applied with a rigid and ahistorical logic that works to inferiorize targeted groups (Ramirez-Berg, 2002), ethnic and racial minorities have sought to combat stereotypes and denigrating images (Bender, 2003; Boskin, 1986; Kibler, 2009). For instance, groups such as the Anti-Defamation League (ADL), the NAACP, and the Involvement of Mexican-Americans in Gainful Endeavors (IMAGE) organized to successfully challenge degrading and stereotypical images of Jews, African Americans, and Latinos at different points during the twentieth century. Comedians also played a role in the struggle over representation by rearticulating the use and focus of degrading stereotypes and words (Haggins, 2007; Weaver, 2011). Berger (1999) suggests that by the early 1990s ethnic and racial stereotypical humor by whites declined in mass media and in the public domain as a result of opposition by ethnic and racial minorities. However, the struggle over stereotypes and representation is not over, and some suggest racial and ethnic stereotyping by whites is reemerging in popular culture (Bonilla-Silva & Ashe, 2014; Pérez, 2013). Therefore, the quest for diversity and social justice is a daily struggle that requires an educated and engaged public that is willing to challenge "common sense" notions of ethnic and racial inequality.

Raul Nguyen-Perez

References

Bender, S. (2003). *Greasers and gringos: Latinos, law, and the American imagination.* New York: NYU Press.

Berger, A. A. (1999). *An anatomy of humor.* Edison, NJ: Transaction Publishers.

Bonilla-Silva, E. & Ashe, A. (2014). The end of racism? Colorblind racism and popular media. In S. E. Turner & S. Nilsen (Eds.), *The colorblind screen: Television in post-racial America.* New York: NYU Press.

Boskin, J. (1986). *Sambo: The rise & demise of an American jester.* New York: Oxford University Press.

Brodkin, K. (1998). *How Jews became white folks and what that says about race in America.* New Brunswick, NJ: Rutgers University Press.

Davies, C. (1990). *Ethnic humor around the world: A comparative analysis.* Bloomington, IN: Indiana University Press.

Feagin, J. R. (2014). *Racist America: Roots, current realities, and future reparations.* New York: Routledge.

Haggins, B. (2007). *Laughing mad: The black comic persona in post-soul America.* New Brunswick, NJ: Rutgers University Press.

Ignatiev, N. (2008). *How the Irish became white.* New York: Routledge.

Kibler, M. A. (2009). Paddy, Shylock, and Sambo: Irish, Jewish, and African American efforts to ban racial ridicule from stage and screen. In Marc Howard Ross (Ed.), *Culture and belonging in divided societies: Contestation and symbolic landscapes.* Philadelphia, PA: University of Pennsylvania Press.

Lippmann, W. (1932). *Public opinion.* Edison, NJ: Transaction Publishers.

Madon, S., Guyll, M., Aboufadel, K., Montiel, E., Smith, A., Palumbo, P., & Jussim, L. (2001). Ethnic and national stereotypes: The Princeton trilogy revisited and revised. *Personality and Social Psychology Bulletin, 27*(8), 996–1010.

Omi, M. & Winant, H. (1994). *Racial formation in the United States: From the 1960s to the 1990s.* New York: Psychology Press.

Pérez, R. (2013). Learning to make racism funny in the "color-blind" era: Stand-up comedy students, performance strategies, and the (re)production of racist jokes in public. *Discourse & Society, 24*(4), 478–503.

Ramirez Berg, C. (2002). *Latino images in film: Stereotypes, subversion, and resistance.* Austin, TX: University of Texas Press.

Roediger, D. R. (1999). *The wages of whiteness: Race and the making of the American working class.* Brooklyn, NY: Verso.

Tajfel, H. (1982). Social psychology of intergroup relations. *Annual Review of Psychology, 33*(1), 1–39.

Weaver, S. (2011). *The rhetoric of racist humour: US, UK and global race joking.* Burlington, VT: Ashgate Publishing, Ltd.

ETHNIC STUDIES

Ethnic studies is an interdisciplinary and multidisciplinary field that critically interrogates questions of power and race/ethnicity, historically and presently. It centers generative questions about the changing meaning of race/ethnicity across space and time. Ethnic studies, furthermore, examines how dominant, interlocking structures of domination—white supremacy, capitalism, (hetero)patriarchy, and other systems—inform the everyday experiences of aggrieved communities. Beyond simply contributing to new academic literature on underrepresented histories and experiences, the field of ethnic studies aims to produce transformative academic knowledge by demonstrating the way power operates, problematizing dominant discourses, and providing alternative understandings of social phenomena. Challenging notions of "objectivity" and "universality" in the social sciences, ethnic studies produces academic knowledge from multiple vantage points (Fong, 2008).

The field of ethnic studies is a political project. It charts multiples structures of domination, theorizes social possibilities, and fosters social action and change. It has its origins in social activism, fostering a conscious commitment of active engagement with grassroots communities. Its activist legacy has paved the way for a growing presence of activist-scholars, intellectuals whose transformative scholarship contributes to the academy and who are also social change agents in their communities (Pulido, 2008). To that end, many ethnic studies professors and students blend, or attempt to do so, scholarly pursuits, politics, and activism as they undertake research or community projects.

The field originated as a result of mass mobilizations led by student and community leaders. Their collective efforts of social protest characterized civil rights struggles of the times. During the 1968 to 1969 academic year, leaders of the Black Student Union and a broad coalition of participants formed the Third World Liberation Front. By leading a historic strike against the administration at San Francisco State College (now known as San Francisco State University), activists successfully pressured officials to institutionalize an ethnic studies department, the first unit of its kind at an institution of higher education in the United States

(Yang, 2000). Relatedly, students and community members, across college campuses in the United States, expressed frustration with the dominance of Eurocentric perspectives in the social sciences, humanities, and other disciplinary areas. College courses neglected, or outright excluded, the histories, experiences, and voices of people of color and members of other marginalized communities. To help make sense of the struggles of people of color worldwide, students fought for the implementation of ethnic studies units where students could learn about underrepresented and often painful histories, such as genocide, conquest, and slavery.

The fight for ethnic studies has occurred alongside other demands, such as the recruitment and retention of students, staff, and faculty of color in higher education. The existence of ethnic studies units is attributed to the struggles, efforts, and dedication of different generations of leaders pushing the project forward. For many, organizing for ethnic studies came at a great cost. Activists often experienced varying degrees of retaliation, harassment, and violence from state actors, university officials, and peers. Some students faced suspensions, expulsions, or other forms of disciplinary action. In the end, many sacrificed their own education so that future generations could benefit from a critical ethnic studies curriculum.

In response to student activism, many college and university officials have institutionalized varying forms of ethnic studies curricula. The struggle for ethnic studies is not a phenomenon of the past. Today, student activists continue to fight for the creation of ethnic studies units—or defend its resources, space, and overall vitality—at their respective institutions. Ethnic studies units oftentimes find themselves on the line of possible elimination. They have resisted administrative efforts, under the guise of budgetary concerns, of being collapsed or lumped into larger ones. Particularly, during times of economic uncertainty and political unrest (as in the current moment), ethnic studies units struggle to sustain its institutional vitality.

Reflective of the historical and political context of its genesis, there are different models of naming and structuring ethnic studies programs and departments. Historically, student activists fought to create multiple, free-standing, ethnic-specific units: African American Studies, Asian American Studies, Latina/o Studies, Native American Studies, and others. Some also worked to ensure that these curricular areas would not be absorbed by area studies, such as African Studies, Asian Studies, and Latin American Studies. On the other hand, some colleges and universities have bridged ethnic studies with area studies by creating units, such as Latin American and Latina/o Studies or African and African American Studies. In some cases, the mergence of ethnic studies units within larger departments of area studies has led to their marginalization. In other cases, these new configurations have generated rich, theoretical inquiries centered at the crossroads of ethnic studies and area studies.

The official naming of ethnic studies units carries political weight and significance. For example, naming a unit Latina/o Studies versus Latino is a conscious effort to avoid subsuming the experiences of Latinas under the broader, masculine label of Latino. Debates over the naming of the units Indigenous Studies or Native American Studies over American Indian Studies also exist. A central concern is to name and structure the program in such a way to highlight the particularities in the diversity of individual, indigenous, and tribal experiences and responses to colonialism. For some, Indigenous Studies is attentive to the heterogeneity of native identities, and expressions within and beyond what we know as the United States of America. It also situates various indigenous experiences with a global framework. For others, the label of American Indian Studies invokes a colonial lexicon that relies on a Eurocentric understanding of native identities and experiences. Still, others argue that the adoption of American Indian Studies is a frame to deepen the study of tribal nations and communities in the United States.

Adopting a comparative and relational approach to the study of race/ethnicity is another structural model as departments organize their curriculum thematically. Under this thematic model, ethnic-specific studies are incorporated within the larger umbrella of ethnic studies or sometimes organized as an area of concentration within the program or department. At times, Native American Studies, however, has been organized as a stand-alone program because American Indian nations face

sovereignty issues (Butler, 2001). By drawing on comparative and relational methods in research and teaching, ethnic studies as a field has moved from nationalist framings and projects to one attentive to the transnational dimensions of academic inquiries. Structured in this way, ethnic studies units can theorize possibilities and take action, as sociologist Michael Omi (2012) has stated, to "undo racial injustice and generate broader racial equality" (p. 327). In other cases, some ethnic studies programs and departments have adopted a new name in response to new theoretical understandings and political pressures. For example, some Chicana/o Studies and Boricua Studies programs and departments have added Latina/o Studies to their departmental names, reflecting the demographic revolution of Latina/o populations from a rich and heterogeneous background (Hu-De Hart, 2001).

Certainly not limited to colleges and universities, the educational movement for the creation and preservation of ethnic studies curricula has also taken place at the elementary, middle, and secondary levels. The Tucson Unified School District (TUSD), for example, has ethnic studies programs in operation. In recent years, however, the ethnic studies curriculum at TUSD has faced intense scrutiny, defamation, and opposition with a passage of a controversial law. In 2010, the Arizona state legislature passed House Bill (HB) 2281, a law prohibiting public school instruction of ethnic studies programs that promotes the overthrow of the U.S. government, advocates ethnic solidarity, fosters racial hatred, and those customized for a particular ethnic group. Drawing on this alarmist language, HB 2281 targeted and criminalized the Mexican-American Studies (MAS) Program at one of the high schools. Consequently, school officials had to dismantle the MAS program. Ethnic studies advocates challenged the constitutionality of the administrative decision to shut down the program in the middle of the school year. The federal and state courts have reviewed and ruled on different aspects of HB 2281.

As evident in the Arizona case, administrative constraints and political turmoil exacerbate the precarious working conditions that many ethnic studies faculty members experience. They often encounter multiple sources of pressure inside and outside of the academy. For faculty of color, in particular, stress may be compounded by micro-aggressions and elusive forms of racism, at the university (Davis, 1989; Solórzano, Ceja, & Yosso, 2000). These subtle manifestations of institutional racism operate alongside other practices of oppression, such as sexism, classism, and homophobia. Faculty members of color, especially women of color (within and outside the field of ethnic studies), often have to negotiate internal and external pressures to assume additional responsibilities, including university service on diversity issues and mentoring students from marginalized communities (Gutiérrez y Muhs, Flores Niemann, González, & Harris, 2012).

Integrating questions of power and race/ethnicity and the intersectionality of other social categories—including gender, sexuality, and class—is the goal of ethnic studies scholarship and teaching. By fostering critical consciousness, and a lifelong passion for social justice, ethnic studies prepare students to positively impact their communities by encouraging them to play a role in removing socially constructed barriers. Ethnic studies scholarship and teaching encourages students to think more critically about systems of hierarchy and inequality and how power relationships create and reproduce inequalities. The curricula prompt students to think about and beyond their own lives—and to make local, regional, and transnational connections. By drawing on intersectionality as an analytical lens to tease out how socially constructed categories work together, ethnic studies classes make visible the differentiated ways that overlapping systems of power operate within and across communities. It provides an important intellectual space for students from various backgrounds to experience transformative learning, and to develop a critical consciousness that will serve them well into the future as they navigate complex systems of hierarchies empowering students to value the complexity in the United States.

Myrna García

References

Butler, J. E. (Ed.). (2001). *Color-line to borderlands: The matrix of American ethnic studies.* Seattle, WA: University of Washington Press.

Davis, Peggy C. (1989). Law as microaggression. *The Yale Law Journal, 98*(8), 1559–1606.

Espiritu, Yen Le. (1999). Disciplines unbound: Notes on sociology and ethnic studies. *Contemporary Sociology, 28*(5), 510–14.

Fong, Timothy P. (Ed.) (2008). *Ethnic studies research: Approaches and perspectives.* Lanham, MD: AltaMira Press.

Gutiérrez y Muhs, G., Flores Niemann, Y., González, C. G., & Harris, A. P. (Eds.). (2012). *Presumed incompetent: The intersections of race and class for women in academia.* Boulder, CO: University Press of Colorado.

Hu-De Hart, E. (2001). Ethnic studies in U.S. higher education: The state of the discipline. In J. E. Butler (Ed.). *Color-line to borderlands: The matrix of American ethnic studies* (pp. 103–12). Seattle, WA: University of Washington Press.

Omi, M. & Winant, H. (2012). Conclusion racial formation rules: Continuity, instability, and change. In D. M. HoSang, O. LaBennett, and L. Pulido (Eds.), *Racial formation in the twenty-first century.* Berkeley, CA: University of California Press.

Pulido, L. (2008). FAQ: Frequently (un)asked questions about being a scholar activist. In C. R. Hale (Ed.), *Engaging contradictions: Theory, politics, and methods of activist scholarship* (pp. 341–65). Berkeley, CA: University of California Press.

Solórzano, D., Ceja, M., & Yosso, T. (2000). Critical race theory, racial microaggressions, and campus racial climate: The experiences of African American college students. *The Journal of Negro Education, 69*(1/2), 60–73.

Yang, P. Q. (2000). *Ethnic studies: Issues and approaches.* Albany, NY: State University of New York Press.

ETHNIC STUDIES

Ethnic studies is a dynamic interdisciplinary field of scholarly inquiry that connects African American, Asian American, Chicano/Latino, Native American, and (most recently) Arab and Muslim American Studies. The country's first College of Ethnic Studies was established at San Francisco State College in 1969. That same year, the Department of Ethnic Studies was established at the University of California at Berkeley. Over the course of four decades, ethnic studies programs have developed at numerous colleges and universities across the country, such as Bowling Green State University, Washington

State University, University of California at Riverside, University of Colorado at Boulder, Brown University, and Ohio State University (to name a few). Ethnic studies graduate programs offer graduate certificates, terminal MA degrees, and the PhD. At the undergraduate level, ethnic studies majors, such as those at Mills College, develop skill sets that enable them to enter a variety of fields such as education, union organizing and youth work, marketing, law, environmental justice, and public health. The National Association for Ethnic Studies—originally the National Association of Interdisciplinary Studies for Native American, Black, Chicano, Puerto Rican, and Asian Americans—was founded in 1972.

One of the central goals of ethnic studies is to sustain a long memory of the experiences of people of color (racialized minorities) in the United States (Berry & Blassingame, 1982). On one hand, ethnic studies seeks to sustain a long memory of innovative scholarship and cultural work that examines local and global dimensions of U.S. racism. Some examples include the eloquent interdisciplinary sociological imagination of W. E. B. Du Bois, the groundbreaking plays of Lorraine Hansberry, the heartbreaking poetry by detained Chinese immigrants etched on the prison walls of Angel Island, and the ethno-biographical literary radicalism of Carlos Bulosan. On the other hand, ethnic studies seeks to sustain a long memory of collective forms of resistance against slavery, colonization, and genocide. This twin task of "re-memory" (to borrow from Toni Morrison) not only positions ethnic studies as a critical repository of collective memory but also compels scholars in the field to create unique methodological approaches to examining the complexity of race, racial difference, and racism within U.S. society.

Pioneering ethnic studies scholar Ronald Takaki (1992/1994) demonstrates an ethnic studies approach to understanding racism as a deeply structural form of inequality and oppression in "Reflections on Racial Patterns in America." As a response to sociologist Nathan Glazer's "postracial" interpretation of the Civil Rights Act of 1964, Takaki lays out a methodology for examining the historical and structural nature of racism, which frames the unequal distribution of resources, wealth, and power between whites and nonwhites as unequal social groups in U.S. society. For Takaki, racism is embedded in the economic foundation of the United States (slavery serves as the cornerstone of U.S. capitalism) and in the construction of whiteness as the pathway to national belonging (the 1790 Naturalization Law provided citizenship for free whites only). Takaki's reading of the Civil Rights Act of 1964 calls for a renewed attention to "[s]tructures of inequality such as poverty, inferior education, occupational stratification, and inner-city ghettos" that "require the government to act affirmatively and to promote opportunities for racial minorities based on group rights" (Takaki, 1994, p. 9).

A distinguishing feature of ethnic studies is the development of methodological approaches for scholarly research informed by a commitment to racial and economic justice in the larger society. Takaki developed a comparative multicultural approach to examining historical experiences of a multiracial U.S. working class within a shared context of oppression, exploitation, and resistance (Takaki, 1993, p. 10). This interdisciplinary approach uses a variety of cultural texts (from scholarship in the field to oral traditions of storytelling) to uncover histories of interethnic working-class solidarity between people of color (Mexican and Japanese farm laborers in early twentieth-century California) and between working-class European immigrant groups and communities of color (Jewish Americans and African Americans during the civil rights movement) (Takaki, 1993, pp. 9–11). The development of new methodological approaches that broaden, enrich, and diversify the scholarship on U.S. history (politics of representation) was informed by movements for social justice that challenged the unequal distribution of resources, wealth, and power (politics of distribution).

Emerging out of a profound and transformative shift within mass movements for social justice in U.S. society, the student-led strike for ethnic studies on the working-class campus of San Francisco State College in the late 1960s illustrates how ethnic studies at its inception envisioned diversity as inextricably interconnected with movements for social justice. The multiracial student coalition of "African American, Latino, American Indian, and Asian American campus groups"—called the Third World Liberation Front—organized the "longest student strike in U.S. history, which won the nation's first School of Ethnic Studies" in 1969 (Omatsu, 1994, p. 25). This multiracial struggle for ethnic studies in the academy was rooted in the advancement of the movement for Black Liberation (Omatsu, 1994; Bloom & Martin, 2013). Pushing against the civil rights campaign's emphasis on integration, while simultaneously advancing Dr. Martin Luther King Jr.'s critique of the U.S. war on Vietnam and analysis of racialized economic inequality in U.S. society, the movement for Black Liberation articulated a critical worldview that connected African American struggles for racial and economic justice with anticolonial movements for self-determination occurring around the globe in the "Third World"—what is now referred to as the Global South (Brown, 2001; Bloom & Martin, 2013).

Asian American studies scholar Glenn Omatsu highlights key features of the multiracial student strike for ethnic studies at San Francisco State College that firmly situated the notion of diversity within the context of social justice. Drawing on a long memory of collective resistance of communities of color against oppression and exploitation, students used strategies of "mass mobilization and militant direct action" (Omatsu, 1994, p. 26). Students also linked their demand for ethnic studies in the academy with the concerns of working-class communities outside of the campus. Second, the student-led strike for ethnic studies drew inspiration from movements for national sovereignty in the "Third World"—Asia, Africa, Latin America, and the Middle East. Third, the demand for diversity within the curriculum (ethnic studies) was informed by the larger goal of transforming the function of educational institutions within class society. The struggle of oppressed and colonized peoples around the world for self-determination framed the specific demands placed on the academy—"open admissions, community control of education, [and] ethnic studies" (Omatsu, 1994, p. 26).

The case of ethnic studies at San Francisco State sheds light on the interconnectedness between mass movements for social justice and the creation of new methodologies for scholarly research. Not only did the student strike for ethnic studies signal a shift in the African American movement, but it also signaled the birth of the Asian American movement (Omatsu, 1994; Bloom & Martin, 2013). The emergence of new movements for social justice, and new forms of collective consciousness among people of color, opened spaces for new methodological approaches to examining the ways in which communities of color in the United States constituted an "internal Third World" or "internal colony" (Blauner, 1972). In addition, scholar-activist Angela Davis reminds us that ethnic studies developed a comparative global framework at its inception: "Ethnic Studies . . . has always involved . . . a bridge-building process inviting us to identify with the struggles and accomplishments of oppressed people of color around the world" (Davis, 1990, p. 186).

Two major challenges for ethnic studies programs that have emerged over the past decades are interconnected: the decline of mass movements for social justice in the late 1970s and early 1980s and the rise of neoliberal globalization. Both have served to usher in a severe backlash against the gains of mass movements for social justice in the late 1960s and early 1970s (Omatsu, 1994; Duggan, 2003). While COINTELPRO was integral to the dismantling of mass movements, the rise of transnational corporations and neoliberal globalization intensified the level of poverty among African Americans and people of color. Historian Vincent Harding identifies the 1970s as marking the emergence of the Winter of Civil Rights (Omatsu, 1994). This was a period in which we witnessed a far-reaching backlash against the gains of the civil rights movement—from the dismantling of mass movements for social justice to attacks on affirmative action programs; from the deindustrialization of major cities to the evisceration of social services (Marable, 1983). By 1990, nearly one-half of African American children were living in poverty (Omatsu, 1994). By 2011, the racial wealth gap was at its widest in a quarter century (Lui et al., 2006; Kochhar, Fry, & Taylor, 2011).

In the absence of mass movements, a central concern for ethnic studies programs became institutional survival, which includes the struggle for academic legitimacy. In the process of institutionalization, ethnic studies programs developed new and academically sophisticated methods for examining racism, difference, and power. Influenced by the cultural turn in the academy (or what feminist theorist Teresa Ebert calls post-ality), ethnic studies incorporated elements of postcolonial, postmodern, and poststructuralist literary and cultural theories—all of which enabled ethnic studies to highlight the multiplicity and heterogeneity of the lived experiences of people of color as well as the complexity of everyday forms of survival/resistance. While the cultural turn opened a new frontier for ethnic studies to examine a variety of topics from the fluidity of identity, culture, and power to individual forms of agency enacted through body politics or the consumption of popular culture, senior scholars/cultural critics in ethnic studies (and in related interdisciplinary fields such as women's studies and cultural studies) expressed deep concern about the ways in which post-al methodological approaches diversify the curriculum at the expense of engaging class analysis and contributing to movements for social justice in the United States and in the Global South (San Juan, 1992; Ahmad, 1992; Mackay, 1993; Saadawi, 1997; Aguilar, 1998; Eagleton, 2003; Okihiro, 2010).

Gary Okihiro (2010), another pioneering scholar in the field, suggests a return to two key concepts: the notion of social formation and the centrality of class analysis. For Okihiro, the concept of social formation, "which Marxist writings posit as the form and stage of society . . . its structure and changes over time," provides a corrective to the post-al cultural turn in ethnic studies (para. 16). Within this framework, race is analyzed as a social and historical formation that functions as a "purposeful design of those who hold and wield power to maintain privileges and poverties" (Okihiro, 2007, para. 7). In other words, analyzing race as a social formation enables one to develop an historical understanding of structural racism and the role it plays in class society: in the division of labor and the unequal distribution of resources, wealth, and power.

Howard Winant (2005), who coined the term *racial formation* with his colleague Michael Omi, also provides suggestions for revitalizing the field of ethnic studies with his essay titled "Teaching Race and Racism in the Twenty-First Century: Thematic Considerations." The themes inventoried speak to a renewed interest in the relationship between race and the development of global capitalism. Winant's list includes the following: "world-system's development as a racially instituted process, diaspora/globality/migration as racialized processes, legacies of conquest and slavery, race and revolution, race/gender as co-constitutive in modernity, and whiteness as a central theme" (pp. 19–21). Several major scholars and writers in the field provide useful examples for productively engaging these themes to reinvigorate ethnic studies in the twenty-first century.

In *Racism and Cultural Studies* (2002), E. San Juan Jr., a pioneering scholar in the fields of ethnic studies and Asian American studies, provides an innovative ethnic studies/cultural studies approach to examining the world-system's development as a racially instituted process. San Juan uses Charles Mills's notion of racial polity in *The Racial Contract* (1997) to open new spaces to advance the race-class dialectic central to the work of W. E. B. Du Bois, C. L. R. James, and Eric Williams. In his other works, San Juan provides a critical examination of U.S.-Philippine colonial and neocolonial relations and the subsequent racial and national subordination of the Filipino people. This approach enables us to see the formation of the Filipino diaspora as a "racialized process" (2008).

Vijay Prashad's *Everybody Was Kung Fu Fighting* (2002) pushes against the distorting logic of color-blind racism and its fraternal twin, commodified multiculturalism (two central ideologies of difference in the post–civil rights period), in order to examine vibrant cultural formations that emerged out of antiracist grassroots struggles within the African and Asian diasporas: from the cultural work of Paul Robeson to the South Asian roots of Carnival in the Caribbean. Delia D. Aguilar's pioneering feminist scholarship has contributed to a rich tradition of Filipino feminism grounded in progressive anticolonial struggle. Her recent theoretical work reminds readers of the ways in which the notion of "triple jeopardy" coined by second-wave women of color feminists is anchored in an analysis of global capitalism (2012). Scholars and writers such as David Roediger, George Lipsitz, John H. Bracey Jr., and Tim Wise have opened new spaces to examine the social construction of whiteness in relation to the development of capitalism (Rothenberg, 2012; Bracey, 2013; Davis & Wise, 2012).

Patricia Hill Collins and John Solomos assert in their finely researched and thoughtfully organized collection titled the *SAGE Handbook of Race and Ethnic Studies* (2010) that "the field of race and ethnic studies is poised to become a broadly defined, theoretically robust and empirically rigorous field of inquiry in the twenty-first century" (p. 528). While the collection documents the ways in which ethnic studies has become an extremely fertile field of scholarly inquiry, it also sheds light on the need to "place greater emphasis on anti-racist theory and practice" (p. 526). Recent developments such as the formation of the Critical Ethnic Studies Association, which combines scholarship and activism, and the organized antiracist movement to support ethnic studies and Chicano studies in Arizona and Texas remind us that a new generation of scholars, teachers, and activists are building upon ethnic studies' long memory of collective struggle to sustain the connection between diversity and social justice.

Jeffrey Arellano Cabusao

References

Aguilar, D. D. (1998). *Toward a nationalist feminism.* Quezon City, Philippines: Giraffe Books.

Aguilar, D. D. (2012). Tracing the roots of intersectionality. *Monthly Review/MR Zine.* Retrieved from http://mrzine.monthlyreview.org/2012/aguilar120412.html.

Ahmad, A. (1992, 1994). *In theory: Classes, nations, literatures.* London and New York: Verso Press.

Berry, M. F. & Blassingame, J. W. (1982). *Long memory: The black experience in America.* New York and Oxford: Oxford University Press.

Blauner, R. (1972). *Racial oppression in America.* New York: Harper and Row.

Bloom, J. & Martin, W., Jr. (2013). *Black against empire: The history and politics of the Black Panther Party.* Berkeley, Los Angeles, and London: University of California Press.

Bracey, J., Jr. (2013). *How racism harms white Americans.* [Film]. MA: Media Education Foundation.

Brown, E. (2001). *New age racism.* [YouTube lecture]. University of California Television, UC Santa Barbara.

Collins, P. H. & Solomos, J. (2010). *The SAGE handbook of race and ethnic studies.* Los Angeles, London, New Delhi, Singapore, Washington, DC: SAGE.

Davis, A. (1984, 1990). Ethnic studies: Global meanings. In *Women, Culture, & Politics.* New York: Vintage Books.

Davis, A. & Wise, T. (2012). *Vocabulary of change: In conversation with Angela Davis and Tim Wise.* [Film]. United States: SpeakOut.

Duggan, L. (2003). *The Twilight of equality? Neoliberalism, cultural politics, and the attack on democracy.* Boston: Beacon Press.

Eagleton, T. (2003). *After theory.* New York: Basic Books.

Ebert, T. (1996). *Ludic feminism and after: Postmodernism, desire, and labor in late capitalism.* Ann Arbor: University of Michigan Press.

Glazer, N. (1975, 1994). The emergence of an American ethnic pattern. In R. Takaki (Ed.), *From different shores: Perspectives on race and ethnicity in America* (pp. 11–23). New York and Oxford: Oxford University Press.

Kochhar, R., Fry, R., & Taylor, P. (2011). Wealth gaps rise to record highs between whites, blacks, Hispanics. *Pew Research Center.* Retrieved from http://www.pewsocialtrends.org/2011/07/26/wealth-gaps-rise-to-record-highs-between-whites-blacks-hispanics/.

Lui, M., Robles, B., Leondar-Wright, B., Brewer, R., Adamson, R., & United for a Fair Economy. (2006). *The color of wealth: The story behind the U.S. racial wealth divide.* New York and London: The New Press.

Mackay, M. (1993). Ama Ata Aidoo. [Interview]. *Belles lettres: A review of books by women, 9*(1) (pp. 32–35).

Marable, M. (1983). *How capitalism underdeveloped black America.* Boston, MA: South End Press.

Mills, C. (1997). *The racial contract.* Ithaca and London: Cornell University Press.

Okihiro, G. (2007). The history of ethnic studies. *Columbia Daily Spectator.* Retrieved from http://www.columbiaspectator.com/2007/10/15/history-ethnic-studies.

Okihiro, G. (2010). The future of ethnic studies. *The Chronicle of Higher Education.* Retrieved from https://chronicle.com/article/The-Future-of-Ethnic-Studies/66092/.

Omatsu, G. (1994). The "four prisons" and the movements of liberation: Asian American activism from the 1960s to the 1990s. In K. Aguilar-San Juan (Ed.), *The state of Asian America: Activism and resistance in the 1990s* (pp. 19–69). Boston: South End Press.

Prashad, V. (2002). *Everybody was kung fu fighting: Afro-Asian connections and the myth of cultural purity.* Boston: Beacon Press.

Rothenberg, P. S. (2012). *White privilege: Essential readings on the other side of racism.* New York: Worth Publishers.

Saadawi, N. E. (1997). *The Nawal El Saadawi reader.* London and New York: Zed Books.

San Juan, E., Jr. (1992). *Racial formations/critical transformations: Articulations of power in ethnic and racial studies in the United States.* New Jersey and London: Humanities Press.

San Juan, E., Jr. (2002). *Racism and cultural studies: Critiques of multiculturalist ideology and the politics of difference.* Durham and London: Duke University Press.

San Juan, E., Jr. (2008). *From globalization to national liberation: Essays of three decades.* Diliman, Quezon City: The University of the Philippines Press.

Takaki, R. (1992, 1994). Reflections on racial patterns in America. In R. Takaki (Ed.), *From different shores: Perspectives on race and ethnicity in America* (pp. 24–35). New York and Oxford: Oxford University Press.

Takaki, R. (1993). *A different mirror: A history of multicultural America.* New York and Boston: Little, Brown, and Company.

Winant, H. (2005). Teaching race and racism in the twenty-first century: Thematic considerations. In M. Marable (Ed.), *The new black renaissance: The souls anthology of critical African American studies.* Boulder and London: Paradigm Publishers.

ETHNOCENTRISM

Ethnocentrism is a social and psychological phenomenon related to ethnicity and culture. The term *ethnocentrism* is composed of the Greek word *ethno*, which refers to a nation, people, or cultural grouping, and *centric*, the Latin word meaning "center." The first scholar to use and conceptualize the term *ethnocentrism* was William Graham Sumner in 1906. In his study of social groupings, Sumner wanted to understand an individual's affiliation, sense of belonging, and social attachments. He defined *ethnocentrism* as a universal tendency for "human beings to differentiate themselves according to group membership" (Brewer, 2007, p. 248). More specifically, ethnocentrism is "the tendency to view the world through one's own cultural filters" (Matsumoto & Juang, 2008, p. 376). This also involves believing one's group is better than others (Whitley & Kite, 2006).

The study of ethnocentrism has a long history in the human and social sciences. Various scholars such as anthropologists, political scientists, social psychologists, and conflict resolution specialists have explored the dimensions of ethnocentrism and sought to address the challenges associated with this phenomenon. Ethnocentrism is closely associated with the universal tendency within societies for people to make distinctions between in-groups and out-groups. In addition, ethnocentrism relies upon the enculturation process both to learn who is part of one's in-group and to learn what is normal and good (Matsumoto & Juang, 2008). As a result of enculturation, individuals who are affiliated and have a sense of belonging to an in-group feel loyalty and preference. Loyalty is important for those individuals who have membership in groups because they are more likely to subscribe to group norms and to trust fellow in-group members. The characteristic of preference is associated with pride and a sense of community within in-groups. Thus, ethnocentrism can be seen as in-group preferential treatment and favoritism.

While the loyalty and preference of ethnocentrism influences individuals to express a cooperative orientation, in relation to fellow in-group members, these same characteristics contribute to prejudice, and a competitive orientation, toward individuals who do not belong to one's in-group or are considered to be members of out-groups. In other words, an ethnocentric approach tends to view the in-group's beliefs, culture, and worldview positively and to evaluate outsiders negatively (McLean & McMillan, 2009). Franz Boas and Bronislaw Malinowski studied the issue of ethnocentrism from an anthropological perspective. They stressed the need for ethnographic fieldwork in order to better understand cultural differences (Eller, 2009). In the 1950s, T. W. Adorno and his colleagues suggested a link between the prejudice that is related to ethnocentrism and authoritarian personalities (Hebl & Madera, 2010). More recently, scholars have demonstrated that, under conditions of intergroup competition, conflict, or threat, individuals may be more likely to have increased in-group identification and out-group hostility (Hebl & Madera, 2010).

Due to the process of enculturation, ethnocentrism is a transgenerational problem. Ethnocentric stereotypes and attitudes can be nurtured and reinforced from various sources over the years. The ethnocentric stereotypes may be passed down from generation to generation through the process of socialization. Those individuals who do not communicate, or have contact with other groups, may not understand and appreciate cultural differences. Members of a social or cultural in-group can, and are more likely to, develop a feeling of self-centeredness that is characterized by the sense of group moral superiority and negativity for outsiders (Brewer, 2007).

As a result of the universal process of enculturation, individuals or groups will be prone to evaluate and judge the world through the lens of their own culture. Likewise, ethnocentrism will shape the views of individuals who identify themselves as a member or product of the same culture and ethnicity. Loyalty toward, and preference for, one's own culture, in comparison to others, can have a positive impact on individuals valuing their cultural heritage and promoting their cultural values. However, oftentimes, individuals use their own cultural standards to judge others' behaviors, customs, beliefs, and attitudes (Hebl & Madera, 2010). When individuals make assumptions about other people's backgrounds and strongly believe that the standards, norms, and values within their own culture are the only acceptable norms, and must be adopted universally, this can lead to social conflict.

Ethnocentrism poses a challenge in society for those who are promoting understanding of, and appreciation for, cultural differences. Ethnocentrism creates walls of separation and misunderstanding among various groups, and it hinders cooperation. Ethnocentrism influences people to resist learning how people from various backgrounds, including those of different ethnicity and culture, see the world and why they behave as they do. However, the understanding of the phenomenon of ethnocentrism itself can begin to alleviate cultural prejudice, as one recognizes the social and psychological dynamics at work that reinforce "us versus them" thinking. The conceptualization of

ethnicity itself, among scholars, has moved from a rather primordial, biologically based perspective to a more constructionist view, in which there is growing recognition that ethnic categories are not fixed and bounded but rather fluid and evolving (Banks, 1996; Jenkins, 1997; Waters, 1990). This understanding, too, can contribute to a greater willingness to reject ethnocentric tendencies.

Blerim Shala
Robin Cooper

References

Banks, M. (1996). *Ethnicity: Anthropological constructions*. New York: Routledge.

Brewer, M. B. (2007). Ethnocentrism. In J. M. Levine & M. A. Hogg (Eds.), *Encyclopedia of group processes and intergroup relations (1)* (pp. 247–52). Thousand Oaks, CA: Sage.

Eller, J. D. (2009). *Cultural anthropology: Global forces, local lives*. London: Rutledge.

Hebl, M. R. & Madera, J. M. (2010). Ethnocentrism. In R. M. Baumeister & K. D. Vohs (Eds.), *Encyclopedia of social psychology (1)* (pp. 314–15). Thousand Oaks, CA: Sage.

Jenkins, R. (1997). *Rethinking ethnicity: Arguments and explorations*. London: Sage.

Matsumoto, D. & Juang, L. (2008). *Culture and psychology* (4th ed.). Belmont, CA: Thomson Wadsworth.

McLean, I. & McMillan, A. (2009). *The concise Oxford dictionary of politics*. Oxford, England: Oxford University Press.

Waters, M. C. (1990). *Ethnic options: Choosing identities in America*. Berkeley, CA: University of California Press.

Whitley, B. E., Jr. & Kite, M. E. (2006). *The psychology of prejudice and discrimination*. Belmont, CA: Thomson Wadsworth.

ETHNOCENTRISM

Ethnocentrism manifests in biased judgment of other cultures solely based on the values and norms of one's own culture. *Ethnocentrism* is defined as "assuming that the worldview of one's own culture is central to all reality" (Bennett & Bennett, 2004), as much as it is also the failure to comprehend others' cultures. As such, ethnocentrism is related to a lack of tolerance for others' cultures, values, and behaviors.

Ethnocentrism can be found wherever cultural pluralism may be found. Cultural pluralism exists when minority cultures are present within a context of a larger dominant culture. In a culturally plural environment, minority or enclave cultures are permitted to exist provided that they do not violate the major culture of the dominant group.

Although it may seem ordinary for a person to discern the world based on one's own cultural norm, ethnocentrism carries a negative connotation because of its destructive potential to lead to negative bias, judgment, and treatment of others different from oneself. For example, Kevin—who is from America—is horrified to discover that Lily—who is from China—has tried dog meat and is not opposed to dog meat consumption. Kevin asks Lily how she could even fathom doing such a morally vile thing and call herself a good person. Kevin fails to realize that it may be perfectly normal in Chinese culture for humans to breed for and consume dog meat, just as Americans do with cows and pigs. Kevin should not judge Lily or her culture to be morally inferior to his, as morality and norm are relative notions that vary from culture to culture.

Possible Origin of Ethnocentrism

Ethnocentrism might have originated in order to avoid disease that could be contaminated from out-groups. An extensive quantitative review (i.e., meta-analysis) study (Terrizzi, Shook, & McDaniel, 2013) found that individuals who fear contamination or are sensitive to disgust tend to adhere more to socially conservative beliefs. The psychological mechanisms that promote fear of contamination, sensitivity to disgust, and disease avoidance—called *the behavioral immune system strategies*—are related to socially conservative beliefs, such as right-wing authoritarian, social dominance orientation, religious conservatism, collectivism, and ethnocentrism (Terrizzi et al., 2013). This indicates that socially conservative values may have functioned as evolutionary disease-avoidance strategy, promoting social exclusivity, tradition, and avoidance of out-group members (e.g., other races) who had been historically perceived as a source of contamination. The behavioral immune system strategies

may regulate social relationships by fostering value systems that protect individuals from out-group members who may pose a disease threat.

In addition to the threat of contamination, individuals may also adhere to socially conservative values because out-group members have posed a threat in terms of predation and competition for limited resources. Further, beyond protecting individuals from these potential out-group threats such as predation, disease threat, and competition for resources, social conservatism may have developed as a means for encouraging in-group cohesion and group functioning and for deterring defection by in-group members (Terrizzi et al., 2013). The behavioral immune system strategies may have lead to socially conservative value systems in order to encourage in-group's prejudice and avoidance of the out-group (Terrizzi et al., 2013).

Religious Individuals' Ethnocentrism

Religious people are expected to be accepting of others. However, a meta-analysis study (Hall, Matz, & Wood, 2010) found that strong religious in-group identity is associated with putting down racial out-groups. This indicates that highly religious individuals tend to express more racial prejudice than nonreligious individuals (Hall et al., 2010). This difference may be attributed to the idea that religious individuals might treat other races as out-groups because religion is practiced mostly within race; Martin Luther King Jr. once stated that Sunday is the most segregated day in America.

Religious people are taught to accept others, but their humanitarianism is expressed mostly toward in-group members. Even intrinsically religious individuals—those who are committed to religion as an end in itself—express tolerance in *direct* measures of racism yet not in *indirect* measures of racism, such as choosing to engage in interracial interactions that implies covert prejudice (Hall et al., 2010). Because training in a religious in-group identity may promote ethnocentrism, religious groups may increase ethnocentrism by differentiating themselves from nonbelievers through identifying nonbelievers with moral inferiority (Hall et al., 2010).

Agnostic individuals who question religion, do not participate in organized religion, or do not have a strong belief in God are more racially tolerant than religious individuals. In addition, women tend to have stronger benevolent values that promote religiosity and show stronger tolerance toward out-group members than men do (Hall et al., 2010).

Individuals who are religious for reasons of social conformity and tradition tend to show intolerance of other races; this indicates that religious racism is beget from notions of social conformity and tradition upkeep. Such individuals are more likely to accept established racial divisions in society. Conservative and conventional life values promoting both religiosity and racism show consistency across different cultures and different religions, such as Christianity, Catholicism, Judaism, Islam, and others (Hall et al., 2010).

Differences in Ethnocentrism within Religious Individuals

Another meta-analysis study divided *Christians* into two categories (McCleary, Quillivan, Foster, & Williams, 2011): fundamentalist Christians and religious questers. *Fundamentalist Christians* are those who claim that the Bible holds the one ultimate, absolute truth about God and human life that must be defended against skeptics' attacks at any costs. In contrast, *religious questers* search for and embrace a continuing reevaluation of religious truth that is complex and tentative; while leaving open the possibility of absolute truth, they express skepticism about the absolute claims of the Bible (McCleary et al., 2011).

Authoritarian individuals submit to authorities, aggress against those inclined to challenge authorities, and embrace societal standards established by authorities. McCleary et al. (2011) found religious fundamentalism is most strongly associated with authoritarianism, indicating both fundamentalist Christians and authoritarian individuals believe in absolute truth and unquestioned submission. In contrast, a strongly negative relationship between religious quest and authoritarianism indicates that religious questers do not share the same belief with authoritarian individuals (McCleary et al., 2011).

A strongly positive relationship between religious fundamentalism and ethnocentrism may indicate that fundamentalist Christians' absolute religious truth is based on the same belief as ethnocentric individuals' good versus bad dichotomy. This might

be because ethnocentric individuals see the world based on in-group versus out-group (McCleary et al., 2011).

A positive relationship between religious fundamentalism and militarism indicates fundamentalist Christians' advocacy of military power in forging change in other societies. There was no study in the meta-analyses that investigated the relationship between religious quest and ethnocentrism or between religious quest and militarism (McCleary et al., 2011).

The relationship between religious fundamentalism and homophobia is stronger than the relationships between religious fundamentalism and other kinds of prejudice against communists, women, and people of color; this may indicate fundamentalist Christians' fear or discrimination against out-groups, especially homophobia. In contrast, the negative or no relationships between religious quest and prejudice indicate religious questers' tolerance of out-groups. The findings that fundamentalist Christians tend to hold in-group versus out-group (e.g., us versus them) mentality, with prejudice against groups whose ethnicity, values, or sexual orientations deviated from fundamentalist norms, whereas that religious questers tend not to hold that mentality, might suggest that not all religious individuals are more ethnocentric than agnostic individuals.

Possible Commonality between Ethnocentric Individuals and Individuals with Militaristic Mentality

In addition to religious individuals' tendency toward ethnocentrism, individuals who have a militaristic mentality also have the tendency toward ethnocentrism. Another meta-analysis (McCleary & Williams, 2009) study found a positive relationship between militarism and personality traits such as (a) punitiveness, (b) authoritarianism, (c) dominance–power, (d) masculinity, and (e) ethnocentrism (in this order of correlation strengths).

A strong positive relationship between militarism and punitiveness indicates that individuals with militaristic mentality tend to emphasize strict and harsh discipline such as capital, corporal, or severe punishment, even torture, in order to restrict crime and to produce submission, especially from its enemies such as prisoners and enemy combatants (McCleary & Williams, 2009).

A strong positive relationship between militarism and authoritarianism indicates that individuals with militaristic mentality tend to accept one directional communication and hierarchical social relationships—power, authority, submission—and they tend to emphasize fixed rules and wariness to trust others (McCleary & Williams, 2009).

A strong positive relationship between militarism and social dominance and power indicates that individuals with militaristic mentality tend to accept inequality between social groups (i.e., their in-group should control out-groups) and masculinity (i.e., males' desire to rule the community and politics, and to have the final authority on decisions; and tend to emphasize status and power such as prestige, respect from others, and accumulation of wealth and social control) (McCleary & Williams, 2009).

A positive relationship between militarism and masculinity indicates that individuals with militaristic mentality tend to accept traditional male roles and characteristics such as respect, admiration, competitiveness, aggressiveness, dominance, and being the breadwinner (McCleary & Williams, 2009).

A positive relationship between militarism and ethnocentrism indicates that individuals with militaristic mentality tend to believe that their in-group members are intellectually, emotionally, and morally superior and preferable to other races (McCleary & Williams, 2009).

The positive relationships between militarism and a variety of personality traits including ethnocentrism indicate that individuals who have militaristic mentality tend to see the world in a simplistic way; that is, looking at people, problems, and solutions in one single term (McCleary & Williams, 2009). This might be because they are confused by complexity and thus prefer simplicity to complexity. Thus, they advocate one single solution for very complex problems; for example, they believe that the country will be safe by a strong military, and thus the most important institution in society is military because it is the ultimate guarantor of freedom and safety (McCleary & Williams, 2009). This might also indicate that ethnocentric individuals also tend to see the world in a simplistic way, either *we* or *they*.

Implications

The need for cultural tolerance is becoming increasingly important in this world, as groups and individuals of many disparate backgrounds must cooperate as a global community in order to overcome global issues such as politics, wars, and climate change. Communities should encourage multicultural consciousness by educating people to be aware and sensitive of others' disparate cultures. Sensitivity and appreciation of other cultures and multiculturalism could play a large, beneficial role in reducing ethnocentric mind-sets. Dong, Day, and Collaco (2008) found that emphasizing and increasing education of intercultural communication sensitivity and multiculturalism specifically might help to overcome ethnocentrism. Overcoming oneself of all ethnocentrism is difficult and demands continuous, conscious effort. There is still a need for more longitudinal empirical studies that examine the specific factors that help reduce ethnocentrism.

Harmony Onyu Lee
Kyung-Hee Kim

References

Bennett, J. M. & Bennett, M. J. (2004). Developing intercultural sensitivity: An integrative approach to global and domestic diversity. In D. Landis, J. Bennett, & M. Bennett, *Handbook of intercultural training* (pp. 147–65). Thousand Oaks, CA: Sage.

Dong, Q., Day, K., & Collaco, C. (2008). Overcoming ethnocentrism through developing intercultural communication sensitivity and multiculturalism. *Human Communication. 11*(1), 27–38.

Hall, D. L., Matz, D. C., & Wood, W. (2010). Why don't we practice what we preach? A meta-analytic review of religious racism. *Personality and Social Psychology Review, 14*(1), 126–39. doi: 10.1177/1088868309352179

McCleary, D. F., Quillivan, C. C., Foster, L. N., & Williams, R. L. (2011). Meta-analysis of correlational relationships between perspectives of truth in religion and major psychological constructs. *Psychology of Religion and Spirituality, 3*(3), 163–80. doi: 10.1037/a0022208

McCleary, D. F. & Williams, R. L. (2009). Socio-political and personality correlates of militarism in Democratic societies. *Peace and Conflict: Journal of Peace Psychology*, 15(2), 161–87. doi: 10.1080/10781910902837248

Ousey, G. C. & Unnever, J. D. (2012). Racial-ethnic threat, out-group intolerance, and support for punishing criminals: A cross-national study. *Criminology*, *50*, 565–603. doi: 10.1111/j.1745-9125.2012.00275.x

Terrizzi, J. A., Jr., Shook, N. J., & McDaniel, M. A. (2013). The behavioral immune system and social conservatism: A meta-analysis. *Evolution and Human Behavior*, *34*(2), 99–108. doi: 10.1016/j.evolhumbehav.2012.10.003

EUROCENTRISM

Eurocentrism and the Social Construction of Race

Eurocentrism is a paradigm rooted in global colonization and capitalism that privileges a European way of knowing and being. It is a set of doctrines and ethical positions that derive from a European context (Wallerstein, 2006) and are presented as neutral, scientific, and universal. In its development, eurocentrism led to an ideological and tangible reordering of the world through ways of knowing that substantiated Western dominance. The development of eurocentrism is marked by the interrelated processes of a) the legitimation of particular peoples and knowledge and the simultaneous illegitimation of other peoples and knowledge, b) the establishment of the global control of labor via colonization and imperialism, and c) the social construction of the idea of "race" (Wallerstein, 2006). Eurocentrism constructed a sense of time and progress that represented the West as the present and the future and the rest of the world as the undeveloped and antiquated past (Tibebu, 2011).

The idea that Europeans were predisposed to racial prejudice prior to the slave trade is contested among scholars. The dissenting argument is that a racist ideology *developed* to accompany and to rationalize the enslavement of Africans and Southeast Asians as the enslavement of Europeans declined (Frederickson, 2002; Wolf, 1982/1997). Therefore, a global racist ideology resulted from the necessity to maintain control of production and labor in a developing capitalist system, particularly in the realms of European industry and plantation. Though capitalism did not form all of the distinctions of race, the process of labor organization, under capitalism, imparted racial distinctions and the establishment of an ideology of European superiority within the system of colonial rule. This colonial system expanded across the globe via wealth derived from production, the expansion of armed forces to enforce colonization and enslavement, and transcontinental alliances formed among European fortune seekers. Colonizers used several strategies to establish and maintain power. Dehumanization was a strategy that Frantz Fanon (1963) equated to turning the colonized into an animal through the use of language to describe their physical, moral, and behavioral characteristics as barbaric and animalistic. These strategies established and reinforced the relationship between the alleged cultural and intellectual inferiority of the colonized and the supremacy of European beliefs, values, and customs—the binary of the European and "Other."

Scholars' assertions regarding the temporal location of the concept of "race" vary greatly. For example, David Goldberg (2006) argued that the sixteenth century marks the rise of race consciousness while George Frederickson (2002) identified fifteenth-century persecution of New Christians and Christian attitudes toward Jews in Medieval Europe, based on the idea of purity of blood. Most scholars agree, however, that the fundamental aspects of modern racism are rooted not in the medieval period, but in the modern period (Frederickson, 2002; Winant, 2001). Nevertheless, it is crucial to consider that racially defined discourses existed long before a clear and so-called scientific concept of "race" was constructed to identify and rank groups of human beings.

Studies have demonstrated that it was in the latter part of the eighteenth century, during the Enlightenment period and the rise of modernity, that the idea of "race"—based on discrete and observable phenotypical traits—came into being (Dussel, 1993; Roberts, 2011). During a time when Europe constituted itself as a cohesive entity by exploring, conquering, and colonizing an "Other," it created an image of itself in superior opposition to the "Other." Philosophers of the day, such as Kant, believed that

Europe's Enlightenment illustrated progressive movement away from the laziness, cowardice, and immaturity of the "Other" (Dussel, 1993). Likewise, Hegel connected the global process of Enlightenment to a universal world history in which movement from the East to the West indicated progress and where Western Europe epitomized the realization of absolute truth, *the* place where Christianity had been fully realized (Hegel, 1975; Tibebu, 2011). In the face of this, it was believed that no other peoples or places could hold rights over this absolute right of history and truth, and most certainly, no other peoples or places could offer anything substantive from which Western Europe could learn. Thus, Hegel's, and arguably Kant's, positions on the global process of development and enlightenment exemplified a sense of superiority that well illustrates the European-superior state of mind at the beginning of the nineteenth century, a sense of superiority that continued to justify European conquest, "discovery," and colonization. Moreover, this privileging of temporal and shifting geographical progress established the powerful binary determination of which societies/peoples qualified for the status of civilization/progress and which societies/peoples were considered archaic/barbaric. An important consequence of this Eurocentric and strict representation of shifting geographical progress is the fixing of racial and ethnic markers belonging to specific territories/peoples labeled as inferior or superior.

From the seventeenth through the nineteenth centuries, the merging of philosophical thought with scientific explanations of racial categories by European physicians and academics, such as Bernier, Linnaeus, and Blumenbach, fashioned the idea that races are natural, primordial, and enduring, and further justified European imperialism and colonization (Aronson, 2007; Roberts, 2011). On a global scale, the shade of a people's skin, and other phenotypical characteristics, served as a determinant of that people's location on the social and economic hierarchies. These dynamics were shaped by a privileging of whiteness, where the cultural practices of those with lighter skin became normative and superior while the practices of those with darker skin were considered and treated as problematic and inferior. In the United States, the racial

theories of Thomas Jefferson were influential in both sociopolitical and scientific contexts (Aronson, 2007; Roberts, 2011). He espoused Africans' inferiority to whites in regard to intellect, civility, and sexual behavior. These philosophical, scientific, and political explanations of racial inferiority instigated the institution of pseudoscientific techniques to support the claim of classifying individuals into discrete races and to justify the enslavement, physical and cultural genocide, and the exclusion of those perceived as deficient and inferior.

Scientific racism continued through the early twentieth century, but racial categorization shifted from calculations related to physique to calculations related to intelligence (Adelman, 2003; Roberts, 2011). Dualisms of the past continued to work to organize people through reference to the racial superiority of Europeans, but the focus during this period shifted toward intelligence. American psychologists assumed that intelligence was inherited; they often confused cultural differences with innate properties and assumed that differences in intelligence between groups were the products of heredity, despite profound social inequality. Lewis Terman (1916), the father of the intelligence quotient, focused his attention on the alleged mental defects of people of color in the early twentieth century and recommended their segregation into special classes to make them efficient workers. The Eurocentrism of the past that relegated the "Other" to colonial domination and slavery had taken a new form of relegation of the "Other" to inferior educational tracks and to their production as efficient workers. Although the explicit association between race and intelligence in the scientific literature eventually shifted, scholarship and practices around gifted education as we know it today have subsumed Terman's theories around intelligence. In fact, Terman is still referenced as the progenitor of gifted education (Borland, 1997). Consequently, it is the implicit references to race and class that are the silent mechanisms by which whites continue to be positioned as superior.

What survived over time, and remains prevalent today is an underlying presumption of a superior white Western self. Eurocentrism, and the dualistic properties it labels on non-European countries, cultures, and peoples, organizes cultural, geographical, and linguistic differences into value-laden categories that privilege European norms and marginalize the beliefs and practices of "Others" under the pretense of neutrality and objectivity. This hegemonic configuration reproduces a frame of social reality that masks the problematic history that has produced it (Leonardo, 2009). This, in turn, further reinforces a belief in the "Other" in binary opposition to an implicit and unexamined Eurocentric "we." Eurocentrism, then, is an epistemology (Delgado Bernal, 2002) of race, racism, history, knowledge, and power that remains "a pervasive condition of thought" (Rabasa, 1993, p. 18).

Brandy S. Wilson

References

Adelman, L. (Executive Producer). (2003). *Race: The power of an illusion*. San Francisco, CA: California Newsreel.

Aronson, M. (2007). *Race: A history beyond black and white*. New York: Ginee Seo Books.

Borland, J. (1997). The construct of giftedness. *Peabody Journal of Education, 72* (3–4), 6–20.

Delgado Bernal, D. (2002). Critical race theory, Latino critical theory, and critical raced-gendered epistemologies: Recognizing students of color as holders and creators of knowledge. *Qualitative Inquiry, 8*(1), 105–26.

Dussel, E. (1993). Eurocentrism and modernity (Introduction to the Frankfurt Lectures), *boundary 2, 20*(3), 65–76.

Fanon, F. (1963). *The wretched of the earth*. New York: Grove Press, Inc.

Frederickson, G. M. (2002). *Racism: A short history*. Princeton, NJ: Princeton University Press.

Goldberg, D. T. (2006). Racial Europeanization. *Ethnic and Racial Studies, 29*(2), 331–64.

Hegel, G. W. F. (1975). *Lectures on the philosophy of world history*. Cambridge University Press.

Leonardo, Z. (2009). Race, whiteness, and education. New York: Routledge.

Omi, M. & Winant, H. (1994). *Racial formation in the United States from the 1960s to the 1990s* (2nd ed.). New York: Routledge.

Rabasa, J. (1993). *Inventing A-M-E-R-I-C-A: Spanish historiography and the formation of Eurocentrism*. Duncan, OK: The University of Oklahoma Press.

Roberts, D. (2011). *Fatal invention: How science, politics, and big business re-create race in the twenty-first century*. New York: The New Press.

Smedley, A. (1999). *Race in North America: Origin and evolution of a worldview* (2nd ed.). Boulder, CO: Westview Press.

Terman, L. M. (1916). *The measurement of intelligence: An explanation of and a complete guide for the use of the Stanford revision and extension of the Binet-Simon intelligence scale*. New York: Houghton Mifflin.

Tibebu, T. (2011). *Hegel and the Third World: The making of Eurocentrism in world history*. Syracuse, NY: Syracuse University Press.

Wallerstein, I. (2006). *European universalism: The rhetoric of power*. New York: The New Press.

Winant, H. (2001). *The world is a ghetto: Race and democracy since World War II*. New York: Basic Books.

Wolf, E. R. (1982/1997). *Europe and the people without history*. Berkeley, CA: University of California Press.

FAIR ASSESSMENT

Fair Assessment of Educational Institutions across Cultural Boundaries

Institutional assessment in an educational setting historically was an evaluative process with a summative judgment made by a recognized accrediting agency that the evaluated institution complied with the standards of membership of the accrediting agency. The cultural context for such evaluative systems is Western, specifically Anglo-American, and rooted in the rationalization and bureaucratization of Western society and institutions both public and private (Weber, 1928, trans. 1978). With imperialism of the nineteenth century, and the emergence of many independent international schools in the twentieth century, especially after World War II, British and American forms of institutional assessment began to have a broader reach and application than just within the United Kingdom and United States. As these forms of assessment reached across cultural boundaries, questions arose about how the process of institutional assessment can be achieved fairly and in a fashion that respects cultural diversity.

American processes of institutional evaluation through accreditation reflect the unique nature of American educational systems built on the traditions of local control, local- and state-level funding, and numerous competing curricula reflecting local, state, and regional values and priorities. Until very recently, a unique aspect of the American educational landscape was the absence of a national curriculum or evaluation system. American models of institutional assessment have been applied to international schools with an American orientation. An international school offering a recognized American high school diploma must receive accreditation through one of the regional accrediting bodies in the United States. Schools must comply with standards and processes characteristic of American practice,

but a specific national mandate from a national, centralized system does not exist. The Office of Overseas Schools (OOS) of the Department of State of the U.S. government further reviews international schools located where children of employees of the U.S. government posted abroad go to school. The OOS evaluation is informal and formative rather than summative in nature. The agency cannot command a school to adopt certain practices because the schools involved are private and independent rather than state funded. Project AERO (American Education Reaches Out), the curriculum and instruction arm of the Office of Overseas Schools, does not require a specific curriculum but only recommends a curricular approach and instructional models.

The British approach, consistent with what emerged in Europe generally, is based on a nationalized, centralized system of aligned curriculum, national assessment of both students and institutions, and external assessment of institutional fitness. In many developing countries, largely as a function of colonial legacies, the nationalized, centralized system became the norm for many international assessment models. The growth of the International Baccalaureate Diploma Programme likewise extended an assessment model based upon a centralized system of aligned curriculum.

Both the American and British approaches to defining educational quality dovetail with respective systems of higher education, particularly the elite educational institutions with postsecondary and postgraduate programs. The formal assessment of K–12 institutions and the nature and priorities of K–12 educational institutions reflect the hierarchy of values of elite institutions of higher education: Ivy League schools in the United States; Oxford, Cambridge, and other Russell Group universities in the United Kingdom; and elite institutions across Europe. The creation of regional accrediting bodies in the United States began in the late nineteenth century as a self-referential process when university and major secondary school leaders created accrediting practices by identifying and codifying valued ideas or practices of the best schools or colleges. Thus, the definition of quality in education was aligned with elite institutional ideals and values, though not without protest from John Dewey and other critics who felt that education should directly serve the needs of citizenship and the marketplace.

The question of defining educational institutional quality and purpose was a backdrop for the most important debate in American education related to social justice in the early twentieth century. Booker T. Washington advocated education as a tool of economic uplift and with educational institutions designed to provide vocational education and craft skills to its students. W. E. B. Du Bois, a former member of Washington's "Tuskegee Machine," advocated education for what he called the "talented tenth." The talented tenth were the top 10 percent of African American students who, according to Du Bois, should receive elite educations and demonstrate through their quality that the rationales for Jim Crow laws were untenable. For both of these theorists, quality education and quality schools were tools of societal and legal transformation.

A significant difference between American and European and other international educational systems in terms of evaluation, both institutional and individual, is found in their respective attitudes toward resources and resource allocations in education. In the United States, the relative abundance of resources available to education in the latter half of the twentieth century, along with the increased demand for postsecondary education, meant that American educational rhetoric, and the systems created, emphasized opportunity for all or at least for most. The European and international models, on the other hand, are based on evaluation and assessment as tools of effective or efficient resource allocations. If one does not demonstrate a sufficient level of educational performance or promise in most educational systems around the world, pathways to higher education are unavailable.

Since World War II, international engagement with education has been based on the assumption that education is a primary route to national development, a mechanism for the enhancement of the quality of life, and a pathway toward the realization of social justice. Those beliefs stand behind major educational initiatives by international bodies. Prominent among such initiatives are the United Nation's Millennium Development Goals, UNESCO's Education for All and Capacity Development for Education for All (CapEFA), and a number of World Bank projects. Such programs bring to life the operational assumption that "education is fundamental to development and growth" (World Bank, 2014, n.p.). With such programs comes the need to demonstrate effects at a number of levels ranging from the individual to the institutional to the regional and national. This need to demonstrate creates additional economic incentives to develop useful, and culturally sensitive, assessment instruments and processes.

The two traditional models of institutional assessment, the decentralized approach of the United States and the centralized approach in Europe, have strengths and weaknesses with respect to educational assessment across cultural boundaries. The decentralized American model respects diversity of local conditions. In that sense, it offers promise of honoring diversity and different cultural settings. However, the circumstances in the United States reflect the fundamental weakness inherent to noncentralized systems. In the United States, many stakeholders in American K–12 education, especially the elite universities and the students who want to attend them, want national benchmarks to legitimate their status. In the absence of a national curriculum, and in light of the perceived need for demonstrations of educational quality, a de facto national curriculum and evaluative process have emerged with the Advanced Placement (AP) program created by the College Board in collaboration and consultation with schools and universities. Students and secondary schools rely on these exams to demonstrate their worthiness for admission to elite universities, and universities use AP results as an important measure of quality when assessing applicants. AP exams allow students from all over the United

States and at international schools from around the world to sit for the same exams where all students are evaluated using a standard scale.

Weakening the case for uniform centralized scales of measurement is the fact that they typically produce unsurprising results: students from families with economic, social, or educational capital, or schools that serve advantaged children, perform well individually and in aggregate, whereas students from economically, socially, or educationally disadvantaged circumstances, and the schools that serve them, do less well, sometimes significantly so. Centralized systems, whether official or de facto, serve the purposes of the dominant pedagogy. Based upon the work of Bourdieu and Passeron (1977), the concept of dominant pedagogy is that dominant discourses have the power to define legitimacy for all members of society and do so in a way that maintains and reinforces existing social, economic, and political arrangements (Worsham, 2001). Two conclusions can be drawn. First, in the absence of a centralized system of measurement, a de facto one, like AP exams, will emerge. Second, any centralized system compromises to some degree the aim of social justice by creating a system whereby the already privileged can legitimate their elite status.

This compromise to social justice exists at the levels of individual students and institutions but also on significantly larger orders of magnitude. Recent European efforts regarding institutional evaluation are framed by the Bologna Declaration of 1999. The declaration captures the rationale for action, linking education to social development, economic capacity, citizenship, and cultural values. The Declaration opens nobly "A Europe of Knowledge is now widely recognized as an irreplaceable factor for social and human growth" (Bologna Declaration, 1999, para. 2). Nevertheless, the Bologna Declaration aims to reinforce European power and authority: education is "an indispensable component to consolidate and enrich the European citizenship, capable of giving its citizens the necessary competences to face the challenges of the new millennium" (Bologna Declaration, 1999, para. 2). In the United States, the real aims of improving education are more baldly expressed in terms of economic and national interests. The American values can be seen through the stated desires to improve institutional assessment,

which began in earnest following the 1983 publication of the Carnegie Foundation Report *A Nation at Risk: The Imperative for Educational Reform*. Institutional assessment was given renewed emphasis in the United States by the passage of the No Child Left Behind Act of 2004 and the Race to the Top initiative of 2009. Each of those elements asserted that American education was underperforming compared to peer nations, and that such a situation would, over time, lead to competitive disadvantages for the American workforce and economy. Each initiative required attention to performance defined as outcomes validated by external measures as the appropriate demonstration of educational quality. This approach was originally applied to institutional judgments of quality, with failing or low scores triggering response mechanisms up to and including school closure in serious cases, while over time the evaluation of quality has expanded to include assessments of individual teachers.

In the United States, evaluative processes in education are often tightly linked to economic success. The Baldrige Performance Excellence Program was created by an act of Congress (The Malcolm Baldrige National Quality Improvement Act, 1987) to enhance the competitiveness of U.S. businesses. The program expanded its scope to education in 1999. The Baldrige Performance Excellence Program has three purposes: (1) to identify and recognize role-model businesses, (2) to establish criteria for evaluating improvement efforts, and (3) to disseminate and share best practices (Baldrige Program, 2010). The Baldrige Program highlights several distinctive features common to current institutional assessment trends. Its original impetus came from concerns about global competitiveness. Its operational assumptions and processes derived from business models, and it places a premium on the alignment of planning, measurement, and adjustment to improve results. Additionally, it is a partnership project between the public and private sectors. This partnership approach has emerged in the United States to meet the need for additional resources, provided to the public by the private sector, and to provide both additional revenue potential and the benefit of the perception of serving the public good for business. The explosive growth of charter schools and online and hybrid education models and schools as business organizations in the United States has its roots in the perceived failures, costs, and resistance to change ascribed to public education at both the school and university levels.

Education is in a period of evolution under the pressures of cost and the emergence of credible educational technology as a force in changing the educational landscape. Institutional evaluation in education is also in a period of transition from an emphasis on quality assurance through standards compliance to continuous improvement models adapted from business with quality demonstrated through performance-based results. A major effect of this transition is a growing emphasis on school quality performance measures (QPMs) as a principal indicator of institutional quality (Muriel & Smith, 2011). Internationally, the landscape features a number of regional and global projects designed to foster improvements in educational assessment as a precursor to educational quality improvement. The International Network for Quality Assurance Agencies in Higher Education (INQAAHE) was established in 1991 to improve practices of institutional accreditation. The International Association of Educational Assessment was created in 1976 and links assessment improvement efforts in the United States to those around the world.

Contemporary assessments of institutional effectiveness reflect four distinct pathways or frameworks for analysis. First, a new field, "edumetrics," has emerged that blends the fields of economics, specifically mathematical analytic modeling, and education. The major development in this work is the development of "value-added" calculations. Mathematic models are used to predict student performance, perform an analysis of the obtained student performance, and statistically calculate the value or weight of confounding variables such as social and economic status. The remaining growth in performance is compared to gains predicted by the model. Differences in real performance, compared to predicted performance, are asserted to represent the "value-add" of the teacher, or, in aggregate, a school. Teachers or schools with high positive value-add results are assumed to be high-performing individuals or institutions. Such metrics are proving very attractive to public authorities, given their claims to objectivity and validity, and are used to warrant job action in the case of poorly performing teachers as well as radical school reform in the case of poorly performing schools.

Second, an increasingly influential and informal mechanism of institutional assessment is public opinion shaped by the mass media. A common form of this approach is the annual reporting of national examination results by schools, providing the public a comparative basis for judgment based on those scores. This popular method of assessment has simple mechanisms—the publication of national examination results in a list—and much more complex methods, as in the case of ranking schools, universities, or graduate schools. Ranking schools has proven to be a lucrative undertaking for a number of media organizations.

A third mechanism of institutional evaluation represents a blending of marketing and educational interests acting in an era in search of objective measures of institutional quality. The College Board established in 1899 (SAT, PSAT, Advanced Placement test products); the Educational Testing Service founded 1947 (Graduate Record Exam and Test of English as a Foreign Language); the American College Testing founded in 1959 (ACT and PLAN); and the International Baccalaureate Programme founded in 1968 (IB Diploma Programme, Certificate Programme, Middle Years Programme, and Primary Years Programme) are each nonprofit organizations established to provide quality assessment instruments, processes, and programs to educational consumers and institutions. Performance scores on those tests are often used as proxies for demonstrating institutional quality. Universities and secondary schools commonly use the scores on such tests as part of their branding as an institution of quality and by media groups in calculating quality ratings or rankings for schools and universities. Schools and universities commonly claim themselves to be "competitive" based on the scores earned by current students in secondary schools and by incoming freshman at universities.

The fourth emergent approach is an educational outgrowth of globalization and national concerns about international economic competitiveness and workforce preparedness. Tests such as Trends in International Mathematics and Science Study (TIMSS) and the Programme for International Student Assessment (PISA) focus on providing comparative results for participating nations. In 2012, sixty-five nations participated in the round of testing (Pisa 2012 Results). These results, and research reports based on these results, are playing increasingly prominent roles in discourse concerning educational quality at particularly the national level (though PISA has recently launched an initiative designed to provide student assessments at the level of an individual institution).

Each of these four elements exists and operates outside of the formal mechanisms of accrediting agencies or governmental authorities, and they have become omnipresent aspects of evaluative judgments about educational institutions. Many stakeholders—parents, administrators, students, teachers, press—and policymakers are using such informal evaluation mechanisms and data to assess institutions and programs.

A critical question is whether the formal or informal systems of institutional assessments contribute to achieving goals of social justice or the provision of access to quality educational paths and improved life and career opportunities. To date, the answer is unclear. The measures of educational institutional quality, both formal and informal, appear inadequate to the tasks assigned them, unequal to the quality claims they make or imply, and colored by their conflicted interests—namely, they all have either tests to sell or results to sell. Perhaps even more fundamentally, the existing consensus of agencies such as UNESCO and the World Bank concerning the relationship of education and national development, and by extension assertions about education as a mechanism of social justice and equity, remains an open question based on history and empirical research.

Charles H. Skipper
Robert A. Pierce

References

Baldrige Program. (2010, March 25). Baldrige performance excellence program. Retrieved from http://www.nist.gov/baldrige/.

Bologna Declaration. (1999). *The Bologna Declaration of 19 June 1999*. Retrieved from http://europa.eu/legislation_summaries/education_training_youth/lifelong_learning/c11088_en.htm.

Bourdieu, P. & Passeron, J.-C. (1977). *Reproduction in education, society and culture*. London and Beverly Hills, CA: Sage Publications.

Muriel, A. & Smith, J. (2011). On educational performance measures. *Fiscal Studies*, *32*(2), 187–206.

Pisa 2012 Results. (2012). Retrieved from http://www.oecd.org/pisa/keyfindings/pisa-2012-results.htm.

Weber, M. (1978). *Economy and society*. (G. Roth & C. Wittlich, Trans.). Oakland, CA: University of California Press. (Original work published 1928.)

Wilson, J. Q. (1989). *Bureaucracy: What government agencies do and why they do it*. New York: Basic Books.

World Bank. (2014). *Education*. Retrieved from http://www.worldbank.org/en/topic/education

Worsham, L. (2001). Going postal: Pedagogic violence and the schooling of emotion. In H. A. Giroux and K. Myrsiades (Ed.), *Beyond the corporate university: Culture and pedagogy in the new millennium* (pp. 229–37). Lanham, MD and Boulder, CO: Rowman & Littlefield.

FOOD JUSTICE

Social Injustice in Our Food Systems Contributes to Food Insecurity and Obesity

One can define social injustice of our food system as the lack of an individual's access to high-quality nutritious foods. Food systems interconnect where our food comes from, who produces it, and finally who ultimately consumes it. Along this path, there are many stakeholders, and some are driven by profitability rather than nutrient quality. There are many policies in place to support production capacity, consumer education, and food safety. However, nutritional quality of the food system has not always been of paramount importance. Parameters including the consumer's genetic and physiological makeup, economic status, and geographical location can contribute to this social injustice of denying high-nutrient, quality food to individuals. These parameters are manifest in the increasing numbers of households who do not have enough nutritious food to eat (food insecurity) and those where less nutritious foods are abundantly available that contribute to obesity and its related diseases. While it may appear at first glance that food insecurity and obesity are incompatible with hunger, they are actually highly correlated as forced consumption of cheap, high-caloric/low-nutritional-value foods drives obesity in individuals. In response to public health concerns associated with food insecurity and obesity, there has been increased awareness in grassroot communities and legislative bodies to find methods to mitigate the long-term costs in medical care and productivity that social injustices in our food system propagate.

Obesity among adults in the United States has increased from 30.5 percent in 1999 (Flegal et al., 2002) to 33.8 percent in 2007 (Flegal et al., 2010), and currently resides at approximately 35 percent (Ogden et al., 2013). During the same time, the number of U.S. households struggling to get enough food has also dramatically risen. Food insecurity is defined broadly by the U.S. Department of Agriculture (USDA) as "limited or uncertain availability of nutritionally adequate and safe foods or limited or uncertain ability to acquire acceptable foods in socially acceptable ways" (Report, 1990). Across the United States, 14.5 percent of households were food insecure in 2012, and 5.7 percent experienced very low food security and disruption in their ability to consume adequate amounts of food (Coleman-Jensen, Nord, & Singh, 2013). For historical perspective, in 1999 a total of 9.7 percent of U.S. households were food insecure or very insecure (Andrews et al., 2000). While food insecurity has increased between 2007 and 2012, obesity rates among adults have remained at high levels.

Logically, poverty or low income is highly correlated with food insecurity (Coleman-Jenson, Nord, & Singh, 2013; Dirks, 2003). However, surprisingly, 20 percent of obese adults had incomes less than 130 percent of the federal poverty level between 2005 and 2008 (Ogden et al., 2010). Among women, lower socioeconomic status correlates with the increasing prevalence of obesity, particularly among non-Hispanic white women (Ogden et al., 2010). For men as a whole, there is no correlation between socioeconomic status and obesity (Ogden et al., 2010). For some populations, the rate of obesity is highest among food-insecure households (Adams,

Grummer-Strawn, & Chavez, 2003; Townsend, 2006). Nackers and Appelhans (2013) found that households with low and very low food insecurity had the highest amounts of obesogenic foods (such as sugar-sweetened beverages, snacks, candy, and desserts) in their households. Concern for obesity is due to its contribution to a wide range of ill health effects including diabetes, heart disease, and hypertension as well as the high associated cost of treatment (Cai et al., 2010).

In the overwhelming majority of cases, obesity results from consumption of more calories than the body burns. However, not all obese individuals have control over all of the factors that result in their overconsumption. In fact, it is the social injustice of many aspects of our food system that influence the human behaviors that contribute to the obesity epidemic, and these factors converge disproportionately on low-income populations. Among these factors are the human innate preferences for acquiring and/or storing physiologically valuable and naturally scarce nutrients (fats and sugars), economic forces that make fat and sugar ingredients inexpensive to manufacture and consume, and environmental factors that affect access and availability of different types of foods.

Humans are hardwired to desire nutrients that, on an evolutionary time scale, have been scarce and required considerable effort to obtain for survival. Among these nutrients is glucose, a monosaccharide that is predominantly the only form of energy used by our most vital organ system, the central nervous system. In the food supply, glucose can be readily identified by its sweetness, and all humans are born with an innate preference for sweet flavors (Ventura & Mennella, 2011). Sweetness increases the likelihood that glucose will be consumed and acts as an energy source for the brain. Fat is the most concentrated energy source in our foods and is the preferred form of energy storage within our bodies. Fat is an energy source that can be used for nearly all physiological systems in the body. Our fat stores are a savings account of energy for the body for those times when food is scarce. An adaptive mechanism for humans has been to seek out these key nutrients (i.e., glucose and fat), and the calories contained in them, whenever they are currently available (Drewnowski & Almiron-Roig,

2010). Historically, these nutrients could become very scarce with the slightest environmental change. Humans still have innate preferences for fats and sweets even when we live in an environment where fats and sweets are comparatively abundant. Food manufacturers and purveyors of human cravings capitalize on these innate preferences to entice consumers to purchase high-fat and sugar-containing products. Although this may put the unknowing consumer at risk of overconsumption and developing obesity, it makes sound business sense to make food products that people will desire.

When it comes to the development of obesity, the innate and learned behavior of the individual is a strong influence. As a person executes the act of overconsuming foods/energy, they may do so unknowingly. Unfortunately, evolution did not give us a calorie counter, only a drive to seek out fat and sugar, among other key essential nutrients (i.e., vitamins and minerals). Evolutionarily, we still have the same drive of our earliest ancestors to consume and store nutrients for those periods of time when they may become scarce. Regrettably, sugars and fats contain calories that our bodies can store in unlimited quantity, and fat leads to obesity. Among people who become obese and manage to reduce their caloric intake to levels below those they expend, the ability to maintain the resulting weight loss is fleeting; only approximately 20 percent of the individuals are able to keep these calories off their body in the subsequent years (Shai & Stampfer, 2008). Recent research suggests that there are permanent biochemical changes that our bodies undergo once they have experienced excess accumulation of body fat (Rossmeislova et al., 2013; Sainsbury & Zhang, 2010). These hormonal changes are not within our cognitive control and pose very powerful stimulators of behaviors that seek to maintain excess caloric stores in the body (Sainsbury & Zhang, 2010). From an evolutionary perspective, these changes in metabolism were beneficial in times of food scarcity. Our modern technologies, however, are evolving at a much faster pace than our genetics, and we are, in many ways, falling victim to our environment and genetic programming. Our innate preferences and our physiological resistance to weight loss have placed us at a disadvantage when inexpensive foods formulated to our tastes are abundantly available.

The social injustice associated with food consumption comes to light when we look at some of the factors driving the composition of refined foods. Economies of scale drive the methods used to produce commodity crops including corn, soy, and wheat; more tons per acre mean greater profit. The economic factors that direct production have little or nothing to do with the nutrient content of the final food products. Achieving this outcome has resulted from modern technologies for developing the best strain of plant to grow, the cheapest and most effective fertilizer to add, and the machinery that reduces labor cost. These technologies have resulted in the largest production of commodity crops than at any other time in history (Dowswell, 2009). Further augmentation of our food supply in the United States has been supported by legislative action such as the Farm Bill (Imhoff, 2012). Taxpayer investment in supporting the production of commodity crops and cushioning the risks associated with agriculture maladies has made commodity crops less expensive to the consumer.

The combination of abundance and low cost has provided opportunities for food science researchers to develop new techniques for processing these crops and to make new ingredients for foods. For example, refining these crops has given us inexpensive ingredients such as high fructose corn syrup, hydrolyzed vegetable protein, and partially and fully hydrogenated vegetable oil. We find these outputs in centralized food-service operations, such as national brand restaurants, and in a wide variety of snack foods, beverages, and pre-prepared foods in grocery stores. Their tastiness and long shelf life make them profitable to the vendor and manufacturer and affordable and enticing to the consumer. Couple this with abundant research devoted to advertising and marketing, and the result is a cash cow that makes nearly everyone happy; that is, until you begin to look at the potential nutritional consequences (Nestle, 2007). Together our physiology and economic environment contribute heavily to our risk for obesity. This is compounded when consumer education may be inadequate to help people be resourceful at avoiding refined foods. This negative outcome can be exasperated by the lack of proximity to alternative foods such as fresh produce.

The USDA has expressed the awareness of disparities in access to unrefined in maps of food deserts (USDA, 2014b). Food deserts can be defined by the proximity to healthful foods, income resources for obtaining it, and transportation access (Ver Ploeg et al., 2012). Research has supported the observation that many of the low-cost foods abundantly available are often refined and processed with a high content of added sugars and fats (Walker, Keane, & Burke, 2010). A relationship between reliance on such foods and the prevalence of obesity and poor health has also been identified in many studies, with much of the burden carried by low-income populations (CCPHA, 2008). It is ironic that the very agency that developed the maps is also charged with establishing standards for healthy dietary planning (USDA, 2014a). Among the dietary recommendations are that half of all foods should come from plant sources such as fruits and vegetables. Many low-income adults struggle with finding whole fruits, vegetables, and grains or fresh sources of lean meats and dairy products in close proximity to their households. These same households identify high cost of some of these types of foods as a barrier to avoiding less-expensive refined and processed options (Jetter & Cassady, 2006).

It seems very unjust that the people who harvest much of the nutritionally valuable produce in our country are paid wages so low that they cannot themselves afford to purchase those foods on the retail market. A recent documentary by director and producer U. Roberto Romano describes the lives of immigrant families who work in fields across the United States. He highlights the estimated four hundred thousand children of these laborers also working in the fields and their struggles with the migrant lifestyle and living conditions (Romano, 2011). In the southern central valley of California, a significant amount of the nation's produce is grown (USDA Natural Agriculture Statistics Service, 2014c). Per capita personal income in 2010 was $29,227 in this area, 30 percent less than the state's per capita income. This region

also has many food deserts (USDA, 2014b). Social injustice is found when the people living in this rich farming region cannot access or afford the dietary recommendations for fruits and vegetables associated with best health outcomes (USDA, 2014a).

In response to these issues, and many other social injustices within our food systems, both nationwide and local grassroots movements are underway. Some examples include: establishing Food Day to build awareness and advocacy (CSPI, 2014), creating local committees of stakeholders for affecting policy change (ValleyVision, 2014), and establishing nonprofit organizations for nutrition education (CFLC, 2014). Lawmakers at all levels are also trying out new policies such as taxation of select refined foods, regulating the maximum size of sugar-sweetened beverages, subsidies for fruits and vegetables, or facilitating the use of food stamps at farmer's markets. While not consistently studied, the manipulation of the human environment can have an impact on eating behaviors. A recent review showed that some approaches can be successful (Thow et al., 2010); however, these assessments have been done with relatively small sample sizes, making it difficult to be extrapolated nationwide. These efforts are encouraging from a public health perspective due to the goal of reducing the development of obesity and improving health. More discussion is needed about methods for improving access to the most healthful foods in all communities. Only time will tell if these approaches will be successful at working within the limitations of our genetics to reduce the human cost associated with the overconsumption of refined foods.

Lynn A. Hanna

References

Adams, E. J., Grummer-Strawn, L., & Chavez, G. (2003). Food insecurity is associated with increased risk of obesity in California women. *Journal of Nutrition, 133*(4), 1070–74.

Andrews, M., Nord, M., Bickel, G., & Carlson, S. (2000). Household food security in the United States, 1999. *Food Assistance and Nutrition Research Report, 8.*

Cai, L., Lubitz, J., Flegal, K. M., & Pamuk, E. R. (2010). The predicted effects of chronic obesity in middle age on Medicare costs and mortality. *Med Care, 48*(6), 510–17. doi: 10.1097/MLR.0b013e3181dbdb20

CCPHA. (2008). Designed for disease: The link between local food environments and obesity and diabetes. Retrieved from http://www.publichealthadvocacy.org/PDFs/RFEI%20Policy%20Brief_finalweb.pdf.

CFLC. (2014). California food literacy center. Retrieved from http://californiafoodliteracy.org/.

Coleman-Jensen, A., Nord, M., & Singh, A. (2013). Household food security in the United States in 2012. *Economic Research Report, 155.* U.S. Department of Agriculture, Economic Research Service.

CSPI. (2014). Food day: Center for science in the public interest. Retrieved from http://www.food-day.org/.

Dirks, R. (2003). Diet and nutrition in poor and minority communities in the United States 100 years ago. *Annual Review of Nutrition, 23*, 81–100. doi: 10.1146/annurev.nutr.23.011702.07334101170 2.073341 [pii]

Dowswell, C. (2009). Retrospective. Norman Ernest Borlaug (1914–2009). *Science, 326*(5951), 381. doi: 10.1126/science.1182211

Drewnowski, A. & Almiron-Roig, E. (2010). Human perceptions and preferences for fat-rich foods. In J. P. Montmayeur & J. le Courtre (Eds.), *Fat detection: Taste, texture, and post ingestive effects* (chapter 11, n.p.). Boca Raton, FL: CRC Press. Retrieved from http://www.ncbi.nlm.nih.gov/pubmed/21452472.

Flegal, K. M., Carroll, M. D., Ogden, C. L., & Curtin, L. R. (2010). Prevalence and trends in obesity among US adults, 1999–2008. *JAMA, 303*(3), 235–41. doi: 2009.2014 [pii] 10.1001/jama.2009.2014

Flegal, K. M., Carroll, M. D., Ogden, C. L. & Johnson, C. L. (2002). Prevalence and trends in obesity among US adults, 1999–2000. *JAMA, 288*(14), 1723–27. doi: joc21463 [pii]

Imhoff, D. (2012). *Food fight: The citizen's guide to the next food and farm bill.* Healdsburg, CA: Watershed Media.

Jetter, K. M. & Cassady, D. L. (2006). The availability and cost of healthier food alternatives. *American Journal of Preventative Medicine, 30*(1), 38–44. doi: 10.1016/j.amepre.2005.08.039

Nackers, L. M. & Appelhans, B. M. (2013). Food insecurity is linked to a food environment promoting obesity in households with children. *Journal of Nutrition Education and Behavior, 45*(6), 780–84.

doi: S1499-4046(13)00581-2 [pii] 10.1016/j.jneb.2013.08.001

Nestle, M. (2007). *Food politics: How the food industry influences nutrition and health.* Berkeley, CA: University of California Press.

Ogden, C. L., Carroll, M. D., Kit, B. K., & Flegal, K. M. (2013). Prevalence of obesity among adults: United States, 2011–2012. *NCHS Data Brief, 131*, 1–8.

Ogden, C. L., Lamb, M. M., Carroll, M. D., & Flegal, K. M. (2010). Obesity and socioeconomic status in adults: United States, 2005–2008. *NCHS Data Brief, 50*, 1–8.

Report. (1990). Core indicators of nutritional state for difficult-to-sample populations. *Journal of Nutrition, 120*(Suppl 11): 1559–600.

Romano, U. R. [Director]. (2011). *The harvest: The story of the children who feed America.* http://theharvestfilm.com/.

Rossmeislova, L., Malisova, L., Kracmerova, J., Tencerova, M., Kovacova, Z., Koc, M., Siklova-Vitkova, M., Viquerie, N., Langin, D., & Stich, V. (2013). Weight loss improves the adipogenic capacity of human preadipocytes and modulates their secretory profile. *Diabetes, 62*(6), 1990–95. doi: 10.2337/db12-0986

Sainsbury, A. & Zhang, L. (2010). Role of the arcuate nucleus of the hypothalamus in regulation of body weight during energy deficit. *Molecular and Cellular Endocrinology, 316*(2), 109–119. doi: 10.1016/j.mce.2009.09.025

Shai, I. & Stampfer, M. J. (2008). Weight-loss diets—Can you keep it off? *American Journal of Clinical Nutrition, 88*(5), 1185–86.

Thow, A. M., Jan, S., Leeder, S., & Swinburn, B. (2010). The effect of fiscal policy on diet, obesity and chronic disease: A systematic review. *WHO: Bulletin of the World Health Organization, 88*(8), 609–14. doi: 10.2471/BLT.09.070987

Townsend, M. S. (2006). Obesity in low-income communities: Prevalence, effects, a place to begin. *Journal of the American Dietetic Association, 106*(1), 34–37. doi: S0002-8223(05)02037-7 [pii] 10.1016/j.jada.2005.11.008

USDA. (2010). *Agricultural charts and maps.* Retrieved from http://www.nass.usda.gov/Charts_and_Maps/index.asp.

USDA. (2014a). *Choose my plate.* Retrieved from http://www.choosemyplate.gov/.

USDA, ERS. (2014b). *Food access research atlas.* Retrieved from http://www.ers.usda.gov/data-products/food-access-research-atlas/go-to-the-atlas.aspx#.Uv6ZdfmcJfE.

USDA Natural Agriculture Statistics Service. (2014c). Agricultural charts and maps. Retrieved March 1, 2014, from http://www.nass.usda.gov/Charts_and_Maps/index.asp.

ValleyVision. (2014). *Valley vision*. Retrieved from http://valleyvision.org/.

Ventura, A. K. & Mennella, J. A. (2011). Innate and learned preferences for sweet taste during childhood. *Current Opinion in Clinical Nutrition & Metabolic Care, 14*(4), 379–84. doi: 10.1097/MCO.0b013e328346df65

Ver Ploeg, M., Breneman, V., Dutko, P., Williams, R., Snyder, S., Dicken, C., & Kaufman, P. (2012). Access to affordable and nutritious food: Updated estimates of distance to supermarkets using 2010 data. *USDA Economic Research Service, 143.*

Walker, R. E., Keane, C. R., & Burke, J. G. (2010). Disparities and access to healthy food in the United States: A review of food deserts literature. *Health Place, 16*(5), 876–84. doi: 10.1016/j.healthplace.2010.04.013

FOODSCAPE

Within the past decade, the concept of foodscapes, though not yet universally defined (Freidberg, 2010), has culminated into a vast array of research on food consumption (Winson, 2004), the influence of structure on the formation and makeup of the food environment (Burgoine et al., 2009), and even in urban planning, food policy, and geospatial studies (Smith et al., 2010). Generally speaking, foodscapes are institutional sites for the marketing, merchandising, and consumption of food (e.g., Winson, 2004) or the areas of land, physical domain, or areas of community (e.g., neighborhood environment) in which most food acquisition or consumption takes place.

With a rapid increase in the prevalence of chronic illness (see, for example, Wang et al., 2006; Giskes, 2009), particularly among the African American population, much research has been conducted assessing foodscapes, food environments, and food access issues. Further, literature suggests that the food environment and neighborhood foodscape have much to do with the diet of its residents and that healthy eating is one of the core contributors

to disease prevention (Galal et al., 2010; Shepherd et al., 2006). Therefore, the cycle continues: food decisions in urban cultures are shaped by the foodscape and food access within one's geographic boundary, and these food decisions are maintained and supported by the very same foods that are available.

Structural Influence and Total Food Environment Benefits

The influence of structure (place and space) on decisions surrounding food has been a long-standing epicenter of urban environment and food research. Foodscapes and urban food environments are heavily influenced by its structure (see, for example, Coveney, 2004; Smith et al., 2010), economic status, and social culture, thereby greatly influencing the space and composition of a neighborhood. Individual choices on food consumption are contextual. In an urban area, structural, economic, and social barriers limit healthy food access and create "food deserts" (see Figure F.1). Understanding how these urban areas and total food environments function is useful in grasping the dynamics and interactions of "collective" and "individual" (Power, 2004). The study of health inequalities and cultural aspects of food will allow for greater understanding of healthy eating and food practices, thus facilitating the amelioration of increasing rates of chronic illness (Power, 2004).

Melinda Laroco Boehm
Christopher M. Boehm

References

Burgoine, T., Lake, A. A., Stamp, E., Alvanides, S., Mathers, J. C., & Adamson, A. J. (2009). Changing foodscapes 1980–2000, using the ASH30 Study. *Appetite, 53,* 157–65.

Coveney, J. (2004). A qualitative study exploring socio-economic differences in parental lay knowledge of food and health: Implications for public health nutrition. *Public Health Nutrition, 8*(3), 290–97.

Freidberg, S. (2010). Perspective and power in the ethical foodscape. *Environment & Planning, A, 42*(8), 1868–74.

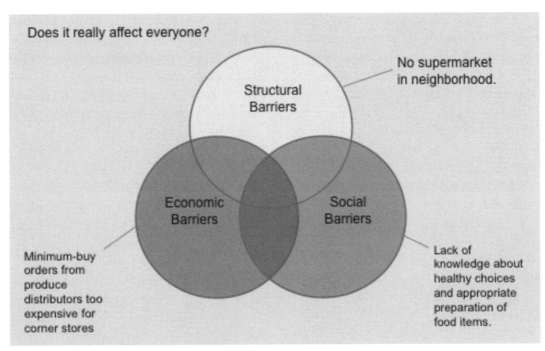
Figure F.1   Total Food Environment Overview

Galal, O., Corroon, M., & Tira, C. (2010). Urban environment and health: Food security. *Asia-Pacific Journal of Public Health*, *22*(3), 245S–261S.

Giskes, K., van Lenthe, F. J., Kamphuis, C. B. M., Huisman, M., Brug, J., & Mackenbach, J. P. (2009). Household and food shopping environments: Do they play a role in socioeconomic inequalities in fruit and vegetable consumption? A multilevel study among Dutch adults. *Journal of Epidemiology & Community Health*, *63*, 113–20.

Power, E. M. (2004). *The determinants of healthy eating among low-income Canadians*. Report prepared for The Office of Nutrition Policy and Promotion, Health Canada, 1–80.

Shepherd, J., Harden, A., Rees, R., Brunton, G., Garcia, J., Oliver, S., & Oakley, A. (2006). Young people and healthy eating: A systemic review of research on barriers and facilitators. *Health Education Research: Theory & Practice*, *21*(2), 239–57.

Smith, D. M., Cummins, S., Taylor, M., Dawson, J., Marshall, D., Sparks, L., & Anderson, A. S. (2010). Neighbourhood food environment and area deprivation: Spatial accessibility to grocery stores selling fresh fruit and vegetables in urban and rural settings. *International Journal of Epidemiology*, *39*, 277–84.

Wang, M. C., Gonzalez, A. A., Ritchie, L. D., & Winkleby, M. A. (2006). The neighborhood food environment: Sources of historical data on retail food stores. *International Journal of Behavioral Nutrition and Physical Activity*, *3*, 15.

Winson, A. (2004). Bringing political economy into the debate on the obesity epidemic. *Agriculture and Human Values*, *21*(4), 299–312.

FREEDOM OF SPEECH

Freedom of speech is the right of individuals to express their opinions on any subject freely through communication. It is counted as one of the fundamental human rights by the United Nations Universal Declaration of Human Rights of 1948 (UN, 1948). Although the term has gained popularity, especially in the last century, the scope of it is still controversial. Most of the people of the world clearly state their support for freedom of speech in principle; however, their reactions to specific examples may change case by case, especially when considering unfavorable statements about the values they believe in, their identity, and the groups that they belong to. In some cases, freedom of speech may also be accepted as a threat to national security.

The proponents of freedom of speech mostly lean on the arguments of John Stuart Mill. According to Mill (1978), freedom of speech involves freedom of thought, feeling, conscience, opinion, sentiments, press, association, and the freedom to publish and express opinions. He claims that free debate and discussion improve one's ideas. Collecting responses of others enables one to develop clearer, stronger ideas. Therefore, the community must allow all ideas to rise since no one can make sure whether an idea is really false or not. So, both individuals and society take the advantage of the differing views, even if the others are wrong.

Mill also draws the limits of the freedom through his well-known Harm Principle. The principle simply states that "the only purpose for which power can be rightfully exercised over any member of a civilized community, against his will, is to prevent harm to others" (Mill, 1978, p. 9). The limit set by the principle may be applied to any type of freedom and draws the line in between clashing rights and values. The conflicts between freedom of speech and hate speech or pornography are probably the most popular examples of this controversy. The people who support restrictions on freedom of speech put emphasis on the harms of unrestricted freedom. With respect to hate speech, the opponents of free speech focus on the silencing effect of hate speech. They claim that the victims of hate speech experience an assault resulting in the humiliation and hesitation to participate in free discussion.

Yusuf Yüksel
Ayhan Akbulut

References

Mill, J. S. (1978). *On liberty*. Indianapolis, IN: Hackett Publishing.

United Nations. (1948). *Universal declaration of human rights*. Retrieved from http://www.un.org/en/documents/udhr/.

FREEDOM SCHOOLS

The Mississippi Freedom Project of 1964 was borne out of the U.S. civil rights movement (1950s to 1960s) through the collaborative efforts of the Student Non-Violence Coordinating Committee (SNCC), the Southern Christian Leadership Conference (SCLC), and the Council of Federated Organizations (COFO). In 1963, Charles Cobb, a field secretary for SNCC (pronounced "snick"), drafted a prospectus calling for the addition of an educational component to the already established project that included a voter registration drive and the creation of community centers. A six-week education program called the Freedom Schools began during the summer of 1964 and operated in twenty counties throughout Mississippi. The purpose of Freedom Schools was to create an educational experience for students that would make it possible for them to become leaders in African American communities and who would challenge the myths of society, perceive more clearly its realities, and find alternatives—ultimately new directions for action (Agosto, 2008). According to a Freedom Schools volunteer, Otis Pease helped to develop the curriculum guide at a March curriculum conference in 1963 (Freedom School Curriculum Materials Transcript; Lynd, 2003). Historian Howard Zinn also developed sections of the curriculum guide (Chilcoat and Ligon, 1999). The director of the Freedom Schools, Staughton Lynd, reported that "[i]ts constituent parts came from many sources" (Lynd, 2003). In 1992, the Children's Defense Fund (CDF) began to offer Freedom Schools with a revised curriculum emphasizing literacy, parent involvement, conflict resolution, and social action (Children's Defense Fund, 2012). Like the Freedom Schools of 1964, the teachers in the CDF Freedom Schools today (or servant-leader interns) are generally college students and are located in about half of the states in the United States. Following in the tradition of the original model, the CDF Freedom Schools' model provides a yearly National Day of Social Action that supports student involvement in community service and social justice advocacy.

Vonzell Agosto

References

Agosto, V. (2008). Intratexturealities: The poetics of the Freedom Schools. *Journal of Negro Education*, 77(2), 168–79.

Chilcoat, G. W. & Ligon, J. A. (1999). "Helping to make democracy a living reality": The curriculum conference of the Mississippi Freedom Schools. *Journal of Curriculum and Supervision, 15*(1), 43–68.

Children's Defense Fund. (2012). *CDF Freedom Schools program.* Retrieved from http://www.childrensdefense.org/programs-campaigns/freedom-schools/.

Freedom School Curriculum Materials Transcript. J. Ellin & N. Ellin Freedom Summer Collection 1963–1988. Civil Rights in Mississippi Digital Archive, University of Southern Mississippi.

Lynd, S. (2003). The Freedom Schools: What were they, what happened? *The Rouge Forum, 11.* Retrieved January 15, 2008, from http://www.rougeforum.org.

GAY-STRAIGHT ALLIANCE (GSA)

A Gay-Straight Alliance (GSA) is an organization, typically based at a school or university, that involves youth members who support peers who are lesbian, gay, bisexual, transgendered, and questioning (LGBTQ). GSAs are an important resource for LGBTQ youth who often deal with bullying and harassment in schools. Open to gay and straight youth alike, these groups help to counter the homophobia and heterosexist norms by challenging the language used and policies enacted at their institutions. The first public school GSA was started at Newton South High School in 1998 in Newton, Massachusetts. Today there are more than four thousand registered GSAs in all fifty states, Puerto Rico, and the U.S. military bases. Yet this is still less than one-quarter of all public schools. GSAs are far less common in rural areas and in the South.

GSAs may work on a number of projects both in and out of their schools or universities. Most participate in some way in national campaigns, such as the Day of Silence and National Coming Out Day. Many receive support in the form of resources or funding from the Gay, Lesbian, and Straight Education Network (GLSEN) and the Gay-Straight Alliance Network. Both organizations offer tools for organizing, recruiting members, hosting events, and more. The Human Rights Campaign (HRC) also offers a wealth of resources about discrimination against LGBTQ persons. HRC also has a program called Welcoming Schools that provides resources for elementary schools and educators designed to ensure that the educational climate is a welcoming one for all.

Research is clear that LGBTQ students are among the most vulnerable when it comes to bullying and harassment in schools and on campuses. In extreme cases, the bullied students are killed or commit suicide, also referred to as bullycide. High-profile examples of homicides and bullycides, such as the shooting death of Lawrence "Larry" King on February 12, 2008, and the suicide of eighteen-year-old Rutgers University student Tyler Clementi on September 22, 2010, have helped propel schools to take action to prevent and respond to harassment. The formation of a GSA can be one important part of those efforts.

Research comparing schools having GSAs with those that do not has found that fewer LGBTQ students hear homophobic remarks daily (57 percent versus 75 percent), feel afraid of their physical safety (61 percent versus 68 percent), and are less likely to miss school because of harassment and fear (26 percent versus 32 percent). Further, students in schools with GSAs or similar student clubs are two times more likely than students without such clubs to say they hear teachers at their school make supportive or positive remarks about lesbian and gay people (24 percent compared to 12 percent).

Additionally, LGBTQ students who report having supportive faculty and other school staff report higher grade point averages and are more likely to say they plan to pursue postsecondary education than LGBTQ students who do not have supportive school staff. Finally, LGBTQ students in schools with a GSA have a greater sense of belonging to their school community than students without a GSA.

Some schools have been hesitant to adopt GSAs, as they fear that parents and community members will object due to their religious beliefs. In 1999, a federal court ruled in *East High Gay/Straight Alliance v. Board of Education of Salt Lake City School District* (81 F. Supp.2d 1166, 1197 [D. Utah 1999]) that schools are in violation of the Equal Access Act when they deny students the right to form GSAs. This Act ensures that schools receiving public funds allow students to use facilities for extracurricular activities.

The Obama administration has supported the work of GSAs. In a letter written on June 14, 2011, Secretary of Education Arne Duncan acknowledged that bullying and harassment of LGBTQ students is far too common in K–12 schools, noting that more than 90 percent of LGBTQ youth in grades six through twelve reported being verbally harassed. Duncan further commented that while GSAs largely focus on supporting LGBTQ youth, those who are perceived to be LGBTQ, and those with family members who identify as LGBTQ, efforts to build school cultures based on respect and acceptance are beneficial to all. He reminded all school districts of their obligation not only to allow GSAs to form and convene on school grounds but also to ensure that they receive equitable resources and support from administrators. Additionally, Duncan announced that the Department of Education's General Counsel, Charlie Rose, had developed legal guidelines to assist school districts in ensuring that they protect the rights of all students. On January 24, 2012, Duncan released a Public Service Announcement (PSA) in commemoration of the first GSA Day.

Laura Finley

Additional Reading

Duncan, A. (2011, June 14). *Key policy letters from the Education Secretary and Deputy Education Secretary*. Retrieved November 4, 2013, from http://www2.ed.gov/policy/elsec/guid/secletter/110607.html.

Gay-Straight Alliances. (n.d.). *GLSEN*. Retrieved November 3, 2013, from http://glsen.org/gsa.

GLSEN. (2007). *Gay-straight alliances: Creating safer schools for LGBT students and their allies* (GLSEN Research Brief). New York: Gay, Lesbian and Straight Education Network.

Human Rights Campaign Foundation. (2012). *Welcoming schools*. Retrieved from http://www.welcomingschools.org.

GENDER

Gender is a "social category" (like race, social class, and sexual orientation) with characteristics that are constructed, represented, and interpreted within the context of various cultures and societies. Just as discourses of race, class, and sexual orientation have certain social meanings, historical contexts, and consequences, so do discourses about gender. Mass culture, for example, generates images and interpretations of masculinity and femininity that are reinterpreted by people in everyday conversations and social institutions, such as schools, workplaces, and communities, which have a gendered character to their formal and informal operations.

The line between biological sex and gender can be confusing. Gender refers to social categories and characteristics that are related to but not identical to biological sex. Biological sex, or sex, refers to the genetic or biological division of the species into "male" and "female." Sex differences between people take place because of physiological phenomena such as the arrangements of chromosomes in a fertilized human egg. Gender differences between people occur because of social and cultural phenomena. Ergo, gender may be viewed as the interpretation of the significance of sex.

Gender roles are organized and ritualized patterns of behavior we follow that are based on our interpretation of the significance of biological sex. They structure our choices and guide our behavior in ways that our particular society or culture deems "gender appropriate" (Sapiro, 1986, 72). For example, Quantz (2011) describes a scenario in which young men at a high school graduation are required to wear blue robes and young women are required to wear white robes and carry a red rose; these young people are participating in a celebration, a performance, and a ritual that marks their transition into adulthood, but at the same time, they are also gendered. That is to say, the graduates are marked by sex to take their different places in society. Each is assigned a role and is expected to dress for (or display the symbols of) and to "perform" within a particular gendered role (Butler, 1990).

The association of sex and gender into socially prescribed gender roles is very powerful in all cultures and societies (Mead, 1935). Contemporary intersections of sex and gender are pervasive within every aspect of Western culture—from the way in which boys and girls are treated in school, to the ways in which parents/guardians raise their children, to the ways in which men and women approach the world and address problems.

A contemporary feminist perspective on gender and gendered roles sees the social construction of gender roles in cultures and societies as particularly problematic because these sexist roles limit the potential growth of individuals and restrict the nature of relations between heterosexual, homosexual, bisexual, and transexual people (Fine & McClelland, 2006). A contemporary feminist analysis would therefore argue that the intersection of race, class, gender, and sexual orientation must be considered in order to explain the construction of gendered, raced, and sexed identities that can position some people in positions of powerlessness and other people in positions of dominance in a culture or society (hooks, 1990). Thinking about intersectionality is key to discourses about how various forms of "difference" are socially constructed, including those of gender, race, class, and sexual orientation (Hill Collins, 2005).

Susan Schramm-Pate

References

Butler, J. (1990). *Gender trouble: Feminism and the subversion of identity*. New York: Routledge.

Fine, M. & McClelland, S. I. (2006). Sexuality education and desire: Still missing after all these years. *Harvard Education Review, 76*(3), 1–32.

Hill Collins, P. (2005). *Black sexual politics: African Americans, gender, and the new racism*. New York: Routledge.

hooks, b. (1990). *Yearning: Race, gender, and cultural politics*. Boston, MA: South End Press.

Mead, M. (1935). *Sex and temperament in three primitive societies*. New York: Morrow.

Quantz, R. (2011). *Rituals and student identity in education: Ritual critique for a new pedagogy*. New York: Palgrave Macmillan.

Sapiro, V. (1986). *Women in American society*. Palo Alto, CA: Mayfield Publishing Company.

GENDER BIAS

Gender Essentialism

Gender essentialism is the view that people have inherent and immutable personal characteristics based on their sex and that these characteristics give rise to gender-specific experiences. This notion is often linked with the "difference" model of feminism (contrast with the "equality" or "social constructivist" model), both of which posit that fundamental dissimilarities between men and women explain their material and social differences. Some gender essentialists may argue that women are naturally more peaceful, nurturing, communicative, and moral than men, thereby affecting their personal relationships and careers. Other essentialists focus on women's shared social conditions rather than their attributes, and emphasize their marginalization within the economy and family unit (e.g., the gender wage gap). More specifically, some essentialists find that women's childbearing alone fundamentally defines their social role and status.

Gender essentialism has been espoused by those who wish to undergird and explain role differentials among men and women as well as by gender-equality activists wishing to create solidarity among women. The latter claim that certain generalizations can be made about "womanhood," "motherhood," and "the family," and that these serve to further global standards for the status of women. Gayatri Spivak unintentionally began a movement toward "strategic essentialism" when she speculated that marginalized groups may find it advantageous to temporarily act as if their identities are stable and homogenous in order to achieve their political goals.

In response to essentialism, antiessentialists maintain that all aspects of gender are socially constructed. Particular contexts create the class, race, and cultural differences among women's interests. They charge that essentialism is marred by ahistorical, racist, classist, and heterosexist elements. Postmodern, particularly black, feminists emphasize that every perspective is socially situated and charge that essentialists fail to see the "intersectionality" of discrimination. Coined by Kimberle Crenshaw, the study of intersectionality examines how biological, social, cultural, and economic categories interact on multiple levels in order to create inequality; intersectionality is at odds with gender essentialism. Some postcolonial/Third World feminists have charged that, in trying to avoid gender essentialism, antiessentialists have, in turn, actually engaged in a form of "cultural essentialism," defining women's identities and experiences not by their gender but rather by their nationality or culture.

Laine Strutton

GENDER DISCRIMINATION

Significant progress has been made in the last sixty years in terms of women's equality. The Civil Rights Act of 1964 was the landmark legislation in the United States prohibiting discrimination on the basis of race, color, religion, sex, or national origin. This act was initially directed toward racial discrimination, but it was eventually expanded to include the word *sex*. While the act ended the unequal application of voter registration requirements and racial segregation in schools, public facilities and in workplaces, a significant area of intervention was racial and gender discrimination in employment practices. Section 703 (a) of the final legislation made it unlawful for an employer

(1) to fail or refuse to hire or to discharge any individual, or otherwise to discriminate against any individual with respect to his compensation, terms, conditions or privileges or employment, because of such individual's race, color, religion, sex, or national origin; or (2) to limit, segregate, or classify his employees in any way which would deprive or tend to deprive any individual of employment opportunities or otherwise adversely affect his status as an employee, because of such individual's race, color, religion, sex, or national origin.

Title VII of the act created the Equal Employment Opportunity Commission (EEOC) to oversee the implementation of this legislation. Most employers with at least fifteen employees, most labor unions, and employment agencies are covered by the EEOC's mandate. The EEOC enforces laws that apply to all types of work situations, including hiring, firing, promotions, harassment, training, wages, and benefits. The EEOC deems it illegal to discriminate against a person because the person complained about discrimination, filed a charge of discrimination, or participated in an employment discrimination investigation or lawsuit.

Prior to the Civil Rights Act, in the late nineteenth and early twentieth centuries, gender-related legislation involved statutes for the protection of labor, such as regulation on maximum hours. As Rhode (1991, p. 38) points out, however, the central difficulty lay in policymakers' inability to recognize not only that working women faced special disadvantages but also that sex-based protections often exacerbated these disadvantages. Therefore, even as gender-specific regulations curbed some of the exploitative conditions to which female employees were vulnerable, such protective legislation provided employers with the justification to avoid hiring women altogether (since women were perceived to be more expensive) and thus limited their entry into occupations considered desirable by male competitors. Women were locked into overcrowded, sex-segregated employment, with limited bargaining power, low or no unionization, and high turnover, making them even more vulnerable to exploitation. Judicial and public attitudes endorsed the *separate spheres doctrine*, by which men inhabited the public sphere—that is, the world of government, law, trade and commerce—and women's roles within the home (the private realm) were glorified. Paid work performed by women in the so-called feminine occupations (such as teaching and nursing) and other unpaid charitable work were considered extensions of women's nurturing duties within the home. The separate spheres doctrine worked to bar women from exercising economic or political sovereignty and assigned them to subservient roles in a patriarchal order. It rationalized this subordination by deeming women's confinement to matters of the home or family as "biologically given" or "natural."

The separate spheres doctrine continued despite women's equal right to vote, passed in 1920. Women were discouraged from holding public office, serving on juries, obtaining higher education, joining certain professions (such as the law), or owning businesses. In the postwar period, with an increasing number of women joining the labor force, ideological and cultural notions of women's roles began to change (Rhode, 1991). By 1960, 38 percent of all women were in the workforce. Changing postwar demographic realities were demonstrably out of sync with the traditional roles prescribed for women under the separate spheres doctrine. Women's increasing education and participation in the workforce meant their increased consciousness. Feminist political action sought not only to deconstruct notions of the idyllic household by pointing to housewives' isolation and lack of fulfillment, but also brought into focus problems faced by the working woman, such as discrimination, harassment, lack of advancement, and occupational sex segregation. In 1961, President Kennedy established the Commission on the Status of Women, which recognized that "prejudices and outmoded customs act as barriers to the full realization of women's basic rights which should be respected and fostered as part of our Nation's commitment to human dignity, freedom, and democracy" (Executive Order 10980, 1961). The mandate of the Commission was to go beyond extant protective legislation and recommend steps that actively promoted women's equal rights. The Commission recommended the Equal Pay Act of 1963, requiring that women and men performing equal work be paid the same salaries.

Catalyzed by developments such as the Civil Rights Act of 1964 and the formation of the Commission on the Status of Women, political action by women led to the creation of the National Organization for Women (NOW) in 1966. NOW was headed by feminist activist and author of *The Feminine Mystique*, Betty Friedan. The organization launched itself not only toward the implementation of Title VII, but also persuaded President Lyndon Johnson to pass Executive Order 11375, requiring all federal contractors to end discrimination on the basis of sex in hiring and employment. In 1972, Congress passed Title IX of the education amendments to address sex discrimination in educational programs receiving federal funding.

Despite these legislative developments, concerns remain with regard to overt or insidious discriminatory practices and unfavorable treatment of individuals on the basis of their gender. Even after the passage of the Civil Rights Act in 1964, the EEOC continued, for instance, to allow sex-classified job advertisements until the intervention of the Supreme Court in 1973. Although legal statutes assure women and men equal pay for the same work and have broken some barriers to women's employment, empirical studies have demonstrated the continuation of unequal pay for equal jobs, occupational segregation, and the concentration of women into relatively low-status, low-paying vocations.

In 1963, when the Equal Pay Act was signed, women made fifty-nine cents on average for every dollar earned by men (based on Census figures of median wages of full-time, year-round workers). In 2010, female full-time workers made only seventy-seven cents for every dollar earned by men, a gender wage gap of 23 percent (Hegewisch & Williams, 2011) and a decline in the wage gap of less than a half percent every year. Further, women earn less than men in every single occupation for which an earnings ratio can be calculated (Hegewisch, Williams, and Harbin, 2012), consistent across all racial and ethnic groups (U.S. Census, 2011). Over a working lifetime, this wage disparity costs the average American woman and her family an estimated $700,000 to $2 million, impacting Social Security benefits and pensions (National Committee on Pay Equity, 2013).

Added to the gender wage gap within occupations is the gender wage gap *between* occupations. Not only are women more likely to work in low-wage, "pink-collar" jobs such as teaching, child care, nursing, cleaning, and waitressing (Boushey, 2009), but male-dominated occupations tend to pay more than female-dominated occupations at similar skill levels, particularly at higher levels of educational attainment (Hegewisch, Williams, & Harbin, 2012), perpetuating gender inequalities across occupations. In the professions, barriers to women's advancement in the workplace—including the "glass ceiling"—persist despite comparable age, experience, and occupational qualifications.

The persistence of discrimination in the labor market is a concern that has occupied economists and sociologists alike. The issue of wage discrimination has, in particular, received much attention in these disciplines since wages are both observable and measurable. Wage discrimination is defined as equally productive workers receiving unequal wages. Textbook models of neoclassical (mainstream) economic theory argue that in perfectly competitive markets, wage discrimination is simply eroded away. If all workers have the same productivity, a firm choosing to discriminate on the basis of gender or race, rather than employing the most productive, lowest-cost worker, would face a cost disadvantage in comparison with nondiscriminating firms. The higher-cost, discriminating firm would face a downward pressure on the price level from its nondiscriminating rivals and would eventually be driven out of business. The best course of action for a rational firm interested in longer-term survival, therefore, is nondiscrimination. A corollary here is that discrimination can only persist if there are factors limiting the amount of competition in the labor or product markets.

In real-world labor markets, however, differential wages are observed between women and men. Two perspectives emerge within mainstream economics on whether these differential outcomes are a result of discrimination. Scholars focusing on labor supply use the human capital theory to argue that the wage disparity between women and men may simply be a reflection of their differing productivities, rather than of gender discrimination. Productivity is taken to be a function of investments made by the worker in education and training, and in gaining experience through job tenure. If women themselves, as workers or suppliers of labor, have opted for lower human capital investments on education, training, or experience in anticipation of their social reproduction responsibilities (child rearing or care work), then the observed differences in wages would simply reflect gender differences in the levels of investment on human capital. Since women's own choices have led to their lower wages, the wage disparity is not regarded to be a result of gender discrimination.

On the other hand, scholars focusing on the demand side within neoclassical economics ascribe the presence of wage discrimination to employer preferences; for example, to the fact that employers may have an irrational "taste for discrimination" (Becker, 1957) developed outside of the labor market. The "employer taste" model predicts that discrimination exists because employers might be reluctant to employ certain groups of workers (women, minorities) and will only be induced do so if these workers are paid lower wages than those paid to workers in general. Through employer "tastes," a situation may arise where equally productive workers are paid different wages. In contrast, the theory of statistical discrimination argues that

discrimination might be a rational response among employers. Since employers might not have complete information on the potential productivity of future workers at the time of hiring, generalized gender and racial characteristics serve as proxies or screening devices to select the best applicants. For instance, if a general perception prevails that women are more likely to work less due to balancing their paid work with their household responsibilities, employers will likely discriminate against women at the time of hiring.

Critics of neoclassical economic theories of discrimination—most notably feminist economists and sociologists—have been frustrated by its myopic emphasis on the labor market, ignoring socialization processes that occur *before* women's entry into the labor market. Human capital theory, in particular, fails to explain the persistence of sexual stereotypes that keep women disadvantaged, despite remarkable progress in female education and experience in the past few decades. For instance, England (1982) points out that gender differences in human capital only seem to explain 50 percent of the gender wage gap. For another, the human capital theory treats labor market discrimination as a separate issue from gender discrimination in other spheres; indeed, prelabor market socialization—which may lead to labor market discrimination as well as to self-perpetuating cycles reinforcing labor market inequalities—is regarded as completely exogenous. Arguing that women's own choices lead to their lower wages obscures the constraints on individual choice imposed by gender norms, social structures impinging upon the workplace, and long-standing discrimination. Since women have always earned lower wages in traditionally "feminine" occupations, while facing significant barriers to advancement in nontraditional ones, it makes economic sense for a household to give priority to the man's more promising career and assign the lion's share of the housework to women. Being assigned these household responsibilities in turn encourages women to make lower human capital investments. Thus, the gender division of labor in the home perpetuates gender divisions in the workplace. Figart (1999, p. 237) therefore proposes a broader, more realistic definition of gender discrimination in the labor market as a "multidimensional interaction of economic, social, political, and cultural forces in both the workplace and the family, resulting in differential outcomes involving pay, employment, and status."

Feminist scholars of the labor market also disagree with the contention that discrimination is irrational or unprofitable by arguing that it can be profitable if it is generalized practice (see, for instance, Bergmann, 1974). Indeed, if labor markets are segregated such that only certain groups have access to certain kinds of labor markets (i.e., occupational segregation), then individual and sectoral wage differentials can continue unabated. For instance, institutional perspectives on the labor market argue that labor markets are divided into a primary sector—where jobs are considered skilled, offer opportunities for advancement, and are also protected by legislation or unionization—and a secondary sector—where jobs are low-wage, exploitative, insecure, and offer no means of advancement (Blau & Jusenius, 1976). Women and people of color tend to overwhelmingly concentrate in the latter. Marxian approaches take the segmentation hypothesis further by arguing that it is not only employers who benefit from the division between "skilled/primary" and "unskilled/secondary" workers in the labor market, but also white male workers who seek to maintain their positions of privilege in the labor market (Rubery, 1978; Williams, 1987). As such, certain jobs become defined as "unskilled women's work," justifying low pay and exploitative conditions.

Feminist sociologists examine how noneconomic factors—customs, norms, and relationships between labor market players—may impact the operation of labor markets and, in turn, shape economic outcomes. Viewing labor markets as complex social institutions means that economic factors behind discrimination can constitute only a partial picture. Work in sociology has therefore focused on the societal mechanisms reinforcing discrimination and sex segregation (Acker, 1990; Reskin, 1988; Bielby & Baron, 1986), as well as their relationship to positions of authority and privilege within organizations (Budig, 2002; Smith, 2002). Nonwage forms of workplace discrimination have also received attention within sociology. Mackinnon (1979) points to sexual harassment at work as a form of discrimination since it is grounded upon women's subordinate position in society, can affect an individual's performance at work, and consequently impact their earnings and employment opportunities. Feminist scholars' contribution to the labor market lies, therefore, in unpacking the processes by which gender interacts with social and economic institutions, such as the household and the workplace, and impacts individual economic agents.

The struggles of the 1960s and 1970s helped to reshape the terrain of discourse around gender discrimination in the United States. Legislative, executive, and judicial branches have played a huge role in spearheading changes, from the passage of the Civil Rights Act in 1964 to the Lilly Ledbetter Fair Pay Act signed into law by President Obama in 2009, the latter of which resets the 180-day statute of limitations under the Civil Rights Act for filing an equal pay lawsuit with each new paycheck affected by the discriminatory action. Legislation has addressed a wide variety of issues pertaining to gender discrimination, such as violence against women, sexual harassment in the workplace, reproductive rights, and equal pay.

Despite these promising steps, challenges remain on many fronts, especially since the changes brought about by legislation have only been gradual and incremental. The liberal framework of regulation and law fails to confront larger social structures resulting in women's unequal and disadvantaged status. Rhode (1991, p. 2) argues, for instance, that "a determination that the sexes are not 'similarly situated' only begins the discussion," and that it is more useful to talk about gender *disadvantage* than difference. A focus on disadvantage, she argues, enables people to ask broader questions on the nature and sources of inequality. Feminist scholars have embarked on such projects through exploring the interrelationships between women's production and reproduction, the limitations of existing policy frameworks, and the nature of the economy/marketplace itself that perpetuates discrimination. Such research will enable the development of cohesive strategies in the realms of gender-based discrimination that are beyond the reach of legislation.

Smita Ramnarain

References

Acker, J. (1990). Hierarchies, jobs, bodies: A theory of gendered organizations. *Gender & Society, 4*(2), 139–58.

Becker, G. S. (1957). *The economics of discrimination.* Chicago: University of Chicago Press.

Bergman, B. (1974). Occupational segregation, ages and profits when employers discriminate by race or sex. *Eastern Economic Journal, 1*(2), 103–10.

Bielby, W. T. & Baron, J. N. (1986). Men and women at work: Sex segregation and statistical discrimination. *American Journal of Sociology, 91*(4), 759–99.

Blau, F. & Jusenius, C. (1976). Economic dimensions of occupational segregation. *Signs, 1*(3), 181–99.

Boushey, H. (2009). The new breadwinners. *The Shiver report. A woman's nation changes everything.* Washington, DC: Center for American Progress, 30–67.

Budig, M. (2002). Male advantage and the gender composition of jobs: Who rides the glass escalator? *Social Problems, 49*(2), 258–77.

England, P. (1982). The failure of human capital theory to explain occupational sex segregation. *Journal of Human Resources, 17*(3), 358–70.

Figart, D. (1999). Theories of discrimination. In J. Peterson & M. Lewis (Eds.), *The Elgar companion to feminist economics.* Northampton: Edward Elgar.

Hegewisch, A. & Williams, C. (2011). *The gender wage gap: 2010.* Retrieved August 13, 2013, from http://www.iwpr.org/initiatives/pay-equity-and-discrimination.

Hegewisch, A., Williams, C., & Harbin, V. (2012). *Gender wage gap by occupation.* Retrieved August 13, 2013, from http://www.iwpr.org/initiatives/pay-equity-and-discrimination.

MacKinnon, C. A. (1979). Sexual harassment of working women: A case of sex discrimination. New Haven: Yale University Press.

National Committee on Pay Equity. (2013). *The wage gap over time: In real dollars, women see a continuing gap.* Retrieved from http://www.pay-equity.org/info-time.html.

O'Leary, A. & and Boushey, H. (2009). *The Shriver report: A woman's nation changes everything.* Retrieved from http://shriverreport.org/special-report/a-womans-nation-changes-everything/.

Reskin, B. (1988). Bringing the men back in: Sex differentiation and the devaluation of women's work. *Gender & Society, 2*(1), 58–81.

Rhode, D. L. (1991). *Justice and gender.* Cambridge: Harvard University Press.

Rubery, J. (1978). Structured labour markets, worker organisation and low pay. *Cambridge Journal of Economics, 2*(1), 17–36.

Smith, R. (2002). Race, gender, and authority in the workplace: Theory and research. *Annual Review of Sociology, 28*, 509–42.

U.S. Census Bureau. (2011). *Current population survey: Annual social and economic supplement.* Retrieved August 21, 2013, from http://www.census.gov/hhes/www/cpstables/032011/perinc/new02_061.htm.

Williams, R. (1987). Capital, competition, and discrimination: A reconsideration of racial earnings inequality. *Review of Radical Political Economics, 19*(2), 1–15.

GENERATIONAL DIFFERENCES

Generational Differences, Generations of Western Society, Managing Multiple Generations in the Workplace

Generational differences in societies are characteristics generally attributed to people's age that constitute a sociocultural phenomenon. Divisions in the generations differ across nations and extend even to civilizations. Perception and recognition of the different characteristics of each generation affect the cooperation between people in social, political, and economic capacities, and subsequently extend to entities in the public, informal, commercial, and nongovernmental sectors. From the perspective of social justice, it is important to draw attention to how workplace management techniques are used to promote equal opportunities among representatives of various generations.

Generational Differences

Generation defines a community of individuals belonging to an age group of people born around the same time period (usually within one year). Generations are often perceived as "historical" communities with a certain hierarchy of values, attitudes, and common momentous experiences such as war, change(s) in the social system, and economic crises.

The concept of generational differences dates back to the early twentieth century (Schaie, 2007). Sociologist Karl Mannheim drew attention to the conflicts between the generations, particularly between children and young people against their parents. These conflicts are based on a failure to understand the other because of differences in experiences, opinions, habits, and behavior as well as the transmission of values. The concept was similarly adopted in psychology by Charlotte Buhler and Raymond Kuhlen. Developmental psychologists pointed out that the age of the individual has to be analyzed in conjunction with the social changes that affect behavior.

Studies on generational differences resumed in the 1960s with the rise of the "generational gap" or "generational conflict" phenomenon. Clashes between younger and older people surfaced after World War II due to rapid changes in the social, economic, and cultural characteristics of societies, which included changes in fashion, lifestyles, electoral behavior, work expectations, and values. Generational gap was observed mainly in the United States and Europe and described the cultural differences between the baby boomers and their parents (Mendez, 2008). This largely unprecedented situation was the result of many older people increasing their power and social influence and, at the same time, many young people rebelling against social norms. Perception of the gap became tied to hippie fashions and values, religious and cultural diversity, music festivals, sexual freedom, and drug use. Generation gap was also the result of a decrease in multigenerational households where three or more generations lived together. The gap can thus be understood as children having fewer opportunities to understand and relate to their parents, grandparents, and great-grandparents.

Another important term in generational differences is an *intergenerational hierarchy boundary* (Gillmore, 2008). This term refers to the observation that family members can only play the roles assigned to them by others. These boundaries not only provide an organized system through which family needs are met, but they also form a means of transmitting affection, values, and knowledge to future generations. For example, a few centuries ago, the boundaries in traditional families led to the idea that children should be treated as adults due to the need for labor. Moreover, parents had relatively less time to raise children, leaving

grandparents to impart their time and experience on children and grandchildren. However, industrialism and technological advances have led to a new situation, in which children are recognized as adults later in life and their entrance into the workforce is delayed. Consequently, the age at which adults are likely to have children has shifted, and with it the age difference between children and parents has increased. This age gap between child and parent could hinder parents' ability to identify with their children, which may result in less involvement. Other differences could arise from a decrease in children's respect for grandparents due to changes in work and living environments, geographical mobility, rising divorce rates, and "age segregation"—for example, when older people reside in age-specific housing or communities while children are raised in nurseries and schools. Sociological and anthropological studies indicate that differences in intergenerational boundaries and hierarchy occur across cultural and ethnic groups (Mead, 1970).

The negative or positive valuation of different generations may be described as "generationism" (Bard & Söderqvist, 2002). This belief holds that certain generational features are better or worse compared to other generations, and like "age-ism," it is a summative judgment of others not typically grounded by verifiable data. Generationism manifests mainly on the negative valuation of currently living generations with respect to past (e.g., negative assessment of ancient cultures as "primitive") or future (e.g., negative assessment of young people behavior) generations.

Generations of Western Society
Several generations in contemporary society have been delineated and described by business fields such as marketing and human resources management (Patterson, 2010). The most prominent generations observed in Western societies are: Traditionalists, Baby Boomers, Generation X, Generation Y/Millennials, and Generation Z. However, it should be noted that the characteristics of each generation depend on the country or society under consideration (for example, Poland in the twentieth century underwent three transformations of its political and economic system, which significantly

contributed to much more complex generational differences). Also, those features may not be as readily applied to civilizations characterized by different traditions and perceptions of social justice (e.g., Eastern cultures). Lastly, those generational differences have been further criticized as middle-class characteristics that cannot sufficiently describe generation members from low- and high-income families.

The Traditionalist generation includes people born between 1920 and 1940. They are often described as conservative, consistent, and reliable. Having survived hard economic times, they are generally patient and hard working, holding patriotism, dedication, and sacrifice in high regard. They typically respect hierarchical structure, earned status, and authority. As employees, they were committed to a particular career for a lifetime. As the name suggests, traditionalists value law, slow change, and the continuity of traditions.

Baby boomers were born between 1946 and 1960. They are generally optimistic and idealistic, but they also see authority and rules as elements that can be questioned and manipulated. They value democracy and teamwork, but they tend to ignore interpersonal conflicts. As employees, they are characterized by a strong work ethic, dedicated to a job and quality outcomes, but they often need to receive performance feedback and be recognized for their personal contributions. Boomers possess a strong desire for individuality and personal gratification and are thus motivated by money, title, material success, health, and wellness.

Generation X encompasses those born between 1961 and 1980. They are characterized by a tendency toward resourcefulness, self-reliance, adaptability, and flexibility. They are often skeptical about the world and are economically conservative, but they are still willing to learn and take risks. However, they tend to undermine teamwork and distrust institutions. They are more interested in their own development and well-being than that of the organization. Consequently, Xers tend to build portable careers as an extension of their attachment to freedom, informality, and a balance between work and leisure.

Generation Y/Millennials are people born between 1981 and 2000. They have never experienced a world without digital technology, in particular the Internet and mobile phones. They are characterized by an interest in higher education and creativity. They were often raised in child-centered, democratic families and tend to appear sociable, optimistic, and self-assured. They are present-oriented, often refusing traditions while embracing diversity. Generation Y members need meaningful work, supervision, and feedback from those who have expertise. They are multitaskers who prefer teamwork but avoid difficult people in the work environment. This generation needs achievements and builds parallel careers.

There is no agreement on the exact birth dates of Generation Z members, although estimates place them somewhere between the late 1990s and the mid-2000s. They were raised not long after the September 11 terrorist attacks, which influenced the politics regarding mobility and data privacy in many countries. Because Generation Z members use many communication technologies, they have been aptly nicknamed "digital natives." They seek out jobs that can be performed in multiple locations, from home to office to café, but they fear the lack of a permanent job and owning homes. They often maintain critical attitudes toward higher education, social security, and state responses to economic crises.

Managing Multiple Generations in the Workplace
The concept of promoting social justice among the generations was introduced in the 1980s as part of "diversity management." It is based on the assumption that an age-diverse workforce should be seen as a competitive advantage (Gilbert, Stead, & Ivancevich, 1999). However, the concept also presumes that modernization—with its increased mobility and age-specific institutions—has reduced most people's opportunities to interact constantly with others outside of their age group. Consequently, many professionals may have little or no exposure to the experiences of different generations, and thus they do not understand their values and expectations.

"Intergenerational social integration" involves activities aimed at the consolidation of individuals and groups representing different generations, thereby increasing the strength and solidarity of relationships between generations (Klimczuk, 2013). These activities help to raise awareness of generation interdependence and highlight how the choices and actions of one generation affect others. Integration policies can occur at different societal levels: at the state level (macro), in family or company (micro), as well as between different generations in local communities, political parties, nongovernmental organizations, and professional associations (meso).

Human relations management in public, commercial, and nongovernment entities may use techniques to increase the benefits derived from multiple generations coordinating in the workplace. One method, often known as "age management" (Walker, 1997), seeks to promote equity and combat age barriers in employment through public policy or collective agreements. Age management involves the implementation of good practices along a few dimensions, namely:

1. Job recruitment (e.g., elevation of maximum age limit; elimination/absence of particular age barriers; positive discrimination of age groups/generations; employment exchange/job center for older workers)
2. Training, development, and promotion (e.g., development of training and educational programs, in particular for older/aging workers; creation of learning environments and workplace mentorships for older workers; promotion of age-specific policy in work organizations)
3. Flexible work practices (e.g., flexible working hours/age-related working time; age-related leave; part-time jobs; flexible retirement/early exit scheme)
4. Ergonomics, job design, and prevention (e.g., improvement of work conditions and workload; mixing younger and older workers; age-related health and/or wealth control; older workers excluded from shift labor)
5. Changing attitudes within organizations (e.g., research related to aging and performance; programs to change attitudes and opinions toward older workers)
6. Changes in exit policy (e.g., elevation of minimum age of early exit; elevation of normal retirement age)
7. Using of other policies (e.g., establishing general age-related policy; seniority programs; sectoral age-related policy as result of collective agreements)

Andrzej Klimczuk

References

Bard, A. & Söderqvist, J. (2002). *Det globala imperiet (The global empire)*. Stockholm, Sweden: Bonnier Fakta.

Gilbert, J. A., Stead, B. A., & Ivancevich, J. M. (1999). Diversity management: a new organizational paradigm. *Journal of Business Ethics*, *21*(1), 61–76.

Gillmore, J. (2008). Intergenerational hierarchy boundary. In S. Loue & M. Sajatovic (Eds.), *Encyclopedia of aging and public health* (pp. 472–73). New York: Springer.

Klimczuk, A. (2013). Analysis of intergenerational policy models. *Ad Alta: Journal of Interdisciplinary Research*, *3*(1), 66–69.

Mead, M. (1970). *Culture and commitment: A study of the generation gap*. New York: Natural History Press.

Mendez, N. (2008). Generation gap. In S. Loue & M. Sajatovic (Eds.), *Encyclopedia of aging and public health* (pp. 386–87). New York: Springer.

Patterson, C. (2010). Generational differences. In C. Clauss-Ehlers (Ed.), *Encyclopedia of cross-cultural school psychology* (pp. 477–78). New York: Springer.

Schaie, K. W. (2007). Generational differences: Age-period-cohort. In J. E. Birren (Ed.), *Encyclopedia of gerontology* (pp. 601–10). Oxford, UK: Elsevier.

Walker, A. (1997). *Combating age barriers in employment. European research report*. Dublin: European Foundation for the Improvement of Living and Working Conditions.

Additional Reading

Gravett, L. & Throckmorton, R. (2007). *Bridging the generation gap: How to get radio babies, boomers, Gen Xers, and Gen Yers to work together and achieve more*. Franklin Lakes, NJ: Career Press.

Hannam, S. E. & Yordi, B. (2011). *Engaging a multigenerational workforce: Practical advice for government managers*. Washington, DC: IBM Center for the Business of Government.

Johnson, M. & Johnson, L. (2010). *Generations, Inc.: From boomers to linksters—managing the friction between generations at work*. New York: AMACOM.

Kunze, F., Boehm, S., & Bruch, H. (2011). Generational leadership—how to manage five different generations in the workforce. In S. Kunisch, S. A. Boehm, & M. Boppel (Eds.), *From grey to silver: Managing the demographic change successfully* (pp. 87–100). Heidelberg, NY: Springer-Verlag Berlin Heidelberg.

Martin, C. A. & Tulgan, B. (2006). *Managing the generation mix: From urgency to opportunity*. Amherst, MA: HRD Press.

McCrindle, M. & Wolfinger, E. (2009). *The ABC of XYZ: Understanding the global generations*. Sydney: UNSW Press.

Newman, S. M., Larkin, E., Friedlander, D., and Goff, R. (Eds.). (2012). *Intergenerational relationships: Conversations on practice and research across cultures*. Hoboken: Taylor & Francis.

Parry, E. & Urwin, P. (2009). *Tapping into talent: The age factor and generation issues*. London: Chartered Institute of Personnel and Development.

Salkowitz, R. (2008). *Generation blend: Managing across the technology age gap*. Hoboken, NJ: John Wiley & Sons.

Zemke, R., Raines, C., & Filipczak, B. (1999). *Generations at work: Managing the clash of veterans, boomers, xers, and nexters in your workplace*. New York: AMACOM.

GENOCIDE

The history of humanity has been littered with several devastating cases of genocide, an act that is rightfully described as "the supreme crime" (Campbell, 2001, p. 25). In the past five hundred years, examples of genocide have included the American Native genocide (death toll of one hundred million), Atlantic slave trade (death toll of up to sixty million), the Armenian genocide (death toll of up to 1.8 million), the Holocaust (death toll of over thirteen million), Cambodian genocide (death toll up to 2.2 million), Kurdish genocide (death toll nearly two hundred thousand), the Bosnian genocide (death toll of two hundred thousand), the Rwandan genocide (death toll up to one million) and various other genocides that are currently happening across the globe (Springer, 2006, pp. 120–24). However, despite the prevalence of the act of genocide,

the term itself did not emerge until the end of the Second World War. The term *genocide* was originally coined by the prominent legal scholar Raphaël Lemkin (1900–1959) by combining the Greek word *genus*, meaning "people or race" with the Latin word *cide*, meaning "killing or murder." Lemkin defined *genocide* as "the destruction of a nation or of an ethnic group" (1944/2005, p. 79). This original focus on a national group or ethnicity has prompted scholars to rethink the contentious term and provide it with a more expansive definition.

In the past several years, the meaning of the word *genocide* has been further elucidated by an array of scholars from different academic fields. The historian Henry Huttenbach (1988) put forward one of the more broad definitions of *genocide*, and he described it as "any act that puts the very existence of a group in jeopardy" (p. 297). This definition, while compelling in its own right, provides little detail as to the possible groups that can be subjected to genocide. The political activist Ward Churchill explains genocide as "the destruction, entirely or in part, of any racial, ethnic, national, religious, cultural, linguistic, political, economic, gender, or other human group, however such groups may be defined by the perpetrator" (Churchill, 1998, p. 432). The incorporation of several types of identifiable groups significantly expands the scope of the term, making it more applicable to modern conflicts.

The various victim groups that can be subjected to genocide have been established with Churchill's definition. However, the possible perpetrators of genocide have not been identified. The historian Frank Chalk and the late sociologist Kurt Jonassohn (1990) also provide more explanation on the identity of the perpetrator in their definition of genocide as "a form of one-sided mass killing in which a state or other authority intends to destroy a group, as that group and membership in it are defined by the perpetrator" (p. 23). The role of the state in committing genocide is echoed by the sociologist Irving Horowitz (1980), who contends that genocide is the "structural and systematic destruction of innocent people by a state bureaucratic apparatus" (p. 17). Again, the state appears in this definition, but focusing exclusively on the state renders the definition of genocide somewhat limited. An ideal definition of genocide must take into account other nonstate actors that can also commit genocide. The political scientist Martin Shaw (2007) appears to realize that the state is not necessarily the only perpetrator of genocide, considering his definition argues that genocide is "a form of violent social conflict, or war, between armed power organizations that aim to destroy civilian social groups and those groups and other actors who resist this destruction" (p. 154). Shaw's definition realizes that the perpetrators of genocide need not always be state actors, but rather can be those who have become self-empowered to carry out various atrocities against an identifiable group.

The concept of genocide did not remain confined to academic circles, but it was shortly incorporated into international law. In 1946, the drafting process for a convention on genocide began. In late 1948, the UN General Assembly voted to approve the Convention on the Prevention and Punishment of the Crime of Genocide (Springer, 2006, p. 19). The convention considers genocide an attempt "to destroy, in whole or in part, a national, ethnical, racial or religious group" (Article 2). The convention did not include political groups in the definition reportedly because certain nations were concerned that their aggressive policies toward radical political groups might violate the convention (Hirsch, 2002, p. 3). However, despite its exclusion of political groups from its articles, the convention clearly lists several acts that constitute genocide, including through mass murder, physical and mental damage, reduction in standards of living, preventing procreation, and forced displacement (Article 2). The convention does not prescribe a specific penalty for committing any of these crimes. Instead, the convention states that those alleged to have broken one of these laws will be brought before "a competent tribunal" (Article 6) in the national or regional jurisdiction in which the crimes occurred. However, a trial and subsequent conviction of a handful of criminals responsible for the genocide will not restore the lives of the individuals affected by the genocide.

The international convention, while important in its own right, was too late to prevent or attempt to prevent the genocides that preceded it. In addition, despite its enactment, the convention has also failed to prevent genocides in Cambodia, East Timor, Iraq, Bosnia, Rwanda, and Sudan. This inability has prompted scholars to look for warning signs that can alert international organizations, other governments, and citizens of an impending genocide. In 1996, Gregory Stanton, one of the leading scholars of genocide and the founder of the organization Genocide Watch, presented a paper that outlined eight different stages of genocide, including classification, symbolization, dehumanization, organization, polarization, preparation, extermination, and denial. The continuum presented not only outlines the stages of genocide but also explains what concerned parties can do to ensure that genocide is stopped and not allowed to advance to the later, more deadly stages (Stanton, 1996, pp. 2–4). The recognition of the signs of genocide is only valuable when the entire international community takes notice, quickly organizes, and moves to prevent this crime against humanity from destroying the lives of countless innocent people.

John Cappucci

References

Campbell, K. J. (2001). *Genocide and the global village.* New York: Palgrave.

Chalk, F. & Jonassohn, K. (1990). *The history and sociology of genocide: Analyses and case studies.* New Haven, CT: Yale University Press.

Churchill, W. (1998). *A little matter of genocide: Holocaust and denial in the Americas, 1492 to the present.* Winnipeg: Arbeiter Ring Publishing.

Hirsch, H. (2002). *Anti-genocide: Building an American movement to prevent genocide.* Westport, CT: Praeger.

Horowitz, I. L. (1980). *Taking lives: Genocide and state power.* New Brunswick, NJ: Transaction Books.

Huttenbach, H. R. (1988). Locating the Holocaust on the genocide spectrum: Towards a methodology of definition and categorization. *Journal of Genocide Studies, 3*(3), 289–303.

Lemkin, R. (1944/2005). *Axis rule in occupied Europe: Laws of occupation, analysis of government, proposal for redress.* Clark, NJ: Lawbook Exchange.

Shaw, M. (2007). *What is genocide?* Cambridge: Polity.

Springer, J. (2006). *Genocide.* Toronto: Groundwood Books/House of Anansi Press.

Stanton, G. H. (1996). The 8 stages of genocide. *Genocide watch*. Retrieved from http://www.genocide-watch.org/images/8StagesBriefingpaper.pdf.

United Nations General Assembly. (1948). Convention on the prevention and punishment of the crime of genocide. Retrieved from http://www.hrweb.org/legal/genocide.html.

GHETTOS

According to the Oxford English Dictionary, the word *ghetto* first appeared in English in Thomas Coryat's descriptions of Venice's Jewish communities in his travelogue *Coryat's Crudities* (1611). Although the precise etymology of the word *ghetto* remains the subject of scholarly debate, it is commonly assumed that the term represents a derivation from the Italian words *borghetto* (the diminutive of *borgo*, delineating an urban district) and *gietto* (referring to Venice's iron foundry, the original location of the city's Jewish neighborhood). Alternative etymological genealogies trace the term back to the German word *gitter* (referring to bars, carrying both protective and restrictive connotations) or the Talmudic Hebrew *get* (relating to the concept of divorce or separation). The Venetian ghetto Coryat describes had been established when Venice, like other medieval towns in Europe, allocated a particular district to their Jewish populations. Initially meant to grant these minorities some autonomy and offer them a degree of protection, their confinement to these neighborhoods became compulsive in the context of heightened xenophobia that followed in the wake of the crusades. Responding to widespread fears that saw Jewish bodies as carriers of disease, the Venetian Senate in 1516 decreed that the city's Jews be restricted within the *Ghetto Nuevo*, which they were allowed to leave during the day in order to pursue their trade but to which they were confined by guards at night. Consecutive centuries saw the proliferation of this model in cities throughout Europe. This development was accompanied by the formation of organizational, economic, and social parallel structures within these ghettos to address the state of seclusion, enclosure, and oftentimes scarcity that had been imposed on these Jewish communities. Most famously, the *Judenstadt* of Prague operated its own town hall and flew its own flag, symbolizing the district's advanced autonomy.

Most central for our current usage of the word *ghetto* are two historical contexts in which the term had been used widely in the twentieth century—namely, the persecution of European Jews under Nazi rule and the sociology of black inner-city neighborhoods in the United States. In Europe, the term *ghetto* thus gained particular notoriety during the Second World War. About three hundred ghettos were established in German-occupied Poland alone, most notably, but not limited to, Warsaw (with a population of about 450,000 confined to 1.3 square miles), Łódź (approximately 200,000 inmates), and Lwów (ca. 150,000). Sealed off from the rest of the city, conditions of living were calamitous in these ghettos. Imposing forced labor on the confined populations, Nazi Germany exploited these ghettos for the production of military supplies and economic gain. Systematic overcrowding, mass starvation, and epidemic diseases, due to the lack of running water or sewage systems, killed hundreds of thousands. Frequently, these ghettos were directly connected via various deportation routes to other ghettos and ultimately to major Nazi concentration and extermination camps. The Warsaw ghetto was thus inextricably linked to Treblinka and the Łódź ghetto to Auschwitz and Chelmno. Outside of Europe, during the Japanese occupation of Shanghai during the Second World War, about twenty-three thousand Jewish refugees from Europe, along with longtime Jewish city residents, were subjected to living in a ghetto measuring approximately one square mile in the Hongkou District.

Within an American context, the term *ghetto* has undergone a number of crucial permutations throughout the twentieth century. As Loïc Wacquant has outlined, while *ghetto* throughout the nineteenth century referred to Jewish concentrations in cities across the Northeast, the Progressive Era saw a widening of the concept to encompass both populations of recent immigrants and growing African American communities during the early years of the Great Migration, groups that were both socially pathologized by the Chicago School of Urban Sociology. With the acceptance of Jews and other ethnic groups into the folds of whiteness and their departure from city centers, abetted by various discriminatory government policies, the term *ghetto* after the Second World War began to almost exclusively call attention to predominantly African American urban enclaves in northern industrial cities. In other words, after expanding around the turn of the century, the conceptual perimeter now narrowed again. These so-called ghettos rose to particular prominence in the mainstream American perception as the localities of urban uprisings that rocked major American cities in the late 1960s and the consequent activism of the Black Panther Party—both in the form of social-democratic programs and as politics of self-defense. Following the conservative backlash of the 1970s and the neoliberal onslaught on menial jobs in the United States, the term *ghetto* in the United States came to signify the blight of black urban neighborhoods, now routinely depicted as pathological sites marked by mass unemployment, drug use, and crime. In their shared design to contain or warehouse those demographic groups rendered undesirable or even redundant by the neoliberal makeover of America, Wacquant (2001) argues the crisis in the black ghetto shares a profound kinship with the rise of the prison in American political and social life.

Today, Loïc Wacquant (2012) argues that the term *ghetto* is conceptually loose and is often applied interchangeable with related but by no means conterminous concepts pertaining to other localities of social stigma—such as the French *banlieues*, the Latin American *barrios*, and the widely used *slum*. Seeking a more analytic concept of ghettos, Wacquant holds that neither poverty nor segregation nor ethnic seclusion itself constitutes sufficient preconditions for the phenomenon of the ghetto. Instead, he advances that *ghettoization* functions as a complex and dynamic process in which the ghetto is best understood as an instrument of ethnic/racial control based on the simultaneous economic exploitation of the respective enclosed communities and their exclusion from social life. In this sense, the ghetto as an institution, beyond extracting labor while simultaneously ostracizing ethnic outcasts, symbolically reproduces the very stigma upon which its establishment was based in the first place. Yet in doing so, the ghetto, whose population's spatial separation also grants a degree of autonomy and cross-social integration, engenders strong group solidarities and fosters articulations of new collective identities.

Balthazar Becker

References

Calimani, R. (1987). *The ghetto of Venice* (K. S. Wolfthas, Trans.). New York: M. Evans.

Wacquant, L. (2001). Deadly symbiosis: When ghetto and prison meet and mesh. *Punishment and Society*, *3*(1), 95–134.

Wacquant, L. (2012). A Janus-faced institution of ethnoracial closure: A sociological specification of the ghetto. In R. Hutchison & B. D. Haynes (Eds.), *The ghetto: contemporary global issues and controversies* (pp. 1–31). Boulder, CO: Westview.

GHETTOS

The word *ghetto* is a loan word that likely emerged from the Italian word *borghetto*, meaning "little borough," although there are other possible etymological origins (Haynes & Hutchison, 2012, pp. vii–x). It is also possible that the word *ghetto* is a derivative of the Hebrew word *get* or divorce (Debenedetti-Stow, 1992, p. 79). However, like its etymology, the precise definition of a ghetto is also a matter of debate in scholarly circles. One of the earliest definitions of a ghetto was put forward by Louis Wirth of the Chicago School. In his influential work on the Jewish ghettos of America, Wirth (1928/1960) defines a ghetto as "the area of first settlement" (p. 4) by immigrant groups. This focus on immigration is limiting, as it does not take into account nonimmigrant groups that have been ghettoized, such as African Americans and Native Americans. The sociologist Robert E. Forman (1971) is more expansive in his definition, as he describes a ghetto as "any area in a city which is inhabited primarily by a racially or culturally distinct group as a result of either voluntary or involuntary segregation" (p. 3). This definition is more inclusive, but it is somewhat narrow. The groups living in a ghetto need not solely share a common racial or cultural heritage, but they can also include additional groups that are susceptible to ghettoization, including religious and sexual minorities. The contemporary age requires that any definition of the word *ghetto* recognize and incorporate additional marginalized groups in modern society. The urban planner Peter Marcuse seems to understand the limiting nature of previous definitions and describes a ghetto as a physical space where the dominant powers of society have regulated an undesirable or unwanted community (2005, p. 17). The notion of stigmatized communities being forced to reside in a specified part of the city remains a consistent feature of the many historical examples of ghettos in both the Old and New Worlds.

The first modern ghetto was formally established in the sixteenth century by the Senate of the Venetian Republic in order to confine the city-state's Jewish population (Calimani, 1985). Less than forty years later, Pope Paul IV (r. 1550–1559) established the Roman ghetto with the purpose of not only confining the Jewish population but also attempting to force their conversion to Catholicism. The Roman ghetto remained in place until the collapse of the Papal States in the late nineteenth century. The ghetto shortly reemerged in the twentieth century during World War II with the notorious Warsaw ghetto. Following the occupation of Poland, the Warsaw ghetto was created by the Nazis in order to restrict the Jewish population before they were forcibly relocated to a concentration camp. The concept of the ghetto should neither be viewed as a structure solely identified with the Jewish community nor a European phenomenon. In time, ghettos started to enclose other communities in the New World.

In the United States, the term *ghetto* was initially used to describe the Jewish immigrant neighborhoods in several parts of the country (Ward, 1982, p. 257). However, the term expanded and slowly started to denote other non-Jewish immigrant communities of nineteenth-century America, particularly those from Southern and Eastern European countries. The ghettos formed by the arriving immigrant communities from Europe were not the only ghettos to develop in the country. In light of the labor demands produced during World War I, African Americans from the rural South began to move to the industrial cities of the North. This period marked the beginning of the "Great Migration" and quickly witnessed a substantial rise in the number of African Americans arriving in major industrial cities, such as Detroit, Cleveland, and Chicago (cited in Weaver, 1967, p. 26). The mass relocation of African Americans during the Great Migration resulted in the establishment of "black ghettos" (Forman, 1971, p. 13) throughout the northern regions of the country. Many of these ghettos established following the Great Migration continue to exist today.

The idea of the ghetto not only has a complex and long history but also remains a major concept within the social sciences. In addition to its historical significance and scholarly importance, the image of the ghetto has managed to permeate into various forms of artistic expression, including Israel Zangwill's play *Children of the Ghetto* (1892), Elvis Presley's song "In the Ghetto" (1969), John Singleton's film *Boyz n the Hood* (1992), and Bertice Berry's book series *Sckraight from the Ghetto* (1996), and *You Still Ghetto* (1997). The prevalence of the ghetto in both academic and popular circles demonstrates that it will remain an integral concept well into the twenty-first century.

John Cappucci

References

Calimani, R. (1985). *Storia del ghetto di Venezia* [History of the Venice ghetto]. Milan: Rusconi Libri.

Debenedetti-Stow, S. (1992). The etymology of the "ghetto": New evidence from Rome. *Jewish History*, 6(1/2), 79–85.

Forman, R. E. (1971). *Black ghettos, white ghettos, and slums*. Englewood Cliffs, NJ: Prentice-Hall.

Haynes, B. D. & Hutchison, R. (2012). Introduction. In B. D. Haynes & R. Hutchison (Eds.), *The ghetto: Contemporary global issues and controversies* (pp. vii–xliii). Boulder, CO: Westview Press.

Marcuse, P. (2005). Enclaves yes, ghettos no: Segregation and the state. In D. P. Varady (Ed.), *Desegregating the city: Ghettos, enclaves, and inequality* (pp. 15–30). Albany: State University of New York Press.

Ward, D. (1982). The ethnic ghetto in the United States: Past and present. *Transactions of the Institute of British Geographers*, 7(3), 257–75.

Weaver, R. C. (1967). *The Negro ghetto*. New York: Russell & Russell.

Wirth, L. (1928/1960). *The ghetto*. Chicago: University of Chicago Press.

Additional Reading

Gutman, Y. (1982). *The Jews of Warsaw, 1939–1943: Ghetto, underground, revolt* (I. Friedman, Trans.). Bloomington, IN: Indiana University Press.

Hilfiker, D. (2003). *Urban injustice: How ghettos happen*. New York: Seven Stories Press.

Lerner, L. S. (2002). Narrating over the ghetto of Rome. *Jewish Social Studies*, 8(2/3), 1–38.

Stow, K. R. (1992). *Alienated minority: The Jews of Medieval Latin Europe*. Cambridge, MA: Harvard University Press.

GLASS CEILING

The term *glass ceiling* refers to the unbreachable barriers a subordinate group (women, minorities) might face in rising up the ranks of hierarchical organizations in the corporate world. The "glass" metaphor refers to the fact that even as these groups may be able to see the path to the top of the organization clearly, the barriers they face in getting there remain somehow invisible or intangible. Alongside other aspects of gender discrimination and inequality in the workplace—namely, the wage gap, occupational segregation, sexual harassment, and women's "double day"—the glass ceiling draws attention to women's unequal opportunities in rising through corporate ranks and disproportionately low returns to their investments in education, experience, or on-the-job training. These barriers may not be ostensible—indeed, there may be no outward policies preventing women's advancement or statements regarding their ineligibility—but much evidence points to the difficulties women continue to face in advancing to senior management positions (Hesse-Biber & Carter, 2000). The phrase is attributed to Gay Bryant, who first used it in her book, *The Working Woman Report*, published in 1984. Two years later, reporters Carol Hymowitz and Timothy Schellhardt at the *Wall Street Journal* popularized the term in an article describing factors that block women's access to the highest echelons of power in the corporate world. Citing a mix of long-standing corporate tradition and subtle prejudice keeping women from rising to the topmost positions, the authors point to a "caste system of men at the top and women lower down" in much of corporate America (Hymowitz & Schellhardt, 1986).

In 1991, under Title II of the Civil Rights Act, a twenty-one-member, bipartisan Federal Glass Ceiling Commission (FGCC) was created. The Commission, chaired by Secretary of Labor, Robert B. Reich, was tasked with identifying internal and external barriers that prevented women and minorities from holding key positions of authority and decision-making portfolios within corporate hierarchies. It presented its findings and conclusion in the form of a report titled *Good for Business: Making Full Use of the Nation's Human Capital* in 1995. This report was followed by the publication, *A Solid Investment: Making Full Use of the Nation's Human Capital*, also in 1995, which contained recommendations on the ways in which the glass ceiling could be dismantled. For both documents, the Commission undertook extensive research and information gathering in the form of conducting public inquiries, collecting background information, commissioning research papers, surveying chief executive officers, and interviewing focus groups. In its reports, the Commission looked into the under-representation of not only women but also minority men at the highest levels of corporate America. Statistics presented in the reports pointed out that senior managers in the Fortune 1000 industrial and Fortune 500 were overwhelmingly white (97 percent), and male (95 to 97 percent) (FGCC, 1995b, p. 9). The picture remained dismal when Fortune 2000 industrial and service companies were scrutinized, with women (most of them white) occupying only 5 percent of the top managerial positions. African Americans held a small proportion of top position (2.5 percent), and the number of Hispanics in senior management (0.4 percent) was severely disproportionate compared to their presence in the work force (8 percent) (FGCC, 1995b, p. 9). These numbers were put in context by the fact that two-thirds of the population in the United States—and 57 percent of workers—were women, minorities, or both at the time of the Commission's surveys (FGCC, 1995a, iv). Men were eight times more likely to become CEOs than women more than a decade after they had graduated from the Stanford University of Business School (FGCC, 1995a, iv). Women and minorities also earned significantly less than their white male counterparts in the same positions, holding the same degrees in the same job categories.

The case made by the Commission for companies to develop active strategies toward dismantling the glass ceiling was couched in the language of the bottom line (i.e., that diversity was good for business, allowing for the fullest use of human resources, thereby ensuring business success, profitability, and competitiveness in the global economy) (FGCC, 1995b, p. 10). Akin to the economic argument against workplace discrimination, this instrumental approach stemmed from the pragmatic recognition that corporate firms might not rethink existing barriers to the glass ceiling unless it also made good business sense. The Commission appealed, therefore, to aspects such as the necessity of managing diverse workforces in a global economy, maximizing the ability to tap into many segments of the consumer market, and being able to resist activist consumer groups.

Research into the experiences of women executives undertaken by the Commission, as well as by other groups (Morrison, 1992; Catalyst 1994, 1996), point to external or societal barriers as well as factors internal to the firm producing the glass ceiling. Societal factors include supply barriers arising from limited opportunities for training and education of the type needed for corporate career advancement and difference barriers arising from biases related to gender, race, or ethnicity (FGCC, 1995a, p. 10). Despite external or structural factors, however, arguably the bigger barriers arise from within the firm. Morrison (1992) surveyed seventy-six top women executives in the Fortune 100 companies and concluded that a "wall of tradition and stereotype" still separated them from the top executive level (Morrison, 1992, p. 14). The 1994 study by Catalyst, *Cracking the Glass Ceiling: Strategies for Success*, cites male stereotyping and preconceptions (such as assuming women might not be as committed to their careers as men, would not work long hours, are not as tough, are too emotional, would make ineffectual leaders, etc.) and management aversion to taking risks with women in areas of line responsibility, exclusion of women from informal networks of communication, lack of careful career planning and mentorship, and counterproductive behavior of male colleagues. A large survey performed by Catalyst in 1996 of 1,251 women executives, *Women in Corporate Leadership: Progress and Prospects*, in the Fortune 1000 companies, adds credence to this view. While the interviewed male CEOs argued that it was supply-side barriers that were largely responsible for the scarcity of women and minorities at the top of the pyramid, women executives believed male stereotyping and preconceptions to be the most significant issue (52 percent), in addition to exclusion from informal networks (49 percent), lack of management/line experience (47 percent), inadequate time spent "in the pipeline" (29 percent), and a generally inhospitable corporate culture (35 percent) (Catalyst, 1996, p. 37). The 1996 report also points out that even as women were underrepresented in the corporate structures of power, white women's experience is considered the representative one since the numbers of women of color in executive positions are too small to warrant definitive conclusions.

The FGCC broadened the "glass ceiling" metaphor to include not only women but also minority men. Some debate has emerged on the inclusion of minority men into the purview of the glass ceiling. Morrison and von Glinow (1990), reviewing other studies, did find that men from minority groups were also impacted by the presence of the glass ceiling, and indeed, that statistics on the racial composition of management ranks showed even less progress for minority men than for women. More recently, however, Cotter, Hermsen, Ovadia, and Vannemann (2001) defined four criteria that must be met in order for glass ceiling inequalities to exist with respect to gender or race:

1. It must be unexplained by other job-relevant characteristics of the employee.
2. It must be greater at higher levels of an outcome than at lower levels of an outcome.
3. It must appear in the chances of advancement into higher levels, not merely in the proportions of each gender or race currently at those higher levels.
4. Its effects must increase over the course of a career.

When these criteria were considered, the authors found a glass ceiling with regard to women's advancement, but not with respect to minority men.

The 1994 Catalyst study also pointed to different spheres the glass ceiling operates in—namely, academia, the professions, and the government. In academia, the issue relates to unequal rates of tenure or promotion that women obtain in comparison to men who have similar academic credentials. The Catalyst study notes the lack of mentorship for women of color—especially African American women—who must deal with a double whammy of being women and from a minority group. It has been argued that the problem is exacerbated in the sciences, where Hopkins (1999) collected significant evidence that fifteen tenured women faculty members at MIT received lower salaries and fewer resources for research than their male counterparts. A 2002 National Science Foundation (NSF) Report attributed the roadblocks faced by women, not to their innate capabilities as determined by sex (a controversial opinion made famous by Harvard president Larry Summers in 2005), but to institutional barriers supported by male administration and workplace bias. In the professions, Foster (1994) discusses the disproportionately few partnerships that women hold in law firms. She attributed the glass ceiling in the legal profession to "the profession's one-dimensional behavioral paradigm" that focuses almost exclusively on career development, the persistence of myths relating to the practice of law, and sex-based stereotyping that prizes "male" roles much more, and therefore, relegates women to the role of secondary players if family life or motherhood enters the picture (p. 1633). In the case of government jobs, a study by Naff (1994), for the U.S. Merit Systems Protection Board, argues that while women held around half of all white-collar jobs in the executive branch, their lack of advancement to top positions was due to assumptions about women's career commitment, often creating a "mommy track" for women employees with families. Naff's research also pointed to the problematic perception of affirmative action, where women who have obtained positions of authority are seen as interlopers who reached these positions not by virtue of competence but because of affirmative action.

Intensive research on the different barriers that bolster the glass ceiling, and proposals to remedy higher-tier corporate exclusion, have admittedly led to improvements in recent times. Catalyst reports (1994, 1996) have observed successful efforts by businesses to tackle the issue, including setting up mentoring programs to promote women's leadership; systematic approaches to encouraging workforce diversity, including affirmative action; a shift in emphasis to performance-based contribution rather than face time or seniority; and setting up some work/family initiatives. Affirmative action has especially benefited women of color, resulting in their heightened visibility; indeed, women of color were significantly more likely to state that affirmative action had a positive or at least a mixed (positive and negative) impact on their careers. Recently, Wirth's (2008) study, for the International Labor Organization (ILO), pointed to improved access to education and training for women, coupled with a broadening of their study and occupational choices, both which go a long way to ameliorate supply barriers. Systematic research has also dispelled many of the myths about women's commitment to their careers and exposed stereotyping; for instance, surveys have found that women did not take more time off work than did men, did not refuse relocation at a greater rate than men, and worked the same number of hours as did men (Wirth, 2008, p. 102).

The shift from manufacturing to service-oriented sectors has also increased women's numbers and visibility in upper management. Despite some progress, much still needs to be done. Women still find it difficult to gain access to traditionally male-dominated spheres, such as line management and executive positions. Wirth's comprehensive list of suggestions includes making procedures around recruitment, job assignment, and promotion objectives structured and transparent so women have a better chance.

The glass ceiling metaphor has led to several variations on the theme and to the emergence of related concepts. One such phenomenon is that of the "glass elevator." While women moving into male-dominated occupations face the glass ceiling, research has demonstrated that men entering traditionally feminine occupations (such as nursing or teaching) rise to managerial and executive levels at much faster rates. The glass elevator is attributed to cultural mores that assign men positions of leadership and women to positions of subordination. The "concrete ceiling" is a powerful metaphor for the complete lack of access that minority women have to managerial/executive power; while the glass ceiling may be broken from time to time by Caucasian women, it is argued that the concrete ceiling is much more unyielding and opaque in cases of women who have to battle both racism and sexism in the workplace. Women are more likely to be assigned to "glass cliffs" (i.e., assigned difficult jobs where the risks of failure are very high). The "sticky floor" exists in direct contrast to the glass ceiling. Unions, advocacy groups, and feminist economists point to the concentration of women in low-paying, low-mobility jobs that constitute the sticky floor and the factors that keep them there.

The glass ceiling and related concepts have found their way into the international lexicon of words related to gender or racial discrimination. These words are part of a call for greater diversity in the workplace. It was significant that one of the areas the Beijing Platform for Action sought to focus on at the United Nations' Fourth World Conference on Women was the underrepresentation of women in decision-making positions. The report notes that "women's equal participation in decision-making is not only a demand for simple justice or democracy but can also be seen as a necessary condition for women's interests to be taken into account" (point 180). The report also notes that women's underrepresentation in positions of authority have also prevented them from having a significant impact on many key institutions. Much research is still needed on the implications of the "glass ceiling" for political change and social transformation.

Smita Ramnarain

References

Catalyst. (1994). *Cracking the glass ceiling: Strategies for success.* New York: Catalyst.

Catalyst. (1996). *Women in corporate leadership: Progress and prospects.* New York: Catalyst.

Cotter, D. A., Hermsen, J. M., Ovadia, S., & Vannemann, R. (2001). The glass ceiling effect. *Social Forces, 80*(2), 655–82.

Federal Glass Ceiling Commission. (1995a). *Good for business: Making full use of the Nation's human capital.* Washington, DC: US Government Printing Office.

Federal Glass Ceiling Commission. (1995b). *A solid investment: Making full use of the Nation's capital.* Washington, DC: US Government Printing Office.

Foster, S. Elizabeth. (1994). The glass ceiling in the legal profession: Why do laws firms still have so few female partners? *UCLA Law Review, 42*(6), 1631–90.

Hesse-Biber, S. N. & Carter, G. L. (2000). *Working women in America: Split dreams.* New York: Oxford University Press.

Hopkins, N. (1999). MIT and gender bias: Following up on victory. *Chronicle of Higher Education.* Retrieved from http://www-sop.inria.fr/members/Juliette.Leblond/Parite/doc-mixite/Women%20Faculty%20at%20MIT.pdf.

Hymowitz, C. & Schellhardt, T. (1986, March 24). The glass ceiling: Why women can't seem to break the invisible barrier that blocks them from the top jobs? *Wall Street Journal.*

Morrison, A. M. (1992). *The new leaders: Guidelines on leadership diversity.* San Francisco: Jossey Bass Inc., Publishers.

Morrison, A. M. & von Glinow, M. A. (1990). Women and minorities in management. *American Psychologist, 45*(2), 200–8.

Naff, K. C. (1994). Through the glass ceiling: Prospects for the advancement of women in the Federal Civil Service. *Public Administration Review, 54*(6), 507–14.

Wirth, L. (2008). *Breaking through the glass ceiling: Women in management.* Geneva: International Labor Office.

GLOBAL CITIZENSHIP

Global citizenship, a concept that emerged out of the global education movement, is not citizenship in the traditional sense, as no country exists to issue a global identity card or passport. Rather, global citizenship is an idea: that people who consider themselves global citizens will focus on pan-national, transnational, and global problems such as environmental degradation, poverty, human rights violations, and many other contemporary issues. A major premise is that students can be educated to be global citizens, with global loyalties, rather than merely be citizens of their passport country.

Since antiquity, various writers have referred to themselves or others as "citizens of the world." The contemporary concept of global citizenship, however, has much more recent origins. The idea began to emerge slowly after World War II. Yet to many people, the Cold War made world harmony and cooperation seem unlikely and distant. After the collapse of the Soviet Union, support for the idea grew rapidly. For some, the term *global citizenship* reflects a desire for a meaningful world government capable of addressing pan-national, transnational, and global problems. To these thinkers, use of the term *global citizen* is paving the way for the creation of world government. To others, the notion of global citizenship is passive: all humans are global citizens because the world today is fully integrated. From this perspective, regardless of whether individuals want to be, everyone is already a global citizen. To others still, being a global citizen requires a commitment to certain ideals and requires action. This perspective is in the tradition of the British charity Oxfam. Initially, the ideals of Oxfam included global awareness, respect for diversity, and outrage at social injustice. Oxfam also emphasized that global citizens take action, locally, nationally, and globally, and work to make the world a more equitable place. Oxfam stresses that individuals must take responsibility for their actions, thus emphasizing individual action (Roberts, 2009).

In the twenty-first century, focused above all else on social justice, Oxfam (2014a) extended its vision to include specific knowledge and understandings, skills, and values and attitudes. Oxfam lists the following knowledge and understandings it deems necessary for global citizenship: social justice, diversity, globalization and interdependence, sustainable development, and peace and conflict. In terms of skills, Oxfam lists critical thinking, ability to argue effectively, ability to challenge injustice and inequalities, respect for people and things, and cooperation and conflict resolution. Finally, it lists values and attitudes: sense of identity and self-esteem, empathy, commitment to social justice and equity, value and respect for diversity, concern for the environment and commitment to sustainable development, and belief that people can make a difference. Together, these knowledge and understandings, skills, values, and attitudes add up to Oxfam's vision statement: "Oxfam's vision is a just world without poverty. We envision a world in which people can influence decisions which affect their lives, enjoy their rights, and assume their responsibilities

as full citizens of a world in which all human beings are valued and treated equally" (Oxfam, 2014b, #1). This ambitious statement is an eloquent appeal for social justice.

For several reasons, schools, especially international schools, have been important incubators for the idea of global citizenship and the idea of global education. International schools themselves are the result of the very global processes driving globalization. The idea of international understanding is a central part of the vision of most international schools. With students who often come from many parts of the globe, and who often have parents of two different nationalities, international schools have a built-in constituency with higher levels of global knowledge and awareness than students in schools in their passport country. Many international schools, as well, offer programs of the International Baccalaureate (IB), the ideals and values of which closely align with the global citizenship movement. The IB recently published a volume titled *Educating for Global Citizenship* (Roberts, 2009). A final factor is the educators themselves in international schools. Usually expatriates from their passport country, teachers and administrators have a stake in the "international" way of life and in understanding people with different backgrounds from their own. Even when schools are not international and are, instead, state schools partially or wholly fulfilling a national educational mandate, teachers, in general, embody the optimism and hope that is inherent in the global citizenship movement.

Today the idea of global citizenship is very popular, with a significant turn occurring around 1990 that reflected broader shifts in global consciousness. For example, the number of humanitarian international nonprofits increased from a few hundred in the 1970s to over twenty-nine thousand by the early 1990s (Standish, 2012). Perhaps more significantly, with the politics of the Cold War over, Western powers were willing to take international military intervention with explicitly humanitarian aims: in Iraq (1991), Somalia (1992), Rwanda (1994), Bosnia-Herzegovina (1995), Kosovo (1999), and East Timor (1999). Further, Western governments began to tie humanitarian aid to human and civil rights objectives. Many nonprofit groups, universities, and even American public school systems began to adopt curricula and agendas aimed at promoting the concept of global citizenship. The United States was not alone. In the United Kingdom, a similar constellation of groups began to promote global education and, with it, global citizenship (Standish, 2012). Finally, since most international schools have either an American or British orientation, the ideals of global education and global citizenship, originating in the United States and United Kingdom, have spread to many international schools throughout the world. As a result, the call for educating for global citizenship has become common.

Criticism of global citizenship and educating for it has come from three different fronts. The first is that educating for global citizenship will not produce individuals with "a clear sense of national identity and a powerful belief in the necessity and right to protect national interests" (Grygiel, 2013, n.p.). This perspective focuses on the fact that citizenship exists in relation to a specific country (the country of one's passport) and that individuals and countries benefit when students are educated with the ideal of solving their own country's problems and advancing their own country's interests. Homogenizing all issues and problems into global issues deprives problems of their local and meaningful contexts and of meaningful solutions. Homogenization also fails to create the meaningfulness needed to genuinely solve problems. This criticism of global citizenship is grounded in the ancient ideals of the polis and has lived on in traditional statecraft and international affairs.

A second criticism of global citizenship hews closely to the first but is focused specifically on education for global citizenship: the global education movement. According to Standish (2012), the global education movement directly blurs boundaries such as the difference between education and social reform and the responsibilities of adults and those of children. In other instances, even when not directly causing a blurring of traditional boundaries, such as the distinction between public life and private life, the global education movement has grafted onto the change rather than resisted it, which to Standish is an abrogation of the traditional role and responsibility of education. For example, across the West, but especially in the United States and the United Kingdom, the decline in vigorous public life through political parties, labor unions, and community groups has increasingly led people to define themselves through private choices, including consumption and individual action, very much along the lines of Oxfam's mandate for individual action. However, because individual action alone has limited political force, the global education movement has contributed to a further decline in vigorous public political action (Standish, 2012). From this perspective, the idea of global citizenship is actually a renunciation of the responsibilities of citizenship.

A final criticism stems not from the ideals but rather from the educational philosophy underpinning most approaches to educating for global citizenship: Reconstructionism. The term *Reconstructionism* originated during the Great Depression when some American left-wing educators called for radical reconstruction of the economic and social order through world government. The Reconstructionist approach, however, is timeless. It involves a teacher introducing students to a grave, serious, or stark social or economic problem, usually couched in terms of a crisis. When the students are in a state of cognitive dissonance or even shock, the teacher guides them intellectually and affectively toward the teacher's political aims—some resolution to the crisis (Duck, 1981). Many programs in global education, the primary conduit for the concept of global citizenship, are Reconstructionist. Even when teachers try not to be overtly political, they almost never can be neutral (Kneller, 1964). The Reconstructionist approach toward any political goal is coercive, and therefore, fundamentally compromises students' rights (Kneller, 1964; Pierce, 2009).

Thus, in terms of diversity and social justice, global citizenship is highly contested. Because the concept *global citizenship* emerged out of the global education movement, which was partly in reaction to globalization and the horrors of the twentieth century and the inequalities and problems of industrialization and modernization, the stated aims of global citizenship seem to support diversity and to advance social justice. Very few people and very few educators would argue against social justice, environmental sustainability, eradication of poverty, and the many other noble aims of the global citizenship movement. However, the movement has critics. Citizens are from specific countries and are best served by having a national point of reference that will solve more problems than appeals to distant global problems. In terms of diversity, strong and coherent national identities provide some bulwark against the homogenizing trends of globalization, and national citizenship may actually better preserve diversity by preserving national identities and languages. Closely related to this criticism is the assertion that blurring boundaries actually collapses moral communities. To be a community requires boundaries; communities typically define who they want in and who should not be in. Thus, a diffuse global identity may eradicate the hierarchy of values required for meaningful communities and cultures. A final criticism of global citizenship is operational and focuses on the strategies whereby teaching for global citizenship is done. By drawing on what are arguably scare tactics, teachers may actually be depriving their students of human rights while claiming to champion them. Teachers may be defending some types of exterior diversity (race, ethnicity, sexual orientation, etc.) but not allowing for diversity of opinion or values.

Robert A. Pierce

References

Duck, L. (1981). *Teaching with charisma: A teaching styles overview*. Burke, VA: Chatelaine Press.

Grygiel, J. (2013, December 6). There's no such thing as a global citizen. *Washington Post*. Retrieved from http://www.washingtonpost.com/opinions/theres-no-such-thing-as-a-global-citizen/2013/12/06/2924cae6-5d0a-11e3-bc56-c6ca94801fac_story.html.

Kneller, G. F. (1964). *Introduction to the philosophy of education*. New York: John Wiley & Sons, Inc.

Oxfam International. (2014a). *Key elements of global citizenship*. Retrieved from http://www.oxfam.org.uk/education/global-citizenship/key-elements-of-global-citizenship.

Oxfam International. (2014b). *Oxfam's purpose and beliefs*. Retrieved from http://www.oxfam.org/en/about/what/purpose-and-beliefs.

Pierce, R. A. (2009). The error of Reconstructionism. In B. Roberts, *Educating for global citizenship: A practical guide for schools* (p. 25). Cardiff, UK: International Baccalaureate.

Roberts, B. (2009). *Educating for global citizenship: A practical guide for schools*. Cardiff, UK: International Baccalaureate Organization.

Standish, A. (2012). *The false promise of global learning: Why education needs boundaries*. London and New York: Continuum International.

GLOBAL EDUCATION

The term *global education* should be conceived in two different ways. First, spelled in lower case, global education refers to various authors, perspectives, and curricula (that have arguably existed since antiquity) whereby the main premise is to understand human history and the human condition in the context of the entire known globe. Closely linked to international education or education for international perspectives, global education embraces the view that students should have some understanding of the entire world. Second, one can also speak of *Global Education*, denoted as a proper noun, which came into existence in the twentieth century and experienced significant growth after World War II. Unlike its lowercase peer, Global Education has a very narrow set of concerns stemming from the global conflicts of Imperialism, World War I, World War II, and the Cold War, as well as from many of the consequences of other elements of modern life, including capitalism and industrialization, environmental degradation, nationalism, and racism. The different natures of the two intellectual programs have also elicited different criticisms.

In antiquity, a rich tradition of global inquiry existed in numerous cultural contexts. Best known in the West are the works of Herodotus (484–425 BCE) and Thucydides (460–395 BCE). Both of these Greek scholars were interested in what constituted the known world. Rome produced the historians Polybius (c. 200–118 BCE) and Livy (59 BCE–17 CE), who were also interested in the world beyond Roman borders. A global perspective was not limited to the Greeks and Romans, however. The Chinese historian Sima Qian (c. 140–86 BCE) examined and assessed documents from both earlier periods in Chinese history and distant lands (Manning, 2003). Of course, the purposes of these histories varied: Herodotus, for instance, used his work to make clear that the Greeks, unlike the Persians, lived under a rule of law (Pagden, 1999).

However, these histories shared a common assumption that knowing beyond the local and parochial deepened human understanding.

During the Middle Ages and early modern period, scholars continued to engage in studies of distant lands and foreign perspectives. China, for example, produced historians such as Liu Chih-chi (d. 721) and Ssu-ma Kuang. Most of the other great civilizations of the classical and postclassical era also produced histories with some claim to a global focus: Al-Tabari (d. 923) and Al-Mas'udi (d. 956) of the Abbasid dynasty, and Ibn-Khaldun in the Arab West (d. 1406). In Persia, Ala'iddin Ata-Malik Juvayni (1226–1283) wrote a history of the Mongolian Empire titled *Ta' rīkh-i jahān-gushā* (*History of the World Conqueror*) (Manning, 2003). When the Ottoman Empire rose to prominence, Mustafa Ali (d. 1599) wrote a universal history and geography beginning with Adam. In the West, Desiderius Erasmus (1466–1536), who late in his life saw Europe torn apart by the Reformation, argued in *The Education of a Christian Prince* for the benefits of a broad liberal arts education in cultivating a sensibility toward and an understanding of human affairs. In his extensive writings on Amerindians, Bartholomé de las Casas (1484–1566) made an appeal, in effect for humanitarian purposes, for the study of distant and exploited people. One of the most influential works among this breed of scholars was Bernard Piacart and John Frederic Bernard's *Cérémonies et coutumes religieuses de tous les peuples du monde*, appearing from 1723 to 1743, which profoundly reshaped the course of modern history by generating a new understanding of religion, both European and non-European (Hunt, Jacob, & Mijnhardt, 2010). The High and Late Middle Ages were periods of travel and exploration for Europeans, Muslims, and Chinese, all of whom sought to increase their knowledge of distant lands and peoples. These voyages helped to advance a new genre, the travel narrative, which gave people access to foreign places without ever leaving home. While travel narratives were already fairly popular prior to the print era, the invention of the printing press expanded their audience of readers tremendously.

During the nineteenth century, many new forces and many more scholars, especially Western scholars, further expanded our understandings of distant parts of the globe. However, what was occurring in schools was rather different. In the eighteenth and nineteenth centuries, modern school systems served the perceived needs of nation-states. In the West, these centuries were characterized by stark nationalism, and schools were seen as instruments of national identity. Through schools, Great Britain sought to create a docile and productive working class and the United States sought to reinforce republican ideals and homogenize immigrants into Americans (with a largely English-American identity), while France, Italy, and Germany sought to inculcate national identities. Granted, the West was not alone in its local or national outlook. Despite compelling need for change, Imperial China clung to its examination system with ethnocentric assumptions and a Confucian focus. Even when education was not expressly nationalistic, in most parts of the globe, systems of education focused on the local and practical: vocational training for future laborers, religious training for future religious leaders, and medical training for future doctors.

Though some attempts at international education were made in the nineteenth century, the real impetus for education to provide an international understanding began in the twentieth century. Initially, attempts to foster international understanding through education emerged out of the cataclysms of imperialism, World War I, and World War II. In 1919, the Institute for International Education was founded in New York. In 1924, the International School of Geneva was founded. In a 1932 address to the National Education Association in Atlantic City, New Jersey, Augustus Thomas, then secretary general of the World Federation of Education Associations, called for an educational plan that would foster cooperation and understanding among nations through an international curriculum and teachers with an international perspective (Standish, 2012). After World War II, international education, and thus global education, gained momentum not solely in reaction to war, other catastrophic events, and modernization and industrialization. For one, the United States now had a global footprint through diplomatic, military, and economic channels, and many Americans viewed global education as a means to support the national enterprise. Equally powerful were commercial linkages and the growth of multinational corporations, not just those headquartered in the United States. All of these forces combined led to an increased desire for global education. One of the most important ways in which this desire for global understanding was satisfied was through the growth of world history as a subfield among professional historians. Consequently, the tradition of world or global inquiry saw a new school of practitioners in the twentieth century: Oswald Spengler, H. G. Wells, Arnold J. Toynbee, and William H. McNeill all produced grand syntheses of world history. McNeill's *The Rise of the West* (1963) was especially influential and led to the formal recognition of world history as a professional field (Manning, 2003).

If changes in world conditions and scholarly perspectives led to a desire for global education from above, changing demographics was a force from below. In the twentieth century, the world experienced dramatic migrations, probably the largest ever in human history, across the globe. Comparatively homogeneous ethnic populations began to experience a far greater degree of diversity than ever before. The United States stood at the forefront of these changes, and American K–12 social studies education evolved significantly in response. During the early part of the twentieth century, at the peak of Eastern and southern European immigration to the United States, students typically studied Greek and Roman history, European history, English history, and American history. At the time, the "melting pot" theory of American identity prevailed, and a major purpose of this curriculum was to educate all Americans under an Anglo-American identity. By the mid-twentieth century, many of these immigrants and their American children had a greater say in local affairs, social studies education softened its stress on Anglo-American identity and strived to be of greater relevance to people of European descent. Students would study ancient history (which included Mesopotamia and Egypt as well as Greece and Rome), European history, and American history. This education allowed Americans to understand fellow Americans of different European lineages and to better comprehend the European affairs that had led to both World Wars.

By the 1960s, a third shift was underway. Most immigrants to the United States after World War II were Asian or Hispanic, and the figurative face of an American was becoming global rather than being almost entirely descended from Europeans or Africans. To reflect these shifts, social studies curricula changed again. Today in the United States, most ninth-graders take Ancient World History (or geography), tenth-graders take Modern World History, and eleventh-graders take American History. In 2002, the College Board Testing Service began offering an AP World History examination, and now more than twice as many students take that exam compared to those who take the AP European History examination (College Board, n.d.). This momentum for world history has been felt outside the United States, too. Now, the International Baccalaureate Diploma Programme offers World History as an option within Group III subject History. In IB schools all over the world, students are devoting considerable time to world history.

Global Education, denoted as a proper noun, emerged in the 1960s as an outgrowth of older forms of global education. Thus, some of the reasons for Global Education include those outlined above: the cataclysms of Imperialism, World War I, and World War II and the conditions around the world that stemmed from capitalism, industrialization, and modernization. After World War II, additional forces came into play that increased general interest in world history and global affairs. For instance, modern media were bringing world affairs into people's homes on a daily basis, at the very time that the United States was fighting a major war halfway around the world in Vietnam. Beginning in the 1960s, a new sense of activism for the globe spread across the Western world. Rachel Carson's *Silent Spring* (1962) ushered in a new era of concerns over the environment and breathed new life into the expression, "Think globally, act locally." The 1960s also saw the origin of the Peace Corps, the coming-of-age of baby boomers, the women's rights and civil rights movements, and concerns for social justice. Together, these and other forces generated a youth political movement that stressed globalization and environmental responsibility, alongside social, economic, and political reform.

These movements had a sense of urgency and eventually worked their way into education. The main elements of Global Education went beyond intercultural education and fostering of intercultural and global understanding. Global Education came to include such fields as peace studies, developmental education, human rights education, foreign policy and area/regional studies, world studies, environmental education, sustainability education, and education for a global market (Standish, 2012). Each of these subfields within Global Education goes beyond traditional global education in that their aims are to prepare students for concrete action: to foster peace, to aid the developing world, to advance human rights, to assist in peaceful and noncoercive foreign policies, and to promote environmental and other forms of sustainability. Programs for Global Education have been advanced in the United States, the United Kingdom, in international schools around the world, and in various different ways in a host of other countries. Common to all of these Global Education programs is a commitment to social reform achieved through education. In recent decades, an extension of Global Education has been the Global Citizenship movement (see **Global Citizenship**).

In terms of educational philosophy, global education is rather traditional. It is rooted in the idea that education seeks to enhance students' knowledge and refine their thinking. It is innovative only in that it asks teachers and students to look beyond the local, the parochial, and even beyond the national or continental as they think about history, geography, and the human condition. Not all teachers have liked the shift from Western history to world history, as it requires them to rethink how they imagine the past. Students have sometimes complained that world history lacks the deep treatment of subjects that they find rewarding. These kinds of concerns will probably soften as teachers grow more accustomed to teaching world history and learn to uncover depth in the study of comparative history and transnational processes. On the other hand, Global Education is far more radical. In terms of educational philosophy, it is rooted in the tradition of the Reconstructionists (see **Reconstructionism**). As their name suggests, the Reconstructionists wanted to remake or reconstruct the world through education. Rather than simply promote the traditional aims of education—that is, increasing knowledge and refining thinking—Reconstructionists aim to change students' attitudes and values in order to prepare them to take political action.

Robert A. Pierce

References

College Board. (n.d.). *The Advanced placement program*. Retrieved from http://apcentral.collegeboard.com/apc/public/program/index.html.

Hunt, L., Jacob, M. C., & Mijnhardt, W. (2010). *The book that changed Europe: Picart & Bernard's religious ceremonies of the world*. Cambridge, MA: Belknap Press.

Manning, P. (2003). *Navigating world history: Historians create a global past*. New York: Palgrave Macmillan.

McNeill, W. H. (1963). *The rise of the west: A history of the human community*. Chicago: University of Chicago Press.

Oxfam. (2014). *Key elements of global citizenship*. Retrieved from http://www.oxfam.org.uk/education/global-citizenship/key-elements-of-global-citizenship.

Pagden, A. (1999). Prologue: Europe and the World Around. In E. Cameron (Ed.), *Early modern Europe: An Oxford history* (pp. 1–28). Oxford: Oxford University Press.

Roberts, B. (2009). *Educating for global citizenship: A practical guide for schools*. Cardiff, UK: International Baccalaureate Organization.

Standish, A. (2012). *The false promise of global learning: Why education needs boundaries*. London and New York: Continuum International.

GLOBAL EDUCATION

A transdisciplinary approach to research, teaching, and learning, global education has continued to expand since its incarnation in England during the 1950s and entry into the American educational discourse during the 1970s. While global education involves learning about histories and cultures of the world, it is predicated on learning about and from people around the world in order to disrupt biased and incomplete narratives of how the world came to be, so students develop informed, culturally relevant solutions for our shared future.

Though he never uses the term *global education*, Robert Hanvey's (1976) *An Attainable Global*

Perspective is often cited as the seminal work for conceptualizing and studying global education. According to Hanvey, developing a global perspective requires: educating people to develop cross-cultural awareness; raising one's consciousness regarding the "deep and hidden layers of perspective" that exist and inform people's choices around the world; and developing a stronger "state of the planet awareness" that includes attention to how the world works (global dynamics), so that the "strangeness" of how people live becomes less strange (pp. 163–65). Other early conceptualizations claimed global education includes any effort taken to provide young people with opportunities to cultivate the knowledge, skills, and attitudes necessary for learning from and coexisting with people around the world.

In addition to learning about how issues and problems experienced in one place affect people and their environment in another, global education involves developing one's perspective consciousness: the acknowledgment that people will vary in how they view and respond to events and issues based on their cultural views, beliefs, values, and norms. Fostering perspective consciousness helps students understand not only that people have differing perspectives but also why another person might see, react, and behave differently.

Engagement in rational reflection and consideration of evidence provided from multiple sides of any global issue is integral to the development of perspective consciousness and can lead to the development of open-mindedness; arguably the starting point of becoming a globally minded individual. Other goals of global education include the development of empathy for others and the need to resist stereotyping by refraining from imagining and "othering" places and people (Said, 1978).

Global education also involves teaching about interconnectedness and interdependence. Often rooted in environmentalism, achieving these goals requires that teachers and students examine how one's actions affect the lives of others and reflect on personal responsibility as inhabitants of a shared planet. Teaching and learning about such concepts, and the development of habits of mind around these issues, can overlap with human rights education, peace education, futures education, sustainability education, and global citizenship education.

Teaching about culture within global education requires moving beyond the surface representations of what people do, eat, and wear to a more substantive understanding of "internal culture" that includes the use of language and the interpretation of events, beliefs, and values (Merryfield & Wilson, 2005, p. 2). Developing more complex understandings of culture can be a difficult process for students to endure and can often result in fear, xenophobia, nationalism, and other forms of resistance to cultural practices different from their own. Adopting a global education approach to teaching about culture involves opportunities for cross-cultural, experiential learning so students learn to think of culture as a process rather than a fixed concept or practice. Global education aims to develop an understanding of global perspectives among students in order to humanize the "others" they see on television and interact with at an increasing rate in schools, their community, and on the Internet.

Technology not only offers opportunities for intercultural experiences to be shared by students despite geographical distance but also allows people in various parts of the world to speak for themselves and allow students to learn firsthand what their fellow global citizens think about the world. Such learning opportunities help to disrupt stereotypes and generalizations that often form out of racist depictions and translations conveyed through media and school curricula.

At the start of the twenty-first century, global education research began to incorporate a postcolonial framework in order to highlight the perspectives possessed by the underrepresented members of society who are often omitted from school curricula, mainstream media, and textbooks. Since then, global education has taken a theoretical turn, incorporating postmodern and postcolonial readings of the world, along with a more critical eye toward cultural studies, state-of-the-planet awareness, race, power, gender, citizenship, global issues, interconnectedness, and more. The development of more critical approaches to what constitutes global education includes: (a) complicating history and contemporary situations by investigating the processes that have conspired to define legitimate knowledge, (b) thinking beyond the nation-state to instead conceptualize and teach about global issues as transnational and interconnected, (c) disrupting narratives constructed around colonialism and stereotypes so that the subaltern may speak, and (d) developing a more globally minded approach to curriculum that includes complexity and subaltern knowledge (Subedi, 2010). The increased inclusion of indigenous perspectives, the adoption of more critical approaches to understanding the relationship between social injustice and geography, the relationship between spirituality and interconnectedness, and the role technology plays in expanding how students imagine and interact with people across multiple places constitute emerging lines of inquiry in global education scholarship.

By providing space for more voices and views to be represented in classrooms, globally minded educators and students are better able to examine issues of inequity related to race, gender, sexuality, class, and ethnicity by learning about religion, art, science, mathematics, language, geography, music, history, and literature in a global rather than just a local or national framework. Students then understand the need for diversity of thought when solving global problems and the responsibility they share beyond their classroom and local community for critically examining inequity and racism across multiple places.

Jason R. Harshman

References

Hanvey, R. (1976). An attainable global perspective. *Theory into Practice*, 21(3), 162–67.

Merryfield, M. M. & Wilson, A. (2005). *Social studies and the world: Teaching global perspectives.* Silver Spring, MD: National Council for the Social Studies.

Said, E. (1978). *Orientalism.* New York: Vintage Books.

Subedi, B. (Ed.). (2010). *Critical global perspectives: Rethinking knowledge about global societies.* Charlotte, NC: Information Age Publishing.

GLOBAL JUSTICE

Global justice is a very new phenomenon. It has a different meaning than "international justice" and "the law of nations." Global justice, in short, is related to the question of how the inequalities between inhabitants of the globe can be justified. States should promote equality both nationally and globally; however, nonstate actors can be more effective in dealing with global inequality problems.

Global justice is seen as the next step of globalization. On the one hand, globalization has undermined the Westphalian state sovereignty because of the international integration of economic activity through international trade, foreign direct investments (FDIs), multinational corporations (MNCs), capital flows, and technological developments. The power of the states shifted toward the markets in the last century. The prominent actor of this shift in the state-market balance of power is the accelerating pace of technological advances. States are not able to control both their national economies and cross-border economic activities. In this regard, the state's role and power has been significantly altered by economic globalization. The emergence of economic interdependency around the globe, the end of the Cold War, the spread of democracy, and advances in new technologies have had profound impacts on the diversification of actors in world politics. A wide range of nonstate actors have emerged and challenged states' conventional power. Thus, nonstate actors have become one of actors in global governance. The international institutions, such as the World Bank, the International Monetary Fund, and the World Trade Organization, have played a key role for the functioning of the world economy since their creation. International institutions and nongovernmental organizations have their own rules and mechanisms, and they can compel national governments to take action and change their policies. It is evident that global problems require global participation and global governance. In this respect, nonstate actors' roles will be more important in terms of global justice.

On the other hand, it is argued that globalization has widened the rich-poor gap. The income ratio between the top 10 percent and the bottom 10 percent is about 273:1. Moreover, there are more than one billion people in the world who do not have enough to eat. In this respect, poverty is at the core of the global inequality problem. In our globalized world, "[r]oughly one third of all human deaths, 18 million annually, are due to poverty-related causes, easily preventable through better nutrition, safe drinking water, cheap rehydration packs, vaccines, antibiotics, and other medicines" (Pogge, 2010, pp. 11–12).

Global justice is of utmost importance in terms of global security. This is because the inability to fulfill basic needs can often lead people, groups, or even states into deep tensions. According to Paul Collier et al. (2003), civil wars are concentrated in the poorest countries of the globe because poverty "increases the likelihood of civil wars." In this regard, prevention of poverty is a fundamental precondition for global security and global justice.

Hakan Aydogan

References

Collier, P., Elliott, V. L., Hegre, H., Hoeffler, A., Reynal-Queral, M., & Sambanis, N. (2003). *Breaking the conflict trap: Civil war and development policy*. Washington, DC, New York: World Bank; Oxford University Press.

Karns, M. P. & Mingst, K. A. (2004). *International organizations: The politics and processes of global governance*. Boulder, CO: Lynne Rienner Publishers.

Ohmae, K. (1996). *The end of the nation state: The rise of regional economies* (1st pbk. ed.). New York: Free Press Paperbacks.

Pogge, T. W. M. (2010). *Politics as usual: What lies behind the pro-poor rhetoric*. Cambridge, UK; Malden, MA: Polity.

Scholte, J. A. (2005). *Globalization: A critical introduction* (2nd ed.). New York: Palgrave Macmillan.

Spar, D. L. (2008). National policies and domestic politics. In A. M. Rugman (Ed.), *The Oxford handbook of international business* (2nd ed., pp. 205–27). New York: Oxford University Press.

Stiglitz, J. E. (2007). *Making globalization work*. New York: W. W. Norton & Co.

Strange, S. (1996). *The retreat of the state: The diffusion of power in the world economy*. New York: Cambridge University Press.

GLOBAL JUSTICE

Global justice is the belief and political philosophy that states that all citizens of the world should be free to pursue their social, political, religious, and economic ambitions free from lacks and limitations, injustice, discrimination, and imprisonment. Helena de Bres (2012), in an article titled "The Many, Not the Few: Pluralism about Global Distributive Justice," argues that global distributive justice has a close kinship to pluralism in all of its forms. Pluralism is part of the solution to global inequality; however, greater research is needed in order to cure the ever-pressing ills of the world.

Global justice addresses the divide between developed and developing countries. It identifies how powerful countries and international policies underdeveloped some geographic areas while supporting others in their growth and prosperity. Case in point: Some people from around the world are starving while others are complaining about overeating and obesity. Can a pluralist society solve the many woes in the world? Can pluralism help countries realize peace and positive global partnerships with former enemies? Is pluralism a system that can usher in an era of collective decision making, as well as mutually beneficial political and economic enterprises? These are questions that have to be tackled if answers to global justice are to be found.

Most often oppressive practices are conducted by wealthy, powerful individuals and undemocratic governments that use violence and domination as their instrument of control. It is the belief of some social scientists that the world is suffering inequality largely because of the conditions wealthy individuals have imposed on people throughout the world. In Thomas Pogge's book *Politics as Usual: What Lies Behind the Pro-Poor Rhetoric*, he argues that ordinary citizens of affluent countries bear significant moral responsibility for world poverty (Pogge, 2010).

There is a powerful and purposeful movement across the world concentrated on finding lasting peace and economic justice among the people of the world. They have many agendas, but they share the same passion—to build sustainable communities across the world where peace flourishes and where an end to injustice, war, tribal conflicts, discrimination, and violence is realized.

Social media has had an impressive impact on spreading the word about global justice initiatives. This model has shown that it can be a strategic communication tool and a source of news. Lest we think, however, that this use of social media is revolutionary in its influence, it is important to remember that other forms of digital technology devices have had an impact on mobilizing people and influencing collective action toward deliberative global justice efforts.

Global justice goals are not simple propositions. Gaining peace, eliminating poverty, promoting education, curing and preventing diseases, and developing a common interpretation among the world's populations about ethical practices, justice, and moral values requires nothing less than a miracle. Nonetheless, the global justice movement is working to realize these goals. The challenge of improving the condition of people throughout the world is being waged by millions of individuals and organizations. Their intentions are serious, and their voices are gaining recognition among international governmental organizations.

The scope, depth, and determination of the global justice movements to promote global justice is far reaching. Their practices are intended to significantly transform societies around the world during this century. This is not a movement for a one-world government; instead, it embraces a perspective that recognizes, respects, appreciates, and celebrates human differences around the world. Arguably, global justice advocates are determined to influence global politics and pressure international agencies to work toward building a better world free from the pain and suffering that is commonplace today. Global justice seeks to establish justice, equality, human rights, good governance, right to food, and personal security around the world.

Sherwood Thompson

References

De Bres, H. (2012). The many, not the few: Pluralism about global distributive justice. *Journal of Political Philosophy, 20*(3), 314–40. doi:10.1111/j.1467-9760.2010.00389.x

Pogge, T. (2010). *Politics as usual: What lies behind the pro-poor rhetoric?* Hoboken, NJ: John Wiley & Sons, Inc.

H

HATE CRIME

The term *hate crime* has many different definitions that have been put forth by academics from various fields, civil rights and advocacy groups seeking to protect vulnerable populations, and anti–hate crime legislation passed by nations around the globe. In the most basic sense, a hate crime generally targets "stigmatized and marginalized groups" (Perry, 2001, p. 10) in society. The perpetrator of a hate crime can target individuals based on an array of factors, including religion, ethnicity, culture, gender, identity, sexual orientation, political beliefs, age, socioeconomic status, and physical and mental abilities. There have been countless instances in history in which individuals have been harassed, assaulted, and murdered simply because they possessed one or more of these traits. However, despite the prevalence of these types of attacks in history, it was only fairly recently that legislation emerged to track the nature and frequency of hate crimes in the United States.

The Hate Crime Statistics Act of 1990 requires the attorney general to gather empirical data and information on hate-motivated crimes in the United States. The difficult task was placed under the auspices of the Federal Bureau of Investigation's Uniform Crime Reporting Program, which continues to publish annual reports on hate crimes. The purpose of the act is to collect data in order to design better strategies for dealing with hate crimes in the United States. It is important to note that the Hate Crime Statistics Act is not a piece of criminal law that describes offenses and specifies punishments for hate-based crimes. A law that prescribed severe punishments for hate crimes emerged shortly thereafter with the passage of the Hate Crimes Sentencing Enhancement Act of 1994. This law allowed judges to impose tougher punishments on offenders who committed serious crimes that were deemed to be motivated by hate. However, this Act's major

drawback was that it only applied in cases in which the federal government had jurisdiction. This limitation was clearly noticed in cases in which the hate crimes took place within a state's jurisdiction.

There are two cases in the United States that not only garnered considerable national and international attention but also clearly showed lawmakers that comprehensive anti–hate crime legislation was required. In 1998, James Byrd Jr. (1949–1998), an African American male living in Texas, was brutally killed and decapitated after he was chained to a truck and dragged several miles by a small group of white supremacists (Levin & McDevitt, 2002, pp. 9–10). In the same year, Matthew Shephard (1976–1998), a gay university student from Wyoming, was tied to a fence and mercilessly tortured to death by two males (Levin & McDevitt, 2002, pp. 13–14). However, despite the bigoted nature of these two cases, the states of Texas and Wyoming did not charge the perpetrators with a hate crime. These major failures in the justice system needed to be remedied by national hate crime legislation.

In 2009, President Barack Obama signed the Hate Crime Prevention Act, also known as The Matthew Shepard and James Byrd Jr., Hate Crimes Prevention Act. The law includes the characteristics of "gender, sexual orientation, gender identity, or disability" (National Defense Authorization Act for Fiscal Year 2010, section 4707) in order to protect a much broader array of individuals. The law also provides federal assistance, both financial and otherwise, to help state and local authorities in investigating and prosecuting perpetrators of hate crimes (National Defense Authorization Act for Fiscal Year 2010, sections 4704–06). The act seems to have had little effect on the number of hate crimes in the United States. In 2009, there were 6,604 reported hate crime incidents in the country (USDJ, 2010). The number of hate crimes slightly increased in 2010 with 6,628 incidents reported (USDJ, 2011), and it slightly decreased in 2011 with 6,222 incidents reported (USDJ, 2012), although the number is still comparable to previous years. The inability of the Hate Crime Prevention Act to reduce significantly the amount of hate crimes in the United States suggests that other measures need to be implemented in order to ensure that hate crimes are eliminated by the end of the twenty-first century.

John Cappucci

References

Levin, J. & McDevitt, J. (2002). *Hate crimes revisited: America's war on those who are different.* Boulder, CO: Westview Press.

National Defense Authorization Act for Fiscal Year 2010, Pub. L. No. 111-84, §4701-13, 123 Stat. 2835-44 (2013). Retrieved from http://www.gpo.gov/fdsys/pkg/PLAW-111publ84/pdf/PLAW-111publ84.pdf.

Perry, B. (2001). *In the name of hate: Understanding hate crimes.* New York: Routledge.

U.S. Department of Justice (USDJ). (2010). Incidents and offenses. *Uniform criminal report: Hate crime statistics, 2009.* Washington, DC: Federal Bureau of Investigation. Retrieved from http://www2.fbi.gov/ucr/hc2009/incidents.html.

U.S. Department of Justice (USDJ). (2011). Incidents and offenses. *Uniform criminal report: Hate crime statistics, 2010.* Washington, DC: Federal Bureau of Investigation. Retrieved from http://www.fbi.gov/about-us/cjis/ucr/hate-crime/2010/narratives/hate-crime-2010-incidents-and-offenses.pdf.

U.S. Department of Justice (USDJ). (2012). Incidents and offenses. *Uniform criminal report: Hate crime statistics, 2011.* Washington, DC: Federal Bureau of Investigation. Retrieved from http://www.fbi.gov/about-us/cjis/ucr/hate-crime/2011/narratives/incidents-and-offenses.

Additional Reading

Jenness, V. (2011). Hate crimes. In M. Tonry (Ed.), *The Oxford handbook of crime and public policy* (pp. 524–46). Oxford: Oxford University Press.

Jenness, V. & Grattet, R. (2001). *Making hate a crime: From social movement to law enforcement.* New York: Russell Sage Foundation.

Lawrence, F. M. (1999). *Punishing hate: Bias crimes under American law.* Cambridge, MA: Harvard University Press.

Levin, J. & McDevitt, J. (1993). *Hate crimes: The rising tide of bigotry and bloodshed.* New York: Plenum.

HATE GROUPS

The United States Federal Bureau of Investigation defines a hate group as an organization whose primary purpose is to promote animosity, hostility, and malice against persons of or with a race, religion, disability, sexual orientation, ethnicity, gender, or gender identity which differs from that of the members or the organization, e.g., the Ku Klux Klan, American Nazi Party. (FBI, 2012)

As such, hate groups are extremely diverse and cover a range of issues from racism to Holocaust denial. Hate groups are not a new phenomenon; in the United States, broadly defined hate groups have long been hostile to immigrants and citizens not representative of the white, Protestant population, ranging from the early hostility toward Southern and Eastern European immigrants of the Know-Nothing Party of the 1850s to the violence against freedmen during Reconstruction. The term *hate crime* emerged in the 1980s to define bigotry motivated by criminal activity; similarly, *hate group* is a relatively new term even if prejudiced organizations have always existed.

Most hate groups identified by the Southern Poverty Law Center (SPLC), a leading watch group of hate in the United States, are rhetorical and law abiding in nature. Activities of such groups include organizing politically and publishing media to support their agenda. Marches, rallies, meetings, and other forms of nonviolent and legal activities provide these groups with protection under the law and legitimacy in the public eye. A smaller number of hate groups advocate criminal and violent activity, leading to the commission of hate crimes against targeted groups. Hate groups do not necessarily advocate or commit hate crimes. Most hate crimes committed in the United States are not hate group affiliated, but hate groups can progress toward violence as the membership grows in radicalism. According to an FBI study of white supremacist groups, hate groups increase hostile rhetoric in order to maintain their identity against and anger toward the other, the other being the targeted group (Schafer & Navarro, 2003). White supremacist groups represent the largest number of active hate groups in the United States, but a number of nonwhite hate groups also exist. The problem facing authorities concerning the regulation of hate groups is the large amount of overlap between movements, the high turnover rate of membership, and the varying levels of criminality among the hate groups. However, all hate groups present bigoted ideas, no matter the target, and most hate groups define race, sexuality, gender, and religion on very narrow terms (Gerstenfeld, 2004). A major cause of the continuation of hate groups in a post-civil-rights-era society is the competing views that the civil rights movement failed, either to incorporate minorities into American society in a manner that emphasizes Protestant white culture, or failed in the sense to provide adequate social justice in a society oppressed by the Protestant white majority. Racial separatist groups on both sides of the color line present bigoted racial views, but they overlap into other forms of discrimination, typically based on religion or gender identity (Oppenheimer, 2005). Hate groups rely upon stereotypes to project differences between groups, emphasize the in-group belonging, and to encourage common goals against the other. By relying on stereotypes, hate groups remove individual identity of targeted groups and replace that with a false, antagonistic image that is easily scapegoated or despised. Relatively stable during normal times, crisis and upheaval trigger the use of prejudices to create scapegoats on who the blame for trouble can be placed (Tsesis, 2002).

Hate groups present a dilemma to concerned watch groups and the state. Most organizations espousing hate do so in a legal manner, protected by the rights to free speech, religion, and assembly. They are visible, have active voices, and relate their messages in a manner that appeals to members of society that may be predisposed to embrace prejudice. While such activities are legal, the negative messages involved have an influence upon the population beyond the active hate groups and encourage divisions within society (Gerstenfeld, 2004). The United States' poor history of government persecution of extremist groups, both left and right, demonstrate the difficulties of policing hate groups, particularly nonviolent ones. The subjective question of what

groups should be targeted for aggressive prosecution remains debated, with the memories of past violations of constitutional rights and civil liberties by the government being judged against the benefits of police action (Jacobs & Potter, 1998). The control of hate groups and hate speech is complicated by the use of media and the Internet to spread prejudice. Hate groups use the freedom and anonymity of the Internet to disseminate propaganda, recruit membership, organize political action, and to otherwise undermine out-groups. Simultaneously, the nature of online interaction encourages fragmentation rather than consolidation, which leaves the many hate groups of similar themes without central leadership. The dispersed nature of hate groups makes the elimination of groups an immense challenge because there is no leadership to focus the scarce resources on. The question of freedom of speech online is in debate as critics argue the ideals spread through such messages are harmful to certain portions of the population in the real world, and the metaphor for a "marketplace for ideals" is inherently inegalitarian (Tsesis, 2002). Others argue that censorship is a threat, and hate speech, so long as it is not acted upon, remains protected (Gerstenfeld, 2004).

As of 2012, the SPLC identified 1,007 known hate groups operating in the United States, up from some 70 percent since 2000. Anger over the economic woes, immigration, and antigovernmental sentiment fueled the explosion in hate groups over the decade (SPLC, 2014). Identity politics, mainstream media bias, and the continuing disillusionment in the United States create a climate ripe for the continued existence of hate groups.

James S. Barber

References

FBI. (2012). *Hate crime data collection guidelines and training manual* (Ver. 1.0).

Gerstendfeld, P. (2004). *Hate crimes: Causes, controls, and controversies*. London: Sage Publications.

Jacobs, J. & Potter, K. (1998). *Hate crimes: Criminal law & identity politics*. New York: Oxford University Press.

Oppenheimer, M. (2005). *The hate handbook: Oppressors, victims, and fighters*. New York: Lexington Books.

Schafer, J. & Navarro, J. (2003). The seven-stage hate model. *FBI Law Enforcement Bulletin, 72*(3), 1–7.

Southern Poverty Law Center. (2014). *Hate and extremism*. Retrieved from http://www.splcenter.org/what-we-do/hate-and-extremism.

Tsesis, A. (2002). *Destructive messages: How hate speech paves the way for harmful social movements*. New York: New York University Press.

HATE GROUPS

Like any group, a hate group is a collection of individuals who interact, influence one another, and perceive their own membership as part of a group (Myers, 2002). However, the distinguishing feature of a hate group is its organization around a shared, and often extreme, dislike or hatred for a group of individuals who share a specific salient feature or characteristic. Although there is no limit to the list of potential demographic characteristic that may lead to the identification of an individual as a member of a despised group, hate groups have largely targeted individuals based on their ethnic or racial identity, national origin, immigration status, religious affiliation, or sexual orientation. Members of a hate group also engage in a range of behaviors that are intended to foster ongoing prejudice, discrimination, and oppression of the target hated group. These behaviors include, but are not limited to: the distribution of propaganda, attempts to influence public policy and legislation, hate speech, public protests and demonstrations, interpersonal violence, and acts of terrorism.

Psychology of a Hate Group

In an effort to better understand and predict the behavior of these hate groups, researchers have examined the psychological characteristics that motivate individuals to seek out, join, and participate in these groups. Two prominent themes emerged from this examination, indicating that hate group membership appears to satisfy both an individual's need for affiliation/belonging and a need for power (Smith, 2008). This need for affiliation is satisfied through increased access to in-group social interaction and is further supported by the use of shared symbols, rituals, and ceremony, while an increased sense of power and perceived status result from favorable comparisons to members of the target hated group who have been subjugated to lower status (Schafer & Navarro, 2006).

Prevalence

The presence of hate groups within the United States is well documented. Both the Southern Poverty Law Center (SPLC) and the Anti-Defamation League (ADL) closely monitor both the presence and activities of known domestic hate groups, and they make this data available to both law enforcement and the public. In 2011, SPLC identified 1,018 active domestic hate groups, and they have catalogued almost one hundred incidents of domestic terrorism enacted by members of these hate groups between 1995 and 2012 (Southern Poverty Law Center, 2012). The U.S. Federal Bureau of Investigation (FBI) also monitors the activity of domestic hate groups and publishes a yearly report on hate crimes statistics that is made available to the public (U.S. Federal Bureau of Investigation, 2013).

The existence of hate groups is not limited to the United States but is a global concern. Any consideration of international hate groups may evoke historic images of systematic genocide, such as that observed under Nazi-occupied Germany during World War II or the 1994 civil war in Rwanda. However, international hate groups continue to be both active and prolific. The September 11, 2001, attack on the United States by an extreme fundamentalist Islamic group led by Osama Bin Laden marked the beginning of a more widespread concern regarding global vulnerability to acts of violence resulting from fundamentalist Islamic extremism. In addition to monitoring domestic hate group activity, the ADL also monitors the activity of international terrorist groups. International efforts to respond to acts of terrorism and reports of human rights violations currently fall under the purview of the UN Security Council and the International Criminal Court. Other international human rights organizations, such as Human Rights Watch and Amnesty International, also help assess the international community for human rights violations.

Larry W. Carter II

References

Myers, D. G. (2002). *Social psychology* (7th ed.). New York: McGraw-Hill.

Schafer, J. R. & Navarro, J. (2006). The seven-stage hate model: The psychopathology of hate groups. *Cultic Studies Review*, 5(1), 1–9.

Smith, A. G. (2008). The implicit motives of terrorist groups: How the needs for affiliation and power translate into death and destruction. *Political Psychology*, 29(1), 55–75. doi: 10.1111/j.1467-9221.2007.00612.x

Southern Poverty Law Center. (2012). *Terror from the right: Plots, conspiracies, and racist rampages since Oklahoma City*. Retrieved from http://www.splcenter.org/sites/default/files/downloads/publication/terror_from_the_right_2012_web_0.pdf.

U.S. Federal Bureau of Investigation. (2013). *Hate crime statistics, 2012*. Retrieved from http://www.fbi.gov/about-us/cjis/ucr/hate-crime/2012/hate-crime.

HEGEMONY

Hegemony is a term popularly used in the social sciences to denote leadership or predominant influence exercised by a country or social group. In basic terms, it indicates the dominance of a group or a person over the others. Originally derived from the Greek word *hegeisthai* (to lead), it has extended beyond to culture and gender, acquiring political undertones. The source of the term goes back to ancient Greece and was first used in 1567 during the Peloponnesian War between Athens and Sparta to describe their struggle for power. It is often employed in the field of international relations to refer to the power politics and the social, cultural, ideological, or economic influence exerted by a prevailing country to achieve world domination. Such dominant power is called a *hegemon*. Sometimes *hegemon*, *empire*, and *imperial power* are used as interrelated concepts; however, many scholars and political scientists, including Zbigniew Brzezinski, contend that there is a clear-cut difference between a hegemon and an empire/imperial power. The hegemon does not acquire colonies based on the European model, but rather establishes its authority based on the consent of the governed by using its military, economic, or political resources. The intellectual origin of the concept of hegemony is generally attributed to Antonio Gramsci, an Italian neo-Marxist thinker. According to Gramsci, power could be exercised subtly rather than forcefully through political, economic, and cultural means. For instance, the bourgeoisie, the dominant upper- and middle-class group in Europe in the eighteenth century, leveraged the means of mass communication and art in order to produce mainstream ideas in line with its own ideology. The hegemonic group usually prefers to use subtle instruments rather than coercive measures such as the government, the army, or the police to establish the proposed social structure. In this sense, establishing hegemony depends on the consent of the society under the control of the ruling class. Such hegemonic discourse is embedded in a culture, and for political theorists, such as Ernesto Laclau and Chantal Mouffe, it is an essential element of a democratic society to achieve a form of consensus and strain away from divisions and conflicts. In international relations, there are three main categories of hegemony to explain how dominant countries, as well as groups or individuals, maintain their power through these means.

Political Hegemony

This is the type of hegemony international relations is most concerned about. Hegemony, or global hegemony, refers to the role of a country acting as a dominant power in a particular region or in the international arena. The country exercises its supremacy through establishing institutions, norms, and values. Such *hegemonic dominance* derives from the country's military or economic power, yet it mainly rests on nonmilitary means. *Hegemony* may be used as an interchangeable term for *empire*; however, most scholars agree that they are two distinct concepts, hegemony denoting specifically a country's prevailing influence without making any claims to the territories or resources of other countries. The Cold War (1945–1990) is a clear example of a battle for political hegemony between the United States and the Soviet Union. Since then, hegemony is a term used to describe the role of the United States as a world superpower in global politics. However, John Mearsheimer, a prominent proponent of offensive realism, points out the unattainability of global hegemony by any single country because no great power in the world possesses the economic or military capacity, and the international political system is too anarchical and chaotic to be controlled alone.

Cultural Hegemony

This type of hegemony refers to the relationship between culture and power through direct and indirect manipulation beyond the psychological or social norms, values, and semiotics. It is a process whereby a social group gains their power with the cooperation of institutions, including religious and educational. By using culture, such dominant groups control the masses, or the subaltern groups, by stripping them of their consent to choose and preventing them from considering alternatives to their socioeconomic realities and other ways to think about them. Antonio Gramsci explained that through the control of culture, a group could exercise control over shaping popular beliefs and worldviews in a society. Rather than using violence or coercion, the dominant class constructs generally accepted myths upon the masses that their subordination is universal and natural. It is possible to see such hegemonic dynamic, also known as *hegemonic masculinity*, in the supremacy of male domination and the predetermined definition of gender roles in a given society. Male attribution of a dominant and leading role is embedded in cultural hegemony and shapes social relations in all parts of the societal order. In this context, hegemony is maintained through its discourses or articulation rather than entities within the political and cultural sphere of society. These myths then serve as a vehicle for the dominant elites to convince subaltern groups that their interests equal the interests of society at large. In other words, by manipulating the use of culture and formal institutions of the state, the elites can create a set of foundational myths that define the national imagination of a country.

Monetary Hegemony

This type of hegemony is also known as *financial hegemony* or *currency supremacy*. It denotes the influence of a particular country in the international economic system. The intellectual origin of the term is often attributed to Michael Hudson, a professor of economics, who argued that the dollar enjoyed unchallenged status of world-competing currency, more than the Euro or the Yen. Dollar hegemony means that most countries in the globe keep their currency reserves in dollars. In the aftermath of World War II, the U.S. power to set up new norms and values in the international system significantly improved. With the establishment of various international organizations, including the United Nations, Bretton Woods institutions, the International Monetary Fund (IMF), the World Bank, and the General Agreement on Tariffs and Trade (GATT) system, the United States ascertained its economic hegemony in the international system. With the dollar's reserve status in the global economy, the dollar emerged as the primary reserve currency globally, dominating central banks, financial institutions, and exchanges of international trade. Washington became the leader of international trade and world macroeconomic policies, and the dollar symbolized the power of American economic supremacy.

Elcin Haskollar
Onur M. Koprulu

Additional Reading

Bocock, R. (1986). *Hegemony*. New York: Ellis Horwood and Tavistock.

Hudson, M. (1972). *Super imperialism: The economic strategy of American empire*. New York: Holt, Rinehart and Winston.

Laclau, E. & Mouffe, C. (2001). *Hegemony and socialist strategy: Towards a radical democratic politics*. London: Verso.

Lears, T. J. (1985). The concept of cultural hegemony: Problems and possibilities. *American Historical Review*, 90(3), 567–93.

Mearsheimer, J. (2001). *The tragedy of great power politics*. New York: W.W. Norton & Company.

HEGEMONY

Countering Hegemony with Leadership for Social Justice

DEFINING HEGEMONY Hegemony is a phenomenon in which groups with perceived positions of power consciously and unconsciously assert their social, political, and economic ideologies of what is considered normal in order to marginalize others (Gramsci, 2011). According to Giroux (1997), the dominant group within any given sociocultural context (e.g., schools, neighborhoods, nations) institutes "systems of practices, meanings, and values" in order to legitimize their interest as common sense or the status quo (p. 6). Invoking Gramsci (1971), Tooms, Lugg, and Bogotch (2010), define *hegemony* as "a sociopolitical construct explaining how groups of people are subjugated through metamessages of what is normal" (p. 98).

Giroux (1997) delineates two forms of hegemony: ideological and cultural. *Ideological hegemony* is deeply embedded in the fabric of society and is a form of control that manipulates one's consciousness and shapes daily behaviors. No Child Left Behind (NCLB), Common Core State Standards (CCSS), and Interstate School Leaders Licensure Consortium (ISLLC) standards are just a few among an array of policies that ideologically dictate the way in which school leaders engage with teachers and facilitate student learning. The CCSS are a national movement to provide consistent and clear understandings of what a student should know and demonstrate (Porter, McMaken, Hwang, & Yang, 2011). The ISLLC provides a framework for defining school leadership through standards for educational leaders (Murphy & Shipman, 1999). Several scholars argue that while these aforementioned policies were designed with the intent of increasing student achievement, the underlying ideology of these policies, in reality, is insufficient and places certain student groups (primarily students of color, economically disadvantaged students, English-Language Learners, and students with disabilities) as the root cause of school maladies (Leonardo, 2007; Valencia, Valenzuela, Sloan, & Foley, 2001).

Cultural hegemony is the mechanism in which dominant groups reproduce their power by inequitably distributing what is considered to be the *right* kind of knowledge (i.e., cultural capital), and this legitimatized knowledge is deemed the knowledge of power (Giroux, 1997). Hence, cultural hegemony drives social and cultural reproduction (Giroux, 1997). The inequitable distribution of cultural capital manifests in many forms within K–12 school settings. Students of color and language minority are overrepresented in lower-track courses (Oakes, 2005) and special education (Artiles, Trent,

& Palmer, 2004; Blanchett, 2009), and black and Latina/o students, specifically, have a higher incidence of disciplinary referrals and suspension rates (Skiba, Michael, Nardo, & Peterson, 2002). Scholars connect this latter phenomenon to the orchestration of the prison industrial complex, given that black and Latina/os are overrepresented in federal and state prison systems (Alexander, 2010; Raible & Irizarry, 2010).

Finally, Gramsci (2011) argues that culture should be recognized as artificial social constructs that must be deconstructed and reconstructed to uncover ulterior motives. Without critically challenging the practices and beliefs of society, intellectual liberation for the oppressed is not possible, and therefore, the oppressed are unable to foster their own culture. Since schools are complex intersections of cultural, social, and political power, it is the responsibility of educational leaders to courageously challenge the status quo and to provide safe spaces for all students, particularly students of color and students of poverty.

Dismantling Hegemony with Critical Pedagogy
Critical theorist Paulo Freire (1970) crafted the idea of critical pedagogy in his seminal work, *Pedagogy of the Oppressed*, to aid the proletariat in an effort to achieve liberation from the shackles of hegemony. Critical pedagogy is "an educational movement, guided by passion and principle, to help students develop consciousness of freedom, recognize authoritarian tendencies, and connect knowledge to power and the ability to take constructive action" (Giroux, 2010, p. 1). Cultivating an awareness of the intricate web of power relations and understanding how some benefit more than others lies at the epicenter of critical pedagogy; similarly, the sociopolitical forces governing the power are brought to light and critiqued (Freire, 1970). The process of deconstructing and reconstructing knowledge occurs when policies, procedures, organizations, and the broader sphere of politics are critically examined by asking provocative questions, such as: "Who benefits? Who is excluded? Who has the power? Why is this policy framed this way?" (Young, Diem, Lee, Mansfield & Welton, 2010). Questioning the status quo challenges the inherent power embedded in politics.

If educational leaders do not challenge the status quo, the hegemonic norms of the local schools continue to oppress students. Freire (1970) argues that the traditional models of education promote the "banking model," where teachers make regular deposits into students and where students are reduced to vessels to be filled. Rather, teachers and students should work together to co-construct knowledge through dialogue, reflection, and praxis to deconstruct and understand how the status quo functions. In this instance, principals should work with teachers to co-construct knowledge and work to become teacher-principals and principal-teachers.

Connecting Critical Pedagogy to Educational Leadership

Institutional leadership is highly influential, if not the strongest factor, in the promotion and realization of school success, particularly in championing historically marginalized students (McKenzie & Schuerich, 2004, 2007; McKenzie, Skrla, & Scheurich, 2006; Reyes, 2005; Reyes & Wagstaff, 2005; Shields, 2006; Skrla & Scheurich, 2001; Skrla, Erlandson, Reed, & Wilson, 2001; Skrla, Scheurich, Garcia, & Nolly, 2004). Activist-oriented school leaders take risks to challenge school-sponsored oppression (Marshall & Anderson, 2009) in order to foster a positive school culture and cultivate "critically conscious" school personnel, students, and parents who work in concert to destabilize hegemonic school structures, policies, and procedures (Freire, 1970).

Central to the challenges of promoting critical consciousness are the complex and messy intersections of power that exist in schools. The efforts social-justice-minded school administrators make to create safe spaces for teachers, students, parents, and community members to challenge the status quo are continually at odds with a myriad of interests, including: locally elected school boards, local community organizations, state and federal mandates, and local businesses and multinational corporations. Each of the competing agendas influences school culture, local curriculum, and learning (student and adults).

For Macedo, education is not neutral, nor is it nondirective (Freire, 1970). Or put differently, there is a hegemonic culture of power that is suffused within the school culture and within the curriculum (Apple, 2004). Therefore, it is a fundamental responsibility of critical pedagogues (both teachers and principals) to illuminate alternative viewpoints through the use of dialogue to dismantle hegemony. Freire (1970) writes that his conception of dialogue is an epistemological relationship. Dialogue is far more than acknowledging another person's perspective; it occurs because it is an indispensable facet of learning and knowing. Dialogical teaching involves theorizing about the experiences of both partners' experiences in the process of dialogue. Here is an example that illustrates this point: Let us suppose the principal of an elementary school is communicating student test scores from locally developed benchmark tests. Scores vary widely across demographics. Rather than speaking in vague platitudes or sidestepping the issue entirely, the critically oriented and socially just principal will ask pointed questions, for instance: "Why do you feel our Latino males continue to miss benchmarks?" or "Why do our free and reduced-price lunch students continue to underperform compared to their non-free and reduced-price lunch counterparts?" But the questions do not stop at this cursory examination; the questions are linked to the sociopolitical context of the community. For example: "Did you know that only 25 percent of our low-income students have health insurance? What are the implications for learning?" Acknowledging differences of power is not enough for critical pedagogues. Critical educators are also advocates for change and reflection. This process, which Skrla, Scheurich, Garica & Nolly (2004) define as an equity audit, is a leadership tool that can be used to uncover, understand, and change inequities that are inherent in schools and districts to improve teacher quality, educational programs, and to promote student achievement.

Activism suffused with critical reflection is the genesis of praxis (Freire, 1970). It is only when the oppressed recognize the inequitable power structures, reflecting on their own personal experiences, can liberating agency transpire. Agency is not simply "talking about" how the sociopolitical forces impact traditionally marginalized students, the socially just leader reallocates resources, alters structures within the organization, changes the school schedule, and does everything in his or her power to support students in need (see Theoharis, 2007; Shields, 2010 for further discussion). In our previous example, if only 25 percent of low-income students have health care, the socially just principal could forge a relationship with a local public health clinic to bring services to the school. Establishing a health clinic within the school to ensure regular checkups, physicals, and dental and eye exams could be ways to mitigate some of the health-related challenges students face. Although addressing health concerns connects to how students learn and achieve, housing a health clinic will most likely not disrupt the cyclical pattern of oppression traditionally marginalized students face because it does not disrupt the sociopolitical structures. However, educators, parents of students, and community members could see the benefits of the health clinic reflected within students and shift their thinking in how access to health care can improve student learning, which may in turn disrupt the reproduction of inequities. The principal is an activist; the commitment to providing the best opportunities for students cannot end at having fruitful conversations. Leaders committed to social justice and critical pedagogy must act.

Illuminating issues of hegemony, facilitating dialogue, promoting critical reflection, and engaging in praxis and activism are components of critical pedagogy and can help the oppressed become more critically conscious. Principals must engage in issues of race and social class to demystify differences and deconstruct assumptions to promote spaces where students feel safe and valued (Swanson, 2012). If principals are to be visionary leaders to promote academic success for all students, it is imperative for all students to feel like a valued member of the educational community.

Jason Swanson
Anjale Welton

References

Alexander, M. (2010). *The new Jim Crow: Mass incarceration in the age of colorblindness.* New York, NY: The New Press.

Apple, M. (2004). *Ideology and curriculum.* New York & London: Routledge.

Artiles, A. J., Trent, S. C., & Palmer, J. (2004). Culturally diverse students in special education: Legacies and prospects. In J. A. Banks & C. M. Banks (Eds.), *Handbook of research on multicultural education* (2nd ed., pp. 716–35). San Francisco, CA: Jossey-Bass.

Blanchett, W. J. (2009). A retrospective examination of urban education: From *Brown* to the resegregation of African Americans in special education—it is time to "go for broke." *Urban Education, 44*(4), 370–88.

Freire, P. (1970). *Pedagogy of the oppressed.* New York: Herder & Herder.

Giroux, H. (1997). *Pedagogy and the politics of hope: Theory, culture, and schooling.* Boulder, CO: Westview Press.

Giroux, H. (2010, October 17). Lessons from Paulo Freire. *Chronicle of Higher Education.* Retrieved from http://chronicle.com/article/Lessons-From-Paulo-Freire/124910/.

Gramsci, A. (1971). *Selections from the prison notebooks.* London: Lawrence and Wishart.

Gramsci, A. (2011). *Prison notebooks (vol. 1, 2, 3)* (J. Buttigeig, Ed. & Trans.). New York: Columbia University Press.

Leonardo, Z. (2007). The war on schools: NCLB, nation creation and the educational construction of whiteness. *Race Ethnicity and Education, 10*(3), 261–78.

Marshall, C. & Anderson, A. L. (2009). *Activist educators: Breaking past limits.* New York: Routledge.

McKenzie, K. B. & Scheurich, J. J. (2004). Equity traps: Useful construct for preparing principals to lead schools that are successful with racially diverse students. *Education Administration Quarterly, 40*(5), 606–32.

McKenzie, K. B. & Scheurich, J. J. (2007). King Elementary: A new principal plans how to transform a diverse urban school. *Journal of Cases in Educational Leadership, 10*(2), 19–27.

McKenzie, K. B., Skrla, L., & Scheurich, J. J. (2006). Preparing instructional leaders for social justice. *Journal of School Leadership, 16*(2), 158–70.

Murphy, J. & Shipman, N. (1999). The interstate school leaders licensure consortium: A standards-based approach to strengthening educational leadership. *Journal of Personnel Evaluation in Education, 13*(3), 205–24.

Oakes, J. (2005). *Keeping track: How schools structure inequality* (2nd ed.). New Haven, CT: Yale University Press.

Porter, A. C., McMaken, J., Hwang, J., & Yang, R. (2011). Common Core Standards: The new US intended curriculum. *Education Researcher, 40*(3), 103–116.

Raible, J. & Irizarry, J. G. (2010). Redirecting the teacher's gaze: Teacher education, youth surveillance, and the school-to-prison pipeline. *Teaching and Teacher Education, 26*(5), 1196–1203.

Reyes, A. (2005). Reculturing principals as leaders for cultural and linguistic diversity. In K. Téllez & H. C. Waxman (Eds.), *Preparing quality educators for English language learners: Research, policy, and practice* (pp. 145–65). Mahway, NJ: Lawrence Erlbaum.

Reyes, P. & Wagstaff, L. (2005). How does leadership promote successful teaching and learning for diverse students? In W. A. Firestone & C. Riehl (Eds.), *A new agenda for research in educational leadership* (pp. 101–18). New York: Teachers College Press.

Shields, C. M. (2006). Creating spaces for value-based conversations: The role of the school leaders in the 21st century. *International Studies in Educational Administration, 34*(2), 62–81.

Shields, C. M. (2010). Transformative leadership: Working for equity in diverse contexts. *Educational Administration Quarterly, 46*(4), 558–89.

Skiba, R. J., Michael, R. S., Nardo, A. C., & Peterson, R. L. (2002). The color of discipline: Sources of racial and gender disproportionality in school punishment. *Urban Review, 34*(4), 317–41.

Skrla, L. & Scheurich, J. J. (2001). Displacing deficit thinking in school district leadership. *Education and Urban Society, 33*(3), 235–59.

Skrla, L., Erlandson, D. A., Reed, E. M., & Wilson, A. P. (2001). *The emerging principalship*. Larchmont, NY: Eye on Education.

Skrla, L., Scheurich, J. J., Garcia, J., & Nolly, G. (2004). Equity audits: A practical leadership tool for developing equitable and excellent schools. *Educational Administration Quarterly, 40*(1), 133–61.

Swanson, J. (2012). *Transformative dialogue: Raising issues of race and social class*. University Council for Educational Administration Convention, Denver, CO.

Theoharis, G. (2007). Social justice educational leaders and resistance: Toward a theory of social justice leadership. *Educational Administration Quarterly, 43*(2), 221–58.

Tooms, A. K., Lugg, C. A., & Bogotch, I. (2010). Rethinking the politics of fit and educational leadership. *Educational Administration Quarterly, 46*(1), 96–131.

Valencia, R. R., Valenzuela, A., Sloan, K., & Foley, D. E. (2001). Let's treat the cause, not the symptoms: Equity and accountability in Texas revisited. *Phi Delta Kappan, 83*(4), 318–21.

Young, M. D., Diem, S., Lee, P., Mansfield, M., & Welton, A. (2010). *Exploring the nature and contributions of critical policy analysis*. American Educational Research Association, Denver, CO, April 30–May 3, 2010.

HETEROGENEOUS ABILITY GROUPING

Social Justice Essentials of Effective School Leadership
Today's public school leaders face indomitable challenges of building local capacity from limited resources in their respective schools in order to enable all students, especially high-need students, to meet formidable expectations articulated in the Common Core curriculum. To ensure that school leaders elevate the performance levels of high-need students to meet curricular expectations, these leaders must possess key essential traits that epitomize the principles of social justice. Therefore, the purpose of this entry is to elaborate, in some detail, the essential social justice principles that define and summarize effective public school leadership. These social justice principles will be explained within the context of Standard One from the National Council for Accreditation of Teacher Education (NCATE) professional standards, featuring that all school leader preparation candidates exhibit expected knowledge, skills, and professional dispositions (NCATE, 2008). The aforementioned conceptual context of this entry acknowledges a widely accepted definition of social justice "as using the means available to us as members of society and as scholars to strive toward the elimination of bias and oppression based on race, class, sexual gender, [disability], etc. . . . and all other forms of subordination and to actively work toward securing full, democratic participation for all members of society" (Rodriguez & Rolle, 2007, pp. 1–2).

Knowledge
The essential social justice knowledge proficiencies that school leaders must exhibit require a thorough understanding of student placement that promotes success for students who have been historically marginalized. Stated more specifically, school

leaders must know the research findings on inclusion, tracking, and ability grouping. The research findings on inclusion will enable school leaders to become strategic on how they schedule and support handicapped students as well as English-Language Learners, in both classes and other instructional settings, so that these respective student groups experience success (Theoharis, 2007). School leaders also must know the process of Response-to-Intervention (RTI) and must ensure that their respective faculty and staff understand this process to identify and to remediate proactively students with extraordinary learning needs. Additionally, school leaders must rely on the research findings that state that heterogeneous ability grouping is more positively related to higher levels of student achievement than that of homogeneous ability and that limited aspects of homogeneous ability often accompanied with looping may be warranted in unusual instructional situations. Finally, social justice leaders must have insight regarding how to restructure state and school district curricula to promote instructional programming that emphasizes cultural pluralism over ethnocentrism and that embraces diversity over social conformity (Jean-Marie, 2008). Therefore, social justice school leaders must excel in knowledge proficiencies, for which they become agents, which equalize student conditions to elevate high-need students to be on the same playing field as affluent students.

Skills

School leaders championing the tenets of social justice must have exceptional skills in data analysis, interpersonal communication, recruitment, and managerial supervision. Social justice school leaders are adept at using data to analyze the particular learning problems of marginalized students. They use the analysis of data to formulate and institute problem-solving solutions undergirding critical theory convictions that result in improved performance for high-need students. Moreover, these school leaders analyze data not merely to improve student achievement but also to ensure that higher student performance shows gains and learning-gap reduction between student subgroups.

The ability of school leaders to communicate is an essential skill to student groups representing varied social needs as well as to their parents and other constituents. This ability enables school leaders to equip their faculty and staff through case-study reflection and instruction regarding what constitutes various student needs and the effective methods to address these needs. Likewise, the ability of school leaders to convey an appreciation of cultural relativity among varied student groups and to showcase the success of model representatives from these subgroups provides high-need students tangible examples that they can emulate.

Social justice school leaders are deliberate and strategic in whom they recruit. They possess refined personnel skills in hiring faculty and staff members that espouse their social justice tenets; provide culturally relevant pedagogy; and champion the success of high-need, low-performing students. These leaders also ensure that hired faculty and staff are equipped with the ability to differentiate teaching and learning in order to meet the unique needs of students from diverse backgrounds. Quite naturally, these leaders recruit employees that originate from these high-need student groups and concurrently are exemplars of how students from these respective groups can be successful. Social justice school leaders operate within the faculty assigned to them, use strategically and purposefully those that espouse their social justice tenets and beliefs, and expand their reach through these in disseminating cultural relativism into the instructional program.

Practicing administrators advocating social justice convictions exhibit a set of managerial and supervisory skills that monitor faculty and the instructional program to internalize and disseminate effective teaching and learning among all students. These managerial skills consist of the ability to devise the master schedule and individual faculty schedules to educate and value a diverse student population. This skill set also suggests that the school administrator creates service delivery and staffing patterns, facilitates student class placement, operates within negotiated faculty and staff contracts, uses release time, and creates relevant and ongoing professional development to promote the celebration of student diversity and equity.

Dispositions

Effective school leaders promoting social justice principles in their supervision must exhibit a set of dispositions that effectuate meaningful educational change for all students. The chief disposition that a school leader must have is to exhibit a *bold vision* that seeks to actualize universal success of even the most marginalized students. The second disposition that a school leader must have is that of a *risk taker*: a change agent that motivates all faculty and staff to perform beyond their expected or standard capacity. Another important disposition that an effective school leader must exhibit is *resilience*. Resilience requires the ability of the school administrator to exhibit sustainable leadership to stay the course of celebrating diversity, of differentiating instruction and learning, and of educating all students in the face of resistance and opposition from staff and constituents that seek to reward only students of privilege and high standing (Hargraves, 2005). These first three dispositions necessitate that the school leader possesses an uncanny ability to establish *high teacher quality standards* to serve all students with outstanding pedagogy. This instructional quality does not settle for students to perform on a normal distribution curve featuring wide achievement measures of range, variance, and standard deviation. Instead, this instructional quality calls for culturally relevant pedagogy that raises bottom-rung-achieving students to at least the median and that empowers high-flying, high-need students to perform two or three standard deviations above the school's mean. So rather than having the normal distribution curve reflect student achievements ascribed by subgroup student profiles, the variance of student performance celebrates diversity and values high-flying minority student achievers. A final disposition of an effective social justice school leader consists of an educational vanguard that institutes both strategic school-community partnerships and vibrant school-parental relations. With strategic school-community partnerships, the school leader is able to establish harmonious relations with all sectors of the larger community to establish a relevance of the school program to these community sectors. Stronger school-parental relations promote greater parental participation and parental monitoring, which results invariably in higher levels of student achievement for all students.

Conclusion

This entry explained, in some detail, the social justice principles that define an effective educational leader in the context of NCATE's professional Standard One: knowledge, skills, and dispositions. The social justice profile of these combined knowledge, skills, and dispositions makes an educational leader transformational and transformative. *Transformational* means that that the educational leader empowers the school institution to change in enhancing student performance for marginalized students and not merely establish success for ascribed layers of students that reflect the larger community's social and wealth stratification. *Transformative* refers to the educational leader's ability to effectuate a change that reconstitutes the community at large, which subsequently causes changes within the school institution (Shields, 2004). Through transformational and transformative leadership, the social justice school leader institutes an enduring and positive educational change, in both the school institution and educational community, that celebrates culturally relevant teaching, learning, and academic success for all students.

Tyrone Bynoe

References

Jean-Marie, G. (2008). Leadership for social justice: An agenda for 21st century schools. *Educational Forum—Kappa Delta Pi, 72*, 340–54.

Hargraves, A. (2005). Sustainable leadership and social justice: A new paradigm. *Independent School, 64*(2), 16–24.

National Council for Accreditation of Teacher Preparation. (2008). *Professional standards for the accreditation of teacher preparation institutions.* Washington, DC: NCATE.

Rodriguez, G. & Rolle, A. (Eds). (2007). *To what ends and by what means? The social justice implications of contemporary school finance theory and policy.* New York: Routledge–Taylor & Francis Group.

Shields, C. (2004). Dialogic leadership for social justice: Overcoming pathologies of silence. *Educational Administration Quarterly, 40*(1), 109–32.

Theoharis, G. (2007). Social justice educational leaders and resistance: Toward a theory of social justice leadership. *Educational Administration Quarterly, 43*(2), 221–58.

HETERONORMATIVITY

Heteronormativity is a term coined by social theorist and literary critic Michael Warner in 1991 to identify the ways in which social institutions and dominant culture are oriented around the assumed normal, natural, and ideal logic of heterosexual attraction and unions. Heterosexuality itself is premised upon the idea that there are two distinct sexes (male and female) and associated genders (masculine and feminine) that are inherently opposite and complementary for the purpose of reproduction and the organization of life activities. The presumed "naturalness" of heterosexuality is bolstered by the social construction of penile-vaginal penetration as the pinnacle of sexual activity. Heteronormativity rests upon the assumption that sexual behaviors can be tied to definable sexual *identities*. It is important to note that this idea of a stable sexual identity or orientation as a key feature of personhood has a relatively short history, which is evidenced through the development of terms such as *heterosexual* and *homosexual* (Katz, 2007; Foucault, 1978; Weeks, 1989). More generally, conceptions of sexuality must be considered in relation to historical approaches to defining—and often conflating—"natural," "normal," and "healthy" (Durkheim 1895/1966).

Warner (1991) argued that many social science frameworks and concepts were developed based on the assumed social centrality of male-female reproductive unions. Therefore, it was insufficient to simply "add" the presence of gays and lesbians to existing social science theories; rather, the grounding of these theoretical approaches necessitated radical alteration. Warner also noted a terminological shift away from "gay" toward "queer" occurring both in individual identification and in scholarly emphasis, moving beyond the idea of tolerance for sexual minorities in favor of a critique of the normative construction of social life. Although the boundaries of "sexuality" remain blurry, personal, and variable depending on context (see Jackson, 2006), "heteronormativity" provides a valuable conceptual lens for thinking beyond individual-level discrimination (often conceptualized as "homophobia"). Conversely, "heteronormativity" offers an avenue to further consider the ways in which social institutions—such as education, religion, the family, health care, the economy, and politics—are organized based on heterosexual logic. Approached through this perspective, the concept of heteronormativity enables a deeper understanding of the various ways in which heterosexual privilege permeates the social world, subordinating LGBTQ (lesbian, gay, bisexual, transsexual, queer) sexualities that challenge or destabilize its boundaries.

Warner's (1991) work builds upon a rich body of gender and sexuality scholarship in the social sciences and humanities, with important roots in 1980s feminist theory. A feminist scholar of particular note is poet and essayist Adrienne Rich (1980). Rich used the concept of "compulsory heterosexuality" to refer to an enforced system of social organization rather than conceptualizing heterosexuality merely as a personal sexual preference. From this perspective, heterosexuality is understood as a political and cultural system that is inseparable from gender inequality. According to Rich, compulsory heterosexuality reinforces gender inequality by ensuring that men have access to women's energy and life activities in all capacities, including—though not limited to—sexuality, children, labor, movement, creativity, and knowledge. This system is "compulsory" yet not explicitly coercive precisely because heterosexuality continues to be presented as unquestionable, and therefore, appears natural rather than systemic. Simultaneously, the historical existence of alternative sexual expressions and relations are routinely erased.

Rhetorician, philosopher, and gender theorist Judith Butler (1990) built on Rich's (1980) notion of "compulsory heterosexuality" and Monique Wittig's (1980) related conception of the "heterosexual contract" with her identification of the "heterosexual matrix" (p. 208, n. 6). Butler developed the notion of "heterosexual matrix" to "designate that grid of cultural intelligibility through which bodies, genders, and desires are naturalized" (Butler, 1990, p. 208, n.6). Here, Butler refers to the dominant way in which people and their bodies come to be understood within a system in which sex assignment as "male" or "female" at birth is presumed to correspond with gender identity as "man" or "woman," gender performance as "masculine" or "feminine," and opposite-sex attraction (Butler, 1990, p. 208, n. 6). Within this "matrix," the emotions, activities, personal connections, and self-expressions of individuals are both limited and regulated. The historical operation of the "heterosexual matrix" is profound, with same-sex desires, activities, and relationships having been institutionally defined and treated as immoral, criminal, and pathological (Foucault, 1978). Recent research demonstrates that LGBTQ persons and couples are still subject to discrimination in various areas of their life, such as work (Williams & Guiffre, 2011) and school (Taylor et al., 2011), and they often do not have the opportunity to see reflections of themselves in mainstream media (Barnhurst, 2007; Carl, 1990; Smith & Brown, 1997, p. 40; Walters, 2001).

More recent scholarship has supported Butler's (1990) insight that the boundaries established by heteronormative practices and institutions regulate both sexuality *and* gender (Jackson, 2006). Those who do not conform to all aspects of the heterosexual matrix have historically been, and often continue to be, subjected to administrative and physical violence as well as employment discrimination and social stigma. The regulative function of heteronormativity is most visible in the marginalization of those who transgress the boundaries of heteronormativity, including people who are trans and gender nonconforming, who engage in non-normative relationship models such as nonmonogamy, and to a lesser extent, people who violate prevailing norms even within heterosexual interactions.

It is critical to recognize that heteronormativity does not operate in isolation from other axis of systemic inequality; it intersects with various forms of privilege and oppression. Using an intersectional perspective that acknowledges these complexities, Patricia Hill Collins (2005) engaged in a critical discussion of black sexuality in the United States. Hill Collins conceptualized heteronormativity as having permeated Western discourse regarding black sexuality. Understood as hypersexual and promiscuous, racialized constructions of black sexuality also encompass assumptions of uncontrolled procreation, bolstering an understanding of black sexuality as implicitly *hetero*sexual; being black is constructed as inherently incongruous with homosexual behavior. Consequently, black LGBTQ people are perceived as being "less authentically" black. Through such discourses, the compounded

influence of heterosexism and racism both invisibilized and oppressed black LGBTQ people. Additionally, alongside the influence of racialized Western discourse, Hill Collins implicated the black community as contributing to this oppression; while members of the black community who "pass" for white are considered to be denying their true selves, LGBTQ members of the black community are essentially encouraged to "pass" for heterosexual. Furthering her intersectional critique, Hill Collins argued that social class significantly influences the extent to which black LGBTQ people may be able to resist these systems of oppression.

Through a variety of social mechanisms (including institutions, culture, and daily interactions), heterosexuality is so consistently presented as normal and unquestionable that its omnipresence is largely invisible to those privileged by it—namely, cisgender heterosexuals (i.e., heterosexual-identified individuals whose gender identity and gender presentation is considered to "match" the sex they were assigned at birth) (Dudley et al., 2005; Jordan & Deluty, 2000; Kitzinger & Wilkinson, 2004; Simoni & Walters, 2001). However, while much research has focused on the negative ways in which LGBTQ people are adversely affected by the heteronormative construction of society, scholarship has also made the argument that heterosexuality itself is constrained by heteronormativity. While heteronormative logic elevates heterosexuality above divergent LGBTQ sexualities, it simultaneously dictates an ideal heterosexuality with rigid gender and sexual expectations. This includes the sexual double standards delineating "permissible" male and female heterosexual behavior (Reiss, 1967), the normative heterosexual "scripts" that encompass gendered roles for the progression of heterosexual encounters (Gagnon & Simon, 1973), and the idealization of lifelong monogamous dyads with traditional gender arrangements (Parsons, 1943/1954; Richardson, 2005). Stevi Jackson (2006) suggested the conceptual utility of "heteronormativity"—as well as Rich's (1980) conceptualization of "compulsory heterosexuality"—is significantly limited by scholarship that neglects to consider the ways in which heteronormativity not only marginalizes those outside of its boundaries but also governs those *within* the realm of heterosexuality.

Nonetheless, the ways in which heteronormativity restrains heterosexuality does not discount the presence of heterosexual privilege (although heterosexual individuals' access to and awareness of this privilege does vary).

Katherine Lyon
Misha Dhillon

References

Barnhurst, K. (2007). *Media q, media/queered: Visibility and its discontents*. New York: Peter Lang.

Butler, J. (1990/1999). *Gender trouble: Feminism and the subversion of identity*. New York: Routledge.

Carl, D. (1990). *Counseling same-sex couples*. New York: W. W. Norton & Co.

Dudley, M. G., Rostosky, S. S., Riggle, E. D. B., Duhigg, M. J., Brodnicki, C., & Couch, R. (2005). Same-sex couples' experiences with homonegativity. *Journal of GLBT Family Studies, 1*(4), 61–78.

Duggan, L. (2003). *The twilight of equality? Neoliberalism, cultural politics, and the attack on democracy*. Boston: Beacon Press.

Durkheim, E. (1895/1966). *The rules of sociological method*. New York: Free Press.

Foucault, M. (1978/1990). *The history of sexuality*. New York: Vintage Books.

Frohard-Dourlent, H. (2012). Working to "increase respect and reduce stigma": Thinking through the possibilities and limits of an antihomophobia education program in Paris. *Journal of LGBT Youth, 9*(1), 1–21.

Gagnon, J., & Simon, W. (1973). *Sexual conduct: The social sources of human sexuality*. Chicago: Aldine Books.

Hill Collins, P. (2005). *Black sexual politics: African Americans, gender, and the new racism*. New York, NY: Routledge.

Hindman, M. (2011). Rethinking intersectionality: Towards an understanding of discursive marginalization. *New Political Science, 33*, 189–21.

Jackson, S. (2006). Gender, sexuality and heterosexuality: The complexity (and limits) of heteronormativity. *Feminist Theory, 7*, 105–21.

Jordan, K. M. & Deluty, R. H. (2000). Social support, coming out, and relationship satisfaction in lesbian couples. *Journal of Lesbian Studies, 4*(1), 145–64.

Katz, J. (2007). *The invention of heterosexuality*. Chicago: University of Chicago Press.

Kitzinger, C. & Wilkinson, S. (2004). Why we got married instead of registering a civil partnership. *Feminism and Psychology, 14*(1), 127–50.

Parsons, T. (1943/1954). Sex roles in the American kinship system (selection from the kinship system of the contemporary United States). In *Essays in sociological theory*. New York: Free Press.

Reiss, I. (1967). *Premarital sexual standards in America*. New York: Free Press.

Rich, A. (1980). Compulsory heterosexuality and lesbian existence. *Signs, 5*(4), 631–60.

Richardson, D. (2005). Claiming citizenship? Sexuality, citizenship and lesbian feminist theory. In C. Ingraham (Ed.), *Thinking straight: New work in critical heterosexuality studies* (pp. 63–85). New York: Routledge.

Seidman, S. (2002). *Beyond the closet: The transformation of gay and lesbian life*. New York: Routledge.

Simon, W. & Gagnon, J. (1986). Sexual scripts: Permanence and change. *Archives of Sexual Behaviour, 15*(2), 97–120.

Simoni, J. M. & Walters, K. L. (2001). Heterosexual identity and heterosexism: Recognizing privilege to reduce prejudice. *Journal of Homosexuality, 41*(1), 157–72.

Smith, R. B. & Brown, R. A. (1997). The impact of social support on gay male couples. *Journal of Homosexuality, 33*(2), 39–61.

Taylor, C. & Peter, T., with McMinn, T. L., Elliott, T., Beldom, S., Ferry, A., Gross, Z., Paquin, S., & Schachter, K. (2011). *Every class in every school: The first national climate survey on homophobia, biphobia, and transphobia in Canadian schools. Final report*. Toronto, ON: Egale Canada Human Rights Trust.

Vaid, U. (1995). *Virtual equality: The mainstreaming of gay and lesbian liberation*. New York: Anchor Books.

Walters, S. D. (2001). *All the rage: The story of gay visibility in America*. Chicago: University of Chicago Press.

Ward, J. (2008). *Respectably queer: Diversity culture in LGBT activist organizations*. Nashville: Vanderbilt University Press.

Warner, M. (1991). Introduction: Fear of a queer planet. *Social Text, 9*(4:29), 3–17.

Weeks, J. (1989). *Sex, politics and society: The regulation of sexuality since 1800* (2nd ed.). London: Longman.

Williams, C. & Giuffre, P. (2011). From organizational sexuality to queer organizations: Research on homosexuality and the workplace. *Sociology Compass*, 5(7), 551–63.

Wittig, M. (1980/2003). One is not born a woman. In C. R. McCann and S. K. Kim (Eds.), *Feminist theory reader: Local and global perspectives* (pp. 244–51). New York: Routledge.

HETEROSEXISM

Heterosexism, and its related term, *heteronormative*, convey and reinforce dominant ideologies about sex, gender identity, and social interactions. *Heteronormative* is a term made popular by Michael Warner (1993), who defined it as the sociocultural assumption that heterosexual relationships, sexual practices, and identities are the norm. Heteronormativity understands the gender binary of "male" and "female" and "man" and "woman" as a natural order. This understanding precludes other gender and sexual identities, rendering the people they belong to invisible and discounted. *Heterosexism*, then, is a system of discrimination that supports heteronormativity by marking nonheterosexuality as abnormal, deviant, and threatening to this natural order (Jung & Smith, 1993). Cramer (2002) defines heterosexism as:

> The expectation that all persons should be or are heterosexual. The belief that heterosexual relations are normal and the norm. These expectations and beliefs occur on individual, institutional, and cultural levels. The behavior manifestations of heterosexist beliefs include denying marriage licenses for same-sex couples and restricting health and retirement benefits to those in heterosexual marriages. (p. 2)

Heteronormativity and heterosexism pervade social institutions such as the law and affect how sexual violence is socially constructed to refer only to acts between men and women (Herek, 1992; Nakayama, 1998).

By identifying certain social and institutional practices as heterosexist, systems of discrimination and even violence against the LGBT community are open to challenge. Heterosexism in the law has been increasingly challenged with the Supreme Court ruling the Defense of Marriage Act unconstitutional, the repeal of the military policy Don't Ask, Don't Tell, and with eighteen states at the time of the writing of this entry embracing marriage equality. However, heterosexism within other legal frameworks continues to persist. Sodomy laws are still in existence in fourteen states, including Idaho, Louisiana, and Mississippi. These laws, despite being ruled invalid by the Supreme Court's 2003 decision in *Lawrence v. Texas*, reflect a continued hostility to sexual practices that have been associated with the LGBT community, despite their existence in heterosexual communities as well. Such heterosexist discrimination has led to the persistent marginalization of LGBT people.

Sara Carrigan Wooten

References

Cramer, E. P. (2002). *Addressing homophobia and heterosexism on college campuses.* Binghamton, NY: The Haworth Press.

Herek, G. M. (1992). Psychological heterosexism in the United States. In A. R. D'Augelli & C. J. Patterson (Eds.), *Lesbian, gay, bisexual identities over the lifespan: Psychological perspectives.* New York: Oxford University Press.

Jung, P. B. & Smith, R. F. (1993). *Heterosexism: An ethical challenge.* Albany, NY: SUNY Press.

Nakayama, T. K. (1998). Communication of heterosexism. In H. L. Hecht (Ed.), *Communicating prejudice.* Thousand Oaks, CA: SAGE Publications.

Warner, M. (1993). *Fear of a queer planet: Queer politics and social theory.* Minneapolis, MN: The University of Minnesota Press.

HIDDEN CURRICULUM

The term *hidden curriculum* refers to attitudes, behaviors, and knowledge that are covertly or unintentionally learned through the schooling process. The construct began appearing in educational research in the 1960s when Jackson (1968) asserts schooling set in motion a set of processes that aim to train, construct, and normalize students according to the requirements of the powerful. The hidden curriculum is said to police the power relations between teachers and students, reinforcing existing differences between social identity groups, and to privilege the cultural values and patterns of the dominant group and tends to ignore or diminish the value of cultural differences that exist in schools (Jackson, 1968; Illich, 1971; Warner, 1999). School climate and culture play a large part in determining what is reinforced in the hidden curriculum of a school and in individual classrooms; the identity and values of each individual teacher impacts the hidden curriculum. Ultimately, the hidden curriculum plays a socializing or normative role in education, providing students with an example of "normal" or accepted behaviors, attitudes, and beliefs (Illich, 1971; Warner, 1999).

Critical analyses of the hidden curriculum, by progressive educators, have included calls to reform schools in ways that acknowledge uniqueness in social identity groups as differences untethered to an assigned value of one relative to another because the hidden curriculum codes some differences as "normal" and others as "abnormal." When it is allowed to operate unfettered by critical analysis, members of especially nondominant social identity groups are forced to conform or resist, and both responses have negative impacts on identity formation, which impact personal, academic, and professional success (DeJean, 2007; Friere, 1970; Bartolome, 2004). It is important to note that, while the hidden curriculum favors dominant group members, it can still negatively impact members of these groups for whom hegemonic constructs also limit their individual, intellectual, and/or career expressions—for example, the white person who is inclined to become an antiracist educator. From a critical analytical perspective, schools are then normative socializers of society, in the views of the mainstream, of the hegemonic establishment. Inevitably, this hidden curriculum of schooling creates and perpetuates prejudice and discrimination and extends the privilege of others.

By way of example of how the hidden curriculum operates, Queer theorists have sought to reveal how this normative nature of schooling manifests as heteronormativity in educational environments in which students are taught through the heterosexual assumption: that heterosexuality is the assumed normal sexual orientation in all aspects of life. Anything that is not heterosexual (gay, lesbian, bisexual) and, by extension of gender identity and expression, anything that does not promote traditional images of masculinity in men and femininity in women

(transgender, transsexual, intersex) is dubbed "queer," and therefore, seen as not normal, deviant, and wrong (Warner, 1993, 1999; Jackson, 2006; DeJean, 2007). Heteronormativity includes those punitive rules—social, familial, and legal—that force members of society to conform to hegemonic, heterosexual standards for identity. Therefore, at school heteronormativity is pervasive as part of the hidden (and sometimes hyperovert) curriculum impacting classroom dynamics, instruction, extracurricular activities, and teaching as a profession.

Ultimately, the hidden curriculum in schools and schooling is a manifestation of the "transparency" of dominant group identities (Bartolome, 2004; Friere, 1970). While these manifestations are highly visible to outsiders to the dominant group, dominant group members, whose interests these manifestations are perceived to represent, often operate as though these manifestations do not exist—as if they are invisible—and/or as if these manifestations are, simply, the way things are for everyone: universally normative.

Zaid M. Haddad

References

Bartolome, L. I. (2004). Critical pedagogy and teacher education: Radicalizing prospective teachers. *Teacher Education Quarterly*, *31*(1), 97–122.

DeJean, W. (2007). Out gay and lesbian K–12 educators: A study in radical honesty. *Journal of Gay and Lesbian Issues in Education*, *4*(4), 59–72.

Freire, P. (1970). *Pedagogy of the oppressed*. New York: The Continuum International Publishing Group, Inc.

Illich, I. (1971). *Deschooling society*. New York: Marian Boyars.

Jackson, J. (2006). Removing the masks: Considerations by gay and lesbian teachers when negotiating the closet door. *Journal of Poverty*, *10*(2), 27–52.

Jackson, P. (1968). *Life in classrooms*. New York: Holt, Rinehart & Winston.

Warner, M. (Ed.). (1993). *Fear of a queer planet: Queer politics and social theory*. Minneapolis, MN: University of Minnesota Press.

Warner, M. (1999). *The trouble with normal: Sex, politics, and the ethics of queer life*. Cambridge, UK: Harvard University Press.

HIERARCHICAL INFLUENCE

The term *hierarchy* refers to a classification system in which various objects are ordered. When applied to a society, this kind of ordering happens as a result of factors because of larger social structural factors. For example, social class, race, gender, sexual orientation, age, and more are all ways in which society organizes its members. This kind of organizing is called *social stratification*. As a result of social stratification, individual behavior changes depending on his or her place within a social strata (one part of the social stratification system).

Origins of Hierarchy and Hierarchical Thinking

The word *hierarchy* comes from the Greek word *hierarches*, or "leader of sacred rites." Both Greek society and philosophy were permeated with discourse on hierarchy. In Greek society, women and slaves were property. Greek social stratification was mirrored in its philosophy. In philosophy, for instance, Plato is known for discussing how people were classified as having a "gold, silver, bronze, or iron" soul. These souls were what determined one's station in Greek society. In other words, for the Greeks, there was some kind of extraworldly "essence," or core, about a person that justified his/her position within a society. This would provide the framework for how the Western world developed hierarchical schemas that would change throughout history. In Medieval Europe, peasants were bound to vassals. These vassals would then be controlled by an aristocracy. These aristocrats would then be subjects of nobility, gentry, and finally, the monarchy. The monarch's justification to rule was largely granted by the Church. In other words, during this time period, the social order was justified largely by the divine right of kings, or the idea that God ordained the monarchy to rule over the different strata within his kingdom. As the Age of Industrialism emerged, the factory brought about a different social stratification system based on wealth, privilege, and education. It is during the Industrial Era that scientific theories surrounding hierarchical behavior began to emerge.

Eighteenth-to-Nineteenth-Century Theories on Hierarchical Influence

Thinkers during the eighteenth to nineteenth century were beginning to explore different understandings of how hierarchies were formed. As a result, these understandings had an effect on the development of Western social stratification. One school of thought that developed during this era was pseudoscientific research on hierarchies. In terms of the pseudoscientific research, authorities on the emerging framework of science (e.g., scientists) began to develop classification systems that placed human beings into different categories via the scientific method. One of the most infamous classification systems developed around this time period was a classification system based on race. This classification system essentially placed the white, Anglo-Saxon male as the apex of human development, while members of other races were categorized as inferior and animallike. It was these pseudoscientific frameworks that partially laid the framework for social stratification in contemporary Western society. Likewise, other thinkers also applied scientific frameworks to society and hierarchies. For example, engineer Herbert Spencer developed the notion of social evolution in which "lower forms" of society were always destined to be eliminated by higher forms of society. For Spencer, issues, such as "poverty," were products of a social version of natural selection and that the poor are socially inferior to the rich, are socially unfit, and are naturally designed to be used as laborers to serve those in higher positions.

In both these examples of racial and social classification systems, people's inferiority to others was somehow biologically "naturalized." That is, there was some biological core that made people naturally inferior to others. Consequently, if these people were naturally inferior, it was not only natural for those in superior positions to have and maintain their social position, but it was also natural for these groups to express dominance over others. For instance, laws that advocated racial, economic, and gendered separation began to emerge. These laws placed white, economically privileged men at the center of the public sphere as the natural leader of this hierarchy for decades following the turn of the nineteenth century. This meant that white, economically well-off men were given primary access to institutions that ensured their position in society. In other words, this particular social position was granted privileged access to government, media, education, and other types of social institutions. In addition to instructions, white, economically privileged men were also able to define culture in the Western world. Given this intellectual history and the consequences that arose from this hierarchy, contemporary thinkers have developed frameworks that explain behaviors that are the result of social hierarchy.

Psychological Effects of Hierarchy and Social Dominance Theory

In the mid-1990s, Jim Sidanius and Felicia Pratto developed their theoretical framework called *social dominance theory*, giving a context of a stratified society on age (older people have more power than the young), sex (men have more power than women), and arbitrary boundaries (since stratification varies by society and culture). This theory holds that a group in power, or the "hegemonic group," maintains its power via three mechanisms: social privilege, mythology, and discriminatory action. Social privileges essentially involve systematic advantages in which the dominant groups benefit from the social structure. For example, men enjoy male privilege in that their views are represented, and held as a priority, in politics, media, and more. The mythology component involves ideologies that justify the dominant group's privilege; for example, the notion of meritocracy. The idea of a meritocracy maintains that people who have a certain amount of wealth have earned it even though most wealth is inherited. These myths allow discriminatory acts (or harmful actions) against subordinate groups to take place. For example, in Nazi Germany, the belief in German ethnic superiority and nationalism led to a mass genocide of Jewish people based on the idea that they were inferior beings. Through three mechanisms, the hegemonic group places itself as the reference point for other groups and acts accordingly.

Omar Mushtaq

Additional Reading

Andersen, H. & Kaspersen, L. B. (2000). *Classical and modern social theory*. Malden, MA: Blackwell.

Babbitt, S. E. & Campbell, S. (1999). *Racism and philosophy*. Ithaca, NY: Cornell University Press.

Bishop, S. & Weinzweig, M. (1979). *Philosophy and women*. Belmont, CA: Wadsworth Publishing Company.

Danziger, S. & Gottschalk, P. (1993). *Uneven tides: Rising inequality in America*. New York: Russell Sage Foundation.

Sidanius, J. & Pratto, F. (1999). *Social dominance: An intergroup theory of social hierarchy and oppression*. Cambridge, UK: Cambridge University Press.

HIGH CONTEXT

The concept of high context is most often attributed to anthropologist Edward T. Hall's (1976) theory of high and low context cultures. This theory focuses on the varying role culture has in shaping diverse communication styles. Hall argues that context carries great importance in all interactions, and understanding the level of context in these interactions is instrumental in effective cross-cultural or intercultural communication. By introducing the concepts of high context and low context, Hall presents a way of understanding differences in culture and communication by examining the significance of context in achieving understanding and avoiding miscommunication.

Cultures and communication in which context is of great importance to structuring actions is referred to as high context. High context defines cultures that are relational and collectivist, and which most highlight interpersonal relationships. Hall identifies high-context cultures as those in which harmony and the well-being of the group is preferred over individual achievement. In addition, tradition, ceremony, and history are also highly valued and, because of long-standing relationships and connections, many aspects of cultural behavior in high-context cultures, such as individual roles and expectations, do not need much overt or thorough explanation.

In relation to communicative behavior, high-context cultures value context more than they do words spoken. Thus, a speaker's tone of voice and nonverbal communicative features, such as facial expressions and gestures, are significant markers that define an interaction. High-context communication carries most of the information within these physical features or internalized pieces of information that are already known about the situation or individuals. Moreover, someone who is an outsider in a high-context situation may miss the subtle messages and meanings embedded within this kind of communication. Because higher context cultures greatly involve the contextualization of messages and decoding of those messages, high-context communication is also characterized by interpretive and emotional messages in addition to the close personal networks and familial histories of those cultures. Some of the countries Hall and Hall (1990) identify as high-context cultures are Japan, Arabic countries, and Latin American countries. Although Hall (1976) acknowledges that cultures are not static, and that differences across generations and time can cause shifts and changes in culture, taking into consideration characteristics that may define a culture or situation as high context may account for differences and diversity across social groups. As a result, identifying where context lies along a continuum from low to high leads to more positive outcomes for intercultural relationships, negotiations, conflict resolution, and in general, the avoidance of miscommunication.

D. Carolina Ramos

References

Hall, E. T. (1976). *Beyond culture*. Garden City, NY: Anchor Press.

Hall, E. T. & Hall, M. R. (1990). *Understanding cultural differences*. Yarmouth, ME: Intercultural Press.

HIJABIPHOBIA

Muslim women in hijab (hijabis), as the most obvious affiliates of Islam, are at times victims of verbal and physical abuse in Western countries. An extreme case of violence against a hijabi occurred in 2009 in a German courtroom where a man was attempting to appeal the fine he had been issued for calling Marwa el-Sherbini a "terrorist" and an "Islamic whore" in a Dresden park. El-Sherbini, a pregnant thirty-two-year-old hijabi, was stabbed by the man eighteen times in front of her husband, who was also injured in the attack, and her young son (Connolly & Shenker, 2009). Another pregnant hijabi in Massachusetts had the hijab ripped from

her head and was beaten until she lost consciousness while walking on the street with her toddler (Ibish, 2008).

American middle school and high school students, like Hannah in Florida, have had the hijab pulled from their heads (CAIRtv, 2007). Other hijabis have been publicly humiliated by school employees for refusing to remove the hijab; such was the case with a student from Oklahoma who was suspended on several occasions because the school staff could not distinguish between a scarf worn to denote religious affiliation and one intended to demonstrate gang affiliation (Ibish, 2008) Some hijabis reported being afraid to go to school after 9/11 due to numerous threats of violence. University students are also not immune to discrimination due to their conspicuous religious attire. Slma Shelbayah was harassed by a professor at Georgia State University. The professor continually linked Shelbayah's hijab to terrorism and bombs. Shelbayah claims that after she filed a complaint with the EEOC in 2008, her university employment was canceled and she was disenrolled as a doctoral student (Muslim Discrimination, 2009).

Hijabis also face discriminatory hiring practices, or they may be terminated after they are hired, as was the case with Hani Khan, who was fired from Hollister Company in 2010 (Huffington Post, 2011). Even in American metropolitan areas with large Muslim populations, such as Detroit-Dearborn, women have been denied employment at McDonald's (CAIRtv, 2010). Hijabis are aware of the Western stigma attached to their hijabs so they tend to avoid applying for jobs in which they will have a lot of interaction with the mainstream public (Ghumman & Jackson, 2010).

The courtroom is not necessarily a place where hijabis can seek justice from the discrimination to which they are subjected in other institutions and in the public sphere at large. There were two recent cases in Detroit: a woman was asked to remove her hijab in court (CAIRtv, 2009), and the small claims case of a woman in niqab was dismissed because she refused to remove her face veil (Associated Press, 2008). In Georgia in 2008, Lisa Valentine was one of several women who were held in contempt for refusing to remove her hijab in a courtroom. Valentine was jailed for ten days (CAIRtv, 2008). It is not surprising that the courts reflect the same prejudices of the greater society. In fact, according to a 2007 CAIR report, government agencies were the most problematic spaces for upholding the civil rights of hijabis, followed in descending order by "workplaces, mosques/community organizations, schools and prison" (Ghazali, n.d.).

Although the voices of hijabis are noticeably absent from mainstream media, even when they are the topic of discussion, hijabis in the social media often claim that the hijab is a source of empowerment for them (Robinson, forthcoming). However, mainstream America continues to view this garment as a tangible manifestation of the subjugation of Muslim women; therefore it, as well as the women who wear it, remains stigmatized.

Rebecca S. Robinson

References

Associated Press. (2008, December 17). U.S. judge jails Muslim woman over head scarf. *Crime & Courts* on NBCNews.com. Retrieved from http://www.msnbc.msn.com/id/28278572/#.TxI4NoF4dpc.

CAIRtv. (2007). Sixth grade FL student says she is scared to go to school. YouTube. Retrieved from http://www.youtube.com/watch?v=9nOvu8Nm-0w&feature=relmfu.

CAIRtv. (2008). CAIR: Muslim woman jailed for not removing head scarf. YouTube. Retrieved from http://www.youtube.com/watch?v=_Iv621TCrG8&NR=1&feature=endscreen.

CAIRtv. (2009). CAIR-MI: Muslim to file suit over judge's hijab ban. YouTube. Retrieved from: http://www.youtube.com/watch?v=Higt6rgArx4&NR=1&feature=endscreen.

CAIRtv. (2010). CAIR video: McDonald's accused of hijab discrimination. YouTube. Retrieved from http://www.youtube.com/watch?v=XvNwiMLEqXI.

Connolly, K. & Shenker, J. (2009). The headscarf martyr: Murder in German court sparks Egyptian fury. *The Guardian*. Retrieved from http://www.guardian.co.uk/world/2009/jul/07/german-trial-hijab-murder-egypt.

Ghazali, A. S. (n.d.). *Islam & Muslims in the post-9/11 America*. Abdus Sattar Ghazali.

Ghumman, S. & Jackson, L. (2010). The downside of religious attire: The Muslim headscarf and expectations of obtaining employment. *Journal of Organizational Behavior, 31*, 4–23.

Huffington Post. (2011, June 27). Hani Khan: Woman "shocked" over Abercrombie & Fitch headscarf firing. *Huffington Post Religion*. Retrieved from http://www.huffingtonpost.com/2011/06/27/hani-khan-shocked-over-headscarf-firing_n_885621.html.

Ibish, H. (2008). *Report on hate crimes and discrimination against Arab American, 2003–2007*. Retrieved from http://www.issuelab.org/resource/20032007_report_on_hate_crimes_and_discrimination_against_arab_americans.

Muslim discrimination on campus. (2009). YouTube. Retrieved from http://www.youtube.com/watch?v=4mDD1_rdUL4&feature=related.

Robinson, R. (forthcoming). Sexuality, difference, and American hijabi fashion bloggers. In A. Piela (Ed.), *Muslim women digital geographies*. Leiden, the Netherlands: Brill Publishers.

HINDUISM

Hinduism is one of the world's oldest, largest, and most complex religions. The precise date of foundation is difficult to ascertain, leading some scholars and devotees to refer to the religion as *sanatana dharma*, meaning "the eternal teaching." This alternative name seems more appropriate considering the word *Hindu* is a Persian word meaning "Indian." In addition to having difficulty determining a precise date of establishment and agreeing upon a proper name for the religion, Hinduism also lacks a central founding or prophetic figure that was responsible for revealing the faith to the world. These issues have not hindered Hinduism from attracting adherents or spreading throughout the world. Although the Hindu religion remains largely concentrated within the Indian subcontinent and greater area, there are also significant Hindu communities in North America, the Middle East, Africa, and Europe (Pew Forum, 2012, p. 28). In a recent estimation, there are over one billion Hindus worldwide, placing Hinduism as the third largest religion in the world following Christianity and Islam (Pew Forum, 2012, p. 9). However, despite the vast size and diversity of the religion, there remains a common purpose shared by all Hindus.

The primary or ultimate goal in Hinduism is to adhere to *dharma*, or one's religious or moral duties, in order to achieve *moksha*, or liberation from the cycle of rebirth. Typically, before one is liberated from the cycle of rebirth, one is reincarnated several times. The notion of liberation is associated with *karma* or actions, with emphasis on the cause and effect of one's actions in life and its effect on future lives. The quality of these future lives is determined by one's *karma*, with positive actions or *punya* resulting in rewards in this life or the next, and negative actions or *papa* producing punishment. In order to achieve complete liberation, one must essentially have no *karma*, which in turn dissolves the *jivatman* or individual personality, allowing the *atman* or divine essence to return to *Brahman*, the absolute reality and truth. This focus on the individual's personal actions should not give the impression that Hinduism does not provide an important role for deities.

There are countless gods and goddesses in Hinduism, but Hindus do not worship every single god and goddess within the pantheon. Instead, Hindus worship the Supreme Being, who takes on the form of different deities. Of the many deities, there are three gods that are particularly recognized in Hinduism. The Hindu *trimurti* or trinity is comprised of Brahma, the creator god; Vishnu, the sustainer god; and Shiva, the recreator god (Narayanan, 2010, p. 51). In addition to the *trimurti*, there are several other deities that are popular among Hindus, including Sarasvati, the goddess of wisdom and consort of Brahma; Lakshmi, the goddess of fortune and the consort of Vishnu; Parvati, known as the goddess and consort of Shiva; and Ganesha, the beloved elephant-headed deity (Narayanan, 2010, pp. 47–50). In order to worship these gods and goddesses, Hindus will often create shrines of various sizes within their own homes. This practice of *puja* or devotion provides Hindus with an opportunity to venerate their chosen god or goddess within the comfort of their own homes. The diversity of the Hindu pantheon is complemented with a rich corpus of sacred literature that continues to inspire and guide Hindus today.

In Hinduism, the most sacred texts are the *Vedas*, a term meaning "knowledge" in Sanskrit. The earliest Veda was composed between 1500 and 1200 BCE, though there are several early and later dates put forward by scholars. In contrast to other Hindu texts, the Vedas are often referred to as *shruti* or "that which was heard" (Narayanan,

2010, p. 36). The Vedas are comprised of four different collections, including the *Rig Veda*, *Sama Veda*, *Yajur Veda*, and *Atharva Veda* (Knott, 1998, p. 16). Each of the four Vedas are divided into four parts, including the *Samhitas* containing a series of hymns, the *Brahmanas* describing proper sacrificial rites, the *Aranyakas* offering a mystical explanation of the previous two sections, and the *Upanishads* comprised of divine teachings imparted to several sages over the centuries. These revealed texts are supplemented with other texts known *smrti* or "that which is remembered" (Narayanan, 2010, p. 43). The *smrti* texts include the two major epics of the *Ramayana* and the *Mahabharata*. Within the *Mahabharata* is the famous *Bhagavad Gita* or the "Song of the Lord." The *Bhagavad Gita* recounts the discussion between a warrior named Arjuna and his charioteer, Krishna, an avatar of Vishnu. In this discussion, Krishna emphasizes the importance of doing one's religious duty even in the face of adversity. The two major epics are accompanied by the *Puranas*, which contain mythological tales about the various gods and goddesses. There are also the six *darshanas* or religious-philosophical schools in Hinduism, one of which is the famous yoga school. While the scriptural works and philosophical traditions of Hinduism garner significant scholarly and popular attention, the festivals and celebrations in Hinduism are also of great interest.

In Hinduism, there are several festivals and holy days that are celebrated throughout the globe. One of the most conspicuous festivals on the Hindu liturgical calendar is *Holi*, celebrated in the spring. In order to commemorate an evil king's son's conversion, Hindus celebrate Holi by throwing vibrantly colored powder in the air. Another festival of importance is *Divali* or *Dipavali*, the festival of lights. On this occasion, which typically occurs in the fall, Hindus will display lights around their homes and exchange gifts. There are also other festivals that celebrate one god or goddess, including *Shivaratri* for Shiva, *Krishna Janamashtami* for Krishna, *Ganesh Chaturthi* for Ganesha, and *Navaratri* or "Nine Nights" for the Goddess (Knott, 1998, pp. 61–62). While these more social aspects of the religion are joyous occasions, Hinduism is still consumed by a controversial social system that continues to attract attention and invite criticism.

The social order of Hindu society has been historically defined by a rigid caste system that describes the duties of and relationship between members of the faith. The origins of the classes or *varnas* can be traced to the *purusa* or cosmic body that was dissected by the gods into four parts. The head is associated with the Brahmin or priestly class, the arms represent the Kshatriya or ruling class, the legs signify the Vaishya or merchant class, and the feet are linked with the Shudra or peasant class. There are also the untouchables who do not belong to one of the four classes but comprise 20 percent of Indian society. The untouchables, also called *dalits* or "oppressed" and *harijan* or "children of God," are viewed as being religiously unclean or polluted (Young, 2010, p. 64). The untouchables are still ostracized, harassed, and violently attacked, despite the existence of laws to protect them from these crimes. It is uncertain as to whether the caste system will dissipate in the near future or remain a feature of modern Hinduism.

In the future, Hindu beliefs, social mores, and rituals will likely remain a defining feature of Indian society. However, the religion is challenged from both sides of the spectrum. On one hand, the reformers wish to distance themselves from the more contentious belief systems and abolish the more antiquated and exclusionary practices that remain in Hindu society. On the other hand, the traditionalists vigorously strive to preserve their religious identity by retaining the beliefs and rituals practiced by their ancestors. Hinduism will endure the challenges posed by these two forces considering that this struggle has emerged before in the long history of this ancient faith.

John Cappucci

References

Knott, K. (1998). *Hinduism: A very short introduction*. Oxford: Oxford University Press.

Narayanan, V. (2010). Hindu traditions. In W. G. Oxtoby & R. C. Amore (Eds.), *World religions: Eastern traditions* (pp. 28–103). Don Mills, ON: Oxford University Press.

Pew Forum on Religion & Public Life. (2012). The global religious landscape: A report on the size and distribution of the world's major religious groups as of 2010. Washington, DC: Pew Forum on Religion & Public Life. Retrieved from http://www.pewforum.org/2012/12/18/global-religious-landscape-exec/.

Young, W. A. (2010). *The world's religions: Worldviews and contemporary issues* (3rd ed.). Upper Saddle River, NJ: Prentice Hall.

Additional Reading

Bhaskarananda, S. (1994). *The essentials of Hinduism: A comprehensive overview of the world's oldest religion*. Seattle: Viveka Press.

Flood, G. (1996). *An introduction to Hinduism*. Cambridge: Cambridge University Press.

Fowler, J. (1997). *Hinduism: Beliefs and practices*. Brighton, UK: Sussex Academic Press.

Pandit, B. (1998). *The Hindu mind: Fundamentals of Hindu religion and philosophy for all ages* (3rd ed). Glen Ellyn, IL: B & V Enterprises.

Rodrigues, H. P. (2006). *Introducing Hinduism*. New York: Routledge.

Zaehner, R. C. (1966). *Hinduism* (2nd ed.). Oxford: Oxford University Press.

HIP-HOP MUSIC AND CULTURE

The first thing that is important to remember about hip-hop is that hip-hop is more than just music. Hip-hop is a culture. Richie Colon, also known as Crazy Legs and a member of the world-renowned New York break-dancing team, the Rock Steady Crew, asserts there are four elements of hip-hop: graffiti, b-boying, DJ'ing, and rap (also known as MC-ing or master of ceremonies) (Colon in Malone, 2003). Although commonly thought of as rap music, hip-hop music and culture has evolved into one of the most popular art forms in the world. In the words of the influential MC KRS-One, "Rap is something you do, Hip Hop is something you live!" (KRS-One, 2010, track 2).

History

Although there are others, it is commonly accepted that there are three founding fathers of hip-hop: Clive Campbell, Kool DJ Herc; Joseph Saddler, Grandmaster Flash; and Afrika Bambaataa, collectively known as Herc, Flash, and Bam. Bam is credited for the phrase *hip-hop* (George, 2012). Hip-hop music and culture evolved during the 1970s in Bronx, New York, by disenfranchised youth who suffered from school fine arts cutbacks. Bam, a former gang member, was inspired to organize a gang truce in New York after visiting Zulu chieftains in Africa. Once back in the states, Bam promoted hip-hop as a way for youth and gang members to have a positive creative outlet (George, 2012). Zulu Nation embraced all ethnicities in the five boroughs of New York, bringing together a multicultural collective of innovation, creativity, and love that is hip-hop music and culture and that has influenced the world.

Graffiti

While graffiti has been around for centuries, the genesis of the stylistic approach to large spray-painted art pieces on subway trains that influenced what came to be known as hip-hop graffiti art was influenced by Taki 183. In addition to his prolific bombing, Taki's popularity was largely due to the 1971 *New York Times* article "'Taki 183' Spawns Pen Pals." It was one of the first articles ever written about the aesthetics of graffiti art, and it brought national attention to the genre. Just one year later, in 1972, the *New York Times* printed an article about a public war on graffiti by New York City officials including Mayor John Lindsay. Demonized in society, the top graffiti artists became so popular in the underground that they were recruited to design flyers for hip-hop parties (George, 2012). Soon, graffiti writers, also known as "taggers," strived to "get up" All-City. That meant having their spray can art pieces on subway trains that went all over the city. Notoriety is important to youth who are otherwise ignored by society. Taggers received street credit for volume (the amount of graffiti), size, and color as well as the degree of difficulty or danger it took to get their pieces on subway trains, overpasses, and buildings. Later in 1980, the *New York Times* printed another article about a newer generation of graffiti artists—NE, T-Kid, and emerging hip-hop graffiti artist Seen, who was the subject of the first ever hip-hop documentary *Style Wars*.

Style Wars brought national attention to hip-hop graffiti art. However, in 1981 the *New York Times* printed additional articles detailing how patrol dogs and barbed wire were used in an attempt to curb graffiti painters (Castleman, 2012). The anger toward graffiti, coupled with the simultaneous appreciation, mirrors hip-hop itself. Just as controversial as it was in New York, hip-hop graffiti art has become popular all over the globe. Hip-Hop graffiti art is found on buildings, cars, clothing, CD covers, and sometimes even in art galleries. Graffiti pushed the boundaries of what is considered nuisance and what is considered art.

B-boying

The movie *Flashdance* was released in 1983 and featured a scene with members of the New York dance group the Rock Steady Crew break dancing in the park. The world has not been the same since. While hip-hop dance moves commonly known as "break dancing" imploded in New York in the 1970s, hip-hop and break dancing exploded across the United States and then internationally. Break dancing's popularity waned in the United States in the 1990s, but in places such as England, France, Germany, Japan, and Korea, it never stopped. Performed by b-boys (and b-girls), break dancing is a dance done both standing up and spinning on the ground. B-boys often use flattened-out, large paper boxes as makeshift dance floors whenever smooth surfaces are unavailable. Herc coined the phrase *b-boy*—short for *break*—when he called dancers, who were waiting on the side of the crowd, to perform as he repeated the drum breaks of songs back and forth between two turntables (George, 2012). This technique extended the time b-boys could form circles and dance with flair and exuberance in a manner that would be impossible in a regular dance crowd. B-boys substituted actual fights with dance competitions to represent their neighborhoods and to gain respect. The "uprock" (fancy moves done in a rocking fashion), the "downrock" (fancy footwork done with hands on the floor), and the "backspin" (also called the "windmill," where dancers spin in rapid circles on their backs) are just some of the moves commonly associated with b-boying.

Hip-hop resists a separation between stage and audience, and crowds often stand around performers in circles. This is largely because, in hip-hop, the audience is part of the performance and not just spectators. Clapping, chanting, shouting, and nodding your head to the rhythm of the dancers as well as the DJ are part of the collective energy that is hip-hop music and culture. The only rule in a break dance circle is that you allow others to take a turn.

DJ-ing

In 1974, Flash said he stopped a vinyl record on a turntable with his hand to manipulate the sound of the music (George, 2012). This seemingly accidental act gave birth to the idea that a turntable could be used as an instrument. The early days of hip-hop were outdoors in parks and block parties. Innovation was not only common; it was a necessary part of the process. DJs had to set up outside wherever they could, often making their own equipment from scratch and "borrowing" power from whatever electrical source they could find (George, 2012). Laptops, iPads, MIDI, DJ software, and MP3 files did not exist at the birth of hip-hop, and DJs had to carry large, plastic crates of records from event to event. Unlike at a nightclub, people did not pay to come and listen to a DJ at a park; if the crowd did not like the music, they were free to walk away. In the early days of hip-hop, a DJ's skill was based on how many different records were played in an hour. Hip-hop DJs are accountable for not only keeping the past alive by playing records that were popular in the past (old school), they are also responsible for playing what is currently popular and new (new school). For example, Herc used his Jamaican roots as an influence for the musical selections he played, often mixing African-influenced music with popular R&B. He also used the Jamaican oratory style of toasting, bragging, and rhythmic chanting when he talked on the microphone. In fact, during the beginning of hip-hop, DJs were the MC's, the forerunner of the rapper. DJs were the ones responsible for motivating the crowd and generating the excitement. As DJ-ing equipment became more available and techniques more complicated, an additional person was needed as a voice of hip-hop, hence the rapper was born (George, 2012). Today, DJ-ing has remained the centerpiece of influence and musicology on which hip-hop culture spins. Just as a good DJ in the past had to know his audience's wants and needs, as well as the right time to let the b-boys dance, the modern DJ must be able to read a crowd in order to select the right music for an ever-changing audience with diverging musical tastes.

Part of hip-hop's popularity is its musical adaptability. African drums playing over an R&B guitar riff, jazz piano, and bass played simultaneously with Gregorian vocal chants, even Asian harvest prayers sung over conga beats, are all acceptable in hip-hop. In fact, hip-hop music questions what is considered music and what is not. Popular cultural critics and professors of hip-hop culture describe sampling in hip-hop music as "postmodernist activity that merges disparate musical forms to communicate an artistic message" (Dyson, 1993, p. 67). Taking small samples from many different songs and putting them together into a new creation challenges whether a recording on vinyl or CD is actually a finished product or merely open to be reinterpreted into another musical collage.

Rap

While it has been argued that the 1979 release of Sugarhill Gang's "Rapper's Delight" (Sugarhill Gang, 1979, track 1) was not the first rap recording, one thing that critics agree on is that it was the first popularly successful rap record. Consequently, "Rapper's Delight" is one of the most influential rap songs in history. Almost everyone knows at least the first few lines of the song, "I said a hip-hop, hippie to the hippie, the hip, hip a hop, and you don't stop, a rock it to the bang bang boogie, say, up jump the boogie, to the rhythm of the boogie, the beat (Sugarhill Gang, 1979, track 1). Rappers have been compared to the African grio, travelers who carry messages and cultural stories and news from place to place; shamans, who help us to remember the past; and signifiers, who help people understand what is and what is not important in life. The hip-hop rapper is, in some ways, all of these and more. Originally, a rapper was called an MC, which is short for either "master of ceremonies" or one who's moving a crowd (George, 2012). Rapping is rhythmical rhyming to the tempo and rhythm of a musical beat. The two most commonly used examples in hip-hop are the last words of a verse in a sentence being emphasized and syllables stressed within a verse. Distinct and separate from spoken word, rap is performed to either music or a steady beat.

Rappers talk about many things, but they often talk about what they know. While "Rapper's Delight" (1979) was primarily a dance/party rap song, rap music quickly became known for being laced with razor-sharp realism. In 1982, Grandmaster Flash and the Furious Five released a record called the "The Message," which was a social commentary on living in urban New York (Grandmaster Flash and the Furious Five, 1982, track 1). By 1988, West Coast rap group N.W.A. released *Straight Out of Compton* (N.W.A., 1988, track 1) about living in Los Angeles. N.W.A., along with Public Enemy, characterized the serious, and often militant, tenor of rap music that is characteristic of West Coast rap. What brought public attention to the differing styles of East Coast and West Coast rap was the 1991 video for the songs "You Could Be Mine" and "Live and Let Die," in which rock 'n' roll artist Axl Rose wore a N.W.A. baseball cap (Raul, 2010). When music executives realized that N.W.A. had sold hundreds of records out of the trunk of their cars, commercialization, including the labeling of East Coast/West Coast styles, became prominent. Oversimplified into rivalries between East Coast rapper Biggie and West Coast rapper Tupac (although born in New York), hip-hop acknowledges regional identification but rejects being boxed into East/West classifications. Since the 1970s, distinct lyrical and music styles have been identified from the South, Chicago, St. Louis, and Florida. Currently, rap music in France, Germany, and Korea are also characterized by not only party music but also the U.S. style of social commentary of their local communities. In fact, Princeton University professor Imani Perry explains that the MC is "the everyman or everywoman of his or her [neighbor]hood" (Perry, 2012, p. 504).

The Future of Hip-hop

Bakari Kitwana (2002), former editor of the acknowledged authority on hip-hop culture and youth politics, *Source Magazine*, describes five ways that hip-hop could become a formal, unified front. First, it can challenge the American political system to challenge race relations and elect more black officials. Since the first African American president, Barack Obama, was elected to the White House in 2009, this seems more like a prediction than a suggestion. In fact, President Obama has been called the president of the hip-hop generation. In the words of rapper Ice-T, "Rap made Barak Obama the president. If it wasn't for rap, white people wouldn't have been so open to vote for somebody like Barack Obama" (2012). Second, it can use its multiethnic appeal to narrow racial divides outside of the United States. Third, hip-hop artists can pool their resources together to help strengthen local communities. Fourth, it can encourage rap artists to be more socially responsible. Finally, hip-hop can do more, in regard to economic development, to benefit those who created the genre as well as those who make the music (Kitwana, 2002).

Since hip-hop was created by American youth from many ethnicities who were reacting against social and economic conditions, the popularity of hip-hop is unlikely to diminish any time soon. When it began, few people believed hip-hop would be around for more than five years, let alone fifty-five. Hip-hop is appealing because of its adaptability, its hybridity, and its ability to be made expressively in multiple contexts. Visual, physical, musical, and auditory, hip-hop music and culture speak to many artistic styles simultaneously. More than just music, hip-hop music and culture are a reflection of life imitating art.

Theodore S. Ransaw

References

Belafonte, H. & Picker, D. (Producers). (1984). *Beat street* [Motion Picture]. Los Angeles: Orion Pictures.

Castleman, C. (2012). The politics of graffiti: Hip-hop founding fathers speak the truth. In M. Forman and M. Anthony Neal (Eds.), *That's the joint!: The hip-hop studies reader* (2nd ed., pp. 14–21). New York: Routledge.

Chalfant, H. & Silver, T. (Producers). (1983). *Style wars* [Documentary]. Brooklyn, NY: Public Art Films.

Dyson, M. E. (1993). African American cultural criticism. In M. Forman and M. Anthony Neal (Eds.), *That's the joint!: The hip-hop studies reader* (1st ed., pp. 61–68). New York: Routledge.

George, N. (2012). Hip-hop's founding fathers speak the truth. In M. Forman and M. Anthony Neal (Eds.), *That's the joint!: The Hip-hop studies reader* (2nd ed., pp. 44–55). New York: Routledge.

Grandmaster Flash and the Furious Five. (1982). *The message.* (Vinyl). Raleigh, NC: Sugar Hill Records.

Ice-T. (June, 2012). *The art of rap* [Television broadcast]. Today Show: MSNBC.

Kitwana, B. (2002). *The hip-hop generation: Young blacks and the crisis in African American culture.* New York: Basic Books.

KRS-One. (2010). Hip hop vs. rap lyrics. On *Sound of da police.* (Vinyl). London: Zomba Label Group.

Lyne, A. (Producer). (1983). *Flashdance* [Motion Picture]. Hollywood, CA: Paramount Pictures.

Malone, B. (2003, August). Chief rocka. *The Source Magazine: The Magazine of Hip-Hop Music, Culture & Politics (15th Anniversary Jumpoff), 167,* 130–33.

New York Times. (1971, July). "Taki 183" spawns pen pals. *New York Times.*

N.W.A. (1987). *Straight outta Compton.* (Vinyl). Compton, CA: Ruthless Records.

Perry, I. (2012). My mic sounds nice: Art, community, and consciousness. In M. Forman and M. Anthony Neal (Eds.), *That's the joint!: The hip-hop studies reader* (2nd ed., pp. 504–17). New York: Routledge.

Raul. (2010, January 15). Dr. Dre was shocked when Axl Rose wore N.W.A. hat in video. *Feelnumb.* Retrieved from http://www.feelnumb.com/2010/01/15/dr-dre-was-shocked-when-axl-rose-wore-nwa-hat-in-video/.

Sugarhill Gang. (1979). *Rappers delight.* (Vinyl). Raleigh, NC: Sugar Hill Records.

HISPANIC

Hispanic: Un Mestizaje

The task of defining or determining criteria for an identity is always difficult. For some, it is where you have come from, for others it is where you are now, and others will argue, it is both the past and the present—shaped by the journey. The following entry offers three distinct perspectives on the Hispanic identity. The first one celebrates the cultural *mestizaje*, or mixture of the identity; the second uses an historical lens to trace a more distinct development of the identity and its shifts; and the third questions the political implications of the term *Hispanic.*

What does it mean to be Hispanic? In order to answer this question, one must first come to understand the significance of *mestizaje*—a mixture of cultures—and its relationship to the syncretic experiences of the diverse groups of people from Mexico, Puerto Rico, Cuba, Central or South America, and their encounters with one another, and with those of Spain, Portugal, and the United States of America. This new identity, that bares no common characteristics, but instead is what Anzaldúa (1999) referred to as a "transcendence of dualities," occurred through colonization and postcolonization (p. 102). Using this lens of *mestizaje*, it is evident that this cultural practice takes on multiple subjectivities. Garcia's (2005) work continues with this notion of multiplicities, arguing that the identity of Hispanics cannot be defined by any particular characteristics. Instead, he points out that the Hispanic identity is one that has resulted from a mixing of different racial and cultural elements that coexist with the original racial and cultural identity that existed before the hybridization occurred.

Another consideration for understanding the meaning of Hispanic takes an historical perspective. Although criticized for its simplicity, Tammelleo (2011) suggests a before-during-after approach. In "Continuity and Change in Hispanic Identity," he traces three significant historical periods that contribute to developing the Hispanic identity: (1) colonization, (2) nationalization, and (3) immigration. Beginning with the Colonial Hispanic identity, Tammelleo concentrates on the "submission of the people of Latin America" (p. 541). The identity then changed to that of a National Hispanic identity due to "the Latin American wars of liberation that resulted in the creation of independent nation states starting in the 1820s" (p. 541). Now in its current state, Tammelleo argues that the Hispanic identity has actually changed. With historical ties to the Treaty of Guadalupe, the Mexican American War, and the Spanish American War, he points out that the immigration of Hispanics created a new Latino/a identity.

Similar to Tammelleo, Alcoff (2005) takes a historical approach to tracing the development of the Hispanic identity, but with a more political focus. For her, 1898 represents a significant shift in the colonial rule of Latin America, from that of Spain to the United States. Alcoff (2005) argues that by using the term *Hispanic* to refer to a group of diverse people, it causes them to be "de-nationalized, de-linked, to the multi-national region of the world that represents the group history . . . and that, to the extent it reminds us evocatively of a colonialism" (p. 441). Her research found that *Hispanic* is a term that is preferred by the political right and is favored by the Anglo middle class. She also emphasizes that the continuation of using the term *Hispanic*, as a means of identity, may cause a loss in political unity and will perpetuate the current colonial rule by the United States.

Exploring the meaning of the term *Hispanic* uncovered neither a specific answer nor a common set of properties that one could use to identify an individual, much less a group of people. This is because the Hispanic identity is one that has been formed, and continues to still be formed, by a hybridization of cultures in the context of dynamic and life-changing historical events associated with colonization of new worlds and new experiences. For some, the Hispanic identity is that of a family whose identity changes with every new addition of a member. For others, it is an identity in flux that is influenced and shaped by historical events and political agendas of colonial power. Regardless of which one is more appropriate or accurate, the fact still remains that the Hispanic identity is *un mestizaje*.

Estanislado S. Barrera, IV
Angelica M. Fuentes

References

Alcoff, L. M. (2005). Latino vs. Hispanic: The politics of ethnic names. *Philosophy & Social Criticism, 31*(4), 395–407. doi: 10.1177/0191453705052972

Anzaldúa, G. (1999). *Borderlands/La frontera: The new mestiza* (2nd ed.). San Francisco, CA: Aunt Lute.

Garcia, J. (2005). *Surviving race, ethnicity, and nationality: A challenge for the 21st century.* Oxford, England: Rowman & Littlefield.

Tammelleo, S. (2011). Continuity and change in Hispanic identity. *Ethnicities, 11*(4), 536–54. doi: 10.1177/468796811419058

HISPANIC AMERICAN CULTURES

Cultural Complexities: Understanding Hispanic American Cultures

Individuals and groups of individuals constantly create and recreate culture and cultural meanings. Spradley (1980) has observed that culture is derived from patterns in behavior, actions, talk, and tools that people from a setting have learned or created.

Culture is reflected in what groups of individuals have collectively deemed appropriate and acceptable, which is ever changing. Over time, individuals interpret their experiences, and in turn, produce behaviors. Individuals share these experiences and behaviors with other individuals, and then collectively experiences are interpreted and behaviors are produced.

Hispanic American cultures are complex and multileveled. Hispanic Americans are comprised of different types of people from different countries, races, and historical and political backgrounds. There is no one culture shared among Hispanic Americans, but rather a multitude of cultures among a multitude of different Hispanic groups that coexist in the Americas and more specifically, the United States. Communities of different groups of Hispanic Americans who share commonalities produce culture. Among the many groups of Hispanic Americans, culture is reflected in their behavior, actions, talk, and tools.

In the U.S. context, *Hispanic* generally refers to anyone of Latin American or Spanish heritage. The term *Hispanic* is rather new to the U.S. political landscape. In the 1970 U.S. Census, the only two racial identifying terms were *White* and *Negro*. The term *Negro* was also reported as *Negro/Other*. The term *Hispanic* was not included in the 1970 U.S. Census. In the "Origins" section of the 1970 census, respondents could choose among several "Spanish" origins (Mexican, Puerto Rican, Cuban, Central or South American, or Other Spanish). In an effort to capture a more disaggregated picture of the U.S. population in the 1980 U.S. Census, the term *Hispanic* was introduced as a partner descriptor to the racial identifying term *Spanish*. According to the 1980 U.S. Census, a person is of "Spanish/Hispanic" origin or descent if the person identifies his or her ancestry with one of the listed groups—that is, Mexican, Puerto Rican, Cuban, Central or South American, or other Spanish. Origin or descent may be viewed as the nationality group, the lineage, or the country in which the person or the person's parents or ancestors were born.

Even though Hispanics are often referred to in a general sense, they are heterogeneous in almost every sense. However, one common identifying factor among Hispanic groups is the use of the Spanish language, but more recently, there has been a focus on groups of Hispanics, mostly second- and third-generation U.S. citizens who do not speak Spanish, or rather speak variations of Spanish, such as code-switching and border Spanish.

One way to aid in defining American Hispanic cultures is to consider the work of postcolonial theorist Bhabha (1995), who stated that when two cultures, usually the colonizer and the colonized, are brought together in identity, hybridity occurs. He defined *hybridity* as a "third space," where heterogeneous lifestyles and practices coexist with homogenizing everyday scenarios of everyday life, and where there is no "originality" or "purity" of cultures. These cultures have "no primordial unity or fixity," but instead have a fluidity of movement from all sides (p. 208). The "third space" that Bhabha identified consists of an ongoing struggle or shifts of cultures. A pure Hispanic American culture does not exist. Language, socioeconomic status, assimilation, acculturation, history, and more all play into the "fluidity" of cultures that belong to the many groups of Hispanic Americans. Defining Hispanic Americans involves a multitude of factors. At what point did an individual, who is considered Hispanic American, enter the United States, and under what conditions? Was the Hispanic American born in the United States, and if so, was he or she born to U.S. citizens, recent immigrants, or non-U.S. citizens? At what level did the Hispanic American assimilate to other cultures, or was acculturation at play?

American Hispanic cultures exhibit varying levels of assimilation. To illustrate this point, Rumbaut (1997) found minorities, such as Hispanic Americans, shifted toward an identity reflecting their national origin, even for those born in the United States, and aligned to their parents' immigrant nationality, rather than assimilating American identities. Rumbaut argued that a turn away from assimilative American identities indicated a rise in ethnic identification. While reflecting on the experiences of white European immigrants and their descendants in the United States, Rumbaut suggested that ethnicity can be "optional and recede into the social twilight" as it did for white Europeans, or it can be a "resilient resource, or an engulfing master status" (p. 501). Ethnic and cultural identity-seeking processes happen at varying degrees among Hispanic Americans, which, in turn, influence culture.

Angelica M. Fuentes
Estanislado S. Barrera, IV

References

Bhabha, H. K. (1995). Cultural diversity and cultural differences. In B. Ashcroft, G. Griffiths, & H. Triffin (Eds.), *The post-colonial studies reader* (pp. 206–9). London, England: Routledge.

Rumbaut, R. G. (1997). Paradoxes (and orthodoxies) of assimilation. *Sociological Perspectives*, *40*(3), 483–511.

Spradley, J. (1980). *Participant observation*. Fort Worth, TX: Harcourt Brace Jovanovich.

U.S. Census Bureau. (1970). General population characteristics. *Census of Population and Housing*. Washington, DC: U.S. Government Printing Office. Retrieved from https://archive.org/details/1970censusofhous00unit.

U.S. Census Bureau. (1980). *1980 Census of population: Characteristics of the population*. Washington, DC: U.S. Government Printing Office. Retrieved from http://www.archive.org/details/1980censusofpopu8011u.

HOMOPHOBIA

Homophobia refers to antigay attitudes or behaviors. Coined in the late 1960s by psychologist George Weinberg, the term is meant to encompass the fear, dislike, or hatred of gays and lesbians, of being perceived as gay, or of one's own gay desires or behaviors. Homophobia tends to exist most strongly in cultures that hold strict expectations and stereotypes regarding gender and sexuality. Homophobic individuals see any deviance from these norms as a threat to the social order. In recent years, some individuals and organizations, including the Associated Press, have criticized the word *homophobia* for its clinical or pathological roots and implied diagnosis, and have suggested terms such as *antigay*, *sexual prejudice*, or *heterosexual bias* as replacements.

Antigay attitudes or behaviors can be institutionalized, interpersonal, or internalized. Institutionalized homophobia refers to heterosexist biases embedded in social organizations or institutions;

for example, a school's tolerance of antigay language or legislation that denies same-sex couples the right to marry. In 2013, seventy-seven countries have laws that criminalize sexual activity between lesbian, gay, bisexual, or transgender people. These countries are most commonly located in less developed nations in and around the Middle East, Southeast Asia, and Africa. Interpersonal homophobia includes name calling, physical harassment, and "gender policing." For example, the use of antigay language such as "that's so gay," or calling someone a "fag" or "dyke," overtly expresses homophobia, as does physical, relational, or verbal sexuality-based bullying. Gender policing refers to the monitoring and enforcement of normative gender expressions (the idea that men should look and act traditionally masculine and that women should look and act in a traditionally feminine role). Hate crimes or violent attacks on individuals who are, or are perceived to be gay or lesbian, are another form of interpersonal homophobia. While reasons for such attacks vary, some common explanations for such behaviors are to demonstrate one's heterosexuality, as a form of male bonding, to purge one's own same-sex desires, or for thrill-seeking motivations. Finally, internalized homophobia refers to the fear, hatred, or dislike of one's own same-sex desires or behaviors, such as having low self-esteem because of one's sexuality.

Homophobic expressions can be overt or covert. Many of the above examples are overt expressions of homophobia, including physical violence or laws that prevent gays and lesbians from enjoying full equality. However, much homophobia is hidden, sometimes invisible, and includes what some scholars and activists have called "microaggressions." Sue (2010, xv) defines *microaggressions* as "the constant and continuing everyday reality of slights, insults, invalidations, and indignities visited upon marginalized groups" that express prejudice and discrimination, often inadvertently or unconsciously. For example, assuming a woman is in a relationship with a man may be well intentioned, but it reinforces heteronormativity and may make a woman who does not identify as heterosexual uncomfortable revealing her sexuality. Similarly, microaggressions also occur when individuals assume that all gay men or lesbians are alike or share particular characteristics.

Many scholars have argued that such microaggressions are just as damaging to those who identify as LGBT as overt expressions of homophobia.

Homophobia has many negative implications. On a micro level, gay and lesbian individuals are at greater risk for depression, loneliness, increased drug use, suicide, isolation, and difficultly in school. On a larger scale, homophobia has negative impacts on the economy. Victims of homophobia are at risk for lower rates of education, poorer health outcomes, and poverty, which can lead to low labor force participation and higher health care costs.

Many factors are related to whether someone is homophobic, but there is a strong correlation between homophobia and a general lack of support for equality between men and women. In terms of demographics, homophobia is more common among men, older people, those with less education, and those residing in geographic areas where negative attitudes represent the norm (for example, rural areas or the midwestern or southern United States). Homophobia is also correlated with frequent religious service attendance and orthodox religious beliefs, such as belief in the literal truth of the Bible. About personality and attitudinal characteristics, homophobic individuals are more likely to display higher levels of psychological authoritarianism and describe themselves as less sexually permissive. Similarly, they tend to hold rigid sex-stereotyped beliefs and "traditional" family beliefs, generally do not support equality between the sexes, and are more supportive of traditional gender roles. Homophobic individuals are more likely to believe that a lesbian or gay sexual orientation is freely chosen, and they are less likely to have had close, personal friends or family members who are openly lesbian or gay.

In the United States, acceptance of LGBT individuals has been increasing over time. The General Social Survey (GSS) has included questions to measure attitudes toward sexual relations between two adults of the same sex for over forty years According to the GSS, in 1980, over 70 percent of Americans believed that same-sex relationships were "always wrong" and only 14 percent believed them to be "not wrong at all." Thirty years later, in 2010, just 43 percent of the population believed same-sex relationships to be "always wrong" while 40 percent believed them to be "not wrong at all."

Mary Nell Trautner
Meghan Murphy

Additional Reading

Nagoshi, J. L., Adams, K. A., Terrell, H. K., Hill, E. D., Brzuzy, S., and Nagoshi, C. T. (2008). Gender differences in correlates of homophobia and transphobia. *Sex Roles*, 59, 521–31.

Pharr, S. (1997). Homophobia: A weapon of sexism. Berkeley, CA: Chardon Press.

Sue, D. W. (2010). Microaggressions in everyday life: Race, gender, and sexual orientation. Hoboken, NJ: John Wiley & Sons.

HOUSING DISCRIMINATION

Housing discrimination takes many forms. It occurs when an individual or family is hindered from or denied the ability to finance, buy, rent, or sell a home based on race, gender, class, religion, national origin, familial status, and disability. Primarily, such discrimination has the harmful effects of housing and spatial inequality and segregation—certain groups are isolated, having a less desirable space, and less of it. The impact, however, does not stop there. It precipitates exclusion from high-quality schools and vital public services and causes exposure to higher rates of crime. Consequently, it exacerbates disparities in education, health, and wealth between groups. Further, property acquisition, typically a tool used to build wealth, has the inverse effect of stripping wealth from minority homeowners who are disproportionately faced with predatory loans or loan terms.

To understand the prevalence of housing discrimination, one can look at the number of complaints reported by the U.S. Department of Housing and Urban Development (HUD), by state and local Fair Housing Assistance Program (FHAP) agencies, and the Department of Justice (DOJ). A conservative estimate puts the occurrence of such discrimination at four million every year. It is important to note, however, that this data only reflects instances of housing discrimination that are reported (*Modernizing the Fair Housing Act*, 2013). HUD, in years past, estimated that less than 1 percent of violations of fair housing laws were reported.

History of Housing Discrimination Legislation

> A racially restrictive covenant is an agreement entered into by a group of property owners, subdivision developers, or real estate operators in a given neighborhood, binding them not to sell, lease, rent, or otherwise convey their property to specified groups because of race, creed, or color unless all agree to the transaction.

Legislation protecting against housing discrimination began to appear in the early 1900s, soon after the abolition of slavery. Upon the institution of Jim Crow laws, the standard of separate and unequal propagated widespread discrimination against racial and ethnic minorities. City and county ordinances enforcing discriminatory practices in housing were prevalent (Klarman, 2004). It wasn't until the landmark case *Buchanan v. Warley* (1917) that the U.S. Supreme Court deemed such racial zoning ordinances unconstitutional. This decision, while quite an advancement in the state of the law, did not apply to private agreements, thus giving rise to racially restrictive covenants.

Following the rise in popularity of restrictive covenants, the advancements in protection against housing discrimination was stagnant for several years. In fact, the Supreme Court ruling in Corrigan v. Buckley (1926) affirmed the legality of such covenants. The Court found that, while states were prohibited from creating race-based legislation, this same prohibition did not apply to private deeds or plat maps containing racial restrictions (Jones-Correa, 2000–2001). The National Housing Act of 1934 also propagated restrictive covenants by introducing the practice of "redlining." This practice essentially designated black neighborhoods as risky or even ineligible for lender support. Land developers, realtors, and current owners were encouraged to institute restrictive covenants to prevent neighborhoods from being redlined (Bratt, Stone, & Hartman, 2006). Redlining flourished yet again with the 1936 creation of the Federal Housing Administration (FHA). The FHA, while touted for revolutionizing home ownership and establishing our current mortgage system, also produced a lending structure that perpetuated segregation and endorsed redlining as part of its underwriting guidelines. The 1938 FHA Underwriting Manual included assumptions about the allure of neighborhood homogeneity and the malignant influence of black home ownership on property values (Jones-Correa, 2000–2001).

More than ten years passed before the Supreme Court decided in *Shelley v. Kraemer* (1948) that racially restrictive covenants were legally unenforceable as they were in violation of the Equal Protection Clause of the Fourteenth Amendment. Despite this ruling, the presence of such covenants was still allowed in private deeds, and their pervasive use continued (Jones-Correa, 2000–2001). The next year, the Housing Act of 1949 set a national goal of providing "a decent home and suitable living environment for every U.S. family." Over ten years later, however, the 1960 census made it apparent that the county was far from realizing this goal. At that time, 46 percent of nonwhites as compared with 14 percent of the white urban population lived in substandard housing. Additionally, over three times as many nonwhites lived in homes that were overcrowded ("The Federal Fair Housing Requirements," 1969).

> Racial steering involves directing white home and apartment seekers into white areas while steering equally creditworthy black prospects into black and racially diverse areas.

Finally, with the Civil Rights Act of 1968, the federal government made a decisive move toward regarding all types of housing discrimination, individual and systematic, as unconstitutional. Title VIII of this Act is known as the Federal Fair Housing Act of 1968 (the Act). The Act unambiguously prohibits specific discriminatory practices such as filtering information about availability, racial steering, blockbusting, and redlining. It applies not only to landlords and real estate companies but also to banks and other lending institutions, municipalities, and homeowners' insurance companies. Many other housing-related activities are also specifically included, such as advertising, zoning, and new construction design.

> Blockbusting techniques included the repeated—often incessant—urging of white homeowners in areas adjacent to or near black communities to sell before it was "too late" and their property values diminished.

The passage of the Act was hard fought, and it ultimately came about when President Lyndon Johnson used the assassination of Reverend Dr. Martin Luther King Jr. as a call to arms—he saw the Act as a fitting tribute and urged congressional approval. While initially focusing on discrimination based on race, color, nationality, and religion, the Act has been amended several times to include other protected classes: gender (1974) and people with disabilities and families with children (1988) ("History of Fair Housing," 2014).

> **Paired-Testing Methodology**
>
> More than eight thousand tests were conducted in a nationally representative sample of twenty-eight metropolitan areas. In each test, two trained individuals—one white and the other black, Hispanic or Asian—contacted a housing provider to inquire about a housing unit randomly selected from recently advertised homes. The two testers in each pair were matched on gender and age, and both presented themselves as equally and unambiguously well qualified. Each tester independently recorded the treatment he/she experienced, including information about all the homes recommended and shown. The test doesn't account for differences in advertising practices that may limit knowledge about available housing options. It also can't measure differences in treatment that might occur after the initial inquiry.

The Current State of Housing Discrimination
Following the passage of the Fair Housing Act of 1968, HUD has conducted several studies in which it meticulously monitored trends in racial and ethnic discrimination in both the housing rental and sales markets. HUD conducted the fourth

such study in 2012 and applied the paired-testing methodology to measure the occurrence and forms of discrimination faced by black, Hispanic, and Asian renters and homebuyers at three stages of their search: (1) ability to make an appointment; (2) availability of units; and (3) agents' willingness to show units. The study shows that the most blatant "door-slamming" discrimination—outright refusal to meet with or provide information about available units, has declined since the first study in 1977, but that other more covert forms persist. Taking all three stages of the home search process into account, minority *renters* were told about and shown fewer homes and apartments than equally qualified whites. Similarly, black and Asian homebuyers were told about and shown fewer homes than equally qualified whites. The overall differences in treatment for Hispanic homebuyers, however, did not prove to be statistically significant (Turner et al., 2013). Findings of other research indicate that when testers pose as more marginally qualified homeseekers, even more discrimination occurs (Hunter & Walker, 1996).

The New Unprotected Classes of Concern

The aforementioned testing, like most fair housing legislation, focuses mainly on discrimination against racial and ethnic minorities, and it does not address discrimination based on source of income, age, sexual orientation, gender identity, or marital status. These classes of people are not protected by the Fair Housing Act and consequently have seen growing incidence of discrimination. While individual states may have protections against such discrimination, there are no federal prohibitions against them.

In 2013, or the first time in history, the Supreme Court heard cases regarding same-sex marriage. This unprecedented occurrence illuminates the fact that issues affecting lesbian, gay, bisexual, and transgendered (LGBT) people are taking a more prevalent position within the political landscape. Accordingly, recent studies have shown a growing trend toward discrimination in the housing market based on LGBT status. Transgender and gender nonconforming people are particularly susceptible to outright housing discrimination and are often forced into homelessness (*Modernizing the Fair Housing Act*, 2013). While not a federal mandate, significant headway was made on March 5, 2012, when HUD established that all housing providers receiving HUD funding are prohibited from discriminating on the basis of sexual orientation or gender identity (Equal Access, 2012).

It is now incumbent upon policymakers, civil rights activists, and organizations to follow in the footsteps of HUD by expanding their focus to include these marginalized groups. Fortunately, the scope of fair housing legislation has expanded over the decades. As recently as March 2013, we celebrated a major advancement—a person claiming discrimination no longer has to prove that the opposing party acted with the intent to discriminate, but now only must show that the practice or act had a discriminatory effect, regardless of the intent (Discriminatory Effect, 2013). Even still, there continues to be room for significant improvements in relevant laws and practices. The Fair Housing Act still has to become more inclusive and adapt to address the patterns of discrimination that persist.

Aminah M. Thompson

References

Bratt, R. G., Stone, M. E., & Hartman, C. (2006). A right to housing: Foundation for a new social agenda. PA: Temple University Press.

Buchanan v. Warley, 245 U.S. 60 (1917).

Corrigan v. Buckley, 271 U.S. 323 (1926).

Discriminatory Effect Standard, Final Rule. 24 C.F.R. pt. 100.500 (February 15, 2013).

Equal Access to Housing in HUD Programs Regardless of Sexual Orientation or Gender Identity 24 C.F.R pts. 5, 200, 203, 236, 400, 570, 574, 882, 891, and 982 (February 3, 2012).

Fair Housing Act, 42 U.S.C. §3601 (1968).

Federal Fair Housing Requirements: Title VIII of the 1968 Civil Rights Act. (1969). *Duke Law Journal 1969, 4:* 733–71. Durham, NC: Duke University School of Law.

History of Fair Housing. (2014). Retrieved December 13, 2013, from http://portal.hud.gov/hudportal/HUD?src=/program_offices/fair_housing_equal_opp/aboutfheo/history.

Hunter, W. & Walker, M. B. (1996). The Cultural Affinity hypothesis and mortgage lending decisions.

Journal of Real Estate Finance and Economics, 13(1), 57–70.

Jones-Correa, M. (Winter 2000–2001). The origins and diffusions of racial restrictive covenants. *Political Science Quarterly, 115*(4), 541–68.

Klarman, M. (2004). *From Jim Crow to civil rights: The Supreme Court and the struggle for racial equality.* New York: Oxford University Press.

Modernizing the fair housing act for the 21st century: 2013 national fair housing trends report. (2013). Washington, DC: National Fair Housing Alliance.

Shelley v. Kraemer, 334 U.S. 1 (1948).

Turner, M. A., Santos, R., Levy, D. K., Wissoker, D., Aranda, C., Pitingolo, R., & the Urban Institute. (2013). *Housing discrimination against racial and ethnic minorities: Executive summary.* Washington, DC: U.S. Department of Housing and Urban Development, Office of Policy Development and Research.

HUMAN RIGHTS

Human rights are the fundamental and inalienable rights held by all persons, regardless of their race, ethnicity, gender, national origin, religion, or other characteristics. These rights are considered to be universal and non-derogable, meaning they are not to be denied under any circumstances. States bear the responsibility for promoting and respecting human rights.

Although there were earlier precedents, such as the concept of natural rights that evolved during the Enlightenment, the modern notion of human rights largely emerged as a result of World War II and the global concern that nothing like the Holocaust should happen again. In 1948, the UN General Assembly met in Paris and, chaired by First Lady Eleanor Roosevelt, drafted the Universal Declaration of Human Rights (UDHR), a set of guidelines, articulated in thirty articles, which delineated the basic rights of humanity. The Preamble to the UDHR provides a statement of purpose: "Whereas recognition of the inherent dignity and of the equal and inalienable rights of all members of the human family is the foundation of freedom, justice and peace in the world." The UDHR was unanimously adopted, although there were eight abstentions (the Soviet Union, Ukrainian SSR, Byelorussian SSR, People's Federal Republic of Yugoslavia, People's Republic of Poland, Union of South Africa, Czechoslovakia, and the Kingdom of Saudi Arabia). In commemoration of the adoption of the UDHR, December 10 has been designated as International Human Rights Day.

Generally, the human rights described in the UDHR, and further explicated in subsequent international human rights treaties, recognize two broad types: civil and political rights and economic, social, and cultural rights. These categories of rights, however, are understood to be interwoven and interdependent. Whereas the UDHR is not binding because it is not a treaty, subsequent international treaties are binding when states both sign and then ratify them.

The UDHR, together with the International Covenant on Civil and Political Rights (ICCPR) and its two Optional Protocols, and the International Covenant on Economic, Social and Cultural Rights (ICESCR), are referred to as the International Bill of Human Rights. The ICCPR and the ICESCR were adopted on December 16, 1966. The Optional Protocols further articulate how the provisions of the treaties are to be achieved. Later international human rights treaties considered by the United Nations to constitute the core of human rights provisions include the ICCPR and ICESCR, the International Convention on the Elimination of All Forms of Racial Discrimination (ICERD), the Convention on the Elimination of All Forms of Discrimination Against Women (CEDAW), the Convention on the Rights of the Child (CRC), the International Convention on the Protection of the Rights of All Migrant Workers and Members of Their Families, the International Convention for the Protection of All Persons from Enforced Disappearance, and the Convention on the Rights of Persons with Disabilities (CRPD). Groups designated to oversee states' enforcement of these rights typically meet annually. Some of the international treaties, such as ICERD, require parties to issue annual reports to these committees in which they detail their progress and challenges.

One concern about actualizing the human rights protections enshrined in these treaties was the absence of any form of international police or courts. On July 17, 1998, the Rome Statute of the International Criminal Court was signed and entered into force on July 1, 2002. This Statute created the International Criminal Court (ICC), located in The Hague, Netherlands, as a mechanism to indict and try persons for genocide, war crimes, crimes of aggression, and crimes against humanity. As of May 2013, 122 countries have ratified the Rome Statute. The United States is not one of them.

Critics contend that the UDHR and other international human rights treaties largely reflect a westernized view of these complex issues. The former prime ministers of Singapore and Malaysia asserted in the 1990s that the UDHR did not adequately reflect the culture and values of Asia. Additionally, criticism focuses on the fact that some of the countries with the worst human rights records are indeed party to various treaties, thus suggesting that their ratification is only symbolic. A more recent trend involves countries that sign and ratify but do so after issuing declarations, reservations, and understandings. These are a form of exception to what is written in the treaty. It is a country's way of stipulating that they disagree, and will not abide by, certain specifications. The United States has been the leader in issuing declarations, reservations, and understandings under the administration of George W. Bush. Critics contend that this waters down the international treaties and negates the true purpose.

While the UDHR and international treaties provide legal requirements regarding human rights, other organizations offer guidelines and resources. The United Nations, which was created by charter on June 26, 1945, is devoted to peacekeeping, developing friendly relations between countries, helping improve the lives of the poor, the hungry, the ill, and marginalized persons globally, and encouraging respect for the rights and freedoms of all of humanity. It has headquarters in New York, Geneva, and Vienna. Specific to human rights, much of the work is coordinated by the UN Human Rights Council.

Other nonprofits and nongovernmental organizations (NGOs) help monitor global human rights and raise awareness about violations. Amnesty International (AI) and Human Rights Watch (HRW) are perhaps the biggest and longest-acting organizations doing human rights monitoring.

Since its founding in 1961 by Peter Berenson, Amnesty International has been a grassroots organization devoted to ensuring the actualization of human rights across the globe. It now has more than three million supporters, members, and activists in 150 countries and territories. AI issues an annual State of the World's Human Rights report as well as regular reports, news updates, blogs, and resources related to global human rights issues. Although initially committed to individual prisoners of conscience, the organization now campaigns on a variety of civil and political issues, such as ending torture and abolishing the death penalty, as well as social, cultural, and economic issues like maternal mortality and slums.

Human Rights Watch started in 1978 as Helsinki Watch, an organization devoted to ensuring that the Soviet government was in compliance with the 1975 Helsinki Accords. It emerged in 1988 as an inclusive organization that represented a number of regional bodies devoted to monitoring abuses perpetrated by governments, in violation of international human rights treaties. Using a strategy of "naming and shaming," HRW uses media coverage to identify and put pressure on human rights abusers. In 1997, HRW shared the Nobel Peace Prize as a founding member of the International Campaign to Ban Land Mines. Today, HRW also issues an annual human rights assessment as well as numerous investigative studies, news reports, videos, and other forms of advocacy.

Human Rights First is another organization that focuses on some of the same human rights abuses. Founded in 1978 as the Lawyers Committee for International Human Rights, Human Rights First is devoted to promoting laws and policies that advance universal rights and freedoms. Its work is eclectic, addressing everything from torture to asylum to LGBT rights.

People must be taught what their human rights are in order for them to be fully enacted. A number of nonprofit organizations and NGOs are devoted to human rights education. Both AI and HRW have some human rights education materials, as does the UN and other NGOs. Such materials emphasize the importance of understanding one another and ensuring that all peoples are treated with dignity and respect.

Laura Finley

Additional Reading

About Us. (n.d.). *Human rights first.* Retrieved November 11, 2013, from http://www.humanrightsfirst.org/about-us/.

History of Amnesty International. (2013). *Amnesty International.* Retrieved November 11, 2013, from http://www.amnesty.org/en/who-we-are/history.

Our History. (2013). *Human rights watch.* Retrieved November 11, 2013, from http://www.hrw.org/node/75134.

United Nations. (n.d.). Available at http://www.un.org/en/index.shtml.

United Nations Human Rights Office of the High Commissioner. (n.d.) What are human rights? Retrieved November 5, 2013, from http://www.ohchr.org/EN/Issues/Pages/WhatareHumanRights.aspx.